ISBN 978-1-331-93697-8
PIBN 10256872

PUBLICATIONS

OF THE

SCOTTISH HISTORY SOCIETY

VOLUME IV

———•———

ST. ANDREWS KIRK SESSION REGISTER

PART I

FEBRUARY 1889

TOMBSTONE OF JOHN WYNRAM

IN THE CHAPEL OF ST. LEONARD'S COLLEGE, ST. ANDREWS.

[See p. lix]

REGISTER OF

THE MINISTER ELDERS AND DEACONS
OF THE CHRISTIAN CONGREGATION OF

ST. ANDREWS

COMPRISING THE PROCEEDINGS OF THE KIRK
SESSION AND OF THE COURT OF THE SUPERINTEN-
DENT OF FIFE FOTHRIK AND STRATHEARN.

1559-1600

PART FIRST : 1559-1582

Transcribed and Edited from the Original
Manuscript with Preface and Notes by

DAVID HAY FLEMING

EDINBURGH

Printed at the University Press by T. and A. CONSTABLE
for the Scottish History Society

1889

REGISTER OF
THE MINISTER ELDERS AND DEACONS
OF THE CHRISTIAN CONGREGATION OF
ST. ANDREWS

COMPRISING THE PROCEEDINGS OF THE KIRK
SESSION AND OF THE COURT OF THE SUPERINTEN-
DENT OF FIFE FOTHRIK AND STRATHEARN.

1559-1600

PART FIRST : 1559-1582

Transcribed and Edited from the Original
Manuscript with Preface and Notes by

DAVID HAY FLEMING

EDINBURGH

Printed at the University Press by T. and A. CONSTABLE
for the Scottish History Society

1889

PREFACE.

THE importance of the Reformation is so great that every authentic record must be welcome, which throws light on its origin, progress, or results. And among the surviving Registers of Kirk Sessions that of which the first part is now printed is entitled to a prominent place, because of the early period it covers and the district with which it is connected. It contains two documents of considerable interest relating to pre-Reformation times; it emphasises the fact that the yoke of the Papacy was cast off in this country at an earlier date than is usually imagined; it embodies the recantations of many of the old clergy, while their former faith was still nominally the established religion of the nation; it reveals the deplorable state into which the people had been allowed to sink, and the earnest and unflagging efforts of the Reformers to cure the festering sores; and altogether it presents a faithful picture of the inner working of the new Church during the first forty years of its existence. In one respect, perhaps, this *Register* stands alone. For eleven years after Wynram's appointment as Superintendent of Fife, it preserves the record of his court as well as of the Kirk Session, and consequently embraces transactions concerning people and places far beyond the bounds of the parish of St. Andrews.

Previous to the Reformation St. Andrews could not only boast of a long line of ecclesiastical dignitaries, the representatives of that foreign hierarchy by which the earlier Celtic Church had been supplanted, but it contained an Augustinian Priory, 'the first in rank and wealth of the Religious Houses of Scotland,' and monasteries of both the

Black and Grey Friars, and was likewise the seat of Scotland's oldest University. Here, in the national headquarters of the Papacy, the reformed opinions had been introduced and nourished by a devoted band of martyrs and confessors, five of whom had been burned to ashes in presence of the citizens in the vain hope of suppressing the living doctrine they taught. The fruit of the seed sown by Paul Craw in the first half of the fifteenth century may have been scanty, but his labours helped to prepare the unpromising and uncongenial soil, which was so vigorously cultivated by Patrick Hamilton, during his brief but ardent ministry in the earlier part of the next century, and whose efforts were aided by the secret importation of Tyndale's translation of the New Testament. From the hour of Master Patrick's martyrdom the cause for which he died took such deep root that all efforts to extirpate it only hastened its spread and triumph. The cruel death of George Wishart was speedily followed by that of his relentless persecutor, with whom fell the political power of the Papacy in Scotland. The public preaching and disputations of Knox and Rough in St. Andrews, in the summer of 1547, in some respects more resembled the work of autumn than of spring-time, but that season was short. The heroic martyrdom of Walter Mill in 1558, however, wonderfully hastened the ripening process, and when Knox returned to the city in June 1559 the harvest was ready.

At the time of his arrival the old order seemed outwardly as strong, perhaps stronger than ever in its various organisations, and its majestic buildings had never been more numerous nor looked more imposing; but its inner life and strength had been eaten out by the gross debauchery and crass ignorance of its officials, and it had deservedly lost its hold alike on the affections and respect of the people. Despite the presence of an armed force in the town and French troops in the neighbourhood, the preaching of Knox was immediately followed by a thorough-going external reformation, the monasteries being overthrown, and, in the language of the day, the churches purged of all monuments of idolatry, only a mutilated Madonna having been spared to modern times. This reformation was carried out with as much formality as was possible in the circumstances, the Lords of the Congregation approving, the Prior and Sub-Prior consenting, the Provost and bailies lending their assistance, and all the citizens with few exceptions heartily concurring. In all probability Wynram was not the only one among the clergy who had long sympathised with the new views, and these now openly declared their convictions, while many followed their example without delay and others more tardily. Writing on the 23d of June, Knox says:—'Diverse channons of Sanct Andrewes have given notable confessiouns, and have declared themselves manifest enemies to the Pope, to the masse, and to all superstitioun.'[1] In January 1571-2 fourteen of those who had been canons of the Priory of St. Andrews are mentioned as Protestants, twelve of them being then parish ministers of the Reformed Church;[2] and, besides these, other thirty-one of the clergy had joined the Reformers by the 17th of March 1559-60. Many members of the University also forsook their former faith, for the first General Assembly deemed twenty-one 'in St. Androes' qualified 'for ministreing and teaching,' and with few exceptions these were professors or regents; so that, as Principal Lee has well said, 'this city was at that time the chief nursery of the Church.'[3] The General Band or Covenant which was 'maid betuix the Lordis and Baronis of Congregatioun,' at Edinburgh, on the 13th of July 1559, and of which no copy seems to have been

---

[1] Laing's *Knox*, vi. 26.

[2] *Booke of the Universall Kirk*, Ban. Club, i. 222. Robert Stewart, Bishop of Caithness and Commendator of the Priory, and John Wynram, are included in the fourteen. Martine says that 'fourteen turned preachers, after the Reformation, at certaine kirks of the Priorie, and some continued still about the monasterie till their death' (*Reliquiae Divi Andreae*, pp. 169, 170).

[3] *Booke of the Univ. Kirk*, i. 4: Lee's *Lectures*, i. 227-232.—John Wynram is mentioned among the twenty-one, but not John Douglas.

preserved elsewhere, was adopted in St. Andrews as 'the
letteris of junctioun to the Congregatioun,' and was signed
here by three hundred and thirty-one men. The exact date
on which the Kirk Session was constituted is unknown, but
in 1559 Adam Heriot,[1] assisted by a large staff of elders and
deacons, entered on the arduous work of practical reformation, and this *Register* of their proceedings begins on the
27th of October in that year.

Even in those early days, while Popery was still established
by law, the Session dealt freely with all sorts of cases that
came before it, hesitating not to judge in claims of marriage
and divorce. There was no feeling of usurpation in this, for
the body of the citizens had voluntarily placed themselves on
the side of the Reformation, and the Session naturally took
up the work that had previously fallen to the ecclesiastical
courts. If further proof of the practically unanimous change
of opinion were required, it is to be found in the action of the
craftsmen. The oath of the Hammermen of St. Andrews
bound them to be 'leill and trew to the honor of God and
Haly Kirk,' and to the weal and good of the altar of St. Eloy.
They were sworn to observe certain rules, under the penalty of
a pound of a wax to the weal of their altar and craft; and
disobedience 'to be pundit' involved the payment of 'ane half
stayne' of wax, besides the 'unlaw' to the bailies. By
one of the rules every brother of the craft had to 'gif ane
plak at the tyme of the deceass of ony brother or sister of the
said craft, sa sonne as the corps cumis to the erd, or within
xxiiij howris thairefter to the dekyne or the positour, to dispence amangis puir chaipillanis, for to pray for the saul of the
said brother.' But on the 28th of July 1560, the craft convened to recast their rules, and every reference to the poor
chaplains, to St. Eloy, his altar, and his wax, was struck out

---

[1] On the authority of Spottiswoode, it is stated (P. 3, n.) that Heriot had
been an Augustinian canon ; and M'Crie, Scott, and Lee have said the same;
but he is not named among those mentioned as still alive in January 1571-2.

at once and for ever.[1] It is no wonder that next month the rulers of the nation acted with promptitude and unanimity. The country was already gained. 'On the face of the parliamentary record,' says Hill Burton, 'it would seem as if the Reformation in Scotland were the work of one day. On the morning of the 25th of August 1560, the Romish hierarchy was supreme; in the evening of the same day, Calvinistic Protestantism was established in its stead.'[2] But this is inaccurate and misleading. Parliament ratified the *Confession of Faith* on the 17th of August, and abolished the Pope's jurisdiction on the 24th of that month. In one of the Acts of the latter day, it was said :—' Notwithstanding the reformatioun already maid according to Goddis Word, yit nottheles thair is sum of the same Papis kirk that stubburnlie perseveris in thair wickit idolatrie, sayand mes and baptizand conforme to the Papis kirk, prophanand thairthrow the sacramentis foirsaidis in quiet and secreit places.'[3]

Reference has already been made to the profligacy and ignorance of the pre-Reformation clergy. Proofs and illustrations are more than abundant in the pages of Knox, of Sir David Lindsay, of their own champions, in the *Acts of Parliament*, and in the canons of their own councils, nor are they lacking in this *Register* and the foot-notes. Nevertheless, regarding their ignorance, the additional and unimpeachable testimony of Archibald Hay, who in the year of Cardinal Beaton's death was Principal of St. Mary's College, may be here adduced :—'I often wonder what bishops thought when they allowed such persons as hardly knew the order of the letters to handle the most holy body of the Lord !'[4] The effects of such ignorance, and of the pernicious lives of the

---

[1] *Bouk of the Hammermen of Sanctandrous*, MS., in St. Andrews University Library.

[2] *History of Scotland*, revised ed., iii. 383.

[3] *Acts of the Parliaments of Scotland*, ii. 534, 535.

[4] *Ad Illustriss. Tit. S. Stephani in Monte Coelio Cardinalem D. Dauidem Betoun gratulatorius panegyricus*, Paris, 1540, fol. xxxiiii.

clergy on the people, combined with the evils which had arisen
from the extension of the Levitical prohibitions of inter-
marriage, were the chief heritage which the Reformers derived
from their predecessors. Yet they set themselves to teach the
nation and to instil into it the principles of a high-toned
morality. No doubt the population was much less then than
now; but the country was as large, the means of transit were
infinitely inferior, and the supply of suitable men was miser-
ably small. Emboldened, however, by the goodness of their
cause, and trusting for strength to the Most High, they right
resolutely undertook the task.

At present I am only concerned with their plans and modes
of procedure as carried out by the Kirk Session and Superintendent. Some of these, it must be confessed, seem harsh in
the light of the nineteenth century, and they were doubtless
felt to be so by those who had been so long accustomed to an
easy laxity of manners. Indeed, obstinate sinners occasionally
refused to comply with them, but in the end they had to
submit. The apparent harshness can only be justified by the
necessity of the times. And the perusal of the *Register* is far
from leaving the impression that the office-bearers meant to be
cruel. Although determined to put down sin, tenderness was
often shown for the feelings of the transgressor, and a manifest
reluctance to proceed to extremities is not rarely revealed. In
the words of a citation issued against a notorious offender, the
Session was 'willing to wyn synneris wyth quietnes rather nor
sevirite to repentans, evir hoping from day to day willing
obedience and satisfaction.'[1] The proceedings are pervaded
by a spirit of strict impartiality, the decisions in difficult cases
were evidently prompted by sincerity, and a remarkable shrewd-
ness is frequently observable in the receiving of suspicious
evidence. The recent words of a writer well versed in the
subject are very appropriate to the period on hand:—'Kirk

---

[1] P. 473.

Sessions in those days were not content with scratching the surface of scandals. They probed to the very core.'[1] As it would be impossible, within the due compass of a preface, to direct attention even briefly to all the interesting points in the first part of this *Register*, it must suffice to deal specially with those things which could not be so well treated in the foot-notes, and to refer more or less generally to some of its most prominent features and outstanding cases.

The articles of heresy with which Sir John Borthwick was charged, and the sentence pronounced by Cardinal Beaton against him, in 1540, are embodied in the process which led to the reversal of the sentence in 1561. The foot-notes may give some idea of the characters of those who sat in council against him, of the number of them who afterwards professed the faith for which he was condemned, and of the clerical antipathy to the reading of the Scriptures. Wynram had the distinction of sitting with the Cardinal in 1540, and of presiding in that court, in 1561, which declared that the givers of the sentence against Borthwick had ' schawynn tham selfis tharby mere ignorant of Godis Word and lawis, and plane inemeis to his trewth.'[2] In the process betwixt John Forret of that ilk, and Elizabeth Leslie, Lady of Nydie, a Papal dispensation was produced in evidence, and was engrossed in the *Register*.[3]

None of the names of the fourteen canons of the Priory mentioned as Protestants in January 1571-2 is to be found among those who signed the General Band of 13th July 1559.[4] Probably they had left the district before it was adopted.

---

[1] Edgar's *Old Church Life in Scotland*, first series, p. 263.

[2] Pp. 89-104. This process has been previously printed in the *Bannatyne Miscellany*, i. 251-263, and in Lee's *Lectures*, i. 327-334; but in both a line has been omitted, and in both Borthwick is described as of *Cenerie* instead of *Ceverie*. In 1556, 'John Burtwick, knight, and John Kellye his page,' were received into the membership of 'the Englishe churche and congregation at Geneva,' and in that same year Borthwick was married there to 'Jane Bonespoir of Britagne' (Professor Mitchell's *Livre des Anglois*, pp. 8, 14).

[3] Pp. 116-123. Some of its peculiarities are pointed out in the note on pp. 115, 116.   [4] Pp. 6-11.

On the 3d of February 1559-60, ten priests 'of there awin fre motyve willis' ratified the Band, and formally renounced idolatry, superstition, the mass, the Pope, and all his traditions;[1] but this renunciation does not appear to have been considered altogether satisfactory, for in that month eight of them, with other six, made a much more emphatic and detailed recantation.[2] And eight priests, who had joined the congregation after the former ten, also with other four, made a still fuller recantation on the 10th of March.[3] Besides these, there is the special recantation of 'Dene Jhone Wilsoun, vicare of Kingorne,' and 'umquhile channoun of Halyrudehows,' which he made in the parish kirk of St. Andrews, in presence of the Admiral and Vice-Admiral of England.[4] And there is also the recantation of John Gresone, who had been Provincial of the Order of Black Friars in Scotland for fully thirty years, which he openly made in the parish church on the 17th of March.[5] The master hand of Knox is distinctly traceable in these recantations, and the fiery vehemence with which he denounces the Pope and all his abominations will still, no doubt, be refreshing to some ardent Protestants. He was in St. Andrews from the beginning of November 1559 until the end of April 1560, and during part of that time, at least, acted as minister of the parish.[6] On the 13th of March another priest signed the recantation of the former twelve.[7] With the exception of Wilson, probably all were local men.[8]

---

[1] Pp. 10, 11.   [2] Pp. 13, 14.   [3] Pp. 11, 14, 15.   [4] Pp. 11, 13.
[5] Pp. 16-18.   [6] P. 27, n.   [7] P. 15.

[8] Information concerning some of them will be found in the notes. Of the others, Thomas Wemys (pp. 11, 15) may perhaps be identified with Sir Thomas Wemyss, chaplain at Leuchars (*New Statistical Account of Fifeshire*, p. 223). John Zoung, junior (p. 11), or Johne Zoung (p. 14), is perhaps the 'Sir Jhone Zoung chaplane,' who was charged with being an accomplice in the Cardinal's slaughter (*Acts of Parliament*, ii. 467). 'Johannes Kinloqwhye' (p. 15) may be the 'Schir Johne Kenlowy' mentioned on pp. 411, 412. Thomas Kynneir (p. 15) might have been confounded with the unworthy successor of John Melville in the ministry at Crail; but that Thomas Kynneir had been chosen minister of Crail, with consent of the Superintendent, more than seven months before the date of the recantation (Scott's *Fasti*, ii. 415; Lee's *Lectures*, i. 336, 337). It was long

In 1573, it was stated that 'the most part of the persons who were channons, monks, and friars within this realme, have made profession of the true religion.'[1]   Many of these, no doubt, were sincere converts, men who had felt the power of religion in their own souls, but it would be an unnecessary and unwarrantable stretch of charity to believe that they were all actuated by the same high motives.   While a few were conscientiously attached to the old faith, and tenaciously adhered to it, many, like Gallio, cared for none of these things, and would with little hesitation join the side in connection with which they hoped to be able to continue their indolent or sensual lives ; and this *Register* shows that, of those who recanted at St. Andrews, several, like the sow that was washed, returned to wallow in the mire.   According to Bishop Lesley, the 'sharp statutes' of the General Provincial Council, which met at Edinburgh in the spring of 1558-9, 'was the princepall caus that a gret nomber of younge abbottis, priors, deanis, and benefest men assisted to the interprice and practise devysed for the ourthrow of the catholicke religeon, and tumult aganis the Quene and Frenche men, fearing tham selffis to be put at.'[2]   But it may well be questioned whether any of these men, with the experience of the past behind them, were induced to overthrow their old faith through fear of such threatened reforms.   And those who came over, after the battle was won, in the expectation of living in their lusts as before, must have been grievously disappointed.   So early as the 4th of April 1560, Mr. John Todrick was. dealt with for adultery, but he showed 'na signe of penitence'; and in 1568 he was suspected of fornication.[3]   Mr. John Setoun, who had become reader of Creich, was deprived of his office in 1562, and letters

customary for any one who had taken the degree of Master of Arts to write *Mr.* before his name ; and those priests who had merely obtained the Bachelor's degree were styled *Sir*, but it was not an academical title (Laing's *Knox*, i. 556).

[1] *Booke of the Universall Kirk*, i. 280.
[2] Lesley's *History of Scotland*, Ban. Club, p. 271.   [3] Pp. 28, 309.

of excommunication were decerned against him and Helen Nicholl.[1] On the 12th of January 1563-4, letters of excommunication were likewise decerned against 'Schir James Stanis, sumtym Papist preist and recanted.'[2] 'Alexander Car, sumtym called Schyr Alexander Car, and Madde Sanderis, ald fornicatoris, huyrmongaris rather,' in Balmerino, were compelled to marry in 1562;[3] next spring, 'Jobane Zeasteris, sumtym monk in Balmerinach,' and 'Eleyn Bunche' were constrained to do the same;[4] and in 1564, 'Jobane Anderson, sumtym vicar of Glesche,' and 'Eufame Pattone' had to follow their example.[5] Probably these incorrigible fornicators would not have escaped the demerits of their deeds, although they had remained outside of the Reformed Church. In July 1563, Sir David Donaldson, 'ane stubburn Papist,' and 'manifest indurit huyr-mongar,' was summoned before the Superintendent, but appeared not. He evidently adhered to his old faith, as well as his old morals. The minister of Monimaill was ordered to command 'all Cristianis fearyng God' to abstain from his company, and his 'vicius lyff and inobedience' were to be made known to the Justice Clerk.[6] Letters of excommunication were decerned against 'Schyr Alexander Gaw and Catren Nesche, huyrmongaris and adulteraris,' in April 1564. At the same time, Dean John Wilson, who had made such a solemn recantation, was summoned with other two priests for saying and hearing mass; and, not appearing, they were excommunicated.[7] In October of that year, Sir Patrick Fergy was summoned for presuming 'to prech and minister the sacraments wythowtyn lawfull admission, and for drawyng of the pepill to the chapell of Tulebarne fra thar parroche kyrk.' On the same day, 'Schyr Johane Moreson, efter his recantacion admittit reader in Mithyll,' was summoned 'for ministracion of baptisme and mariaige efter the Papisticall fasson, and that indifferently to all personis.' He had also

---

[1] P. 172.   [2] P. 188.   [3] P. 146.   [4] P. 180.   [5] P. 194.
[6] Pp. 183, 184.   [7] P. 193.

abused the Lord's Supper, dispensing it in private houses, in
the kirk-yard, and 'about the kirk-yard dykis,' receiving a
penny from each communicant. On the previous Pasche day
he had ministered it to a hundred persons. With him, Sir
John Stephyn was summoned 'for dayly ministracion of the
sacramentis and solemnizacion of mariageis on the Papisticall
fasson in the chapell of Sanct Gormoo, ane prophane hous suspendit; and also for mantenyng of ane huyr in his cumpanye,
quhai hes born to hym twa barnis, as yit unbaptisit except it
be by hymself or sum other Papist prest.'[1]

In the recantation made by the fourteen priests in February
1559-60, they confess, 'We haif ower lang abstractit ourselfis,
and beyne sweir in adjuning us to Christes Congregatioun.'
But others were much more 'sweir,' and the receiving of converts was spread over thirteen years. Knox, in describing the
reformation of Perth, in a letter written on the 23d of June
1559, says that the priests were 'commanded, under paine of
death, to desist frome their blasphemous masse.'[2] But there
is nothing in this *Register* to show, or to raise the suspicion,
that any of the recantations, preceding the 18th of March
1559-60, were extorted. No force was used to gain them except
the force of reason; and seemingly the refractory were liable
to no penalty save obloquy, unless the dread perhaps of losing
their livings, and if they were driven over so early by that, it
would be difficult to find a better proof of the strong hold
which the reformed doctrines had already obtained. The
provost and prebendaries of the Kirk-heuch having been summoned to appear before the Superintendent, the provost appeared on the 25th of April 1561, and after showing that he
and one of the prebendaries had joined the congregation, they
were 'admittit and decernit to be ansuerit of thar frutis';
but the deacons were ordained to uplift the fruits of the other
three prebendaries.[3] In the following June the case of John

---

[1] Pp. 226, 227.   [2] Laing's *Knox*, vi. 23.   [3] Pp. 76, 77.

Kipper comes up in a very different manner. He is first mentioned in connection with his piteous petition for reconciliation,
directed from the castle of St. Andrews, in which he was
warded.[1] As it is not said that Kipper had broken that Act
of Parliament, which forbade the saying or hearing of mass
under the pain of confiscation of goods, and corporal punishment at the discretion of the magistrates, for the first offence,
banishment for the second, and death for the third, it is probable
that he was warded, under some local regulation, for his active
opposition in ' defending and mantenyng of idolatrie, supersticion and Papistrie ;' more especially as in his zeal he had
been guilty of ' blasphemyng of Cristis religion, Superintendent,
and ministeris of Godis Word.' Even now obstreperous
individuals who indulge in violent language are liable to imprisonment. Kipper was of mature age, having nearly reached
fourscore, but the next recalcitrant Papist who was tackled
was made of sterner stuff. In the following August Mr.
Thomas Meffen, one of the disobedient prebendaries of the
Kirk-hench, when warned to appear before the Superintendent
and ministry, replied, ' that he was nether ane Papist nor ane
Calvynist, nor of Paul nor of Apollo, bot Jesus Cristis man ;
he wald nocht cum to tham nor to thar hows ; bot gyf the
Superintendent or the minister had ocht to do wyth him, at
thar request he wald cum to thar chalmer and speik tham.'
Again he was summoned, but only sent a substitute ; nor did he
appear until January, and then he protested that they were
not his judges. Two days later he again appeared, but ' under
protestacion of nocht admitting ony present his jugis.' From
that day's proceedings it is learned that he had ' beyn chargit
divers tymmis to recant and adjone hymself to Cristis congregacione, als weyll oppynlie in the essemble be Adame Heriot
minister, as particularlie be commissaris tharto deput be the
Lordis of Congregacione.' From the date of Heriot's appointment to Aberdeen, the public charges by him cannot well have

---

[1] P. 81.

been later than July 1560, probably they were earlier. It
further appears that a cause which Meffen had brought before
the magistrates was repelled, because he was not joined to the
congregation ; and that ' ane testimoniall' to that effect had
been sent to Dundee. Mr. Thomas, still undaunted, insisted
that he was not ' ane member of the congregacion'; on which
Wynram protested that ' be frequenting and dayle residence
mackeyn in this cite contrary to the proclamacion mayd aganis
kyrkmen,' he should therefore ' incur the painis thretnet in the
sayd proclamacion.'[1] It was ordained that a supplication be
directed to the magistrates, ' ether to caws hym obeye the
ordor of the kyrk and subject hym to disciplynn, or ellis to
exclud hym this citie, that na perturbacion of the unitie and
ordor be brokyn by him.'[2] After a lapse of more than seven
years, he was accused for not being present at the communion,
excused his absence by the extreme illness of a friend, ' and
opinlie protestat that he imbrased alreddye the religion now
resavit and mentenit, and promittit faithtfullie to communicat
wytht the rest at ministration of the communion ; and abhorrit
and detestit al superstition and Papistrie and abusing of the
sacramentis in tyme bipast, wytht transubstantiation, impanation, and al utheris erroris in tyme bipast.'[3] In August 1562
a rumour having reached the city that Mr. William Cranston
was to return, arrangements were made for his reception. He
was to be asked ' quhat religion he is of,' and if he professed
himself ' ane Papist or of his ald and wonted religion, that he
be ernistlie required and requested to depart fra this citie,' with
intimation ' gyf he wyll nocht obey the request, that all the
membris of this congregacione salbe oppynly inhibit and forbyddyn to intercommone or cumpany, by or sell, wyth hym,
under pane of excommunicacione.' Should he on the other
hand declare himself a Protestant he was to be charged ' to gev

---

[1] The proclamation may have been such an one as that indicated, p. 137,
n. 1 ; or perhaps that of which the essential part is given, p. 270, n.

[2] Pp. 135-138.   [3] Pp. 317, 318.

confessione of his fayth, and to subscryve the articulis of
recantacione commonly used.' If he desired to preach he was
only to be allowed on certain conditions, one of which was that
at the end of his sermon he should 'confes treuly (accordyng
to his conscience and testimone tharof) that ether ignorantly
or of malice' he taught wrong doctrine in the last sermon he
made in this kirk.[1] On the 29th of March 1564, James Lyell,
'sumtym Papist prest,' who had recanted four years before,
came under a new obligation.[2] In September 1567 John
Kinloqwhye signed the recantation, and next month Thomas
Kynneir did the same.[3] There is nothing in the *Register* to
show that they were even asked to do this; but in June 1568
two procurators, Mr. David Dischington and Mr. James
Rolland, were requested to give confession of their faith, 'that
according to Act of Parliament, we mycht understand quba
kepit ane uthir face of religioun.'[4] Neither of them was prepared for instant compliance, and as Rolland, after giving in
'sum ansuers in write,' drops out of sight, he had probably
left the town. With Dischington, however, there was some
trouble. At his third appearance he stoutly refused to
give his answers to the articles in writing, nor would he
acknowledge theirs to be the true religion, 'allegeing that
gyf he gaif his ansuere in wryte that it wald be blawdit
in the pulpet quhair the preacheris ralis by thair text:
and sa departit wytht fume and anger; nochtwythstanding the seat promist that his writting sould nocht be

---

[1] Pp. 169-171.   [2] P. 191.   [3] P. 15.

[4] P. 296.—In writing the note on that page, I overlooked the Act of 1567, to
which special reference was evidently made. In response to one of the articles
proponed by the Kirk, Parliament 'declarit and grantit jurisdictioun to the said
Kirk: quhilk consistis and standis in preicheing of the trew Word of Jesus Christ,
correctioun of maneris, and administratioun of haly sacramentis; and declaris
that thair is na uther face of kirk, nor uther face of religioun, than is presentlie
be the favour of God establischeit within this realme; and that thair be na uther
jurisdictioun ecclesiasticall acknawlegeit within this Realme, uther than that
quhilk is, and salbe within the same Kirk, or that quhilk flowis thairfra concerning the premissis' (*Acts of Parliament*, iii. 24, 25).

blawdit, bot he sould have sufficient ansuere in wryte wytht quietnes.' Had the session been tyrannically disposed, his answer and anger would have evoked hasty and high-handed procedure. ' Yit being of mynd to repres his stubburnes and be al meanis posseble to wyn hym,' it was simply resolved to warn him to appear five days later with his answers in writing, ' and gyf he comperis nocht the minister to proceid to public admonesing of hym, according to the ordour appointed be the kirk.'[1] But no further action seems to have been taken for nearly ten months, when, after some explanations by the Superintendent and the minister regarding the Lord's Supper, he ' adjunit hym faithtfullie to the religioun and imbrased the sam,' and promised to partake of ' Christis communione at the nixt ministration thairof.'[2] He did not fulfil his promise, however, but excused his absence by ' seiknes and alteration of his bodie.'[3] On the next occasion he made a very different answer :—' Quhen I maid the promis I lukit for ane uthir thing nor I see, for ever ilk ane of thame wald cut utheris throtis quha gaes to that communioun, and thairfoir I wil nocht keip promis.' This was on the 19th of June 1571, and again ample time was allowed for reflection. On the 7th of November he renewed his former promise, and the seat decerned that if he failed, ' it sal be procedit aganis hym to excommunicatioun, wythout forthir calling.'[4] Laurence Dalglesche was more easily managed. He seems to have joined without the least hesitation in June 1569, and next August explained that ' he baid nocht fra the communioun of set purpos nor hypocriticallie.'[5] In February 1572-3, John Forret, vicar of Swinton, recanted, but the form has not been copied into the *Register*.[6] On the 8th of March 1572-3, the Session ordained, ' that the namis of the Papistis wythin this congregatioun be serchit and gevin in bil to the minister, that ordour ma be takin wytht

---

[1] P. 297. [2] Pp. 319, 320. [3] P. 322.
[4] Pp. 352, 353. Pp. 318, 323. [6] P. 375.

them according to Act of Parliament.'[1] The search had
either been very superficial or the delinquents were few in
number.   Only five individuals are mentioned, including Sir
David Muir, one of the old chaplains of the Lady Altar in the
parish church, 'ane Papist unrecantit and obstinet.' The
mere fact that such a man had been allowed to hold out so
long, speaks volumes for the practical tolerance of the Session.
On the 25th of the same month, 'that all suspitioun of Papistrie
in this reformat congregatioun be removit,' it was ordained,
'That the heal preistis that brukis ony fundatioun wythtin
this citie compeir this day xv dayis, of new to gyf confession of
thair faitht, and to ansueir to sic thingis as sal be sperit and
askit of them, concerning the pointis of religion and observing
of the preaching and doctrine.'[2] But so far as the *Register*
shows no one appeared.

In this age, permeated with what in the *Solemn League
and Covenant* is termed 'detestable indifferency,' these dealings of the Session with obstinate Papists will doubtless be
regarded as flagrant infringements of the liberty of conscience,

---

[1] P. 376.—The Act here referred to was passed on the 26th of January
1572-3.   It was ordained, 'that the lauchfull archebischoppis bischoppis superintendentis and commissionaris of the dioceis and provinces of this realme be
thame selfis, and the ministeris and reidaris serving at the kirkis within thair
charges respective, with all diligence efter the publicatioun of this present Act,
note the names of the persounis asweill men as wemen suspectit to be Papistis,
or that hes not communicat with the sacramentis as thay ar now trewly ministrat
in the Reformit Kirkis of this realme; and with the lyke diligence lauchfully
admónische thame according to the ordour of the Kirk. . . . And in case of
the contumacie and non comperance of ony persounis swa admonischeit, or
comperand gif thay refuse to obey the admonitioun, and thay quha hes returnit
to thair errouris efter thair confessioun anis gevin, that everie lauchfull archibischop bischop superintendent or commissionar present ane roll and catholog
of the names of the disobedientis obstinat or relaps persounis to our Soverane
Lord and his Regent, betuix and the first day of Junii nixt to cum.' An archbishop or bishop failing to make this return was to lose a year's income, a superintendent or commissioner was to lose the same and his office to boot.   Those
named in the catalogue were, after its publication, to be 'estemit infamous and
unabill to sit or stand in jugement, persew, beir office, nor sall not be admittit
as previs witnessis or assysouris aganis ony professing the trew Religioun, ay
and quhill thay have recounsallit thame selfis to the trew kirk' (*Acts of Parliament*, iii. 71, 72).   [2] P. 376.

or may even be denounced as gross persecution; but they were deeds of kindness compared with the atrocious doings of David Beton, Patrick Hepburn, and John Hamilton in the same city and during the same century. It might have been supposed that men who had suffered persecution would have learned to feel compassion and exercise a spirit of free toleration; but those who had passed through such a struggle could hardly remain neutral, and the Reformers could not afford to give their opponents any undue advantage, whereby their hard-won liberties might have been again wrested from them. They knew something of the plots that were being hatched, and the schemes that were being laid, for their overthrow, and they behoved to be watchful. That their fears were well founded has been recently proved afresh. Nicolas de Gouda, the Pope's legate to Mary Queen of Scots in 1562, thus wrote to the General of his Society:—'The Pope exhorted her in defending the faith to follow the example of Queen Mary of England.'[1] It is almost unnecessary to recall the nature of that example. In 'four years as many as two hundred and eighty-eight persons, of all ranks and orders, perished at the stake, the greater part for their abandonment of Mediævalism and their adherence to the doctrine of the English Reformation.'[2] Gouda's statement may be accepted as correct so far as it goes, although found in a book remarkable for its misrepresentation of facts.[3]

---

[1] Forbes-Leith's *Narratives of Scottish Catholics*, 1885, p. 67.

[2] Hardwick's *History of the Church during the Reformation*, edited by Stubbs, p. 221.

[3] To show that this charge is neither reckless nor unjust, a specimen of the perversions may be given from the introductory sketch. On p. 6, he says :—'On the eve of the Reformation, the Church of Scotland could glory in prelates who were distinguished equally for their talents and virtues.' After mentioning a few of these, he proceeds :—'The inferior clergy could also pride itself on many learned and virtuous priests, who, after undergoing for several years the various trials of a severe persecution, were at last banished ; and who, strangers though they were, acquired, in foreign universities, a high reputation for character, ability, and learning.' Then he adds in a foot-note :—'M'Crie says, "They were to be found in all the universities and colleges. In several of them they held the honourable situation of principal, and in others they amounted to a

If it has been at all tampered with, its strength will have been modified not increased.

In the eighth head of the *First Book of Discipline*, the duties of elders and deacons are clearly laid down, and also rules for their election :—'Men of best knawledge in Goddis Word, of cleanest life, men faithfull, and of most honest conversatioun that can be fund in the Churche, must be nominated to be in electioun ; and the names of the same must be publictlie red to the whole kirk by the minister, geving thame advertisement, that frome amongest these must be chosin elderis and deaconis. Yf anye of the nominated be noted with publict infamye, he aught to be repelled ; for it is not seamlie that the servand of corruptioun shall have authoritie to judge in the Churche of God. Yf anye man knowis utheris of better qualiteis within the Churche then these that beis nominated, lat thame be put in electioun, that the Church may have the choise. . . . The elderis being elected, must be admonischeit of thair office, which is to assist the minister in all publict effares of the Churche ; to wit, in judgeing and decernyng causses ; in geving of admonitioun to the licentious lever ; in having of respect to the manneris and conversatioun of all men within thair charge ; for by the gravitie of the seniouris aught the licht and unbridillit life of the licentious be corrected and bridillit. Yea, the seniouris aught to tak heyde to the life, manneris, deligence, and studye of thair ministeris. . . . The office of the deaconis, as is before declared, is to receave the rentis, and gadder the almous of the churche, to keip and distribute the same, as by the ministerie of the kirk shall be appointed. They may also assist in judgement with the

third of the professors." ' Though his references are usually very full, on this occasion he does not even say which of M'Crie's works the quotation is from ; but it will be found in his *Life of Melville*, first edition, ii. 419 ; second edition, ii. 279 ; third edition, p. 320. Incredible as it may seem, M'Crie is there speaking of the Protestant universities and colleges of France, and, immediately after the passage quoted, adds :—' Most of them had been educated under Melville at St. Andrews.' His teaching there did not begin until twenty years after the Reformation.

ministeris and elderis, and may be admitted to read in the assemblie yf thei be required, and be fund abill thairto.' Though the election ought to be yearly,[1] the same men might be re-elected ; and as to 'how the voitis and suffreigeis may be best receaved, so that everie man may gyf his vote frelie, everie severall churche may tack such ordour as best seameth to thame.' Before the *First Book of Discipline* was prepared,[2] there had been one election of elders and deacons at St. Andrews; and on the 1st of October 1561, 'in the session of Superintendent and ministerie of Sanctandrois,' at which the Provost, bailies and town-council of the city, and the Rector and chief members of the University, were present, regulations were drawn up for future elections.[3] On the 1st of March 1559-60, the minister and elders, in a difficult case, took the advice of John Douglas, John Wynram, William Skene, and John Rutherfurd ;[4] twelve days after his election as Superintendent, Wynram, with the 'holl ministerie,' took the 'consayll of the Provest of Sanctandrois, Rector and chief membris of the Universite, anent the tryall and admissione of ministeris in the hol dioceye ;'[5] and in Borthwick's case many of the University officials were consulted ;[6] but after the meeting in October 1561, two or three members of the University were usually, if not always, chosen elders.

The office-bearers met weekly, and in their joint capacity were generally called the *ministry* until 1568, but afterwards that term was almost entirely superseded by *seat*, *assembly*, and *session*. Sometimes *kirk* is used in the same sense ;[7] and 'consistory '[8] also occurs, as well as 'the consistoriall court of the minister and eldaris.'[9] Occasionally the terms are combined

---

[1] In the English congregation at Geneva the ministers as well as the elders and deacons were elected annually (*Livre des Anglois*, pp. 11, 12). The Protestant congregations in Scotland, while yet without ministers, chose some to exhort, as well as elders and deacons, and in Edinburgh they seem to have done so as early as 1556 or 1557 (M'Crie's *Knox*, 1861, p. 140).

[2] P. 74, n.   [3] Pp. 1, 2.   [4] P. 26.   [5] P. 75.
[6] P. 103.   [7] Pp. 296, 439.   [8] P. 38.   [9] P. 42.

as—'sessione and ministerie,'[1] 'seat and ministerie,'[2] 'sessioun and seniouris,' 'assemblie and sessioun,'[3] 'sessioun and kirk.'[4] In such matters no doubt much was left to the clerk. From several incidental references it is evident that the deacons were not only present at the meetings of session, but were counted members of that body. For example, in 1570, the phrase occurs—'the assemblie of eldaris and deakins of the sessioun of the citie of Sanctandros';[5] and in 1571, 'the heal brethir of the sessioun and membris thairof' are described as 'minister, eldaris, and diaconis.'[6] After election they all seem to have sworn the same oath, and promised to obey the same rules.[7] Although there was a large staff both of elders and deacons in St. Andrews, from 1559 onwards, it might have been supposed that their respective duties had become somewhat mixed up, more especially as the attendance was often meagre; and that from merely being present to receive instructions and give advice, the deacons at length came to be regarded as members of session; but that a distinction of offices, in some measure at least, was still realised, is proved by the continued election of both.[8] In one of the earlier minutes, a culprit is mentioned as having been called before the 'minister, seniouris, and counsall';[9] in another, as before the 'minister, eldaris, and counsall';[10] and at an earlier date than either of these, a summons runs in the name of the 'ministre, eldaris, and diacons.'[11] Perhaps the word 'counsall' in the first two is equivalent to 'diacons' in the third; but all the three are prior to the *First Book of Discipline.* In the earlier minutes the phrase 'minister and elders' is used much oftener than 'minister, elders and deacons'; but the edict for Wynram's election is signed by three of the deacons as well as by the minister and

---

[1] P. 82.   [2] P. 315.   [3] P. 454.   [4] P. 344.
[5] P. 338.   [6] P. 348.   [7] Pp. 369, 370, 400, 413, 420, 432.
[8] Dr. Edgar points out that, 'In Mauchline Parish, and in many other parishes, it was long the custom to ordain men to the office of elder *and* deacon' (*Old Church Life*, second series, p. 6).
[9] P. 29.   [10] P. 38.   [11] P. 22.

seven elders.[1] In 1564, in a case of discipline, a supplication is sent to the magistrates from 'the minister, eldaris and diaconis';[2] and, in 1579, 'the minister, eldaris and diaconis' ordain and decern.[3] Letters of monition also run in their names;[4] and so do sentences in such important cases as the vindication of a condemned heretic,[5] and the commanding of a man to marry a woman against his will.[6] They are even introduced into sentences of excommunication:—'We, minister, eldaris and diaconis of Cristis kyrk and congregacion of Sanctandrois, are called as watchemen ower his flok.'[7] Moreover, there are indications that this practice was not confined to St. Andrews, that it was followed in Kirkcaldy,[8] Kinghorn,[9] and Crail.[10] The General Assembly, too, recognised other duties than the management of alms and revenues as pertaining to the deacons. In 1563, it was ordained that, in large parishes, the minister should ask the elders and deacons to help him in visiting the sick;[11] and in March 1572-3, a complaint having been given in by Mr. Robert Scott against Wynram, the Assembly not only found that the Superintendent had wronged him, but gave 'full power and commission to the ministers, elders and deacons of the congregation of Sanct Andrews, to take cognition, decide and conclude upon the whole rest of the said Roberts complaints yet undecided.'[12] Even after the adoption of the *Second Book of Discipline*, deacons were still regarded in St. Andrews as members of session;[13] and the yearly elections were kept up, with more or less regularity, until 1600; but these points can be better discussed after the second part of this *Register* is in type.

---

[1] P. 75. [2] P. 195. [3] P. 439.
[4] Pp. 261, 264. [5] P. 101. [6] P. 220.
[7] P. 203, see also pp. 274, 311. [8] Pp. 53, 54.
[9] Pp. 249, 250. [10] P. 258, 259. [11] *Booke of the Univ. Kirk*, i. 43.
[12] *Ibid.* i. 264.—In 1567, the 'Convention of the brethren, haldin . . . befor the Generall Assemblie,' thought 'it necessar that every minister, with the elders and deacons, sall search out within ther awin bounds at ther sessiouns' the 'crymes of incest and adulterie' (*Ibid.* i. 111). [13] P. 470.

At first, the weekly meeting of session was held on Thursday, with occasional meetings on other days; but in a short time Wednesday was chosen as the regular day. 'The scoole of Sanct Leonardis College' was, at least, once the place of meeting,[1] and 'the counsal-howse at the Auld College' was similarly honoured.[2] The parish church is mentioned more frequently, and sometimes the particular part of it is more clearly defined as 'the consaill hows wythin the parrochie kyrk,'[3] or 'abone paroche kirk dur,'[4] or 'the consistory hows abone the porche dur of the paroche kirk,'[5] or '*dominicula supra porticum templi parochialis.*'[6] Occasionally it is simply said to have been the council-house, but there can be little doubt that almost from the very first the meetings with few exceptions were in the parish church. In 1561 and also in 1570, two in the afternoon is mentioned as the hour of meeting.[7]

Allusion has already been made to the scant attendance at the meetings of session. Busy men would doubtless find it rather a severe tax on their time to be present at every meeting of session and at week-day preachings too. This was experienced ere the fervour of the Reformation was spent. In May 1561 'the minister elderis and deaconis present' consented that if any of their number were absent on a Wednesday he should pay a shilling; if he came after three o'clock, being in the city or vicinity, sixpence; and if he were only so late that the prayer was ended, threepence. To this there is the mysterious addition, that any one swearing an oath in the seat, 'unrequirit and admittit to sweir,' should pay twopence for each fault. In February 1567-8 this Act was ratified and approved, but augmented so that any one departing before the business was finished, without asking and obtaining leave, should pay threepence.[8] The Act was again ratified in

---

[1] P. 22. [2] P. 23. [3] P. 129.
[4] P. 18. [5] P. 52. [6] P. 61.
[7] Pp. 107, 342. [8] P. 72.

October 1570,[1] but there had evidently been laxity in the application, for in November 1572 the old Act is again copied into the *Register*, with the warning that the penalties are to be 'onforgevin ;[2] and in the following January it was ordained that, unless the absentees had a 'lawful impediment, and the sam apprevit be the sessioun,' they should 'be punisched according to the Act maid of befoir, wythtout exception of personis and forgeving to ony man.'[3] Even this was not enough, for in July 1574, 'in respect of the slaw convening of the brethir of sessioun to the ouklie assemblie,' the minister threatened to admonish them publicly from the pulpit 'to observe the ordour undir paine of excommunication.'[4] The same difficulty was experienced in other places, and quite as early; for, in July 1562, the General Assembly concluded that the minister should require 'his elders, and every ane of them,' to assist him in all his lawful assemblies, and that he should proceed against the negligent by admonitions, and, if necessary, should with the advice of the Superintendent excommunicate them, even although they were magistrates.[5] But in spite of penalty and threat, when an important case was to be tried, 'the haill sessioun' had to be specially warned; and the poor attendance may have been the chief cause why, at some periods, so few meetings seem to have been held. The duties were no doubt felt to be often difficult and delicate as well as arduous, and occasionally those who were elected declined the office:[6] the most notable refusal being that of Archibald Hamilton, who afterwards apostatised.[7]

It was on the 13th of April 1561 that Wynram was elected, in the parish church of St. Andrews, to be 'Superintendent of Fyff, Fotheryk and Strathern,'[8] or, as the extent of his diocese

---

[1] P. 342. [2] P. 370. [3] P. 373. [4] P. 396.
[5] *Booke of the Univ. Kirk*, i. 116. The fining method was adopted by the kirk-session of Aberdeen in 1568, the penalty for being absent was two shillings (*Ecclesiastical Records of Aberdeen*, Spald. Club, p. 14). A similar plan of enforcing attendance was used by the crafts and town-council of St. Andrews.
[6] P. 401. [7] P. 398. [8] P. 73.

is described in the *First Book of Discipline*, 'the hoill schirefdome of Fyffe and Fotheringhame, to Striveling; and the
hoill schirefdome of Perth.' After his appointment he seems
to have been frequently present at the meetings of session.
Generally, as will be noticed, in cases pertaining to the parish
of St. Andrews, the decisions run as before in the name of
the session; while in the cases which came before it from
Wynram's large district the decisions run in his name with its
advice;[1] and once, at least, he empowered it to act for him in
his absence.[2] In a somewhat remarkable case which affected
himself, Wynram handed over the jurisdiction to the minister
and elders ' as to the ministerie of the principall town of his
residence,' and acted himself as complainer. Wardlaw, a son
of the Laird of Torrie, had been parson of Balingry before
the Reformation, and, after Wynram's appointment as Superintendent, dispensed the sacraments without being admitted
by him to do so. On Wynram causing another to 'baptis
ane barin' there, Wardlaw resented the intrusion, and declared ' that he wald not be ane redar to Jhon Knox nor
ony other in Scotland'; and when that minister went to
the parish to celebrate a marriage, he forcibly prevented
him, so that Wynram had to go himself—leaving ' otheris

---

[1] The ministry or session formed in fact his council, pp. 107, 184, 231. While
this session was his lesser council, the synodal assembly of his province was his
greater council; but these were so far from being merely his assessors, that when
occasion required they might be his judges (*Booke of the Universall Kirk*, i. 29;
First Book of Discipline, fifth head). But, in some cases, it seems as if the
Superintendent and session exercised a joint jurisdiction, as, for example, in
the claim of adherence led by Alexander Cuningham against his wife. The
sentence runs in the names of the Superintendent, minister, and elders (P. 133);
but this is perhaps only a parallel to those sentences of the session in which the
deacons are similarly recognised. In the process between John Forret and
Elizabeth Leslie, a commission to examine an infirm witness was given to two
of the elders, by the Superintendent, minister, and elders, under the seal of the
ministry (PP. 123, 124); nevertheless, in the same process, the sentence runs in
the name of Wynram as 'juge in the caws,' and the only references to 'the
ministerie of Sanctandrois' in it are that its 'consall and sentement' was 'heirin
had and heard,' and the closing statement that several of its members were present at the pronunciation (PP. 130, 131).　　　　　[2] P. 321.

gret besines.' Still worse, when the Superintendent admonished him and the parishioners to repair the church, he openly
answered, 'The devill ane penny he wald spend upon the
kyrk!' And on the following day, in presence of the heritors,
he reviled Wynram, saying, 'he wald no nathing in that
behalve, nor obey ony admonision or command of that fals, dissaitfull, gredy, and dissimblit smayk, for he wes ane of tham
that maist oppressed, smored, and held down the Word of
God, and now he is cumin to it, and professis the same for
gredines of gayr, lurkand and watchand quhill he maye se ane
other tym!' He was so hot that he added, 'Or I war not
revenged of that fals smaik, I had lever renunce my part of
the kyrk of God!' He denied part of the articles laid to
his charge, and when the witnesses were produced objected to
them as enemies, although several of them were his near relatives. From the evidence it appears that he was so determined
to stop the minister from officiating in his church that he had
actually provided Jedwood staves in the chancel. A procurator conducted the case for Wynram, and the Session gave
sentence in his favour, and ordered Wardlaw to make public
satisfaction both in the church of St. Andrews and in that of
Balingry, under pain of excommunication.[1]

When an ecclesiastic could use such irreverent and violent
language, what was to be expected from the ignorant herd!
While Popery was still established by law, Agnes McKe was
charged with imputing the dearth that then prevailed 'to the
Word and doctryne now teachet in this cietie.' Her male-
volence, and that of several others at the same time, evidently
arose from their being debarred from the Lord's Supper. That
they were justly excluded is only too plain from the manner in
which they spoke of that sacrament. All their invectives need
not be quoted here, but one man was charged with saying:—
'The divell knok owt Johne Knox harnes, for quhen he wald se

---

[1] Pp. 82-89.

him hanget, he wald gett his sacrament!' and another with
saying;—'The divell ane kirk will I gang to! and, The divell
burn up the kirk or I come into it! and, It wer gude that
Knox war kend the gayt quhare fra he come!'[1] A more un-
disciplined set could hardly be imagined as fitting subjects for
the rigorous jurisdiction of a kirk-session. Yet in other places
the same evil spirit was displayed. The wife of a Crail bailie
rose in her parish church one day, and cried out against the
minister, John Melville, a brother of the famous Principal of
St. Mary's College:—'It is schame to yow that ar gentillmen
that ye pull hym nocht owt of the pulpot be the luggis!'[2]

Even before the appointment of the Superintendent two
cases from other places were brought before the St. Andrews
session. Alexander Lathrisk, indweller in Kirkcaldy, wished
to divorce his wife, but 'the minister, eldaris and diacons' of
that town refused to take up the case without the command of
the Lords of Privy Council. Lathrisk accordingly petitioned
the Lords, and they, perhaps distrusting the Kirkcaldy session
both for timorousness and incapacity, requested 'the ministeris
and eldaris of Sanctandrois' to do justice in the action. As
Lathrisk's wife was a notorious offender, there was little trouble
in proving her guilt. Witnesses were produced, and also a
'testimoniall' from eighteen of the inhabitants of Aberdour,
who, with delightful simplicity, described themselves 'as maist
part of the honestest men of the said toun.' Fortunately,
honesty and education are not necessarily allied, for only a
third of them could write their own names. The session found
that the woman ought to be divorced, and punished by the
magistrates, and that her husband should have liberty to marry
again, but referred 'the pronunciatioun and publicatioun of the
sentence to the minister of Kirkcaldy.'[3] The other case was
brought before the session by the petitioner herself, Alison
Calland, who in January 1558-9 had been contracted and

---

[1] Pp. 33-36.   [2] P. 107.   [3] Pp. 50-59.

married after 'the corrupted Papisticall maner' to James
Alexander, indweller in St. Monans. James proved to be an
unfaithful and cruel husband, and in less than five months
drove her out of his house. She wished to be divorced from
him, and to obtain liberty to marry another husband; and in
approaching the session of St. Andrews thus explained why she
came to it for relief:—'We are destitute of ministeris and
eldares, and in sick cais, for justice to be haid in tymes bypast,
hed ever recours to the said cietie of Sanctandrois as place of
justice.' Probably she had heard of the decision in Lathrisk's
favour, but had evidently dim ideas of the constitution of the
session. She addressed her petition to 'My lordis, minister and
eldares of the Christiane congregatioun of the cietie of Sanctandrois;' and besought their 'lordschipes,' 'with the weale
avysed counsall of the eldaris of this said cietie, to call the said
James Alexander before your lordschipes and them.'[1] A
'libellat citacion' was granted to her; and on the 5th of March,
1560-61, both she and her husband appeared before the session,
'submittyng tham to the jurisdiccione of this ministerie, and
to the disciplin of the kyrk,' each of them finding caution that
they 'sall obey and fulfyll the jugment, determinacion, and
sentence of this present ministerie, in this present caus, under
payn of payment of twenty liƀ., as sowm liquidat to be rasit
and distributit to the puyr.' Fully thirty witnesses were called
and examined; and sentence in Alison's favour was pronounced
in the consistory on the 14th, and publicly in the congregation
on the 18th of May 1561. Before the decision was given
Wynram had been appointed Superintendent, and the session
communicated 'the secretis of the said accione and caws' to

[1] There seems to have been much dubiety even in the city of St. Andrews, in
those early days, as to the proper mode of addressing the session. The following
forms are used :—'Your m. faithfull minister and eldaris of this cietie of Sanctandrois, and your assessouris' (p. 19); 'your wisedomes maist honorabill ministre
and counsale' (p. 20); 'honorabill sirs, minister, eldaris, and diacons' (p. 30);
'minister, eldaris, and counsale of this sette,' 'your nobilitie and wysedomes'
(p. 37); 'richt venerable minister and eldaris' (p. 44); and 'richt worschiphull
minister and eldaris' (p. 47).

him, and obtained ' his avysement and consent;' but the sentence was given by 'the minister and eldaris,' otherwise ' the
ministerie of the reformed kyrk and congregacion of the citie
and parrochyn of Sanctandrois,' and is signed by the minister
and eleven elders.[1]

Wynram's years must have rendered the discharge of his
onerous duties very burdensome, and ever and anon complaints
of his neglect were lodged in the General Assembly. At
length his labour was lightened, in an unexpected and rather
unwelcome manner, by the appointment of the aged John
Douglas to the Archbishopric of St. Andrews. The steps and
motives which led to the erection of Tulchan Prelacy in Scotland are too well known to require recapitulation here. In
the matter of his own exaltation, poor old Douglas was much
more of a helpless tool, than of a designing instrument, in the
hands of the politic and grasping Morton. From 1561 he seems
to have been regularly chosen an elder of this congregation,
and, on the 12th of October 1571, the list of elders is headed by
the name of ' Mr. Johne Dowglas, Archibischop and Rector
of Sanctandros.'[2] Before the latter date he had sat in Parliament as the Archbishop of St. Andrews, but was not yet
inaugurated. Though he is occasionally mentioned after this
in the *Register*, his name does not again appear in the list of
elders.[3] On the 6th of February 1571-2 Mareoun Schewes
and Henry Dikesoun appeared before the session, and they
are the last who are mentioned as having been summoned
' wytht the Superintendentis letteres to compeir befoir hym
and the seat';[4] on the 10th of that month Douglas was

---

[1] Pp. 63-72. The names of the subscribing elders correspond with those
elected in 1560 (P. 4), with one exception : 'Jhon Martyn' has been substituted
for 'Mr. Wilelmus Cok.'   [2] P. 350.

[3] Miles Coverdale, who was promoted to the See of Exeter under Edward VI.,
and ejected under Mary, was elected an elder of the English congregation at
Geneva, on the 16th of December 1558 (Professor Mitchell's *Livre des Anglois*,
p. 12). ' It is noteworthy that of the five English bishops then in exile, three
were members of Knox's congregation at Geneva ' (*Ibid.* p. 10).

[4] P. 361.

inaugurated by Wynram;[1] but, on the 21st, 'the Superintendent, wytht avis consent and assent of the seat,' made a
statute concerning the hours of preaching 'in tyme cuming.'[2]
The General Assembly met in St. Leonard's College, on the
6th of next month, and next day Wynram, of his own free will,
'dimitted the office of Superintendentrie, which he had within
the diocese of Sanct Andrews, in the Assemblies hands, requesting them most earnestly to provide for another in his
room, for the comfort of the Kirk, and visiting the ministers
within the foresaids bounds.' This demission was not accepted.
He was ordained 'to use his awin jurisdictioun as of befoir in
the provinces not yet subject to the Archbischoprick of Sanct
Androes;' and was requested 'to concurre with the said Archbischop, quhen he requyres him in his visitatioun or uther-
wayes within his bounds, quhill the nixt Generall Assemblie.'[3]
On the 12th day of that same 'March, the seat of St. Andrews
is mentioned as having ordained, 'wytht consent of Johne,
Archibischop of Sanctandros,' that all the elders and deacons of
the city should convene that day eight days, to remedy 'the
slaw convening of eldaris and deaconis to the ouklye assemblye.'[4] After this Wynram only appears to have been once
present at a meeting of session, and it was in the capacity of a
witness:[5] the place he had formerly occupied in it was now
taken by Douglas as Archbishop, by whose letters delinquents
from other parishes were summoned,[6] and in the trial of these
delinquents he was the judge, although the advice and consent
of the session were taken;[7] while in purely local cases he acted
with the session,[8] though the judgment seems to have belonged to it.[9] The General Assembly, which met in August
1572, declared that 'the diocie of Sanct Andrews, wheresoever
it lyeth,' pertained to 'the Bishop of Sanct Andrews, and to

---

[1] R. Bannatyne's *Memoriales*, Ban. Club, p. 223.   [2] P. 362.
[3] *Booke of the Univ. Kirk*, i. 239, 242.
[4] P. 362.   [5] P. 392.   [6] P. 366.
[7] P. 381.   [8] Pp. 367, 387.   [9] P. 377.

no other Superintendent to visite and plant kirks.' The
diocese of Douglas, as thus defined, included nearly the whole
of that part of the east coast of Scotland which lies between
the Tweed and the Dee. Staggered by its extent, and the
consequent responsibility, he answered that, because the bounds
were so great, and he was personally unable, he 'desired some
of the godliest and best learned to concurr with him in taking
order how the whole diocie may be served.'[1] Among the
brethren whose counsel he wished are the Superintendent of
Angus and Mearns and the Superintendent of Lothian, but
not Wynram, who however is still named in the proceedings of
this Assembly as the Superintendent of Fife.[2] From a question put at the same Assembly it is evident that the appointment of bishops had already caused some friction between
them and the superintendents.[3] The rules or acts of the
session of the 5th of November 1572 show how the regular
business was conducted, and on that account are worthy of
careful perusal; but one of them is of special interest in this
connection, as it refers to the transaction of business from
beyond the parish, and reveals the uncertainty which the
session still entertained regarding the respective jurisdictions
of the Superintendent and Archbishop.[4] Wynram is denominated 'Superintendent of Stratherne' in the three General
Assemblies respectively held in March 1572-3, August 1573,
and March 1573-4; but, in the seventh session of the latter,
he 'demitted purely and *simpliciter* his office in the hands of
the Assembly';[5] and Douglas died on the 31st of the following July. Wynram is mentioned as 'Prior of Portmook' in
the Assembly held in March 1574-5; in its third session
he received 'commission of a superintendentship . . . in the
bounds of Fife and Stratherne, exeeming the bounds apper-
taining to the Bishop of Dunkeld,'[6] and is thereafter called

---

[1] *Booke of the Univ. Kirk*, i. 243, 244.   [2] *Ibid.* 244, 247.
[3] *Ibid.* 249.   [4] Pp. 369, 370.
[5] *Booke of the Univ. Kirk*, i. 297.   [6] *Ibid.* i. 318.

by his old title—Superintendent of Fife—in that Assembly,
and also in the next, held in August 1575, which continued
him in his office ;[1] but in April 1576 his district was reduced
to 'Fife, from Sanct Andrews to Leven,' and though so much
curtailed he was to have the help of others.[2] The first allusion
in the *Register* to Patrick Adamson, as the successor of *D*ouglas,
is on the 13th of February 1576-7, and it relates to the summoning of a man from another parish 'to compeir befoir my said
Lord Bischop in this seat.'[3] There are other references to his
letters in the same case at a later date. In *D*ecember 1578 he
is termed 'my Lord of Sanctandrois, Bischop and Superintendent.'[4] After presbyteries were erected, there was no necessity
for the session dealing with the inhabitants of other parishes ;
and there is nothing in this part of the *Register* to show that
Adamson made any attempt to encroach on the rights of the
session.

The faithful exercise of discipline was long regarded as of
the highest moment. One of the three notes, by which our
Reformers distinguished the true Church from the false, was
' Ecclesiasticall discipline uprychtlie ministred, as Godis Word
prescribed, whairby vice is repressed and vertew nurished.'[5]
Indeed they went further, including the correction and punishment of offences among the things 'so necessarie, that without
the same thair is no face of ane visible kirk.'[6] 'There was
nothing,' says one eminently qualified to give an opinion, 'in
which the Scottish Reformers approached nearer to the primi-
tive Church than in the rigorous and impartial exercise of
ecclesiastical discipline, the relaxation of which, under the
Papacy, they justly regarded as one great cause of the universal

---

[1] *Booke of the Univ. Kirk*, i. 337.

[2] *Ibid.* i. 359—The exact date of Wynram's death is uncertain. It occurred
either on the 18th or 28th of September 1582 (Wodrow's *Collections upon the
Lives of the Reformers*, Mait. Club, i. 463, 468).

[3] Pp. 421, 422—The term *seat* was also applied to the see or episcopate
(*Booke of the Univ. Kirk*, i. 222, 226).   [4] P. 433.

[5] *Confession of Faith of* 1560, article xviii.

[6] *First Book of Discipline*, ninth head.

corruption of religion. . . . In some instances they might carry
their rigour against offenders to an extreme; but it was a
virtuous extreme, compared with the dangerous laxity, or
rather total disuse of discipline, which has gradually crept into
almost all the Churches which retain the name of reformed.'[1]
It would be difficult to describe the objects of discipline better
than is done in the *Book of Common Order*, or by George
Gillespie, in his definition of 'the end of ecclesiasticall power,
yea the end as well of the ministery itself, as of the godly
minister':—'That the kingdome of Christ may bee set forward, that the pathes of the Lord bee made straight, that
his holy mysteries may bee kept pure, that stumbling-blocks
may bee removed out of the Church, lest a little leaven
leaven the whole lump; or lest one sick or scabbed sheep infect
the whole flock; that the faithfull may so walk as it be-
cometh the Gospel of Christ, and that the wandering sheep
of Christ may be converted and brought back to the sheep-
fold.'[2] No class was exempted from its exercise, for, in the
seventh head of the *First Book of Discipline*, the broad rule
was laid down:—'To discipline must all estaitis within this
realme be subject, yf thay offend, alsweil the reullaris as thay
that are reulit; yea and the preachearis thame selfis, alsweill as
the poorest within the Churche.' The offences of which cognisance was taken, and the early regulations for the guidance of
church-courts in dealing with them, are to be found in that
book, and in those portions of the *Book of Common Order*
entitled *The Order of Ecclesiastical Discipline*, and *The Order
of Excommunication and of Public Repentance*. Practical illustrations of these dealings will be found in abundance in the
following pages.

Dr. Edgar concludes a most interesting and instructive
chapter on 'Marriages in Olden Times' by stating, 'I am
happy to say that the contentions in divorce suits form no part

---

[1] M'Crie's *Life of Knox*, 1861, p. 251.
[2] *CXI. Propositions concerning the Ministerie and Government of the Church*, 1647, p. 28.

of *Old Church Life in Scotland.*[1] The fact of the matter is, however, that, in the first few years after the Reformation, such cases occupied much of the time of the church-courts.[2] Two of these decided in the St. Andrews session have been already referred to; and several cases were taken up by this session while Popery was still established by law. In February 1559-60, William Rantoun lodged a petition, craving the divorce of his wife, Elizabeth Geddy. Proof was led, and in March Knox publicly pronounced sentence in her favour.[3] In May, she moved a claim against her husband, and sentence of divorce was given against him in January 1560-61.[4] Meanwhile a much more interesting case had been raised and disposed of. Margaret Archbald, spouse of David Gudlawde, had left him in 1524, gone over to Denmark, and there married another. David now petitioned the session, and on the 16th of March 1559-60 the minister and elders decerned him ' ane edict in the caus forsaid, upoun four-scoire days.' One copy of this edict, which was written in Latin, was fixed on the door of the parish church, and another despatched to Denmark. In due course a reply was received from ' Jhone Olufson, called Spaidmaker, minister of Lund, in Skonesyde; '[5] but it was in Danish, and the aid of William Christesone of Dundee had to be obtained to translate it, from which it may be inferred that there was then no Danish scholar in the university. Two witnesses were also examined, Scotchmen evidently, who had been abroad and testified what they had seen. Margaret did not appear in answer to the summons, and sentence was pronounced,

---

[1] *Old Church Life in Scotland*, second series, p. 203.
[2] See p. 268, n. 2.　　　[3] Pp. 18-27.　　　[4] Pp. 37, 59.
[5] For the following information concerning Olufsen, I am indebted to my friend, Mr. Maitland Anderson, who has drawn it from the *Kirkehistoriske Samlinger*, Kjöbenhavn, 1849-52, vol. i. pp. 389, 394:—Hans Spandemager was born in Malmö, his right name being Hans Olufsen (in Latin, Johannes Olavi). Before accepting the Reformed doctrines he belonged to the monastery of the Holy Ghost in Malmö. He was the first to join Mortensen in preaching the Reformed doctrines in his native city. He afterwards became parish priest in Lund and likewise Provost of the district of Torne, and died at an advanced age on 4th May 1571.

in November 1560, divorcing her and granting liberty to her
injured husband to marry another wife. This liberty he would
not be slow to exercise, for, in pressing for divorce, he had
urged that in respect of his age he could 'nocht be at ease
allane'; and had plainly stated that he wished to marry
'Catheryne Niesche, ane chaste virgyne past xl yeris of aige';
that he had given his 'faith and promise' to her, and that
their banns were duly proclaimed.[1] This was not the only
occasion on which a fugitive was divorced in absence. James
Martyn deserted his wife, Elizabeth Thecar, and, taking
Janet Alexander with him, crossed the sea to Lubke.[2] As his
departure was notorious, it was not deemed necessary to send
a summons after him; but he was openly cited, on the 18th of
May 1561, in the parish church, and the edict was thereafter
fixed on the principal door of that church. Sixty days were
allowed for his appearance, and in the interval, 'twa Scottismen,' who lived in that country, came here 'to sell the ladnyng
of thar schip.' They intended to leave again before the case
came up for decision, and so their evidence was taken before
two bailies in the Tolbooth. Sentence against Martyn was
given on the 23d of July.[3] It is noteworthy, that although
Wynram was acting as Superintendent before this case was
brought up, the session carried it through, apparently without
even consulting him; Elizabeth Thecar was doubtless a parish-
ioner, and Martyne's absence for five years did not place
him beyond its jurisdiction. Divorce was almost always sued
for on the ground of infidelity, but in one case the plea
was impotence. The procedure in that case, which was tried
before 'the Superintendent and ministery,' was very curious,[4]
but the continued cohabitation which was prescribed to the
parties had been customary under the Canon law.[5] It will
be observed that in every divorce case, the pursuer invariably

---

[1] Pp. 44-50. An application by the General Assembly to the Archbishops of
England concerning a fugitive wife, unlike the above, seems to have elicited no
response (Laing's *Knox*, vi. 534-538).   [2] Lübeck (?)   [3] Pp.77-81.
[4] Pp. 151-155.   [5] Riddell's *Peerage and Consistorial Law*, 1842, i. 536.

pleaded for liberty to marry again. This liberty was in accordance with the *First Book of Discipline;* and one of the things which the subscribers to the *Negative Confession,* of 1580, were bound to 'abhorre and detest' was the Roman Antichrist's ' crueltie agaynst the innocent devorced.' [1]

The divorce cases, which were brought before the session and the Superintendent, were far exceeded in number by the claims of marriage in which they decided. These claims were usually urged by frail maidens against their deceivers; but in one or two cases the petitioners were jilted swains, the fickle flirt having promised to marry two men.[2] Generally the women were victorious, no doubt having right on their side.

The reconciliation of ill-matched or quarrelsome couples was frequently undertaken by the session. It was sometimes, indeed, these well-meant attempts which led to a process ending in divorce; for if a man and his wife were living separately, they were ordered to adhere or show cause why they should not. But the efforts to restore harmony were occasionally crowned with success. One jealous husband, ' in signe of concord, amite, and simple remit of all displesor,' at the request of the venerable John *Douglas,* 'kissid and embraced' his spouse 'and drank to hyr.'[3] In another case, a man's wife, who confessed that she had not been so obedient ' as becam hyr of dewetie toward hyr husband and head,' at his desire on her knees asked him forgiveness, and her father became cautionar that in future she should be 'ane gud and faythfull wyff and servand' to him.[4] Women, too, freely forgave their erring husbands.[5] Nor were those at variance with their neighbours allowed to partake of the sacrament until reconciliation was effected.[6] And two hostile families were not only reconciled,

---

[1] Row's *History,* Wod. Soc. p. 75.—In a pre-Reformation book, traditionally associated with Wynram, it is stated :—' The partising and devorsing, quhilk our Salviour sais may be done for fornicatioun, suld be understand allanerly of partising fra bed and borde, and nocht fra the band of matrimony' (Hamilton's *Catechism,* 1882, fol. clxvii). [2] Pp. 48, 253.
P. 169.   [4] P. 192.   [5] Pp. 245, 284.   [6] Pp. 409, 410.

in presence of the session, 'in the luif and feir of God'; but, 'with thair awin consentis,' were bound that if any one of them should fail towards another, the offender should pay ten merks to the offended, and make public satisfaction in presence of the congregation.[1]

There are several references in the *Register* to hand-fasting, illustrating its forms and significance, and showing that it survived the Reformation. No matter how secretly espousals were made, if followed by copulation, they might annul the subsequent marriage of either party in the lifetime of the other; and therefore by the Synodal Statutes of Aberdeen and of St. Andrews, in the thirteenth century, it was required that espousals should take place before a priest and three or four trustworthy witnesses.[2] The same formula was not always used at these espousals or hand-fastings.[3] In his brief episcopate, 1515-1521, Andrew Forman deemed it necessary that clandestine espousals should be denounced under pain of excommunication, in every church of his diocese, four times a year; and that similar denunciations should be thundered against all those, who, after being hand-fasted, lived as man and wife, without being married in face of the church.[4] In the *Register*

---

[1] P. 477.

[2] *Concilia Scotiae*, Ban. Club, vol. i. pp. clxxxvi, clxxxvii.

[3] In or before 1518, David Johnson was thus espoused to Margaret Abernethy :—'I promytt to yow Begis Abirnethy that I sall mary yow and that I sall nevere haiff ane uther wiff and therto I giff yow my fayth.' Begis made promise to him in the same terms (*Liber Officialis Sancti Andree*, Abbot. Club, p. 21). In 1556, the vicar of Aberdour 'minestrat and execut the office anent the hand-fasting' betwixt Robert Lauder, younger of the Bass, and Jane Hepburn, daughter to Patrick, Earl of Bothwell, 'in thir wordis following :—I Robert Lawder tak yow Jane Hepburne to my spousit wyf as the law of Haly Kirk schawis, and therto I plycht yow my trewht; and siclyk, I the said Jane Hepburne takis yow Robert Lawder to my spowsit husband as the law of Haly Kirk schaws, and therto I plycht to yow my trewth and execut the residew of the said maner of handfasting conforme to the consuetud usit and wont in syk casis' (*Carte Monialium de Northberwic*, Ban. Club, p. 72). The form of words used by the man in marriage was, 'I tak the to my weddit wyfe,' and by the woman, 'I tak the to my maryit husband'; both of them adding—'In the name of the Father, and the Sonne, and the Haly Spreit' (Hammilton's *Catechism*, 1882, fol. clxvii, clxviii). [4] *Concilia Scotiae*, vol. i. p. clxxxvii.

there are instances both of secret [1] and open espousals, some of
the latter made before priests,[2] and others before the minister,
reader, or elders, and other witnesses.[3] Too often the parties
were content with that ceremony, as their forefathers had been
before them, and had to be compelled to celebrate their marriage openly under pain of excommunication. On the other
hand, others would have afterwards resiled had they not been
constrained to complete the band of matrimony. When the
espousals had been followed by copulation, the transgression of
either party with any other was regarded as adultery.[4] In
the case of John Fowlis and Mirabell Brown, the ceremony,
celebrated on a Sabbath-day, in 1563, before witnesses, was
simple enough. After agreeing with his future mother-in-law
as to 'towcher gude,' 'the said Jhon be laying his hand in the
hand of Mirabell promyst to marie hyr, and sche promyst to be
gud servand to hym.'[5] In the case of James Thomson and
Janet Smyth, one witness deponed that he 'promittit of his
gear to the said James iiij lib̄., and Simon Adam promittit
iiij bollis malt;' while another testified 'that he heard and saw
the promis maid and held up handis for performing of the
premissis.'[6] St. Andrews was by no means the only place
where the evil custom which had so long attended hand-fasting
lingered after the Reformation.[7]

---

[1] Pp. 29, 145, 330.   [2] Pp. 182, 285.
[3] Pp. 248, 249, 280. —On one occasion an elder used a most extraordinary
formula ; nothing like it will be found in any manual ancient or modern.
[4] Pp. 61, 246, 253, 255.   [5] P. 230.   [6] P. 316.
[7] In Aberdeen it seems to have been much more prevalent, and steps were
also taken there to make them complete their marriage (*Ecclesiastical Records of
Aberdeen*, Spald. Club, p. 11) ; and in 1568 it was ordained, 'that nether the
minister nor reader be present at contractis off mariage-making, as thai call
thair handfastinis' (*Ibid.* p. 14). From at least the days of St. Malachy until a
much later period, marriages in Ireland 'were usually contracted only by
sponsalia de futuro' (Lanigan's *Ecclesiastical History of Ireland*, iv. 64, 70-72).
Sir Walter Scott refers to a most pernicious custom known as hand-fasting on
the Borders. Avenel thus explains its nature to Warden :—'We Bordermen
are more wary than your inland clowns of Fife and Lothian—no jump in the
dark for us—no clenching the fetters around our wrists till we know how they
will wear with us—we take our wives, like our horses, upon trial. When we

The attention of the session was early directed to the formalities of marriage. An act concerning the proclamation of banns was made on the 20th of June 1560, requiring both the parties, if they lived within the parish, to appear personally before the session-clerk; and if either the man or the woman lived in another parish, and the marriage was in this church, that the stranger should bring a testimonial of the due proclamation of the banns.[1] In 1569 'Maister Andro Kircaldy' was ordered to pass to Kilconquhar church, and there 'upon ane Sunday' to 'ask God and the congregation forgevenes, for solemnizing of mareage of Johne Wemis and Effem Wemis, umquhill Lady of Kilconquhar, by al guid ordour and wythout proclamation of bannis.'[2] In the same summer, and seemingly in the same church, at the proclamation of the banns for the third time between George Dischington and Janet Calland, the Lady of Carmurie and her servant 'interponit thame selves, allegeand that they had sum resonable causis to propone and allege quhy the saidis parteis mycht nocht nor sould nocht proceid to completing and solemnizing of the band of mareage;' but, as they never appeared before the session, though sundry times called on, to give their reasons, the minister of Kilconquhar was ordained to proceed with the marriage.[3] In March 1570-71, the question was put in the General Assembly, 'Is it not expedient and necessar, that an uniform order be observed in all kirks, in making promises of marriages, quhither they shall be made *per verba de futuro, vel verba de præsenti;* or should no promise be made till the solemnization?' The

---

are hand-fasted, as we term it, we are man and wife for a year and day; that space gone by, each may choose another mate, or, at their pleasure, may call the priest to marry them for life—and this we call handfasting' (*The Monastery*, chap. xxv). In the upper part of Eskdale multitudes of each sex are said to have resorted to an annual fair where they were handfasted, went off in pairs, and after living together for a year declared their dislike or approbation of each other at the next fair, when they were either married for life, or the engagement rendered void. It is also stated that this custom prevailed in the Hebrides, that it was practised in the north of Scotland, and that traces of it are found in France (Jamieson's *Dictionary*, where the authorities are quoted).

[1] P. 42.   [2] P. 319.   [3] P. 321.

answer was, 'Promise of marriage *per verba de futuro* sall be made, according to the ordour of the reformed Kirk, to the minister, exhorter or reidar; takeand caution for abstinence till the marriage be solemnizit.'[1] In August 1575 the following question was put in the General Assembly, 'Whether the contract of marriage used to be made before the proclamation of banns betwixt man and woman, should be made be words of the present tyme, the man saying to the woman, I take thee to be my wife, and the woman saying to her husband, I take thee to be my husband; or should there no contract or promise be made while the instant time of solemnization of the marriage?' To this it was answered, 'Let the order observed within the reformed Kirk of Scotland be keeped. Parties to be maried sould come before the Assemblie, and give in thair names, that thair bands may be proclaimit, and no farther ceremonies usit.'[2] If, when espousals were made before witnesses, the man used the words 'I take thee to be my wife,' and the woman, 'I take thee to be my husband,' it is not surprising that many of the people, with their old notions of hand-fasting, should think themselves already married. In February 1576-7, the question came up in the session, as if it had not been already decided by the General Assembly, and it was 'thocht gude that the parteis that ar to mak promis of mareage cum befoir the seat, and gyf up thair names in wryte, quhilk salbe deliverit to the redar, and the promis to be maid *per verba de futuro* in tyme cuming.'[3] And in July 1578, Henry Scot, *alias* Kilmoun, in presence of the seat, made 'promis of mariage to Agnes Meffen, be deliverance of his hand to the said Agnes, and to solempnizat the band and promis of mareage maid be hym to hir in face and visage of the kirk.'[4] This case however was exceptional, as the parties already had a child to baptize; and no ceremony is mentioned in connection with the two

---

[1] *Booke of the Universall Kirk*, i. 195, 196.
[2] *Ibid.* i. 343.   [3] Pp. 421. 422.   [4] Pp. 429, 430.

couples who came before the seat on the 13th of March
1576-7.[1]

The requirements of the *First Book of Discipline*, that
marriage should be celebrated in face of the congregation, and
on Sabbath, were long adhered to rigidly; but in March 1569-
70, because of Patrick Ogilvy's 'grite infirmite and seiknes,'
the session, at the request of his father-in-law, allowed him to
be married on Wednesday.[2] In the General Assembly of July
1579, questions were put concerning marriage on other days
of the week, from which it appears that there was considerable
diversity of practice and therefore ' no small slander among the
people.' The Assembly granted liberty to solemnise it on any
day of the week, provided that there was a sufficient number
of witnesses present, and that the banns were proclaimed on
three Sabbaths.[3] Although one of the questions had been
'proponed be the Synodall Assemblie of Sanct Andrews,' the
session waited until December 1580 before stating ' that it
salbe lesum to marie in all tym cuming upone Wadnisday.'[4]
This delay was the more remarkable as, in 1570, it had been
found necessary to supplicate the magistrates 'for reformatioun of the grite abuse usit be new mareit personis in violatioun of the Sabbat day.' Not only did these persons absent
themselves from the preaching in the afternoon, but after
supper in the evening, to the evil example of others, they per-
turbed ' the town wytht rynning thair throw in menstralye
and harlatrye.'[5] Perhaps the measures of the magistrates had
been so drastic that the bad example was not repeated.

In February 1567-8, for special reasons, liberty was granted
to the Provost of Kirkhill to solemnise his marriage in another
parish.[6] And in 1572 a couple of sinners were married on the
same Sabbath as the woman made her ' satisfaction and repentance.'[7] In June 1575, Elizabeth M^cke, who had alleged, but
failed to prove, that her father compelled her to be hand-fasted

---

[1] P. 423. [2] P. 332. [3] *Booke of the Universall Kirk*, ii. 439-441.
[4] P. 452. [5] P. 341. [6] Pp. 293, 294. [7] P. 363.

with Thomas Read, was ordered to marry Read under pain of excommunication.[1] Neither the marriage nor the penalty was carried out in haste; for, nearly four years later, she was again ordained ' to proceid to mareage witht the said Thomas, undir sic pains as the kirk may lay to hir chairge.'[2] Perhaps one of the most important and salutary enactments concerning marriage was drawn up in 1579. Its importance is stamped in the margin with a double *nota*, and in its first line, running as it does in the name of the ' minister, eldaris, and diaconis.' It ordained, ' that, in tyme cuming, nane be resavit to compleit the band of matrimonye, wythtout thay rehers to the redar the Lordis Prayeris, Beleve, and the Commandementis of God.'[3] It was no doubt because of the session's jurisdiction in matrimonial matters that, in 1562, Eufame Colt asked it to decern that she was the lawful daughter of ' umquhill Jhon Colt and Cristen Kyrk.'[4]

The faults and failings with which the session had to deal were of many kinds, but the sin of fornication outnumbered them all. Strenuous and unremitting efforts were put forth to suppress this vice in all its forms. Over and above the pains of discipline, it was deemed advisable to imprison transgressors in the steeple, the period being increased in aggravated cases.

Death was regarded as the due desert of adultery and incest. Church-courts had no power to inflict such a penalty, but the discipline which penitents of this class had to undergo, ere they were again received into the bosom of the Church, was very severe. St. Andrews was occasionally scandalised by such heinous sins, and when the *fama* broke out, a searching investigation was at once begun by the session.

In the spring of 1568, the session began to exercise a strict vigilance over Sabbath-breakers. The attendance at Sabbath markets was one of the commonest forms of this sin, and one of the most difficult to eradicate.[5] Craftsmen too plied their

---

[1] P. 410. [2] P. 434. [3] P. 439.
[4] P. 147. [5] Pp. 294, 416, 479-481.

avocations on that day, and of these the fleshers were the most
perverse and stubborn.[1] Sins of the harvest were not unknown. One man was taken to task for threshing corn, another
for leading corn, and a third for binding beans.[2] A married
woman was 'decernit in tyme cuming to desist fra keping of
taverine upon the Sabbat day' under pain of forty shillings,
'and to mak public repentence upon the penitent stule.' This
decreet was given forth with her husband's consent as well as
her own.[3] A baker's wife, who had been guilty of 'selling of
candil and braed on Sundays,' of absenting herself from the
church, of 'mis-saying and disobedient to hir husband,' was
ordered to desist in future under the pain of £10, ' and to sit
in the joiggis xxiiij howris.' Nothing is said about her or her
husband's consent to this decreet. Her own would doubtless
have been refused ; and her husband, however willing, would
not have dared to give his. Raw material of her kind would
not be too plastic in the hands of the session. She was likewise delated 'for fliting wytht hir nychtbouris, and selling of
bread tyme of sermon on Sunday.'[4] With all their sternness
the members of session were only human, and once were guilty
of sanctioning Sabbath profanation. The daughter of Thomas
Balfour, a bailie and an elder, was married on the 1st of
August 1574, and the session gave liberty on that occasion ' to
play the comede mentionat in Sanct Lucas Evangel of the Forlorn Sone.' It was stipulated, however, 'that playing thairof
be nocht occasioun to wythdraw the pepil fra heryng of the
preaching, at the howre appointed als weil eftir nune as befoir
nune.'[5] This relaxation was not overlooked by the General
Assembly, and the session did not repeat the experiment. In
the following March, all the inhabitants, 'spetialy yowng men,'
were publicly warned from the pulpit, 'that nane of them
presume nor tak upon hand to violat the Sabbat day, be using

---

[1] Pp. 309, 314, 349, 364, 365, 403.   [2] Pp. 374, 380.
[3] P. 421.   [4] P. 343.
[5] P. 396.

of playis and gemmis publiclie as they war wont to do, contrafating the playis of Robein Huid.'[1]

Closely allied with Sabbath profanation, regarded indeed as
a form of it, was non-attendance at church. This habit had
been very prevalent before the Reformation. 'One canon,'
of the General Provincial Council of 1552, 'sets forth that,
even in the most populous parishes, very few of the parishioners come to mass or to sermon; that in time of service,
jesting and irreverence go on within the church, sports
and secular business in the porch and the churchyard.'[2]
The session tried various plans to remedy this evil. The
absentees were ordered to attend in future under pain of
excommunication;[3] James Makke, who seems to have been
guilty of open violation of the Sabbath as well, was to
pay forty shillings to the poor if he again transgressed;[4]
the help of the Magistrates was implored;[5] and in 1576 a
termagant was informed that if she were again delated as
'ane bannar or blasphemar of hir husband, or not to cum to
the sermon on the Sabbat day,' she should 'sit in the gok stule
xxiiij howris.'[6] Perhaps the most efficacious plan was that
adopted in June 1574, which was meant not only for Sabbath-
preaching, but for week-day services, and which was to be
extended in its application to students, inhabitants, and all
sojourners. Captors were chosen 'to vesy the hail town.' It
was arranged that 'every Sunday thair sal pas and vesy ane
bailye, ane elder, twa diaconis, and twa officeris inarmit wytht
thair halbartis.' Lest these might have been insufficient to
cope with the delinquents 'the rest of the ballies and officeris'
were to be in readiness, 'to assist them to apprehend the
transgressoris, to be punisched conform to the actis of the
kirk.'[7]

It will be observed that in the *Register* for several years

---

[1] P. 406.
[2] *Concilia Scotiæ*, vol. i. p. cli.
[3] Pp. 309, 337, 338.
[4] P. 363.
[5] P. 373.
[6] P. 420.
[7] Pp. 394, 395.

after the Reformation, the Lord's Day is invariably denominated Sunday not Sabbath. The retention of old names is somewhat remarkable, and serves to illustrate the power of habit. Excommunication is sometimes called cursing;[1] and discipline, penance.[2] The former names of special days are frequently used, such as—Rood-day, Michaelmas, St. Stephen's day, Pasch, All-hallow day, St. Luke's day, Mary-day or Marimas, St. James' day, Palm Sunday, Cayr Sunday, Low-Sunday, Mid-Sunday, Fasterennis-e'en, Yule; and also those which are still in common use — Candlemas, Whitsunday, Lammas, and Martinmas. Of these, Yule is generally mentioned only to have its observance denounced. It was not enough that the superstitious customs, which clung tenaciously to it, should be given up; but its devotees must on no account abstain from work on that day, that being a violation of the Sabbath, 'quhilk only sould be kept haly day.' One mason had to promise that if no one employed him, he would 'wirk sum riggen-stanis of his awin.' Another craftsman tried to stir up opposition among his fellows, saying, that 'it becam nocht honest men to sit upon the penitent stule,' and that he was 'ane yowng man and saw Zwilday kepit halyday, and that the tyme may cum that he may see the like yit.' He was very bold, but a fortnight later offered 'to undirlye the correction quhatsumevir the ministerye wil injone to hym.'[3] Possibly this craftsman lived to see the tables turned, for forty-seven years afterwards Archbishop Spottiswoode wrote from St. Andrews:—'I know his Majesty will desire to hear of our observation of Christmas, which in this city was never better keeped, with great confluence of

---

[1] Pp. 36, 41, 308.

[2] Pp. 29, 302.—It is frequently called punishment in the *Register*, but Rutherfurd objected to the use of that term. 'No medicine,' he said, 'is received unwillingly by wise men, and no medicine is a punishment.' See his *Divine Right of Church Government and Excommunication*, 1646, pp. 632, 633.

[3] Pp. 387-390, 404.

people to church, and a generall cessation of people from work, our tailyour excepted, whom I caused punish for his contempt.'[1]

It appears that 'William Stewart, sumtyme Lioun King of Armes,' was tried and burned at St. Andrews, in 1569, for 'witchcraft, nigromancye, and utheris crymes.'[2] And it is certain, that on the 28th day of April 1572, a witch was burned in St. Andrews. James Melville, who was an eye-witness of her execution, says that Knox dealt against her from the pulpit, 'sche being set upe at a pillar befor him';[3] and Richard Bannatyne preserves some details of the tragedy.[4] As there is no reference whatever to either case in the *Register*, they must have been tried before another tribunal, probably a civil court. The first trial for witchcraft before the session did not take place until the 18th of January 1575-6. Before next Wednesday the reputed witch and her husband fled, one witness testifying that the unhappy man had said, 'that for hym self he durst byde, bot yit his wyffe feared, and thairfoir they durst not byde.'[5] She does not seem to have been in custody, nor did she appear before the session, and, so far as the *Register* shows, no attempt was made to capture her. In October 1581, Bessy Robertson was delated 'for nevir cuming to the kirk nor communioun,' and 'for witchcraft.' It was ordained that she should be openly warned by the reader, 'to compeir on Weddinsday nixt to answer befoir the sessioun.'[6] With the warning she apparently did not comply, and no further action seems to have been taken in the matter.

There were many other offences which were punishable by the magistrates as crimes, but of which the session took cognisance so far as the slander was concerned. Of these, references will be found in the *Register* to cases of murder,[7]

---

[1] Gordon's *Scotichronicon*, i. 460.   [2] Laing's *Knox*, vi. 692.
[3] Melville's *Diary*, Wod. Soc. p. 58.
[4] Bannatyne's *Memoriales*, Ban. Club, p. 233.
[5] Pp. 414-416.   [6] P. 455.   [7] P. 422.

slaughter,[1] blasphemy,[2] usury,[3] personal violence,[4] banning,
and slandering.[6] The session was ever ready to help the
weak or oppressed. Having heard that a child had been
burned to death, the parents were called and rigorously
examined;[7] and so were the parents of a child that had been
overlaid.[8] A young man, too, who it was supposed had been
hardly used by his 'gude-fathir,' was called and questioned.[9]
And a young woman, who had been forcibly abducted, applied
to the Superintendent and session for such remedy as they
'mycht of Goddis law mak to hir.'[10]

The session had no hesitation in dealing with 'playaris at
cairtis and dyce.' These were warned that future offences
would necessitate their appearance on the penitent stool, and
the infliction of a fine for behoof of the poor.[11] In those days
there were several drunkards in St. Andrews, as it must be
confessed there are still. One of these was charged in 1574
with his weakness, aggravated by working on Sabbath, and
was 'admonesed to desist and ceas thairfra in tyme cuming,
undir al biest paine that the kirk may lay to his charge.'[12]
This does not seem to have terrified him; for, six months
afterwards, it was resolved that if he should be again delated
for drunkenness, he should sit upon the highest penitent stool,
'witht ane paper about his head, and his falt writtin thairintil.' And the general warning was added for sympathetic
sinners—'This to strek upon al drunkatis.'[13]

The last-named punishment seems absurd enough, but it was
not unprecedented. In 1564 a man, who had two years before
contemned 'the ministerie of Carnbe,' and had since been
excommunicated, was ordered 'to compeir' on the following

---

[1] Pp. 439, 440.   [2] Pp. 43, 44, 482.   [3] P. 309.
[4] Pp. 329, 447, 478.   [5] Pp. 225, 343, 420.   [6] Pp. 176, 399, 451.
[7] P. 424.   ·   [8] P. 468.   [9] P. 418.
[10] P. 343.
[11] Pp. 314, 432.—A curious obligation to abstain from cards, dice, chess, and
tables for a year will be found in the Appendix to the *Carte Monialium de
Northberwic*, Ban. Club. pp. 70, 71.
[12] P. 403.   [13] Pp. 409, 410.

Sabbath, 'at the kyrk of Carnbe ane hour befoyr the prechyn, and thar at the kyrk dur space foyrsayd stand in the jogis, wyth ane papar abowt his head, contenyng wryttyn tharupon, BEHALD THE CONTEMPNAR. And siclyik to stand in sum public place of the kyrk of Carnbe, wyth the paper abowt his head duryng the tym of the prechyng, and at the end tharof confes his offence,' etc.[1] In 1579, an erring husband, who had grievously injured his wife, was condemned 'to sitt down upone his kneis,' in presence of the congregation, and, holding 'his awin tung in his hand,' pronounce the words :—'Fals tung thow leid.'[2]

The commonest form of punishment inflicted was a more or less protracted appearance on the penitent stool, penitent seat, or stool of repentance, as it is called. One poor wretch is mentioned as having sat 'bot ten Sundais,' and he was 'yit to sit ten several Sundayis.'[3] That it was no commonplace stool, or anything resembling those still preserved in the parish church, is quite evident, from the references to the different elevations on which penitent sinners of the various classes had to sit. Once the phrase occurs, 'the umest penitent stuil,'[4] and again, 'the umest stuil of repentence';[5] and from these it might have been inferred that there were various stools of different heights; but in other places these expressions are found, 'the penitent stuill and mid gre thairof,'[6] 'the hieest of the penitentis saiet,'[7] 'the penitent stuill, in the adultraris place and gre,'[8] and 'the adultraris place of the penitent stuill.'[9] But with all its shame, the penitent stool could hardly be considered a punishment to some vile offenders, one of those already mentioned was admonished to 'ascend and discend thairupone moderatlie.'[10]

---

[1] P. 229.

[2] P. 441.—In 1610, a woman in Aberdeen was ordained to use similar words, but was not asked to hold her tongue while doing so (*Ecclesiastical Records of Aberdeen*, Spald. Club, p. 75). This and most of the other punishments, adopted in St. Andrews in particular cases, were inflicted in Aberdeen under 'certane actis and statutis' devised by Heriot and the session in 1562 (*Ibid.* pp. 5-12).

[3] P. 402.   [4] Pp. 409, 410.   [5] P. 426.   [6] P. 378.
[7] P. 385.   [8] P. 452.   [9] Pp. 463, 476.   [10] P. 441.

There are more than a dozen references to sackcloth as the
special garb of the penitent, one to 'the gown maid for adultereris,'[1] and another to a penitent in linen clothes.[2] Wealthy
sinners would gladly have paid a pecuniary penalty to escape
part of the humiliating public satisfaction; but the General
Assembly, in 1573, declared that 'Na superintendent nor commissioner, with advyse of any particular kirk of thair jurisdictioun, may dispence with the extremitie of sack-cloth prescryvit
be the acts of the generall discipline, for any pecuniall sowme
or paine *ad pios usus.*'[3] In March 1563-4, an adulterer was
ordered to pay a sum, not exceeding £10, for the poor, or
'kyrk-work;'[4] and next year a fine was imposed on two inces-
tuous persons.[5] It is not said that the rigour of discipline was
to be mitigated in consequence, and in the latter case it was
certainly severe.

Some kinds of transgressions were visited with pecuniary
penalties over and above the regular satisfaction on the stool.
These were fornication,[6] not revealing sin,[7] Sabbath-breaking,[8]
being a Papist and maintainer of Papistry,[9] absence from communion and examination,[10] and slander.[11] In the last case the
money thus exacted was to be devoted to 'the commoun wark
of this citie;' but generally all such penalties were destined for
the poor. Besides these fines, men were ordered to 'tocher'
women they had wronged and would not marry,[12] and others
were decerned to support their illegitimate offspring.[13] In
August 1573, it was asked in the General Assembly :—
'Whither if the Assembly may lawfully impone pecuniall
pains to the committers of drunkenness, fornication, breach of
the Sabbath, and such like, or not.' It was answered :—'The
Assembly ordains, That, anent fornication, and the breach of
the Sabbath, the Acts of Parliament be putt in execution: as

---

[1] P. 444.   [2] P. 401.   [3] *Booke of the Univ. Kirk*, i. 284.
[4] P. 191.   [5] P. 233.   [6] Pp. 232, 378.   [7] P. 400.
[8] Pp. 363, 421.   [9] P. 333.   [10] Pp. 317, 409.   [11] P. 451.
[12] Pp. 186, 322, 358.   [13] Pp. 304, 486.

for drunkenness, They should give admonitions, which being disobeyed, they shall be repelled from the table of the Lord; yet magistrates may inflict a pecuniall pain for the same, while order be tane in Parliament.'[1]

Imprisonment was also resorted to as a terror to evil-doers. In February 1568-9, Andro Alexander, *alias* Gossept Andro, was admonished by the Superintendent and seat that in future he should 'suffer na opin cairting and dysyng, nycht walking and drynking in his hows, under paine of excommunication and impresoning of his persoun.'[2] In every other case, perhaps, where imprisonment is mentioned, it was to be inflicted for adultery or fornication. Others than citizens might be received to discipline for these sins, but were not liable to imprisonment; they were sometimes asked, however, to remember the poor instead.[3] In April 1576, it was statute and ordained by the session 'that fra this furtht that al transgressoris, sic as fornicatoris and adulteraris, be impresoned in the steple of the parroche kirk of this citie, thair to remain according to the ordour.'[4] Evidently solitary confinement in the steeple could only be secured by imprisoning one transgressor at a time.[5] In October 1577, the session was so well ·satisfied with the 'gude service' of the beadle 'in keping of the presoun hows,' that it was ordained that every one—man or woman—imprisoned in future should pay him two shillings before they were released.[6] Yet mercy was mixed with judgment, for one woman, 'in respect of the vehemensie of the storme,' was released in the midst of her term, caution being found that she would afterwards re-enter.[7]

Banishment was adopted for some heinous offenders. In October 1562, a man was ordered to find cautioners, and to

---

[1] *Booke of the Univ. Kirk*, i. 284.　　[2] Pp. 313, 314.
[3] Pp. 363, 477.　　[4] P. 417.
[5] Pp. 462, 463, 471, 484. In 1579 a couple of fornicators were ordered to enter into prison on the same day (P. 444), but that does not appear to have been tried again.
[6] Pp. 427, 428.　　[7] P. 466.

have the obligation entered in the Sheriff Books of Fife, that
if he were again convicted of his sin he should be banished
from the county for life.[1] And in March 1581-2, a woman
was ordained to leave the parish within fifteen days; and
supplication was to be directed to the magistrates to that
effect.[2]

In March 1563-4, a confirmed harlot was condemned to
'ane hour in the jogis' at the Market Cross.[3] Reference has
already been made to a man suffering this punishment at
Carnbee in 1574,[4] and to a baker's wife, who was threatened
with it in 1576.[5]

Still another form of punishment was behind all these. In
1574 a married woman who had 'heavely sclanderit' a neigh-
bour was warned that, if she did the like again, she should
'sitt in the gok-stuil duryng the magistrattis will.'[6] And, in
1576, a woman, who was outrageous to her husband, and did
not attend the church, was threatened that if she repeated
either offence she should 'sit in the gok-stule xxiiij howris.'[7]

That imprisonment, the most frequently inflicted of these
punishments, was not regarded by the session as forming any
part of ecclesiastical discipline is clearly implied in several
passages, where entering into prison is distinguished from
satisfying the church.[8] But the question naturally arises, If
these penalties formed no part of church discipline, what right
had the session to impose them? Or, it may be asked, Were
the civil and ecclesiastical jurisdictions confounded? It might
be answered that the church courts had no power to inflict
such penalties; and that, to a cursory reader, they apparently
usurped civil authority. In the *Second Book of Discipline* the
two jurisdictions are distinguished with great precision, and
there are many incidental statements in this *Register* which
show that from the very first the session recognised that civil
punishments belonged to the civil magistrates. Offenders are

---

[1] Pp. 173, 174. [2] P. 475. [3] P. 191. [4] P. 229.
[5] P. 343. [6] P. 399. [7] P. 420. [8] Pp. 358, 467.

frequently committed, or remitted to the bailies for civil correction;[1] and in pronouncing sentence against an adulterer,
whose crime was deemed worthy of death, it is expressly said
of the magistrate, 'to quhome we will that this our sentence
prejudge nathing.'[2]   Supplications were sent to the magistrates not only asking them to punish evil-doers for the civil
aspect of their offences,[3] but for their disobedience to the
session ;[4] or requesting them to cause the obstinate to submit
to discipline ;[5] and the mere fact that the aid of the magistrates had to be invoked shows that the session had no power
to enforce civil pains.   Long after this period, Principal
Baillie, in reply to Bishop Maxwell, says : ' No church-
assembly in Scotland assumes the least degree of power to
inflict the smallest civill punishment upon any person ; the
Generall Assembly it selfe hath no power to fine any creature
so much as in one groat: it is true the lawes of the land
appoint pecuniary mulcts, imprisonment, joggs, pillories, and
banishment for some odious crimes,[6] and the power of putting
these laws in execution is placed by the Parliament in the
hands of the inferiour magistrates in burroughs or shires, or of
others to whom the Counsel Table gives a speciall commission
for that end ; ordinarily some of these civill persons are ruling
elders, and sit with the eldership : so when the eldership have
cognosced upon the scandall alone of criminall persons, and
have used their spiritual censures only to bring the party to
repentance, some of the ruling elders, by vertue of their civill
office or commission, will impose a mulct, or send to prison or
stocks or banish out of the bounds of some little circuit.'[7]
Dr. M'Crie states that, in all instances recorded in *The Buik of
the Kirk of Canagait*, where any civil penalty is added to the

---

[1] Pp. 41, 58, 150, 168, 324, 374, 377, 478, and many others.
[2] P. 60.
[3] Pp. 223, 247, 251, 315, 353, 423, 440.   [4] Pp. 245, 448, 465, 467.
[5] Pp. 138, 149, 373, 459.   [6] See p. 451, n.
[7] Baillie's *Historical Vindication*, 1646, pp. 17, 18.   See also Gillespie's *Nihil
Respondes*, 1645, p. 24 ; and his *Male Audis*, 1646, pp. 43, 44.

ecclesiastical, the expression is used—' the baillies assistane the assemblie of the kirke ordains,' &c.[1]   If this distinction was always kept in view in the kirk-session of St. Andrews, the clerks have frequently failed to observe it; but in justice it must be added that, from the very beginning, there always appear to have been two or three bailies in the session; and in one case at least their civil office was clearly recognised—' the Superintendent and ministerie committis the saidis Jhon Duncan and Bege Mychell in the handis of the baillies present, to be civile correckit and punist.'[2]   Still two stubborn facts remain—the transgressors were imprisoned, not in the tolbooth, but in the church-steeple; and the jailer was not a town-officer, but the beadle.

Many interesting references will be found in the *Register* to the dispensation of the sacraments, including the examination which preceded the Lord's Supper, and a very early notice of communion tokens; to the care and relief of the poor; to the repelling and receiving of witnesses and procurators; to the length of sermons; to fasting; to the systematic visitation of the town; and to the custom of taking caution.   The names of ministers and readers too will be found who are not mentioned in Scott's *Fasti*, nor probably elsewhere.

Among the more interesting and prominent cases are those of John Bicarton, whose defection began by refusing to present his own child to baptism, and whose stubborn and outspoken defiance led to his excommunication; of the aged Lady Lindsay who wished to marry again after her husband's death; of her daughter, the widow of the gallant Norman Leslie, who married a Cupar merchant against the will of her parents, and kept his booth for him, but afterwards denied that she was his wife; of Joanna Hepburn, a natural daughter of the Bishop of Moray, who was forced into a promise of marriage, but was released by the session; and of Janet Wemyss, who wished to be divorced from Robert Boswell, and who threatened, in

---

[1] M'Crie's *Melville*, 1824, i. 474.   [2] P. 141.

presence of the session, 'to caus ding owt' all his 'harnis,' who was accompanied by a number of 'barronis, gentyllmen and frendis,' and who afterwards, in connection with Mr. Jhon Dalglesh, gave the session ten times more trouble than before.

The original *Register* is a foolscap folio containing 300 leaves, but four of the pages are blank. The 27th of October 1559 is the earliest date prefixed to an entry, and the last is the 7th of October 1600. David Spens had boldly written the title high on the first page, the list of office-bearers of 1559 on the second page, and then passed on to the third page. The space, which he reserved under the title for some preliminary entry, has been utilised by a later clerk. This part embraces the first 309 pages. The handwriting varies very much, some of the clerks writing a clear bold hand, others preferring letters almost microscopically small; some have written very carefully, others very hurriedly. Few have made the slightest attempt at punctuation, and capitals are used in the most arbitrary manner. Some of the earlier scribes have tried to keep all the entries on each case together. Like many similar volumes it was long given up as lost, and it still bears traces of the neglect and bad usage to which it had been subjected, but is now safely preserved in the University Library.

The process concerning Borthwick was printed from it, in the *Bannatyne Miscellany*, in 1827, under the care of Principal Lee; and, under the same eye, nearly the whole of the other proceedings before August 1563, except the process of Forret and Leslie, were printed in the *Maitland Miscellany* in 1843. It has been thought necessary, however, for various reasons, to reproduce these proceedings here; but throughout, the transcript for the press has been made from the original, with which also, to ensure accuracy, the proofs have been very carefully compared. In four cases some of the grosser details have been omitted, compressed, or modified.[1] More might have

---

[1] Calland against Alexander (pp. 64, 66, 67, 69), Hyllok against Gyb (pp. 151-155), the process against Forbes of Reres (p. 164), and Thomson against Downy

been done in this way, but an anxious desire to preserve every-
thing throwing light on the manners of the past, and on
the forms of procedure in the session, coupled with the feeling that the passages so treated might have been considered
coarser than they really are, forbade anything like wholesale
condensation. To save useless repetition a few other passages
have also been compressed.[1] In no case has any such liberty
been taken with the text without due acknowledgment, nor
has the name of any one been omitted. Deleted words, which
seemed of the slightest importance, have been restored within
brackets. Contracted words have been extended, and, for the
reasons given by Hill Burton,[2] the inversion of ' u,' ' v,' and ' w,'
and of 'i,' and 'ʲ,' have been corrected, 'th' has been substituted for 'ʸ' when necessary, and 'ʸ' for 'z,' except in the
names of persons and places. Otherwise the spelling has been
rigidly adhered to.[3] In some parts of the *Register*, especially at
the beginning and end, the outer edges of the leaves have been
so frayed that the letters at the ends of the lines are completely
gone, and occasionally the ends of the lines on the inner side of
the page have been imprisoned by the binder; these have been
supplied within brackets, and so have a few letters, here and
there, which have been quite worn out. When a word is required to complete the sense, it is supplied in the text, but in
brackets, and is marked in a footnote as 'omitted.' In the
earlier sheets evident blunders in the original are retained in
the text with the addition of (*sic*), and where the meaning is
obscure the proper reading is given below; but, as the later
scribes are more careless, it was deemed better to give the

(P. 482). Of these the first three were thus dealt with the more readily as they
are fully printed in the *Maitland Miscellany ;* and in the fourth only one clause
has been omitted.

[1] Pp. 44, 200, 201, 203, 370, 476.

[2] *Register of the Privy Council*, vol. i. pp. xlviii-lii.

[3] The first two syllables of *minister* have frequently been written with eight
perpendicular strokes, as often perhaps with six; but these and a few similar
mistakes have been disregarded. The spelling of the original has not been
rigorously followed in this Preface.

correct reading in the text, and the erroneous in a footnote. Occasionally the paragraphs have been broken up. Most of the entries in the original have marginal notes, a few of which afford additional information; nearly all are intended to facilitate reference, some have been supplied by later clerks, and others are now added within brackets.

It need hardly be explained that, during the period covered by this *Register*, the year began on the 25th of March, and the clerks have dated their entries accordingly; yet, curiously enough, one passage seems to imply that popularly the year was held to begin on the 25th of December.

All attempts to find any document, with the seal of the session or Superintendent, have hitherto been fruitless. An accurate idea of the handwriting of some portions of the original, and of the signatures of some of the priests who recanted, is furnished by the four facsimiles. The frontispiece shows the present state of the tombstone of John Wynram, which lies in the floor of the roofless chapel of St. Leonard's College, and which has suffered much from exposure to the weather. When the chapel was cleared of rubbish in 1838, the stone was uncovered, and at that time the whole of the inscription was legible except two words. *Round the border:*—M · JOHANI · WYNRAMO · CŒNOBIARCHÆ · CONVERSIS · REBVS · FIFANORVM · EPISCOPO · ANN · ÆTATIS · SVÆ · 90 · OCCVMBENTI · POSITVM · *Above the shield:*—[VITA ·] PIETATE · [INSIGN]IS · GENERE · AMPLA · PROPINQVIS · CONSILIO · NVNC · TVMVLI · REPPERIT · ACTA · MODVM · *Under the shield:*—MVLTA · CVM · DEAMBVLAVERIS · DEMVM · REDEVNDVM · EST · HAC · CONDITIONE · INTRAVI · VT · EXIREM ·[1] Dean Stanley was inclined to make merry over the '*conversis rebus.*'[2]

In conclusion, I have to express my indebtedness to Dr.

---

[1] Grierson's *Delineations of St. Andrews*, 1838, pp. 251, 252; Lyon's *Ancient Monuments of St. Andrews*, 1847, fig. 7.

[2] Stanley's *Church of Scotland*, 1872, p. 100; and his *Addresses and Sermons at St. Andrews*, 1877, p. 16.

Mark Anderson for great and unwearied help ungrudgingly given, to Professor Mitchell for finally revising the Papal Dispensation, furnishing the notes on the *Sancti Quatuor Coronati* and on the two legates, and for several corrections, to Mr. William Aitken of the Madras College for much assistance, and to Mr. Law for many valuable suggestions.

D. H. F.

ST. ANDREWS, 27*th December* 1888.

CORRECTIONS

Page 5, n. line 2, *for* ii. *read* iii.

,, 76, margin, *for* prebendarics *read* prebendaries.

,, 99, line 12, *for* pocuis *read* pocius.

,, 160, ,, 10, *for* desposicionis *read* deposicionis.

,, 161, ,, 3, *for* desposicione *read* deposicione.

,, 175, margin, *for* Mrio. *read* Mri.

,, 208, line 7, *after* kyrk *insert* [1].

,, 209, ,, 7, *after* [allegis] *insert* [1].

,, 224, margin, *for* Cyllok *read* Wyllok.

,, 313, line 11, *for* conten   n *read* contenit in.

,, 318, ,, 2, *for* imparation *read* impanation.

,, 362, ,, 29, *delete* of.

,, 369, n. line 6, *for* bec us *read* becaus.

,, 385, line 23, *for* de *read* die.

,, 393, ,, 1, *for* lxiiij^{to} *read* lxxiiij^{to}.

LIBER REGISTRI

ENORMIUM DELICTORUM CORRECTORUM
PER MINISTRUM SENIORES ET DIACONOS
CONGREGATIONIS CHRISTIANAE CIVITATIS

SANCTI ANDREAE

Liber regvi enormium delictorum correctorum
per ministrum seniores et diaconos congregationis
christianae civitatis Sanctdandreae feliciter
Incipit 1559. ☞ men 2.t

Liber Registri enormium delictorum correctorum per ministrum seniores et diaconos congregationis Christianae civitatis Sancti Andreae fæliciter incipit 1559. Amen, etc.

Die xxv[to.] Julii anno Domini etc. lx.

The quhilk daye, the minister and eldaris, havand respect [Statute of to the inlayk of almos, and multitud of misterfull to be helpit almos.] therwyth, and [also that] divers strangeris mackis requestis and producis byllis for support of the sayd almos, heyrfor divisis and statutis that in tym cuming na stranger be ansuerit of ony part of the sayd almos, in ony tym cuming, uther particularlie nor manifestly, bot negatyve ansuer to be gevyne indifferentlie to all stranger.

Die 1 Octobris, anno Domini, etc. lxj.

The quhilk daye, in the session of Superintendent and [Statute anent ministerie of Sanctandr[ois], being present the Provest of the the eleccion of said cite, ballies and consayll, the Rector of [the] Universite, eldaris and and cheif membris of the sam, for ordor to be takyn anent the diaconis.] [eleccion] of the eldaris and diaconis, thai have statut and assignit yearlie,[1] [in] tym cuming, the daye of eleccion to be upon the secund Frydaye efter [the] eleccion of the Provest and ballies, and to proceid in this ordor, [viz.,] the Rector of the Universite for the tym, wyth the avys of his consayll, [sal geve] in wryt the names of sex qualefeit men of the thre

---

[1] According to the eighth head of the *First Book of Discipline*, elders and deacons ought to be elected yearly, ' least that by long continuance of suche officiaris, men presume upoun the libertie of the Churche.'

A

Collegis [to the] Provest, quhai, wyth the avyis of the consayll of the town, sal [geve] ane sufficient numer of the maist
qualefiet men of the citie [also] in wryt, jonit wyth the
personnis gevyn in to hym be the Rector, q[uhilk] salbe
deliverit to the minister upone the Sunday preceding the
[daye] of eleccion, and salbe publest in the essemble, thar
namis an[d] daye of eleccion, according to the ordor. And
upone the daye of eleccion, efter the prechyng at the minister
hes used al detfu[ll] circumstancis requirit of his part, sal
conveyn the Provest, ba[llies], consayll, and communite of fre
burgessis, togethyr wyth the Rector and [the] membris and
regentis of the Universite, in the Towbuth, q[uhen], be thar
mutuall consentis and eleccionis, the eldaris a[nd] diaconis salbe
chosyn and elecced furth of the numer [gevyn] in wryt befoyr
rehersed. According to the quhilk elleccion, follo[wis] eldaris
and diaconis elecced :—

Seniores.

[Eldaris and
diaconis
elected in 1561.]

Mr. Jhon Dowglas, Rector [1]　　Mr. Martyn Gedde
Mr. Alan Lawmonth　　　　　　Mr. William Cok
Mr. Jhon Rutherfurd, college [2]　Jhon Moffat
Thomas Martyne　　　　　　　Mr. Robert Pont [4]
Mr. James Wylkie, college [3]　　George Broun
Mr. Thomas Balfoir　　　　　　Jhon Motto.[5]
Jhon Wod

---

[1] Douglas, who was a descendant of the Douglasses of Pittendreich, appears
as a determinant in 1515, being then in the second class of St. Leonard's with
Wynram, Dunkanson, and Alesius. He was a licentiate in 1517, and thirty
years later was elected Provost of St. Mary's College. For twenty-three succes-
sive years he was Rector of the University, and was appointed the first tulchan
Archbishop of St. Andrews in 1571. Laing's *Knox*, i. 286 ; ii. 455.

[2] Rutherfurd was Provost of St. Salvator's College. James Melvill (*Diary*,
Wod. Soc., p. 27) characterises him as 'a man lernit in philosophie, bot
invyus, corrupt.' See an account of him in M'Crie's *Melville*, 1824, ii. 367-371.

[3] Wilkie, who succeeded Buchanan as Provost of St. Leonard's College in
1570, is described by Melvill (*Diary*, p. 27) as 'a guid, peaceable, sweit auld man.'

[4] The well-known Robert Pont. See *Wodrow Miscellany*, pp. 304-306 ;
Brunton and Haig's *Senators of the College of Justice*, pp. 151-153 ; and Lee's
Lectures, i. 230.

[5] The *Black Book of St. Andrews* bears on its title-page that it was 'begun
be Jhone Motto, commone clerk off the said cite,' in 1550.

Diaconi.

Thomas Wolwod
Charlis Guthre
James Robertson
Alexander Narne

Charlis Gedde
George Blak
William Zowll
William Mayne.

Adamus Heriot [1] *minister ecclesiae parochialis Sanctiandreae.*

[*Minister, seniores, et diaconi,*] *anno Domini millesimo quingentesimo quinquagesimo nono, etc.*

Seniores.

Magister Alanus Lawmonth
Valterus Geddy
Magister Thomas Balfowr
Thomas Martyne
Joannes Martyne
Joannes Motto
Dauid Walwod

[*Dauid Carstaris* erased]
Magister Robertus Pont
Joannes Moffat
Georgius Browne
[*Alexander Smyth* erased]
Magister Martinus Gedde
Joannes Wod.

Diaconi.

Thomas Walwod
Alexander Narne
Magister Dauid Russall
Vilelmus Mayne

Magister Thomas Fermour
Carolus Geddy
Georgius Blak
Dauid Spens.

---

[1] Heriot, who had been an Augustinian canon in St. Andrews, was 'an eloquent preacher, and well seen in scholastic divinity.' He was probably one of those canons who made 'notable confessiouns' before the 23d of June 1559. I cannot find the precise date of his election or appointment as minister of St. Andrews, but he did not remain long here, for Knox, in recording the events of July 1560, says : 'Heirefter war the commissionaris of bruchis, with sum of the nobilitie and barronis, appoyntit to see the equall distributioun of ministeris, to change and transport as the maist pairt sould think expedient. And sua was Johne Knox appointit to Edinburgh ; Christopher Gudman, (quha the maist pairt of the trubillis had remanit in Ayre,) was appointit to Sanctandrois : Adame Heryot to Abirdene' (Laing's *Knox*, ii. 87). After labouring fourteen years at Aberdeen, Heriot died on the 28th of August 1574, 'greatly beloved of the citizens for his humane and courteous conversation, and of the poorer sort much lamented, to whom he was in his life very beneficial' (Spottiswoode's *History*, Spot. Soc. ed., ii. 198). He appears to have retained the vicarage of St. Andrews until his death (*Wodrow Miscellany*, p. 361).

[*Minister, seniores, et diaconi,*] *anno Domini millesimo quingentesimo sexagesimo.*

Crostoferus Gudman[1] *minister ecclesie parochialis Sanctiandree in absencia Adami Heriot.*

Seniores.

Mr. Alanus Lawmonth
Mr. Thomas Balfour
Joannes Moffat
Mr. Robertus Pont
Mr. Wilelmus Cok
Thomas Martyne

Mr. Martinus Gedde
Dauid Wolwod
Joannes Wod
Wilelmus Monepenny
Joannes Motto.

Diaconi.

Thomas Wolwod
Alexander Narne
Carolus Gedde

Wilelmus Mayne
Georgius Blak
Dauid Spens.

[Eldaris and diaconis chosyn in 1562.]

Cristoher Gudman minister.

Eldaris the sexty twa.

Mr. Jhon Dowglas, Rector
Mr. Thomas Balfour, balie
George Brown, balie
Mr. James Wylkie
Mr. Alan Lawmonth, citiner
Mr. William Cok, citiner

Mr. William Ramsay[2]
Mr. William Scot
Dauid Wolwod, citiner
Thomas Wolwod, citiner
James Robertson, citiner
Johan Motto, citiner.

Diaconis.

William Zowill
Charlis Gedde
Robert Murray
Wiliam Ferre

George Blak
Walter Mackesone
Andro Motto
Wyliam Mayne.

---

[1] Goodman, who was a native of Chester, had been Knox's colleague at Geneva. As mentioned in the preceding note, he was appointed to St. Andrews in July 1560. He was one of its representatives in the first General Assembly, and returned to England in 1565, where he died in 1601. See M'Crie's *Knox*, note III.

[2] Ramsay was second principal master in St. Salvator's College. He was also admitted minister of Kilmany in 1564, and translated to Kemback before 1570 (Scott's *Fasti*, ii. 496). Richard Bannatyne says he was 'a learned and a guid man, but seducit be the Hammiltounes factione' (*Memoriales*, Ban. Club, p. 259). See notice of him in M'Crie's *Melville*, ii. 371, 372.

Cristofer Gudman minister.

Eldaris chosyn in the kyrk the lxiij year.

Mr. Jhon Dowglas	Mr. Thomas Balfour
George Brown, balie	Jhon Moffat
Mr. William Cok, balle	Mr. Martyn Gedde
Mr. William Ramsaye	James Robertson
Mr. Alan Lawmonth	William Monepenny
Mr. James Wylke	Jhon Motto.

Diaconis.

Charlis Gedde	Thomas Dagles
William Zowll	Alexander Rowch
George Blak	Alexander Myllar
William Ferre	Thomas Greg.

Veneris.

The xxvij day of October, 1559.[1] Robert Roger, schip- *Penitentia* wrycht, cittiner of Sanctandrois, in presence of the congrega- *Roger.* tioun, in the paroche kirk of the said ciete than to heir Godis Word convenit, beand comprehendit ane .oppin adulterar, declared himself penitent, of the forsaid cryme of adultery, to God and the said congregatioun, at the tyme of ten houris or therby, before none, the sermon beand endit, immediatlie, to the exemple of uthiris to commit nocht the lyke, at decrete of the minister and eldaris of the said citte, &c., gevin furth be thame ther upoun xxvj day of the said moneth.

Jovis.

Upoun the secund day of November, 1559, James Reky, *Decretum* tailyeour, delatate to the minister and eldaris of this congrega- *contra* Reky.

---

[1] This is the earliest dated entry in the volume. In the *Maitland Miscellany*, ii. 209, it is erroneously given as the 26th of October, and the same mistake has been made in lettering the back of the *Register*. Writing to Mrs. Anna Lock, from St. Andrews, on the 2d ˋof the preceding month, Knox says: 'Christ Jesus is preached even in Edinburgh, and his blessed sacraments rightlie ministred in all congregatiouns where the ministrie is established; and they be these:—Edinburgh, Sanct Andrewes, Dundie, Sanct Johnstoun, Brechin, Montrose, Stirline, Aire' (Laing's *Knox*, vi. 78).

tioun, for the manteyning and fostring of Margaret Edname,
and ressate of William Rantoun, adultereris, in his howss, to the
great and manifest sclander of the congregatioun. He hes
confessit that the brute of ther adultery beand knawin to him,
therefter, at desyre of the freindis of Margaret, he ressavit hir
to buyrding in his hows, nevertheles tholeit and gaif place to
Williame to repair oppinlie to his howss, to eit and drink, diverss
tymes. And now, the wechtines of his offenss delatate to him,
he is becumin penitent and obedient, and, as he was commandit,
hes expellit Margaret fra his howss. Yit, becawse the sclander
wes public to this congregatioun, and also to the intent that
utheris tak nocht occasioun to fortife sic abominatioun, James
is decerneit oppinlie to confess his falt, and to ask God and the
congregatioun forgevens, an[d] to desist fra all sic in tyme
cuming.

Veneris.

*Penitentia
Reky.*

The thrid day of the forsaid November, the said Jame[s], in
presence of the congregatioun gatherit in the paroche kir[k] to
heir the sermon, declareit oppinlie himself penitent according
to the said decreit.

Mercurii.

*Penitentia
Rantoun.*

Upoun the xxij day of November, 1559, William Rantoun,
delat[ate] with Margaret Aidnam for the cryme of adultery, in
presen[ce] of the congregatioun schew signe of repentence,
oblysa[nd] him in tymes cuming, under all hyeast payne of
correctio[un], to abstiene fra the elyke, &c.

The tennour of the lettres conteynand the names of all
them that are adjoynet to the congregatioun within
this cietie.

The letteris [o]f
junctioun to the
Congregatioun,

WE quhais names ar underwrittin juness us in all thinges
conforme to the Generall Band maid betuix the Lordis and
Baronis of Congregatioun, at Edinburgh, the xiij day of *Julii*,
anno, etc. lix, to the Congregatioun and memberis therof, to
assist in mutuall support with the said Congregatioun, with our

bodies, geir and force, for maynteyning of the trew religioun of Christe, and downe putting of all superstitioun and idolatrie, conforme to the said Band, quherof the tennour followis and is this :—WE QUHAIS names ar underwrittin, quhilkis hes subscrivit thir presentes with our handis, haifand respect to our dewties in setting fordwart the glorie of God, and knawand alswa that we are commandit to june ourselfis togiddir as memberis of ane body, for the furtherance of the samyn, dois, in the name of Christe Jesus, unite ourselfis, that we, in ane mynde and ane spirite, may endivour us, with our haill power and diligence, to walk fordwart in the waiis of the Lord, laboring to destroy and put downe all idolatrie, abhominationess, superstitioness, and quhatsumever thing dois exalte the self against the majestie of our God, and maynteyn and sett up the trew religioun of Christe, his Word and sacramentes, and alswa assist and defend the trew ministeris therof. And as we be sones of ane Father, parttakeris of ane Spirite, and beyris of ane kingdome, swa sall we maist hartlie, faythfullie and trewlie concur togiddir, nocht onlie in the materis of religioun, bot sall lykewise, at our utter poweris to the waring of our labouris, substance and lyves, assist, defend and maynteyne every ane ane uthir, against quhatsumever that troubles, persewis or invades us, or ony ane of us, in our lyves, landis, gudeis, heretageis, offices, benefices, pensiones, or uthir thinges quhatsumever, praesentlie in our possessioness, or quhilkis justlie we possesset at the begynning of thir praesent trowblis for the religioun, or ony uthir causs praetendit upoun religioun, or persewit under praetenss of the samyn. And, for observing of the premissis, we bind and obliss ourselfis, in the praesence of our God, of his Sone Jesus Christe, calling for the Haly Spirite to strenth us to performe the samyn. At Edinburgh the xiij of Julii, the yeir of God, j^m v^c fifty nyne yeris.[1] Quhilk band we approve in all pointtis, and adjoynis ourselfis for mutuall defenss to the haill adheraris therto.

---

[1] Although both Knox and Calderwood have engrossed the Bands of December 1557, May 1559, August 1559, April 1560, and September 1562, yet neither mentions this Band of July 1559; nor can I recall the slightest reference to it in the pages of any of their contemporaries.

Follows the names.

Patrick Lermonth of Darsy, Provest,[1] Maister Alane Law-
month, Johne Muffatt, baillies ; Thomas Broun, George Brown,
Thomas Martyne, Dauid Carstaris, Johne Martyne, Maister
Williame Cok, Johne Dalglesche, Mr. Martyne Gedde, Charles
Guthere, Mr. Robert Pont, Henry Cairnes, Mr. Dauid Meldrum,
Andro Meffen, Alexander Narne, Johne Wode, eldar, James
Robertsone, Patrick Knox, Williame Mayne, James Ruther-
furde, Andro Motto, Williame Aidname, Robert Lermonth,
Thomas Braidfute, Alexander Walcar, Andro Thomsone, Walter
McKesone, Walter Lany, Dauid Spens, Johne Wod, youngar,
Leonard Williamsone, Williame Pringill, Johne Symsone, mer-
chand, Andro Wricht, Henry Balfour, Thome Aidname, Alex-
ander Napar, William Giffard, Robert Hew, Williame Neche,
Mr. Dauid Russall, Mr. William Skene, Johne Kembak, Mr.
Richard Jacksone, James Ramsay, Johne Watson, Robert
Murray, Alexander Nory, ester, Williame Zwle, James Browne,
eldar, Thomas Meffen, Archbald Mwre, Alexand[er] Brydy,
Johne Wylie, Williame Dalglesche, James Gedde, William
Rantoun, Andro Gudelawde, Johne Gudelawde, Johne Kowcace,
Thomas Flemyng, Thomas Lockard, Walter Ade, Johne Broun,
Dauid Gray, Thomas Leiche, Stephin Gibsone, Thomas Peblis,
James Thomsone, yongar, Robert Sountar, George Legate,
Robert Mwdy, Dauid Baverych, Andro Nicholsone, Dauid Smart,
Robert Bruce, Alexander Smyth, Walter Gedde, Alane Mal-
vill, James Brog, Robert Rayt, Robert Kilgour, Dauid Ade,

---

[1] Patrick Learmonth's father, Sir James of Balcomie and Dairsie, was Provost
of St. Andrews at the time of Beaton's assassination, and for many years previously (Laing's *Knox*, i. 174). In the *Black Book of St. Andrews*, Patrick is
mentioned as Provost so early as 1550. He sat in various Parliaments, including that of 1560, by which the *Confession of Faith* was ratified, and that of
1585, when he represented the burgh of St. Andrews (*Acts of the Parliaments
of Scotland*, ii. 526 ; iii. 381). Queen Mary knighted him on the 8th of February 1561-2, the marriage day of her brother, afterwards the Regent Moray
(*Diurnal of Occurrents*, pp. 70, 71). He was one of those who were 'wardit in
the Northland' in the troublous year of 1565 (*Register of Privy Council*,
i. 369, 405). In the MS. copy of Wyntoun's *Cronykil* preserved in the St.
Andrews University Library, there is written at the bottom of a page in
Book vi., chap. 137—
'Patrik Lermontht
of Dersy knycht this bouk pertines of ry[cht].'

Henry Duncansone, Henry Small, Henry Mwre, Johne Bicker-
toun, Andro Moffat, smyth, Maister Thomas Gilcryste, James
Brydy, Duncane Leche, Johne Blak, Andro Symsone, junior,
James Gilrwfe, Thomas Branche, Charles Cuthbert, William
Balfour, eldar, Williame Gedde, Alexander Kircaldy, Dauid
Banis, James Clwny, Hugo Lockard, Dauid Bruce, Johne
Brabanar, Jame[s] Steill, Duncane Dauidsone, Johne Smyth,
maltman, Andro Watso[ne], Alane Watsone, James Smyth,
George Pate, Alexander Rudman, Alexander Millar, Andro
Browne, Dauid Walwod, Mr. George McKesone, Mr. Johne
Dalglesche, Williame Arthour, Alexande[r] Rowcht, Alexander
Duncane, Dauid Zongar, James Reky, Andro Cromy, Williame
Grenelaw, Dauid Bruce, William Lathangy, Williame Mychel-
sone, Andro Kenzow, George Myllar, Thomas Hammyltoun,
Charles Hagy, James Bet, Robert Wyle, Alane Dewar, James
Broun, George Vteyne, Thomas Wilsone, merchand, Robert Law,
Johne Cowpar, Williame Walcar, Alexande[r] Nory, eldar,
Andro Smyth, Thomas Tailzeour, Johne Kelle, Henry Fayrfull,
Alexander Ramsay, tailyeour, Sir Walter Bowsy,[1] Johne Syb-
bald, James Myretoun, James Broun, junior, Maister Thomas
Balfour, Johne Husband, James Bennett, Thomas Dicksone,
Andro Moffat, baxtar, James Dudingstoun, Johne Henrysone,
Williame Dewar, Robert Jacsone, Dauid Myles, Johne Russall,
Williame Callendar, Johne Tailzeour, William Horsburgh,
Williame Carstaris, Williame Swyne,[2] Andro Meffen, tail-
yeour, Andro Monypenny, Williame Mories, youngar, Dauid
Wawch, Thome Baxtar, James Alane, Andro Barclay, Peter
Thomsone, Andro Trunblay,[3] Thome Reif, Thome Duncane,
Patrick Smyth, Johne Scharp, Thome Lodean, Thome
Cryste, Dauid Gudelawde, Williame Downy, Thom Walcar,
Sir Walter Lawsone, Mr. Johne Bonkle, Johne Meffen, Andro
Grief, with my hand, Richard Bell, Andro Turnour, Williame and names
Henrysone, Johne Walcar, Andro Lundy, Williame Herman, adjuned, &c.
Dauid Rantoun, Thome Henrysone, Robert Crag, Williame
Mortoun, Robert Dewar, Dauid Bell, Robert Dick, yongar,
Johne Lokard, Thome Olypliant, Williame Wan, Williame

---

[1] Sir Walter Bousey is mentioned in 1547 as procurator for the Choristery of
St. Andrews (*Abstract of the Writs of St. Andrews*, No. 273).
[2] Swinton.   [3] Perhaps Trimblay.

Layng, Johne Andersone, Andro Gibsone, Alexander Powtie,
George Castaris, Thome Wilsone, George Hagy, Williame
Cryste, Robert Swordy, Williame Dwne, Johne Wan, Johne
Williamsone, Johne Moncur, Williame Rynd, Robert Peblis,
Laurence Talzeour, Johne Zoung, Dauid Mortoun, Robert
Fortoun, Sir Walter Mar,[1] Johne Moffet, Mr. Andro Wilsone,
Johne Daijs, James Broun, Thome Dwry, James Sountar, Henry
Wilsone, James Haye, Alexander Walcar, George Crawfurde,
Mr. Thomas Paty, Robert *D*ick, eldar, Thome Broun, Andro
Symsone, eldar, Williame Bell, eldar, Michaell Smyth, Alex-
ander Wat, Thomas Wilsone, George Saige, Mr. Johne
Homyll, Johne Kembak, Symone Millar, Andro Forrett, George
Stevinsone, Dauid Millar, Dauid Wilsone, Andro Forrett, junior,
Williame Balfour, junior, Henry Millar, Johne Blak, Dauid
Mories, Johne Dalglesche, Andro Coleyne, Williame Heriott,
James Logy, Thome Broun, Thom Wemys, Andro Symsone,
Mr. Thomas Bell, Mr. Thomas Fermour, Thomas Lyell, George
Philp, James Myllar, Dauid Watsone, Walter Bawne, George
Blak, Mr. Andro Inche, Richard Robertsone, Alane Rayt,
Robert Roger, Robert Mayne, Alexander Daijs, Thom Wod,
Johne Small, Alexander Murray, Williame Tailzeour, Dauid
Cowper, Thome Broun, James Crawfurde, Thome Banys, Mr.
James Walcar, Thome Wemys, Henry Dempstar, Hugo Mows,
Mr. George Nycholsone, Mr. Dauid Wod, Johne Thomesone,
Robert Criste, Alexander Ade, Charles Gundy, Henry Braid-
futt, Johne Fayrfull, Johne Trayll, Ambrose Schevez, Williame
Stevinsone, James Zong, Thomas Walwod, Williame Mylne, &c.

[Chaplanes
quhai wes
adjoynet to the
congregatioun.] *Die tertio Februarii, anno lix*, comperis thir chaplanes efter
writtin of there awin fre motyve willis (the professioun abone
writtin being red in there praesence) ratifies the samyn, and

---

[1] Sir Walter Marr was a presbyter in 1548; and, as chaplain of the altar of
St. Katharine in the parish church of St. Andrews, in 1556, he mortified a
tenement and several annual rents and feus to his brethren the chaplains and
choristers, for the performance of certain masses, which if they failed to celebrate regularly, the revenue was to be divided among citizens who had fallen
back in their circumstances, but had not spent their meens in bad management,
gluttony, or drunkenness (*Abstract of the Writs of St. Andrews*, Nos. 128, 106).

singularlie, be themselfis, adjoynis them to the congregatioun, affirmes the doctryne presentlie techet in this cietie, and daiis bypast sen Witsounday, to be Goddis trew Word, renunceis all idolatrie, superstitioun, the mes, the Paip, and all his traditiones, and professis the administratioun of the sacramentis as thei ar taucht and practiset be the ministeris to be conforme to Goddis Word. And in witnes of that professioun forsaid hes consentit that ther names be under wryttin as the same hed beyne subscrivit be there awin handis.

Followis the names of the priestis.

Robert Smyth, Mr. Johne Todrick, Thomas Durward,Thomas Braidfute, Johne Thomsone, elder, Henry Guling, Dauid Frostar, John Zoung, junior, Robert Dauidsone, junior, Johne Thomsone, junior.

Followis certane names of uthir priestis quhai wes adjoynet efter the forsaid. [Uthir priestis quhai wes adjoynet.]

Joannes Balfour, Hugo Bontaveroun, Joannes Broun, Robertus Marschell, Thomas Wemys, Joannes Thomsone, James Symsone, Andro Baxtar.

Followis certane laymen names adjunit to the Congregatioun efter the forsaid. [Certane laymen adjunit efter the forsaid.]

Johne Mortoun, James Thomsone, James Lyell, Johne Wodcok, Alexander Gibsone, Patrick Ramsay, with my hand, Alexander Dempstertoun, Dauid Dempstertoun, Mr. Alexander Sybbald.

I, Johne Wilsone, umquhile channoun of Halyrudehows, presentlie renunceis, and from thence furth sall utterlie renunce, refuse and forsaik, the Bischop of Rome, callet the Pape, his authorite, power and jurisdictioun. And I sall never consent nor aggree that that lecherouss swyne the Byschop of Rome (quhai hais rutet up the Lordis vyneyard sa far as in him was) The recantatioun of Dene Jhone Wilsoun vicare of Kingorne maid in the Paroche Kirk of Sanctandrois, upoun Sounday the

[*blank*] day of
Februar 1559,
in presence of
the Admirall
and Vice-ad
(*sic*) admirall
of England.[1]

sall practise, or exerce, or haif ony maner of authorite, jurisdictioun, or power, within Christes Kirk heir in this realme, or
ellisquhare; bott sall resist the samyn at all tymes, to the
uttermast of my power. An[d] alls I renunce and refuss all
maner of idolatrie, superstitioun and hypocrisie, and espetiall
the mess, as maist abhominable idolatrie, contrarious and repugnant to Christes dead and passioun. And als, I renunce all
veneratioun of sanctes and purgatorie repugnant t[o] the samyn,
and frome thencefurth will onlie accept and repute Jesus
Christe, the Sone of the leving God, the Redemar of me and
all mankynde frome syn, hell, dead and damnatioun, to be the
onlie head, rewlar, and gydar of his Kirk, alss weill militant as
triumphant. And to my cuning, wit, and uttermast of my
power, without hypocrisie or dissimulatioun, I will observe
keip and maynteyne the hale effectis and contentis of the New
and Auld Testament, as the onelie rewle to atteyne to salvatioun, to avance the glore of Gode, and to the extirpatioun and
extinguissing of the Antichristes authorite. And attour, I
abhor and detestis all veneratiou[n] of idollis and imagies, and
all traditiones of men sett owt to thirle the consciences of
Goddis people aganis his holy lawes. And this I wil[l] do
aganis all maner of persones of [quhat][2] state, dignite, degre or
conditio[un], they be of. And I protest, in presence of God
and of this his congregatioun, that I sall never, fra this tyme
furth, practise or exerce, oppinlie or privatelie, say, do, speak, or
be ony uthir meane consent to the injust and usurpet power of
the Antichriste of Romme, be ony maner of pretenss. And in

---

[1] It was while a body of French troops were marching, in the midst of a
snow-storm, by the Fife coast, to St. Andrews, that the first eight ships of the
English fleet, under William Winter, arrived in the Forth on the 22d of January
1559-60. On learning their nationality, the French hurriedly retired by Stirling
to Leith. In Queen Elizabeth's instructions to Winter he is called 'Master of
the Ordnance of her Majesty's Admiralty' (Keith's *History*, Spot. Soc., i. 408).
But in Thorpe's *Calendar of State Papers*, and elsewhere, he is frequently
designated Admiral Winter. Knox says he was 'a man of great honestie, sua
far as ever we could espy of him' (Laing's *Knox*, ii. 56). 'The English men
landed for their refreshment. Especially in Fyfe they were thankfully receaved
and well entreated, with such quietnes and gentle entertainment betwixt our
nation and them, as no man would have thought that ever there had beine any
variance' (*Wodrow Miscellany*, p. 78).

[2] Omitted.

caiss ony [aith or promise][1] be maid, or hes beyne maid, be me,
to ony persone or persones, in maynteynance, defens or favour of
the Pape of Romme, that innimye to Christe, or his authorite, I
repute, takis and haldis the samyn as vayne, and of nane effect,
strenth nor force, sa help me God throwch Jesus Christ[e].

And heir, in presence of God and this his congregatioun, I
confessis and granttis that I haif faltet greatlie aganis God and
his said congregatioun, in thocht, worde and deid, and spetialie
in blasphemows wordis, for the quhilkis I ask God mercie, and
the haill congregatioun forgivenes, for Christes saik.

Followis the subscriptioun,

Johne Wilsone abone writtin with my hand.

We confess with our hart unfenyeatlie, withowt ony respect to particular profict, movet alanarlie be the feare of God and his Word, that we haif ower lang abstractit ourselfis, and beyne sweir in adjuning us to Christes Congregatioun, setting furth his honour and glorie, of the quhilkis we ask God mercie and this congregatioun [forgivenes].[1] *Item*, we hartlie reniunce the Pape, quhai is the verray Antichriste and suppressour of Godis glorie, with all diabolic inventioneis as be purgatorie, the mess, invocatioun of sanctis and prayaris to them, worschipping of images, prayeris in strange language, and multipliing of them to certane numer, and all ceremonies useit in Papistrie, as be hallowing of candellis, watter, salt, and bread, with all there conjurationes ; and, finalie, all authorite asweill of the wicked Paip as uthiris that suppressis Goddis law and stoppis his Word, and planelie maynteynes idolatouris and idolatrie, with all lawes and traditioness, inventiones of men maid to bind and thrall mennis consciences ; and promiseis, in tyme cuming, to assist in word and wark, with unfenyiet mynde, this congrega-tioun efter our powar, and never to contaminate ourselfis with the forsaidis idolatr[ie] and superstitiones, nothir for profict nor feer. And we haif contrare our consciences, Goddis gloir and his Word, grevouslie offendet in thir forsaidis. We ask God and his holy congregatioun mercie, &c.

Sounday the [blank] day of Februar, 1559, recantet thir priestes under-writtin, &c.

---

[1] Omitted.

Followis the names of them quhai recantet.

Robertus Smyth, *manu propria*, M. Joannes Toddrick, Thomas Durward, Johne Zoung, Dauid Frostar, Johne Thomsone, eldar, Henry Gwling, Jacobus Lyell, Thomas Braidfute, Robertus Dauidsone, junior, Walter Bowsy, Adame Gibsone, Magister Joannes Browne, *manu propria s[cripsit]*, Alexander Lowsoan.

Sounday, the
10 of Marche,
1559, recanted
thir priestes
under-writtin,
&c.
We, quhais names ar under writtin, presentlie renunceis fra thyne furth, and sall utterlie renunce, refuse and forsaik the Bischop of Romme, called the Paip, his cursed and usurped authorite, power and jurisdictioun, opinioun, traditioneiss, and lawes, and in spetiall the law of him quhilk saiis, that it behuiffes us to trow in the Kirk of Romme as nedefull to our salvatioun ; and we sall never consent, assent, nor aggree, that that odiouse beast and lechorouss swyne (quhai hais worted and ruted up the Lordes vyneyard sa far as in him was) sall practise, or exerce, or haif ony maner of authorite, jurisdictioun or power, within the Kirk of Christe, heyr in this realme or ellisquhare.   And als, we renunce and refuse all maner of idolatrie, superstitioun and hypocrisie, and espetiall the mess, as maist abhominable idolatrie, contrarious and repugnant to Christes death and passioun.   And als, we renunce and refuse all veneratioun or worschipping of sanctes, and purgatorie, contrare and repugnant to the to the (*sic*) samyn ; and frome thyne furth will onlie accept and repute Jesus Christe, the Soone of the aeternall and everliving God, the Redemar of us and all mankynde frome syn, hell, death and damnatioun, to be onlie the hiead, rewlar and guidar of his Kirk, als well militant as triumphant.   And to our cuning, witt and uttermaste of our powar, without hypocrisie, or dissimulatioun, or regard haiffing to ony eardlie respect, bott of onlie luffe favour affectioun and zeale to the glorie of God and his aeternall veritie uttered to us in the bluide of Christe Jesus, we sall observe, keip and maynteyne, the haill effectes and contentis of the New and Auld Testament, as the onlie rewle to attaine to salvatioun, to avance the glorie of God, and to the extirpatioun and extinguissing of the kingdome and authoritie of the Antichriste ; and attour, abhorres and detestis all veneratioun of

And gen... purposes of god and this congregation not confess and
grauntit that in as far as no... fallen against gods ministre...
of his... and his said congregation in word and deed...
... bretheren wordes for the... word god...
the said congregation forasmuch for... christes...
follow... named

Johannes Ball... man...
... Mr... Thomas...
... James...
... Thomas...
... Sand...
...
...
... Joannes...

idoles, images, and all traditions of men sett owt to thirle the
consciences of Goddis people aganis his holy lawes.   And this
we will do aganis all maner of personeis, of quhat estate,
dignitie, degree, conditioun, thei be of.   And protestes, in praesence of God and of his heir gathered congregatioun, that we
sall never, fra this tyme furth, practise or exerce, oppinlie or
privatlie, say, do, speak, or by ony maner of way consent, to
the injust and usurpet powar of the maist odiowse and execra-
bill Antichriste of Romme, by ony maner of praetenss.   And in
caiss ony aith or promise be maid, or hais beyne maid be us, to
ony persone or persones, in maynteynan[ce], defenss, or favour
of the Paip or Bischop of Romme, that inimye to Chris[te],
or his authoritie, we repute, takis and haldis the samyn as vane,
and of nane effect, strenth nor force.   Sa help us God throwch
Jesus Christe.

And heir, in praesence of God and this congregatioun, we
confess and granttis that, in sa far as we haif falted aganis God,
his ministeris of his Kirk, and his said congregatioun, in thocht
word and deed, spetialie in blasphemows wordes, for the quhilkis,
we ask God mercie and the hale congregatioun forgivenes, for
Jesus Christes saik, &c.

Followis the names.

Joannes Balfour, *manu sua scripsit*, Hugo Bontaveron, Joannes
Broun, *subscripsit*, Robertus Marscheall, *subscripsit*, Thomas
Wemys, *manu sua*, Joannes Thomsoun, *manu propria*, James
Symsone, Andro Watsone, with my hand, Andro Baxter, with
my hand, Thomas Smyth, Alexander Balfour, *vicarius de Kil-
many*,[1] Magister Joannes Lawmonth, *manu propria*.

The 17 day of September, anno 1567 yeiris, this onder
scription wes mayd in this assemblye.

Johannes Kinloqwhye
manu propria scripsit.

Thomas Kynneir, with my hand.

xv[to] *Octobris*, 1567, Thomas Kinneir subscrivit.[2]

The xiij day of March, anno etc. *l nono*, I Maister Niniane
Cwke affirmes all the premissis *teste manu propria etc.*

---

[1] This had originally been written, ' vicar of Kilmany.'
[2] These entries of the 17th September and 15th October 1567 have been

Sounday the
xvij day of
Marche 1559.

Followes the rectantatioun of Freire Gresone,[1]
Priour Provintiall Generall of all the freris Pre-
dicatouris in Scotland, be him playnlie, in the
faice of the congregatioun, within the paroche
kirk of Sanctandrois, day and yeir forsaid, maid.

The recanta-
tioun of Freir
Gresone, and

Heir, in presence of almichty and everliving God and of this
holy congregatioun, I grant and confess, that in tyme bypast,

afterwards inserted at the bottom of the page, and they contain the first autograph signatures in the volume.   Kinloqwhye has written, 'Johannes Kinloqwhye *manu propria scripsit*,' and Kynneir, ' Thomas Kynneir, with my hand.'
The clerk has written the rest.

[1] Griersoun or Gresone was Prior of the Predicant Friars at Aberdeen in 1516,
and was reckoned ' one of the men of learning and piety who adorned the early
years of the University of that city ' (*Liber Collegii Nostre Domine*, Mait. Club,
p. liii.).   He was Prior of the convent at St. Andrews in 1517 (*Register of the
Great Seal*, iii., No. 229).   That *Register*, and the *Abstract of Writs of the City
of St. Andrews*, show that Dempster is rather under than over the mark in saying
that he was Provincial of the Order in Scotland for thirty years.   He was in the
Provincial Council of 1549 (Robertson's *Concilia Scotiae*, ii. 84).   Foxe includes
him among the persecutors of Patrick Hamilton, the proto-martyr of the Scottish
Reformation ; and also names him in the *concilium malignantium* convened
against Walter Mille, the last Protestant martyr in Scotland (Cattley's *Foxe*,
iv. 558 ; v. 645).   He must therefore have been an old man when he made this
recantation.   Knox preached his famous sermon, on the ejection of the
buyers and sellers from the temple, in St. Andrews, on the 11th of June
1559, and occupied the pulpit on the three following days.   The reformation of the city apparently began on the 11th (Laing's *Knox*, i. 349, with vi.
25, and *Wodrow Miscellany*, p. 60), when the churches were 'purged' of
their altars and images, and the monasteries of the Black and Grey Friars
were destroyed.   The *Abstract of Writs*, No. 41, shows that on the 21st
of June—only ten days afterwards—Gresonè, with consent of the Prior and
Order in St. Andrews, disposed of the yard of the monastery to William
Morrice, citizen, his two sons, William and Andrew, George Swine in Methel,
and John Bickerton in St. Andrews, for their gratitude and many services per-
formed to the friars, and for paying them a certain sum of money after they
were expelled from their monastery and the same destroyed.   It was to be
held of the Prior and Convent for the yearly feu of fifteen merks, and was
not to be sold without their consent.   From the same *Abstract of Writs*, No. 44,
it further appears that, on the 1st of August 1559, Gresone, as Provincial, trans-
ferred an annual rent, which had been founded for the Order at St. Monans,
to the heirs of the donor, because religion had ceased in the kingdom.   At the
sale of the Osterley Park library, the University of St. Andrews secured a copy
of Major's *Historia*, with Gresoun's name boldly inscribed in two places.
According to Dempster he lived until 1564 (*Historia Ecclesiastica*, Ban. Club,
i. 330).

I haif maynteynet and defendet diver[se] kyndes of supersti- Provintiall of
tioun and idolatrie, by[1] the lawes and ordinances of almichty the Freiris Pre-
dicatouris in
God, and hais remanet ower lang at the opinioun and defens Scotland, &c.
of sick thinges; and repentis the samyn fra the bodowme of
my hart; and is content, in tyme to cum, to instit[ut] and conforme my lyfe to the Word and doctryne of the aeternall God,
set furt[h], explicate and declared be his prophetes, and the
apostolis of our onlie Salvio[ur] Christe Jesu, in the Auld
Testament and the New; and thinkes that the Kirk and Congregatioun of God may be sufficientlie instructit to inchew syn,
dead, and hel[l], and quhow they may cum to everlesting lyfe,
be they thingis quhilkis ar reveled to us, be the Haly Gaist,
in New and Auld Testament; and therfore I reject, renunceis
and abhorris all uthiris doctrynes and traditiones of men,
quhilkis are contrarious to Goddis haly Word, and is set owt
to thirle mennes conscienses, to obliss them under the payne of
deadlie syn.

And in spetiall, I renunce the Pape to be head of the Kirk,
and als, I renun[ce] him, and all his traditiones and lawes
repugnant in ony sort, or makand dirogatioun, to Goddis lawes
or libertie of the samyn.

Item, I renunce the mess as it hais beyne uset in tymes
bypast, and the fenyiet and inventet purgatorie, as pestiferous
and blaspheming thingis, and as contrarious thinges to the
merites, dead, passioun, and omnisufficient sacrifice offered
upoun the croce, be our Salviour Christe for the redemptioun
of mankynde.

Item, I grant that na graven image suld be maid and wor-
schippet in the Kirk of God, and that na honour suld be gevin
therto, and that all exhibitioun of sick honour, exhibite, or to
be exhibite, to sick stokkis or stanes, is verray idolatrie, and
against the expres command of God.

Item, I grant that we haif na command of God biddand us
pray to ony sanctis at[2] are departet, bott onlie to him quhai
is Sanct of all sanct[is] viz. Christe Jesu, our onlie Salviour,
Mediatour, and Advocate, everlevand, and perpetualie makand
intercessioun to his Father, for all his faithfull people and

---

[1] Against.   [2] That.

B

membiris of his body. And siclyke, I grant that we haif na
command to pray for them that are departet.

Item, as I grant that to them that hais the gift of chastitie it
is gude and godlie to lief in chastitie, evin sa I grant, according
to Sanct Paules doctryne, that it is lauchfull to all men and
wemen to mar[y] quhai hais nocht the gift of chastitie, nochtwithstanding ony vow maid to the contrary; bott give thei be
vexed and urnet with ustioun[1] and urgent appetites of the
flesche, they ar bound be the commandement 'of the apostle
to mary.

Item, I deny all transsubstantiatioun in the sacrament of the
body and blude of our Salviour Christe Jesu; and, that auri-
culare confessioun is necessar for the salvatioun of man.

Thir forsaid, and all uthiris ungodlie opinioness and inventes
of men, quhilkis ar contrariowss to God and his holy Word, I
detest, abhor, and renunceis, for now and ever. And of my
lang adherence to the samyn, I ask God mercie, and this his
haly congregatioun forgivenes, &c. &c.

Followis the tennour of the subscriptioun,

Frater Johannes Gresone *manu propria.*

Followis the proces betuix Williame Rantoun and
Elizabeth Geddy his spows, in the quhilk Williame
persewes Elizabeth of divorce for, be him against hir
allegeat, adultery as the process conteynes, &c.

Abone paroche kirk dur.

Rantoun   *Primo Februarii*, 1559. The quhilk day, Williame Rantoun
gaif in ane petitioun of divorce against Elizabeth Gedde. The
minister and eldaris sett to ansuer therto this day fyvetene
daiis, and ordeinet the said Elizabeth to be warnet therto,
agane the said day.

Gedde   *Decimo quinto Februarii*, 1559, *loco predicto.* In the caus of
divorce betuix Williame Rantoun and Elizabeth Gedde, in the

---

[1] Tortured with burning.

terme statut to ansuer to the said Williames petitioun, compered Elizabeth, and gaif ane ansuer conteynand in effect that
sche purgeit hir, and deniit his clame and petitioun.   And the process.
ministeris and eldaris hes statute Williame to prieve his clame,
and bring his witnes, and he and Elizabeth warned therto,
the twenty ane day of this instant moneth of Februar.

Followis the tennour of Williame Rantones clame,
and Elizabeth Geddeis ansuer therto.

Unto your m. faithfull minister and eldaris of this cietie of
Sanctandrois, and your assessouris, humelie menes and schawes
Williame Ranto[un], citiner of the said cietie, that quhare, at the
plesour of God, I, the said Williame, mariet and tuke to wyfe
Elizabeth Gedde, in the moneth of September, in the yeir of
God, &c. xlviii yeris, and, conforme to the samyn band, did my
devour and dewtie to triet and interviney hir, according baith
to Goddis law and manness, untill the tyme that, incontrare
Goddis law and the sai[d] band, the said Elizabeth, nocht onlie
defowlyiet my bed in the abhominabill sy[n] of adultery, with
Andro Olyphant and uthiris diverss, in the moneth of Novem-
[ber,] the yeir of God, &c. fifty sevin yeiris, bott alswa therefter,
proceding to forthir malice and abhominatioun, hes conspiret
cruellie and ungodlie my dead, murder, and destructioun, with
parttaikaris and complices of adultery.   Beseikand your m. Rantoun
ansuer heirintill, to tak cognitioun in the said mater, for setting
fordwart of Goddis Word and law, the premissis, sa far as neid
beis, beand sufficientlie provin, to decerne the said Elizabeth
to haif brokin and violatet the said band of matrimony betuix
me and hir, and, conforme to the law of God, that I therfore
aucht and suld be fre fra the samyn band, and that I may haif
fredome and libertie in God to mary in the Lord quhome I
please, according to Goddis law Christes Evangell and the
richtuousnes therof, and yo[ur] m. ansuer humelie I beseik &c.

Followis the tennour of Elizabeth Geddies ansuer.   Gedde

Ye are nocht ignorant (maist honorabill ministre and counsale of this cietie) of the contryvet accusationes, presentate to

your,wisedomes in wryte, be my husband Williame Rantoun, be
the quhilkis he alleages that, till I had plaiit the harlot, he
entrietet me accordinglie. He proceades specifieng the yeir
and moneth, yea and names ane amanges mony uthiris, with
quhome he alleages I defyled his bed ; and, nocht content to
have farcet[1] his letter with thir maist manifest lies, he con-
tinewes accusing me to haif conspyret his dead. I pray your
wisedomes maist honorabill ministre and counsale (according
to his desyre) to tak cognitioun in the mater, and gif his accu-
sationess be provin of trewth, be famose and honest men, then I
pray your wysdomes, nocht onlie to condescend to the divorcement (quhilk he maist earnestlie wisches), bot also mak me
suffer sick punischement as his oppin and manifest adulter[y]
hes deserved, and daylie dois deserve. To oppin the mater to
your wisedomes, he wald that I suld justlie purches that thing
quhilk he wranguiselie procures ; bott, I am nocht deliberate to
do swa, althocht the greatnes of his offenss, first to God and to
his Kirk, secundarlie towardes me, dois merite no les. To
importune your wysdomes with langar wryting wer. superfluos,
therfore referring the haill mater to the tryall, and to your
discretiones, I pray the aeternall God to mak yow the instrument of ane mutuall lufe betuix my husband and me.

process.

Your wisedomes maist humil and obedient oratrice,

Elizabeth Gedde, &c.

Ultimo Februarii, 1559. In the causs of divorce betuix
Williame Rantoun and Elizabeth Gedde, as ane terme to
Williame to prief his clame, the causs being suscitate at the .
actes in presence of parties, to preif, as said is, the actioun be
Williame : in the quhilk terme compered Williame, and pro-
duceit Thomas Myretoun, Bege Grahame, Alexander Rudeman,
Andro Symsone, Robert Craig; and[2] [produceit][3] Jonet Watsone
subornate and seducet be Williame, and the[n] repellet—be

----

[1] Stuffed.
[2] Here two blank leaves have been inserted by the binder. In the *Maitland
Miscellany* (iii. 224-226) the next leaf has been reversed.
[3] The upper part of this word has been cut off by the binder.

hir awin confessioun maid be hir in Williames presence—be
the judges. And the judges decernes Margaret Moncur, in [Rantoun]
A[n]struthir, Agnes Lessellis, in Fawkland, and Margaret Steyn,
in the Erlisferry, to be summond, and Andro Baxtar, against
this day fyvetene daiis; and decernes lettres of summondis, at
the instance of the [said] Williame, in presence of Elizabeth,
warnet bayth to that day.

> Followes the depositioness of witnes, produced the day
> forsaid, examinate in Sanctleonardes Scoole.

Thomas Myretoun, cietiner of Sanctandrois, baxtar, examin- Gedde
ate in the causs forsaid, upoun the pointtis of Williames libel-
late bill, the deponar beand admittet, sworne, and ressavit, be his
great aith sworne, depones that he knawis nathing in the causs
of adultery, nor of the crymes conteynet in the clame, except
that in *December* twa yeir[is] bypast, or therby, the deponar
remembyris in the said Williames awin howss, quhare James
Rutherfurde dwelles instantlie, that he and his wyfe wes wrasland
togiddir, and in the meyntyme that sche bait him in the arme,
quhilk he belevis wes nocht of malice, Margaret Lawsone beand
present in the chalmer, *plus nescit, etc.*

Andro Symsone, dwelling in the Sowthgait, be west the kirk, process.
ane maltman, examinate upoun his aith, depones that he knawis
nathing in the mater or caus, except that he seis Alexander
Rudeman haunt to the hows of Elizabeth Gedde, eatand,
drinkand, and quhiles sowpand, *plus nescit, etc.*

Robert Craig, dwelling nixt nichtbour to Elizabeth Gedde,
knawis na thing of the crymes conteynet in the bill. &c.

Margaret *alias* Bege Grahame, examinate betuix Williame
Ranto[un] and his wife, knawis nathing, except sche saw Andro
Olyph[ant] cast his cloyk abowte Elizabeth Gedde, and kis hir,
upoun [hir] awin stayr, dwelland than quhare James Rutherfurde [dwelles], and that thre yeris bigane, or therby : sche
knawis na fo[rther] of the crymes conteynet in the bill, &c.

Alexander Rudeman *conformis est Roberto Craig i[n omnibus]*.[1]

---

[1] Two corners of this leaf—an inner and an outer—have been torn off, but
the probable words are here supplied in brackets.

Decimo quarto Marcii, 1559. In the actioun and causs [of divorce moved] be Williame Rantoun against Elizabeth Gedde, as [ane term to] Williame assignet, for forther probatioun of h[is clame and to mak] diligence for Margaret Moncur, in Anstruthir, A[gnes Lessellis, in] Fawkland, and Margaret Steyn, in Erlisfe[rry: in quhilk terme] Williame produceit the saidis Margaret S[teyn, Agnes Lessellis,] and Margaret Moncur, quhilk Margaret [wes allegit be Elizabeth] to be ane kynniswoman to William &c. The [judges decernis Andro] Baxtar to be ressavit on Setterday n[ixtocum the xvj of Marche] at twa efter none. Parties war[neit to the said day.]

Followis the tenno[ur] of the summondis [quhairby the witnes] expressed in the act precedent wes su[mmond.]

Rantoun,
Gedde, process. The ministre, eldaris, and diacons, of the Christiane congregat[ioun of the] paroche of Sanctandrois, to all ministeris, eldaris, and diacons, of [the Christiane] congregatioun of Anstruthir, and Fawkland, to quhais knawleages thir [present] litteris sall come, be grace, mercie, and peace fra God our Father, and the Lo[rd] Jesus Christe ; requyreing yow, in the name of the eternall God, and of his Soone, Jesus Christe our Lord, for mutuall societie and company to be nuriset amangst us, as becummis brethren, the membyris of Christes Body, as perchaunce it sal happin yow in the elyke caiss requyre us, for sercheing furth of the veritie, to the maynteynance of virtew, and extinguissing of vice, for avancement and upsetting of the kingdome and glorie of God, to quhome onlie be all prayse, honour, triumphe, and glorie for ever. So be it. That ye summond warne and charge Margaret Moncur, in Anstruthir, Agnes Lessellis, in Fawkland, Margaret Steyn, in Erlisferry, and Andro Baxtar, to compere before us, in the Scoole of Sanct Leonardis College, within the cietie of Sanctandrois, the fourtene day of this instant moneth of Marche, at twa howris efter none, or therby, to beyr leill and suthfast, in ane actioun and caus of divorce and partysing, moved before us be Williame Rantoun, cietiner of Sanctandrois, against Elizabeth Gedde, his spous, for suspitioun of adultery, as thei will answere to

God, upoun the dreadfull day of his last judgement, quhen the secreetes of all man and women salbe disclosed ; certifiand them, gif thei compeir nocht, the said day and place, we will use all compulsioun against them, quhilk the law of God permittis us, that is cursing and excommunicatioun of the congregatioun of Christe. And this ye do, as ye sall in lyke maner requyre us in tyme cuming, gif it sal happin yow to haif the elyke càus before yow, the quhilk to do we committ to yow our full power, conjunctlie and severalie, be thir our letteres, dewlie execute and indorsate, delivering them agane to the beirar, gevin under the seill, quhilk we use in this and the lyke caussis, and the subscriptioun manuall of our scribe, at Sanctandrois the xj day of Marche, 1559.

> Dauid Spens,[1] ane of the diacons and scribe in the said caus, with my hand subscrivit.

> Followis the depositiones of the said witnes, examin-a[t] the xiiij day of Marche, 1559, in the counsal-howse at the Auld College, &c., comperand be the summondis.

Margaret Moncur, ane of the witnes ressavit in the causs, sum[mond], sche beand speret quhat sche kend of Williame Rantownes wyfe, the deponar testifies that sche come to Sanct-androis toun, four daiis before Sanctandrois day, ane yeir bigane at Sanctandrois day [las]t bypast, and sche beand ludged in Williame Rantownes, [with] hir sister, Besse Moncur, and Agnes Lessellis, than servand [in Will]iame Rantoun hows. Efter that sche wes in hir bed [with her] sister, sche raiss efter nyne houris to hir eies, sche saw ane candell licht in the chalmer Rantoun that gangis throw the hall to the galla[ry], to the baksyde, throw the lok of ane dur, sche lukeand in beheald and saw ane

---

[1] David Spens was one of the three representatives of St. Andrews in the first General Assembly, which met at Edinburgh on the 20th December 1560, and was one of those whom that Assembly considered qualified 'for ministring and teaching' (Peterkin's *Booke of the Universall Kirk*, pp. 1, 2). He was appointed minister of Monimail, from whence he was translated to Carnbee, in 1566 or the following year, and there he died in August 1575 (Scott's *Fasti*, ii. 411, 501). All the earliest entries in the *Register*, with few exceptions, are in Spens' autograph.

young man, quhilk sche weynd haid beyne Williame Rantoun
himself, and, becaus sche trowet it haid beyne the said Williame,
sche desyred nocht in to the chalmer, and this sche beheald the
space of ane half howr, be ane throwch lok, the key beand owt
of the dur. And thei haid fische that nicht to there supper.
The said man haid rede hoyse and ane dosk beyrd, lyke Maister
Robert Ki[n]pontt,[1] quhais beyrd sche lykenet the mannes
beyrd unto, quhilk Mr. Robert ane of the senioris wes present
at hir examinatioun. Sche affirmes it wes Andro Olyphant,
and sche past to hir bed sa schoun as sche saw his hoiss

Gedde   drawen of; bot the uthir twa remaneit still the quarter of ane
hour efter hir; and sche and hir marrowis rais at sex houres;
and the gude wyfe wes up before them, and hir servand called
Jonet. Sche knawis nathing of imaginatioun of his death.
And thir thingis sche saw in Robert Lermonthtis ludgeing, on
the north syde of the Sowth Gait off Sanctandrois; and there
wes nane in the chalmer, bott the man and the gude-wyfe, and
that sche drew of his hois, and therefter blew owt the candell,
and sche knew nocht gif that Elizabeth past to the bed or
nocht. &c.

process.   Agnes Lessellis, summond and sworne, sche confessis that
sche hais borne ane bayrne in huyrdome to [Wi]lliame Cowpar,
ane walcar dwelland in Edinburgh. Twa yeir bigane at Sanctandrois day, sche lay in Williame Rantones howse, beand [then
in] company with Margaret Moncur alanerlie, witnes forsaid,
in [the] gallary, within ane ludgeing of Williames, at Argailles
port on the so[uth] syde of the gate. There is nocht ane hows
betuix the gallary and the h[owse], quhilk sche and Margaret
Moncur lay in; and Margaret Moncur called upoun hir, and
sche raiss, beand walked b[e] Margaret, and luket at the dur,
beand sett up a char be Margaret Moncur; and thei luket
bayth in at the dur at aneis; and sche saw ane [man] with ane
payr of rede hoyse; and Margaret Moncur wes up befor[e]
Agnes, and remanet efter hir at the dur; and the candell wes
p[ut] owt or sche lay doun; the dur wes oppin; and sche
and Margaret Moncur raiss upoun the morne at sevin or aucht

---

[1] Best known as Robert Pont; see references in note 4, p. 2. This page of
the *Register* is so defaced that much of it is almost illegible.

houris, and the gu[de]-wyfe raiss evin then. And sche knew
nocht the man, nor yit kna[wis] him nocht; and sche saw
nocht Elizabeth pass to the bed with the m[an]. Sche remembyris nocht quhat thei had that nicht to ther suppe[r]. Sche
knawis nocht the machinatioun of death be Elizabeth to
Williame, and sche beleves Elizabeth to be ane hones[t] woman,
and never saw the contrar therof.

Margaret Stevin, summond and sworne, purges hirself of
subornaci[oun], beand demandate of hir aith, sche knawis na
thing of Elizabeth Gedd[e], Williame Rantones wyfe, bot that
sche is ane honest woman, a[nd] hais nocht pollutet his bed.
Sche deniis that ever sche saw on[y] suspitioun betuix Andro
Olyphant and Elizabeth, and sche hais seyne Andro Olyphant
ly in William Rantones howse; bott never uthirwyse bot
quhen William Rantoun wes at hayme: and .sche knawis na
uthir thing in this caus.

xvj Marcii.

Andro Baxtar, witnes, summond and sworne, in the causs of Rantoun
Williame Rantoun against Elizabeth Gedde, his spows, he
knawis na thing to Williame Rantones wyfe, bott that sche is
ane honest woman, and in spetiall betuix Andro Olyphant and
hir, and he knawis never machinatioun of `dead be hir to
him. &c.

Decimo sexto mensis Martii, 1559. In the causs of divorce
of Williame Rantoun against Elizabeth Gedde, as in the terme
to produce Andro Baxtar, witnes in the said actioun, the said
Andro beand produceit, and examinate as is abone conteynet
in his depositioun, the minister and eldaris, judges, hais statute
to pronunce in the said causs, parties being warned to that
effect, to Thurisday nixtocum &c.

Vigesimo primo mensis Martii predicti, 1559. In the actioun
and causs off divorce, proponet be Williame Rantoun against
Elizabeth Gedde, his spows, as in the terme statute be the
minister and senioris to pronunce in the said causs, haiffand
the assistence and counsall of Mr. Johne Dowglas, Rectour of Gedde
the Universitie of Sanctandrois, and Johne Wynrame, Suppriour

of Sanctandrois, Mr. Williame Skene and Maister Johne Ruthirfurd, hais pronunceit ane sentence absolvatour for Elizabeth Gedde, to be put in forme, and t[o] be publicate in the pulpate upoun Sounday nixtocum, viz. xxiiij Marche, the seniouris beand present there to affirme the samyn. The parties summond to heir and see the said sentence publicate. &c.

process.

The sentence in forme as it wes red oppinlie be Johne Knox minister in presence of the congregatioun, &c. &c. &c. &c.

With incalling of the name of the everliving God, and of his Sonne Jesus Christe, quhai beiris lele and anefauld witnessing to our consciences, we, the minister and seniouris of this our Christiane congregatioun within the parochin of Sanctandrois, judges in the actioun and causs moved and intented before us be Williame Rantoun, cietiner of this cietie and brother of the said congregatioun, against Elizabeth Gedde, his spowss, for the alleaget committing of adultery be his said spows with Andro Olyphant, and divers utheris (in generall saying), lyke as the petitioun be him before us produced mair at lenth beares in effect &c.: the said petitioun with ansuereing therto, reasones, jures, allegationess, with testimonies and depositiones of witnes, and all thinges concerning baith the saidis parties, in presence of Mr. Johne Dowglass, Rectour of the Universitie of Sanctandrois, Johne Wynrame, Suppriour, men of singular eruditioun and understanding in the Scriptures and Word of God, with Masteris Williame Skene and Johne Ruthirfurde, men of cuning in sindry sciences (with quhome we communicate[d] the secretes of the meritis of the said actioun and caus), being be us and them hard, seene, consyderet, and ryplie understand: and find-and na causs, of thei thinges produced before us, and be us consyderet and seene, as said is, quherfore the said Elizabeth suld be divorcet fra the said Williame; bot in tyme cuming, and fra thyne fur[th], that sche suld be absolvet fra his petitioun forsaid, and crymes therin layd to hir charge injustlie, and to be intertineyt and trietet be him in maner following: (we haiffand onlie God before our eies), be this our sentence

The sentence pronunced for Gedde, &c.

Sentence pronunced for Gedde, &c., &c.

Sonny was exhortit and promittit my the consistorie ettand

Judgis Jndicatur apony Symunday the XII day of the

month of march — 2.73.9.

David Spens ane of the diacons of the christiane

congregatioun of Sanctandrois and Scribe my the actionis

and causs forsaid vritt my hand

27.1

diffinityve, pronuncess, decerness, and declaress, the said Elizabeth innocent of the crymes layd to hir charge, conteynet in the
petitioun forsaid, and absolves hir therfra; and that the said
Williame Rantoun sall maynteyne, triet, and intertiney, the
said Elizabeth Gedde, his spows (quhome, nochwithstanding
ony thing alleaget or produced be the said Williame before us
against hir, we find to be ane honest woman), as becummis ane
husband on all behalfis to triet his wyfe, in bed and buyrd
and all uthir thinges, according to the law and commandment
of God, be this our sentence diffinityve, publiclie heir red and
manifestate in the presence of God and yow heyr gathered and
conveyned congregatioun, this Sounday the xxiiij day of the
moneth of Marche, lykeas the samyn wes decerned and pronunced in the consistory, settand judges juditialie, upoun
Thurisday the xxj day of the samyne moneth of Marche, 1559.

> Dauid Spens, ane of the diacons of the Christiane
> congregatioun of Sanctandrois, and scribe in the
> actioun and causs forsaid, with my hand subscrivit.

Ultimo Marcii, 1560.　Margaret Aidnam askit God and the
congregatioun forgivenes of the adultery committed be hir
with William Rantoun, publiclie in the paroche kirk of this
toun, Johne Knox beand at that tyme minister, &c.[1]　☞ *nota.*

---

[1] This entry is partly written in the margin, opposite the signature of Spens.
The Protestants of Edinburgh had elected Knox as their minister on the 7th of
July 1559; but as it would have been dangerous for him to have remained there
after the treaty with the Queen Regent, the Lords of the Congregation constrained him to leave his flock under Willock's charge before the end of that
month; and sent him as a commissioner to explain their cause to the English,
in order to obtain help (*Wodrow Miscellany*, pp. 63, 65; Laing's *Knox*, i. 388;
ii. 32).　On the 2d of the following September he wrote from St. Andrews:—
'Notwithstanding the fevers have vexed me the space of a moneth, yitt have I
travelled through the most part of this realme, where (all praise be to his blessed
Majestie) men of all sorte and conditiounis embrace the truthe' (Laing's *Knox*,
vi. 78).　He appears to have visited St. Andrews frequently about this time, for,
besides the foregoing letter, he wrote from it on the 15th of August, 21st of September, and the 15th of October.　The result of the skirmish at Restalrig, on
the 6th of November, caused the Lords to retire to Stirling, where, on the 8th,
they resolved to separate.　Several went to Glasgow, and the others to St.
Andrews, Knox accompanying the latter (Laing's *Knox*, i. 465, 473; ii. 5;
Spottiswoode's *History*, i. 307).　He remained at St. Andrews until the end of
April 1560, when he returned to Edinburgh (M'Crie's *Knox*, 1861, p. 205);

Decimo sexto Marcii, 1559. The quhilk day, Andro Lummisden called for nocht adhering to Besse Smyth his spows. He confessis that he hais nocht adheyred to hir in bed this twelf yeir bigane. In respect of his confessioun, and delatioun past therupoun, the ministers and eldaris decerness him to adheyre in bed and buyrd, within fourty aucht houris, to his said spows; and to lat the samyne adheyreing be notified to the minister and eldaris forsaid, within aucht daiis efter the said xlviij houris, be the said Besse Smyth his spows, and uthiris ther nychbouris, under the payne of all severe ecclesiasticall discipline that may be layd to his charge, with the incalling of the civile powaris hand, &c.

Die Jovis quarto mensis Aprilis, 1560. The quhilk day, M. Johne Todrick[1] and Margaret Ramsay being called, for the

---

but, as already mentioned (footnote, p. 3), it was three months later ere he was formally appointed to that charge by the Commissioners of Burghs. Besides occasional visits, he must have been about five months continuously in St. Andrews. Over and above its importance as, still in name at least, the ecclesiastical capital of the country, and the seat of the oldest and principal Scottish University, this city had peculiar personal attractions for Knox. Here he had been called to the ministry by John Rough in 1547; and next year, when a sickly captive in the French galleys, and nigh to the gates of death, he exclaimed: 'I see the stepill of that place, whare God first in publict opened my mouth to his glorie, and I am fullie persuaded, how weak that ever I now appear, that I shall nott departe this lyif, till that my toung shall glorifie his godlie name in the same place' (Laing's *Knox*, i. 228). At the General Assembly in December 1565 'the commissioners of Sanct Andrews requested that Mr. Knox might be transplanted and placed in Sanct Andrews, which was refused. The Assemblie willed them to choice one out of their own Universitie in place of Christopher Gudman, who latelie departed into England' (Keith's *History*, iii. 127, 128). When Kirkcaldy of Grange received the Hamiltons into Edinburgh on the 4th of May 1571, Knox's position became very critical; and, to please his friends, he left next day. He first went to Abbotshall, and in July to St. Andrews, where he remained until August 1572. His love to it as the place where first ' he gave the rout

'Till Antechrist that Romische slave,'
and his visit to it
' Quhen he was not far fra his grave,'
are referred to by John Davidson in his *Schort Discurs of the Estaitis quha hes caus to deploir the deith of this excellent Servand of God*, reprinted by M'Crie in the supplement to his *Life of Knox*, by Maidment in Davidson's *Poetical Remains*, and by Dr. Rogers in his *Three Scottish Reformers*.

[1] Mr. John Todrick is mentioned in 1530 as chaplain of the altar of St. Thomas the Martyr in the parish church of St. Andrews, and in 1540 as a chaplain in

cryme of adultery, before minister, seniouris, and counsall, to haif ressavit pennance for the said syn, and findand na signe of penitence in them, are suspendet for forther trying of there syn, to the effect that signes of worthie repentance may be brochon in them be prayeris and commoun supplicationes in the congregatioun.

The tennour of the clame of Catheryne Tweddell clamand mariage of Walter Ramsay lorymar[1] in the Auld College.

Minister, eldaris, and counsall, of the Christiane congrega- Tweddell, tioun of this cietie, reformed now toward the religioun of Ramsay. Christe Jesus, unto your wysedomes, humelie menes and schawis Catheryne Tweddell that, quhare be the seductioun of Walter Ramsay, lorymar in this cietie, I haif gevin my body to be useit be him, quharethrow I haif conceved and borne ane bayrne to him, and all this I haif done because, in the presence of God onlie, he gaif me his fayth that he suld fulfill the band of mariage in faice of the congregatioun, or Haly Kirk, quhilk promise he diverss tyme iterate and renewed to me, be giving me his rycht hand, before I wald consent to his desyres; and now the said Walter deniis the said his faythfull promise of mariage maid to me and purposis nocht to complete the samyn with me, except he be compelled. Beseikand your wysedomes heirfor to causs and compell him him (sic) to fulfill that, quhilk he hes maid, ane faythfull promise of mariage to me, according as the law of God will.

Undecimo die mensis Aprilis, anno Domini, 1560. The quhilk Tweddell, day, Walter Ramsay being clamed be Catheryne Tweddell for Ramsay, &c. mariage, to be complieted with hir in the faice of Haly Kirk, according to his promise to hir maid, the minister and eldaris, according to the law of God, decerness the said Walter to compliete the said band with the said Catheryne, becaus the

---

the aisle of that church (*Abstract of the Writs of St. Andrews*, Nos. 3, 165). He also occurs as a notary public on the 16th of March 1540-41 (*Records of the Priory of the Isle of May*, p. xcvi.). On the 3d of February 1559-60 he joined the congregation by approving the band, and he was one of those who likewise made a formal recantation that month (*supra*, pp. 11, 14).

[1] Saddler, or bridlemaker.

woman alleaget hir to haif beyne ane virgine or he gat hir, and
he culd say na thing in the contrare therof, tyme and place
being offered to him to object to the contrare and prief the
samyn, and Walter Ramsay being demanded give he wald use
ony forthir defenss in this mater, and give he knew ony lauchfull
caus quhareby he mycht be absolved fra hir petitioun, he said
he wald use na thing against hyr. &c.

The tennour of the clame of Besse Millar clamand mariage of Alexander Adie.

Myllar, Adie.

I, Besse Millar, servand to Dauid Coling, alleages promyse
of mariage maid to me be Alexander Adie, quharefore he may
nocht compliet the band of mariage with Marioun Ogilvy, or
yit ony uthir woman, be reasone of mariage promiseit to me,
before ony promise maid be him to the said Marioun Ogilvy,
or ony uthir woman, heirfore desyres the minister to causs tryall
be takyn in the matter, and justice be ministrate to bayth the
parties, according to the will of God and gude conscience, &c.

Answer therto followis.

Myllar, Adie.

Honorabill sirs, minister, eldaris, and diacons, of the Christiane congregatioun of this cietie, unto your m. humelie menis
and complanes I, Alexander Adie, and Marioun Ogilvy my spows,
upoun Besse Millar, that quhare I, to haif avoydet fornicatioun,
contracted and handfast the said Marioun Ogilvy, to haif hir
to my lauchfull wyfe, and promitted faythfullie to solemne the
band of mariage with hir, in faice of the congregatioun, and
to that effect caused the minister to proclayme the bannes, as
use is; and now the said Besse Millar wranguislie, with[out][1]
ony promise of me maid to hir of mariage, clames me, I never
makand hir promise of mariage, nor yit hes sche ony bayrnes
to me, nor yit promiste I to hir ony of my gayr. And suppos
I had carnall daill of hir of before, committand therby fornicatioun with hir, to evade that syn I cheset to me the said
Marioun to be my lauchfull wyffe, quhai before the said con-

---

[1] Omitted.

tract convened the said Besse, and requyred of hir give I haid maid ony promise to the said Besse to haif mariet hir, quhai ansuered and said, Marioun I pray God that every ane of yow haif gude of ane uthir, for I haif nathing to say to him nor yow, bot I wald ye war als weill as myself. And in harvesd last wes, the said Besse granttes that I promiste never mariage to hir, and discharget me becaus ther wes na promise betuix me and hir. And, as I sall ansuere before the aeternall God, I promiset never to mary the said Besse, nor yit to give hir ony of my gayr. And in sa far as I had carnall dayll with hir, it come of hir seiking, and nocht of myne; and sche come to me onsend for quhen ever I haid dayll with hir; quhilk syn I repent fra the boddoum of my hart, and askis God mercie, and sall never in tyme cuming God willing committ siclyke. Quherfore, I beseik your m. to caus the said Besse mak me and spous forsaid ane sufficient amendis, for the oppin sclandering of me before the haill congregatioun, sayand that I suld haif promiste to hir mariage, quhilk I did never, as I call and tak God to witnes. And your m. ansuer heirintill humelie I beseik. &c. &c.

Dicto die undecimo mensis Aprilis, 1560. The quhilk day, in the caus moved be Besse Millar, clamand mariage of Alexander Adie, at the desyre of the said Alexander, it is admitted till him, be the minister and eldaris, to prief his byll. He named twa witnes, thai ar to say, Beatrice Buge and Jhone Ewene. Beatrice Buge being produced and examinate, it is statute to Alexander to mak diligence for Johne Ewene upoun Thurisday nixtocum, Alexander haifand na ma witnes to produce bott Johne onlie, in presence of parties warned to the said day.

> The depositiones of witnes produced be Alexander Ad[ie] against Besse Myllar, togiddir [with][1] Alexander Adies aw[in] confessioun in presens of minister and eldaris maid, &c.

Beatrice Buge, sister to Johne Buge, wricht and cietiner of [*Depositio* this cietie, being sworne and examinate, be hir great aith Buge.]

---

[1] Omitted.

sworne, sche knawes nathing of talking of mariage betuix
Alexander Adie and Besse Myllar; and being demandet
quhidder give sche ever hard Besse Myllar discharge ony
promise of mariage maid be Alexander Adie, sche saiis sche
hard never hir say that sche had ony promise of mariage of
him, nor yit discharge ony promise; bott upoun the harvesd
field, sche being scorned with uthiris, sche said, Quhat scorne
ye me with Alexander Adie, I haif nocht ado with him, God
send him ane gude wyfe, or ellis never ane. As to Marioun
Ogilvy, that nicht that Marioun wes handfast with Alexander
Adie, the deponar past to Dauid Colingis howss, and Marioun
desyred Besse Millar to gang and drink with hir father, and
Besse Millar said, Forsuith Marioun I will nocht gang with
yow, I haif nocht to say to yow, mekle joy mott ye haif of
him. And sche knawis na forthir. &c.

Confessio
Adie.

Alexander Adie confesis tha[t] he knew never of Besse Millar
bot sche wes ane maden; and he never maid promise to hir,
nor never gaif hir gayr, nor yit tuke gayr fra hir.

Die vigesimo quinto Aprilis, 1560. The quhilk day, the
caus of Alexander Adie against Besse Millar suscitate and
newlie walkynnet, as haifand the desyre to mak diligence for
Johne Ewene, witnes named be Alexander Adie, for the probatioun of his bill. Johne Ewene being produceit, sworne, and
examinate, the minister and eldaris hais statute Thuristay, the

ii. Maii.

secund day of Maii to pronunce in presence of parties warned
to that day.

Followis the tennour of Jhone Ewenes depositioun.

Depositio
Ewene.

Johne Ewene, witnes produced for Alexander Adie against
Besse Millar, being sworne and admitted, depones that he hard
never ony promise of mariage nor commowning of mariage
betuix them, bot fairn-year[1] in harvesd, upoun the harvesd
field, that Besse Millar said to the deponar, schawand to hir
that Alexander Adie suld mary Marioun Ogilvy, and sche said,
God give every ane of them gude of uthir, for I haif na quhite

---

[1] Last year.

thried to quyte him out. Nane beand present bott he and
sche and the hors, &c. He knawis na mayr.

Jovis.

Die secundo mensis Maii, 1560. The quhilk day, in the actioun
and caus moved be Besse Millar against Alexander Adie ane[1] the
clame of mariage, as in the terme statute be the minister and
eldaris to pronunce, thei haif continewed the mater for forther
avisement to be haid therintill quhill Thuirsday the xvj day *Jovis, xvj. Maii,*
of Maii, in presence of parties warned to the said day. *ad pronuntian-
dum.*

Followis ane dilatioun against Agnes McKe that sche, mur- Macke, Adie,
murand against Gods Word, imputtis the wyte, to the Word &c.
and doctryne now teachet in this cietie, of the darth presentlie
regnand in this cuntrey : quhilk sayingis ar provin be [*blank*]
Erskin spouss to Johne Watsone, *alias* Irische Jocke, and Agnes
Symsone. And alswa that sche said, God lat them never haif
mayr part of the joy of Heaven, then they leit hir haif of the
communioun : provin be Mr. Johne Dowglass, Rectour, and Mr.
Robert Hammyltoun,[2] regent of the New College, &c.

---

[1] Should be *anent.*

[2] Mr. Robert Hammiltoun, as rector of Torrens, witnesses à charter of Archbishop Hamilton's in 1558 (*Register of Great Seal,* vol. iv., No. 1742). Knox
includes him among the 'zelous men,' who that year exhorted their brethren,
when they had 'na publict ministeris of the Worde' (Laing's *Knox,* i. 300).
And, in 1559, he accompanied Knox in his mission to solicit aid from the English.
They probably set out about the end of July. Knox's narrative seems to imply that
he left Edinburgh with the Lords of the Congregation, on the 26th of July, for
Linlithgow ; from whence they went to Stirling, where they subscribed a band
on the 1st of August, and sent 'ane or twa messingeris' to prove the English,—
Sir Henry Percy having asked Knox to meet him at Alnwick, and Cecil having
arranged to meet him at Stamford (*Ibid.* i. 381, 382 ; ii. 32). But Knox can
hardly have been at Stirling on the 1st of August, for he and Hamilton sailing
from Pittenweem arrived at Holy Island, and there learning that there was some
uncertainty as to Percy's whereabouts, they addressed themselves to Croft, Captain
of Berwick, and Warden of the East Marches, who advised them to proceed no
further ; 'the said Jhone and Maister Robert followed his counsall,' and remained
two days with him in Berwick Castle ; yet Knox was back again in Stirling by
the 6th of August (*Ibid.* ii. 32-34 ; vi. 63, 64). Hamilton appears to have been
in hearty agreement with Knox for some time after this, for he was one of the
principal ministers who insisted, in 1561, that the mass should be taken from the
Queen (*Ibid.* ii. 291). He afterwards became the minister of St. Andrews, and
Principal of St. Mary's College.

Adie.

Walter Adie delatat with thir wordis, Wille Mayne,[1] will ye give me ane techet [2] to be served the Divellis

---

[1] One of the deacons.

[2] A ticket or token. Steuart of Pardovan speaks synonymously of 'tickets,' 'warrants,' or 'tokens,' and also more specifically of 'the parish lead ticket' (*Collections and Observations*, 1709, p. 138). Long before his time, they seem to have been commonly made of metal; but it may be doubted whether the 'twelf stand of cairts to be tikkits' for the communion in Edinburgh, in 1578, were not rather some sort of stiff paper or cardboard, even although a goldsmith was employed 'for stamping of thame' (Lee's *Lectures*, i. 392); and the communion tickets of St. Andrews, in 1656, can scarcely have been metal, seeing they were to be 'written by the clerk' (*Ibid.* p. 401). When the Lord's Supper was first dispensed to the Secession Congregation at Ceres in 1743, two thousand tokens were distributed; and 'according to tradition, these tokens were circular pieces of leather, about the size of a shilling, with a hole perforated in the centre' (Mackelvie's *Annals and Statistics of the U.P. Church*, pp. 126, 127). The first Presbyterian Church of the city of Charleston, U.S., used paper tickets until the beginning of this century, when elaborately engraved silver tokens were adopted (*Notes and Queries*, fifth series, xi. 14). The reference in the text is probably the earliest on record to the use of communion tokens in the Reformed Church of Scotland. Indeed, it is so early that it confirms the conjecture, that it was one of those usages of the Romish Church which were continued; and the supposition is further strengthened by the fact—here stated on the authority of my friend, the Rev. Andrew Fleming of Blairs College— 'that the custom of giving tokens or tickets to those going to communion at Easter, "when all Catholics are obliged to go,"' was observed 'in the Catholic Church of St. Andrew's, Glasgow, some forty years ago, but is now abolished.' He also informs me that 'tokens or rather tickets' are still used in Rome; 'but they are given to the communicants at Easter, after they have been at the communion, and not before.' Mr. Cochran-Patrick mentions a Scottish token dated 1622, and expresses the opinion that 'probably some of the undated ones are earlier.' He further says that 'leaden counters were used in the Catholic churches before the Reformation;' and adds, 'I have some in my collection with emblems on them which could hardly have been in use in the Presbyterian Church in the seventeenth or eighteenth century' (*Notes and Queries*, fifth series, xi. 515). In an earlier number of the same journal, another writer states his conviction that what are known as 'Abbey tokens'—which are made of lead or pewter, and quite distinct from the copper coins known as 'Abbey pieces'—were. given to the frequenters of the sacraments. He refers to the tokens still presented to the members of many (if not all) of the Roman Catholic confraternities on their reception; to those of the Templars and secret societies of the Middle Ages; to the traces of their use as badges of membership in the mysteries of Paganism; and sees an allusion to an old custom in the Scriptural promise of 'a white stone, and in the stone a new name written, which no man knoweth saving he that receiveth it' (*Ibid.* i. 201, 202). When the General Assembly met at Glasgow in 1638, 'the churche durris wes straitlie gardit by the toune, none had entress bot he who had ane taikin of leid, declairing he wes ane covenanter' (Spalding's *Memorialls of the Trubles*, Spald. Club, i. 117). In the

dirt?[1]   I sall by[2] ane poynt of wyne and ane laif, and I
sall haif als gude ane sacrament as the best of them all sall
haif.   Provin be Mr. Johne Ruthirfurd, William Mayne, and
George Blak, &c.

The minister and eldaris decernis Agnes McKe and Walter   *xxvj Aprilis,*
                                                            1560.
                                                            Macky, [Adie.]

Booke of Common Prayer, intended for the Church of Scotland, and written
in the reign of James the Sixth, it is ordered that, 'So many as intend to be
partakers of the holy communion, shall receive there tokins from the minister
the night before' (*Scottish Liturgies of the Reign of James VI.,* 1871, p. 65).
And Dr. Sprott, in one of his editorial notes, says that tokens 'have always
been used too in the Episcopal congregations of old standing in the north of
Scotland' (*Ibid.* p. 107).   They were also used in England.   Cardinal Pole is
said to have employed them in Queen Mary's time, in order to know who con-
formed and who did not; but I have been unable to find the authority for this
statement.   The evidence however of their use in that country at a later period
is abundant.   The token-books of St. Saviour's, Southwark, extending from
1592 or 1593 to 1630, are still preserved.   'The street name is given as a heading or in the left margin, and the names of the communicants run in column.'   In
1596, '2200 tokens are accounted for at 2d. each;' and in 1620, '1862 tokens
at 3d. each' (*Notes and Queries,* fifth series, x. 108,109).   They are mentioned in
the churchwardens' book of the parish of Newbury in 1658; and in the parish
account book of St. Peter, Mancroft, Norwich (*Ibid.* xi. 14, 515).   Perhaps the
most interesting reference to their use in England occurs in the trial in 1634 of
John Richardson, Esq., who farmed the tithes and oblations of 'the chaplerie of
Sct. Margaret's in Durham.'   He was charged with disturbing divine service on
Palm Sunday, Good Friday, and Easter Day, by his irreverent manner of col-
lecting the dues.   One witness deponed that, at Easter time and on communion
days, Richardson's predecessor 'tooke Easter reckeninges of such people as
received the holie communion, and there accompted with them, and delivered
and received tokens of them as is used in other parishes, as examinate beleveth.'
Another testified that Richardson, or his under-farmers, usually write down
'the names of all the then communicants not householders, and att the tyme of
writinge there names dow deliver them tokens, which in the tyme of the administracion of the sacrament,' they 'call for againe, to the end they may knowe
whoe doe pay their Easter offeringes and whoe doe not.'   And another explained
that. sixteen or twenty years previously he had seen 'Richardson at Easter time
goe upp and downe amongst the communicants, and in time of receiving the
holie communion receive of some communicants some monies, and take in
certaine leade tokens (as the use of the parish is) from such as had formerlie by
there maisters reckened and payed.'   And that he had 'seene all whoe were
under-farmors to Richardson since that tyme . . . doe the like' (*Acts of the High
Commission Court within the Diocese of Durham,* Surtees Society, pp. 82-100).
The Presbyterian Church has never charged dues for the sacraments nor sold
her tokens.

   [1] Divellis dirt was evidently used to express the greatest contempt.   In For-
farshire, asafœtida pills are widely known as devil's dirt pills !   [2] Buy.

Adie to be fraternalie corrected, efter ecclesiasticall disciplyne, and supplicatioun to be directit to the ballies and civile magistrates, for forthir correctioun civilie to be put to the saidis personeis, and proces deduced in the consistory extracted and send to the saidis magistrates, the said personeis being be the minister judicialie monysed to absteyne in tyme cuming fra sic blasphemous sayingis, under paynes of cursing.

xxvj Aprilis.
[Murdow.]

Margaret Murdow delatate for blasphemous sayings against the sacrament of the body and blude of Christ, sayand thir wordes in the oppin fische mercat, Ye gif your supper quhome to ye pleass: I traist to God ye salbe fayne to steale fra that supper and dennar, or[1] this day tolmonth. Provin be Margaret Carstares on Thursday *secundo Maii*. To prief be uthir witnes, Setterday *quarto Maii*, 1560.

Probanda Jovis,
2 (sic) Maii.

Die secundo
Maii, 1560.
[Law.]

Johne Law said, The *D*ivell knok owt Johne Knox harnes,[2] for, quhen he wald se him hanget, he wald gett his sacrament. Johne Law granttis that he said, God give Knox be banget.

Die secundo
Maii, 1560.
[Petillok.]

Williame Petillok, dwelland be este Thomas Martynes, said, The *D*ivell ane kirk will I gang to! and, The *D*ivell burn up the kirk or[1] I come into it! and, It wer gude that Knox war kend the gayt quhare fra he come! Williame granttes thir wordes, The *D*ivell cayre[3] the kyrk! *Probanda ulterius Jovis nono Maii proxime futuro.*

Jovis, 9 Maii
probanda.

[Thomsone.]

Elene Thomsone, the spous of Johne Dryburgh, ane playne contemner of the Word of God, nethir cummes to preaching nor prayeris, ane evill speaker of the ministeris, and espetialie of Johne Knox, and ane blasphemar of the Sacramentes. *Probanda Sabbato[4] quarto Maii.*

Sabbatum, 4
Maii.

[Howburne and Downe]
continuatur ad
Jovis, 9 Maii.

Andro Howburne and Margaret Downe, fornicatouris, continewed ther correctioun quhill Thuirsday the nynte day of May, in hope of mariage to be compleitit amangst them. *Interim,* that thei absteyne frome all societie and mutuall company, under the panys of ecclesiasticall disciplyne.

---

[1] Ere.   [2] Brains.   [3] Rake up.   [4] Here used for Saturday.

Followis the clame of Elizabeth Gedde, conteynand
the intenting and moving of ane actioun against
Williame Rantoun, hir husband, for adultery be him
committed, for divorcement, &c.

Minister, eldaris, and counsale, of this sette, unto your wysedomes humelie meynis and compleynes your daylie oratrice,
Elizabeth Gedde, upoun Williame Rantoun, that quhare we
beand copuled and juned in lauchfull mariage, and the said
Williame ressavand the sowme of twa hundreth markis, usuall
money of this realme, in tocher gude fra my father and uthiris
friendes, I treatet, obeyed and served the said Williame accordingly as become me of dewtie, conforme to the institutioun of
that holy band, unto the monethis of November and December,
in the yeir of God, &c. fifty aucht yeris, quhen the said
Williame abstracted him fra my company, leavand me al
uterlie destitute of his solace and interteyneing as he aucht to
haif done on the uthir syde. And nevertheles the said Williame,
contrare to the command of God, and his faythfull promise
lauchfullie maid to me the tyme of the solemnizatioun of the
said mariage, tuke ane chalmer, in the este end of the Sowth
Gait of this cietie, on the north syde therof, perteyning to
Master Thomas Meffen ; quhare in the saidis monethes and yeir,
and diverss uthir tymes sensyne, [he][1] held Margaret Aidname
with him in company, sumtymes by the space of xv or xx daiis
togiddir, and committed the abhominable cryme and syn of
adultery with hir ; quhilk abhominatioun, committed with the
said Margaret, he hais confessed judicialie before your wysedomes, and also in presence of the haill congregatioun of this
cietie ;[2] quharethrow, of the law of God, I acht and suld be
separated and divorced fra him, and libertie to be granted to
me to mary in the Lord, as maist gudelie may seyme expedient,
and alss the said sowme of twa hundreth markes gevin with me
in tocher refoundet, restored, and payed, agane to me : be-
siekand your nobilitie and wysedomes heirfor, maist humelie,
the premissis beand sufficientlie provin as accordis, to pronunce

Rantoun,
Gedde.

---

[1] Omitted.   [2] *Supra*, p. 6.

and decerne me to be divorced and separated *simpliciter* fra the
societie and company of the said Williame in all tymes cuming,
and libertie granted and given me to mary in the Lord,
togiddir with restitutioun of the said sowme of twa hundreth
markes gevin to the said Williame in tocher tyme of the contract of mariage forsaid, according to equitie and justice.   And
your gude ansuer heirin, maist humelie, I beseik, &c. &c.

   Secundo die mensis Maii, 1560.   The quhilk day, Williame
Rantoun being warned to compeir in the consistory, before the
minister, eldaris and counsall, at the instance of Elizabeth
Gedde, his putative spous, the saidis Williame and Elizabeth
judicialie compearand, the said Elizabeth produced the petitioun and clame preinserted, and, conform to the samyn,
proponed ane actioun of divorce (for adultery done and
committed be the said Williame with Margaret Aidnam)
against the said Williame ; quhilk adultery libelled the said
Williame hes judicialie confessed, and the ressait of aucht
scoyr merkis of tocher gude, and the residew of the clame.   It
is statute be the ministeris, eldaris, and counsale, to prief
forthir be witnes, in the actioun and caus of divorce and
adultery.   And the saidis Williame and Elizabeth hais chosin
Masteris Williame Skene,[1] Johne Ruthirfurde, and Robert Pont,
with Johne Motto, amicable compositouris equalie amangst
them.   And Mr. Johne Dowglas, Rectour, and Mr. Johne

---

[1] Skene has been already twice mentioned in the text ; namely, as one of
those who joined the congregation by approving the 'band,' and as a man 'of
cunning in sindry sciences,' consulted by the session in the case of Rantoun
against his wife (*supra*, pp. 8, 26).   He was a brother of the more famous Sir
John Skene, who collected the Acts of Parliament.   William appears to have
studied abroad, and was incorporated in St. Mary's College in 1556 ; the General
Assembly of 1560 deemed him fit for 'ministring and teaching,' but it is uncertain
whether ' he ever had any particular charge ; ' he was Conservator of the Privi-
leges of St. Andrews University, and was elected Dean of the Faculty of Arts
in 1565 (M'Crie's *Melville*, ii. 373, 474; Peterkin's *Booke of the Universall
Kirk*, p. 2 ; Lee's *Lectures*, i. 228).   He was at the same time the teacher of
law in St. Mary's, and the Commissary of St. Andrews.   James Melvill says that
he went to the Consistory, ' whar the Comissar wald tak pleasour to schaw us the
practise, in judgment, of that quhilk he teatched in the scholles.   He was a man
of skill and guid conscience in his calling, lernit and diligent in his profession,
and tuk delyt in nathing mair nor to repeat ower and ower again to anie schollar
that wald ask him the thingis he haid bein teatching' (*Diary*, Wod. Soc. p. 29).

Wynrame, Suppriour, ower men for decideing of the matter of tocher gude, &c.   And witnes to be produced upoun the divorce on Setterday, fort day of Maii, in presence of parties warned therto.

Setterday. 4 Maii.

Quarto mensis Maii, 1560.   The quhilk day, in the actioun and causs of divorcement, moved and intented be Elizabeth Geddy, against Williame Rantoun, hir praetended husband, as in the terme to prief forthir in the said causs be witnes, compered Elizabeth Geddy, in presens of Williame, and produced sex witnes, viz. Cristyne Burell, Mathew King, and Jonet Cuninghame his spows, Andro Meffen, tailyeour, Alexander Smyth, doctour of the Sang Scole in the Abbay, and [*blank*] his wyfe; quhilkis, beand admitted be William, he useand na exceptioun against them, haiffand place and tyme offerred therto, wer sworne and exexaminated (*sic*), as efter followis in ther depositiones under inserted.   And with consent of parties, the minister and eldaris hes statute to pronunce on Thurisday nixt to come, *nono Maii*.

Jovis, 9 Maii.

Followis the depositiones of witnes in the caus of William Rantoun, examinated the said ferd day of Maii 1560, and Elizabeth Gedde, his spous putative, &c.

Cristyne Burell examinated in the causs of Williame Rantoun. Sche knawis nathing, bot that upoun ane nicht the deponar past to the stare of hir hows quhare sche dwellis, and there fand the dur snecked and unbarred, and sche barred the dur; and, efter that, Margaret Aidnam come to the dur, and culd nocht gett it oppin, and therefter sche past away and brocht Williame Rantones quhingar and oppynned the dur; quhilk quhingar, the deponar fand under ane almery, and sche speirit at at (*sic*) Margaret Aidnam, and sche said it wes Williame Rantones quhingar, and sche grantted sche wes that nycht in his chalmer.

[Depositiones of witnes in the caus of Rantoun and Gedde.]

Mathew King depones, that quhen he dwelt on the stare,

quhare the clerkis chalmer wes, in Mr. Thomas Meffens land, in the est-end of the Sowth Gait, that he dwelland under, and Williame Rantone abone, saw Margaret Aidnam in Williame his chalmer, and [she][1] wald be there xv or xx daiis; and Williame grantted that he had hir, and wald part with his wyfe and mary hir, and desyred the deponar nocht to revele his secrete.

Jonet Cuninghame the said Mathewes wyf is conforme to Mathew hir husband *in omnibus, etc.*

Andro Meffen, tailyeour, depones that he hes seyne Margaret Aidnam in the bed with Williame Rantoun anes, and divers tymes hir allane lyand in his bed, in his chalmer forsaid.

Alexander Smyth, doctour of the Sang Scole in the Abbay,[2]

---

[1] Omitted.

[2] In treating of pre-Reformation times in Scotland, Cosmo Innes says, 'There were schools for teaching singing and chanting in the different cathedral cities, and the term "sang-school" is not yet forgotten in the North, where the choral school has often been the ground-work of our burgh grammar schools. The education, even of the chorister, required a knowledge of reading, not a very valuable acquisition for the laity when books were so scarce; and to this was added instruction in the principles of grammar, and the beginning of classical learning' (*Scotland in the Middle Ages*, pp. 135, 136). In 1527, a choir was appointed in the parish church of St. Andrews for singing psalms at five o'clock in the morning in summer, and at six during winter, and a mass at one o'clock every day (*Abstract of Writs of St. Andrews*, No. 105). The earliest definite reference to the sang-school of St. Andrews, which I have seen, is in 1545 (*Ibid.* No. 126); but as the one mentioned in the text is described as 'in the Abbay,' they were probably different institutions. Although music was not allowed to usurp the supreme place in the services of the Church as before, yet the Reformers were neither forgetful of its importance, nor insensible to its charms; but they wished the service of praise to be truly congregational, and their providing a complete metrical psalter by 1564 shows that they were thoroughly in earnest. In 1560 they had declared that 'Men, wemen, and children wald be exhorted to exercise thameselvis in the Psalmes, that when the Churche convenith, and dois sing, thai may be the more abill togither with commoun heart and voice to prayse God' (*First Book of Discipline*, ninth head). 'The Psalter or "Psalm-book" became the great treasury of vocal praise, and the musical genius of the religious community found sufficient occupation in adapting all the Psalms to congregational use' (Hill Burton's *History of Scotland*, 1876, iv. 352, 353). The Scottish Psalter of 1566, though still in MS., is a monument to the taste of the Prior of St. Andrews—afterwards the Regent Moray—who suggested it, to the skill of David Peables—one of the canons of St. Andrews—who harmonised it, and to the enthusiasm of Thomas Wode—afterwards Vicar of St. Andrews—who carried it through. Several beautiful facsimile specimens of its pages are in the

and [*blank*] his wyf, are conforme to Mathew King and hi[s] wyfe in all thingis.

Margaret Murdow granttis the sclanderous wordis layd to [*Monitio*] Murdow. hir charge, or, at the liest, sick wordis in effect, therefor the minister hes moniste hir to absteyne fra sick sayingis in tymes cuming, under panes of cursing; reservand civile correctioun to the magistrates of the toun; and supplicatioun to be directed with this proces to the Provest and baillies, *in uberiori forma*.

Nono Maii, 1560. Elene Thomsoun confessis in lyke maner [*Monitio*] Thomsone. hir delatioun, and namlie the injurious wordes spokin to Johne Knox, quharfor the minister moniste hir to desist fra sick say-

---

seventh volume of the *Proceedings of the Society of Antiquaries of Scotland*, and in Macmeeken's *History of the Scottish Metrical Psalms*. James Melvill bears testimony to the ardent study of music in his time, in Montrose, St. Andrews, and Glasgow (*Diary*, pp. 22, 29, 79). Nevertheless, Parliament was convinced in 1579 that the art of music and singing was 'almaist decayit,' and therefore requested the provost, bailies, council, and community of the most special burghs, and the patrons and provosts of colleges where 'sang scuilis' are founded, to erect and set up 'ane sang scuill with ane maister sufficient and able for instruction of the youth in the said science of musik' (*Acts of the Parliaments of Scotland*, iii. 174). In 1627 and also in 1632 there was paid 'to the maister of the musik scholl [in St. Andrews], and for taking up of the Psalme at preaching and prayeris, of fie ijᶜ li.' (Livingston's *Scottish Metrical Psalter*, p. 22). James Melvill undoubtedly refers to the 'Doctour of the Sang Scole' mentioned in the text, when he says, 'In these yeirs I lerned my music, wherin I tuk graiter delyt, of an Alexander Smithe, servant to the Primarius of our Collage, wha haid been treaned upe amangis the mounks in the Abbay. I lerned of him the gam, plean-song, and monie of the treables of the Psalmes' (*Diary*, p. 29). Servant or servitor was often used then to signify clerk, secretary, or man of business. In his preface to the edition of the *Scottish Psalter*, printed at Edinburgh in 1635—the first published with the tunes harmonised—Edward Miller says :—' I acknowledge sinceerely the whole compositions of the parts to belong to the primest musicians that ever this kingdome had, as Deane Iohn Angus, Blackhall, Smith, Peebles, Sharp, Black, Buchan, and others, famous for their skill in this kind' (Livingston's *Scottish Metrical Psalter*). As the two last thus mentioned, viz., Black and Buchan, were the respective masters of the sang schools of Aberdeen and Haddington, it is very probable that Smith was Alexander Smith of St. Andrews, more especially as Peebles, who is named with him, was David Peebles of this city. I possess nn old MS. collection of songs and music bearing the signature :—' Alexr. Smith, St. Andrews, Febrewarie the fy[ft], 1722.' Perhaps he may have been a descendant as well as a namesake of the old 'doctour.'

ingis in tymes cuming; reservand civile correctioun as is before
said of Margaret Murdow *in omnibus.*

Jovis 23 Maii.   Continuatur causa Rantoun ad pronunciandum et Gedde
Jovis xxiij Maii in praesentiis partium.

Ramsay,   *Die decimo sexto Maii.* Patrick Ramsay is obliste to tak the
Small.   bayrne gottin upoun Besse Small fra the said Besse, and provide ane nuryce to the samyn; and the woman oblist to pay
xx s. yerelie, at Mertymes and Witsomday, till the barne be
sevin yeris auld; and the nurice to be gottin, and the bayrne
takin fra hir, betuix this and Sounday nixtocum.

Actum de   *Die Jovis vigesima Junii,* 1560. The quhilk day, the minis-
bannis.   ter and eldaris, of this cietie reformed, statutes and ordeynes
that all bannes of them, quhai ar contracted, or hes maid promise of mariage, be ressaved be the scribe of the consistoriall
court of the minister and eldaris of the said cietie, bayt the
parties being præsent before him (gif thai bayth remane within
the paroche of Sanctandrois); and gif the ane party remanes
in ane uthir and salhappin come to this kirk to be maryed, that
party sall bring ane testimoniall fra that part quhare thai
remane of the lauchfull proclamatioun of there bannes in there
paroche kirk; lyke as, gif the ane party remanand heyr sall take
ane testimoniall heyr of this kirk, being perchance maryed in
ane uthir. And heirupoun the saidis minister and eldar[is]
interponis there decrete and ordinar authorite, &c.[1]

---

[1] The proclamation of banns of marriage on three Lord's days was enacted by
David de Bernhame, Bishop of St. Andrews, in a Synod held at Musselburgh in
1242 (*Concilia Scotiae,* ii. 58, 59); and the Synod of Aberdeen decreed in the
same century that no priest was to presume to celebrate marriage unless the
parties had been publicly and solemnly proclaimed on three several occasions,
according to the form of the Fourth Lateran Council, that he who wished and
was able might offer any lawful objection (*Ibid.* ii. 37, 270). The latter Synod
further ordained in that century that no persons may contract marriage without
three separate proclamations solemnly made in the church where they live, if
they stay in the same parish; if in different parishes, that they be proclaimed in
both; and that marriage do not take place without faithful and lawful witnesses
(*Ibid.* ii. 42). These regulations were practically adopted at the Reformation,
for the English Congregation at Geneva declare, in their *Order* of 1556, that the
banns are to be 'publisshed three severall dayes in the congregation, to the intent

Die decimo sexto mensis Julii, 1560.   Andro Howburne, being *Monitio Howburne.*
before the minister and eldaris accused for blaphemows (*sic*)

that if any person have interese or title to either of the parties, they may have
sufficient tyme to make theyr chalenge' (Laing's *Knox*, iv. 198); and the same
words are found in the *Book of Common Order* (*Ibid.* vi. 326, 327). Again,
'for avoiding of dangers, expedient it is that the bannes be publickly proclaimed
three Sundayes, unlesse the persons be so knowne that no suspicion of danger
may arise, and then may the time be shortned at the discretion of the ministry'
(*First Book of Discipline*, ninth head). In 1565, the General Assembly followed
the example of St. Andrews Kirk Session:—'The haill Assembly, with one
voyce, statutes and ordaines, That no ministers hereafter receave the parochiners
of ane uther parochine to be married, without ane sufficient testimoniall of the
minister of the parochine wherefrae they came, that the bands are lawfullie proclaimed, and no impediment found, so that the order that has been taken be the
Kirk, in sic affaires, be dewlie observed under the paine of deprivation frae his
ministrie, tinsell of his stipend, and uther paines, as the Generall Kirk shall
hereafter think to be imponed' (Peterkin's *Booke of the Universall Kirk*, p. 39).
As 'mariage without proclamation of bans,' in 'these years bygone, hath
produced many dangerous effects,' the General Assembly, of 1638, 'discharge the
same, conforme to the former acts, except the Presbyterie in some necessarie
exigents dispense therewith' (*The Principall Acts of the Solemne Generall
Assembly*, 1639, p. 38). The Westminster Divines provided that the 'purpose
of marriage shall be published by the minister three severall Sabbath dayes in the
congregation, at the place or places of their most usuall and constant abode respectively. And of this publication, the minister, who is to joyn them in
marriage, shall have sufficient testimony, before he proceed to solemnize the
marriage' (*Directory for Publike Worship*, 1645, p. 48). In 1690, the General
Assembly again forbade marriage 'without due proclamation of bans, according
to order, three several Sabbaths in the respective parishes,' and recommended
presbyteries 'to censure the contraveeners' (*Principal Acts*, 1691, pp. 10, 11).
And in 1699, to remedy 'several abuses' which had 'crept in,' the Assembly
further ordained, 'That, before any proclamations be made, the names and designations of the persons to be married, and their parents, tutors, or curators, if they
any have, be given up to the minister of the bounds in which any of them live
and reside, that thereby it may be known, if their parents and friends give consent
thereto;' that the persons proclaimed have their 'names and full designations,
such as they are designed by in writes or contracts of marriage,' 'fully and
audibly expressed; and that, where there are more churches collegiat in the place
or town, the proclamations be made in all and every one' where they or either
of them reside, 'and this to be attested to the minister who marries them' (*Principal Acts*, 1699, p. 9). 'By a recent Act of Parliament, a secular substitute for
banns has been legalised, and the General Assembly in 1879 authorised ministers,
"if they see fit, to receive, as a valid notice of marriage, a registrar's certificate."
At the same time it modified the old regulations of the Church, by enacting that
"proclamation of banns shall, in ordinary cases, be on two separate Sabbaths"
instead of three ; and that, "it shall be in the power of the minister to complete
the proclamation on a single Sabbath"'(Sprott's *Worship and Offices of the
Church of Scotland*, 1882, pp. 144, 145).

saying aganis the sacrament of the body and blude of Christe, sayand that he suld hallow ane laif[1] and ane pynte of aill, and mak als gude ane sacrament as thai mak, and had als mekle power to do that as thei had, mening the ministeris; and also sperand vayn questiones, scornfull aganst the majestie of the Trinitie, *videlicet*, Quhidder come the Fathir frome the Sone? or the Sone fra the Father? and quharefra come the Haly Gaist? Quhilkis premissis being provin to haif being spokin be the said Andro, in presence of George Wilsone, Thomas Broun, cutlar, and Dauid Watsone, malman,[2] cietineris, suorne befoir the eldaris in presence of Andro Howburne, the minister monysed, be avise of the eldaris, the said Andro to desist fra sic lyke in tymes cuming, under the payne of excommunicatioun, reservand forthir punischement to the civile sworde, &c.

Statute of almows.

[Here follows the 'Statute of almows,' which has been copied on the first page of the *Register*, immediately under the title, and which only differs from that copy in the spelling, and in the few following words:—' *vigesima sexta*,' for ' *xxv*^{to}'; 'day,' omitted; 'statutes and ordeynes,' for 'divisis and statutis;' and the addition of three final *etceteras*.]

Petitio Dauid Gudelawde, &c.

Richt venerable minister and eldaris, unto your wisedomes, humilie menis and schawes, Dauid Gudlawde, That now it is not unknawin that Margaret Archbald, my spous for the tyme, and Cristyne Petbladow hir moder, spous to umquhile Andro Archbald then on lyfe, in the yeir of God м° v° xxiiij yeris, departed furth of this realme, by[3] the knawlege or consent of ony of us ther said husbandis, being baith suspected adulteraris, as the died hes schawin in the said Margaret, be defyling of my bed, takin ane uthir party in praetended matrimony xxxv yeris bipast. In quhilk tyme I haif led ane continent lyfe, withowtin ony suspicioun imputed to me. And now, haifand respect to my aige that I may nocht be at ease allane, and findand Catheryne Niesche, ane chaste virgyne past xl yeris of aige, hes procured hir consent to be juned with me in the band of matrimony; and therupoun hes gevin my faith and promise be wordes of the præsent tyme, according to the custome used in

---

[1] Loaf. [2] Should be *maltman*. [3] Without.

tymes bipast. Beleving na impediment to haif beyne maid to the completing, we haif conversed together, tresting also, as yit I trest surelie, the said Margaret is decessed; and also our bannes being proclamed dewlie, na persone come to schaw ony impediment knawin to us, except that we are informed that friendis of the said Margaretis solistes to differ our actioun. Heirfor, I beseik your wisedomes to grant to me ane edict, to be executed in sick public maner, as is maist decent upoun sa few daiis as the law provydes; and that onlie for the weale of the woman, that standis in great displeassour and melancoly, becaus sche is cumin to sa great aige withowtin reproche, and now is deceved by[1] baith our knawleges. Forder lang dilay may be praejuditiall to our caus, in sa far as I haif bott twa witnes in this realme; and gif ony of them sall inlaik, I am not of puissance to procure probatioun furth of far cuntreyes; albeit commoun voice and fame is the same, gif that wer sufficient.

Decimo sexto Marcii, 1559.

The quhilk day, the minister and eldaris of this reformed kirk of Sanctandrois decernis ane edict in the caus forsaid, upoun fourscoire daiis, with intimatioun to the party to be summond; with certificatioun, gif the party summond compere or nocht, that the saidis minister and eldaris will procede be public edictes to actes judiciall, as salbe nedefull in the said cause, to the finall sentence geving; and that James Brand and Alane Steill witnes be produced in the meantyme, and examin-ated *ad futuram rei memoriam propter metum mortis aut alius diutinae absentiae.*

Mandant et praecipiunt minister et seniores ecclesiae Chris-tianae apud civitat[em] Sanctiandreae in regno Scotiae, consis-tentis, per hujus edicti publici januae templi parochialis civitatis praemissae affixionem, citari prout re ipsa citant Marg[a]ritam Archbald sponsam (priusquam se ab illius con-tubernio separaret) Dauidis Gudelawde civitatis praedictae civis quod compareat coram eis in loco ad jura reddenda et

Edictum Gudelawde.

---

[1] Against.

causas audiendas, intra civitatem ipsam jam sepius dicta[m]
destinato, octuagesima die juridica citationem hujuscemodi
ipsorum proxime et immediate sequente, si dies illa juridica
fuerit, alioqui die juridica inde proxime sequutura ad videndum
et audiendum causam et actionem divorcii, propter adulterium
per ipsam Margaretam patratum (quoniam ut refertur ipsam,
Dauide viro suo in humanis agente, adhuc et superstite, alteri
viro intra partes Datiae[1] sese copulasse, tertium praeceptum
secundae tabulae, ubi scriptum est, ne adulterat[o] transgredi-
endo) pro parte ipsius Dauidis, contra ipsam, ut ob hoc simpliciter separentur disjunganturque, actis et terminis judicialibus,
juxta ordinationem juris divini, servatis, moveri et intentari,
certam reddentes ipsam, quod sive in termino superius limitato,
ad effectum praemissum comparuerit, sive se contemptim et
contumaciter absentaverit, ipsi minister et seniores, in causa
et actione praedicta, ad instantiam Dauidis usque ad finaem
diffinitivae prolatione inclusive juxta ordinationem juris divini
procedent, ut sententia lata libera Dauidi in Domino nubendi
potestas concedatur : proviso quod Margaretae personalis in-
timatio si apprehendi possit publicum fiat sinminus in urbe
aut villa ubi magis continue moram trahere dinoscitur apud
domicilium (si quod habuerit) de praemissis certior reddatur
has vero edicti litteras huic januae affigi mandarunt, ne veri-
simile sit apud quempiam incognitum remanere, quod tam
Gudlawd. publice et patentur cunctis est manifestatum.   *D*atum sub
sigillo quo in similibus utimur et subscriptione scribae ipsorum
ministri et seniorum, apud civitatem Sanctiandreae, die decimo
sexto mensis Martii, et secundum supputationem ecclesiae
Scoticanae anno *D*omini M⁰ v^c quinquagesimo nono.

> Dauid Spens diaconus in ecclesia praedicta ac scriba
> coram ministro et senioribus praedictis manu mea
> exaravi, etc.

Sequitur tenor executionis edicti praemissi etc.

Die decima septima Martii anno quo supra ego Georgius
Blak diaconus ecclesie et congregationis Christianae reformatae

---

[1] *Daciae*, Denmark.

apud civitatem Sanctiandreae accessi ad principalem januam
templi parochialis ejusdem ex parte australi ipsius templi con-
stitutam et ibidem valvis dictae januae praesens edictum affixi
ipsumque per totum tempus sermonis in dicto templo habiti
stare permisi Margaretam Archbald supradictam secundum
tenorem ejusdem citavi coram Magistro Joanne Lawmonth,
Thoma Flemyng, et Dauide Spens, testibus rogatis et requisitis.

Georgius Blak manu propria.

Richt worschiphull minister and eldaris, of the Christiane Gudelawd.
congregatioun within the cietie of Sanctandrois, unto your wisedomes humilie menis and compleanes Dauid Gudelawde, cietiner
of the said cietie, upoun Margaret Archbald : that, quhare I
being joyned with the said Margaret in the band of matrimony,
and keipand to hir ane gude, trew part, conforme to the law of
God, nochtheles, in the yeir of God 1524, withowt my consent
or knawlege, sche departed over see to the realme of Denmark,
and ther juned and gaif hir body to Hanis Boukle, *alias*
Buckijlis, defyled my bed, committed adulterie, buyr twa
bayrnes ; quharthrow is permitted to me, be the law of God,
to be divorced and separated fra the said Margaret, and
absolved and relaxed of the band and contract maid and
solemnized betuix us in matrimony, with fredome and libertie
to contract and solemnized matrimony with ane uthir lauchfull
woman according to Goddis Word : heirfore, I beseik yowr
wisdomes to ressave my probationes, and witnes upoun the
premissis, quhilk being sufficientlie provin, that ye decerne be
yowr sentence the said Margaret ane adulterar, and me therfor
to be divorced and separated frome hir, relaxed and absolved
fra all band and contract of matrimony maid betuix us, and
fredome and libertie to contract and solemnized matrimony
with ane uthir lauchfull woman, according to Goddis haly
Word, &c.

Die vigesimo nono Augusti, 1560.   *Per ministrum et seniores.*

The quhilk day, compered Dauid Gudlawde, and produced Gudelawde.
ane summondis, executed upoun the kirk dur of Sanctandrois,

under forme of edict, the xvij day of Marche, 1560; and ane
wryting fra the minister of Lund, in *D*enmark, interpret furth
of *D*anis language in our vulgare toung be Williáme Christesone,[1] minister of *D*undee, makand mentioun that the said
minister haid ressavit the said citatioun to be intimate to
Margaret Johne Buklys; and desyred witnes to be ressavit
upoun the pointtis of his abone writtin clame; and produced
Alane Steill, quhei wes sworne and examinated as his depositioun forsaid makis mentioun. Therfore it is statute be
eldaris to produce uthir witnes *literatorie*, in presence of Dauid,
and in peane of contumace and nocht compéarence of Margaret,
summond, be the edict before inserted, the xvij of Marche
abone writtin.

Eodem die etc.[2]

Decretum.
Baveryche,
Phenisoun,
Seres.

The quhilk day, compeared James Baveriche, cordiner in this
cietie, and Elizabeth Phenisone, as in the terme assigned to
decide the matter *et* caus betuix the saidis James and Elizabeth
and Andro Seres, anent th[e pro]mise of mariage maid first to
James Baveriche, and therefter to the said Andro. And now
the caus being rypelie consydered and seyne be the minister
and eldaris, Mr. Knox being consulted heirupoun, hes founden
the said Elizabeth to bé the wyfe of James Baveriche, and therfore to adhere to him, and therfor the said Andro Seres to be
fre to mary quhome he pleassis, in the Lord. This beand
decreted in judgement, the said Elizabeth to compere on
Sounday nixtocum, and ask God and the congregatioun forgevenes of the offens and sclander, done be hir in making the
secound promise to Andro Seres.

---

[1] Christesone was appointed to Dundee in July 1560—the same time as Goodman was to St. Andrews. He was a member of the first General Assembly
in the following December, and attended thirty-eight of the sixty succeeding
Assemblies, and was Moderator in July 1569 (Scott's *Fasti*, iii. 684). He
died in 1603 (Maxwell's *Old Dundee*, p. 129).

[2] These words are the last on a leaf; and 'the quhilk day' are the first on the
next page, which seems at some time to have been the outer page of the volume,
as it is much soiled, and has suffered from damp; but there does not appear
to be anything wanting.

Responsum ministri de Lund in Datia.

Jhone Olufson, called Spaidmaker, minister of Lund, in Gudlawde. Skonesyde, confessis that he hes ressavit ane litter of summondis, writtin in Sanct Androis the 17 of Marche, 1559, frome ane called Williame Raa, burges in Elsinger, concerning ane woman called Margaret Johne Bucklijs, the quhilk he promissis to praesent in judgement before *capitulo Lundensis juridice,* the Monday efter *Joannis Baptiste,* and swa to send the same litter of summondis hither with ane sure ansuer to the same, &c. Interprete owt of *D*enis languaige be Williame Cristesone, minister of *D*undee.

The quhilk day, viz., *xxix Augusti,* Alane Steill being produced be Dauid Gudlaud witnes in the said caus, sworne and examinated, depones and clearlie priefis the contentes of the bill and summondis forsaid to be trew. *Causam scientie reddit* that he wes in Margaret Archbaldis hows thre quarteris of ane yeare, and hard hir confes as is libellated.

Die Jovis quinto mensis Septembris, 1560.

The quhilk day, in the actioun and caus of divorce moved Gwdelawd. be Dauid Gudelawde against Margaret Archbald, *alias* Johne Buklijs, to prief forther in the caus forsaid, compered Dauid, produced James Brand witnes in the said matter, quhai, being sworne and examinated, depones conforme to Alane Steill as to the pointtis libellet; therefor it is statute to pronunce *literatorie.*

Sententia Gudlawde.

With incalling of the name of the lyving God, we, minister [*Sententia*] and eldaris of this Christiane congregatioun of the cietie and Gudelaude. parochin of Sanctandrois, judges in the actioun and caus of divorce, moved before us be Dauid Gudelawde, cietiner of the said cietie and membir of the said congregatioun, against Margaret Archbald his spows; for hir departing over sea to ane fare countrey, fra the said Dauid withowttin his consent and knawlege, to the realme of *D*enmark, in the yeir of God ane thowsand fyve hundreth twenty four yeris; and ther continualie remaning hes, under pretens of matrimony, ad[j]oyned hirself

D

and gevin hir body to Johne Boukle, conceved and borne
to him thre bayrnes, defyled the bed of the said Dauid, committing the filthy syn of adultery ; as at lenth is conteyned in
the said Dauidis petitioun before us produced against hir ; the
forsaid Margaret beand lauchfullie summond be our publict
edict, upoun the præmunitioun of fourscore dayes, to compeir
before us at certane day and place, at the instance of the said
Dauid, to ansuer in the said caus of divorce, to the finall end
and sentence geving therin, in all dietes and actes judiciall ;
and lauchfull intimation therof maid be the minister of the
kirk of Lund, in Denmark, quhare the said Margaret makes
residence : we with detfull ordour haif proceded, and being
rypelie advysed with the said petitioun, together with the
testimony and depositioneis of famose witnes, and all uthiris
deduced in the said caus, findis . the forsaid petitioun, and
adultery committed be the said Margaret, sufficientlie provin :
haiffand heirfore God onlie befoir our eies and the testimonie
of his Word, be this our sentence diffinityve pronunces, decernis and declares the said Margaret Archbald ane adulterar,
and therfore the saidis Dauid and Margaret to be separated
and divorced ; as be this our sentence we divorce and separate
them simplie and perpetuallie ; and libertie to the said Dauid
in the Lord to contract and mary ony uthir lauchfull woman,
as he micht haif done before he wes conjoyned with the said
Margaret.   Pronunced upoun Thuirsday, the sevin day of
November, in the yeir of God mᵒ vᵒ and thre scoir yeris, at the
instance of Dauid Gudlawde, and in peane of nocht compearence
of Margaret Archbald, heirto summond in maner forsaid, &c.

Followis the proces of Alexander Lathrisk in Kircaldy.

Request of the
Lordis of
Secrete Coun-
sale for Alex-
ander Lauth-
risk in Kirk-
caldy.
My Lordis of Secret Counsale unto your lordschipes humelie
menis and schawis I, your servitour, Alexander Lathrisk,
indwellar in Kirkcaldy : that, quhar it is notour and manifest
to all sick as knawis Besse Symsoun, sumtyme my spous, that
sche dissociate hirself of my company nyne yeris syne with the
mayr, and sensyne hes used hirself maist viciouslie, gevand the
plesur of hir body alsweale to strangearis oppinlie and com-
mounlie præsent in this realme for the tyme, as to sindry the

natyve lieges therof; and hes borne bairnes to sindry persones; quherthrow sche maist ungodlie and falslie hes brokin and violated hir promise of mariage to me, and swa, be the ordour of Goddis Word plainlie reveled, partising aucht to be led betuix us be the Kirk of God, and I releved and fred of hir, and sche to be left to condigne punischement of the civile magistrat; nochttheles, the minister, eldaris and diacons, of the said toun of Kirkcaldy, refussis to tak the caus before them, withowt command of your lordschipes; beseiking heirfor your lordschipes that ye will gif command to them to tak tryall in the mater and decyde therin, as Godis Word dois ordeyne, to his glorie and gude exemple of uthiris to eschew sick filthynes, but[1] stop or dilay, and your lordschipes ansuer humilie I besiek.

Deliberatio dominorum.

Apud Edinburgh, secundo Decembris, anno etc. lx°. The Lordis requestes the ministeris and eldaris of Sanctandrois to procede and do justice [in][2] this actioun within writtin, to baith the parties within expremed conform to the Word of God.

> Jamis.[3]
> James Stewart.[4]
> R. Boyde.[5]
> Wchiltre.[6] Cunnyghamhed.[7]
> Johne Erskyne.[8]
> Jhone Wischert.[9]

---

[1] Without. [2] Omitted.

[3] James, Duke of Chatelherault, who had been Regent of Scotland after the death of James the Fifth.

[4] Best known as the Regent Murray. [5] Robert, fourth Lord Boyd.

[6] Andrew, second Lord Stewart of Ochiltree. In the text the scribe has at first written 'Walter,' doubtless supposing that it was Cunnyghamhead's Christian name, but it has been afterwards altered into 'Wchiltre.' According to the Treaty of Edinburgh, 6th July 1560, the ensuing Parliament was to nominate 'twenty-four able and sufficient persons,' from whom the Queen was to elect seven and the States five 'to serve as an ordinary Council of State during her Majesty's absence' (Keith's *History*, i. 301). All those named in the text save Ochiltree are included in the twenty-four (*Ibid.* i. 326); but he was one of the twenty-nine from whom the Council of Protestants were chosen in October 1559 (Thorpe's *Calendar of State Papers, Scotland*, i. 119; Keith's *History*, i. 236). The *Register of the Privy Council* is blank from January 1553-4 to Sept. 1561.

[7] William Cunningham of Cunninghamhead.

[8] More probably the Laird of Dun than Lord Erskine. [9] Of Pittarrow.

Citatio
Lawthrisk.

The minister and eldaris of the reformed kirk and congregatioun of Sanctandrois, to the ministeris, eldaris and diacons of
the alsua reformed kirkis and congregationes of Kirkcaldy and
Aberdour, wisched grace, mercie and peace fra God our Fader
and the Lord Jesus Christe, so be it. Forsamekle as be the
Lordis of Christiane Congregatioun and Secrete Counsale therof
hes, be ther letteres of request directed to us under theris or
[at]¹ least certane of ther subscriptiones manuall, requested us
to procede and do justice in this under writtin actioun and
caus of divorce, intented and moved be Alexander Lawthrisk,
in Kirkcaldy dwelland, against Elizabeth *alias* Besse Symsone
his pretended and alleaged spous, for committing the filthy
cryme and syne of adultery, brekand the thrid command of
the secound table, quher it is writtin, Thow sall nocht commit
adultery. And we, willing to obey the saidis Lordis requestes,
in sa far as we may of equitie and justice according to the law
of God ; and that the veritie, be just tryall in the said matter
taking, may be searched owt diligentlie and maid knawin to us,
and the faythfull kirkes and congregationes abone exprimed ;
that ignorantlie as blind judges we procede nocht to ony act
judiciall, in this sa ponderous and wechty causs, withowt trew
cognitioun tayne rypelie in the same : heyrfore, consultatioun
haid before, be mature deliberatioun therefter following, think-
and it ressonable and maist conforme to justice, to procede
ordourlie be ane summondis præceding all act judiciall heirintill be us to be observed, will we that the said Elizabeth *alias*
Besse Symsone forsaid, be the tennour of this our edict to be
publiclie affixed to the kirk durres of Kirkcaldy, upoun ane
Sounday, the tyme of the preacheing or commoun prayaris to
stand ther, be summond, warned and atteached; quhom we alsua
summond, warne and atteache be the tennour of thir presentis,
anese, twyse, thrise, peremptourlie, to compear personalie before
us, in the consistory hows abone the porche dur of the paroche
kirk of Sanctandrois, upoun Weddinsday, the aucht day of the
moneth of Januar nixtocome, in the houre of caus, quhare
judgement is to be gevin and caussis to be heard ; and ther to
heare and see cognitioun and tryall takin and proces led in the

---

¹ Omitted.

actioun and caus forsaid of adultery moved and intented be the said Alexander against hir, witnes ressaved, sworne and to examinatioun admitted, and to finall conclusioun and determinatioun in the same to be hed heirin, in sa fare as the law of God sall licentiate and permitte us; with certificatioun that albeid the said Elizabeth *alias* Besse Symsoun compeare the said day and place, or nocht, we will procede in the said matter, and minister justice according as Goddis law sall permitt, as said is, to our finall judgement heirintill, and in tymes cuming will use na forther summondis in youris kirkes forsaid; bott, gif it salbe thocht expedient, we will use edictes upoun our consistory and hows of justice dur, sa oft as neid salbe. And the causs of this our maner of summoning is be public edict, becauss we are certanelie advertysed the said Elizabeth *alias* Besse Symsone to be ane vagabound haiffand na certane dwelling place; bot gif sche ony certane place of residence suld haif beyne [assignit][1] to hir, the same suld haif beyne in Kirkcaldy, quhare praesentlie the said Alexander remanes. Attour, that ye summond lauchfullie James Nicoll, Robert Cant at the Griene Hied, Thomas Turnour, to compeare day and place forsaid; to beare leale and suithfast witnessing in the premissis, in sa far as thei knaw of ther conscience to be of veritie, as thei sall ansuer to God. The quhilk thinges to do, we committe to yow and ilk ane of yow our full plane power, be hir[2] our letteres and edict public, be yow dewlie execute and indorsate, agane delivering them to the bearar. Gevin under our sele quhilk we use in sick caus, and subscriptioun manuall of our minister, at Sanctandrois, the xiij day of December, 1560.

Christophor Goodman, minister.
Mr. Alane Lawmontht.
Johne Motto.
Dauid Walwod.

Tenor executionum edicti praeinserti.

Upoun Sounday, the xv day of December instant, we, Lawthrisk. minister, eldaris and diacons, of the reformed kirk and con-

---

[1] Omitted.   [2] Should be *thir*.

gregatioun of Kirkcaldy, publiclie in the paroche kirk of the same, in tyme of commoun prayaris, haif summond, warned and atteached Elizabeth *alias* Besse Symsone abone writtin, and affixed this present edict upoun the dur of the said kirk, according to the tennour of thir presentes, be thir our subscriptiones manuall, &c.

> Georgè Scott, minister.[1]
> Johne Quhyt, eldar.
> Dauid Hay, eldar.
> George Bawcanquell, eldar.

The xxij day of *D*ecember, I, Johne Patersone,[2] minister in Aberdour, upoun thir abone writtin James Nicholl, Robert Cantt and Thomas Turnour, dwelland within the paroche of Aberdour, efter the tennour of this present, I haif summond the said persones oppinlie before the congregatioun : this I haif done under my subscriptioun manuall, and summond the said Besse, and affixed this edict on the kirk dur, efter the tennour heirof. Johne Patersone, minister, &c.

Lawthrisk. *Octavo die mensis Januarii,* 1560. *Secundum supputationem ecclesiae Scoticanae.* The quhilk day, compeared, in presence of minister and eldaris, Alexander Lathrisk, in Kirkcaldy, and produced the edict forsaid, execut and indorsate against and upoun Besse Symsone, in Kirkcaldy and Aberdour kirkes, the xv and xxij days of *D*ecember last bypast, in payne of contumacie and nocht compeerence of Besse, summond lauchfullie in maner forsaid ; and produced ane testimoniall of the inhabitantes and maist honest men of Aberdour, subscryved with ane notar ledand ther handis in ane part, and partlie subscryved with some of ther awin handes, recognosced be James Nichol-

---

[1] George Scott, brother of Thomas Scott of Abbotshall, was translated to Dysart in 1574 and died in 1582 (Scott's *Fasti,* ii. 514, 534). He was one of those appointed 'to represent the chapter in the Reformed Kirke' at the election of John Douglas to the Archbishopric of St. Andrews, and was present ; but 'tuike ane instrument that he condiscendit not' (Richard Bannatyne's *Memoriales,* Ban. Club, pp. 222, 223).

[2] So late as 1574, 'Johnne Patersoun' is mentioned as 'reidare at Abirdour,' with a stipend of £10 (*Wodrow Miscellany*, p. 363).

soun in Aberdour &c. And als the said Alexander produced thre witnes, viz. James Nicholsone forsaid, Robert Cant, taillyeour, and Thomas Turnour, in Aberdour dwelland; quhilkes witnes being produced and sworne wer examinated, as followes heyrefter, &c. The inserting of the testimoniall forsaid of quhilk the tennour followis.

The testimoniall, &c.

Till all gude Christiane people, to quhais knawleage thir Lawthrisk. presentis sal [happin][1] to come, the inhabitantis and nichtbouris of the toun of Aberdour sendis greting in God everlesting: since meritoriouss it is, and to all gude Christianes of dewtie perteanes, to bear record and witnessing in matteris concerning the commoun weale, specialie to the suppressing of vice and oppin and manifest offendaris; swa it is that Elizabeth, *alias* Besse Symsoun, nominat to be spous to Alexander Lathrisk, being notourlie knawin ane harlot of hir body to Frensche, Inglis, and Scottismen; and being apprehended within the toun of Aberdour, in the monethis of Junii or therby last bypast, was put in ane cart and harlet throw the samyn and banist our boundis in tyme to come. We therfor be this write charitabillie requyres all gude people to use and handill the said Besse, quhare ever sche be apprehended, in lyke sort, that sick oppin transgressouris have na refuge. In witnes quhareof, we undersubscrivand, as maist part of the honestest men of the said toun, hes subscrived thir presentis, with our hand, at Aberdour, the xxiiij day of October, the yeir of God J^m v^o and sextie yeris.

Sir Walter Patersone, vicare of Aberdour, with my hand. Lawthrisk.

Johne Robertsone, officer of Aberdour, with my hand on the pen led be the notar underwrittin.

Alexander Hay, *notarius de mandato dicti Joannis.*
Robert Wardin, with my hand at the pen.
Walter Robertsone, with my hand at the pen.
Thomas Dictioun, with my hand at the pen.
James Williamsoun, baillie of Aberdour.

---

[1] Omitted.

Joannes Patersone, minister of Aberdour.
Willi Ramsay.
Johne Wardane, with my hand at the pen.
Robert Crag, with my hand at the pen.
Robert Cant, with my hand at the pen.
James Smyth, with my hand at the pen.
Jhone Fyn.
Walter Cant, with my hand at the pen.
Williame Alexander.
Francisce Cwke, with my hand.
Johne Boid, with my hand at the pen.[1]
Johne Gibsone, with my hand.

---

[1] Considering the state of education and the difficulty of acquiring it previous to the Reformation, it was no discredit to 'the honestest men' of Aberdour that so many of them could not write their own names. It would be easy to multiply instances of more culpable ignorance, but two must suffice. In signing a charter in 1544, the Prioress and Prioress-elect of North Berwick were constrained to add to their names, 'wyth my hand at the pen;' and opposite the names of the twenty subscribing nuns are the equally significant words, 'wyth all our handis leid at the pen' (*Carte Monialium de Northberwic*, Ban. Club, p. 60). And in 1566 the Countess of Huntly displayed the same inability in signing the marriage contract of her daughter (Stuart's *Lost Chapter in the History of Mary Queen of Scots Recovered*, p. 100). Probably Sir Walter Scott did the great Earl of Angus, otherwise known as 'Bell-the-Cat,' no injustice when he represented him as exclaiming :—

> 'Thanks to Saint Bothan, son of mine,
> Save Gawain, ne'er could pen a line.'—*Marmion*, Canto vi. 15.

In those days great numbers were unable even to read, and many of whom better things might have been expected were far from being proficient in the art. In one of the satirical pieces of the Reformation it is asserted :—

> 'The Curat his creid he culd nocht reid.'
> *Gude and Godlie Ballates*, 1868, p. 180.

Alexander Seaton, the fugitive Prior of the Black Friars of St. Andrews, in his letter to James the Fifth, avers that 'some of thame cane not read thair matynes who ar maid judgeis in heresye' (Laing's *Knox*, i. 49). And by the General Provincial Council, in 1552, 'the clergy were enjoined to exercise themselves daily in reading' Hamilton's *Catechism*, 'lest their stammering or breaking down might move the jeers of the people' (*Concilia Scotiae*, vol. i. p. cliv). Such ignorance on the part of religious teachers would have been inexcusable even before the invention of printing, but on the eve of the Reformation was highly blameworthy. 'The learning of the Scotch Convent may not have been carried to a high pitch; but such learning as there was, was always found there. . . . Kelso had schools in the town of Roxburgh in the time of William the Lion, and Dunfermline had endowed

James Nicholsone, witnes abone exprimed,[1] produced, sworne Lawthrisk.
and examinated, depones, he wes present with uthiris divers,
quhen thei tuke Besse Symsone owt of Thomas Turnouris hows
of Aberdour, being companied with Johne Gibsone and uthiris
divers, quhom to sche wes ane quhore, to Inglismen and Scottis
soldiouris; and put hir in ane cart and caried hir throwch the
toun of Aberdour, quhai nochtwithstanding hir careing sche
thocht na schame therof, and said sche wald abuse hir bodi
and be ane huyr, and[2] thei wer all hanged, &c.

Robert Cant, tailyeour, in Aberdour dwelland, depones conforme to James Nicholsone; and that sche wes in company
with Inglismen in Halyfald, be the sea syde in the Hewches
betuix the Brount Ileand and Aberdour.

---

schools in the city of Perth at least as early' (*Scotland in the Middle Ages*, p.
135). The schools of St. Andrews reach back to a still more remote date, for
they 'appear to have been of note as early as A.D. 1120' (*Concilia Scotiae*, ii.
290). But it was two centuries after the death of William the Lion ere the
University of this city was founded, and for many years it had no buildings of
its own. In 1496 the earliest Scottish Education Act ordained 'that all barronis
and frehaldaris that ar of substance put thair eldest sonnis and airis to the sculis
fra thai be aucht or nyne yeiris of age, and till remane at the grammer sculis
quhill thai be competentlie foundit and have perfite Latyne; and thereftir to
remane thre yeris at the sculis of art and jure' (*Acts of the Parliaments of Scotland*, ii. 238). When such men had to be compelled to send their eldest sons
and heirs to school there must have been few scholars. Immediately before the
Reformation there are said to have been more than three hundred pupils at
Andrew Simson's grammar school in Perth (Row's *History*, Wod. Soc. p. 8).
But this must have been a very exceptional case, for in 1562 Ninian Winzet,
the uncompromising opponent of Knox, declares that he had marvelled greatly
how in times past, amid so much liberality towards religion and science in Scotland, 'sa litle respect hes evir bene had to the grammar sculis . . . that in
mony townis thair is not sa mekle providit thairto as a common house: and in
nane almaist of al ane sufficient life to ane techear' (*Certane Tractatis*, Mait.
Club, p. 26). There was a striking contrast between the Act of 1496 and the
scheme propounded by the Reformers in 1560. They insisted 'that everie
severall churche have a schoolmaister appointed,' and 'that no fader, of what
estait or conditioun that ever he be, use his children at his awin fantasie, especiallie in thair youth-heade; but all must be compelled to bring up thair children
in learnyng and virtue' (*First Book of Discipline*, fifth head). Yet long afterwards scholars had occasionally to contend with difficulties which are undreamt
of in these days of School Boards. In 1715 the boys attending the grammar
school of St. Andrews, were, for want of benches, 'necessitat to wreatt upon
ther floor, lying upon ther bellies' (*Minutes of St. Andrews Town Council*,
vol. v).

[1] Expressed.   [2] Although.

Thomas Turnour ressaved, sworn and admitted, depones conforme to James Nicholsone *in omnibus, etc.*

Quhilkes witnes, being produced, sworne and examinated, as is abone conteyned, decerned are testimoniales [1] be the minister and²eldaris forsaid, in forme and effect as efter followes.

Lawthrisk.

The name of Christe·Jesus, Sone of the eternall God, being incalled, quhai beares testimonie to our consciences the thinges following to be of veritie, we, minister and eldares of Christes kirk and congregatioun within the cietie of Sanctandrois, being requested and charged be the Lordis of Secrete Consale, and ther commissioun in wryte directed to us therupoun, haif takin cognition and tryall in the causs of divorce, moved be Alexander Lathrisk in Kirkcaldy against Besse Symsone his putative spouss, for the filthy cryme of of (*sic*) adultery be hir committed. The merites of the causs seyne and consydered, and we rypelie and maturelie avysed with certane depositiones of certane famows witnes, dewlie summond, compearand, ressaved, sworne, admitted, and examinated be us, in peane of nocht comperence of the said Besse, be our public edict to that effect lauchfullie summond ; together with ane testimoniall in wryte, subscryved be ane notar and certane honest men of Aberdour and partis therto adjacent, dewlie recognosced : findes that the said Besse Synsone (*sic*) [is]² ane polluted and filthy adulterar, sa comprehended, gevand hir body to diverss men, in the towne and parochin of Aberdour, withowttin ony signe of repentance schawin be hir ; and heirfore, be the law of God, maist justlie the saidis Alexander and Besse to be dyvorced,

Lawthrisk.

separated and divided, and libertie to the said Alexander to mary in the Lord ; and the said Besse to be committed to the civill magistrates, to be punisched as Goddis law praescryves : referring and committing the pronunciatioun and publicatioun of the sentence to the minister of Kirkcaldy, to be publiced and pronunced in the congregatioun committed to his cure, as becomes him of his dewtie toward the membyris of his flok.

---

[1] Their decision was doubtless thus designated because the sentence was not formally published by them.
² Omitted.

Thir thinges to be sa in died, as are abone specified, we testifie
be thir presentes, subscryved with our handis, and the hand of
our scribe notar under writtin, at Sanctandrois, the ix of
Januar, 1560, &c.

Sententia Elizabeth Gedde *contra* Villiam Rantoun.

With incalling of the name Christe Jesus, Sone to the eter- *Sententia,*
nall and everleving God, quhai is the way, the veritie, and the Rantoun,
lyfe, quhome we, the minister and eldaris of this reformed kirk *divorcii.*
of Sanctandrois, takes to witnessing of our consciences, that
we, takand cognitioun in the actioun and caus of divorcement
or partysing, moved and intentated by Elizabeth Gedde against
Williame Rantoun hir prætended husband, for the filthy and
abhominable cryme and syne of adulterie committed be him
with Margaret Aidnem; the parties petitioun, ansueringes,
richtes, reasones, jures, and allegationes, with the testimonies
and depositiones of witnes, and all uther thinges concerning
the said matere, before us produced in præsence of men of great
eruditioun, with quhome we communicated the secretes of the
said caus and matter, and with us and them being heard, seyne,
consydered, and rypelie understand ; haiffand respect to the
dilatioun gevin in to us before the moving of this causs, upoun
the filthy cryme forsaid of adulterie committed be the saidis
William and Margaret, and the said William, being called
and therof accused and examinated upoun his aith, perjuradlie
denyed the same, and nevertheles therefter the saidis Williame
and Margaret oppinlie, singularlie, and lamentablie, in the
faice of the congregatioun assembled within the paroche kirk
of Sanctandrois, confessed the forsaid cryme of adulterie betuix
them committed ; like as the said Williame also hes also confessed the [like][1] in this caus judicialie before us ; and sa be
confessioun of partie and depositioun of famos witnes, we fynd
the said William gyltie, and the said Elizabeth innocent, and
justlie of the law of God aucht and suld be divorced and *sim-*
pliciter partysed fra the said Williame hir praetended husband ;
and heirfore, be this our sentence diffinityve, pronunces, decernes,

---

[1] Omitted.

and declares, the said Williame ane perjured adulterar, and the said Elizabeth innocent divorced, and fre of the company and societie of the said Williame, with full power to hir according to the law of God to mary in the Lord ; and the said Williame to be haldin and reputte ane dead man, worthy to want his lyfe be the law of God, quhen ever it sall pleas God to stirre up the heart of ane gude and godlie magistrate to execute the same with the civile sworde; to quhome we will that this our sentence prejudge nathing, bott committes the same to him, quhen it salbe thocht expedient and ganand[1] tyme to tak forther triall and cognitioun heirintill, according to the law of God forsaid : be this our sentence diffinityve, subscryved with our handes, pronunced judicialie the thrid day of Januar, and publiced in the faice of the congregatioun the twelft of the samyn, 1560.

Followis the process in the causs of divorce betuix Alexander Clerck against Agnes Schevez.[2]

The Petitioun, &c.

Petitio
Clerk.

Worschiphull minister and eldares of the congregatioun Christiane of this reformed cietie of Sanctandrois. Unto your wisedomes humilie menis and schawis your Christiane brother Alexander Clerck, upoun Agnes Schevez sumtyme my spous : that quhare, in the yeir of God J^m fyve hundreth fourty seavin yeris, promise of mariage wes maid betuix me and the said Agnes, and the same alreadie completed before God albeit

---

[1] Suitable, fit.

[2] This is the first entry on the page, but there is a considerable space left blank above it, and there is also a blank space at the bottom of the next page, where this case ends. It may therefore be inferred that some at least even of these continued cases were inserted in the *Register* on the respective dates which the various entries bear. And the isolated position of the entry immediately preceding the above confirms the inference, for if the clerk had not begun to record the ' clame of Elizabeth Gedde' (*supra* p. 37) until the sentence was pronounced, the whole of the case would have appeared together. On the other hand, the short entry on p. 27 must have been written at a date subsequent to that which it bears—hence its position, partly in the margin, and hence too its statement, 'Johne Knox beaud at *that* tyme minister.'

solemnizatioun therof wes nocht haid before the congregatioun, nevertheles, I standing ever trew and anefald[1] to hir, sche, immediatlie efter the said mariage betuix me and hir contracted as said is, brekand the thrid command of the secound table, committed adulterie with Henrie Balfour; quhilk adultery is evidentlie declared, in that ther is ane bairne gottin betuix them. Beseikand heirfore your wysedomes to inquyre diligentlie and tak probatioun heirupoun, and, gif sa beis founden as I haif alleaged, to decerne and declare the said Agnes to haif brokin mariage and committed adulterie; and therfore me and the said Agnes to be separated and put syndry, with power to me agane to mary in the Lord God, as his maist haly law permittes: this of your juditiall authoritie implorand maist humelie, &c.

Die Mercurii xix[no] Februarii, 1560. Per ministerium ecclesiae reformatae Sanctiandreae in dominicula supra porticum templi parochialis. The quhilk day, compered Alexander Clerk and produced the petitioun forsaid, in peane of contumace of Agnes Schevez, and in hir absence the ministerie forsaid decerned the copy therof to hir, to ansuer therto on Fryday nixtocome, with certificatioun to hir beand warned to compere the said day or nocht, thei procede and ministre justice in the said matter, according to the law of God, and receve probationes upoun the said petitioun, quhidder sche compere or nocht. And immediatlie heirefter, the said Agnes, the dayt heirof, comperand, confessed the contentes of the said petitioun toward the thinges therin laid to hir charge; and therfore the said ministerie, judges on this behalf, hes set and statute Fryday nixtocome, for to pronunce for the part of the said Alexander, becaus of the confessioun forsaid, and notorietie of the cryme be hir committed being maist manifest, &c.

Die Veneris vigesima prima mensis Februarii, 1560. The quhilk day, in the actioun and caus of Alexander Clerk and Agnes Schevez tending to divorce, the minister and eldares decernes them to be separated, be reasone of adulterie committed be the said Agnes, with licence to the said Alexander

---

[1] Upright, guileless.

to mary in the Lord agane; and warnes the parties Alexander
and Agnes to compear on Sounday nixt to come, the xx3 of
Februar, to hear the sentence of divorce publiced in the faice
of the congregatioun *in uberiori forma, etc.*

Sententia Clerk *contra* Schevez, &c.

*Sententia.
Clerk, Schevez.*

With incalling the name of Christe Jesus, Sone of the
aeternall and everleving God, quhai beares leale and suthfast
witnessing to our consciences, we, the ministerie of the Christiane congregatioun of this reformed cietie of Sanctandrois and
parochin therof, judges in the actioun and caus of divorce,
moved and intentated before us be Alexander Clerk against
Agnes Schevez his prætended spous, for the cryme of fornicatioun or adulterie committed be hir with Henry Balfour, to
quhome sche hes borne ane bayrne, transgressing the the (*sic*)
thride commandment of God in the secound table, quhare it
is writtin, Thow sall nocht commit adulterie: lykeas the said
Alexanderis petitioun, gevin in before us therupoun, at mayr
lenth proportes and beares in effect. The said petitioun, with
ansuering, ther reasones and allegationes, with probationes,
and namelie the said Agnes confessioun maid in our praesence
juditialie, the caus and cryme being manifest and notoriouss,
and all uthir thinges concerning baith the saidis parties being
be us heard, seene, consydered, avysed with all, and rypelie
understand; and we therfore, findand the said caus lauchfullie
provin before us, and sa to be as is be the said Alexander
alleadged and proponed, decernes, pronunces, and declares the
said Agnes, for the cryme forsaid of adulterie be hir committed,
to be cutted of, divorced, and separated fra the said Alexander,
and in tyme cuming nocht to be reputed and haldin for his
spous or wyfe ony mair; to the said Alexander permitting
agane newlie to mary quhome it sall pleass him, sa the same
be lauchfullie in the Lord and according to the law of God:
be this our sentence diffinityve, pronunced in judgement the
xxj of Februar, and decerned heir in praesence of this Christiane
congregatioun to be publiced this Sounday, the xxiij of Februar,
month forsaid, 1560.

The process of Alisone Calland against James Alexan[der].

Petitio Supplicatoria.

My lordis, minister and eldares of the Christiane congregatioun *Petitio.* of the cietie of Sanctandrois.   Unto your lordschipes humilie Calland *contra* Alexander. menis, complenis and schawis, I, your servitrice, Alisone Calland, upoun my pretended spous, James Alexander, induellar in the toun of Sanct Monanis : that quhare we, of the corrupted Papisticall maner, wer contracted and maryed, in the moneth of Januar in the fiftie aucht yere of God ; be virtew of the quhilk, efter the prætended solemnizatioun of the said mariage, I remaned with him to the secound day of the moneth of Maii nixt therefter ; and albeit the said James aucht and wes obliste of the law of God to haif honored, entrietted, gevin and rendered dew benevolence to me, as husband aucht to haif done to his wyfe ; and nocht to beare impyre abone me as ane tyran. Nochtheles abusing the said entrieting daylie and continualie, [he][1] manisched,[2] reproched, and bacbyted me, all my lynage and ofspring, saying that he haid entered amang theves, bordalleris[3] and beggares ; and at tymes, in his furie and anger conceved against me without ony deserving, wald say, with ane proterve[4] and severe visage and cowntenance, with his hand upoun his quhingar, that he wiste quhat held his hand, bot he suld thrist his quhingar throch my cheikes.   Throw quhilk severitie and frawardnes, I wes maid sa affrayed and abased that I durst nocht gudlie, nor yit dar accompany with him, for feare of my lyfe. And albeid the said James, my prætended spous forsaid, the said secound day of Maii, withowt ony occasioun or offenss maid be me to him, maisterfullie repudiate and putt me furth of his hous, denuding me of his company ; and that same nicht and continualie sensyne hes remaned, having with him in company ane servand woman of his awin, called Elizabeth Cwke, quhai lyes continualie and nichtlie in chalmer with him ; and is beloved, be the judgement of nichtbouris nixt adjacent to him, that he entreates the said Elizabeth in bed and buyrd, and

---

[1] Omitted.   [2] Threatened.
[3] Haunters of brothels.   [4] Furious.

schawis sick familiaritie to hir as man dois to his wyfe in all
sorttis. [Here she condescends to several particular charges
against her husband ; but does not repeat all his ' railling and
filthy langage that is nocht to be spokin and recited amangst
Christianes.'] Beseiking your lordschipes heirfore, with the
weale avysed counsall of the eldaris of this said cietie, to call
the said James Alexander before your lordschipes and them ;
becaus, we are destitute of ministeris and eldares, and in sick
cais, for justice to be haid in tymes bypast, hed ever recours to
the said cietie of Ṣanctandrois as place of justice, &c.; and tak
diligent inquisitioun and triall in the premissis. And gif it
beis founden, the said James Alexander to be culpable heirintill, alsweale toward his severitie and frawardnes, as adulterie,
defowling his body as said is, and can nocht lauchtfullie be maid
quite and clene therof be his nichbouris adjacent to him, that
I may be divorciat and asundre fra him, with licence to me
in the Lord God to joyne my persone in lauchfull matrimony
to ane uthir, according to the law of God : and your ansuer
humelie I besiek, &c.[1]

Die quinto mensis Marcii, anno Domini m°v° sexagesimo.

Calland,
Alexander.

The quhilk daye, comperis Alesone Calland and producis
ane libellat citacion, formit according to the tenor of the
peticione befoyr wryttyn, executit and indorsat ; tharin James
Alexander summond, and he comperand, the foyrsaid citacion
red in his presens ; bayth the saidis parteis submittyng tham
to the jurisdiccione of this ministerie, and to the disciplin of
the kyrk : James denyis the libell. The ministerie statutis to
Aleson Wedinsdaye, the xj day of Marcii instant, to preṽ hyr
libell : parteis heirto summond be actis. And at desyr of
Jam[es] Alexander, Thomas Martyn citionar is becumin caucioṅ
for James Alexander that [he][2] sall obey and fulfyll the jugment,
determinacion, and sentence of this present ministerie in this
present caws, under payn of payment of twenty liḃ., as sowm
liquidat to be rasit and distrubutit to the puyr ; and James
Sandelandis of Inuery[3] oblesis hym to relev Thomas Martyn of

---

[1] This is the last entry in the writing of David Spens.   [2] Omitted.
[3] Invery is the old name of St. Monans. Wyntoun relates that ' Saynct
Monane,' one of Adrian's company, chose to lead his life at Invery, ' sa nere the

souertie foyrsayd. In lyik maner, Wiliam Pryngyll cordinar is becumin caucionar for Aleson Calland, under payn of twenty liƀ. ; and James Greg oblesis hym to relev Wyliam tharof.

Die undecimo Marcii anno quo supra.

The quhilk day, as in term assignit to Aleson Calland to preve hyr libell deny[it] be James Alexander, comperis Aleso (*sic*); and, in presens of James, produces ane summondis executit and indorsat upon James *D*wn duelland in Abyrcrumme,[1] Dauid Mayr thar, Male Stewynson spows to James Bynnyn in Sanct Monan[is], Margret Paige spows of Thomas Bynnyn in Sanct Monanis, Aleson Small spows of Iohn Strathaquhen, William Irland, Jhon Steynson, Margret Grundestoun, Margret Castaris, Elizabeth Mwyr, Margret Dyckeson, Janat Maleyn, Annabell Sunter, Jonet Dycson, Cristen Wylson, Thomas Cowpar, Joannes Mwyr, Andro Alexander, Schyr Thomas Symson, Andro Trâyll, Dauid Mwrdo, George Prat, Wiliam Gybson, Margret Cartar, Ihon Brown, Janat Myllar, Margret Bynnyne, Margret Maxtoun, Wyliam Zong, Symon Herreis, Robert *D*uncan ; quhilkis ar sworne and admittit in presens of James, and

Calland, Alexander.

---

sé,' and 'thare endyt he' (Laing's *Wyntoun*, ii. 85, 86). His cell, now converted into a cow-house, is still shown close beside the beautiful church erected by David the Second. But Dr. Skene identifies the saint with the Bishop of Clonfert of the sixth century, and thinks it probable that only his relics were brought to Invery (*Celtic Scotland*, ii. 314). Part of the lands of Inverin was granted to the monks of May by David the First (*Records of the Priory of the Isle of May*, p. x). James Sandelandis, who was laird of Cruvie as well as St. Monans, was in the Parliament of 1560 (*Acts of the Parliaments of Scotland*, ii. 526). In 1565, when it was 'thocht meit and convenient to depute and appoint the keping of the havynnis and commoun passagis' within Lothian, Fife, and Angus, 'to trew and faythfull subjectis,' James Sandelandis was intrusted with those of 'Sanctmonanis,' 'Kilmynnane,' and 'Pettinweme' (*Register of Privy Council*, i. 381). His descendant Sir James Sandilands was created Lord Abercromby in 1647, whose son sold the estate to the famous David Leslie, afterwards Lord Newark (Wood's *East Neuk of Fife*, 1862, pp. 141, 269).

[1] The village of Abercromby, which has dwindled into a few houses, is a mile to the northward of the burgh of St. Monans. In 1647 the Presbytery of St. Andrews disjoined the town and lands of St. Monans from the parish of Kilconquhar, and annexed them to the parish of Abercromby ; and this was ratified by Parliament in 1649 (*Acts of the Parliaments of Scotland*, vol. vi. part ii. pp. 433, 434).

E

singularlie examined in presens of the holl ministerie. And
Margret Rychartson, and James *Dawson*, summond, and
exc[usit] be impediment of seiknes : at desyr of Aleson, and in
presens of James, supplicacion is decernit to the ministerie of
Anstroyer (quhar thai dwell) to examin thaim. And statutis
to Aleson the xxvj of Marcii instant, to reproduce the sayd
suplicacion ; and to bayth the parteis the xiiij daye of Maii
nixt to cum, to compeyr befoyr the ministerie and heir pro-
nuncede in the said caws.

Followis the deposicionis of wytnessis examinated
upon the puntis of the libellat summondis of Aleson
Calland aganis James Alexander.[1]

1 Thomas Dwn, dwelland in Abyrcrumme, ansueris that [he] [2]
hearis common voce and fayme, that James Alexander lyis wyth
Besse Cwyk and at it war gud sche war owt of his hows. He
knawis na mayr.

Dauid Mayr dwelland in Abyrcrumme is conform to Thomas
Dwn wytness precedin[g].

2 Male Symson, spows to James Bynnyn in Sanct Monanis, be
hyr ayth deponi[s] that, upon ane daye sche being in cumpany
wyth James Alexander, hard hym [acknowledge his guilt with
Elizabeth Cwyk ;][3] and that common voce and fam beris record
that James lyis wyth Elizabet Cwyk.

3 Margret Paige, spows of Thomas Bynnyn in Sanct Monanis,
be hyr ayth deponis that sche hard James Alexander confes,
in hyr awyn hows and [in] [2] presens of Male Symson wytnes
preceding, that [he] [2] had lyin wyth Elizabeth Cwyk : and that
common voce and faym beris record to the same.

4 Schyr Thomas Symson, sumtym ane chaplen, in his deposicion
confessis that [he] [2] hard James Alexander confes, in the hows
of James Bynnyn in Sanct Monanis efter departing of Aleson

---

[1] The marginal numbers opposite the witnesses' names are incorrect in the
Register. Though David Mayr occurs twice he is only numbered once. In the
other cases, the mistake has aiisen through the oft-recurring name of James
Alexander beginning the line.

[2] Omitted.   [3] Modified.

Calland his wyf fra his cumpany, that that sam nycht [he had committed adultery,][1] nocht specifiand the nam of the woman.

5   Dauid Mwrdo, servand, dwelland wyth Stephyn Clark in Kylconquhar, deponis that he dwelt ane half year wyth James Alexander sen he was mareit wyth Aleson Calland, and at he and James Alexanderis son wated[2] James Alexander and Besse Cwyk, and saw the thing betuix tham that wes not lyklie.

6   Dauid Mayr, dwelland in Abyrcrumme, deponis that the
7 common voce and fame is that James Alexander hes carnall dayll wyth Besse Cwyk.

8   Margret Grundestown in Sanct Monans is conform to Dauid Mayr wytnes preceding.

9   Margret Castares in Sanctmonans knawis nathing bot common face (*sic*) and fam *ut supra*.

10   Elizabeth Muyr dochter to Margret Castaris is conform to hyr mother.

11   Margret Dyckeson knawis nathing except common voce and fame.

12   Janat Maleyn, spows to Andro Dyschingtoun, knawis nathing bo[3] commone voce and fame.

13   Aleson Small, spows of Ihon Strathaquhen, deponis that the
14 common voce and fame is, that James Alexander lyis wyth Besse Cwyk, and at he makis his ruys[4] therof as sche hard say.

15   Annabill Sunter in Sanct Monanis knawis na forthir bot
16 common voce and fame is that James Alexander lyis wyth Besse Cwyk.

17   Janat Dyckeson relict of Ihon Small knawis na farther bot of common voce and fam *ut supra*.

18   Cristian Wylson, spows to Thomas Cowpar, deponis that sche saw Aleson Calland depa[r]t fra James Alexander gretand; and sayis sche trowis James wyll not deny bot at he put hyr awaye. *Item*, as to his lying wyth Besse Cwyk, the common voce and fame hes beyn sua be the space of twa yeris bypast.

---

[1] Modified.   [2] Watched.   [3] Should be *bot*.   [4] Boast.

19 Thomas Cowpar [1] in Sanct Monanis knawis nathing bot common voce and fame *ut supra*.

20 Jhone Mwyr in Sanct Monanis deponis that he hard James Alexander saye behind Aleson Callandis bak evyll talk of hyr, vidz., that he cam amangis theiffis bordellaris and beggaris. James and Besse Cwyk are evyll schanderit (*sic*) togethyr be common voce and fame.

21 Andro Alexander in Sanct Monanis knawis nathing bot common voce and fame *ut supra*.

22 Andro Trayll, dwelling in Sanct Monanis, deponis that common voce and fam is that the caws of awaye puttyng of Aleson Calland fra James Alexander is Besse Cwyk.

23 George Prat, dwelland in Kylconquhar, deponis that James Alexander and Elizabeth Cwyk ar sclanderit be common voce and fame.

24 Wiliam Gybson in Kylconquhar knawis nathing bot of common voce and fame.

25 Margret Cartar, familiar servand to James Alexander, examinat upon the puntts of summondis, denyis the hayll, except that sche confessis that Elizabeth Cwyk servand also to James Alexander lyis commonlie and nychtlie wyth the deponar, except sum nychtis sche passis and lyis in the chalmer, quhar James Alexander lyis, and in special sche lay thar the Sunday at nycht nixt efter followit Sanct Monanis day now last bypast.

26 Jhon Brown servand to James Alexander knawis nathing bot that ilka body sayis that James Alexander hes carnall dayll wyth Elizabeth Cwyk.

27 Janat Myllar deponis that common voce and fam beris record that James Alexander lyis wyth Besse Cwyk and at he mackis his rus therof.

28 Margret Maxtoun deponis that common voce and fame beris record of all the hayll poyntis and headis contenit in the libillat summondis.

---

[1] In 1828 John Cowper died, in the parish of St. Monans, 'in his ninety-second year, in full vigour both of body and mind, a respectable farmer, whose ancestors and himself had occupied the same farm on the Abercromby estate for nearly 300 years.' 'There is every reason to believe that it is of this stationary family' that William Cowper of Olney writes: 'I am originally of the same shire [Fife], and a family of my name is still there' (*Statistical Account of Fifeshire*, 1845, p. 344).

29 Margret Bynnyne, dochter to James Bynnyn, deponis and sayis, that sche hard James Alexander confes, in hyr motheris hows and hyr presens, that the nycht preceding his confession he had lyin twys wyth Elizabeth Cwyk ; and in this also is conform to Male Symson hyr mother the secund wytnes : and that the common voce and fame beris record that James hes carnall dayll wyth the sayd Elizabet, and at sche lyis nychtlie in his chalmer quhen sche plesis.

30 Wyliam Zong, barber, citiner of Sanctandrois, deponis that now laytle in this last wynter, in the hows of Ihon Caddellis in Anstroyer, being present in cumpany wyth the deponar Ibon Caddellis, Margret Rychardson spows of the said Ihon, and thair servand, James Alexander oppynlie avansit and mayd his rus [that he had been guilty on the preceding night].[1]

31 Symon Herreis deponis and confessis that Elizabeth Cwyk lyis in chalmer wyth James Alexander : *causam sciencie reddit*, the deponar was servand in hows wyth the said James in the symmer half year last bypast. He saw Elizabeth gang ben to thè chalmer quhar James laye and to bed, and saw hyr ryis in the mornyngis and cum but.[2] *Item*, he confessis that common voce and fam beres record that thai have carnall dayll together.

32 Robert Duncan in Sandfurd[3] deponis and is conform to Symon Herreis wytnes preceding in al thingis, vidz., in caus of knawlege as deposicion.

Die xxvj mensis Marcii anno Domini m°v°lxi.

The quhilk daye, as in term assignit to Aleson Calland to reproduce the supplicacion direct to the minister and eldaris of

---

[1] Modified. [2] Come into the outer apartment.

[3] Probably Sandford in Kilconquhar parish, which occurs in the *Inquisitionum Retornatarum Abbreviatio* as ' Sanctfuird,' ' Sanfuird ' and ' Saintfurd,' and in the *Valuation Roll* and best modern maps of Fife as ' St. Ford.' In Blaeu's map of the *East Part of Fife*, 1654, it is marked ' Stanfurd '; and due north near the Tay, he shows ' Stanfurd Narne ' and ' Stanfurd Hay,' which, after being long indiscriminately written ' Sandfurde,' ' Sanctfuird,' or ' Saintfurd,' now bear the name of ' St. Fort,' though still called ' Samfurd ' in the neigh-bourhood. In the adjoining parish of Leuchars there is a place and its surround-ings known as ' Michael's,' but in the *Valuation Roll* and *Ordnance Survey* these appear as ' St. Michael's,' although the name was derived from Michael Irvine— a publican of this century !

the kyrk of Anstroyer, comperis Aleson, and reproducis the sam togethyr wyth the deposicionis of Margret Rychardson and James Dawsone: of the quhilkis deposicionis follouis the tenor heyrunder. The ministerie statutis to the parteis the xiiij of Maii nixt to cum to heyr pronunced in the sayd caws of divorce: parteis heyrto summond.

33 Margret Rychardson, spows of Ihon Caddellis, deponis and confessis sche hard James Alexander say he had actuall conversacion wyth ane woman, bot sche knawis not the woman, nor hard hym not exrem[1] na tym and knawis no may[r.]

34 James Dawson, dwelling in the Wester Wemys, xix yearis of aige *prout asseruit*, deponis and sayis, that he hard James Alexander call his wyff, Aleson Calland, huyr and theif, and said he wes enterit amangis huris and theiffis. And also deponis that Elizabeth Cwyk lay continualie in the hows and chalmer wyth James Alexander, betuix the festis Wytsunday and Martymes last bypast; and at it is suspectit that James Alexander had actuall conversacion wyth the sayd Besse Cwyk, and he hard syndry personnis saye the sam. *Et reddit causam scienċie*, the deponar dwelt and remanit wyth the said Jam[es] Alexander betuix the saydis terms of Wytsundaye and Martymes.

Die xiiij^{to} mensis Maii anno Domini m^o v^c lxj.

The quhilk daye, the minister and eldaris, being avysed wyth the proces of Aleson Calland aganis James Alexander, fundes James ane adulterar; and decernis sentence of divorce to be put in forme, and the sam to be publesit this nixt Sundaye the xviij of Maii instant in the essemble of the congregacion of Sanctandrois, bayth the parteis to be summond to heir the sam pronunct; in presens of Aleson and in payn of not comperance of James heyrto summond.

Sentencia Calland contra Alexander.

Wyth incalling the name of Crist Jesus, Sone to the eternall and everlevyng God, quhai beris leil and suthfast wytnesing to our consciences, we, the ministerie of the reformed kyrk and congregacion of the citie and parrochyn of Sanctandrois, judges in the accion and caws of divorce, moved and intentadet befoyr

---

[1] Should be *exprem*.

us be Alisone Calland aganis James Alexander hyr pretendit
howsband, for the cryme and fylthy syne of adulterye, committed be hym wyth ane woman called Elizabeth Cwyk, in
that transgressing and brekyn the thrid commandiment of God
in the secund tabile contened quhar it is wryttyn, Thow sall not
commyt adulterie : lyikas in the peticion, produced and gevyn
in befoir us therupon for the part of the said Aleson Calland,
at mayr lenth in effect is conteyned ; the said peticion wyth
ansuering therto, reasonis and allegacionis, wyth testimoneis
and deposicionis of mony honest and famose wytnes, befoyr us
summond, produced, sworn and examinated, and utheris thingis
appertenyng and belangyng tharto, and parteis foyrsaidis concernyng, being be us hard, seyn, considered, avysed wythall,
and ryplie understand ; communicating the secretis of the said
accione and caws wyth Maister Jhon Wynram, Superintendent
of Sanctandrois, and wyth his avysement and consent heirto :
we, fyndand the caws alleged and proponed be the said Aleson
conform to hyr peticion lawfullie and fullelie provyn, pronunces, decernis, and declaris, be this owr sentence diffinityve,
the said James Alexander, for the cryme foirsaid of adulterie
be hym committed, to be cutted [of][1] and divorced and seperated fra the said Aleson, and in tym cuming not to be haldyn
and reputed for hyr howsband ony mayr ; permytting the said
Alesone agane newlie to marye quhome wyth it sall pleas hyr,
sa the sam be lawfullie done in the Lord and according to the
Word of God ; gevyng forder execucion and punyschement
heirof, that is of the cryme of adulterie committed be the saidis
James Alexander and Elizabeth Cwyk, to the temporall magistrat, quhai is the Steward of the Regalitie of Sanctandrois, wythin
quhais bowndes and jurisdiccion the said James remanis ; exhorting, and als in the name of the eternall God requiring, hym
that he punysche accordinglie as he maye, and als [he][1] awcht
and suld do of his office at this present ; be this owr sentence
diffinityv[e,] subscrivit wyth owr handis, pronunced in owr consistoriall auditore the xiiij daye of Maii, and publesched in
this congregacion this Sundaye the xviij daye of Maii, in the
year of God m°v°lxj.   Crostopher Gudman, minister, Mr. Alan

---

[1] Omitted.

Lawmonth, Mr. Thomas Balfowr, Jhon Moffat, Mr. Robert
Pont, Thomas Martyn, Jhon Martyn, Jhon Wod, Mr. Martyn
Gedde, Wylliam Monepenny, Dauid Wolwod, and Ihone Motto,
elderis.

Die xxj° Maii anno lxj°.

Anent the
absens fra the
sait.

Nota.

The quhilk day, the minister elderis, and deaconis present
consentis that, quhen ony of thame remanis and absentis thame
selfis fra the sait ony Weddinsday, thai sall pay xij d. for thair
absens ; and quha cumms efter thre houris sall pay vj d., thai
being present in this citee or in the feildis therto adjacent ;
and quha sa beis absent quhill efter the preyar be done in the
saitt ony Weddinsday sall pay iij d. ; and all that sueris ane
aith in the sait, unrequerit and admittit to sueir, sall pay ij d.
ilk falt to the puir.

Die quarto Februarii 1567.[1]

The quhilk day, the act immedietlie preceding ratifeit and
apprevit be the sait, the Superintendent being present ; and if
ony man depart befoir the sait ryis, wythout licience askit and
obtenit, [he][2] sall pay iij d.

Heir followis the forme and tenor of the edict, executit
in chergyn of the inhabitantis of the diocy of Sanctandrois to the eleccion of Maister Jhone Wynram[3] in

---

[1] This and the preceding entry appear to have been written at the same time,
and are at the bottom of a page.

[2] Omitted.

[3] Wynram, whose name has occurred several times in the text already, was
born in 1492. He appears to have entered St. Leonard's College in 1513, and
two years later took the degree of Bachelor of Arts. In 1532 he is mentioned
as a canon-regular of the monastery of St. Andrews, and in 1539 as its Sub-Prior
(Lee's *Lectures*, i. 340-342). Though he early showed his leanings to the new
views, he kept himself out of serious trouble. In 1546 he preached at the trial
of Wishart, and—according to Buchanan, Pitscottie, and Spottiswoode—inter-
ceded for him after his condemnation, but was angrily rebuffed by the Cardinal.
Next year he had a discussion with Knox in St. Leonard's yard (Laing's *Knox*,
i. 193-197) ; and in 1549 was a member of the Provincial Council (*Concilia
Scotiae*, ii. 83). On several occasions he was one of the visitors of St. Leonard's
College, and in 1550 there are ' regulations about altars, copes, surplices, &c.,

the office of ane superintendent, quhai wes elected and chosyn in Superintendent of Fyff, Fotheryk, and Strathern, wythin the parochie kyrk of the citie of Sanctandrois, upone Sundaye the xiij daye of Aprill, in the year of God m°v°lxj yearis, be the common consent of lordis, barronis, ministeris, eldaris, of the saidis bowndis, and otheris common pepill present for the tym, according to the ordor provydit in the Buk of Reformacion.[1]

Seing that it hath pleased the mercy of owr God sa to illuminat the hartis of ane gret part of the consail, nobilitie, and estatis, of this realme, that clearlie thei can discern betuix lycht and darknes; and also sa to move them that, be plane confession of thar fayth, thei have approved the puritie of doctrin and religion contened wythin his holy Word; and last hes gevyn to tham his fatherlie grace to resaive, peruse, and

Eleccione of Maister Jhone Wynram in Superintendent of Sanctandrois diocesye.

---

which do not indicate any great desire on the part of Mr. John Wynram and his coadjutors to relinquish the most useless observances of the Church of Rome' (Lee's *Lectures*, i. 343). The tradition which associates his name with the authorship of Hamilton's *Catechism* is not entitled to implicit belief, although something can be said in its favour (Professor Mitchell's *Historical Notice* prefixed to Hamilton's *Catechism*, 1882, p. xvii); but there can be no doubt that he was present at other three trials for heresy besides Wishart's, namely, those of Sir John Borthwick, Adam Wallace, and Walter Mille (Cattley's *Foxe*, v. 607, 637, 645). The Martyrologist relates that the absurd controversy as to whom the *Pater Noster* should be said was referred ' by the Holy Church to Dean John Winryme'; and he adds in a foot-note, 'This Winram is now become a godly minister in the Church of God, and a married man' (*Ibid.* p. 644). As Superintendent, he had the oversight of ' Fiffe, Perth, Straitherne, Clakmannan, Kynrose and Strevelingschire on the north syde of Forth, with Menteth '; and his stipend was, ' quheit ij chalderis, beir v chalderis, aitis iij chalderis, meill ij chalderis, money v° merkis ' (*Register of Ministers, Exhorters and Readers*, Mait. Club, p. 2).

[1] The duties of the superintendents, and the mode of their election, are prescribed in the *First Book of Discipline.* The form and order used at the election of Spottiswoode as Superintendent of Lothian, on the 9th of March 1560·1, will be found in the *Book of Common Order.* ' The number of persons elected as superintendents never exceeded the five who were first chosen. The office was one of a very arduous nature. It conferred no degree of superiority over their brethren; it had no great pecuniary advantage; while, like other members, they were subject to be censured, superseded, or deposed by the General Assembly. As their number was never increased, the Assembly from time to time appointed commissioners or visitors for special districts ' (Laing's *Knox*, vi. 386).

approve the Buk of Reformacione,[1] offre[d] unto thar honouris
be the ministeris and commissionaris of kyrkis; efter the
approbacion quharof the Lordis of Secreit Consail have directed
thar cherg[e] and commandiment to the ministeris, eldaris, and
diaconis, of Lothyane, Fyff, Mern[is], Glasgow, Argyill, and of
partis adjacent, requiring tham, and every diocy for the self,
to propone be publict edict certan men in the said chearge
specifyed; to wyt, to the diocy of Edinburgh, Mr. Ihone
Spottiswod; to the diocy of Sanctandrois, Mr. Ihon Wynram;
to the diocy of Brechyn, Jhone Erskyn of Dwn; to the diocy
of Glasgow, Jhon Wyllok: to the diocy of Argyill, Mr. Ihon
Carswall; to be elected and appoynted superintendentis and
owersearis, every man to the diocy assigned to his cherge. We,
therfor, the ministeris, eldaris, and diaconis, wythin the
diocy of Sanctandrois, to wyt, of the citie of Sanctandrois,
and of the burrowis of Perth, Cowpar, Craill, Anstroy[er],
Kyrkaldy, Dunfermling, &c., sa mony of us as convenientlie
mycht be essembl[ed], fyrst havyng respect to the gloir of our
God and to the preparacion of Cristis kyngdome wythin this
realme, and nixt to our detful obedience to the superi[or]
poweris, have assigned Sunday the xiij of Aprill nixt to cum,
to the elecc[ion] of the said Jhon Wynram to his foirsaid office
and charge. And tharfor we most humilie requir, and, in
the name of the eternall God and of his Sone Crist Jesus (quhois
onlie gloir in this accion we seik), we charge erlis, lordis, barronis, burgessis, ministeris, eldaris of kyrkis, and all otheris
to quhom vot apperteins in eleccion of sic cheef ministeris,
that thei be present wythin the parrochie kyrk of the citie of
Sanctandrois the daye foirsai[d], immedietlie efter nyne howris
befoir nuyn, to assist the said eleccion, and be ther votis to
consent to the same, or ellis to oppone aganis the lyff and
doctrin of the person nominated: and lyikwyis we requir and
charge the said Jhon Wynram, to be personalie present the same
daye in tym and place above expressed, to accept the chearge

---

[1] The charge to Wynram, Dowglas, Spottiswoode. Willok, Row, and Knox, to
draw up the *First Book of Discipline*, was dated the 29th of April 1560; and
it was ready by the 20th of the following month. The nobility 'did peruse it
many dayis.' Knox has recorded the names of the principal men who subscribed it on the 27th January 1560-1 (Laing's *Knox*, ii. 129, 258-260).

quharwyth the kyrk sall burd[yn] hym : wyth certificacion to
al and syndry that seing, wythowt the cayr [of] superintendentis, neyther can the kyrk be suddenlie erected, neyther
can th[ei] be retened in disciplin and unite of doctrin ; and
farther seing that o[f] Crist Jesus and of his apostolis
we have command and exempill to appoynt me[n] to sic
chergis ; and now last that we have command of the upper
power[is] to put the same in execucione ; we intend to proceid
in the said eleccione according to the ordor of the Buk of
Reformacione, nochtwythstanding the absence of ony personis.
And this we notifie to all and syndrie wythin the said docesye,
be this our publict edict subscrivit wyth owr handis at the citie
of Sanctandrois, upon the twenty daye of the moneth of Marcii,
in the year of God 1560. Cristofer Gudman, minister ; Mr.
Alane Lawmonth, Mr. Thomas Balfowr, Ihone Moffat, Mr.
Martyn Gedde, Jhon Motto, Mr. Robert Pont, Ihon Wod,
eldaris ; Dauid Spens, Thomas Wolwod, George Blak, diaconis
of Sanctandrois.

Die xxv^{to} mensis Aprilis anno domini m^{o}v^{c}lxj.

The quhilk daye, it is provydit, statutit, and ordened, be the [Statut anent
Superintendent and holl ministerie, wyth consayll of the the the tryall and
admissione of
(*sic*) Provest of Sanctandrois, Rector and chief membris of the ministeris, exhortaris, and
Universite, anent the tryall and admissione of ministeris in the readaris.]
hol dioceye, that sa mony ministeris, exhortaris, or readaris, as
ar alredy placed in kyrkis detfullie, that the Superintendent in
his visitacion tak tryall of every ane particularlie, be hearing
of thar doctrin [and]¹ reading, in the kyrke [qubair]¹ thai ar
placed, and inquir of thar lyff and conversacion be inquisicione
amangis thar flok. And as concernyng the admission of
otheris that ar not placed, it is ordened that, in tym cuming,
al sic as pretendis to be admitted to minister in ony kyrk,
wythin the bowndis of Fyff, Fotheryk, or Strathern, sall compeir wythin this cite, at sic daye and place as salbe assignit to
tham be the Superintendent, to be examinated, fyrst privatle
upon the cheaf puntis and headis in controversy, and tharefter
ane porcion of text assignet to the minister to declar in the

¹ Omitted.

pulpat in the essemble, and to the exhortar or reader to reid or exhort in the public assemble.

[Parrochyn of Sanct Leon-ardis.] *Item,* it is also ordened that the parrochyn of Sanct Leonardis salbe adjunit to heyr the word of God, and resaive the sacramentis and disciplyn, in the parrochie kyrk of the the (*sic*) citie of Sanctandrois, in tym cuming, aye and quhille mayr ampill forme of reformacion and religion incres and be had be the stablesched authoritie, and this wythowtyn ony prejudice of profitis pertenyng to Sanct Leonardis College.[1]

[The provestrie of Kirkheuch, or the Kirkhill, or the Lady College Kirk upon the heuch, suspended in all time coming. Its prebendari~s— 1. Lameletham, 2. Kyngask and Kinglassie, 3 Kynkell, *Item,* the Lady College Kyrk upon the hewch is decernit suspendit, and ane prophane hows,[2] and sa to be haldyn in tym cuming.

The quhilk daye all and syndry prebendaris of the Lade College foyrsayd, and Provest of the sam, being lawfullie summond be the Superintendentis letteres, to compeyr this daye and schaw thar obedience gevyn to the Quenis Grace letteres and cherge, anent thar gevyn of thar confession of thar fayth, and subscryving of the articlis, and obtenyng of thar

---

[1] The greater part of the little parish of St. Leonard's is four or five miles from the city of St. Andrews; but that part is, and probably has always been, very sparsely populated. Most of the parishioners live in the detached portions which are in St. Andrews and its outskirts. In his account of St. Leonard's, Dr. Buist gave several reasons for believing that it acquired the character and name of a parish in 1512 when the college was erected (*Statistical Account of Fifeshire,* pp. 498-500), but when he wrote, the *Register of the Priory* had not been printed. That the parish did not originate with the college is quite certain, for on the 22nd of December 1413 Wyntoun, who was a canon of St. Andrews as well as Prior of St. Serf's, produced the *Register* before the Official of the Diocese, '*in ecclesia parochiali Sancti Leonardi infra civitatem Sanctiandree*' (*Liber Cartarum Prioratus Sancti Andree,* Ban. Club, p. 15). According to Hew Scott, James Wilkie, who succeeded Buchanan as Principal of St Leonard's in 1570, became minister of the parish in 1578; from that date until the union of St. Salvator's and St. Leonard's Colleges in 1747, the ministers of the parish with one exception held the Principalship of St. Leonard's in conjunction; and from 1747 to 1824 the ministers were invariably the Principals of the United College (*Fasti Ecclesiae Scoticanae,* ii. 398-401). Since 1759 the congregation has worshipped in St. Salvator's Chapel, which in 1844 the Court of Session disjoined from the parish of St. Andrews and annexed to that of St. Leonard's *quoad sacra tantum,* and the old church of St. Leonard's has long been a roofless and neglected ruin.

[2] That is, decerned to be suspended and declared to be a profane house.

admission, and called comperis Mr. James Lermonth, Provost, 4. Kernis and Cameron— for hymself, and schew that he [and] Mr. Henry Adam[1] Foulis all in the parish prebendar of Lammelethem war adjonit to the congregacion, of St. Andrews at the Reforma- and heyrfor ar admittit and decernit to be ansuerit of thar tion.][2] frutis. And Mr. Thomas Meffen, prebendar of Kyngask and Kynglasse, Mr. James Henrison, prebendar of Kynkell, Mr. Wyliam Ballingall, prebendar of Kernis and Cameron, not comperand ; and understand inobedient to the cherge : the Superintendent, wyth avyis of the consayll, ordenis the diaconis of the kyrk of the citie of Sanctandrois to resave and intromit wyth the frutis of thar[3] foyrsaidis prebendreis, to be distrubutit at the discrecion and sycht of the holl ministerie, and compt randerit therof.

The proces of Elizabeth Thecar aganis James Martyn hyr spows concernyng divorce.

The ministerie of the reformed kyrk of Sanctandrois, be the *Citacio* Thecar tenor of thir presentis, commandis and chargis that James *contra* Martyne. Martyn, pretendit husband to Elizabethe Thecar, be summond,

---

[1] *Adam* is an interlinear addition.

[2] This marginal note is in the *Register*, but is written in a modern hand. Martine preserves a tradition that ' the Culdees of old, at least Regulus and his companions,' had a cell on a rock, ' called at this day our Ladies Craige,' beyond the end of the pier, which on the sea's encroaching they forsook and ' built another house at, or near, the place where the house of the Kirk-heugh now stands ' (*Reliquiae Divi Andreae*, p. 24). There is better evidence to show that towards the end of the sixth century Cainnech founded a monastery about the same place ; that the Abbot, Tuathal, died in 747 ; and that two centuries later Constantine, after resigning the crown, ended his days within its peaceful walls (*Celtic Scotland*, ii. 137, 271, 326, 327). This early Culdean house became a Collegiate establishment and a Chapel Royal—probably the first of either in Scotland—but when these changes occurred is still unknown. Some interesting *Historical Notices of the Provostry of Kirkheugh*, by David Laing, are printed in the *Proceedings of the Society of Antiquaries of Scotland*, iv. 76-86. See also *Concilia Scotiae*, vol. i. pp. ccvi-ccxxvi.

[3] Here the entry concerning the ' Lady College Kyrk ' turns over the page, and the blank space left at the bottom has been so far utilised by a clerk that he has written on it :—

' *Die xxjo Maii anno lxj.*

' The quhilk day the minister elderis and deaconis present '

Then, noticing his mistake, he has turned back a leaf and entered the minutes ' anent the absens fra the sait ' at the foot of it.

lyikas be the tenor heirof thei summond hym, to compeir
befoyr tham in the consistorie hows, wythin the parrochie kyrk
of Sanctandrois, upon the nixt thre scoyr lawfull daye immedietlie efter following the execucion heirof, at twa howris efter
nuyn or tharby, quhilk is the howr of caws for ministracion of
justice, befoyr the said ministerie, to hear and se ane accion
and caws of divorce and partesyng, moved against hym be
the said Elizabeth, for the crym and syne of adulterie committed be the said James wyth ane woman called Janat
Alexander, wyth quhom the said James departed ower se fra
the said Elizabeth his lawful wyff thane, be the space of fyve
yearis or tharby, toward the partis of Dutcheland, and thar
remanand wyth hyr in the town of Lubke, hes gottyn (as is
reported be famos men) thre barnis wyth the said Janat, sen
his departing of this realm fra the said Elizabeth his sumtym
lawfull wyff, brekand the thrid commandiment of God contened
in the secund tabill, quhar it is wryttyn, Thow sall not commit
adulterie: and to hear and se lawful probacionis and wytnes
produced and brocht in, to verefye and mak clear the caws
alleaged, and als to se produced and, to all actes judiciall neidfull to be haid in the said caws, proceded[1] wyth sic intimacione
that this edict and summondis be red publiclie in this parroche
kyrk befoyr the sermon, and tharefter affixed upon the kyrk
dur to stand all the tym of the sermon, sua that nane allege
ign[o]rance of that thing quhilk is so manifestlie publiced and
maid patent. Gevyn under the saill quhilk in sic caussis we
use, wyth the subscripsio[n] of our scrib, is affixit at Sanctandrois, the xvij of Maii, *anno* 1561.

Sundaye, the xviij daye of Maii, the year abov wryttyn, I
George Blak, ane of the diaconis of the reformed kyrk of
Sanctandrois, in presens of the congregacion convenit in the
parrochie kyrk tharof, befor the sermon summond lawfullie
James Martyn foyrsaid, be oppyn proclamacion in the said
kyrk, efter the tenor of the above wryttyn edict, and thare[fter]
the same being red I affixit it upon the principall dur of the
said kyrk. In presens of the congregacion I did thir thingis,

---

[1] There is probably a mistake here in the *Register*; perhaps some words are omitted.

and for farther verificacion heirof hes subscrivit my indorsacion,
Ge. Blak wyth my hand.

Die secundo mensis Julii, anno Domini m⁰vᶜlxj.

The quhilk daye, in presens of honourabill men, Mr. Alan
Lawmonth and Jhon Moffat, ballies of the citie of Sanctandrois, in the towbuth of the same, judiciale comperis Elizabeth Thecar spows of James Martyn, quhai exponis and
schawis to the ballies foyrsaidis, that sche rasit ane citacione
of the ministerie of Sanctandrois, thar[in] caused summond the
said James upon thre scoyr dayes, to hey[r and] se divorce led
betuix hym and hyr for adulterie, committed be the said James
in gevyn his body to Janat Alexander sen his mareage wyth
hyr, betuix quhon (*sic*) thre barnis ar procreat, and wyth
quhom he kepis hows in the toun of Lubke ; and that heir
ar present in [ju]giment, on cace cumin¹ twa Scottismen,
strengearis and inhabitan[tis] in that cuntre, to sell the ladnyng
of thar schip, quhilkis ar wytnessis necessary for probacion of
hyr intent, quhilkis also ar not to remayn in this realm, bot
to depart hastelie and befoyr the diet of hyr summonds sall
cum : heirfor desyris thame to be resavit, sworne, and examinated, *ad futuram perpetuam rei memoriam.* Quhilk desyr be²
thocht ressonabill to the foyrsaid ballies, and be tham grantit,
Elizabeth producis Archibald Duncan and Alexander Gallo-
waye ; quhilkis ar resavit, sworne, and judicialie examinated
upon the foyrsaid alleged adulterie singularle, and in thar
deposicionis ar *conformes ;* vid., thai affirme and grantis in thar
deposicionis that James Martyne, brother to Thomas Martyn
and Ihon Martyn of this citie, kepis hows wyth Janat Alexander in the town of Lubke, and as mareit folkis ar haldyn
and reput thar wyth thar neyghboris, and have procreat betuix
tham twa barnis, borne be the said Janat and acknawleged be
the said James to [be] his barnis. Examinated upon the caws
of thar knawlege, thai ansuer that thai have beyn in the hows
of James Martyn in Lubke, quhar thai have hard and seyn as
befoyr thai have deponit : examinated upon the interrogatoris
of law, thai purge thame.

---

¹ By chance come.   ² Should be *being*.

Die xxiij mensis Julii anno Domini 1561.

The quhilk daye, compiris Elizabeth Thecar and producis the summondis deulie execut and indorsat upon James Martyn, of the quhilk the tenor is befoyr wryttyn. He ofttymmis called and not comperand, Elizabeth, in payn of not comperance of James, being admitted to preve the punctes of hyr summondis, producis the act and deposicionis of wytnes befoyr mencioned in probacione. The ministerie avysed tharwyth, togethyr wyth the notoritie of the cryme and act, pronuncis and declaris the said James ane adulterar, and for his adulterie committ[ed] wyth Janat Alexander, to be cutted of, divorced, and seperated fra the sayd Elizabeth Thecar, and in tym cuming not to be haldyn for hyr spous ony mayr ; wyth liberte to the said Elizabeth in the Lord to marie ony lawfull howsband, according to the law of God. Pronunced at the instance of Elizabeth Thecar, and in payn of not comperance of James Martyn heirto lawfullie summond. This to be publest this nixt Sundaye, and put in dew forme of sentence, and the attentik extract tharof to be deliverit to Elizabeth, &c.

Sentencia divorcii Elizabeth Thecar contra Jacobum Martyne. Wyth incalling of the name of Crist Jesus, Sone of the eternall God, we, minister and eldaris of the Cristiane congregacione of the citie and parrochyn of Sanctandrois, jugis in the caws of divorce moved befoir us be Elizabeth Thecar aganis James Martyn hyr spows, for cryme and syne of adulterie committed be the said James wyth ane woman called Janat Alexander ; wyth quhome the said James departed ower sey to the partis of Almanye, fra the said Elizabeth thane his lawfull wyff ; remanand thar be the space of fyve yearis or tharby in the town of Lwbke, and have procreat betuix thame thre barnis sen thar departyng ; transgressand the thrid command of God in the secund tabill, quhar it is wryttyn, Thow sall not commit adulterie : as at lenth is contened in the libell summondis rased at the instance of the said Elizabeth deulie executed indorsat and befoir us reproduced ; tharin the said James summond upon the premunicion of thre scoyr dayes, and he called, we wyth detfull ordour have proceded ; and being riplie avysed wyth the foirsaid libellat summondis, togethyr wyth the testimonye and deposicionis of famos wytnessis, and all otheris deduced in the said caws, fyndis the foyrsaid crym and syne of adulterie according to the libell sufficientlie provyn ; havand heirfor God onlie befoir owr ees, and the testimone of his Word, by this owr sentence diffinityve, pronuncis, decernis and declaris the said James Martyn ane adulterar, and for his adultery, be hym committed wyth the said Janat Alexander, to be cutted of, divorced and seperated fra the said Elizabeth Thecar; and in tym cuming not to be haldyn for hyr spows ony mayr ; wyth liberte to the said Elizabeth in the Lord to marye ony lawfull howsband, according to the law of God. Pronunced upon the xxiij of Julii, in the year of God 1561, at the instance of Elizabeth Thecar, and in payn of not comperance of James Martyn heirto lawfullie summond.

Die xxj mensis Junii anno 1561.

The quhilk daye, Jhon Kipper, sumtym in Papistrie called *Caucionarii* Schyr Ihon Kipper, wardor [1] wythin the castell of Sanctandrois *Joannes Kyppar.* for contempsione and blasphemyng of Cristis religion, Superintendent, and ministeris of Godis Word, and for defending and mantenyng of idolatrie, supersticion, and Papistrie, caused in his name his mynd, confession, and desyr, under his hand wryt, be presentit to the Superintendent, of the quhilk the tenor followis.

My Lord, unto your Lordschipe humilie and lamenttablie menis I, your Lordschipes orator, Jhone Kypper, sumtym knycht of the Papis kyrk, that quhar I have beyn in my tender yowth blindit be sinister preaching of the trew Euangel[l] of almychty God, and in takyn of the sammyn and heir throucht hes abusit my self, be saying of mes and usand supersticion and idolatrie, belev[ing] salvacion tharin, contrar the institucion of Crist, and in vilepensione of his preciows blud sched for me and mankynd. And now I ame becumin of aige, ane man neir iiij[xx] of yearis, and, prysit be almychty God, persavis the trew Ewangell and Gospell of almychty God trewlie and sincerlie prechit ; quhilk I confes, and wyll byid at to my lyffis end, desyrand your Lordschipe heirfor, and for Ihesus Cristis saik, to

---

[1] Warded.

caws me to be delivered to that effect, that I maye cum befoyr
the hayll congregacion, and thar penetenle mak ane oppyn
amendis for the offence and sclander committed be me heirin-
tyll, and that I maye be adjunit heirto; and your Lordschipes
answar heirintill maist humilie I beseik, be me your Lordschipes orator, Ihon Kyppar, sumtym knycht of the Papis
kyrk. Quhilk wryt being seyn and considerit be the Superintendent, the said Ihon being relaxit and tharby put to libirtie
fre of ward, and the foyrsayd handwryt to hym schawin and be
hym recognesit, in presens of Dauid Wolwod, Ihon Hogistoun,
Jhon Kembak, he is set at libirtie to the effect that he maye
heyr the doctryn for x dayes or langar, as salbe thocht expedient to the Superintendent, minister and eldaris.   And ony
tym, upon xlviij howris warnyng efter the saydis ten dayis
liberte, he to compeyr wythin the citie of Sanctandrois, in the
session of the ministerie, to rander ane confessione of his fayth ;
and as it salbe ordened to hym, be the sentiment of the sessione
and ministerie, to underlie correccion, or to recant and amend
in the public assemble, according to his awyn wryt foyrsayd.
For fulfylling of the quhilkis, Ihone Kembak and George
Wylson, citionaris, conjunctlie and severalie, ar becumin caucionaris for the said Ihon Kippar, under payn of payment of
ane hundreth marchas as sowm liquidat, to be disponit to the
puyr ; and Iohn Kippar oblesis hym to relev the saydis Ihon
and George of the foyrsayd sourte, befoyr wytnes above
expremit.

The proces of accusacion led and deducit aganis Mr.
Alexander Wardlaw, pretendit parson of Balingry,[1]
at the instance of the Superintendent.

Die ix mensis Julii anno domini 1561.

The quhilk daye, comperis Patrik Ramsaye, procurator, and
in naym of Mr. Ihon Wynram, Superintendent, be his mandat,

---

[1] He was a son of Henry Wardlaw of Torrie, and was parson in October
1551 (Scott's *Fasti*, ii. 525). Henry Wardlaw, Bishop of St. Andrews, and
founder of its University, and Walter Wardlaw, Bishop of Glasgow, were of the
same family (Keith's *Catalogue*).

red and admittit, and producis ane summondis deulie executed
and indorsat, tharin summond Mr. Alexander Wardlaw of
Ballingry[1] to compeyr befoyr the ministerie of Sanctandrois, to
ansuer to sic headis and articlis as salbe obeckit (*sic*) aganis
hym for inobedence, contempsio[n], and blasphemows spekyn
aganis the Superintendent of Fyiff, wyth commissio[n] in the
sayd summondis to the sayd ministerie to cognosce in the sayd
caws, to the pronunciacion of the sentence and execucion of
the same. The sayd Mr. Alexander Wardlaw called and comperand be virteu of the sayd summondis, Patrik Ramsaye in
naym foyrsayd producis certan articles in wryt, quhilkis being
red in presens of Mr. Alexander, and be hym denyid as thai ar
signit, the ministerie statutis to the Superintendent the xvj
of Julii instant to prev the denyed. And at desyr of Mr.
Alexander the copy of the saydis summondis and articlis ar
decernit and deliverit to hym, to avyis wythall in the myd
tym.

Die xvj Julii anno domini 1561.

The quhilk daye, as in term stat (*sic*) to Mr. Ihon Wynram,
Superintendent, to preve his articles and headis agans Mester
Alexander Wardlaw and be hym denyed, comperis Patrik
Ramsaye, procurator, in nam of the sayd Mr. Ihon, and producis Peter Watson, minister, James Wardlaw, Mr. Dauid
Ramsaye, Thomas Lodeane, his servand, Martyn Hearyng,
Andro Law, Jhone Jowsie, Henry Wardlaw, Andro Wardlaw,
Ihon Wardlaw, and Barte Mureson, in presens of Mr. Alexander, quhai objecked aganis thaim *inimicicite* (*sic*) and parciall
consell and informacion gevyn in the mater: quhilkis being
admittit to his probacion, he agane referred the same to thar
athis, and thai, sworne, purges thame selfis, and ar resavit,
sworne, and to examinacione admittit. The ministerie statutis
the penult of Julii to pronunce.

---

[1] The clerk has at first written ‘Mr. Alexander Ballingall,’ but has altered
the last word to ‘ Ballingry,’ and inserted before it in the margin ‘ Wardlaw of.’

Followis the articlis and headis quharupon the wytnes ar examinat.

1   *Item*, in the fyrst, It is allegit that Mr. Alexander Wardlaw hes ministrat the sacramentis of baptisme and the supper of the Lord, sen Reformacion and eleccion of the Superintendent, nocht being admittit tharto ; and becaws the Superintendent, in his visitacion of Ballingry, caused ane minister, admittit, baptis ane barin, Mr. Alexander injurit the Superintendent, affyrmand hymself to be minister of that kyrk, lawfullie chosyn and providit tharto, and that he wald not be ane readar to Ihon Knox nor ony other in Scotland.

2   *Item*, Peter Watson minister being deput to support the rowm of ane minister in Balingrye,[1] be the Superintendent in his visitacion, quhill farth[er] provision be had, the sayd Mr. Alexander stoppit hym to frequent thar, manest and bostit hym ; and in speciall, upon the last of Junii by past, be his wryt, he of manesyng stoppit hym to cum to solemnizat

---

[1] Peter Watson, who was a member of the chapter of St. Andrews before the Reformation, was translated to Markinch before 1567, from thence to Dumfries before 1574, and to Flisk about 1580. In 1574 the General Assembly appointed him a commissioner for visiting Nithsdale and Annandale, and for several years this appointment was renewed. He died on the 17th of January 1585 (Scott's *Fasti*, ii. 525, 551 ; i. 567 ; ii. 493). He complained to the General Assembly, in August 1575, 'that the toun of Dumfreis, at Christmasse-day last bypast, seing that nather he nor the reader would nather teache nor read upon these dayes, brought a reader of their owne, with tabret and whissell, and caused him read the prayers ; which exercise they used all the dayes of Yuile ' (Calderwood's *History*, iii. 351). In October 1577, the General Assembly ordained him, for celebrating marriage in a private house, to confess his offence on a Sabbath day, 'in the parish kirk of Disdeir, where the parteis sould have beene maried' (*Ibid*. 386). In 1579 he confessed that he had only visited within six miles of Dumfries, the rest of the country being destitute of ministers, and that a high altar still stood in the New Abbey (*Booke of the Universall Kirk*, Ban. Club, ii. 429). On the 4th of January 158⅘ James the Sixth wrote to the Laird of Barnbarroch : 'We haif send our directioun to Mr. Peter Watson, persoun of Flisk, for the boundis of the diocy of Galloway, according to the ordour and resolution taken be us with avise of the Lordis of our Secreit Counsell upon the secund day of Januar instant, and hes willit him, gif neid sall require, to crave and require your assistance, fortificatioun, and mantenance in all thing that may mak God, us, and our lawes to be obeyit, and our cuntrie retenit in guid quietnes, and gude order' (*Correspondence of Sir Patrick Waus*, 1882, pp. 318, 319).

matrimony betuix two personnis, quharby the Superintendent wes constranit to cum to that solemnizacion hymself fra otheris gret besin[es]; in quhilk tym the sayd Mr. Alexander in oppyn assemble injurit the Superintendent, and sayd he hundit the hayl cuntre aganis hym, and that he wes verray parciall.

3   *Item*, upon the secund daye of Julii, the Superintendent beand in the sayd kyrk of Balingrye, seand gyf the kyrk wes repared conform to the Act of his vesitacion and Book of Reformacione, vidz., partlie upon the expensis of the parrochyn and partlie upon the expensis of the tendis,[1] and the sayd Mr. Alexander and parrochinaris being admonesed tharto be the Superintendent, Mr. Alexander mayd ansuer and sayd, The devill ane penne he wald spend upon the kyrk: gevand evyll exempill and occasion to the parrochinaris to leif undon thar deuete.

4   *Item*, upon the thrud daye of Julii foyrsaid, thar being convenit in the sayd kyrk of Balingrie, for consultacion takyn anent the reparacion tharof, the Lard of Torrie, Andro Wardlaw, brethyr to the sayd parson, Ihon Wardlaw, James Wardlaw, his emis,[2] Barte Mwreson, Thomas Lodean, and Mr. Dauid Ramsaye; thai called upon the sayd Mr. Alexander, as

---

[1] Only three months before the Reformation burst upon the country, the General Provincial Council of 1559 enacted that ruined or decaying churches were to be rebuilt or repaired, the chancel by the rector, the nave by the parishioners (*Concilia Scotiae*, vol. i. p. clix). And next year the Reformers had to exclaim : ' Of necessitie it is, that the churches and places whair the people aught publictlie to convene, be with expeditioun repaired in durres, wyndois, thak, and with such preparationis within, as apperteaneth, alsweall to the majestie of the Word of God as unto the ease and commoditie of the people. And becaus we knaw the slouthfulnes of men in this behalf, and in all other whiche may not redound to thair privat commoditie ; strait charge and commandiment must be gevin, that a certane day the reparationis must be begune, and within another day, to be affixed by your Honouris, that thei be finished : penalteis and soumes of money must be injoyned, and without pardone taken from the contempnaris . . .   The expensses to be lyfted partlie of the people, and partlie of the teindis, at the consideratioun of the ministerie' (*First Book of Discipline*, ninth head).   In 1584 it was matter of lamentation that : ' Be the insatiable sacrilegius avarice of erles, lords, and gentlemen, the Kirk, scholles, and pure, are spulyied of that quhilk sould sustein tham.   The materiall kirks lyes lyk sheipe and nout faulds rather then places of Christian congregationes to assemble into ' (Melvill's *Diary*, Wod. Soc., p. 188).   [2] Uncles.

parson tharof, desyring hym to concur wyth thame according
to the admonicion mayd be the Superintendent: Mr. Alexander
ansuerit and sayd, he wald do nathing in that behalve, nor
obey ony admonision or command of that fals, dissaitfull, gredy,
and dissimblit smayk,[1] for he wes ane of tham that maist
oppressed, smored, and held down the Word of God, and now
he is cumin to it, and professis the same for gredines of gayr,
lurkand and watchand quhill he maye se ane other tym.   And
farther ekit, and sayd befoyr the sam personnis above wryttyn,
Or I war not revenged of that fals smaik, I had lever [2] renunce
my part of the kyrk of God !

Followis the deposicionis of wytnessis.

1   James Wardlaw summond, resaved, sworne, admittit, and
examinat upon the articlis, be his ayth deponis, and confessis,
and affirmis the fyrst artikyll, and also the rest of tham.
Examinat upon his caws of knawlege, he ansueris that he wes
present in the kyrk of Balingry, upon the sext daye of Julii as
he belevis, hard and saw Mr. Alexander Wardlaw stop Peter
Watson minister to preche, to minister baptisme or solemnizat
mariage, and for the sam caws, of set purpos, the parson had
Jedwod staiffis[3] in the qweyr.   *Item,* he saw Mr. Alexander
minister baptisme, efter inhibicion gevyn to hym be the
Superintendent.   *Item,* he hard the ansuer gevyn be Mr.
Alexander to the Superintendent specified in the thrid artikyll.
Item, he wes present in the kyrk of Balingry, hard Mr. Alexander speik the wordis specified in the ferd artikyll.
2   Thomas Lodean summond, resaved, sworn, admitted, and
examinated upon the articlis, in his ayth deponis, and is conform to James Wardlaw, wytnes preceding.
3   Peter Watson, minister, summond, resaved, sworn, and
admitted, examinated upon the articlis, be his ayth deponis,
and in his deposicion confessis the secund artikyll.   *Causam
sciencie reddit,* the manesing and bosting wes mayd to the

---

[1] Mean fellow.   [2] Rather.
[3] A Jedburgh staff was a kind of spear, of which the craftsmen of Jedburgh
were the noted makers.

deponar, hayth in word and wryt, be Mr. Alexander, and also impediment was mayd to hym bayth wyth wordis and wapins, vidz., Jedwod staiffis, provydit in the kyrk, be Mr. Alexander for the nanis.[1]

4 Martyn Hearing, dwelland in Kyrknes,[2] examinat upon the articlis confessis the secund ; and is conform tharin wyth the wytnes preceding. He knawis na mayr.

5 Andro Law duelland in Kyrknes is conform to Martyn Hearyng.

9 (sic.) Jhone Jowsie, dwelland in Balingrie, resavit, sworn, and admittit, examined upon the articlis, ansueris that he hard Mr. Alexander Wardlaw inhibit fra ministracion be the Superintendent ; and hard, be common voce and fam, that tharefter Mr. Alexander baptised ane barn of Jhon Bruc, in Capildra. The thrud and secund articlis he confessis : he wes present, hard and saw as is artikulat. The ferd and last artikyll he confessis to be trew, as common voce and fam of the parrochyn of Ballingre recordis, bot he wes [nocht][3] present hym self tym tharof.

Die penultimo mensis Julii anno Domini m°v°lxj.

Wyth incalling of the name of the Eternall owr God, we, *Sentencia* minister and eldaris of Cristis kyrk and congregacion wythin *co*ntra *Ward-* the citie of Sanctandrois, jugis in the caws, and cognicion *lay de Balin-* takeyn anent the offence, injurie, and blasphemy don and said *grie.* be Maister Alexander Wardlaw, named of layt parson of Balingrie, aga[nis] Maister Jhon Wynram, Superintendent of Fyff, Fotherik and Strathern, be verteu of commissione and cherge direct be the foyrsaid Superintendent to us, as to the ministerie of the principall town of his residence wythin the said

---

[1] Nonce.

[2] Kirkness is in the parish of Portmoak, and was granted by Macbeth and his Queen to the Culdees of Lochleven. It is in the memorandum of this grant that Gruoch's parentage has been preserved (*Liber Cartarum Prioratus Sancti Andree*, Ban. Club, p. 114). In the list of those qualified for 'ministreing and teaching' in 1560, the future Superintendent of Fife occurs as 'Johne Wynrhame of Kirknesse' (*Booke of the Universall Kirk*, Ban. Club, i. 4). Kirkness now belongs to the Marquis of Northampton, and close to the mansion-house traces of the foundations of many small dwellings are still to be seen.

[3] Omitted.

diocye ; and we proceding ordorlie in the foyrsaid caws, efter
divers dietis tharin kepit, the said Maister Alexander lawfullie
summond to the same, and last of al to heiyr pronunced ; and
he comperand in all dietis, his defens lawfull to hym admittit :
we, havand God and the testimonie of his trew word befoyr owr
ees, maturlie and ryplie avysed wyth articles and headis, proponit aganis the said Mr. Alexander, twechyng the foyrsaid
offence, injurie, and blasphemie, his answer mayd tharto, wyth
deposicionis and testimonie of divers famos wytnessis, fyndis
the saidis articles and headis, partlie be Mr. Alexander confessed, and the rest tharof (be hym denyed) sufficientle provyn,
and at the said Maister Alexander, pretending and furthschaw-
ing hymself ane professor of the Ewangell of Crist Jesus, hes,
contrary to that profession, maist ungodlie abused hymself
publiclie, hes injurit, blasphemit, disobeit and contempnit
the said Maister Ihon Wynram, Superintendent, and therby
gevyn evyll exempill and occasion to otheris of contempsion
and inobedience : and heirfor pronuncis and decernis the said
Mr. Alexander to compeyr upon Frydaye, the fyrst daye of
August nixt to cum, in the publict assemble wythin the parroch[e] kyrk of the citie of Sanctandrois, and thar oppinlie
confes his falt and offence don aganis God and the Superintendent, in blasphemyn[g], injuryng, and contempnyng of hym,
and offending of hym injustlie ; and tharof ask God mercy and
the Superintendent forgyfnes.   And also upon Sundaye, the
thrid daye of August foyrsayd, the sayd Mr. Alexander sal
compeyr in lyik maner, in the public assemble wythin the
parrochie kyrk of Balingrie ; and, [in][1] presens of the minister
that salbe appoynted to be thar that daye, publiclie confes the
foyrsaidis offensis, at sic tym as the minister, thar present for
that, sal requir the sam to be don of hym ; and thar ask God
mercy, and the minister in name of the Superintendent forgyfnes, and the hayll congregacion forgyfnes of his sclander gevyn ;
pronunsing and desyring tham in tym cuming to obey all
superioris, and to tak na occasion nor evyll exempill of hym,
by the foyrsaid thingis be hym raschelie and injustle don.   And
thyr premissis to be don be the sayd Mr. Alexander, under the

---

[1] Omitted.

payn of excommunicacion; and gyf he falyeis, excommunicacion to be executed and used aganis hym wyth al severite.[1]
Pronunced in presens of the said Mr. Alexander, in the consistorie hows of the said ministerie, wythin the parroche kyrk
of Sanctandrois, upon Wedinsdaye, the penult daye of Julii, in
the year of God 1561.

Followis the ordor and proces, deducit in the declara-
tor gevyn upon the articles and sentence gevyn aganis
Schyr Ihon Borthuik, of Ceverie, knycht, be umquhill
Dauid, Cardinall, &c.

Die vigesimo mensis Augusti anno Domini m°v°lxj.

The quhilk daye, comperis Schyr Ihone Borthuik, knycht,[2] [Proces. Schyr Jhon Borthuik.]
and producis ane commissio[ne] and supplicacione subscrivit be
the Lordis of our Soveran Ladeis Secreit Consayll, of dayt, at
Edinburgh, the xii of August instant, direct to the Superintendent and ministerie of Sanctandrois, for cognicione takyn
upone the articlis, and sentence tharupon gevyn be umquhill
Dauid, Cardinall, Archbischop of Sanctandrois,[3] aganis the sayd

---

[1] Wardlaw seems to have complied with the 'premissis,' for in 1567 or 1568
he is described as the exhorter of Ballingrye, with 'the thryd of the personage'
as his stipend (*Register of Ministers, Exhorters and Readers*, Mait. Club, p. 25).
And in 1574 he is mentioned as 'persoun, minister' of Ballingarie, 'sustenand
his awin redare' (*Wodrow Miscellany*, p. 364).

[2] Sir John Borthwick, a son of that Lord Borthwick who was slain at Flodden,
was Lieutenant of the French King's Guard, and a favourite attendant of James
the Fifth (Sadler's *State Papers*, i. 19, 22). Certain lands in Wigtown were
granted to him for his good service by James in 1535; and in 1538, as Sir John
Borthwick of Cinery, he was declared next in succession to the free barony of
Borthwick, if the son of William, fourth Lord Borthwick, had no lawful male
heirs (*Register of the Great Seal*, vol. iii., Nos. 1493, 1826). Professor Mitchell
has pointed out that among the youths enrolled as *cives* of St. Andrews University in 1509 were David Lindesay, David Beton, Gavin Logy, Jho. Borthek,
and John Gaw (Gau's *Richt Vay to the Kingdom of Heuine*, Scot. Text Soc.
1888, pp. ix-xi).

[3] The well-known David Beaton—crafty, cruel, and dissolute—got the Abbacy
of Arbroath in 1523; was appointed coadjutor to his aged and enfeebled uncle
in the Primacy on the 5th of December 1538; was created a cardinal fifteen days
later; became Lord Chancellor on the 13th of December 1543, and was slain in
his own stronghold on the 29th of May 1546. Laing says that 'in the Cardinal's absence, who accompanied the King' in his voyage round the Western

Schyr Ihon Borthuik, condempnyng the saydis articlis heretical,
and the said Schyr Ihon tharfor infamit and punissed, &c.: and
to geve thar declarator tharupon, as thai fynd according to the
law and Word of God.   Quhilk commission red and understand
be the saidis Superintendent and ministerie, and thai acceppand
the same, at desyr of Schyr Ihone, thai decern hym ane edict to
summond al havand interes, or pretending interes, in the sayd
caws or ony thing that followed tharupon, to compeyr for thar
interes, upon the fyve daye of September nixt to cum befoyr
thame.   And the sayd Schyr Ihone exhibitis and deliveris to
the ministeris foyrsaid the trewe exemplar of the foyrnamed
articlis and sentence—copied and collacionat be Ihon Mosman,
notar public, and scrib to the schyrref-deputis of Edinburgh,
under his signe and subscripsion, sufficientlie recognoscit be
hym, drawyn furth of the actentik extract of the same, extract
furth of the *Registre* of the sayd umquhill Dauid, Cardinal,
be Maister Andro Olephant,[1] notar public, and secretar to
the sayd umquhill Dauid, Cardinall, under his signe and subscripsion ; and be Ihon Lord Borthuik[2] purchest be compulsatoris, executed upon the said Mr. Andro, and be the sayd
Lord produced befoyr the saidis schyrref deputis—to be seyn,
considerit and discussed in the myd tym ; and also presentlie

---

Isles, 'Gawin, Archbishop of Glasgow, and Lord Chancellor of Scotland,' presided at Borthwick's trial (Knox's *Works*, i. 533). And Dr. Grub avers that
' sentence was pronounced against him in the Cardinal's name ' (*Ecclesiastical
History*, ii. 20). But Dr. Laing has himself shown that the King's eldest lawful
son was born at St. Andrews on the 22d of May 1540, and baptized on the 28th,
the very day of Borthwick's trial, and that the arrangements for sailing were not
completed before the 11th or 12th of June (Knox's *Works*, i. 82). Moreover, the
Earls of Huntly, Marischal, and Arran, who were also appointed to accompany
the King (*State Papers*, v. 179), are proved by the text to have been present at
the trial ; and therefore Beaton could have been there too, so far at least as
the voyage was concerned.   Spottiswoode not only states expressly that he was
present and presided, but gives the substance of his opening speech (*History*,
i. 138).

[1] Andrew Oliphant, vicar of Foulis and Innertig, was twice intrusted with a
mission to Rome, and was accuser in the merry trial of Sandie Furrour, and
the tragic one of Walter Mill.

[2] This, the fifth Lord Borthwick, was a nephew of Sir John's ; and, according
to Knox, one of the three noblemen who in 1560 voted in Parliament against
the *Confession of Faith*, assigning as their reason that they would believe as
their fathers believed, but this is inconsistent with Randolph's statement (Laing's
Knox, ii. 121).

declaris his mynd, in quhat sence he spak the saidis articlis, be .
explicacione tharof. Of the quhilkis articlis and sentence[1] the
tenoris followis :—

Joannes Borthuik, Capitaneus Borthuik wlgariter nuncupa- [Articles, and
tus, suspectus infamatus et convictus per testes omni excepcione upon be um-
majores, anno Domini m°v° quadragesimo, vicesimo octavo Cardinal.]
mensis Maii, in cenobio Sancti Andree, presentibus reverendis-
simis ac reverendis et venerabilibus in Cristo patribus, Gavino
Archiepiscopo Glasguensi, regni Scocie cancellario,[2] Willelmo
Abyrdonensi,[3] Henrico Candide Case, et capelle regie Strewilln-
gensis,[4] Joanne Brechinensi,[5] et Willelmo Dunblanensi,[6] ecclesi-

---

[1] A 'certain friend' having furnished Borthwick with a copy of the process,
he 'thought good to bestow some labour in refelling those articles, which they
could not prove.' Foxe, in the first edition of his *Acts and Monuments*,
embodied the articles and sentence, with the preface and answers of the
accused, and they are reprinted in Cattley's edition. Foxe's inaccuracies may
be corrected by the text. Keith professes to give the process from Foxe, but
omits one of the articles, as well as Borthwick's preface and answers. Calderwood copies the articles and sentence, and also the substance of the answers,
from Foxe. Spottiswoode summarises the articles, but some of them unfairly.

[2] Gavin Dunbar was promoted to the Archiepiscopal See of Glasgow in 1524,
was Lord High Chancellor from 1528 to 1543, and died in 1547. He is praised
by Buchanan, but denounced by Knox. Borthwick's was not the only case of
heresy with which he was concerned, for he took part in the condemnation of the
Vicar of Dollar, and the other four who perished in the same fire; he was
induced to condemn Russell and Kennedy; and he also consented to and wit-
nessed the death of Wishart (Brunton and Haig's *Senators of the College of
Justice*, pp. 1-5; Laing's *Knox*, i. 62-66, 145, 148).

[3] William Stewart was elected Bishop of Aberdeen in 1532, and died in 1545.
'A man,' says Spottiswoode, 'given to virtue, charitable to the poor, and ready
to every good work' (*History*, i. 210).

[4] Henry Wemys was Bishop of Candida Casa, or Whithorn, from 1526 until
his death in 1541. He also held Dundrennan Abbey *in commendam*. His
surname was long uncertain, but is set beyond doubt in Maziere Brady's *Episcopal
Succession*, Rome, 1876, i. 158, 159.

[5] John Hepburn, Bishop of Brechin, died in 1558, in the thirty-fifth year of
his consecration. He was of the family of Bothwell. Friar Arth was buffeted
by him in Dundee, and called a heretic, and Wishart was cursed by him for
preaching in the same town (*Registrum Episcopatus Brechinensis*, Ban. Club,
vol. i. p. xii.; Laing's *Knox*, i. 37, 155).

[6] William Chisholm obtained the See of Dunblane in 1527, and died in 1564.
'A great adversary to the new Reformation, he alienated the episcopal patrimony
of this church to a very singular degree; most of which he gave to his nephew,
Sir James Chisholm of Cromlix. He likewise gave great portions to James
Chisholm of Glassengall, his own natural son, and to his two natural daughters'
(Keith's *Catalogue*).

arum episcopis ; Andree de Melros,[1] Georgio de Dunfermling,[2] Joanne de Pasleto,[3] Joanne de Lundoris,[4] Roberto de Kynlos,[5] et Willelmo de Culros,[6] monesteriorum abbatibus ; Macolmo

---

[1] Andrew Durie was promoted from the Abbacy of Melrose to the See of Whithorn in 1541. Through dread at the 'tragedy of Sanct Geill,' he died in September 1558. According to Knox, he was 'sometymes called for his filthines Abbot Stottikin' (Laing's *Knox*, i. 261).

[2] George Durie, brother of Andrew, was present at Patrick Hamilton's trial, and helped to bring Melville of Raith to the scaffold (Lorimer's *Hamilton*, p. 150 ; Laing's *Knox*, i. 224). James Beaton on Forman's death held the Abbacy of Dunfermline 'a second time *in commendam*, and afterwards styled himself *usufructuarius*, or *administrator fructuum*, while he allowed the name and probably devolved the duties of Abbot on George Dury,' Archdeacon of St. Andrews, who 'styled himself Abbot of Dunfermlin in 1530, and he continued to take the title of Abbot or Commendator, apparently subordinate to the Archbishop, during the life of the latter. After the Primate's death, in 1539, he acted as Abbot or Commendator.' In 1560 'he went to France, and it is uncertain if he ever returned ;' but 'he granted charters, or at least his name is inserted in charters, so late as 1564' (*Registrum de Dunfermelyn*, Ban. Club, pp. xvi, xvii). Nevertheless, Dempster says that he died on the 27th of January 1561, and, absurdly enough, adds that he was beatified on the 6th of August 1563 (*Historia Ecclesiastica*, i. 206). Two of his natural children were legitimated on the 30th September 1543 (Brunton and Haig's *Senators*, p. 68).

[3] John Hamilton, natural son of James, first Earl of Arran, held the Abbacy of Paisley from 1525, succeeded George Crichton in the See of Dunkeld, and Cardinal Beaton in the Primacy, and was hanged at Stirling in 1571. 'A man he was of great action, wise, and not unlearned, but in life somewhat dissolute' (Spottiswoode's *History*, ii. 156). Martine saw 'copies of charters granted by this Archbishop to William, John, and James Hamiltons, his three naturall sones,' borne by Grizzel Sempill (*Reliquiae Divi Andreae*, p. 244). Of these, William and John were legitimated on 9th October 1551, and so was another son, David, on 20th April 1580 (*Register of the Great Seal*, iv., Nos. 637, 3002).

[4] John Philips obtained the Abbacy of Lindores in 1523 (Brady's *Episcopal Succession*, i. 197). At the Reformation he joined the Protestants (Laing's *Knox*, ii. 599).

[5] Robert Reid, whose father fell at Flodden, was educated at St. Andrews, and in 1528 was anointed as Abbot of Kinloss. In 1541 the King wrote to Rome recommending him for the Bishopric of Orkney, designing that he 'should retain all his existing preferments, and that he should provide a pension of 800 marks to his Majesty's natural son, John Stewart.' This arrangement was so far carried out that Reid continued in receipt of their fruits, but his nephew, Walter, was admitted Abbot of Kinloss in 1553 (Stuart's *Records of the Monastery of Kinloss*, pp. xlix-li). He was one of the Scots commissioners who died suddenly in suspicious circumstances at Dieppe in 1558. Knox charges him with avarice, but he was undoubtedly one of the best bishops of the old Church, and may be regarded as the founder of Edinburgh University.

[6] William Colvill, a canon of the Lady College Kyrk (see p. 76), was promoted to the Abbacy of Culross in 1531, which he resigned in 1536 in favour of John

de Quhytirne,[1] Joanne de Pyttynweym,[2] prioribus ; Magistro
Alexandro Balfour, vicario de Kylmane, rectore universitatis
Sancti Andree ;[3] Magistris nostris Joanne Mayr,[4] Petro Càpel-
lano,[5] in sacra theologia professoribus et doctoribus ; Martino
Balfowr, in sacris literis et decretis bachalario, Officiali Sancti
Andree principali ;[6] Joanne Wynram, Suppriore ;[7] Joanne

Colvill, reserving the fruits. Accordingly, in 1541, he is designed 'Commendator
and Usufructuar of Culross,' while in the same document John appears as Abbot.
William joined the Reformers, and signed the *First Book of Discipline* in 1560
(Brady's *Episcopal Succession*, i. 171, 172 ; Laing's *Knox*, ii. 598).

[1] Foxe erroneously calls him 'Mancolme,' and Keith (in his *History*, i. 336)
'Mancolalyne,' from which Parker Lawson, in an editorial note, surmises that
'the real name is Maclellan.' But it rather seems to have been Malcolm
Fleming, who, with Archbishop Hamilton and others, was imprisoned for celebrating mass in 1563. Randolph then characterised him as 'an notable arche-
papyste.' He was put to the horn in 1568, and died in that year (Laing's
Knox, ii. 370, 379 ; vi. 526 ; *Reg. of Privy Council*, i. 629). Forbes-Leith, who
of course describes him as 'an earnest follower of the true religion,' inaccurately
places his death in 1563 (*Narratives of Scottish Catholics*, 1885, p. 94).

[2] John Rowle was Prior of Pittenweem in 1526, was styled 'usufructuar' in
1552, and died in 1553. 'Under Rowle's administration the lands which had
originally been granted to the house of the Isle of May, and had continued in
its possession since the twelfth century, were mostly alienated.' He had four
natural sons legitimated (Brunton and Haig's *Senators*, p. 80 ; Stuart's *Records
of the Priory of the Isle of May*, pp. xxxi-xxxiv).

[3] In 1546 he is mentioned as '*M. Alexander Balfour rectoris de Loncardy et
vicarii de Kilmany*' (*Register of the Great Seal*, iv. No. 36). He was one of the
priests who recanted on the 10th of March 1559-60 (*supra*, p. 15).

[4] John Major, the preceptor of Knox and Buchanan, and the author of the
Historia Majoris Britanniae, was incorporated as a member of St. Andrews
University on the same day as Patrick Hamilton, the 9th of June 1523, became
Provost of St. Salvator's College in 1533, and died in 1552 (Lee's *Lectures*, ii.
345, 346 ; *Concilia Scotiae*, ii. 284).

[5] Peter Cheplane was a bachelor of theology and a canon of St. Salvator's
in 1514, and rector of Dunino and a canon of St. Salvator's in 1517 (*Register
of the Great Seal*, iii. No. 43 ; iv. No. 175).

[6] Martin Balfour concurred in the condemnation of Patrick Hamilton's articles
in 1528, but was too old and weak to appear personally at the Provincial Council of 1549 (Spottiswoode's *History*, i. 125 ; Robertson's *Concilia Scotiae*, ii. 84).
'The Bishoprick of St. Andrews consisted of the two Archdeaconries of Lothian
and St. Andrews proper. . . . The Official of St. Andrews proper, added to his
jurisdiction as judge in the first instance of that Archdeaconry, a jurisdiction of
review of the decisions of the diocesan courts, suffragan to the Archbishoprick,
as well as those of the province of Glasgow' (*Liber Officialis Sancti Andree*,
Abbot. Club, p. xxvii).

[7] Now Superintendent of Fife, and head of that court to which Borthwick had
come for redress.

Annand[1] et Thoma Cwnyngham,[2] canonicis ecclesie Sanctiandree; fratribus Joanne Thomson, Priore Fratrum Predicatorum
civitatis Sanctiandree,[3] cum socio Joanne Tuledaf, Guardiano
Fratrum Minorum dicte civitatis Sanctiandree,[4] et Joanne
Paterson, vicario conventus ejusdem.[5] Necnon presentibus
nobilibus potentibus et magnificis dominis, vidz., Georgio de
Huntlie,[6] Jacobo de Arane,[7] Willelmo, Marescallo,[8] Willelmo
de Montros,[9] comitibus; Macolmo, Domino Flemyng, Camerario

---

[1] Annand was a canon of the Metropolitan Church of St. Andrews in 1518,
condemned Patrick Hamilton's articles in 1528, became Principal of St. Leonard's
College in 1544, opposed John Rough in 1547, and is called by Knox 'a rottin
Papist' (Spottiswoode's *History*, i. 125 ; Laing's *Knox*, i. 188).

[2] Thomas Cunningham appears to have succeeded Gavin Logie as Principal
of St. Leonard's (Laing's *Knox*, i. 36).

[3] John Thomson was still Prior of the Dominicans in St. Andrews in 1544-5
(*Abstract of Writs*, No. 6).

[4] John Tullidaff, Warden of the Franciscans, was one of those who condemned
Hamilton's articles in 1528 (Spottiswoode's *History*, i. 125). Andrew Cottis
was Guardian in 1549 (Robertson's *Concilia Scotiæ*, ii. 84). The Grey Friars'
Monastery in St. Andrews suffered so much at the Reformation that in an Instrument of Sasine, dated 20th September 1559, its site was conveyed to Patrick
Learmonth, Provost, and the community of St. Andrews, as 'a piece of waste
ground demolished in its buildings containing six particates of land in breadth
and lately possest by the Minor Friars lying on the north side of the Mercate-
gate and going north as far as the North Street' (*Abstract of Writs*, No. 293).

[5] John Paterson, General Minister of the Minorites of the Observance, was
present at the Provincial Council of 1549 (Robertson's *Concilia Scotiæ*, ii. 84).

[6] George, fourth Earl of Huntly, was taken prisoner at the battle of Corrichie,
on the 28th of October 1562, by Andrew Reidpeth, 'quha put him upone his
horse to have brocht him to the Quenis Majestie ; bot howsein he was set upoun
horsback, incontinent thairefter he bristit and swelt, sua that he spak not one
word, bot deceissit' (*Diurnal of Occurrents*, p. 74).

[7] The vacillating James, second Earl of Arran, and first Duke of Chatelherault. He signed the *First Book of Discipline* in January 1560-1.

[8] William, fourth Earl of Marischal, befriended George Wishart at Dundee.
In the Parliament of 1560 he declared : 'It is long since I have had some
favour unto the trewth, and since that I have had a suspitioun of the Papisticall
religioun ; but, I praise my God, this day hes fully resolved me in the one and
the other' (Laing's *Knox*, i. 126 ; ii. 122).

[9] William Grahame, second Earl of Montrose, was 'chosin to remane continualie with the Quenis Grace in the castell of Striveling for the suir keiping
of hir persoun,' and therefore Parliament, on 12th Dec. 1543, excused him from
other public duties (*Acts of Parl.*, ii. 442). He was one of the few nobles who were
present at her first mass after she returned to Scotland in August 1561 (Laing's
Knox, vi. 128) ; next month she chose him as one of her Great Council) *Reg. Privy
Council*, i. 157) ; and he was one of those who signed the bond at Hamilton for her
defence immediately after her escape from Loch Leven (Keith's *History*, ii. 809).

Scocie,[1] Joanne, Domino Lyndesaye,[2] Joanne, Domino Erskyn,[3] Georgio, Domino Setoun,[4] Hugone, Domino Somerwyll,[5] Jacobo Hammyltoun de Fynnart,[6] Waltero, Domino Sancti Joannis de Torphichin,[7] militibus ; Magistris, Jacobo Fowlis de Colintoun, S. D. N. regis ac registri clerico,[8] Thoma Ballindyn ejusdem domini nostri regis justiciarie (sic) clerico,[9] et multis atque com-

---

[1] Malcolm, third Lord Fleming, founder of the Collegiate Church of St. Mary at Biggar, was slain at Pinkie in 1547.

[2] John, fifth Lord Lindsay, of the Byres, the 'grandson and successor of the sage Lord Patrick,' held 'the offices of hereditary baillie and seneschal of the regality of the Archbishopric of St. Andrews.' Squire Meldrum, who acted as Deputy-sheriff of Fife and as marschal of Lindsay's household, appointed 'Johne Lord Lindesay my maister special' one of his three executors. When the *Confession of Faith* was ratified by Parliament in 1560 the venerable Lord Lindsay declared, that 'since God had spared him to see that day, and the accomplishment of so worthy a work, he was ready, with Simeon, to say, *Nunc dimittis.*' He died in 1563 (*Lives of the Lindsays,* i. 52, 190, 272, 276; Laing's *Lyndsay's Poetical Works,* 1879, i. 212, 306).

[3] John, fourth Lord Erskine, father of the Regent Mar, and grandfather of the Regent Murray, was excused with Montrose from other public duties in 1543, because he had charge of the infant Queen ; and, for the same reason, he and Lord Livingstone were exempted by the Privy Council in 1545 from serving 'aganis our auld inymyis of Ingland' (*Acts of Parl.,* ii. 442; *Register of the Privy Council,* i. 11). In 1548 he accompanied the Queen to France, and died there in 1552 (Brunton and Haig's *Senators,* p. 40).

[4] George, fourth Lord Seaton, 'ane wise and vertewes nobleman, a man well experienced in all games,' died in 1545 (Brunton and Haig's *Senators,* p. 52).

[5] Hugh, fifth Lord Somerville, is said to have received more of the favour of James the Fifth, and less of his benefits, than any other subject. He was taken prisoner at Solway Moss, and afterwards supported the English interest. He died in 1550 (Brunton and Haig's *Senators,* pp. 50, 51).

[6] In less than three months after Borthwick's trial Sir James suffered a more tragic fate. 'Upone the xvj day of August, the yeir of God jmvcxl yeris, Schir James Hamiltoun of Fynnart, knycht, was convictit be ane assyise, and heidit at the skaffald at the trone of Edinburgh' (*Diurnal of Occurrents,* p. 23).

[7] The wise Sir Walter Lindsay,

> 'Lord of Sanct Johne, and Knicht of Torfichane,
> Be sey and land ane vailyeand capitane,'

was one of Squire Meldrum's executors. He seems to have lived until at least the close of 1545; but he died before the 20th of January 1546-7, as on that day letters of legitimation were granted to James Lindsay, bastard and natural son 'quondam Walteri Domini Sancti Johannis' (Laing's *Lyndsay's Poetical Works,* i. 212; *Lives of the Lindsays,* i. 191).

[8] Sir James Foulis was Clerk Register from 1531 to 1548. He died before the 4th of February 1549.

[9] In 1539 James the Fifth conferred on Thomas Bannatyne, or Ballindyn,

pluribus aliis dominis, baronibus ac honestis personis, in testimonium premissorum rogatis et requisitis etc., hos sequentes
tenuisse errores, publice dogmatizasse, et instruxisse, vidz.

Primo et in specie, sanctissimum dominum nostrum Papam
Jesu Cristi servatoris nostri vicarium, non habere nec posse
exercere aliquatenus majorem authoritatem in Cristianos quam
quicunque alius episcopus vel sacerdos.

Indulgencias concessas a supremo domino nostro Papa nullius esse roboris, efficacie, vel, momenti, sed duntaxat eas ad
populi abusionem et animarum earundem deceptionem fuisse
et esse factas.

Papam esse symoniacum, publicum quotidie vendentem dona
spiritualia; et presbyteros omnes per matrimonium conjungi et
copulari debere.

Omnes hereses Anglicanas wlgo nuncupatas seu saltem earundem majorem et saniorem partem de presenti per Anglos
observatos (sic), fuisse et esse bonas, justas, et a Cristi fidelibus
observandas tanquam veraces et divine legi conformes, quas
eciam publice affirmavit, dogmatizavit, authorisavit diversas et
plurimas personas (sic) ad illas acceptandum persuadendo.[1]

Populum Scoticanum fuisse et esse omnino execatum et
abusum per ecclesiam Scoticanam et ejusdem clerum quos dixit
et affirmavit non habere veram fidem Catholicam, et per hoc
publice affirmavit et predicavit fidem suam fuisse meliorem et
prestanciorem quam fidem omnium aliorum ecclesiasticorum in
regno Sco[cie].

Conformiter ad veteres errores Joannis Wycleif et Joannis
Hws hereticorum in consilio Constanciensi condemnatorum
affirmavit, predicavit ecclesiasticos non debere possidere nec
habere possessiones aliquas temporales, imo. nec eciam habere
jurisdiccionem aut authoritatem aliquam in temporalibus,

'the office of Justice Clerk, a situation which became almost hereditary in his
family.' Knox includes him among 'the men of counsall, judgement, and god-
lynes, that had travailled to promote the Governour, and that gave him faythfull counsall in all dowtfull materis.' He died in 1546 (Brunton and Haig's
Senators, p. 57; Laing's Knox, i. 105, 106).

[1] Spottiswoode has foisted into this article the words 'their new liturgy,' and
several zealous Episcopal writers, without looking into the articles in Foxe or
glancing at Borthwick's answer, have been egregiously misled by the unwarranted
interpolation.

eciam in corum subditos sed [*blank*] ab eis similiter subtrahi
.debere, quemadmodum his diebus fit in Anglia.

Mendose et. contra honorem, statum, et reverenciam sacre
regie majestatis Scotorum dixit, tenuit, et asseruit regem Scotorum nostrum serenissimum Cristiane fidei propugnaculum velle
sibi appropriare contra jura et libertatem ecclesie, possessiones
terras et redditus a progenitoribus et eciam a Cristomet serenis-
simo regi ecclesie datas et concessas et in suos privatos usus
converti, et ad hoc, ut se multiplicitrr (*sic*) ascripsit, eundem
serenissimum dominum nostrum regem toto conamine suasit.

Voluit ac peciit et frequenter ac ferventer ex animo desider-
avit ecclesiam Scoticanam pervenire, et deduci ad idem punc-
tum eorundem et similem finem et ruinam ad quam ecclesia
Anglicana jam actu pervenit.[1]

Publice tenuit, dixit, asseruit et affirmavit ac predicavit et
dogmatizavit leges ecclesie vidz. sacros canones et sanctorum
patrum decreta ab ecclesia sancta catholica et apostolica approbata nullius esse vigoris aut valoris inferendo, propterea,
affirmando eadem fuisse et esse contra legem Dei condita et
emanata.

Pluribus ac multimodis vicibus dixit tenuit et affirmavit et
publice asseruit nullam religionem fore observandam, sed illam
simpliciter abolendam et distruendam fore et esse, sicut nunc
in Anglia destructa existit [*blank*] omnem sanctam religionem
vilependendo et affirmando fore, propter abusionem eorum
habitus per eos delati asseruit eos esse deformes ad modum
monstrorum nichil utilitatis aut sanctitatis pre se ferentes,
inducendo, propter hoc, et suadendo quantum in eo erat omnes
sue opinioni adherentes, ut omnis religio in regno Scocie simpliciter et penitus tollatur, ac distruatur in maximum catholice
ecclesie scandalum et Cristiane religionis diminucionem et
detrimentum.

Plane constat per legitimas probaciones eundem Joannem
Borthuik habuisse et actualiter habere diversos libros suspectos
de heresi, damnatosque tam papali quam regia et ordinaria
eciam authoritatibus lege prohibitos, vidz. specialiter et in

---

[1] Spottiswoode renders this article: 'That the Church of Scotland ought to
be governed after the manner of the English !'

specie, *Nouum Testamentum in wlgari Anglice*[1] *impressum, Ecolampadium, Melanctonem,* et diversos *Erasmi* et diversorum aliorum hereticorum condemnatorum, necnon, et librum *Vnio Dissidencium* nuncupatum, manifestissimos et maximos errores seu hereticos asserciones in se continentes illosque tam publice

---

[1] In his answer Borthwick exclaims : ' O good God ! who can suffer so great a blasphemy? with what a filthy cankered stomach do these Romish swine note the New Testament with heresy ! Who would not judge it a most venomous tongue, which dare pronounce and utter such contumelious words against the holy Gospel of our Saviour Christ ? ' (Cattley's *Foxe*, v. 620.) Buchanan says that in those days reading the New Testament ' was numbered among the most heinous crimes ' (Aikman's *Buchanan*, ii. 351). On the 29th of March 1539 Norfolk wrote to Cromwell from Berwick : ' Dayly commeth unto me some gentlemen and some clerkes, wiche do flee owte of Scotland as they saie for redyng of Scripture in Inglishe ; saying that, if they were taken, they sholde be put to execution ' (*State Papers, Henry VIII.*, vol. v. p. 154). The penalty attached to the possession of the New Testament comes out very clearly in one of *The Gude and Godlie Ballates* (ed. 1868, p. 166)—

> ' Quba dois present the New Testament
> Quhilk is our faith surelie ;
> Preistis callis him lyke ane heretyke,
> And sayis, brunt sall he be.'

And in the Epistle to James the Sixth, prefixed to the *Bassandyne Bible*, it is said : ' The false namit clergie of this realme abusing the gentle nature of your Hienes maist noble gudschir of worthie memorie made it an cappital crime to be punishit with the fyre to have or rede the New Testament in the vulgare language, yea, and to make them to al men mare odius as gif it had bene the detestable name of a pernicious secte, they were named New Testamentares.' In 1533 Alesius printed a pamphlet ' against a certain decree of the bishops in Scotland which forbids to read the books of the New Testament in the vernacular tongue ' ; and in the same year Cochlaeus issued a reply in defence of the bishops (Anderson's *Annals of the English Bible*, ii. 430-441). Archibald Hay —who in 1546 was Principal of St. Mary's College, St. Andrews—testified within eight days of Borthwick's trial that ' those who presided over the Church for many years, acquired very great wealth, [and] boasted that they had not touched a letter of the New Testament ; threatening awful things against all others who most carefully examine the mind of God in the Sacred Writings ' (*Ad Illustriss. Tit. S. Stephani in Monte Coelio Cardinalem D. Dauidem Betoun gratulatorius panegyricus*, Paris, 1540, fol. xxxviii). On the 15th of March 1542-3, while the Cardinal was in prison, Parliament declared it lawful for the lieges to possess and read ' baith the New Testament and the Auld in the vulgar toung, in Inglis or Scottis, of ane gude and trew translatioun,' ' providing alwayis that na man despute or hald oppunyeonis ;' but the Archbishop of Glasgow in name of the prelates dissented against the Act until a Provincial Council of the clergy should express an opinion on the subject (*Acts of Parliament*, ii. 415).

quam privatim legisse, studuisse aliisque presentasse et communicasse atque plures Cristianos in eisdem instruxisse, docuisse et dogmatizasse ad effectum divertendi eos a vera fide Cristiana et catholica.[1]

Eundem Joannem Borthuik in omnibus hiis erroribus et heresibus tam pertinacem esse constat, et indurato animo eosdem sustinuisse, docuisse, dogmatizasse sic, ut nolit eb (*sic*) eisdem diversis suis amicis et personis illum deligentibus et ad fidem sanctam catholicam reducere volentibus, cupientibus, et suadentibus ullo modo divertere, nec a suis erroribus per eorum consilium declinare velle, aut illis sic suadentibus aliquatenus acquiescere, sed pocuis in suis erroribus immobiliter persistere vellet,[2] de quibus omnibus premissis et multis aliis erroribus per eum tentis, dictis, publicatis affirmatis, predicatis, et dogmatizatis est et laborat publica vox et fama, et ita dictus Joannes Borthuik ut hereticus herisiarcha pessime de fide catholica senciens a compluribus personis tenetur, habetur, et reputatur. Propterea, nos, Dauid, Cardinalis, etc., sedentes pro tribunali more judicum judicancium, positis coram nobis sacrosanctis Dei Evangeliis, ut de wltu Dei judicium nostrum prodeat, et oculi nostri videant equitatem, solum Deum et catholice fidei veritatem pre oculis habentes, ejusque nomine sanctissimo primitus invocato, habito in et super hiis et secuto prudencium consilio tam theologorum quam jurisperitorum, prefatum Joannem Borthuik capitaneum dictum de premissis heresibus et dogmatibus iniquis, et multipliciter damnatis, ut premittitur, suspectum, infamatum, et pe[r]legitimas probaciones contra eum in singulis premissis heresibus convictum,[3] et legitime vocatum, citatum et non comparentem, sed profugum et fug[i]tivum[4] absentem tanquam presentem sentenciamus, pronunci-

---

[1] This is the article which Keith has omitted.

[2] Foxe makes the preceding part of this paragraph the twelfth article, and the rest 'the sentence of condemnation.'

[3] Lesley says that his heresy was 'provin be sufficient witnes agayns him' (*History of Scotland*, Ban. Club, p. 159). But Borthwick himself states that, although they had gathered a great number of witnesses, no proof was alleged except their names (Cattley's *Foxe*, v. 607).

[4] He fled to England, and was sent by Henry the Eighth as a Commissioner to the Protestant Princes of Germany (Lesley's *History*, p. 160; Spottiswoode's *History*, i. 139). From a letter of Balnaves to Somerset it appears that Borthwick had been in St. Andrews Castle in April 1547 (Laing's *Knox*, iii. 420).

amus, decernimu[s], definimus, et declaramus vere hereticum et
heresiarcham fuisse, et esse ac penis heretici convicti et heresi-
archi debitis (*sic*), plectendum, puniendum, et castigandum
fore, et propterea curie et potestati seculari trad[en]dum et
relinquendum, prout tradimus et relinquimus, omniaque et
singula ejus bona mobilia et immobilia qualitercunque et
quocunque titulo acquisita, et in quibuscunque partibus exist-
ant ac officia quecunque per eum hactenus habita, salvis tamen
dote et parte, seu porcione bonorum uxori sue incumbentibus, que personis, fiscis, et usibus, quibus de jure et con-
suetudine regni applicari debeant, per presentes confiscamus,
et applicamus ac confiscari et applicari decernimus, et declaramus per presentes : necnon, dicti Joannis effigiem manu
factam et ad ipsius instar depictam et formatam publice
per hanc nostram civitatem Sancti Andree, in curru deve-
hendam, et postea apud crucem foralem ejusdem nostre
civitatis in signum malediccionis aliorumque terrorem et exem-
plum ac sue contumacie et condemnacionis perpetuam memoriam fuisse, et esse conburendam similiter decernimus, non
minus tamen, quod si postea idem Joannis apprehendatur eum
similes penas juxta juris disposicionem heresiarchis debitas subi-
turum similiter decernimus, et declaramus nulla spe miseri-
cordie desuper subsequente, ac omnes et singulos utriusque
sexus Cristi fideles cujuscunque dignitatis status, gradus,
ordinis, condicionis, vel preminencie (*sic*) fuerint, ac quacunque
ecclesiastica vel mundana prefulgeant dignitate tenorum presencium expresse monemus ne abhinc dictum Joannem Borthuik hereticum et heresiarcham convictum et declaratum in
eorum domibus, hospiciis, castris, villis, oppidis, aut aliis quibuscunque locis recipiant seu admittant, aut sibi esculenta
vel poculenta aut aliqua alia humanitatis obsequia et necessaria
ministrant, seu ministrari faciant, aut secum communicet (*sic*)
edendo, bibendo, aut aliquo alio humanitatis solacio eidem
impendendo, aut pertractando, sub simili majoris excommunicacionis pena et cum certificacione quod, si in premissis culpabules
inventi fuerint quod accusabuntur, propterea, ut hereticorum
fautores receptores et defensores et penis eisdem incumbentibus
prout de jure punientur.[1] Lecta, lata et in scriptis redacta

---

[1] The remainder is omitted by Foxe.

fuit, hec nostra sentencia in ecclesia nostra metropolitana et provinciali Sancti Andree nobis inibi in navi ejusdem super scalam et pro tribunali sedentibus sub anno incarnacionis Dominice millesimo quingentesimo quadragesimo, die vero mensis Maii vigesimo octavo.

Die quinto mensis Septembris, anno Domini m°v^clxj.

The quhilk daye, Mester Wyliam Scot comperis as procurator and in name of Schyr Ihon Borthuik, knycht, be his mandat red and admittit, and producis ane edict of the Superintendent and ministerie present, under thar sail, deule executit and indorsat, tharin summond be oppyn proclamacion at the marcat croce of the cite of Sanctandrois, upon the premunicion of xv dayes bypast, al and syndry havand or pretending to have interes in the caws of discussing and declarator gevyn upon the articlis, allegit haldyn be the sayd Schyr Ihon, and sentence condempnator of infame gevyn tharfor upon the sayd Schyr Ihon be umquhill Dauid, Cardinal, Archibischop of Sanctandrois, as at mayr lent is contenit in the sayd edict.   And al and syndry foyrsaydis havand interes, &c., being oft tymis called, and nane comperand to propone or use ony defence of objectione in the sayd caws and stop of the said declarator, the Superintendent and ministerie, ryplie and maturle avysed wyth the saydis artikles and sentence, the consall of godlie lernit men and thar consentis tharto had, pronuncis thar declarator as follows:—To all and syndry to quhais kinawlege thyr presentis sal cum, Maister Ihon Wynram, Superintendent of Fyff, minister, eldaris and diaconis of Cristis kyrk wythin the reformed citie of Sanctandrois, grace, mercie, and peace frome God our Father, throwgh Jesus Crist owr Lord and onle Saluior, wyth perpetuall increas of his Holie Spirit.   It mot be knawyn that we—be verteu of ane commission and supplicacion, direct to us be deliverance of the Lordis of owr Soweran Ladeis Secreit Consayll under thar lordschippis subscripsionis, of dayt, at Edinburgh, the xij daye of August, in the year of God m°v^clxj yearis, purchest and presented befoyr us be Schyr Ihone Borthuik, of Ceverie, knycht—being requested and desyrit to considder certane articles alleged haldyn be the said Schyr

The declarator and retractacione of the sentence of Schyr Ihon Borthuik.

Jhone Borthuik, and quharupone ane pretendit sentence wes gevyn be umquhill Dauid, Cardinall, Archibischop of Sanctandrois, decernand the saidis articlis hereticall, and thar throwgh the said Schyr Ihon to be infamed and punissed, &c.; and, the saidis articlis being fundyn be us ressonabyll, conform to Goddis Word and not hereticall, to declar the said Schyr Jhone not to have falyeit tharintyll, nor to be infamed nor punissed, or to incur ony skayth ther throwgh, bot at he may persew his just accionis befoir quhatsumever jugis, nochtwythstanding the sammyn; and to geve our declarator tharupon, conforme to the law and Word of God. Quhilk commissione being be us resavit, wyth reverence and obedience as efferit, together wyth the trew exemplar of the foyrnamed artiklis and sentence, copeit and collacionat be Ihon Mosman, notar publict, and scrib to the schyrreff deputis of Edinburgh, under his signe and subscripsion; drawyn furth of the actentik extract of the sammyn, extrackit furth of the Registre of the sayd umquhill Dauid, Cardinall, be Maister Andro Elephant, notar publict, and secretar to the said umquhill Dauid, Cardinall, under his signe and subscripsion; and be Jhon Lord Borthuik purchest be compulsatoris, executed upon the said Mr. Andro[1]; and be the said Lord produced befoyr the saidis schyreff deputis, the copeis quharof ar registrat in our bukis; and efter our acceptacion of the foyrsaid commission, all and syndry havyng or pretending to have interes in the said caws, or ony thing that followed tharupon, being summond be our publict edict, and proclamacion of the sam of (sic) the marcat croce of the said citie (and copy tharof affixed upon the said croce), to compeir for thar interes at certan day and place tharin assigned, upon the premunicion of xv dayes warnyng precedeing the said day; and we in the mayn tym havand trial, consideracion and

---

[1] Oliphant had already been subjected to a much more disagreeable experience. Writing on the 4th of February 1559-60, Randolphe says:—'The Duks men took . . . a faithfull chapelein and a paynefull, of the Bishop's of St Andrewe, called Sir Andrewe Olifant, that accompayned the Franches in this voiage, by the commandement of his lorde and maister. Ther was fownd abowte hym a bill of as many as the Byshop had named to be saved from spoiling in Fife; the copie of his inventorye is sent unto my Lorde James, that the Bishops freends may be the better knowen, and he hymself putt into the prison at Glascoughe' (Sadler's *State Papers*, ii. 239, 240).

jugiment, in discussing of the saidis artiklis and sentence, wyth the consail, jugiment and consent of venerabill and godlie lernit men, to wyt, Mr. Ihon Dowglas, Rector of the Universitie of Sanctandrois, and Provest of the New College, Mr. Robert Hammyltoun, regent in the same, Mr. Jhon Rwyerfurd, Principall, Master Wyliam Ramsay and Mr. Dauid Gwyld, mesteris in Sanct Saluatoris College, Mr. Ihon Duncanson, Principall,[1] and Mr. James Wylke, rege[nt], in Sanct Leonardis College, wyth otheris divers ministeris and professoris of Godis Word; the explicacion of the said Schyr Ihon Borthuik, concernyng certan generaliteis contenit into sum of the saidis artiklis, be us hard, considerit and wyth the saidis artiklis conferred and fullelie aggreand: we fynd the saidis artiklis racionabill, not hereticall, bot ma stand wyth Godis Word, and none of tham bot may be interpret to ane gud sence, according to the mynd of the said Schyr Ihon in his explicacion tharof; and heirfor declaris the saidis artiklis racionabyll, and not hereticall, and the said Schyr Jhon Borthuik not to hav falyet tharintyll, nor to have deservit infamite, punischement, nor skayth tharfor; bot he, as ane man of gud fame, may persew his just accionis befoir ony juge competent, notwythstanding the said pretendit sentence; quhilk in the self we declar to be null and wranguslie

---

[1] Probably the same 'Jo. Dunkanson' who, in 1515, was in the second class of St. Leonards with Ninian Bard, John Rowl, John Dowglas, John Wynram, and Alexander Alan, afterwards known as Alesius (*Register of St. Andrews University*). He was a canon of the Augustinian Priory, and 'became Principal of St. Leonard's College in 1556,' and, 'having been converted to the reformed religion, retained his office in the college, as his share of the rents of the convent.' When he 'retired from the principality in 1566, he gave to the college a great cup or maizer, double gilt, and other articles, to the value of 30 pounds, also 20 pounds to purchase coals, 100 pounds to the new work of the college, with 50 pounds of his yearly pension for the abbey of St. Andrews. In addition to these donations, amounting to 200 pounds, he gave two tin flagons for the use of the college, and (what appears to have been much more valuable) all his books, both great and small' (Lee's *Lectures*, ii. 346, 347). Though he thus parted with his books and so much of his money, his course was not nearly run, for he took a prominent part in the affairs of the Church during the next thirty years. He was minister at Stirling in 1563, was afterwards appointed minister of the King's household, and, coming to Edinburgh with the King, continued to preach in the chapel of Holyrood. He died on the 4th of October 1601, being about a hundred years old (Scott's *Fasti*, i. 150; ii. 671; *Wodrow Miscellany*, pp. 455, 456).

gevyn, and the gevaris tharof to hav schawynn tham selfis tharby mer ignorant of Godis Word and lawis, and plane inemeis to his trewth. Pronunced in the consistoriall hows, wythin the parroche kyrk of the citie of Sanctandrois, upon the v daye of September, in the year of God m°v°lxj yearis, as day assigned in our sayd edict, in payne of not comperance of tham havand interes, heyrto summond, called, and not comperand. In wytnes and testimone of the premissis, to thir our present letteres of testimoniall and declarator, subscrivit wyth our handis, the sailis of Superintendent and ministerie foyrsayd ar affixed, year and day foyrsaidis.[1]

Die viij mensis Octobris, anno Domini 1561.

Proces aganis Wyliam Mor- toun of Cammo, and Elizabeth Arnot in Crayll, and Caluartis in Kingisbernis.

The quhilk daye, comperis Johane Malwyll,[2] minister of Cristis kyrk in Crayll, and, in presens of the Superintendent and ministerie, producis ane summondis deulie execut and indorsat, tharin summond Begis Calwart, Robert Calwart, hyr brother, in Kyngisbernis, Wiliam Mortoun, of Cambo, Elizabath [*Bowsie* —deleted] Arnot, spows of Wiliam Bowsie, in Crayll, and the said Wiliam for his interes, to ansuer to the punctis of the saidis summondis respective. And thai called and nocht comperand to ansuer, nochtwythstanding that thai war anis of befoyr summond and nocht comperaind; and now in the secund summondis chergit to compeyr person-alie, wyth deu intimacion gyf thai comperit nocht that the Superintendent wald proceid and resave probacione. According to the tenor of the quhilk summondis, the Superintendent, in payn of thar nocht comperance, admittis the punctis of the foyrsaid summondis to the probacione of the said Ihonie

---

[1] The sentence of excommunication having been thus reversed, the civil sequel followed in due time. On the 28th of February 1562-3 Borthwick was rein-stated in all the possessions and honours he had 'befoir the leding and deducing' of Beaton's 'pretendit sentence aganis him' (*Register of the Privy Seal*, cited in M'Crie's *Knox*, 1861, p. 394). 'This worthie knight ended his age with full-nesse of dayes in Sanct Andrewes' (Calderwood's *History*, i. 123). The exact time of his death is unknown, but it must have been before the 9th of December 1570, for in a charter of that date William Borthwick is mentioned as son and heir of the late Sir John Borthwick of Cineray (*Register of the Great Seal*, iv. No. 1974).

[2] An elder brother of the famous Andrew Melville.

Malwyll; quhai for probacione tharof producis Mr. Wiliam Meldrum, Niniane Hammyltoun, Mr. Alexander Mortoun, Jhone Brown, Robert Grwb, Wiliam Crostrophyn, Dauid Grundestowin, Dauid Wyle, Wiliam Trayll, Wiliam Kaye, and Alexander Bell, quhilkis ar resavit, sworne, and to examinacione admittit, and presentlie examinat upon the punctis of the said summondis, of quhilk summondis the tenor followis.

Maister Johane Wynram, Superintendent of [Fyff],[1] to my lovyttis, minister, readar of Crayll, or ony other being required upon the execucion of thir presentis, greting, for sa mekyll as it is humilie menit and schawyn to me, that quhar Begis Calwart, in the Kingisbernis,[2] oppinlie injurit, diffamit, and sclanderit Janat Bowman, spows of William Crostrophyn, in Kingisbernis, in calling of the said Janat ane huyr, and at sche wes huyr to hyr awyn servand and hyir man: or sic lyik wordis in effect. For the quhilk injuris and sclander, sche wes dilated, accused, and convict, befoyr the minister and eldaris of Crayll, present for the tym in thar assemble; and be thar deliverance ordened to have comperit in the publict assemble of the congregacione of Crayll, upone ane certane Sunday in the moneth of August last bypast, and thar to have maid public satisfaccione to the partie and congregacione offendit. At quhilk daye comperit thar wyth hyr Robert Calwart, in Kyngisbarnis, and mayd plane contradiccione and interrupcione to the minister in the pulpot, saying thir wordis, or syclik in effect, as followis:— Begis Calwart sall mak na amendiment to Janat Bowman, except that Janat ask hyr forgyfnes! Attowr, it is also menit and schawyn to me be Johane Malwyll, minister of Goddis Word in the said kyrk of Crayll, that, upon the foyrsaid Sunday, he, takand occasione be nonpayment of the stipend ordened to have beyn payed to the reader of the said kyrk furth of the frutis and vicaraige, persuaded and exhorted the auditor to answer the said reader, and pay to hym his stipend of the rediest in thar handis, to the support of his gret necessitie, rather than to answer sic as did nothing tharfor. And albeid

---

[1] Omitted.

[2] On the 9th of February 1631 the Commissioners of Teinds ratified an Act of the Kirk Session of Crail erecting Kingsbarns into a separate parish, and Parliament confirmed it in 1633 (*Acts of Parliament*, v. 85).

he maid his protestacion, that na man suld be offended therby,
nevertheles, Wyliam Mortoun, of Cambo,[1] oppinlie in the public essemble, manest, boistit and injurit the said minister in
the pulpot, saying thir wordis following, or sicklyik in effect:
—My brother[2] is and salbe vicar of Crayll quhen thow sal

---

[1] In January 1555-6 William Mortoun, or Myretoun, resigned the lands and
barony of Cammo to his son Thomas, but reserved a free tenement to himself
(*Register of the Great Seal*, iv. No. 1023). 'Myretoun off Kammo' was a member
of Parliament in 1560 (*Acts of Parliament*, ii. 526). According to Wood,
William Myrton of Cambo was twice married. By his first wife he had Thomas
and thirteen daughters, all of whom were married, except the youngest, who
became a nun and died abroad. And by his second wife he had Patrick and
four daughters, all of whom were married—the fourth in 1617 to Robert Maule,
uncle of the first Earl of Panmure. Myrton died shortly before 1581 (*East Neuk
of Fife*, 1887, pp. 460, 461).

[2] In 1517 the parish church of Crail 'was, on the petition and endowment of
Sir William Myreton [vicar of Lathrisk, and a relative of the Cambo family],
with the consent of Janet, Prioress of Haddington, erected into a collegiate
church, with a provost, sacristan, ten prebendaries, and a chorister' (*Register of
the Collegiate Church of Crail*, p. 4). On the 4th of January 1561-2 certain
houses and lands were feued by Mr. David Myrtoun, vicar of Markinch, and
prebendary of St. Catharine's chaplainry in the parish church of Crail, with
consent of Mr. Alexander Myrtoun, apparent heir of Alexander Myrtoun of
Randelstoun, patron of the said prebend (*Register of the Great Seal*, iv. No.
2839). The Myrtouns of Randelstoun, or Randerston, were a branch of the
Cambo family (Wood's *East Neuk*, p. 460). There were still other bonds of
connection between the Myrtouns and the church of Crail. In 1546 Mr. Patrick
Myrtoun was Archdean [? Archdeacon] of Aberdeen and Provost of the Collegiate Church of Crail, in 1570 he was Treasurer of Aberdeen and Provost of
the College Kirk of Crail, and in 1576 Mr. Patrick Myrtoun received a presenta-
tion under the Privy Seal to the Provostry of Crail, then vacant through the
non-compearance of Mr. Patrick Myrtoun, last Provost thereof, to have given
confession of his faith and his oath of allegiance (Conolly's *Fifiana*, 1869,
pp. 143, 151, 153). In 1583 the General Assembly earnestly craved the King
and Council: 'that ane brother of the Laird of Camboes, refuseing to abyde
the judgement of the Kirk, and allowes the breaking of the [King's] lawes concerning his religioun, may be summoned to a particular dyatt, to underly the
law' (*Booke of the Universall Kirk*, Ban. Club, ii. 616). On the 23d of March
1594-5 Father Mortoun, a Jesuit, was arrested at Leith on the very night of his
arrival, finding that he was apprehended he tore his instructions with his teeth,
but the document was taken from him and deciphered. He also brought a
valuable tabernacle or shrine with him. Colville says:—'The man is a folishe
bigot Papist, and hes bein abrod this 10 year: of the bous of Cambo, in Fife.
. . . The superstition and folie of the preist forseid wes much lawchin
at. When he saw his Majestie tak the tabernacle, and that he must neadis part
with it, he craved it for a grace anis to kis it befor he suld want it' (Colville's
Letters, Ban. Club, pp. 150, 151).

thyg[1] thy mayt, fals smayk ; I sall pul ye owt of the pulpot be
the luggis, and chais ye owt of this town ! In lyik maner it wes
menit and schawyn to me, be the said minister, that upone ane
Sunday in the moneth of Junii, in this instant year, he being
in the public assemblie and kyrk of Crayll preachyng Goddis
Word, and, as his tex for the tym ministrat occasion, applyand
his doctrin to the fals bretheren of Papistis, wythowtyn ony
just occasion of offence mayd be hym to ony person, Elizabeth
Arnot, spows of Wiliam Bous[ie],[2] rays in the essemble and
wyth hech voce said aganis hym thyr wordis, or siclyik in effect,
following :—It is schame to yow that ar gentillmen that ye
pull hym nocht owt of the pulpot be the luggis ! Quhilkis
foyrsaidis offencis, so grevoslie tending to the contempt of God
and his most holy Word and ministeris therof, expres aganis
all law and gud ordor, being denunced to me; and I for my
par[t, and] according to my vocacion and dewetie, direct my
otheris letteres of befoyr upon the saidis personnis committaris
of the same, chergyn thame to have comperit befoyr me and
the ministerie of Sanctandrois as principall town of my residence,
at certan day assignit to tha[m], to ansuer to the foyrsaidis ;
and to have hard and seyn tham decernit, be jugimient of the
kyrk, to have falyeit gretumly,[3] and to underly disciplin therfor
accordinglie. Quhilkis letteres, at day appoynted, being repro-
duced befoyr me, deulie executed and indorsat, and the foyrsaidis personnis, oft tymmis called and nocht comperand, ar to
be haldyn therby *contumaces* and nocht obedient. Heirfor I
requir you and every ane of you, in the nam of the eternall
God, that ye laufullie summond, warn and cherge the saidis
Begis Calwart, Rober[t] Calwart, Wyliam Mortoun, Elizabeth
Arnot, and Wiliam Bowsy hyr spows for his interes, to compeyr
befoyr me and the ministere of Sanctandrois, wythin the
parrochie kyrk and consayll hows therof, upone Wedinsdaye,
the viij day of October instant, at twa howris efter nuyn, as

---

¹ Beg.

² William Buse, or Bowsie, was one of the bailies of Crail in 1551 (*Register
of the Great Seal*, iv. No. 2454). As will be seen in a subsequent note (P. 111), he
was deprived of that office in 1567 ; and a Wyliam Bowsie, in Crail, was delated
to the Superintendent for adultery on the 11th of February 1561-2.

³ Greatly.

howr of caus; and ther to ansuer upon the offences foyrsaidis
respective, and to se probacion deduced and takyn tharupon,
and thame and every ane of thame respective decernit to underly
disciplyn and correccion, according to the law of God and
ordor of the kyrk establesched; and to mak sythment[1] to the
parteis offended: makand to tham be thir presentis intimacion
that, quhidder thai compeir or nocht, we wyll procead in the
saydis causis, as the Spirit of God sall inspyr· us, and as we
maye and awcht of the law of God. The quhilk to do we
commit to you power in the Lord, be thir presentis, delivering
the same be you deulie executed and indorsat agane to the
berrer. · Gevyn under the Superintendentis signet and subscripsion, at Sanctandrois, the secund day of October, in the year of
God ane thowsand, fyve hundreth, sexty ane yearis.

Followis the deposicionis of the wytnes in thir foyrsaydis causis.

[Deposicionis
of wytnes.]
    Maister Wyliam Meldrum, sone to the Lard of Newhall,
summond, called, sworne, and examinated upon the poyntis of the
summondis befoyr wryttyn. And fyrst, concernyng the partis
1 of Begis Calwart and Robert Calwart hyr brother, he confessis
the sam as thai ar libellat. Secindlie, concernyng the part of
Wiliam Mortoun of Cambo, the deponar confessis the sam as
it is libellat. And also confessis the part libellat aganis
Elizabeth Arnot. Examinat upon his caws of knawlege, he
ansueris that he wes present in the essemble of Crayll, tym and
place libellat, hard and saw as he hes deponit. Examinat upon
the generall interrogatouris of the law, he purgis hym: and
wald justice triumphit.
2   Niniane Hammyltoun, familiar servand to the lard of Newhall, sworn, and examinat upon the poyntis of the foyrsayd
libellat summondis, be his ayth deponis, and is conform to Mr.·
Wyliam Meldrum, wytnes preceadyng, in all thingis.
3   Robert Grub, servand to the Lard of Newhall, examinat
upon the foyrsaid libell and poyntis tharin contenit. The

---

[1] Satisfaction.

fyrst concernyng Caluartis he denyis. As to the secund, concernyng Wiliam Mortoun of Cambo, he ansueris and deponis
that [he]¹ wes present in the essemble in Crayll, tym libellat,
hard Wiliam Mortoun saye to Ihon Malwyll minister, he being
in the pulpot, that he suld tak hym owt of the pulpot be the
luggis and chais hym owt of the towin. He knawis na mayr
of the libell. Examinated upon the interrogatouris of law, he
purgis hym ; and wald justice triumphit.

4   Maister Alexander Mortoun, eldest sone of Randerstoun,²
summond, called, sworne, and examinated upon the thre headis
and poyntes of the sayd libellat summondis, deponis, and is
conform to the fyrst twa wytnes in al thingis concernyng the
accionis of Calwartis and Wyliam Mortoun of Cambo. *Item,*
as concernyng the part of Elizabeth Arnot, he denyis it, and
grantis that he wes in the kyrk tym libellat, and hard hyr cry
wyth lowd voce ; bot, he wes sa far distant fra hyr, he mycht
nocht heyr the sentence of hyr word.

5   Johane Brown, of layt called Schyr Ihon Brown,³ prebendar
in Crayll, sworn and examinat &c., be his ayth deponis, and is
conform to Mr. Wyliam Meldrum fyrst wytnes in all thingis.

6   Wyliam Crostrophyn, of layt otherwayis called Schyr
Wyliam, prebender in Crayll,⁴ sworn and examinat &c., is
conform to Mr. Wyliam Meldrum fyrst wytnes in al thingis.

7   Dauid Grundestown, wytnes, sworn and examinated &c.,
deponis and is conform to Mr. Alexander Mortoun concernyng
twa headis. The thrid he denyis : he wes nocht present that
daye.

8   Wyliam Trayll, wytnes, sworn and examinated &c., deponis

---

¹ Omitted.   ² See note 2, p. 106.

³ Among the old documents belonging to the burgh of Crail there is an
instrument of sasine, dated 20th January 1550, in favour of Sir John Brown,
chaplain, in five acres of arable land, being parts of the lordship of Cambo,
proceeding on the resignation of Sir William Myrtoun, in consideration of two
hundred merks paid to him by the said Sir John (Conolly's *Fifiana*, p. 144).
He unfortunately married a wife who proved unfaithful (*Booke of the Universall
Kirk*, Ban. Club, i. 396 ; Scott's *Fasti*, ii. 416).

⁴ William Costorphin, priest, is mentioned in 1539 ; and in 1580 he and the
other prebendaries of Crail granted a charter to John Lawson of a tenement in
St. Andrews, to be held for the payment of twenty shillings Scots (*Fifiana*,
pp. 140, 154).

and is conform to Dauid Grundestoun wytnes preceading in al thingis.

9   Dauid Wyle, servand to the Lade Balcome, wytnes, sworn and examinated &c., be his ayth deponis, and is conform to Mr. Wyliam Meldrum fyrst wytnes in all thingis.

10   Wyliam Kaye, in Fawsyd, wytnes, sworn, and examinated be his ayth, deponis and confessis all the poyntis of the libellat summondis. Gevyn his caws of knawlege, that he wes present, hard and saw as is libellat. .

11   Alexander Bell, servand to the Lard of Pytmule, wytnes, sworn and examinated &c., be his ayth deponis, and is conform in all thingis wyth [*Alexander*—deleted] Wyliam Kaye, wytnes preceadyng.

Die xv*to* Octobris, anno Domini m°v*f*lxj.

Sentencia contra Caluartes, Wyliam Mortoun de Cambo, and Elizabeth Arnot.

The quhilk daye, comperis Johan Malwyll, minister of Crayll, and producis ane summoindis of the Superintendentis deulie executed and indorsat, tharin laufullie summond to this daye, Begis Calwart, Robert Caluart, hyr brother, Wyliam Mortoun, of Cambo, Elizabeth Arnot, spows of Wyliam Bowsie, to heyr the sentence pronunced aganis tham respective, for the causes and thar offences specifyed in the libellat summondis registrat in thir bukis the viij of October instant. And thai and every ane of tham called, lauful tym byddyn, and nane of tham compirand, the Superintendent, rypplie and maturlie avysed wyth the sayd libellat summondis and headis tharin contenitt, the deposicionis of wytnes tharupon produced, and al otheris deduced in the sayd caws, fyndes all and hayll the poyntis of the foyrsayd libellat summondis laufullie and sufficientlie provyn: and heirfor, wyth avys and consayll of the ministerie of Sanctandrois, pronuncis and decernis and declaris the saidis Begis Calwart, Robert Caluart, and Wyliam Mortoun, of Cambo, and Elizabeth Arnot, and every ane of tham according to the gravite of thar dilacionis, to have grevoslie offendit aganis the law of the eternall God, the establesched ordor of the Kyrk, and aganis the sayd Johan Maluyll minister, to the havy and grevows sclander of the Ewangell of Crist Jesus and his religion, and evyll exempell to otheris: and heyrfor, the sayd Begis

Calwart to compeir in the public esscmble and kyrk of Crayll, upon Sunday, the xxvij of October instant, and thar mak the satisfaccion for the injurie and sclander be hyr don aganis Janat Bowman, according to the chearge gevyn to hyr be the ministerie of Crayll ; and also confes hyr offence in dissobeying the sayd chearge, and humyll hyrself upon hyr kneis, ask God mercy and the congregacione forgyfnes : and the said Robert Calwart[1] to compeyr, day and place foyrsayd, and confes his offence, humyll hymself in the presens of God one his kneis, ask God mercy and the congregacione forgyfnes : and the sayd Wyliam Mortoun, of Cambo, to compeir day and place foyrsayd, and confes his foyrsayd offence in the presens of God and the congregacion, humyll hymself on his kneis, ask God mercy and the sayd Johan Malwyll in speciall and the holl congregacion forgyfnes : and the said Elizabeth Arnot to compeyr daye and place foyrsayd, and confes hyr offence foyrsayd in the presens of God and his congregacion, humyll hyrself one hyr kneis, ask God mecy (sic) and the sayd Johan Malwyll in speciall and the holl congregacion forgyfnes : ilk person foyrsayd under the payn of excommunicacion, quhilk pane to be put to execucion upon the disobeyaris, gyf ony sall attempt to disobey. Pronunced in presens of the sayd Ihon Malwyll, and in payn of nocht comperans of the saydis Begis, Robert, Wyliam, and Elizabeth, heyrto laufulle summond.

---

[1] Calwart, or Calvart, afterwards got into more serious trouble. He was one of the tenants of ' Maister Thomas Ramsay, heretabill fewar of ane auchtane part of the landis of Kingisbarnis ; ' but although Ramsay obtained a decreet before the Lords of Session decerning his tenants to remove, Calvart refused to leave, even after he was ' denunceit rebell and put to the horne.' Accordingly, ' the said Maister Thomas menit him to the Lordis of Sessioun thairupoun ; and be thair deliverance obtenit utheris lettres, chargeing David Betoun of Creich stewart of Fyff and his deputtis, to serche seik tak and apprehend the said Robert Calvart.' The Stewart duly apprehended the rebel, but while reposing within a dwelling-house at Crail, the inhabitants, warned by ' the sound of ane drum ' and the ringing of the common bell, gathered to the number of four hundred, ' instructit with all maner of wappynis apt for weir,' and headed by three of the bailies, including William Bowsie, and other ringleaders, among whom ' Williame Bowsie youngar' is mentioned ; they broke open the house, and, despite the Stewart's commission, ' straik and dang ' him and rescued the prisoner— ' usurpand the rather the office of princes nor liegis.' On the 7th of October 1567 the Privy Council deprived the three bailies of their office for their offence (Register of the Privy Council, i. 577-579).

The proces betuix Jhon Forret, of that Ilk,[1] and
Elizabeth Leslie, Lady of Nydy.[2]

Die secundo mensis Julii, anno Domini 1561.

[Proces betuix
Jhon Forret of
that Ilk, and
Elizabeth
Leslie, Lady of
Nydy.]
The quhilk daye, comperis befoyr the ministerie Johane
Forret of that Ilk and producis ane summondis of the Superintendentis deulie executed and indorsat upon Elizabeth Leslie,
Lady of Nydy, chergyng and admonesing hyr to adheir to the
said Johane as to hyr lawfull husband, wythin xlviij howris
efter the said monicion; or ellis to comppeir this daye befoyr
the said ministerie, and schaw ane ressonabill caws quhy sche
suld not do the same. And sche called comperis, and be consent of parteis Wedinsday is statut to Elizabeth, to produce
hyr causis in dew forme quhilk sche wyl use. Parteis heirto
summond *apud acta.*

Die ix mensis Julii anno quo supra.

The quhilk daye, as in term assignit to Elizabeth Lesle,
Lady of Nydy, to to (*sic*) produce hyr causis, qualefeit in wryt,
quhy sche suld nocht adheyr to Johan Forret, hyr spows, comperis Elizabeth and producis certan artiklis in wryt, seyn and
considerit be the said Iohan Forret, and be hym denyit and
grantit as is notit. And at desyr of Elizabeth, Wedinsdaye

---

[1] According to Sibbald, the estate of Forret, in the Parish of Logie, belonged
to the Forrets from the time of William the Lion at least (*History of Fife and
Kinross*, 1803, p. 415). On the 19th of October 1555 the Queen confirmed a
charter, granted on the 5th of the preceding August by David Forret ' *de
eodem feodatarii . . . cum consensu patris sui Johannis Forret de eodem usu-
fructuarii,*' in favour of Alan Cowtis and Marjorie Walwod his wife, of half
the lands and mill of Bowhill in Lochoreshire (*Register of Great Seal*, vol. iv.
No. 1005.) ' Jhon Forret off that Ilk' was in the Parliament of 1560 (*Acts of
Parliament*, ii. 526).

[2] Nydie is near the western extremity of the parish of St. Andrews. About
the end of the thirteenth century Hugo of Nidyn granted to the Abbey of Balmerino the use of his quarry and a free road thereto through his land (Campbell's *Balmerino and its Abbey*, pp. 90, 91). Pope Adrian the Fourth confirmed
the mill of Nidin to the Priory of St. Andrews in 1156 (*Liber Cartarum Prioratus Sancti Andree*, p. 52).

the penult of Julii instant statut to hyr, to prev hyr artiklis;
and suplicacionis grantit to hyr, to the Superintendent of
Angus [1] direct, for al probacionis necessar.

Followis the tenor of defencis.

In the fyrst, the said Elizabeth allegis, that gevand that ony [Defencis of Elizabeth Lesle.]
mariaige, *de facto*, had beyn solemnizat betuix hyr and the said
Johan, that the sammyn is and wes onlawfull and aganis the
law of God; becaws the said Johan lang befoir, wythowt ony
knawlege of the said Elizabeth Leslie, had promesed and consented to marye Elizabeth Autherlonye, Lady of Athinlek,[2]
and, efter the same promys maid, had carnall dayll wyth the
said Elizabeth Autherlo[ny], and intreated hyr as his lawful wyff
in bed and burd, be the space of [3] thre yearis or tharby;
and tharefter the said Elizabeth Leslie, nocht knawing ony
promys maid, *de facto et non de jure* mareid the said Johan
Forret. And now, knawyng that of the lawe of God he is
nocht nor may nocht be hyr lawfull howsband, becaws of his
consent and promys maid to Elizabeth Autherlony of befoir,
sche alleagis sche awcht nocht to be compelled, contrary to hyr
. conscience and the law of God, to adheir to hym as hyr lawful
howsband. And for the probacione of the sammyn promes
and consent, the said Elizabeth Leslie producis ane dispensa-

---

[1] John Erskine of Dun.

[2] The old tower of Auchenleck, in Monikie Parish, 'is a square building of
four stories, exclusive of the flag tower and cape-house, and has much the resem-
blance of a Border Peel. The hall and other chambers have circular roofs of
stone, and the old " iron yett" or grated door . . . is in excellent preservation.
The building is of ashler, and seems to belong to the end of the fifteenth, or
beginning of the sixteenth century. The chief apartment is on the third story.
Entering from it are two bed-closets, and a little oratory, all in the thickness of
the wall. In the oratory, which measures seven feet six inches, by six feet two
inches, a benatura, a piscina, and an ambry, still remain, along with some
architectural ornaments, among which is a shield with three lozenges' (Jervise's
Memorials of Angus and Mearns, 1861, p. 331). Having examined the tower
since the foregoing was in type, I must add that Jervise's description is incorrect,
for only one of the stories is vaulted, the oratory is not in the thickness of the
wall, but over the staircase, and the ' iron yett' has disappeared.

[3] *Of of* in MS.

H

cione, under the not and subscripsion of Thomas Spalding, *primo Maii anno m°v^cxlij°,* purchased be the said Johan and Elizabeth Autherlony, makyng mencion that thai, or at the lest in thar name thar procuratouris lawfullie constitut, desirit ane dispensacione to solemnizat mariaige, becaus they[1] desyrit to[2] solemnizat the same, and mycht nocht do the sammyn wythowt ane dispensacion[3] becaws thai war of kyn, and also *sese invicem actu fornicario carnaliter cognoverunt.* And hayth the said Johane and Elizabeth Autherlony, efter mutuall promys of mariaige and carnall dayll had betuix tham, constitut thair procuratouris to purchas and obteyn the said despensacion, as at mair lenth is contenit in the same, and also in the instrument of constitucione of procuratori under the not of Johan Guthre notar public, [quhilk][4] gyf neid beis salbe maid manifest.

Secundlye, promys and consent, of the law of God, specialie confirmit and consummat be carnal dayll following, makis mariaige; and so it is that Johan Forret of that Ilk promised and consented to marye Elizabeth Autherlony, lang befoyr the said Elizabeth Lesle wes maried wyth hym, and confirmit the same, using hyr in all sortis as hys wyff neirhand the space of fouyr yearis; and therfor the said Elizabeth Leslie aucht nocht to be compelled to adheir unto hym, bot to be *simpliciter* divorciat fra hym, lyikas sche ernestlie requiris. And for probacion of the premissis, Elizabeth Leslie producis the dispensacion foirsaid; and, gyf neid beis, requiris ane daye wythin the quhilk sche ma obteyn the Quenis Graces letteres, or other wayes to compell Johan Guthre, notar, mencionat in thé dispensacion, to gev furth the instrument of constitucion of procuratori, to declar the sammyn. And sche desyris the Lady Athinlek to depon heiron, conform to the sammyn.

And in takyn and farther verificacion of the said promys, the said Johan obtenit the said despensacion, and translated the said Elizabeth Autherlony and hyr guddis to hys place of Forret; and usit hyr and thame as his awyn and proper, and so war estemed in the cuntre; and promised to put hyr in conjunct fe of the cottoun of Forret; and tharfor wes never put

---

[1] *The* in MS.   [2] *To to* in MS.   [3] *Dispensasacion* in MS.   [4] Omitted.

in the *D*enis bukis for fornicacion or insest, as was the use of
the cuntre than, bot levyt in mutuall cohabitacion, fruicion
and usage of otheris gayr and bodeis, sche as his maried wyff,
and he as hyr undowted howsband.   And sua the Lady of
Nydy aucht nocht to be compelled to adheir to hym, bot rather
to be devorsit fra hym ; and heirupon desyris the saidis Johan
Forret and Elizabeth Autherlonye to be examinat, upon thar
conscience and athis, &c.   *Item,* albeid thar war may excepcionis
and artiklis produced in wryt be Elizabeth Lesle nor thyr
befoyr wryttyn, thai ar left furth of this *Registre* as superflew,
becaus thai war nocht provyn ; and also al dietis and probacionis produced,[1] f[o]r the sam caus, ar heir omittit, quhilkis
war used concernyng the probacion of the otheris artiklis
omittit.   So that efter the Lady Athynlek had beyn summond
lawfullie to hav comperit as wytnes, and excused be seiknes
and aige ; and at the ayth of Ihon Forret wes decernit to be
takyn upon the artiklis befoyr wryttyn, at desyr of Elizabeth
Lesle, the ayth of Jhon Forret wes decernit to be takyn ; and
ane commission direct to examyn the Lady Athynlek in presens
of Ihon Forret, and he summond to compeyr and se hyr sworn
and admittit.   And now followis the tenor and forme of the
dispensacion produced, the commission of the commissaris, the
deposicionis of the Lady Athynlek and of Jhon Forret.   And
fyrst the dispensacione :—[2]

---

[1] *Produced ar* in MS.

[2] Cosmo Innes, in speaking of the extension of the Levitical prohibitions
of inter-marriage, says :—' It might be curious to trace the gradual extension
of the canonical prohibitions till they reached persons in the *seventh* degree
of consanguinity, as we find was the case in the time of Pope Gregory
the Great, in the beginning of the seventh century, and as it continued till the
enormity of the evil obliged the Lateran Council in 1215 to relax the prohibitions to the fourth degrees of consanguinity and affinity, resting the rule not on
any divine precept, but on the most arbitrary and even whimsical grounds of
convenience.   To this must be added *cognatio spiritualis*, the relationship
through baptism, which affected not only the relatives within the same degrees,
of the *baptizans* and *baptizatus*, but all the connexions within those degrees
created by the relation of god-fathers and god-mothers, and the children
for whom they stood sponsors, to the same extent as if actually parents and
child.   Whatever may have been the motives that induced the Church thus
to extend the prohibitions of the Levitical code, one necessary result was the
great demand for dispensations from the Head of the Church and those wielding
his authority. · · · The Archbishop of St. Andrews, writing in 1554, stated, that

[Despensacio
pro Johanne
Forret et Eliza-
betha Auther-
lonye.]

Universis et singulis sancte matris [1] ecclesie filiis ad quorum noticias presentes litere pervenerint, Johanes Thorntoun [2] ecclesie cathederalis Morauiensis precentor, sanctissimique domini nostri pape et ejus sacre penitentiarie apostolice in hac parte commissarius specialiter deputatus, salutem in Domino sempiternam, ex parte honorabilis viri Joannis Forret de eodem, laici, et Elizabeth Autherlony domine de Adflek, mulieris Sancti Andree diocesis, nuper nobis oblate peticionis series continebat quod ipsi ex certis racionabilibus causis desiderant invicem matrimonialiter copulari, sed quia in tercio et quarto affinitatis gradu

---

such was the connexion between families in Scotland, that it was scarce possible to match two persons of good birth who should not come within the forbidden degrees; and on that account (*ut sunt hominum ingenia semper in vitium proclivia*) many married without dispensation, promising to obtain it subsequent to marriage; but afterwards instead of doing so sought for divorce, or put away their wives on the pretext of the want of dispensation and of the expense of procuring one. . . . For the remedy of these mighty evils, that were sapping the foundations of society, the statesmen of Scotland and Archbishop Hamilton were content to propose, that the Archbishop who was *Legatus natus* should have the power of dispensing for the marriage of persons in the third degree of consanguinity and affinity, and of such as were connected through *cognatio spiritualis*' (*Liber Officialis Sancti Andree*, pp. xx-xxii, xxv-xxvii). Dr. Stuart refers to an instrument of dispensation dated at Edinburgh the 6th of June 1536, granted by John Chesholme, Chancellor of the Cathedral Church of Dunblane, in which 'there is engrossed a commission by Anthonius, cardinal-priest and penitentiary of his Holiness the Pope, dated at Rome 24th June 1534, empowering the said John Chesholme to grant dispensations to the extent of twenty couples.' This licence in Chesholme's favour was qualified by various stipulations, and was only to continue in force for five years. The restriction of time was quite unnecessary, for this dispensation, although granted within two years of the date of his commission, was the nineteenth of the twenty which it empowered him to issue (*Lost Chapter in the History of Mary Queen of Scots*, pp. 68, 69). It will be observed that the document in the text embodies a commission by Cardinal Antonius authorising John Thorntoun to grant dispensations to forty-five couples; and that the one in favour of John Forret and Elizabeth Autherlony was the thirty-ninth, although granted within eleven months after the commission was sealed at Rome! Power to the same effect, but limited to twenty-one couples, had been given to Gilbert Strachquhan in 1527, and he disposed of sixteen within nineteen months (*Illustrations of the Topography and Antiquities of Aberdeen and Banff*, Spalding Club, iii. 331-333).

[1] In MS. m̄r̄s, probably for m̄r̄s. A few manifest blunders in this document have been corrected.

[2] Mr. John Thorntoun, who had two natural sons, Gilbert and Henry, was rector of Ancrum, and built a mansion in Glasgow adjacent to the Bishop's palace. In July 1560 he is described as precentor of Moray and usufructuary of the vicarage of the Parish Church of Aberkirdor. He died in 1564. His nephew,

simplici ex communi stipite sibi invicem simul attinentes,[1] ex eo
perveniente, quod dictus Joannes quandam Elizabeth Kynneir
sui ipsius sponsam, in quarto et tercio consanguinitatis gradu
dicte Elizabeth Autherlonye conjunctam, carnaliter cogno-
verat, et hujusmodi impedimentum ignorantes sese invicem
actu fornicario carnaliter cognoverunt, desiderium similiter
in hac parte perimplere non possunt absque legitima dispensacione apostolica desuper habita et obtenta, quare nos
per discretos viros, dominum Joannem Forret, procuratorem,
et eo nomine dicti Joannis, et Alexandrum Ryddo⁴, procuratorem similiter et eo nomine dicte Elizabeth, de quorum procuratorum mandato per unum instrumentum publicum, signo
et subscriptione discreti viri Joannis Guthre, laici, Brechinensis diocesis sacra authoritate apostolica notarii pub[lici]
subscriptum et signatum, et coram nobis originaliter lucede
constabat, debita cum instancia fuimus requisiti quatenus ad
executionem nostre commissionis instru[cte] scripte et inserte
ac contentorum in eadem procedere, et cum eisdem Joanne et
Elizabeth super impedimento tercii et quarti gradus affinitatis predicte juxta et secundum teno[rem] et formam commissionis et facultatis nostre super talibus impedimentis desuper concessis misericorditer despensare dignaremur :
Nos igitur illorum consulere saluti animarum cupientes et
eorum piis desideriis in premissis benigne annuentes, receptis
primitus de mandato nostro nonnullis testibus fidedignis, ad
sancta evangelia juratis, et per notarium publicum suprascriptum
diligenter examinatis, ex quorum depositionibus et diligenti
inquisicione super noticiam impedimenti predati, comperimus
prefatos Joannem et Elizabeth in hujusmodi tercio et quarto

Mr. John Thorntoun, succeeded him in the vicarage of Aberkirdor, and another
nephew, Mr. James Thorntoun, who 'appears to have been an active and con-
fidential agent of James Beaton, Archbishop of Glasgow,' succeeded him as
precentor of Moray and rector of Ancrum (*Register of the Great Seal*, vol. iv.
Nos. 492, 1963, 2148; Laing's *Knox*, ii. 180; vi. 687). According to the
valuation of 1561 'the rentale of the chantorie of Murray . . . . *in victualibus*,
the maist parte beir, the remanent quheit, will extend to 18 chalderis. The
money that is payit of the said chantorie will extend to the soume of 180 merkis.'
But there is this suggestive *nota* added, 'He grantis it was sett befoir for 440
merkis' (*Registrum Episcopatus Moraviensis*, Ban. Club, p. xx).

[1] *Attingentes* and *attingerent* are the forms usually found in such documents.

affinitatis gradu fore attinentes ac sese invicem actu fornicario carnaliter cognovisse, ipsamque Elizabeth ab aliquo propterea minime raptam extitisse, sed ipsos ad hujusmodi despensacionis gratiam obtinendam alias habiles et ydoneos fore concepimus; idcirco authoritate apostolica nobis commissa, et qua fungimur in hac parte cum prefatis Joanne et Elizabeth, ut matrimonium inter se libere contrahere, illud in facie ecclesie solemnizare, et in eodem, postquam contractum et solemnizatum fuerit, licite remanere possint, et valeant bannis tamen et aliis solemnitatibus in hujusmodi matrimonio et similibus servari solitis et consuetis prius tamen editis et ligitime servatis, juxta tenorem commissionis et facultatis nostre predicte, nobis a sede apostolica dispensandi cum quadraginta quinque copulis super talibus impedimentis desuper concessis, in personas dictorum dominorum Joannis et Alexandri procuratorum prefatorum Joannis et Elizabeth et hujusmodi despensacionem humiliter petentum, misericorditer duximus dispensandum prout tenore presencium, cum eisdem Joanne et Elizabeth in Dei nomine amen dispensamus, dummodo dicta mulier propter hoc ab aliquo rapta non fuerit, ut coram nobis minime extitisse constabat, ac eos ab excommunicacionis sentencia quam propterea eciam per constituciones provinciales et synnodales incurrerunt, incestusque seu fornicacionis reatu et excessibus hujusmodi absolvimus, prolem inter eos respective susceptam, si qua erit, et suscipiendam, legitimam fore decernentes, impedimento predicto in aliquo[1] non obstanti; commissionis vero nostre, de qua supra fit mencio, tenor sequitur et est talis:—Antonius miseratione divina tituli Sanctorum quatuor coronatorum[2] presbyter cardinalis dilecto nobis in Cristo Joanni Thorntoun canonico Glasguensi salutem in Domino: sedis apostolice indefessa clemencia, circum · quaque pervigil ea potissimum circumspicere non desiit,[3] per que animarum perriculis obvietur ac paci et tranquillitati Cristi fidelium consulatur, juris rigorem temperando, ipsorum

---

[1] Supply *modo*.

[2] The *Sancti quatuor coronati* were four brethren of noble birth who suffered under Diocletian, whose story is briefly given in Butler's *Lives of the Saints*, under date November 8th. The church dedicated to them supplied the title of one of the Cardinal-priests. A *martyrium* was erected to them by the successor of Augustine at Canterbury.   [3] Or *desinit*.

Cristi fidelium et temporum qualitatibus prefatis, prout secundum Deum salubriter expedire cognoscit, sane nobis oblate nuper pro parte tua peticionis series continebat quod plures Cristi fideles in regno Scocie et in fide illi subjectis, necnon in provincia Hybernie, ad pacem et concordiam inter se suosque consanguineos et amicos componendam et conservandam, necnon inimiciciis et dissensionibus, que oriri possint, obviandis, ac certis aliis racionabilibus causis moti, interdum cupiunt invicem matrimonialiter copulari, sed consanguinitatis et affinitatis aut cognacionis spiritualis seu publice honestatis justicie vinculis impediti, hoc sacrum nequiunt, absque sedis apostolice dispensacione, et interdum ad sedem ipsam ob illius ab eis notabilem distanciam aliaque varia presertim presertim (sic) hiis temporibus impedimenta, proth dolor, urgencia, pro despensacionibus desuper obtinendis commode aditum seu ad eam recursum habere non possunt, sepeque propterea evenit quod, aut pacis desiderio suo bone hujusmodi frustrantur, aut, impedimentis hujusmodi non obstantibus, invicem copulantur absque alia desuper despensacione in [non]¹ modicum animarum periculum et scandalum plurimorum, et si tibi dispensandi cum eisdem Cristi fidelibus super impedimentis hujusmodi ab eadem sede tribueretur facultas, profecto paci et tranquillitati ac animarum saluti eorundem Cristi fidelium non parum consuleretur, quare supplicari fecisti humiliter tibi et eisdem Cristi fidelibus super hiis per ipsius sedis clemenciam de oportuno remedio misericorditer provideri : Nos igitur, qui pacis et tranquillitatis zelatores sumus, animarum saluti eorundem Cristi fidelium consulere volentes, et attendentes quod tu persona satis fide digna et bene merita existis, de qua in hiis et aliis specialem in Domino fiduciam obtenemus, hujusmodi supplicacionibus inclinati, authoritate domini Pape, cujus penitentiarie curam gerimus, et de ejus speciali et expresso mandato super hoc vivevocis oraculo nobis facto, tibi, ut per te et seu alium vel alios in dignitate ecclesiastica constitutum seu constitutos ad id per te deputandum seu deputandos, hinc ad quintum annum a data presencium computandum, cum quadraginta quinque copulis vidz. quadraginta quinque viris et totidem mulieribus super impedimento quarti

---

¹ Omitted.

gradus consanguinitatis vel affinitatis seu consanguinnitatis et
affinitatis scilicet aut primi secundi tercii vel quarti publice
honestatis justicie aut cognacionis spiritualis, eciam si alter con-
jugum aut contrahere volencium secundo vel tercio, alter vero [1]
simplici vel duplici triplici quadruplici aut multiplici quarto
consanguinnitatis et seu affinitatis aut publice honestatis justicie
gradibus inter se respective essent conjuncti aut se attinerent,
necnon cognacionis spiritualis inter levatum et seu levatam,
ac filios et seu filias levantis in baptisimo et seu confirmacione
exorte, duntaxat eciam si per adulterium absque machinacione
se invicem polluerunt, eciam si omnia impedimenta hujusmodi,
seu eorum pars quecunque insimul concurrerint in matrimoniis
contrahendis, vel eciam clandestine contractis et consummatis
ignoranter, aut contractis scienter et non consumatis, in cognacione vero spirituali, ut prefertur, exorta, et seu publica hones-
tate eciam scienter contractis et consumatis, ut, impedimentis
consanguinitatis affinitatis vel cognacionis spiritualis seu publice
honestatis hujusmodi non obstantibus, quadraginta quinque viri
et totidem mulieres predictum matrimonium inter se, eciam si
impedimenta hujusmodi ignorantes aut scientes ante contractum
matrimonium se actu fornicario seu incestuoso carnaliter cognoverint, seu eciam forsan post contractum ignoranter et con-
sumatum, vel contractum scienter non tamen consummatum,
divorciati fuerint et post sentenciam divorcii sese cognoverint,
de novo respective libere contrahere et in eo postquam contractum fuerit, seu si jam ignoranter eciam clandestine contraxerint, eciam si illud carnali copula consumaverint, seu scientes
impedimenta hujusmodi vel eorum alter sciens, matrimonium
similiter contraxerint clandestine, eciam carnali copula inter eos
minime subsequuta, in eorum contracto matrimonio remanere
necnon in foro consciencie, in eisdem gradibus, ac eciam primo
secundo tercio et quarto affinitatis simplici duplici triplici
quadruplici seu multiplici gradibus ex actu fornicario tam preveniente, et in casibus in quibus negocium hujusmodi penitus
occultum extiterit, matrimonium inter se scienter vel ignoranter
contraxerint, carnali copula inter eos subsequuta, vel non, ut,
eisdem impedimentis non obstantibus, in eorum contracto matri-

---

[1] Or *viro*.

monio remanere, seu illud de novo inter se contrahere et in eo
postmodum similiter similiter (*sic*) remanere libere et licite
possint et valeant (nullis tamen super hiis testibus adhibitis, aut
literis datis, vel processibus confectis) authoritate apostolica,
dummodo dicte mulieres propter hoc ab aliquo rapte non
fuerint, dispensare: Ac eis, qui scienter vel ignoranter et
clandestine contraxerint ac eciam impedimenta scientes vel
ignorantes sese ante contractum matrimonium seu eciam post
sentenciam divorcii, ut premittitur, carnaliter cognoverint, ab
excommunicacionis sentencia quam propterea eciam per constituciones provinciales et synodalcs incurrerint ac incestus seu
fornicacionis reatu et excessibus hujusmodi absolvere, et eis
pro modo culpe penitenciam salutarem injungere, prolemque
inter eos susceptam, siqua erit, et suscipiendam, legitimam
decernere, ac eciam cum eisdem copulis quorum alter contra-
hencium, seu eorum qui jam contraxerunt, secundo et quarto seu
tercio et quarto a stipite communi seu stipitibus communibus
respective gradibus distare noscuntur, si in literis per te seu a
te, ut prefertur, deputandos super dispensacionibus hujusmodi
concessis, mencio secundi seu tercii graduum predictorum facta
non fuerit juxta formam juris et constitucionum felicis recorda-
cionis dominorum Gregorij xj[1] et Clementis vj[ij] Romanorum
pontificum super hoc editarum, declarare libere et licite possis
et valeas, dictique per te deputandi possint et valeant, viris,
existentibus premissis, tenore presencium indulgemus, ac tibi
et deputandis predictis super hoc plenam et liberam concedimus
facultatem, non obstantibus premissis, ac bone memorie Octonis[2]
et Octoboni,[3] olim in regno Anglie, et forsan eciam in dicta pro-

---

[1] Or, x[j], *i.e.* decimi.

[2] Octo, Otto or Otho, Cardinal-deacon of S. Nicolas *in carcere Tulliano*, was
sent in 1237 as Legate to England, Wales, and Ireland, and apparently to Scotland also. In 1237 he held a Council in St. Paul's, London, and enacted a
number of canons for reformation of prevailing abuses. See Wilkins' *Concilia
Magnæ Britanniæ*, vol. i. pp. 649-663. His entrance into Scotland was at
first opposed by the king, Alexander II., but ultimately it was permitted under
certain conditions, and in 1239 he held a Council at Holyrood, in which part at
least of the canons he had enacted at London seem to have been extended to
Scotland (Robertson's *Statuta Ecclesiæ Scoticanæ*, vol. i. p. lviii and note).

[3] Octobonus or Ottobonus, then Cardinal-priest of S. Adrian—afterwards Pope
Adrian v.—was in 1265 sent as Legate to England, Scotland, Wales, and Ireland. In 1269 he too held a Council in St. Paul's, London, and there promul-

vincia, apostolice sedis legatorum, et quibusvis aliis apostolicis, necnon in provincialibus et synodalibus consiliis editis, generalibus vel specialibus constitucionibus et ordinationibus statutis et consuetudinibus regni Scocie et provincie predictorum, eciam juramento confirmacione apostolica vel quavis firmitate alia roboratis, ceterisque contrariis quibuscunque, proviso [tamen][1] quod dupla seu tenores dispensacionum hujusmodi quas vigore presencium per te et seu a te, ut prefertur, deputandos, fieri contegirit, ut premittitur, sub tuo in forma actentica sigillo nobis et officiio penitentiarie apostolice hujusmodi in eo cum aliis illius registris perpetuo, pro utilitate parcium despensaciones hujusmodi concernentium, servanda, infra tempus congruens pro facti qualitate transmittere cures, et numerum quadraginta quinque copularum nulatenus excedas, nec ipsi deputandi excedant nec cum aliquibus ex xlv copulis predictis quorum uterque forsan tercio consanguinnitatis vel affinitatis aut propinquiori gradu a stipite communi distarent, vel cognacione spirituali aliasque, ut prefertur, reperta, seu aliis impedimentis et jure prohibitis [blank] quibusvis gradibus affinitatis ex actu fornicario preveniente, in foro consciencie tamen ubi negocium hujusmodi occultum fuerit, et jam contractum matrimonium extiterit, et nullis, ut prefertur, testibus adhibitis aut literis datis seu processibus confectis ac alias in casibus in hujusmodi facultate expressis dispensare, nec dicta facultate post spacium quinque annorum uti presumas, nec deputandi presumant; et si quid pretextu presencium contra illarum tenorem fieri contegerit, illa et inde sequuta quecunque nullius exeant roboris vel momenti. Datum Rome apud Sanctum Petrum sub sigillo officii penitentiarii 4 non. Junii pontificatus domini Pauli Pape Tercii anno septimo.—In quorum omnium et singulorem fidem et testimonium premissorum has presentes literas nostras sive hoc presens publicum instrumentum processum hujusmodi nostrum in ordine nostrarum dispensacionum trigesimum nonum in

gated certain canons, which are recorded in Wilkins' *Concilia*, vol. ii. pp. 1-19. The Scottish clergy were summoned to this Council, but they only sent four deputies to protest against anything being concluded to their prejudice in their absence. Subsequently at Perth they refused to receive these canons. The Scottish king refused him entrance into his kingdom. See Robertson's *Statuta*, vol. i. p. lxiii and notes).

[1] Omitted.

se continentem fieri fecimus, et per notarium publicum subscriptum subscribi et publicari mandavimus, sigillique nostri jussimus
et fecimus appencioni communiri. Datum et actum infra
opidum Edinburgj, Sancti Andree diocesis, horam circiter
decimam ante meridiem primo die mensis Maii anno Domini
m°v°xlij indictione xv^ta pontificatus sanctissimi in Cristo patris
et Domini nostri domini Paulj, divina providencia Pape
Tercii [1] anno octavo, presentibus ibidem honorabilibus et dis-
cretis viris Thoma Ramsay, Jacobo Alan, Andrea Crawfurd,
cum diversis aliis testibus vocatis et requisi[tis]. Et ego vero
Thomas Spalding arcium magister, clericus Sancti Andree diocesis, sacra authoritate apostolica notarius, gratia predicte
despensacionis [et] [2] concessionis ceterisque premissis omnibus
et singulis, dum, sicut premittitur, agerentur dicerentur et
fierent, una cum prenominatis domino, commissario, et testibus
presens fui, eaque omnia et singula sic fieri vidi, scivi, et
audivi, ac in notam cepi, ideo hoc presens publicum instrumentum despensacionem hujusmodi in se continens manu propria
fideliter scriptum exinde confeci et in hanc publicam formam
redegi, signoque et subscripcione meis solitis et consuetis una
cum appinsione sigilli prefati domini commissarii subscripsi et
signavi, in fidem, robur, et testimonium veritatis omnium et
singulorum premissorum rogatus et requisitus.

Followis the tenor of the commissione.

Maister Jobane Wynram, Superintendent of Fyff, minister [Commissione
and eldaris of Cristis kyrk and congregacione wythin the to M^ris. Robert
citie of Santandrois, to our lovit bretheren, Maisteris Robert Wyliam Cok.]
Pont and Wyliam Cok, eldaris of the said citie, grace, mercy,
and peace for salutacion. Forsamekyll as Elizabeth Autherlony, Lady of Athinlek, being summond be our Sowiran Ladeis
letteres at the instance of Elizabeth Leslie, Lady of Nydye, to
have comperit befoyr us at certan day and place assignit to

---

[1] Paul III., by whom the Council of Trent was convoked, and who sent to
James v. in 1536-7 the 'mystic cap and sword blessed by him on Christmas
night,' and 'profered to him the title of Defender of the Christian faith.'
[2] Omitted.

hyr, to have born wytnes in the caws of ressonis of the said
Elizabeth Lesle aganis Johan Forret of that Ilk, and at the
said daye hyr assonze [1] of aige and infirmite produced befoyr
us; we have decernit owr commission direct to yow to examyn
the said Elizabeth, as be thir presentis we commyt to you
power in the Lord to summond and call befoyr yow the said
Elizabeth Autherlony wytnes foyrsaid, to resave hyr ayth and
deposicione, and to examyn hyr upon the foyrsaidis ressonis
and articles of the said Elizabeth Lesle, in sic place as salbe
thocht maist convenient be you, and ony lawful day betuix this
and the xxiiij day of September instant, quhilk is statut for
produccion; wyth power to you also to summond the said
Johan Forret to compeir the said day and place, to heir and se
the said Elizabeth resavit, sworn and admittit in the said caus,
admitting to hym his lawfull excepcionis and defensis according
to justice. And the deposicion of the said Elizabeth be you
put in wryt, that ye produce the sam befoyr us, the said xxiiij
day of September, wyth thir presentis, gevyn under the sayll
of ministerie foyrsaid, according to our deliverance, at Sanctandrois, the xj day of September, in the year of God m^{o}v^{c}lxj
yearis.

Followis the tenor of the summondis.

[John Forret
summoned by
Wyliam Cok
and Robert
Pont.]

Wyliam Cok and Robert Pont, eldaris of the kyrk of Sanct
Andros, to our lovittis, minister, reader or ane of the diaconis
of the kyrik (*sic*) of Logy, and to Dauid Forret, James Anderson, and every ane of you, grace and peace in the Lord.
Forsamekyll as the commission [2] of the Superintendent in
Fyff and ministere of Sanct Andros, is direct tyl us, to
examyn Elizabeth Autherlony upon certan articles concernyng ane caws, depending befoyr the said Superintendent and
ministerie, betuix Elizabeth Leslie Lady of Nydye and Johan
Forret of that Ilk, as the said [3] commission at mayr lenth
proportis; we requir tharfor and desyris yow, or ony of
you to quhom thir presentis beis presented, as faythfull

---

[1] Excuse.
[2] *As the commission as the commission* in MS.
[3] *As the said as the said* in MS.

membris in the Lord, that ye laufully warn and cherge the said
Johan Forret, of that Ilk, to compeir befoyr us, in the place of
Athinlek wythin the bowndis of Angus, the xvij and xviij daye
of this instant moneth of September, betuix viij howris in the
mornyng and iiij efter nuyn; to heir and se the said Lady
Athinlek ayth of fidelite takyn be us, and sche admitted as
wytnes in the said caws to depon upon the foyrsaidis articlis,
or to allege ane racionabill caws in the contrar, with deu intimacion as efferis. The quhilk to do we commit to you and
every ane of you our ful power be thyr presentis, gevyn under
our signet and subscripsionis, at Sanctandrois, the xiij day of
September, the year of [our]¹ Lord m°v°lxj yearis. Robert Pont,
wyth my hand, Wyliam Cok, wyth my hand. Follows the
indorsacion: The xiiij daye of September, I, James Anderson,
in the parochie of Logy, presentit this present to Dauid
Forret, allegit reader in Logy kyrk, quha red the sammyn, and
als affixit ane cope heirof on the sayd kyrk dur, summondyng
Johan Forret of that Ilk, conform to the tenor of the sammyn,
befoyr the said Dauid and Johan Rowch.—James Anderson.

Followis the examinacion and deposicion of the Lady
Athynlek.

At Athinlek, the xviij daye of September, in the year of [Examinacion
God 1561 yearis, abowt xij howris at nuyn or tharby, the Lady and deposicion
Athinlek underwrytyn wes sworn and admittit to examinacion of the Lady
Athynlek.]
as followis, in absence of Ihon Forret of that Ilk tharto sum-
mond and nocht compirand.

The quhilk daye, Elizabeth Autherlony, Lady of Authinlek,
being summond to compeir day and place abone wryttyn
befoyr us, commissionaris underwryttyn, to beyr wytnes and
declar the virite, in the accion and caws depending befoyr the
Superintendent of Fyff and ministere of Sanctandrois, betuix
Elizabeth Leslie, Lady of Nydy, and Johan Forret of that Ilk,
as the commission direct to us proportis, hes comperit tym and
place foyrsayd, and, hyr ayth of fidelite being resavit to testify
the virite upon the said Lady of Nydeis articlis, deponis as
follows: that is to say, upon the fyrst article, concernyng pro-

---

¹ Omitted.

mys of mariaige betuix hyr and Johan Forret of that Ilk, sche
affirmis it to be trew as it is articulat, and at the sayd promys
of mariaige wes fyrst mayd betuix tham *hinc inde* abowt Fast-
ronis-ewyn,[1] in the year of God, &c. xlj yearis, wythin the place
of Athinlek, and than the said Johan Forret promisit to
solemnizat mariaige wyth hyr at Pasche [2] nixt tharefter following; and tharefter, befoyr that sammyn Pasche, he schew
unto hyr that thai behovit to have ane dispensacione, be resson
of consanguinite betuix hyr and his fyrst wyff, and sche gave
hym ten pundis to rais the said dispensacion at that tym; and
bayth sche and the said Johan Forret constitut procuratoris to
that effect, and tuk instrumentis in Mr. Ihon Guthreis hand
tharupon: and the said dispensacione being schawyn, and red
to hyr in the substanciall puntis tharof, affirmis it to be of
verite, and confessis that sche gav the same to Mr. Ihon Ruyer-
furd, and efter at the said dispensacione wes rasit, vidz., at the
nixt Wytsunday thairefter, the said Johan Forret of that Ilk
caused hyr cum to his place of Forret,. quhar sche remanit [3]
wyth hym the space of ane year in bed and burd, and [wes] [4]
reput as his lawful wyff. Upone the secund artickle, sche
deponis as affoir, ekyng farther that the hayll space at
the said Johan Forret and sche war together, bayth in
Aithinlek and Forret and uther places, wes be the space of
twa yearis; and that he transportit and used hyr and hyr
gayr, as is contenit in the secind part of the secund article,
and also promised to put hyr in the conjunct fe of the cottoun
of Forret; and that sche wes reput as his wyff hayth in Fyff
and Angus; and quhen the said Elizabeth Autherlony wes
called in the consistory of Brechyn, or summond for ony thing,
the said Johan Forret wes summond and called also as hyr spows
for his interes. And als sche deponis that he brocht haym the
said dispensacion owt of Edinburgh hymself; and the hayll tym
that sche was in Forret, sche had the cuyr and administracion of
his hows as his lawful wyff. As toward the rest of the articlis,
sche knawis na thing uther than is above specifyed, except be
report of otheris. And thir premissis sche deponis to be of

---

[1] The eve preceding the first day of the fast of Lent—Shrove Tuesday.
[2] Easter.
[3] *Quhar sche remanit quhar sche remanit* in MS.   [4] Omitted.

viritie, as sche wyll ansuer befoyr God, and desyris justice to have place wythowt fayd [1] or favor.   Followis subscripsionis of the commissaris, Robert Pont wyth my hand *scripsit*, William Cok wyth my hand *subscriptus*.

Followis the confession and deposicion of Ihon Forret party.

Johane Forret of that Ilk sworne in presens of the ministerie, [Confession and be his ayth examinat upon the articles of Elizabeth Lesle and deposicion of J[h]on Forret.] in the caus foyrsayd : to the fyrst article, he ansueris and confessis thar wes ane condicional promys of mariaige betuix hym and Elizabeth Autherlony, Lady Athinlek, mayd tym articulat ; and son efter the said promys the deponar had carnall dayll wyth the said Elizabeth Autherlony, and rased the dispensacion at the handis of Mr. Ihon Thornton.   As to the using of the same, he referris hym to the tenor therof and contentis tharin : the dispensacion to hym schawyn and exhibit to recognosce it, he ansueris that he is nocht letterit nor can reid,[2] bot that dispensacion that he rased he deliverit to the said Elizabeth Autherlony.   Examinat upon the fyrst part of the secund artikill, ansueris as affoyr that efter promys foyrsaid the deponar and Elizabeth Autherlony kepit cumpany divers yearis, and that lang befoyr he mareid Elizabeth Leslie.   The secund part of the secund artikill he confessis, except the promys of inputtyn of Elizabeth in the cottoun of Forret.

Die ultimo mensis Decembris, anno Domini 1561.

The quhilk day, Johan Forret, of that Ilk, summond to [Jhon Forret declar and cleyr his deposicion mayd upon the articlis of cleris his deposicion.] Elizabeth Leslie, Lady of Nydye, and specialie quhar he deponit and confessed ane condicionall promys betuix hym and Elizabeth Autherlony, Lady of Athinlek : for declaracion of that

---

[1] Feud.

[2] Among the names adhibited to the band of the barons and gentlemen of Fife, at St. Andrews, on the 12th of September 1565, obliging them to ' trewlie serve the King and Quenis Majesteis . . . . owther for resisting thair Hienessis rebellis or persewing thame and expelling thame furth of this cuntre, or to resist and invaid Ingland, in caise it sal happin to persew,' occurs ' Johnne Forret of that Ilk, with my hand at the pen led be Alexander Hay, notar ' (*Register of the Privy Council*, i. 367, 368).

word condicional, he sworn deponis that the condicion wes
betuix hym and Elizabeth Autherlony as followis, vidz., that
sche sudd caws hyr son to marie his dochter; and now confessis that this condicione wes mayd to hym be Elizabeth
Atherlony efter the promys of mariaige and carnall dayl
betuix hym and Elizabeth Autherlony. Quhilk confession
wyth the rest preceding Elizabeth Lesle acceptis, and passis
fra al farther produccion. The Superintendent statutis Wedinsday nixt to cum to pronunce. *Partibus citatis.*

Die *vj*[to] *mensis Januarii anno Domini* 1561.

[Elizabeth
Leslie absolved
fra adhering to
Johan Forret.]

The quhilk daye, in the accione and caus of adherence, proponit be Johan Forret of that Ilk aganis Elizabeth Leslie,
Lady of Nydy, to adheyr to hym as to hyr lawful husband,
as desyr of this term statut to pronunce, the Superintendent,
avysed wyth the peticion and desyr of Johan Fo[r]ret, defensis
and articles of Elizabett Lesle concernyng the alleged promys
of mariaig and carnall dayll betuix the sayd Johan and
Elizabeth Autherlony, Lady Athinleik, yit levand, and mayd
befoyr the pretendit mariaig betuix Ihon Forret and Elizabeth Lesle, and confessionis of the sam contenit in the
deposicionis of the sayd Ihon Forret and Elizabeth Autherlony, fyndis that the sayd Jhon Forret had mayd promys
of maruag wyth Elizabeth Autherlony yit on lyve, and
knew hyr carnale efter promys mayd betuix tham,[1] and that
befoyr the pretendit mariaige mayd *de facto et non de jure*
betuix the saydis Jhon and Elizabeth Lesle, and heirfor
absolvis Elizabeth Leslie fra adhering to the said Ihon instantle, in respect of the premissis and of all that is yit
knawyn.

Die *xiiij*[to] *mensis Januarii anno Domini* 1561.

[Elizabeth
Leslie sues for
divorce.]

The quhilk daye, comperis Elizabeth Leslie, Ladye of
Nydye, and produces ane libellat summondis of the Superintendentis of Fyff deulie executed and indorsat, tharin summond
Johan Forret of that Ilk, [quha][2] comperand be verteu of the
sayd summondis confessing hym summond. Of the quhilk
summondis the tenor followis :—

---

[1] *Than* in MS. [2] Omitted.

Maister Johan Wynram, Superintendent of Fyff, &c., to my [Tenor of the Superintendentis summondis.] lovittis, minister or reader in the parrochie kyrk of Logy, or ony other quhilk salbe requirit wyth execucion of thir presentis, grace, mercy and peace from God the Father, throwgh Jesus Crist our Lord and onlie Saluer. I requir yow, in the name of the eternall God, that ye laufullie and peremptorlie summond Johan Forret of that Ilk, to compeir personalie befoyr me or the ministerie of Sanctandrois, in the consaill hows wythin the parrochie kyrk of the citie of Sanct Androis, upone Wedinsday the xiiij daye of Januar instant, in the howr of caws, at the instance of Elizabeth Leslie Lady of Nydye his pretendit spows, to heir and se the matrimony, *de facto et non de jure*, contracted betuix hym and the said Elizabeth, provyn to be and have beyn null fra the begynnyng; becaus the said Johan Forret, lang befoyr the said pretendit mariage, had mayd promys of mariaige wyth Elizabeth Autherlony, Lady of Athinlek, quharupon. follow[it] carnall dayll also betuix the saidis Johan and Elizabeth Autherlony, and cohabitacion kepit betuix thame be the space of divers yearis, thai being haldyn and reput as mareit personnis; albeit the sammyn wes unknawyn to the said Elizabeth Lesle quhill now laytlie wythin thir thre yearis or les, sen the quhilk knawlege sche hes abstracted hyr fra cumpany and cohabitacion of the sayd Ihon, moved of conscience becaus the sayd Elizabeth Autherlony is yit levand, wyth quhom he mayd the fyrst promys: and heirfor the sayd Johan Forret to heir and se the sayd pretendit matrimony, mayd *de facto et non de jure* betuix the sayd Ihon and Elizabeth Lesle, to be and have beyn fra the begynnyng nul, and he to be seperated, divorciat and dividit *simpliciter* fra the said Elizabeth Lesle; and the sayd Elizabeth Lesle to be set at libertie, and put to fredom in the Lord to mare wyth ony lawful husband, according to the law of God; or ellis the said Johan to schaw ane ressonabyll caws quhy the sam awcht not [to][1] be don: wyth intimacion, gyf the said Johan compeir nocht, we wyll proceid in the said caws as we may and awcht of the law of God. The quhilk to do we commyt to you power in the Lord be thir presentis,

---

[1] Omitted.

delivering the same be yow deulie executed and indorsat agane to the herrer :[1] gevyn under the saill of the said ministerie at Sanctandrois, upon the viij daye of *Januarii, anno Domini* 1561.

Quhilk summondis being red in presens of the sayd Johan Forret, and his ansuer required therunto, and gyf he ony defens had or wald use to stop the sayd divorciment, he ansueris that he wald use nan other nor he had used alredy in the proces of adherence. And the summondis and contentis tharin referred to probacion of Elizabeth Lesle, sche, in presens of the sayd Johan, producis and repetis the decreit absalvator, and proces gevyn and led be the Superintendent, in the caus of adherence proponit be Ihon Forret aganis hyr. Nathing thar aganis objecked, the Superintendent statutis Wedinsday nixt to cum, to pronunce in presens of parteis, heyrto chergit be ac[tis].

Die xxj mensis Januarii anno Domini 1561.

Sentencia divorcii inter Johanem Forret et Elizabeth Lesle. Wyth incalling of the name of Crist Jesus, Sone of the eternall and everlevyng God, Maister Ihon Wynram, Superintendent of Fyff, &c., juge in the caws of divorce moved be Elizabeth Leslie Lady of Nydye aganis Johan Forret of that Ilk for nullite of the pretendit mariaige maid, *de facto et non de jure,* betuix the foyrsaid Johan and Elizabeth, in respect that the sayd Johan Forret, lang befoyr the said pretendit mariaige, had mayd promys of mariaige wyth Elizabeth Autherlony, Lady Athinlek, quharupon followed carnall dayll also betuix the saidis Johan and Elizabeth Autherlony, and cohabitacion kepit betuix tham be the space of twa yearis, thai being haldyn and reput as mareit personns, albeit the sammyn wes unknawyn to the said Elizabeth Leslie quhil now laytlie wythin thir thre yearis or les, sen the quhilk knawlege sche hes abstracted hyr fra cumpany and cohabitacion of the sayd Johan, moved of conscience becaus the said Elizabeth Autherlony is yit levand, wyth quhom he mayd the fyrst promys, as at mayr lenth is contenit in the libellat summondis, rased at the instance of the said Elizabeth Leslie, deulie executed and indorsat upon the said

---

[1] *Brrrer* in MS.

Johan and befoyr us produced; quharupon we have procedit
wyth detful ordor, admitting to bayth the saidis parteis thar
just and lawful defences. And we being ryplie avysed wyth
the foyrsaid libellat summondis, ansuer of John Forret therunto
mayd, probacionis therupon producet and repetit be the said
Elizabeth Leslie, and all otheris deduced in the said caws, the
consall and sentement of the ministerie of Sanctandrois heirin
had and hard, we fynd the intent of the sayd Elizabeth Leslie
sufficientle and clerlie provyn : heirfor, havyng God onlie befoir
our ees, and the testimonie of his trew and eternall Word, pronuncis, decernis, and, be this our sentence diffinityve, declaris
the foyrsaid pretendit mariaige *de facto et non de jure* mayd
betuix the said Johan Forret and Elizabeth Leslie to be and to
have beyn fra the begynnyng nul ; and the sayd Johan Forret,
becaus of his prece[ding] promys and carnal dayll and cohabitacion wyth Elizabeth Autherlony following tharupon, to be
divorciat, seperated and dividit fra the sayd Elizabeth Leslie ;
and libertie in the Lord to the sayd Elizabeth Leslie to marye
ony other lawful husband, according to the law of God : committing the sayd Johan Forret to the handis and power of
temporall magistratis havyng pouer to punys hym, according
to the law of God and ordor of this realm. Pronunced in
presens of the saidis parteis, wythin the parrochie kyrk and
consistorie hows of the cite of Sanctandrois, upon Wedinsday
the xxj of Januar, in the year of God m°v°lxj yearis, being
present for the tym Crostopher Gudman, minister, Mr.[1] Ibon
Dowglas, Rector of the Universite of Sanctandrois, Masteris
James Wylke, Alan Lawmonth, &c.

*Sessio domini Superintendentis et ministerie Sancti
Andree, tenta in ecclesia parrochiali ejusdem civitatis,
die decimo Decembris, anno Domini jm°v°lxj.*

The quhilk daye, ane nobill and mychty lord, Andro, Erl of *Decretum Symson.*
Rothes,[2] of his awyn proper confession oblesis hym, as fermorar of [Frutis of the
the frutis of the abbaye of [*Sanctandrois*—deleted] Lundoris, to Abbaye of Lundoris.]

---

[1] *Mris* in MS.
[2] Andrew Leslie, fourth Earl of Rothes, succeeded his father—one of the commissioners who died suddenly at Dieppe—in 1558, and joined the Lords of the

paye to Wyliam Symson, minister in Ebde,[1] yearle at twa
usuall termis in the year, Wytsunday and Martymes, be twa
equall porcionis the sowm of fowyr scoyr liḃ. in money; or[2]
ellis to assigne the sayd Wiliam to uptak sa mekyll victualis
as extendis to the valor of the sayd sowm, according to the
common price of the cuntre, yearle in the moneth of Januar;
begynnand the first term of payment at the term of Martymes
in the sexty ane year, and sa yearlie and termle, contenuand
aye and sa lang as the sayd lord remanis fermorar to the sayd
frutis, and the sayd Wyliam remanis minister in the sayd kyrk,
or [as][3] son tharefter as commodite of tym sal serve.   In lyik

Decretum
Wobstar.

maner the sayd nobyll lord, Andro, Erl of Rothes, of his awyn
proper confession, oblesis hym, as fermorar of the frutis of the
abbay o[f] Lundoris, to paye to Johan Wobstar,[4] exortar in
the kyrk of Collesse, yearlie at twa usuall termis in the year,
Wytsundaye and Martymes, be twa equall porcionis the sowm
of ane hundreth marchas in money; or ellis to assigne the said
Jhon to uptak sa mekyll victualis as extendis to the valor of
the said sowm, according to the common price of the cuntre,
yearlie in the moneth of Januar; begynnand the fyrst term
of payment at the term of Martymes in the lxj year, and sa
yearlie and termle, contenuand aye and sa lang as the sayd
lord remanis fermorar to the saidis frutis, and the said Johan
remanis exortar in the said kyrk, or [as][3] sone tharefter as
commodite of tym sal serve.

Congregation, with whom he acted and suffered ; but he fought for the Queen at
Langside.   It was several years after the date in the text ere John Philip
resigned the Abbacy of Lundores in favour of Bishop Leslie, who was succeeded
in the commendatorship by Patrick Leslie of Pitcairlie, second son of Earl
Audrew, and afterwards first Lord Lindores (Laing's *Knox*, i. 263, 350; ii. 53,
129, 601; *Register of Privy Council*, i. 357, 409; *Historie of King James the
Sext*, Ban. Club, p. 26; Laing's *Lindores Abbey*, p. 403).

[1] Symson was minister of Abdie and Dunbog in 1565 (Scott's *Fasti*, ii. 466).
[2] *Of* in MS.   [3] Omitted.
[4] Webster was reader at Collessie in 1567 or 1568, with a stipend of £20
(*Register of Ministers, Exhorters and Readers*, p. 24).

Heir followis the sentence gevyn be the Superintendent and ministerie in favoris of Alexander Cwnynghame, anent the adheryng of Cristen Wod to hym
as to hyr lawfull husband, nochtwythstandyng the
sentence of divorce, procurit be hyr in Papisticall
maner, fundyn nul, as the proces beris, quhilk is
omittit heir, becaws it is al wryttyn into ane buk
be the self remanand wyth *Regester*, &c.

Wyth incalling of the name of Crist Jesus, Sone of the *Sentencia*
eternall and everlevyng God, quhai is the waye the verite and *Cwnygham*
the lyff, to wytnes wyth our consciences, we, Master Johan *contra* Wod.
Wynram, Superintendent, &c., minister and eldaris of the
reformed kyrk and cite of Sanctandrois, in takyng cognicion
in the complaynt and peticion of ·Alexander Cwnynghame,
fear of Wast Bernis,[1] proponit befoyr the said ministerie,
allegiand that Cristian Wod, wyth quhom he contracted and
solemnizat mariaige in the face of the kyrk, had passed fra
hym wythowtyn ony just caus, had remanit fra hym be the
space of twa yearis or tharby, and wald nocht adheir to hym
as to hyr lawful husband wythowt sche be compelled, desyring
hyr to be caused to adheir to hym according to the law of
God, and owr autorite quhilk we have of the law of God to
be tharto interponit.   The said Cristian heirto laufullie
summond and comperand, the forme of the said peticione red,
sche confessed the mariaige foyrsaid, and for stop of desyr of
adheryng be hyr to Alexander, be waye of excepcione, proponit
and alleged sche wes divorciat fra Alexander and ane sentence
tharupone gevyn.   In discussing of the quhilk excepcione, we
have procedit in examinacione of the said allegit divorciment,

---

[1] Alexander was the son of William Cunninghame of Barns (*Register of Great
Seal*, iv. No. 1700).   It was with one of the fair daughters of this house that
Hawthornden was 'deliriously in love,' and whose untimely death he so piteously
bewails :

> ' I have nought left to wish : my hopes are dead ;
> And all with her beneath a marble laid.'

The scene too of his *Polemo-Middinia*, or *Midden-Fecht*, is laid at the West or
New Barns (Professor Masson's *Drummond of Hawthornden*, 1873, pp. 45-52,
476-484).

proces and sentence tharof, in divers and syndry dietis, the
said Cristian therto lawfully at all tym summond, all lawfull
defensis admittit to bayth the saidis parteis.   And now
finalie, the peticion of the said Alexander, ansuer of Cristen,
proces, sentence of the said allegit divorce, rychtis, juris,
ressonis, allegacionis, probacionis,[1] testimoneis and deposicionis of certan famos wytnessis, and all otheris producit and
deducit in the said caws befoyr us be bayth the saidis parteis,
be us seyn, hard, considerit and ryplie understand, together
wyth the testimonye of the trew and eternall Word of God:
we fynd that the saidis Alexander and Cristiane have contracted and solemnizat matrimonye in the face of the kyrk,
and ar jonit in the band of matrimonye; and at the divorciment, proponit be waye of excepcione be the said Cristiane
for hyr defence and to stop hyr adheryng to the said Alexander, is and wes fra the begynnyng nul, invalid, and na caws
to stop the said Cristiane to adheir to the said Alexander as
to hyr lawfull husband, becaws the pretendit sentence of the
said alleged divorciment wes pronuncit into ane privat and
prophane hows (sa called in Papistre) wythin the reformit citie
of Sanctandrois, and that lang efter the said citie wes reformed
be sinceir preaching and hearing of Goddis trew Word,
all public idolatrie, Papistrie, and Papisticall jurisdiccione
abolesched furth of the same, the consistorie hows dischergit
and stekyt up, the multitud of the inhabitantis of the said
citie be professione and protestacione adjonit into ane Cristiane
congregacione: and also in respect that in the said pretendit
proces is nocht specifyed ony caus of divorce permitted in
the Word and law of God, bot alanerly sic causis of pro-
pinquite of greis of consanguinite and affinite as ar inventit
and statut be Papisticall tradicionis to impeid mariaige; upone
the quhilkis greis (sa monye at the lest as ar provyn in the
said proces) the saidis parteis had obtenit and used Papisticall
dispensacione, quharby the saidis impedimentis and causis war
removed lyik as thai war ordened.   And heirfor declaris and
ordenis the said Cristian Wod to adheir to the said Alexander Cwnynghame hyr lawfull husband, and to obey hym as

---

[1] *Porbacionis* in MS.

becummis of dewetie the lawfull wyff to obey hyr lawfull husband, according to the ordinance and law of God. And letteres of monicione in dew form to be gevyn heirupon, to be executed upon the said Cristiane under pains of excommunicacione; and gyf sche contempnis to obeye, the same pains to be executed aganis hyr. Pronuncit in the consis[to]ry hows, wythin the parochie kyrk of the citie of Sanctandrois, in presens of Alexander Cwnyngham makand instance, and in payn of nocht comperance of Cristian Wod heyrto laufulle summond.

The accusacione and prowd ansueris of Mr. Thomas Meffen wyth decreit aganis hym followis.

Die xxv^{to} mensis Augusti, anno Domini &c. lxj.

The quhilk daye, as in the diet assignit be the Superintendent and ministerie to tak cognicione and tryall anent the conversacione, inobedience and contempsion of divers inhabitantis of this citie, and namle of Mr. Thomas Meffen, and command gevyn to George Blak and Wyliam Mayn, dioconis, to warne hym to compeyr in this essemble, the saydis George and Wiliam, diaconis, varefyis that thai lawfullie chergit the said Mr. Thomas Meffen, personalie apprehendit, in name of the Superintendent and ministerie, to compeyr this daye in thar session and consistorie hows, quhilk Mr. Thomas ansuerit and gave thame in cherge to report for his ansuer: That he was nether ane Papist nor ane Calwynist, nor of Paul nor of Apollo, bot Jesus Cristis man; he wald nocht cum to tham nor to thar hows; bot gyf the Superintendent or the minister had ocht to do wyth hym, at thar request he wald cum to thar chalmer and speik tham. Quhilk answer and report hard be the Superintendent, he affirmis lyik report mayd to hymself be Mr. Thomas as concernyng his cuming befoyr the ministere, and that he wald nocht compeyr befoir the ministerie, desyring hym to have hym excusit for he wald cum to hymself at his desyr. And heirfor the sayd Mr. Thomas is decernit to be called yit anis agane.

[Accusacione and proud ansueris of Mr. Thomas] Meffen.

Die xxvij Augusti, anno quo supra.

Meffen.

The quhilk daye, Mr. Thomas Meffen provyn warnit to this daye, according to the deliverance of the ministerie in the act *xxv Augusti*. Thomas Martyn, in name of Mr. Thomas Meffen, proponis and allegis that Maister Thomas wes informed howe in the last session and diet of this ministerie·it wes divisit that he suld be impresonit, and at Master Thomas had byddyn hym saye: That ane gret part of thame that ar upone the sayt war his inimeis, thai had send ane wrang testimoniall aganis hym to *D*unde; he had also gret knawlege and understanding, bayth in the civil law and in the Scriptur and law of God, as thai or ony of tham had, he wald except nane bot the Superintendent and minister; he wald nocht be jugit wyth tham, nor have ony thing to do wyth tham that war sic inimeis to hym; and also denyis hym to be ane of this congregacione. The Superintendent and ministerie ordenis Mr. Thomas to be chergit be the diaconis to compeyr Wednisday nixt to cum, to justifye his sayingis sa reportit in his name.

Die quinto Januarii, anno quo supra.

Meffen.

The quhilk daye, Mr. Thomas Meffen warnit at command of the Superintendent to compeyr in this session, and he comperand, the [ansuer][1] proponit be Thomas Martyn in his name [2] red to hym, and requirit gyf he wald affirme the same, and also requiret to geve confession of his fayth. Na direct ansuer had of hym and the tym past, the Superintendent be his awyn mowth *verbo* summondis hym to compeyr befoyr hym and the ministerie, Widnisdaye nixt to cum, to geve confession of his fayth, and also to answer be his ayth upon the verite of the [ansuer][1] proponit in his name, be umquhill Thomas Martyn upon the xxvij of August last bypast, under payn of proceding aganis hym be excommunicacione; and Mr. Thomas protestis that he admittis nocht the jugis to be juge to hym.

---

[1] Perhaps omitted.

[2] The words ' his name ' are written as catchwords at the bottom of the page, but the next page begins ' in his name.'

* *Die septimo mensis Januarii, anno Domini* 1561.

The quhilk daye, as in term assignit to Mr. Thomas Meffen *Decretum* to compeyr and gyf confessione of his fayth, and to ansuer be *contra Meffen.* his ayth upon the verite of that proponit in his name be umquhill Thomas Martyn, &c., according to the desyr of act Monenday last wes, comperis Mr. Thomas, under protestacion of nocht admitting ony present his jugis, and fyrst of all producis the copy of ane testimoniall send to *D*unde fra this ministerie, of the quhilk the tenor followis: WE testifye be thir presentis that Mr. Thomas Meffen hes beyn chargit divers tymmis to recant and adjone hymself to Cristis congregacione, also weyll oppynlie in the essemble be Adame Heriot minister, as particularlie be commissaris tharto deput be the Lordis of Congregacione; and as yit hes nocht obeyit in recanting and adjonyng hym to the congregacione; and for the same caws hes beyn repellit in jugiment be the magistratis: in the year of God 1560, &c.—Bye the quhilk testimoniall, the said Mr. Thomas allegis hym injurit be the subscrivaris tharof, in presens of the personnis subscrivaris: quhai for thar partis confessis the gevyn of the sam at the desyr and request of thar faythfull brethern in *D*unde, in wryt send to tham to the sam effect; and desyris the Superintendent, Rector, minister and rest of the ministerie to consydder and trye the sam; and to cal to remembrance quhat thai knaw and hes hard toward the requisicion of Mr. Thomas publicle and particularle; and offerris tham to prev the repelling of Mr. Thomas be the magistratis becaws he wes nocht adjonit to the congregacion, in presens of Mr. Thomas, quhai planlie denyis hym to be ane member of the congregacion or to be adjonit tharto. Quhilk confession the Superintendent acceptis, and protestis tharfor that Master Thomas, be frequenting and dayle residence mackeyn in this cite contrary to the proclamacion mayd aganis kyrkmen, incur the panis theretnet in the sayd proclamacion.[1] And in respect of his ansueris foyr-

---

[1] Knox says that it was an old custom of the provost, bailies, and council of Edinburgh, after their election at Michaelmas, to proclaim the statutes and ordinances of the town; and therefore in 1561 the provost and magistrates ' caused proclame, according to the formar statutes of the town, that no adulterar, [no

saydis, wyth mony otheris recentle spokyn in thar audience of
gret contempsion, the Superintendent and ministerie ordenis
supplicacion [to be][1] direct to the magistratis of this citie,
ether to caws hym obeye the ordor of the kyrk and subject
hym to disciplynn, or ellis to exclud hym this citie, that na
perturbacion of the unite and ordor be brokyn by hym. And
as to the desyr of the subscrivaris of the testimonial be hym
producit, anent the tryall tharof, in respect that it is oppynlie
knawyn to the Superintendent and maist part of the rest of
the ministerie, the sam concernyng the public requisicion be
the minister and particularle the Superintendent and Rector
as commissaris deput be the lordis to[2] the sayd Mr. Thomas to
recant and adjon, and disobeying of the sam be hym; and
also in respect that Ihon Moffat, present, magistrat of this cite
for the tym, confessis and affirmis that he repellit Mr. Thomas
and his caus for the tym in jugment as ane that wes nocht
adjonit; the Superintendent, minister, Rector, and rest of the
hol ministerie nocht participant in subscriving of the sayd testimoniall,[3] decernis the same treule and laufulle gevyn, and
na injury don in gevyn tharof.

Die xxvij mensis Augusti, anno 1561.

[The teynd
schayffis of the
prebendreis of
the Ladye Kyrk
of Hewch.]

The quhilk daye, the teynd schayffis—assignit be the Superintendent to be colleckit and resavit be the diaconis of Sanctandrois, of the prebendreis of the Ladye Kyrk of Hewch, for
inobedience of Mr. Thomas Meffen, prebendar of Kyngask and
Kynglesse, Mr. James Henrison, prebender of Kynkyl, as in the
act xxv[to] Aprilis anno quo supra[4]—ar set for this instant crop,

---

fornicatour,] no noted drunkard, no mess-mongare, no obstinate Papistis that corrupted the people, such as preastis, freiris, and others of that sorte, should be
found within the toun within fourty-aught houris thairafter, under the paines
conteaned in the statutes.' Keith charges both Knox and Buchanan with giving
'a very untrue account' of this affair, but Laing has shown that Keith is in
error (Laing's *Knox*, ii. 289, 290; Keith's *History*, Spot. Soc. ii. 89-94). The
statement in the text seems to imply that a somewhat similar proclamation had
been made in St. Andrews, so far as concerned 'kyrkmen' at least; and that
Wynram wished to act on it, after the Queen had resented it in Edinburgh.

[1] Omitted. [2] *Of* in MS.
[3] *Testioall* in MS., the scribe having omitted the mark of contraction.
[4] See pp. 76, 77.

be avyis of the Superintendent and ministerie, as efter-followis, al havand interes beand summond to compeyr for thar interes this daye and nan compirand.

Item, in the fyrst set to Thomas Monepenny, of Kynkell,[1] *Assedacio Monipenny.* the teynd schaiffis of the hayll landis of Kynkell, wyth the pertinentis tharto contiguo[s] adjacent, for this year and crop of lxj year, for payment of fourty marchas, according to the assedacione alleged mayd to hym of befoyr be Mr. James Henrison prebendar, quhilk xl marchas Thomas oblesis hym and is becumin actitat to paye to the ministerie, and thar collector to be deput tharto, at Candylmes nixt to cum.

Item, set to the sayd Thomas Moneypenny the teynd *Assedacio ejusdem.* schaiffis of his landis of Kyngask wyth the pertinentis, for this instant year and crop of lxj, for the quhilk he oblesis hym and is becumin actitat to paye sexteyn lib., at Candylmes nixt to cum, to the collector deput of the ministerie, securite to be mayd to Thomas of warrandice and releif of sa mekyll as he payis at resayt tharof.

The quhilk daye, Mr. Wiliam Cok, as lauborar and taxman *Assedacio Cok.* of the landis of Kynglasse, is becumin actitat to pay to the collector of the ministerie of Sanctandrois, for the teynd schaiffis of Kynglasse and this crop of lxj year, awcht marchas at Candilmes nixt to cum, provydit that securite of warrandice be mayd to hym be the resavar of his resayt.

Die ultimo mensis Decembris, anno Domini 1561.

The quhilk daye, comperis Gelis Scrymgeor and producis *Scrymgeor contra Dundas.* ane summondis of the Superintendent deulie execut and indorsat, tharin summond Archibald Dundas, in Pote, hyr husband, to heyr and se hym provyne ane adulterar in gevyn

---

[1] In 1434-5 Walter Moneypenny of Kinkell leased the adjoining farm of Easter Balrymonth, 'the tend inclusit,' from the prior and convent of St. Andrews for nine years (*Liber Cartarum Prioratus Sancti Andree*, pp. 423, 424). In 1565 the King and Queen granted to Alexander, son and heir-apparent of Thomas Moneypenny of Kinkell, the lands of Cameron, which Thomas resigned (*Register of Great Seal*, iv. No. 1666). According to Sibbald, Kinkell, which is in the parish of St. Andrews, derived its name 'from the chapel of St. Anna, built here by Kellach, Bishop of St. Andrews, about *anno* 875' (*History of Fife and Kinross*, 1803, p. 348).

his bode in adulterie to Anne Duncane and Catren Cragdenny,
and therfor to heyr and se hyr be decernit seperated and
divorcit fra hym, wyth liberte to hyr to mare in the Lord,
and he to underly disciplyn for his transgression. The said
Archebald comperand, the summondis red in his presens, he
confessis the adulterie foyrsaid, [and][1] submittis hym to the
ordinance and disciplin of the kyrk. The Superintendent
assignis Wednisday to bayth the parteis to compeir and heir
pronuncit in the caws.

Die septimo mensis Januarii, anno Domini quo supra.

Sentencia divorcii inter Scrymgeor et Dundas.

The quhilk daye, in the accione and caws of divorce
intentat be Gelis Scrimgeor aganis Archebald Dundas, hyr
husband, for the fylthy crym of adultery committed be hym
wyth Anne Duncan and Catren Cragdenny, as desyr of this
term set to pronunce, the Superintendent, avysit wyth libellat
summondis of Gelis [and][1] ansuer of Archebald, fyndis the
adulterie confessit be Archebald ; and heirfor pronuncis, and,
wyth the avys and consall of the ministerie, decernis the said
Archebald ane adulterar ; and tharfor accordyng to the law of
God the sayd Gelis Scryngeour seperated and divorciat fra hym,
wyth liberte to hyr in the Lord to mare ony other man,
according to the law of God ; and the said Archebald be
supplicacion to be committed in the handis of his magistrat
quhom to he is subject, vidz., the hallie of Abyrnethe. And
Peter Dundas is becumin caucion for Archebald his father,
that he sall compeir befoyr the said ballie and underly civil
correccione for the foyrsaidis crimis, according to ordor
resavit.

Die xxj Januarii, anno quo supra.

Processus Kay [contra Duncan.]

The quhilk day, Janat Kay, induellar in Sanctandrois, in
presens of Ihon Duncan hyr mareit husband and Bege Mychell,
allegis that the saydis Ihon and Bege hes committit the fylthy
crym of adulterie, in jonyng of thar bodeis be carnal copulacion
and procreacion of ane barn ; and tharfor desyris hyr to be

---

[1] Omitted.

divorciat and seperated fra the said Jhon, and set at liberte
according to the law of God.   Quhilk adulteri being manefest,
the woman wyth child, and be tham both confessit, the Superintendent and ministerie committis the saidis Ihon Duncan
and Bege Mychell in the handis of the ballies present, to be
civile correckit and punist, according to the ordour resavit in
this cite; and statutis to the parteis Wednisday nixt to cum,
to compeyr and heyr pronuncit, or reconsyl in the myd tym.

Die xxviij Januarii anno Domini 1561.

The quhilk daye, in the accione and caws of divorce *Sentencia*
intentat be Janat Kaye aganis Johan Duncan for fylthy *divorcii inter Kaye et*
adulterie be hym committit wyth Bege Mychell, as desyr of *Duncan.*
this term set to pronunce in the sayd caws, the ministerie,
seing na persuasion can mak reconsiliacion and fyndyng the
crym notor and confessit, pronuncis and decernis Johan Duncan
ane adulterar, and Janat Kay divorcit, seperated fra hym, and
at liberte to mare in the Lord, according to the law of God.
Pronuncit in presens of parteis.

Die xxj mensis Januarii, anno quo supra.

The quhilk daye, Johane Zong cordinar delated as suspect Inhibicion of
of adultery wyth Janat Thomson spows of Wiliam Gylcrist, Jhon Zong fra Thomson.
and accused tharof, he denyis and offerris hym to purge hym
of the sam be his ayth; and, becaws na perfyt probacion can
be had, his ayth takyn, and examinat be his deposicion, he
purgis hym of all carnall dayl wyth Janat at ony tym.   And
for evadyng of mayr sclander in tym cuming, and that na
occasion of suspicion be gevyn to hyr husband, John Zong is
diffendit and inhibit and perpetuale dischergit to cum in the
hows of Wyliam Gylcrist, or in ony other suspect place wyth
the sayd Janat, under payn of excommunicacione and committing of hym in the handis of the temporall magistratis to
[be][1] punist as an adulterar: to the quhilk the sayd Ihon
assentit.

---

[1] Omitted.

Die xj Februarii anno Domini quo supra.

Contractus inter Anderson et Syme. The quhilk daye, Robert Anderson and Effe Syme, servandis to Johan Bisset in the Grange besyd Sanctandrois, being delatit and accused for fornicacion committit betuix thame, manifestit be procreacione of ane barne betuix thaim, and be thame both confessed, thai ar aggreit to contenew in service for certan yearis, and, as God sall send to tham prosperows succes in the myd tym, to solemnizat mariaige. And Robert confessis hym dettor of the law of God to marye and tak to hys wyff the sayd Effe, becaws he hes deflored hyr virginite; and oblesis hym sa to do in deid, provydit that gyf sche gevis hyr bodye to ony other in the myd tym Robert to be fre. And bayth the saidis personis to concur, upon thar equall expensis, to the fostering of thar barne in the myd tym foyrsaid. And also thai ar decernit to mak public satisfaccion this nixt Sundaye in the essemble.

Die xj Februarii, anno Domini 1561.

AccusacioBowse adulter. The quhilk daye, Wyliam Bowsie in Crayll delated to the Superintendent for adultery committed be hym wyth Besse Lumisden, and disobeying of the ministerie of Crayll quhen he wes chergit to comper befoyr thaim and underly disciplyn tharfor; and now summond be the Superintendentis letteres to compeyr and ansuer tharupon, befoyr hym and the ministerie of Sanctandrois; and comperand, the delacion red in his presens and he tharof accused, he requestis for ane schort delaye to ansuer. And at his desyr, Setterday is assignit to hym to compeyr befoyr nuyn in the Superintendentis chalmer, befoyr the Superintendent and minister, thar to confes, or resave ane term assignit to hym to compeyr and heyr and se proceid aganis hym.

Die quarto Marcii anno quo supra.

Decretum contra Wm. Bowsie adulterum. The quhilk daye, anent the caws of delacion gevyn in be the ministerie of Crayll aganis Wyliam Bowsie, tweching the adulterie committed be the said Wilzam wyth Besse Lumisden and his inobedience don to the said ministere, and delaye gevyn to hym to ansuer to the accusacion tharof layd agans hym, as in the act xj Februarii last bypast, the Superintendent and minister in trying of his caws foyrsayd wyth hym, thai have resavit plane confession of the sam be his awyn mowth, and therfor it is decernit be the Superintendent, wyth the avyis of the holl ministerie, that the sayd Wylliam Bowse be committit be supplicacion to the minister, eldaris and ballies of Crayll, to be civile corrected and punisched as ane adulterar be the saydis ballies, according to the law of God, or at the lest according to the ordor resavit and usid wythin this realm in reformit burrowis; wyth certificacion to the saidis ballies, gyf thai neclect thar execucion, it salbe complanit of thar parcialite[1] and slewth to the suprem authorite. *Expedita est supplicacio.*

Die xviij mensis Marcii anno quo supra.

The quhilk daye, compiris Thomas Swyntoun and producis ane libellat summondis, tharin summond Margret Robertson to heyr and se hyr decernit to procead to solemnizacion of mariaige wyth the sayd Thomas, becaws of promys mayd betuix tham in presens of the reader of Forgondyne and famos[2] wytnes, and bannis proclamit betuix tham be the sayd reader at both thar commandis, na impediment schawyn nor knawyn to stop, as at mayr lenth is contenit in the said summondis, red in presens of Margret, comperand be virteu of the sayd summondis, and be hyr denyed as is libellat. The Superintendent statutis to the said Thomas Wednisdaye nixt to cum, to preve the punctis of his summondis. Parteis heyrto warnit *apud acta.* *Processus inter Swyntoun et Robertson.*

Die xxv^{to} mensis Marcii, anno Domini 1562.

The quhilk daye, as in term assignit to Thomas Swyntoun to preve the punctis of his summondis denyied be Margret Robertson, comperis Thomas and producis ane summondis execut and indorsat upon Alexander Irland, Archebald Duncan, Wyliam Rollok and Paul Quhit. Thai called and nocht comperand ar notit *contumaces.* The Superintendent decernis ane other summondis upon the saydis wytnes and parte defender, *Swyntoun, Robertson.*

---

[1] See p. 107, n. 2; p. 111, n. [2] *Famor* in MS.

and assignis Wednisday nixt to cum to do deligence be execucion of the sayd summondis.

Die primo mensis Aprilis, anno Domini quo supra.

*Produccio
testium per
Swyntoun.*

The quhilk daye, as in term assignit to Thomas Swyntoun
to do deligence for his wytnes, specifyed in the act Wednisday
last wes, in the caws moved be hym aganis Margret Robertson,
comperis Thomas and for desyr of term producis the summondis
execut upon Wyliam Rollok, Archibald Duncan, comperand,
quhilkis ar sworn and to examinacion admittit in presens of
Margret. And Alexander Irland summond and knawyn seik,
and for expidicion of the caws examinat be Mr. Ihon Row
minister of Perth,[1] his deposicion is producit in presens of
Margret and admittit. And Thomas renuncis all farther probacion of wytnes, and producis ane testimoniall[2] of the reader of
Forgondyne of proclamacion of bannis betuix hym and Margret.
The Superintendent statutis Wednisdaye nixt to cum to pronunce. Parteis heirto summond *apud acta.*

Die vigesimo mensis Maii, anno quo supra.

Decretum
Swynton.

The quhilk daye, comperis Thomas Swyntoun and producis
ane summondis of the Superintendentis deulie execut and indorsat, tharin summond Margret Robertson to this daye, to
compeyr and use hyr defensis, gyf sche ony had, to stop the
solemnizacion of mariaige betuix the sayd Thomas and hyr ;

---

[1] The leading events of Row's life are widely known. Born at Row, near
Stirling, about 1526, and educated at St. Leonard's College, he became agent
for the Scotch clergy at Rome, and was appointed Papal nuncio to repress the
Reformation in his native country, but, having been converted, proved a ' corbie·
messenger.' After preaching for some time at Kennoway, he was appointed to
Perth, where he was the first to teach Hebrew in Scotland. By his learning,
moderation, and ability, he rendered valuable services to the Church. At first
he opposed Andrew Melville's views on Episcopacy, but, forced ' by strength of
reasone and light holden out from Scripture,' confessed his error, and afterwards
'preached doun Prelacie all his dayes.' He died on the 16th of October 1580.
Five of his sons were ministers, and one of them wrote the *History of the Kirk of
Scotland*, which has been printed both for the Maitland Club and the Wodrow
Society (Scott's *Lives of the Reformers*, 1817, pp. 156-197 ; M'Crie's *Knox*,
note PP ; Row's *History*, Wod. Soc., pp. 415, 447-457).

[2] *Testioall* in MS., the mark of contraction being omitted.

wyth certificacion gyf sche comperit nocht or comperit and used
na lawful defensis, the Superintendent wald procead and pronunce in the principall caws. Sche called and nocht comperand,
the Superintendent and ministerie, avysit wyth the summondis
and punctis tharof, ansuer of Margret, probacionis of Thomas,
and al deducit and producit in the sayd caus, findis the promys
of mariaig betuïx the saidis Thomas Swyntoun and Margret
Robertson lawfulle mayd and sa provyn, thar bannis proclamit
and na impediment mayd nor schawyn; and tharfor decernis
the saydis Thomas and Marion [1] to be oblest be lawfull promys
to mare, and tharfor to procead to the solemnizacion tharof,
and to end and perfit the sam wythin xxx^{ti} dayes nixt heirefter,
under pane of excommunicacion to be execut upon the party
contravenand.

Die tercio Junii, anno Domini quo supra.

The quhilk daye, the Superintendent, in takyng cognicione *Decretum inter*
anent the clame of mariaig proponit in his visitacion be Mar- *Andream*
Brown et
gret Steynson wyth Andro Brown parrochinaris in Largo, the *Margretam*
Steynson in
parteis foyrsaidis summond to this daye and comperand, it is *Largo.*
fundyn [be hym],[2] be confession of parteis, that Margret haldyn
for ane virgyn undeflored resident in hyr fatheris hows, [*Thomas*
—deleted] Andro com thar and persewit and tyistit hyr to
grant and consent to his lust; and his persut and tyistyng sche
refused otherwayis to consent, except he wald mak hyr ane
honest woman; and at [*Thomas*—deleted] Andro ansuerit
tharto saying, Is nocht my fatheris sone gud anewch for your
fatheris dochter? and in that instant and pronunciacion of thir
wordis thai jonyt thar handis togethyr, and consequentle thar
bodeis. And [*Thomas*—deleted] Andro, demandit, knawis nor
allegis na thing contrar bot Margret wes ane virgyn at thar
fyrst melling togethyr, never suspect nor knawyn to have man
befoyr hym. The Superintendent, wyth the avys of the ministerie, decernis the said Andro to solemnizat mariage wyth
Margret, wythin xl dayes nixt heirefter, according to the law
of God and hyr clame, under pane of excommunicacione. And

---

[1] *Sic.*   [2] Omitted.

K

as concernyng the allegacion and confession maid be Andro, of carnall dayll had be hym wyth Margret Alan, fyndis the sam ane manifest transgression of the law of God ; and heirfor committis hym to be civile punist, be gentyllmen and eldaris of the parrochyn of Largo. Pronuncit in presens of parteis.

Contractus matrimonii inter Car et Sanderis in Balmerinaucht.

  The quhilk daye, Alexander Car,[1] sumtym called Schyr Alexander Car, and Madd[e] Sanderis, ald fornicatoris, huyrmongaris rather, delated to the Superintendent, summond, comperand and accused, confessis thar gyltines, ar desyrus and contentit to contract and solemnizat mariaige, for avoyding of sclander, mutuall societie and help of ather toward other, and weyll of thar barnis procreat betuix tham. In respect of the quhilk, the Superintendent ordenis tham to compeyr in the essemble of Balmerinaucht parroche kyrk, this nixt Sunday the xiiij of Junii instant, and thar confes thar ald lang transgression and offencis, ask God mercy and the congregacion forgyfnes, and to solemnizat thar mariaige wythin xl dayes nixt heirefter, under pan of excommunicacion.

Die xij mensis Augusti anno Domini 1562.

Decretum Lindesay et Schewes in Byirhillis.

  The quhilk daye, anent the desyr proponit be Thomas Lindesay and Cristen Schewes, in Byirhillis, of baptysing of thar barne, and offence laid to thar cherge in abusing the ordor of the kyrk, to wyt, that efter thai had desyrit thar bannis to have beyn proclamit in this kyrk being membris tharof, and the sam refusit to tham becaus the sayd Cristen wes knawyn to have beyn mareit with ane [*blank*] Lyell, quhais deces wes nocht certan nor knawyn, and albeid sche allegit hyr divorcet fra hym be ordor[2] used in the kyrk Papisticall and for lawfull caws, the sammyn standing undiscussed thai past both to Edinburgh, fenyeit tham to be duellaris thar, and be sinister informacion procurit thar bannis to be proclamit and thar mariage solemnizat thair ; the saydis personis, comperand for satisfaccion of the sayd dowt of divorciment, exhibitis ane proces of divorce

---

[1] Sir Alexander Car, notary, witnesses an obligation at the ' Abbay of Balmorynach' in 1555 (*Liber Sancte Marie de Balmorinach*, Abbot. Club, p. 68).
[2] *Ordo* in MS.

led befoyr Mr. Wyliam Cranstoun, sumtym Officiall of Sanct Androis, at the instance of Cristein aganis the sayd [*blank*] Lyell; quhilk seyn and considerit, it is fundyn the said proces ordorlie led accordyng to law and practyk of Papistri[e] and ane laufull caus of impotencie *ex parte viri* confessed and provyn, and the sentence subscrivit be the sayd officiall. In respect of the quhilk, thai ar decernit for brekyn of ordor to compeyr, upon this nixt Sundaye, in the public essemble of the congregacion, and duryng the tym of prayeris and prechyn syt upon the penitent stuyll; and tharefter schaw public signis of repentance in confessing of thar faltis, aske God mercy and the congregacion forgyfnes one thar kneis; and at efternuyn present thar barne to be baptised.

Die primo mensis Julii, anno Domini 1562.

The quhilk daye, the ministerye, at desyr of Eufame Colt, *Decretum Colt.* decernis ane edict in dew forme to be direct to the minister or reader of Sanct Androis, to summond all havand or pretending interes to compeir befoyr tham, upon Wednisday nixt to cum, in thar session; to heyr and se the said Eufame provyn and decernit laufull begottyn in the band of matrimony, betuix umquhill Jhone Colt and Cristan Kyrk his lawfull spows, thar matrimonye standyng undesolvit betuix thame, quhill the daye of deces of the said umquhill Jhon; and testimoniales tharupon to be gevyn for clearyng of all dowtis tharof in tym cuming.

Die viij mensis Julii, anno quo supra.

The quhilk daye, comperis Eufame Colt and producis ane *Decretum literaru' testimonialium Colt.* edict, under the sayll of the ministerie, laufulle execut and deuly indorsat, tharin summond all and syndry havand or pretending to have interes, to heyr and se the said Eufam provyn and decernit laufull begottyn in the band of matrimony, betuix umquhill Ihon Colt and Cristen Kyrk his lawfull spows, thar matrimonye standing undesolvit betuix thame quhill the day of deces of the said umquhill Jhon, and testimoniales tharupon to be gevyn, &c. Efter produccion of the quhilk, all havand or pretending to have interes being callit and nane comperand,

Eufam in pane of[1] thar contumacite producis certane famos
and unsuspect wytnes; quhilkis being resavit, sworn, admittit,
and instantle examinat, and the intent of Eufame relevantle
and sufficientlye provyn, the ministrie decernis thar testimoniall[2]
tharupon in forme under thar sayll.

Die quinto Augusti, anno Domini 1562.

Peticio Buge
contra Jak.

The quhilk daye, Peter Jak summond be the Superintendentis
letteres at the instance of Besse Budge and comperand, sche
apud acta clamis mariaige of Peter be ressone of promys maid
betuix tham twa privatlie, and also be ressone Peter deflored
hyr virginite. The promys denyed be Peter and referred to
his ayth; and he, sworne and examinat, purgis hym. And as
concernyng the defloryng of hyr virginite, he gaynsayis nocht
that, nor allegis defence lawful to absolve hym fra that part of
hyr clame. And being understand to the Superintendent that
the mother of Besse Budge is levand, he ordenis hyr to consult
wyth hyr mother in this mater betuixt this and Wedinsday
nixt to cum, quhilk daye he statutis to pronunce in this caws
in presens of parteis heirto summond *apud acta*.

Die xij mensis Augusti, anno Domini 1562.

Budge *contra*
Jak.

The quhilk daye, as in term assignit be the Superintendent
to pronunce in the clame of mariaig betuix Besse Budge and
Peter Jak, Peter called and nocht comperand, the Superintendent decernis ane summondis[3] to Besse to summond Peter to
compeir this day xv dayes to heir pronuncit.

Die xvj Septembris anno quo supra.

Inhibicio Jak.

The quhilk daye, Peter Jak summond be the Superintendentis letteres, at the instance of Besse Budge, to heir pronuncit
in the clame of mariaige persewit be hyr, he comperand, the
caws is contenowit to Wednisdaye nixt to cum in presens of
parteis heirto summond. The Superintendent inhibitis and
chergis the said Peter that he procead nocht in solemnizacion

---

[1] *Or* in MS. [2] *Testioall* in MS. [3] *Summodis* in MS.

of mariaige wyth ony other parte oneto the finall end of this caws; wyth intimacion gyf he do in the contrar, he salbe haldyn and reput for ane manifest contempnar of the kyrk, and tharfor be punisched according to disciplyn, wyth invocacion of the support [1] of the temporall magistrat for his punischment.

Die xx° mensis Januarii, anno Domini quo supra.

The quhilk daye, Peter Jak being summond be the Superin- Inhibicoon tendentis letteres, at the instance of [*Peter Jak*—deleted] Besse of Jak. Budge, to heir procead in the caus of mariage persewit be Besse and depending betuix tham, according to the desyr of the last act: the said Peter comperand, he allegis and confessis hymself to have solemnizat mariaige sen the last act wyth ane other woman. Quharfor, the Superintendent [2] understanding the said pretendit mariaig to be unlawfull, and don in prejudice of the said Besse Budge persewar, in als contrary to his inhibicion, chergis the said Peter that he absteyn fra all cumpany and cohabitacion wyth the woman quhilk he allegis hym to have mareit, quhill farther tryall be had in the mater and avys of the Lordis of the Prevy Consayll be socht and had, under payn of excommunicacion; wyth certificacion gyf he obey nocht, his contempsion salbe declared to the Quenis Maiesty and hyr Consayll be ane complaynt.

Die secundo Septembris, anno quo supra.

The quhilk daye, Andro Olephant and Issobell Mortoun Olephant, delated and accused for kepyn cumpany in bed and burd Mortoun. unmareit, to the offence of God and sclander of the congregacione. The saidis Andro confessis thar cumpany kepyn as said is, and allegis thai ar contracked and mayd promys of mariag [3] and ar wylling to solemnizat thar mariaige; and thai also in presens of the holl ministerie professis the religion and doctrin tawcht in this kyrk and thaimselfis membris of this congregacion, and submittis tham to disciplyn. The ministerie ordenis tham to compeir Sunday cum awcht dayes in the

---

[1] *Suppt* in MS.   [2] *Superindent* in MS.   [3] *Mariauag* in MS.

essemble, to mak public satisfaccion as use is, and tharefter
thar bannis to be proclamit, and wythin xxj dayes thai to
solemnizat thar mariage : to the quhilk thae assent.

Die xxvj Augusti, anno·Domini 1562.

Philp *contra* Thomson.

The quhilk daye, Anne Thomson delated and accused of
adultery, being mareit wyff to Archebald Philp hes gevyn hyr
body to Andro Sellar and wyth barne to hym, and hes seperated
hyrself fra societie of hyr said ˙husband be the space of sex
yearis and mayr.   Anne confessis hyr wyth barne to Andro
Sellar, and at sche wes mareit wyth Archebald Philp and hes
beyn fra hym mayr nor sex yearis, and allegis sche wes mareit
wyth hym aganis hyr wyll.   And now comperis Archebald
Philp, and desyris hym to be divorciat and mayd fre fra Anne
Thomson, becaus of adulterie committed and granted be hyr
wyth Andro Sellar to quhom sche is wyth barne.   The
Superintendent ordenis Andro Sellar to be called and his part
to be hard, and contenewis the desyr proponit be Archebald
Philp aganis Anne quhill[1] new warnyng.

Die xx° Januarii, anno Domini m°v°lxij.

Decretum divorcii Philp.

The quhilk daye, the caus of divorce proponit be Archebald
Philp aganis Anne Thomson his spows, for adultery committit
be hyr wyth Andro Sellar, being suscitat at desyr of Archebald
in presens of Anne, accordyng to the desyr of the last act : the
Superintendent, avysed wyth the peticion of Archebald and
confession of Anne Thomson and Andro Sellar, fyndis the sayd .
Archebald and Anne to have beyn mareit and that Anne hes
committit adulterie ; and heyrfor decernis hyr ane adultrix,
and the sayd Archebald to be seperated and divorciat fra hyr,
and liberte to Archebald to mary ony other lawfull wyf
according to the law of God ; and committis the sayd Anne be
supplicacion to the magistratis of this cite, to be punest
accordyng to ordor resavit and used in the same.

---

[1] *Quhilk* in MS.

Processus divorcii inter Joannem Gyb in Strathor et Margretam Hillok.

Upone the xxij daye of Aprill, the year of God m°v°lxij *Peticio Hyllok contra Gyb.* yearis, the quhilk daye, Jhone Gyb in Wester Strathor convenit befoyr the Superintendent and ministery of Sanctandrois, at the instance of Margret Hillok his spows. Margret proponis ane accion of divorce agains hym, and allegis that sche hes beyn his mareit wyf and accumpaneid wyth hyme in burd and bed be the space of twa yearis last bypast, and maist part tharof obeyand hym as becam hyr of dewety to obey hyr husband. [She claimed divorce on the ground that he was 'impotent of natur'; and John, 'efter divers and mony vayn assonyeis,[1] at lenth confessis the same.'] The Superintendent, wyth avys of the ministerie, avysed wyth the allegacion of the parte persewar and confession of Ihon, fearyng desayt to be in the mater, ordenis the saidis Ihon and Margret to coheir and keip cumpany together, and every ane to trayt other, as becummis man and wyff jonit in matrimony, for the space of thre quarteris of ane year at the lest, wyth certificacione to tham that [quha][2] falyeis heirin sall underly disciplyn of the kyrk wyth rigor. [On the 10th of March 1562, Jhon Gyb *Hyllok contra Gyb.* again compeared, having been 'summond be the Superintendentis letteres, at the instance of Margret Hillok, to heyr proceid in the caws of divorce allegit be hyr.' After hearing John's confession and answers concerning 'ane called Dauidson, quhilk womane sum tym dwelt in Strathor,' and also regarding Margret Hyllok, 'the Superintendent wyth avyis of his consayll ordenis the saydis Jhon Gyb and Margret to coheir and keip mutuall cohabitacione, and ether of tham to treit other in bed and burd as becummis lawfull husband and wyf, aye and quhill ane of thame allege and prev ane lawfull caws quhy sa suld nocht be, under pane of excommunicacion, wyth incalling of the temporall power for punischyng of the disobedient: and at thar be na farther delay fund in ony of [the][3] parties, bot wythin xv dayes thai enter and contenew in mutuall cohabitacion.' From the next entry, which is dated 21st April 1563, *Hyllok contra Gyb.*

---

[1] Excuses.   [2] Omitted.   [3] Omitted.

it appears that there was also 'ane other and new charge gevyn
to tham be the Superintendent to conveyn and keip cumpany
as mareit man and wyff in the hows of James Wemys in Cardon,
quhai had promyst reset and treating to tham for certain tym
appoynted to tham be the Superintendent, be his mowth
spekyng to tham and nocht obeyit.' Both parties had been
summoned to appear this day, the 21st of April, but John
failed to compear; and therefore, 'the Superintendent ordenis
ane summondis to be direct to summond both the saydis parteis
to this daye xv dayes; and in the myd tyme ordenis the said
Margret, at the sycht and consayll of Thomas Scot of Abbotis-
hall,[1] to compeyr in sic hows as he sall appoynt to hyr, and thar
keip cumpany in bed and burd wyth the said Jhon for the
space of sex dayis and nychtis at the lest.' To this Margret
consents. 'And the said Thomas Scot acceptis upon hym the
cherge to put the premissis in execucione concernyng his part
at request of the Superintendent. And in cace ony of the
parteis be fundyn inobedient to the place and appoyntment of
the said Thomas, the sam to be excommunicat as ane contempnar of the kyrk and ordinance tharof, providit that Ibon
be adverteist and chergit heyrto be the[2] sayd Thomas Scot,

Hyllok *contra* quhilk he promittis to do.' On the 19th of May 1563, John
Gyb.
and Margret both compeared 'at the cherge and appoyntment of the said Thomas: thai exhibit to the Superintendent
ane myssyve direct to hym fra the sayd Thomas Scot, berand

---

[1] Thomas Scott, of the Balwearie family, was one of the commissioners sent by
the congregation from Perth to Chatelherault and D'Oysel at Auchterarder, in
May 1559, 'to heir quhat appointment the Quene wald offer' (Laing's *Knox*,
i. 341); and was one of those who, in the following January, gave such valiant
and unwearied assistance to Kirkcaldy of Grange against the French (*Ibid.* vi.
106). After the establishment of the Reformation he took part in several
General Assemblies (*Booke of the Universall Kirk*, Ban. Club, i. 38, 50, 203,
271). In September 1565 he is mentioned as 'Baillie of the regalitie of Pettinweme;' and next March his name occurs in the long list of persons charged to
appear before the Privy Council as delated of Riccio's slaughter (*Register of Privy
Council*, i. 368, 437). When Knox left Edinburgh for St. Andrews in May 1571,
he went by way of Abbotshall, and seems to have stayed for some time with
Scott (Richard Bannatyne's *Memoriales*, Ban. Club, pp. 119, 174); who is described as of Petgorno as well as of Abbotshall (*Register of Great Seal*, iv. Nos.
2183, 2897). Petgorno had previously belonged to Thomas Scott, the Justice-
Clerk, whose woful death is recorded by Knox (Laing's *Knox*, i. 69, 70).

[2] *The the* in MS.

in effect that the commission be hym acceppit wes put to
execucion, referryng the rest to be reportit be the parteis.'
They were both 'sworne and examinat in thar conscience and *Deposiciones*
be thar athis;' when, among other things, John declared that *Gyb et Hyllok.*
'he of gud mynd and singular favor had toward Margret foyrsayd wyllinglye jonit wyth hyr in mariaige'; but admitted
'that gyf he war partit and mayd quit of hyr, he is myndit to
mare ane other woman.' '*Item*, he confessis that Margret hes
desyrit of hym (being in thar beddis) to be quit and partit fra
hym, and at he suld consent tharto; and confessis that he
mayd hyr ane grant sa to do, and at he wes desyrus to be qwyt
of hyr.' On the 23d of May 1563, 'the Superintendent, in *Deposiciones*
proceding of tryall in the caus of potency of Ihon Gyb, resavit *testium.*
the athis of Andro Gyb,[1] Andro Inglis,[2] and Donis Dorky,[3] in
presens of Jhon Gyb and Margret Hyllok; na objeccion mayd
aganis thame be ony of the parteis, thai war examinat,' and their
depositions duly recorded. On the 23rd of June 1563, ' bayth *Decretum ab-*
the saidis parteis summond to this daye to heir pronunced in *solvatorium sed*
the said caws and Margret comperand, the Superintendent, *non simpliciter.*
avysed wyth the proces and all tharin deduced, fyndis na caus
of impotencye provyn, and tharfor absolvis Ihon Gyb fra the
instance of Margret as it is intentat, and thar mariaige to have
beyn and [to][4] be lawfull, and sa to remane and be haldyn aye
and quhill sum caws be allegit and provyn: and the parteis
to adheyr to other wythin xl dayes[5] nixt heirefter, except in
the myd tym sum caus be yit allegit and provyn quhy thai
suld nocht sa do; quhilk delay of xl dayis is grantit in respect
of this formar proces, contentis tharof, and at the sam hes
dependit so lang.']

Die septimo Julii, anno Domini quo supra.

The quhilk daye, comperis Margret Hyllok and producis *Hyllok contra*
ane letter summondis of the Superintendent, deuly execut and *Gib ex novo*
capite.

---

[1] 'Andro Gyb, indwellar in Strathor, sone and servand to Cristen Dauidson wedo.'

[2] 'Andro Inglis, mareit man, tenent to the Lard of Balmowto in Strarndeye.'

[3] 'Donis Dorkye, servand woman to Cristen Dauidson wedo in Strathor.'

[4] Omitted.

[5] *And the parteis wythin xl dayes to adheyr to other wythin xl dayes* in MS.

indorsat, tharin summond Ihon Gyb, at hyr instance, to compeyr befoyr the Superintendent and ministery of Sanctandrois,
to heyr and se the sayd Margret allege and prev ane sufficient
caws quhy sche suld nocht adheyr to the sayd Ihon Gyb as to
hyr lawfull spows ; bot sche to be divorciat seperated and
dividit fra hym, for adultery committed and be hym confessed
with Donis Dorke, and liberte to the sayd Margret grantit to
mare wyth ony other lawfull husband according to the law of
God ; wyth intimacion that quhidder he compeyr or nocht the
Superintendent wald proceid in the sayd caws according to the
law. Ihon Gyb called and nocht comperand, lawfull tymm
byddyn, Margret, in pane of nocht comperance of Ihon Gyb,
allegis that the said Ihon is and hes beyn at all tymmis impotent to hyr, and also hes confessit hymself ane adulterar in
gevyng of his body to Donis Dorkye, hes cuttit of hymself fra
hyr, and heyrfor sche awcht and suld be devorciat seperated
and dividit fra the sayd Ihon ; and askis and desyris the Superintendent sa to decern aganis the sayd Ihon, and liberte to hyr
to mare wyth ony other lawfull husband according to the law
of God. And for probacion heirof, and fyrst part of the same,
Margret repetis the confession of Ihon Gyb specifyed in the
actis of proces led betuix the sayd Ihon and hyr in this auditorie, the xxij of April *anno* 1562, and xix of Maii *anno* 1563 ;
and for probacion of the adulteri betuix Ihon Gyb and Donis
Dorke, Margret repetis the confession of Jhon Gyb incertit in
his deposicion examinat upon his ayth as in the act the xix of
Maii *anno* 1563, and deposicione of Andro Gyb and Donis
Dorke examinat in the sayd proces the xxiij of Maii year foyrsayd ; and also producis Alexander Gyb and Donis Dorke
wytnes summond, quhilkis ar resavit sworn and admittit, in ·
payn of nocht comperance of Ihon Gyb. The Superintendent
statutis *literatorie* to pronunce, and that in respect that this
accion hes beyn depending befoyr hym be the space of other
half year and befoyr the act and ordinance of this last Parliament.[1] [Here follows the evidence of ' Alexander Gyb brother

Deposiciones testium.

---

[1] ' Forsamekill as the abominabill and filthy vice and cryme of adulterie hes
bene perniciouslie and wickitlie usit within this Realme in tymes bygane, . . .
It is statute and ordanit, be the Quenis Majestie and the Estatis in Parliament,
That all notoure and manifest committaris of adulterie, in ony tyme tocum efter

german to Ihon Gyb'; and also the statement that the deposition of 'Donis Dorky, servand to Cristen Dauidson, wedo in Wester Strathor,' 'is conforme to hyr fyrst deposicion gevyn the xxiij of Maii last wes.']

Die xxj mensis Julii, anno Domini 1563.

The quhilk daye, Jhon Gyb and Margret Hyllok summond Hillok *contra* be the Superintendentis letteres to this daye to heyr pronuncit Gyb. in the caus of divorce proponit be Margret aganis Ihon, for adultery committ[it] be hym wyth Donis Dorky, according to the desyr set *literatorialie* the vij daye of Julii instant; and bayth comperand, the allegacionis of Margret contenit in the act *septimo Julii instantis* red in presens of Ihon, and he tharupon deligently examinat. [John's deposition is here inserted.] The Superintendent contenewis his pronunsacion in this caus to the xj day of August nixt to cum, in presens of Ihon Gyb and Margret Hyllok heirto summond *apud acta.*

Die xj mensis Augusti, anno Domini 1563.

Wyth incalling of the name of Crist Jesus, Sone of the *Sentencia* eternall God, quhai is the waye the verite and the lyff, Master *divorcii inter.* Jhone Wynram, Superintendent of Fyff, &c., juge in the caus *Gyb et Hyllok* of divorcie movad be Margret Hyllok aganis Jhon Gyb for adultery committit be the said Jhone wyth Donis Dorkye, transgressand the thrid command of the secund tabyll and law of God, quhar it is wryttyn, Thow sal nocht commit adulterye: as at mayr lenth is contenit in the summondis and articlis produced for the part of the sayd Margret, quharupon we have procedit, admitting to bayth the saydis parteis thar just and lawfull defensis according to thar desyris, and being ryplie and maturle avysed wyth the articulis of the sayd Margret, ansuer

the dait heirof [4th of June 1563], salbe punist with all rigour unto the deid, alsweill the woman as the man doar and committar of the samin, efter that dew monitioun be maid to abstene fra the said manifest and notoure cryme ; and for uther adulterie, that the actis and lawis maid thairupone of befoir be put to executioun with all rigour ; and als declaris that this act on na wyse sall prejudge ony partie to persew for divorcement for the crymes of adulterie befoir committit conforme to the law' (*Acts of the Parliaments of Scotland*, ii. 539).

and confession of the sayd Ihon mayd tharto, probacionis and
deposicionis of wytnes, fyndis the intent of the sayd Margret
sufficientlie varefyed; and havyng God onlye befoyr our ees,
and the testimonye of his trew and eternall Word, pronuncis,
decernis, and be this our sentence diffinityve declaris the said
Ihon Gyb to be ane adulterar, and tharby to have cutted of
hymself and to be seperated and dividit and divorciat fra hyr;
and licience and liberte to the said Margret to mary in the
Lord wyth ony other lawfull husband according to the law of
God: committing the said Ibon to the handis and punischiment of the temporall power for the crym. Pronunced in
presens of Margret makand instance, and in pa[ne] of nocht
comperance of Ihon heirto summond, wythin the parro[che
kyr]k[1] and consistory hows of Sanctandrois, upon the xj day
of August, the year of God m⁰ v⁰ lxiij yearis; being present
Crostofer Gudman, minister, Mr. Ihon Dowglas, Rector of the
Universite of Sanctandrois, Masteris William Ramsay, James
Wylke, William Cok, eldaris, &c.

In the sessione of the Superintendent and ministerie
of Sanctandrois, haldyn wythin the parreis kyrk of
the said cite, upone Wedinsday the xxiij of Junii the
year of God 1563.

Processus
Forbes de Reres.

The quhilk daye, Jhone Forbes, apperand of Reres,[2]
delated for nocht adheryng to Barbara Sandelandis his spows
be the kyrk of Lucris, and being summond be the Superintendentis letteres to compeir and heir hymself decernit to adheir to
the said Barbara his spows, as becummis the husband to his

---

[1] Blotted.

[2] Reres, which is in the parish of Kilconquhar, certainly belonged to the
Earls of Fife, and is believed by some to have been the residence of the good
Macduff (Wood's *East Neuk of Fife*, 1887, p. 12). Lord Hailes explains the
remarkable case concerning the ownership of Reres, by which the peace was
ruptured between Edward and Baliol (*Annals of Scotland*, 1776, pp. 225-231).
On the 21st of February 1550-1, the Queen granted to John Forbes, son and
apparent heir of Arthur Forbes, the lands and baronies of Reres and Leuchars
Forbes, which Arthur had resigned, reserving a free tenement to himself and a
reasonable third to Margaret Betoun, his spouse, when required (*Register of the
Great Seal*, iv. No. 584).

wyff, in treatyng hyr accordyng to the law of God and ordinance
of the Superintendent gevyn to hym of befoyr in this caws, and
to contenew tharin or ellis to schaw ane ressonabyll caws quhy
he suld nocht sa do, as at lenth is contenit in the saidis letteres
deuly execut indorsat and reproduced : comperis Ihone, quhai,
for his defence and to stop his adherance, proponis and allegis
adultery committit be the said Barbara wyth Wyliam Huntar
of Balcarros,[1] manifestit be procreacion of ane child betuix
thame, borne in the Westhows[2] in the moneeth of [blank], in
this instant year of sexty thre ; quhilk adultre the saydis Barbara and Wyliam hes confessed divers tymmis befoyr famos
wytnes, quhilk Ihon offeris hym to prev and desyris hym
admittit tharto ; quhilk being provyn he awcht nocht to be
compelled to adheir to the said Barbara bot suld be absolvd
tharfra.   The Superintendent, understanding the excepcione
ressonabyll to be admittit to probacione, statutis to Ihone
Wedinsday nixt to cum to prev his allegacione ; and decernis
hym letteres to summond his wytnes, and Barbara, to heyr the
sammyn resavit and admittit or to schaw caws to stop the same.

Die ultimo Junii, anno Domini m°v°lxiij.

The quhilk daye, as in term assignit to Jhon Forbes apper- [Certan wytnes examinat.]
and of Reres to preve his allegacione and excepcion of adultery
proponit to stop his adherance to Barbara Sandelandis his
spows, and to summond Barb[ara] to heyr his probacionis
resavit and admittit or to schaw caus to stop the same, comperis Ihon and producis ane summondis execut and indorsat
upone Barbara and certan wytnes according to the desyr foyrsayd.   The said Barbara called and nocht comperand, in payn
of hyr nocht comperance Ihon producis Dauid Ramsaye of

---

[1] On the 12th of November 1549, the Queen granted to William Huntar, son
and heir-apparent of David Huntar, and to Grissil Trail, his wife, the lands of
Balcarrowis, which the said David Huntar and his wife, Margaret Wod, had
resigned, reserving a free tenement for their lifetimes (*Register of the Great Seal*,
iv. No. 392).

[2] On the 21st of February 1550-1, the Queen granted to Arthur Forbes of
Reres and Margaret Betoun, his spouse, and John Forbes, his son and heir-
apparent, the lands of Westhous in the barony of Leuchars, which Arthur personally resigned (*Ibid.* No. 585).

Brakmonth, Ihon Vr minister of Lucris, Ihon Gawy, Besse
Barclay, Eufaim Ferre, Mirabell Pont, Janat Pont, Michell
Balfowr of Burle, Mr. James Lermonth, Ihon Nesche, Nycholl
Spittell: quhilkis ar sworne admittit and instantle examinat.
And Mr. Robert Hammyltoun, George Lewyngstoun, Robert
Dauidson, Andro Wod apperand of Largo, Mr. Alexander
Wod, summond and nocht comperand ar notit *contumaces*, and
literatorie statut to Ihon to do deligence for thame.

Die xiiij^{to} mensis Julii anno quo supra.

[Other wytnes examinat.]

The quhilk daye, as in term statut *literatorie* to Ihon Forbes
apperand of Reres to do diligence for Mr. Robert Hammyltoun,
George Lewyngstoun, Robert Dauidson, Andro Wod apperand
of Lairgo, and Mr. Alexander Wod, wytn[es], to prev his excepcion of adultery proponit to stop his adherance to Barbara
Sandelandis, comperis Jhon and producis ane summondis of the
Superintendentis execut and indorsat, tharin summond the
saydis wytnes and Barbara Sandelandis to heyr and se thaim
resavit sworne and admittit. And he producis Mr. Robert
Hammyltoun, George Lewyngstoun, and Robert Dauidson,
quhilkis ar [1] resavet sworne and admittit and instantle examinat,
in pane of nocht comperance of Barbara, and *literatorie* assignit
to the sayd Ihon to do farther deligence for Andro Wod and
Mr. Alexander Wod.

Die xv^{to} Septembris anno Domini quo supra.

[New wytnes to be summond.]

The quhilk daye, comperis Mr. Wyliam Skeyn, procurator
and in name of Ihon Forbes apperand of Reres, and mackis
fayth *in animam constituentis*, according to the constitucione
and power grantit to hym, in presens of the Superintendent,
be the sayd Ibon, that certane new wytnes, necessar to prev the
excepcione of adultery proponit be the sayd Ihone to stop his
adherance, ar new cumin to his knawlege; and heirfor desyris
ane summondis to summond Gressell Trayll, Janat Ihonstown,
Catren Layng, Besse Lawson, Robirt Wobstar, wytnes, and
Barbara Sandelandis to heyr and se thame resavit sworne and

---

[1] *As* in MS.

admittit or to schaw ressonabyll caws quhy sa suld nocht be, accordyng to the common styill and practik of this realm. Quhilk desyr being thocht ressonabyll, the Superintendent grantis letteres according to the desyr.

Die penultimo Septembris anno prescripto.

The quhilk daye, Gressell Trayll, Janat Ihonstoun, Catren [New wytnes *contumaces.*] Layng, Besse Lawson, and Robert Wobstar, wytnes new cumin to knawlege of Ihon Forbes of Reres, necessar to prev his excepcion of adultery proponit to stop his adherance to Barbara Sandelandis, and the sayd Barbara[1] provyn lawfully summond to this daye, thai called and nocht comperand ar notit *contumaces*, and *literatorie* statut to the sayd Ihon to [do][2] deligence farther for the saydis wytnes.

Die xiij Octobris anno Domini m°v°lxiij.

The quhilk daye, as in term assignit *literatorie*[3] to Ihon [New wytnes examinat.] Forbes apperand of Reres to do deligence for his wytnes to preve his excepcion of adultery proponit to stop his adherence to Barbara Sandelandis, comperis Ihon and producis our Souerain Ladeis letteres be deliverance of the Lordis deuly execut and indorsat, tharin sumond Gressell Trayll, Janat Ihonstoun, Catreyn Layng, Besse Lawson, Robert Wobstar; [quhilkis, being][2] called and comperand, ar resavit sworne admittit and examinat, in pane of nocht comperance of Barbara Sandelandis heyrto summond; and Mr. Alexander Wod and Andro Wod apperand of Largo, also summond be our Souarane Ladis letteres and nocht comperand, ar notit *contumaces*. The letteres redeliverit for probacion tharof, and *literatorie* assignit to the sayd Ihon to do farther deligence for the saydis Andro and Mr. Alexander Wod.

Die primo mensis Decembris anno quo supra.

The quhilk daye, comperis Ihon Forbes apperand of Reres [Andro Wod examinat.] as in term statut to hym *literatorie* to do deligence for Andro Wod apperand of Largo and Mr. Alexander Wod; and pro-

---

[1] *Bara* in MS.   [2] Omitted.   [3] *Literatoree* in MS.

ducis the sayd Andro Wod, quhai is resavit sworne and examinat, in pan of nocht comperance of Barbara Sandelandis heyrto summond. And Ihon passis fra Mr. Alexander Wod, and is contentit wyth his wytnes produced, together wyth ane instrument be hym produced, under not of Thomas Malwll notar publict, of dayt the secund of Julii *anno &c. lxiij.* The Superintendent statutis Wednisdaye nixt to cum to pronunce, in presens of Ihon, and decernis his summondis to summond Barbara tharto.

Followis the desposicionis of the wytnes produced be Ihon Forbas apperand of Reres to prev the adultery of Barbara Sandelandis wyth Wyliam Huntar of Balcarros.

[Deposicionis of wytnes.]

1   Dauid Ramsaye of Brakmonth, wytnes, summond, called, comperand, sworn and examinat upon the excepcion of adultery, proponit be Ihon Forbas apperand of Reres to stop his adheryng to Barbara Sandelandis his spous, committit be hyr wyth Wiliam Huntar of Balcarros, be his ayth and in his conscience deponis and affirmis the excepcione trew. Examinat upone the caws of his knawlege, he ansueris and deponis that at twa syndry tymmis, now laytlie sen Wytsunday last wes, the sayd Barbara Sandelandis, in presens of the said Ihon Forbes and the deponar, confessit hyr to have offendit aganis the said Ihon Forbes hyr husband in committyng of the said adulterye, and sat down one hyr kneis askit hyr husband forgyfnes, lamentyng hyr awyn cace and offence. Examinat upon the generall interrogatoris, he purgis hym, except he confessis he haldis his landis of Brakmonth of the ald Lard of Reres [1] father to the producer.

---

[1] 'Arthure Forbes off Reres' was in Parliament in 1560 (*Acts of Parliament*, ii. 526). In 1552 he was chosen one of the 'amicabill compositoris' on the part of Robert Betoun of Creich, to decide the 'deidlie feid' between him and Lundy of Balgony and Fairny of that Ilk ; and in 1569 he was charged with harbouring Robert Betoun of Westhall, a rebel and fugitive because of 'the cruel and abhominabill murthour and slauchter' of James Ramsay (*Register of Privy Council*, i. 126, 655).

2   Jhone Vr,[1] minister of Goddis Word in Lucris, wytnes, sworne
and examinat in the said excepcion of adultery, be his ayth
deponis and in his desposicione affirmis the excepcione trew.
Examinat upon the caws of his knawlege, he deponis that he,
accumpaneid wyth the ald Layrd of Reres, past to Barbara
Sandelandis, saw the barne quhilk laytle wes borne be hyr, hard
the sayd Barbara confes that hyr barne [wes][2] gottyn betuix
hyr and Wyliam Huntar of Balcarros. Examinat upon the
generall interrogatoris, he purgis hym.

3   Jhone Gawy, domesticall servant to Arthur Forbes of Reres,
of perfyt aige, sworne and examinat upon the foyrsayd excepcion of adultry, deponis in his ayth [and][2] conscience the same
to be trew. *Causam sciencie reddit*, he saw the bern of Barbara be hyr laytle borne, hard hyr confes the same barn gottyn
betuix hyr and Wyliam Huntar of Balcarr[os].   Thar was[3]
present wyth hym, Anie Gyll, servand to the sayd Arthur
Forbes. Examinat upon generall interrogatoris, he purgis hym
of all parcialite.

4   Besse Barclaye, spows of James Wemys in Lucris, sworn
and examinat upon the foyrsayd excepcione of adultery, &c., in
hyr conscience deponis that, laytly wythin ane moneth of tym
bypast, sche hard Barbara Sandelandis sayr gretyng confes ane
man child borne be hyr, and lamentyng that Ihon Forbes culd
never get ane lad wyth hyr; and knawis [na][2] mayr of the
excepcione except common voc and fame beris record of the
same. Examinat upon the generall interrogatoris of law, sche
purgis hyr of all parcialite.

5   Eufame Ferre, spows of Ihon Jnche in Pytlathe, sworn and
examinat upon the foyrsaid excepcion of adultery, in hyr conscience deponis that Barbara Sandelandis was ane lang tym in
Pytlathe quhar the deponar also dwelt for the tym, in quhilk
tym the deponar saw Wyliam Huntar resort thar fyrst at
Lammes. He com and careit Barbara Sandelandis away to
help to baptis his barne as cumar,[4] and Barbara remanit absent

---

[1] John Ur, or Ure, had been a canon of the Augustinian Priory of St. Andrews
before the Reformation ; and, therefore, according to the arrangement of the
Leith Convention of 1572, he was a member of the chapter of the revived Archbishopric of St. Andrews (Calderwood's *History*, iii. 186).

[2] Omitted.   [3] *Thai war* in MS.   [4] God-mother.

that tym awcht dayes, and efter that Wyliam Hunter com twys
or thrys agane to Pytlathe; bot the deponar never suspect
evyll betuix thame quhill the word rays that Barbara had
borne ane barne to Wyliam; quhilk be hyr hard, sche past to
Barbara and reprevit hyr in the Westhous, sayand to hyr, God
gyf sche had knawyn sic foly quhen schei saw Wyliam Huntar
com to hyr to Pytlathe, sche suld have mayd hyr doing knawyn.
To quhilk Barbara mayd hyr ansuer and sayd, Quhar to reprev
me of the thing that is done? I can nocht mend it nor bring
it agane now that is done. Examinat upon the generall interrogatoris of law, sche purgis hyr.

6   Mirabell Pont, relict of Ihon Smyth cottar to the ald Lard
of Reres, in Westhows, wytnes, sworn and examinat upon the
excepcion of adultery, &c., in hyr conscience deponis that sche,
deponar, at command of the ald Lady Reres[1] that same nycht
Barbara Sandelandis wes lychtar of her barne in question, com
to the Westhows and resavit the new borne barne fra the said
Barbara, and had the barne thre olkis in hyr hows; and sche
sperit at Barbara gyf the father wald grant wyth the barn
(menyng Wyliam Huntar bot nocht expremit his nam). And
Barbara ansuerit saying, Ye! fayth wyl he! Sche knawis na
mayr in this mater, except that common voce and fame beris
record that the sayd bern is Wyliam Huntaras of Balcarros;
and purgis hyr of all parcialite.

7   Janat [Jhonstoun—deleted] Pont, spows of Peter Ihonstoun cottar to the Lard of Erlishall in the Westhows, wytnes,
sworn and examinat upon the excepcion of adultery, &c., in hyr
ayth deponis that common voce and fame is sa as the excepcion
beris; and at sche gave sowk to ane bern quhilk wes[2] called
and haldyn for the berne of Berbara Sandelandis.

8   Mychaell Balfowr of Burly,[3] wytnes, sworn and examinat

---

[1] 'That Lady Margaret Reres, one of the Beaton family, so called after her
marriage with Arthur Forbes of Reres, and who was one of Mary Stuart's court
ladies, and the nurse of her son, was at an earlier period one of Bothwell's mis-
tresses, rests entirely upon Buchanan's unreliable statement' (Berry's translation
of Schiern's *Life of Bothwell*, p. 53).

[2] *We* in MS.

[3] On the 25th of June 1553, the Queen confirmed to Michael Balfour of
Burlie, and Cristine Betoun his wife, the Mains of Burlie and Terhill (*Register of
Great Seal*, iv. No. 806). And on the 18th of June 1566, the King and Queen

upon the excepcion of adultery, &c., in his ayth and conscience deponis that he wes present in the Westhows, place of the Lard of Reres, upon the Fryday nixt befoyr Wytsunday last wes, quhar he spak face to face wyth Barbara Sandelandis lying in hyr bed; hard hyr planle confes to hym sche had laytleye borne ane barne, quhilk wes begottyn betuix hyr and Wyliam Huntar of Balcarros; and sche desyrit the deponar to labor for hyr at the handis of hyr husband to remit hyr. Examinat upon the generall interrogatoris, he ansueris that the producer is syster sone to his wyf that deponis, and of the rest he purgis him.

9 M. James Lermonth, Provest of Kyrkhyll,[1] wytnes, sworne and examinated upon the excepcion of adultere, &c., in his conscience and ayth deponis that he knawis na thing of the said excepcion, bot that common voce and fame is that Barbara Sandelandis hes borne ane barne to Wyliam Huntar of Balcarios leytle. The deponar sawe ane barne quhilk wes sayd to hym to be the barne gottyn betuix Wyliam Huntar and Barbara Sandelandis, and knawis na mayr in this mater. He purgis hym of all parcialite.

10 Jhone Nesche, gardiner in Pytlathe, wytnes, sworne and examinat upon the excepcion of adultery, &c., in his conscience deponis that [he][2] knawis nat thing of the excepcion, bot at common voce and fame is that Barb[ara][3] Sandelandis hes leytle borne ane barne to Wyliam Huntar of Balcarrows; and at, abowt Zowll or Candylmes last wes, the deponar saw Wyliam Huntar cum to Pytlathe thre syndry tymmis, and remanit the space of ane howr ilk tym or tharby, and wes wyth Barbara in the hows. Quhidder thai war alane into the hows or nocht, the deponar knawis nocht, for he was in the yard and saw Wiliam enter and pas up in the hows quhar Barbara was. Examinat upon the generall interrogatoris, he purgis hym.

11 Nycholl Spittell,[4] minister of Goddis Word, wytnes, sworne

---

granted to him half the lands of Kynloche, and the heritable office of coronership of Fife, which Parliament confirmed on the 19th of April 1567 (*Ibid.* No. 1736; *Acts of Parliament*, ii. 561). He was an arbiter with Arthur Forbes in 1552; and was also charged with him, in 1569, as a maintainer of Robert Betoun. He enjoyed the questionable honour of being father-in-law of Sir James Balfour of Pittendreich (R. Bannatyne's *Memoriales*, Ban. Club, p. 52).

[1] See pp. 76, 77.   [2] Omitted.   [3] Blotted.
[4] Nicol Spittal was minister of Fowlis-Easter in 1563, 'having in 1567 For-

and examinat, &c., in his conscience deponis that, he being in
Pytlathe duelling and the sayd Barbara also, he saw Wyliam
Huntar of Balcarros and ane servand wyth hym cum[1] thar one
horsbak, quhilkis lychtit in the clos of Pytlatehe, and Wyliam
past up alane to the hows quhar Barbara was, levyng his servand wyth the hors, and Wyliam remant thar in the sajd hows
the space of other half howr efter his jugiment. In quhilk
tym the deponar, being offendit tharwyth, past to the wyff of
Ihon Nesche, gardinar of the place, and demandit of hyr quhai
wes up in the hows wyth Wyliam and Barbara; and sche
ansuerit saying, thar wes nabody wyth tham. The deponar
knawis na mayr in this mater, except that common voce and
fame is in the cuntre that Barbara hes borne ane barne to the
sayd Wyliam Huntar. He purgis hym of al parcialite.

12   M. Robert Hammyltown, regent in the New College in
Sanctandrois, wytnes, sworn and examinat upon the excepcion,
&c., deponis as follous : being inquirit gyf Barbara Sandelandis gave hyr body or buyr ane barne to Wyliam Huntar of
Balcarros; ansueris, he knawis nocht. *Item,* he deponis that,
upon Thurisday efter Trinite Sunday at last wes, he cam to
Balcarros and thar efter supper spak wyth Gressell Trayll,
Wyliam Huntaris wyff, quhai mayd ane havy lamentacion to
the deponar that hyr husband gave hys body to Barbara Sandelandis.   And tharefter Wyliam Huntar, passand be the waye
wyth the deponar toward Magas, confessed to hym be the waye
that he had grevosly offendit towardis God and his wyff, quhai
wes sa gud to hym at all tymmis, and at he wald satisfy hyr as
sche plesed for the wyckednes that he had committit, for it
com upon ane sudden chance that ever he had ado wyth that
woman, and no mencion wes mayd of Barbara.

13   [Here follows the evidence of 'George Lewyngstown in
Cragfudy of perfyt aige,' and 'syster sone to Wyliam Huntar.']

14   Robert Dauidson, tenent to Wyliam Huntar in Balcarros, of

---

gound and Benvie also in charge'; he was afterwards translated to Benvie ; from
thence he removed to Longforgan ; and died an indweller at Dundee on the 9th
of April 1576 (Scott's *Fasti,* iii. 712, 715, 719). He was one of those who
signed the letter directed by the General Assembly, in December 1566, to the
bishops of England, entreating them to deal gently with the brethren about the
surplice and other apparel (Calderwood's *History,* ii. 335).

[1] *Cun* in MS.

laufull aige, wytnes, &c., sworn and examinat, in his conscience
deponis that common voce and fame is that Barbara Sandelandis hes born ane barne to Wyliam Huntar; and knawis na
mayr in this mater, and purgis hym of all parcialite.

15   Gressel Trayll, spows of Wyliam Huntar of Balcarros,
     wytnes, sworne and examinat upon the excepcion of adultery of
     Ihon Forbes, &c., in hyr conscience deponis that the brut of the
     cuntra is, and was, thàt Barbara Sandelandis had borne ane
     barnee laytly to Wyliam Huntar, husband to the deponar; and
     at Wylizam Huntar confessit to hyr, wyth his awyn mowth
     spekand, that he had carnall dayll wyth the sayd Barbara and
     tharby had falyeit aganis the deponar, and offerrit hym redy to
     amend to hyr in ony sort at hyr plesur. Sche also deponis
     that sche, for avoyding of pleye and cummaris,[1] send to George
     Lewyngstown in Cragfudy, and caused hym fetche the bern
     borne be Barbara Sandelandis brutit to be hyr husbandis and
     put it to fosteryng one hyr expensis; and gave certan penne-
     worthis to Margret Huntar to pay for the fosteryng of ,the
     same. Sche also deponis that Barbara Sandelandis hes resortit
     to thar hows divers tymmis wythin this other half year.
     ·Examinat upon the generall interrogatoris of law, sche purgis
     hyr.

16   Janat Jhonstown, xviij yearis of aige and mayir, servand to
     Cristen Balfour, relict of Dauid Kynnayr in Cragfudy, wytnes,
     sworne and examinat upon the excepcion of adultery, &c., be
     hyr ayth deponis that sche knawis na thing in this mater nor
     nane of the personis, bot alanerly that the deponar was send be
     George Lewyngstoun, furth of Cragfudy to the Westhows, to
     resave ane barne and bryng to hym, quhilk sche performit;
     indeid resavit ane manchild thar fra ane gentyll woman, quhai
     prayed hyr to do weyll to the barne, quhilk barne the deponar
     brocht to George Lewyngstown to Cragfude, and he caused the
     deponar resave the barne to fosteriyng; and past tharwyth to
     the hows of Janat Smyth, relict of Robert Jhonsone, cottar in
     the cottoun of Cragfudy to Cristen Balfour, and thar kepit
     the barne quhill it decessit: al wes don this year befoyr har-

---

[1] Strife and vexations. The first letter of *pleye* has been altered, and it might
be read *foleye*.

vysd. Examinat upon the generall interrogatoris of law, sche purgis hyr.

17 Catren Layng, relict of George *D*uncan, cottar in the cottoun of Cragfude, wytnes, sworne and examinat upon the excepcion of adultery, &c., be hyr ayth deponis that sche knawis na thing of the excepcion, bot at sche wes present in tym of deces of ane barne in cottoun of Cragfudy the sam symmer, and lowked[1] the barnis eyn and wynd hym; hard thane be common voce and fame, and namly of the keparis of the barne, that the barne foyrsayd wes gottyn betuix Wyliam Huntar of Balcarros and Barbara Sandelandis, Lady of Reres. Examinat upon the generall interrogatoris of law, sche purgis hyr.

18 Besse Lawsone, xx^{ti} yearis of aige, servand to Alexander Olefeyr cottar in Cragfudy, wytnes, sworne and examinat upon the excepcion of adultre, &c., be hyr ayth deponis that sche wes present in cumpany wyth Janat Ihonstown wytnes preceding, in fetchyng of the barne fra the Westhows to Cragfudy, and in that part is conforme to the sayd Janat Jhonstoun in hyr deposicion; and purgis hyr of the general interrogatoris of law.

19 Robert Wobstar, xx^{ti} yearis of aige and mayr, servand domesticall to Wyliam Huntar of Balcarros, wytnes, sworn and examinat, &c., be his ayth deponis that he wes send be Gressell Trayll, wyf of Wyliam Huntar foyrsaid, to George Lewyngstoun in Cragfudy, desyring the sayd George in hyr nam to caws resave ane barne fra Barbara Sandelandis furth of the Westhows, and put it to fosteryng upon hyr expens, quhill sche wyst quhai awcht it: and kennis na mayr in this mater.

20 Andro Wod, apperand of Largo,[2] wytnes, sworne and examinat upon the excepcion of adultery, &c., in his conscience deponis that he hes hard of the confession of Wyliam Huntar of Balcarros, that the said Wyliam Huntar had carnall dayll wyth Barbara Sandelandis, being wyf to Ihon Forbas apperand

---

[1] Closed.

[2] This Andrew Wod was grandson of Sir Andrew Wod, the famous naval commander (Wood's *East Neuk of Fife*, 1887, pp. 72, 74). On the 28th of November 1556, Andrew Wod of Largo sold to Andrew Wod his son and heir-apparent and Egidia Gourelaw his wife the lands of Balbreky (*Register of Great Seal*, iv. No. 1129).

of Reres; and knawis na mayr in the mater, except that common voce and fame is sa as the excepceion beris. Examinat upon the generall interrogatoris, he purgis hym in all, except that he confessis hym to atteyn in consanguinite to the producer and to Barbara, and can nocht declar nor reckyn the decreis. Also he and Wyliam Huntar ar secundis in degreis of consanguinite.

Die octavo mensis Decembris, anno Domini m°v^clxiij.

Wyth incalling of the name of Crist Jesus, Sone of the *Declaracio adulterii Barbare* eternall and everlevyng God, quhai is the way the verite and *Sandelandis.* the lyff, be quhais mercy and gudnes we, Mr. Ihon Wynram, Superintendent of Fyff, being called to that office as ane watcheman ower hys flok to behald examyn and trye (be the law of God) the conversacion lyff and maneris of thoes committed to our charge; and occasion being offerred be delacion gevyn in to us, be the ministery of the kyrk of Lucris, upon Jhon Forbas apperand of Reres for nocht adheryng to Barbara Sandelandis his lawfull wyff, to summond the said Ihon Forbas to ane certan daye, to compeyr befoyr us and the ministerie of Santandrois, to heir and se hym decernit to adheir to the said Barbara his lawfull wyff, to intret hyr accordyng to the ordinance and institucion of mariaige, or to schaw ane ressonabyll caws quhy he suld nocht sa do. The said Ihon being summond and comperand at day and place affixit to hym, he, for his defence and to stop his adherance, proponit be way of excepcion and allegit adultery committit be the said Barbara Sandelandis wyth Wyliam Huntar of Balcarros, manifestit be procreacion of ane child betuix tham, born in the Westhows in the moneth of Maii in this instant year of lxiij; and the foyrsaid adultery also confessed be the saydis Barbar and Wyliam Huntar befoyr divers famos wytnes. We, understandyng the foyrsaid excepcion and defence relevant and consonant wyth the law of God, have admittit the same to his probacion, quha for probacion tharof hes produced honest famos and unsuspect wytnes in detful numer. Quhilkis, being be us laufully summond, comperand ar resavit sworne admittit and deligently examinat, in pan of nocht comperance of the said Barbara

Sandelandis heirto laufully summond. We, being maturly
avysed wyth the foyrsaid excepcion of adultry, deposicionis of
the saydis wytnes, havyng only God befoyr our ees and the
testimony of his trew and eternall Word, the consayll and
sentiment of the ministery of Sanctandrois tharin had and
hard, fyndis the sayd[1] excepcion of adultery relevantly and
sufficiently provyn; and tharby in defalt of the said Barbara
sufficient occasion gevyn to us to ceas fra farther proceadyng
aganis the said Ihon Forbas, or to decern hym to adheyr to
the said Berbara as to his lawful wyff: committing the said
Barbara Sandelandis, wyth hyr criminall caus of adultry, to
temporall magistrat, juge competent to hyr and the said cryme.
Pronunced in the parroche kyrk of the cite of Sanctandrois,
upon the viij of December anno 1563, being present Masteris
Ihon Dowglas, Rector, Crostofer Gudman, minister; Masteris
Wyliam Ramsaye, James Wylke, Alan Lawmonth, and hol
ministerie, in peana contumacii parcium citatarum[2] et non com-
parentum.

In the sessione of the Superintendent of Fyff and
ministerie of Sanctandrois, haldyn wythin the parrochie kyrk of the citie of Sanctandrois, upon the xix
day of August, the year of God m°v° sexty twa yearis.

Mastertoun
contra Boyd.

The quhilk daye, Adam Mastertoun charget and monest, be
the Superintendent and his letteres, to adheir and intreat
Agnes Boyd his spows as becummis the husband to treat his
lawfull wyff according to the law of God, or ellis to schaw ane
ressonabyll caws quhy he suld nocht sa do; comperis Adam and
in presens of Agnes allegis aganis hyr that he is nocht haldyn
to adheir to hyr, and proponis ane excepcion of adultere, as at
lenth is contenit [in][3] the sam, vidz., betuix Agnes and Gilbert
Arskyn. Quhilk wes admittit to his probacion, and divers
dietis kepit in the sayd caus, wytnes produced resavit and
examinat, &c., and finaly, concordit and aggreit as follouis.

---

[1] The sayd the said in MS.
[2] Citatorum in MS.
[3] Omitted. The exception was doubtless in writing.

Die 17 mensis Decembris, anno Domini 1562.   Indicione 6, *Concordia inter* regni Marie regine anno 21, horam circa secundam post meridiem, *Mastertoun et Boyd.* in camera venerabilis et circumspecti viri magistri Joannis Dowglas, Rectoris alme Universitatis Sanctiandree, infra Nouum Collegium civitatis Sanctiandree, coram dicto domino rectore, tamquam uno seniorum ministerii Sanctiandree, et magistris Roberto Hammyltoun et Patricio Constyn [1] regentibus dicti collegii testibus.

Adame Mastertoun exoneris [and][2] remittis all rancor consavit be hym aganis Agnes Boyd his spows, and renuncis the accion and excepcion of adultery proponit be hym aganis hyr, and acceppis hyr in his favoris, and grantis to adheir to hyr as to his lawfull wyff, and requiris hyr as his lawfull wyff to returne and pas wyth hym to thar commone dwelling place. And [in][2] signe of concord amite and simple remit of all displesor, the said Adam, at desyr of the said Mr. Ihon Dowglas, kissid and embraced the said Agnes and drank to hyr.[3] *De super dictus Adam Mastertoun peciit instrumenta a me Joanne Motto notario publico.*   J. Motto *subscribitur.*

Die xix mensis Augusti, anno Domini 1562.

The quhilk daye, the Superintendent and ministerie being *Ordinaciones* consultit anent the cuming of Master Wyliam Cranstown [4] to *erga Magistrum Wm. Cranstoun.*

---

[1] Patrick Constyn, minister of Ceres, and better known afterwards as Patrick Adamson, Archbishop of St. Andrews.

[2] Omitted.

[3] Although this sign of concord and forgiveness may be despised in these days of aggressive Good Templarism, it flourished long among the craftsmen of St. Andrews. For example, it was decreed on the 19th of August 1580, 'that Mathew Clenye suld confess he had maid offence to Alexander Millar and tharfor to drink to him, and to confess him offendit to Johnne Millar and drink to him, and Johne to drink agane to Mathew' (*Bouk off the Statutis and Ordinansis off the Bruderine of. the Hammermen of Sanctandrous*, MS.). So popular indeed was this mode of healing differences that it affected the funds of the craft, and therefore, on the 2d of March 1593, 'It is statute ordanit and decernit, be thame all with ane consent, that quhan ony variance sall happin to fall betwix the maister and his servand, na silver of the craftis be drunkin at the aggreing of thame, bot the servand to pay xiijs. iiijd., and the maister vjs. viijd., quhilk of thame beis fund in the falt' (*Ibid.*).

[4] Mr. William Cranstoune, Provost of Setoun and licentiate in theology, was in the Provincial Council of 1549 (Robertson's *Concilia Scotiae*, ii. 83).   He was

this cite of Sanctandrois, and ordor to be takyn wyth hym at his cuming, for umbeschewing[1] of inconveniencis, thai have thocht gud and consentit and ordened that, sa soone as the said Master Wyliam Cranstoun cummis to the said cite, the Superintendent (gyf he be present in this citie) and the ministerie sall conveyn in session, send and requir the said Mr. Wyliam to compeir befoyr tham, and at his comperance demand of hym quhat religion he is of, and desyr to have confessione of his fayth. And gyf he professis hym ane Papist or of his ald and wonted religion, that he be ernistlie required and requested to depart fra this citie, that na perturbacione of religion be mayd heir be hym, nor suspecion takyn of hym be his residence; wyth intimacion, gyf he wyll nocht obey the request, that all the membris of this congregacione salbe oppynly inhibit and forbyddyn to intercommone or cumpany, by or sell, wyth hym, under pane of excommunicacione; and gyf neid be the sammyn to be execut realy and wyth effect. Otherwayis, gyf he confessis hym ane Protestant and to affirme the religion and doctrin resavit and tawcht in this citie and kyrk, he to be desyrit and cherged to gev confessione of his fayth, and to subscryve the articulis of recantacione commonly used; quhilk gyf he refusis to be reput and used as ane Papist in maner foyrsaid. And gyf he consentis and obeyis the request [and][2] submit hymself to disciplyn, he to be resavit as ane Cristiane membre of the congregacion; nevertheles, nocht to be admittit to preche wythowtyn admissione lawfull. And gyf he desiris

---

also Official of St. Andrews (*supra*, p. 147). Probably it is the same William Cranstoun who is mentioned as professor of sacred literature and Principal of St. Salvator's College on the 4th of February 155⅘ (*Register of Great Seal,* iv. No. 1277). At the Reformation, 'several of the masters in St. Salvator's, including William Cranston, the Principal, adhered to the ancient religion, and left their places' (M'Crie's *Melville,* ii. 344, 345). On the 12th of October 1561, Mary Queen of Scots wrote to Queen Elizabeth, begging 'letters of safe conduct for William Cranstoun, and others, to pass through England to France' (Thorpe's *Calendar of State Papers, Scotland,* i. 175). And on the 24th of September 1562—five weeks after the date of the entry in the text—Randolph wrote to Cecil, from the north of Scotland, 'Mister William Cranstons, that passed latlie by you, a great favorer of Papystes, is happelie ded in thys myschevous worlde' (Laing's *Knox,* vi. 144).

[1] Avoiding.　　　　　　　　　　　[2] Omitted.

admission to preche, it salbe grantit only upon this condicione and obligacione, be promys that he sall confes all the saidis common articulis ; and confut [the false ;][1] and prech the trew and contrary doctrin, concernyng thar articulis, to the Papisticall doctrin, singularly ilk ane be thame self; and at the end of his sermon sall confes treuly (accordyng to his conscience and testimone tharof) that ether ignorantly or of malice he falyeit in teching wrang doctrin the last sermone he maid in this kyrk, anent the reall presence of the body and blud of Crist in the sacrament of the supper of the Lord, and obsecracionis[2] mayd be hym in confirmyne of the said doctrine ; ask God mercy tharof and the congregacion forgyfnes, &c.

Die secundo Septembris anno Domini 1562.

The quhilk daye, Andro Sellar yonger accused for adultery committed wyth Annie Thomson, spows of Archebald Philp in Ballestown, quhai is wyth child to the said Andro. He confessis hym to have had carnall dayll wyth the said Anne, bot he never knew that sche was ane other mannis wyf. In respect of the quhilk, the saidis Andro and Anne ar committed be the ministerie and thar supplicacion, to be civile punist be the Provest and ballies accordyng to the ordor resavit. *Accusacio Cellar et Thomson de adulterio.*

The quhilk daye, Andro Elephant and Issobell Mortoun delated and accused befoyr the ministerie for kepyn cumpany in bed and burd unmareit, to the gret offence aganis God and sclander of the congregacione. Thai confes thar kepyn of cumpany, and affirmis that thai ar contracked in promys of mariaige, and ar wylling to procead to solemnizacion tharof ; and professis thame selfis membris of this congregacione, imbrasaris of the doctrin tawcht in this kyrk, [and][4] submittis thame to disciplin. In respect of the quhilk, the ministerie ordenis thaim to compeir this nixt Sunday in the public essemble, and thar mak public satisfaccion ; and [the][4] same done thar bannis to be proclamit, and wythin xxj dayes nixt tharefter to procead to solemnizacione of thar mariaige ; to the quhilk thai consent. *Accusacio Andree Olephant et Margrete Mortoun.*   *Responsio.[3]*   *Decretum.*

---

[1] Omitted.   [2] Entreaties or protestations.
[3] This word is somewhat uncertain ; the first part of it is contracted, and it seems to end in *eo* or *oo*.   [4] Omitted.

Die xvj Septembris anno Domini 1562.

Decretum contra Gedde meritricem Schryngeor de Dunde. The quhilk daye, Janat Gedde delated called and accused befoir the ministerie for fornicacione, committit wyth Dauid Scrymgeor in *D*unde, and cuming to this cite fugityve fra disciplyn quhar the offence was committit, and bearyng hyr barne wythin this cite. Janat confessis the fornicacion committit in *D*unde wyth Dauid Scrymgeor, and allegis that the caws of hyr cuming to this cite was to serve James Gedde, quhom to sche mayd promys of service befoyr sche knew hyrself to be wyth child. The ministerie decernis hyr to depart wyth hyr barne to *D*unde, and thar wythin viij dayis to underly disciplin and obteyn hyr barne baptised, and nocht to return quhill[1] sche bryng testimoniall[2] of the fulfylling of the same.

Die xxiij mensis Septembris, anno Domini etc. lxij.

Decretum contra Setoun and Nicholl for excommunicacion. The quhilk daye, Mr. Ihone Setoun readar in Creych[3] and Eleyn Nycholl, delated to the Superintendent as huyrmongaris, and the sayd Mr. Ihon for contempnyng and necletyng of his office in the sayd kyrk, and summond be the Superintendentis letteres to this day and session, oft tymmis called and nocht comperand, ar noted *contumaces*, and letteres of excommunicacion descernit to be send and execut upon tham, and the said Mr. Ihon is deprivit fra his office of readar in the said kyrk.

Murdo, Kynayr, adultereris excommunicat. In lyik maner Alexander Murdo and Besse Kynayr, delated and summond for to underly disciplyn for adultery committed betuix tham, non-comperand ar decernit to be excommunicat.

[Balcanquell, Olephant, fornicatoris.] The quhilk day, Johane Balcanquell and Gelis Olephant, fornicatoris, delated called accused and confessand thar delacion, ar ordenit this nixt Sunday in the essemble of the congregacion to syt upon the penitent stul tym of the sermon, and at the end tharof schaw signes of repentance in askyn God mercy and the congregacione forgyfnes upon thar kneis.

---

[1] *Quhilk* in MS. [2] *Testioall* in MS.
[3] John Seytoun, vicar of Creich, witnesses a charter on the 10th of February 1548-9 (*Register of Great Seal*, iv. No. 298).

Die ultimo Septembris anno quo supra.

The quhilk daye, Alexander Lytstar acclamed in mariaige be [Lytstar, Turpy.] Margret Turpy as he that hes deflored hyr virginite. Alexander is chergit to absteyn fra contrackyng and solemnizacion of mariaige wyth ony other person, unto sic tym as the sayd clame be discussed, under payn of excommunicacion, &c.

Die septimo Octobris anno quo supra.

The quhilk daye, in the sessione of the Superintendent and *Declaracio innocentie Dwry* ministerie of Sanctandrois, anent the sclander rased upon *spows Archibald.* Dauid Ballingall and Elizabeth Dwry spows of Dauid Archibald parrochinaris of Kennoquhy, the mater being deligently tryed and examinat be the Superintendent and ministerie foyrsad, thai fynd the said Elizabeth Dwry innocent tharof, and albeid the sayd Dauid Ballingall most wyckedly and ernistlye labored to tyist the sayd Elizabeth Dwry to have consented to his fylthy lust and desyir, sche be the grace of God hes constantly refused and resisted. Quhilk offence done be the said Dauid Ballingall, in schawyng his evyll wyll to have[1] performit and brocht to pas his consavit lust and tentacione, now (moved be the Spirit of God) he hes confessed and schawyn owtward signes *Confessio* of repentance, wyth humil submission of hymself to disciplyn; *Ballingall.* and heirfor is decernit to compeir in the essemble of the congregacion of the kyrk of Kennowy, upon Sunday the xj of October instant, and thar in presens of God at the command of the minister humyll hymself upon his kneis, confes his offence and ask God mercy tharof and the congregacione forgyfnes. And of his occasion of sclander gevyn to tham, and for avoyding of all occasion of suspicion and sclander gevyn for the tym to cum, the said Dauid Ballingall is discherged and forbyddyn to *Decretum et* accumpany wyth the said Elizabeth Dwry in ony maner or sort, *satisfaccio Ballingall.* privatly or oppynlye, bot [to][2] absteyn fra talkyn eatyng drynkyn or other resortyng wyth hyr; to the quhilk he hes consented, and is oblest to keip the same under pane of bannesing hym the bowndis of Fyff for all the dayes of his lyftym; and for fulfill-

---

[1] *Hawo* in MS.   [2] Omitted.

ing of this his promys and obligacion sall fynd gentyllmen
landit caucionaris for hym, actitat in the schyrreffis bukis of
Fyff, that gyf ony occasion of suspicione or sclander be gevyn
or mayd be hym, and he tharof giltye and convicked, that he
sall remove and be bannist the bowndis of Fyff for all the dayes
of his lyff and never to returne. In respect of thyr premissis,
the Superintendent ordenis the minister of Kennowy to moneis
all and syndry personis of his congregacion, that nane of tham
pretend to sclander the sayd Elizabeth Dury, or in thar
talkyng to speik evyll of hyr for ony sic caus; and to exhort
tham to thank and praese God of his grace grantit to hyr to
resist sa constantly sic tentacion, quharof sche is to be prased
and nocht evyll reportet.

Die xj Novembris anno domini etc. lxij.

Matrimoniale decretum inter Pawy et Kynnisman.

The quhilk daye, Mariory Pawy askis Wyliam Kynnisman to
marye hyr, as he that promyst to hyr be his hand gevyn in hyr
hand, and spekyng and saying to hyr, be his hand he layd in
hyrris, he suld marye hyr and never have ane other woman bot
hyr, quhilk promys Mariory referris to the ayth of Wyliam;
quhilk Wiliam refused to sweyr, and referred the allegacion of
Mariory to hyr ayth; and sche, sworne in his presens and
examinat be hyr ayth, deponis the foyrsaid promys alleged be
hyr to be trew. Quharfor, the Superintendent decernit the said
Wyliam to solemnizat his mariaige wyth the said Mariory, and
monesis hym to compleyt the same wythin xl dayes nixt heirefter, under pane of excommunicacione.

Die xxv Novembris anno quo supra.

Matrimoniale decretum inter Dauison et Stewart.

The quhilk day, Jobane Dauidson walcar and Elizabeth
Stewart, for transgression of the ordor of [the][1] kyrk, ar decernit
this nixt Sunday to mak public satisfaccion in the essemble, &c.,
and tharefter thar bannis to be proclamed, and wythin xx^{ti}
dayes nixt tharefter to solemnizat thar mariaige.

---

[1] Omitted.

Die penultimo Decembris anno quo supra.

The quhilk daye, Johane Mortown, servand to Thomas *Matrimoniale* Ramsay in Sanct Nicholes, and Catren Brown in New Grange,[1] *decretum inter Mortowin et* fornicatoris, grantis and confessis promys of mariaige betuix *Browin.* thame, and to performe and solemnizat the same at the farrest at Wytsunday nixt to cum; and to absteyn from all carnall dayll in the myd tym, and to mak public satisfaccion for thar sclander gevyn this nixt Sunday, in the public essemblie of the congregacion, to the quhilk thai ar admittit.

Die xiij Januarii anno quo supra.

The quhilk day, comperis Mr. Wyliam Fayrfull, procurator *Repulsio pro-* for Eufam Murraye Lade of Rasyth be hyr mandiat, tendyng *curatorum domine de* to perseu ane accion of injuris aganis James Mowbray in Dun- *Rasyth et* fermlyng; and in lyik wyis comperis Mr. Ihon Bown, procura- *Mowbray.* tor of the sayd James Mowbray be his mandat, tending to defend and to persew the sayd Eufam for injuris. The Super- intendent and ministerie, tending to keip the ordor of the sayt, refusis to admit procuratoris; and grantis letteres, at the instance of parteis, to summond ilk ane other to compeyr per- sonaly under panis of excommunicacion. And sa the proces ceassed becaus the Lard of Rasyt[2] wald nocht consent to ony persut at instance of his Lady.

The quhilk daye, in the caus of injuris persewit be Johan *Decretum* Brown,[3] reader in Kyngorne Ester, aganis Mr. Dauid Wod, *deprivacionis Mrio. Dauidis Wod et in favorem Brown.*

---

[1] St. Nicholas and New Grange are both in the parish of St. Andrews.

[2] On the 7th of September 1550, the Queen granted to Robert Stewart, son and heir-apparent of Henry Stewart of Rossyth, the lands and baronies of Rossyth, Cragyis, Durrisdeir and Schambody; which the said Henry personally resigned, reserving a free tenement (*Register of Great Seal*, iv. No. 518). On the 26th of March 1553 there is a confirmation in favour of Robert Stewart, '*feodi-tario de Rossyth*,' and Eufamie Murray his wife (*Ibid.*, No. 770.) He was in Parliament in 1560 (*Acts of Parliament*, ii. 526). She was the second daughter of Sir William Murray, of Tullibardine, and was thrice married: first to Stewart, next to Robert Pitcairn, Commendator of Dunfermline, and afterwards to Patrick Gray of Innergourie (Wood's *Douglas's Peerage*, i. 145, 146).

[3] John Brown was exhorter in Kinghorn Wester, or Burnt Island, in 1567, with a stipend of xl merkis, and was reader there from 1574 to 1589 (*Register of Ministers, &c.*, Mait. Club, p. 25; Scott's *Fasti*, ii. 528). His stipend in 1574 was £20 and the kirk-land (*Wodrow Miscellany*, p. 362).

minister of Kyngorne foyrsayd, the Superintendent, avysed wyth
the complant of Johan persewar, ansuer and confession of Mr.
Dauid, deposicionis of wytnes, and al otheris deduced in the
sayd caus, fyndis clerly provyn that Mr. Dauid, oppynle in the
Generall Essembly of the Kyrk of Scotland, in Edynburgh,
and also befoyr the ministerie of Sanctandrois, injuirit and
diffamit Jhon Brown readar, calling and affirmyng hym to be
ane hypocrit, ane idolatar, ane mes mongar; and heirfor
[decernis that][1] instantly befoyr the ministerie the sayd Mr.
Dauid on his kneis ask the sayd Ihone Brown forgyfnes. And
farther decernis and ordenis the said Mr. Dauid, ane of thir nixt
twa Sundayes following, to pas to the kyrk of Kyngorne Est
and thar mak ane sermon, and at the end tharof, in the public
essemble of the congregacion, acknawledge and confes hymself
to have excedit the bowndis of his office in dischergyng of Ihone
Brown fra his office of readyng of the common prayeris, and
calling of hym raschely knayff; and to ask hym and the
congregacion forgyfnis: and fra thyn furth dischergis and
deprivis the sayd Mr. Dauid fra ministracion of the Word, at
the discrecion of the Superintendent, for sic tym as he sall
appoynt to hym, and quhill he obteyn new admission.[2]

Die xx Januarii anno Domini etc lxij.

Accusacio Thome Skyrlyng lectoris in Crayll.

The quhilk daye, Thomas Skyrlyng, readar in Crayll, summond for ministracion of baptisme and mariaige nocht being
admitted, he comperand and tharof accused, for his defence
producis ane commission in wryt, subscrivit be Ihon Maleyn
minister of Crayll, Wyliam Annand, Mr. George Meldrum,
Thomas Bane, and rest of the eldaris of Crayll, for excusyng of
his ministracion [of][3] mariaige. In respect of the quhilk, the
Superintendent ordenis the saydis minister and eldaris to be
summond to compeyr befoyr hym and the ministerie of Sanct-

---

[1] Omitted.

[2] Mr. Dauid does not appear to have been reinstated, for Thomas Biggar, who
'had been a member of the chapter of St. Andrews previous to the Reformation,'
was admitted as his successor in 1564 (Scott's *Fas. i*, ii. 543).

[3] The words *of baptisme and* have been erased—no doubt the *of* by
mistake.

androis this nixt Wednisday. And as to his ministracion of baptisme, he allegis speciall command of the eldaris to minister baptisme, quhilk is statut to hym to prev upon Wednisday nixt to cum. Also the Superintendent inhibitis the sayd Thomas fra using his office in the kyrk, quhill the end of this his offences and tryall tharof.

Die xxvij Januarii anno quo supra.

The quhilk day, as in term assignit be the Superintendent to Thomas Skyrlyng reader of Crayll to prev the command of the eldaris, and as daye affixt to the minister and eldaris to be summond, &c., the Superintendent, efter tryall takyn in the sayd mater, fyndis the sayd Thomas to have gretly offendit in ministracion of solemnizacion of the pretendit mariaige of Peter Jak, wythowtyn laufull autorite or power granted to the sayd Thomas tharto, and the pley also of mariaige intentat be the clame of Besse Buge aganis the sayd Peter depending unde-cidit ;[1] and also in ministracione of baptisme wythowtyn admis-sion being onlye ane readar ;[2] and tharfor dischergis the sayd

Decretum contra Skyrlyng in Crayll.

---

[1] On the 16th of September 1562, the Superintendent had inhibited Peter Jak from marrying any other woman until Besse Buge's claim against him was decided ; but on the 20th of January, the same day that Skyrling was summond, Jak confessed that he had married another woman (see above, pp. 148, 149).

[2] 'To the kirkis qubair no ministeris can be haid presentlie, must be appointed the most apt men, that distinctlie can read the Commoune Prayeris and the Scripturis, to exercise boyth thameselfis and the kirk, till thai growe to greattar perfectioun ; and in process of time he that is but a reader may attain to a farther degree, and, by consent of the Church and discreet ministers, may be permitted to minister the sacraments ; but not before that he be able somewhat to perswade by wholesome doctrine, beside his reading, and be admitted to the ministerie' (*First Book of Discipline*, fourth head). The reader of Crail was by no means the only aspiring member of his order, for, in July 1568, the General Assembly 'ordeaned that superintendents command readers to absteane from all ministra-tioun of the sacraments, under paine to be accused as abusers, and criminall, according to the Act of Parliament' (Calderwood's *History*, ii. 422). In August 1573 the reader at Dalry was enjoined by the Assembly 'to make his publict repentance upon two severall Lord's dayes, becaus, being discharged from all ministratioun of the Lord's Supper, [he] had not the lesse ministred the same, at Kilburnie, the last Easter. It was ordeanned, that this act sall strike upon all readers that sall be found guiltie of the same crime' (*Ibid.* iii. 293). And in October 1576, the Assembly concluded 'that no reader within this realme minister the bolie sacraments, except suche as have the word of exhortatioun in their mouths' (*Ibid.* p. 376).

Thomas fra the office of readyng quhill Sunday the vij of
Februar nixt to cum; and ordenis and commandis the sayd
Thomas Skyrlyng this nixt Sunday to compeir in the public
essemble of the congregacion in Crayll kyrk, and thar oppynly
confes hym to have falyeit and offendit in ministracion of the
pretendit mareaige of Peter Jak, nocht being laufully admittit
to sic office, and the impediment standing in the part of the
said Peter Jak be the clam of mariaige intentat be Bege Buge
undecidit; and tharfor on his kneis ask God mercy for his
offence, and the congregacion forgyfnes of his sclander gevyn,
and this to do under pane of excommunicacione.[1]

Decretum contra Jo. Maleyn ministrum de Crayll.   Upone the ferd daye of Februar, *anno etc. lxij*, the quhilk
daye, cognicione takyn anent the part of Jhon Maleyn, minister
of Crayll, in the solemnizacion of the pretendit mariaige of
Peter Jak wyth ane woman in Crayllis pareis be Thomas
Skyrlyng reader in Crayll, it is fundyn that the said Johane
Maleyn minister was sufficiently adverteist of the impediment
and pleye of mariaige depending betuix the sayd Peter and
Bege Buge, and that he was deuly inhibit to solemnizat
mariage betuix Peter Jak and ony other person quhill decision
of the sayd pley befoyr the Superintendent depending; and
tharfor the sayd Ihon Maleyn minister to be gilty in committyng ony pretendit power to Thomas Skyrlyng readar to
solemnizat ony mariagis in his absence, except he verefy that
he publest the inhibicion foyrsayd gevyn to hym in the essemble
of the congregacion, or ellis mayd excepcion of Peter Jak in
the comission and power committit to the sayd readar. The
rest of this mater and disciplyn is contenewit oneto sic tym as
the Superintendent sall think gud to call the sayd Ihon
Maleyn minister and eldaris of Crayll for this caws.

Peticio Gray contra Ihonstoun.   The quhilk day, Marion Gray, in presens of Iohan Jhonstoun, allegis that the sayd Ihon hes deflored hyr virginite, and
tharfor haldyn of the law of God to marye hyr, and askis hym
to be compelled and decernit to solemnizat mariaig wyth hyr.
Quhilk Ihon allegis for his defence that the sayd Marion was
deflored be James Kynnisman befoyr he knew hyr carnaly, and

---

[1] Skyrling no doubt obeyed the Superintendent's penitential commands, for he
was still reader at Crail in 1567. His stipend was paid by the town (*Register of
Ministers, Exhorters aud Readers*, Mait. Club, p. 23). •

offeris hym to prev the same ; and at his desyr Wednisday the
x day of Februar nixt to cum is statut to hym to prev. Parteis
heirto summond be actis, &c.

Upone the x day of Februar, as in term assignit to Johan *Inhibicio*
Jhonstoin to prev his excepcion aganis Marion[1] Gray, he com- *Johanstoin.*
peris and his wytnes nocht comperand, the Superintendent
offerris to the sayd Ihon letteres to summond his wytnes ;
quhilk he refused to resav, and stubburnly sayd and alleged
the Superintendent culd do na thing to hym bot keip hym
unmareit : he suld tak tham but mariaige that wald tak hym.
In respect of the quhilk, the Superintendent inhibitis the sayd
Johane to contract or procead to mariaig wyth ony other
person, quhill decyding of this clam and caus of Marion persewar, under pan of excommunicacion ; and ordenis inhibicionis
in wryt to be direc to all kyrkis necessar to the same effect.

Die xvij Februarii anno etc. lxij.

The quhilk daye, Andro Angus,[2] reader in Leslye, accused *Decretum contra*
and convict for ministracion of baptisme wythowtyn laufull *Angus[3] reader*
admissione, and also of barnis that war nether presented be *in Leslie.*
father nor mother, in the pareis kyrk of Kynglasse ; and therfor is decernit to absteyn fra all sic in tym cuming under all
heast pane and cherge, and for his offence committit to compeyr
this nixt Sunday in the public essemble of the congregacion of
Kynglasse, and thar oppynle acknawledge his falt foyrsayd, ask
God mercy and the congregacion forgyfnes.

The quhilk day, Dauid Styrk delated, accused, and be his *Decretum con-*
confession convict, of ministracion of baptisme in the kyrk of *tra Styrk in*
Kynglasse, both to the barnis of the same parreson and also *Kynglasse.*
of otheris paresonis, wythowtyn ony lawfull admission ; nor
havand na office in the kyrk also interponit hymself[4] to
read the common prayeris in Kynglasse, and interruppit the
reader tharof laufully admittit tharto. Heyrfor the Super-

---

[1] The last letters have been altered : it seems to have been *Mariory.*

[2] 'Andro Anguse' occurs as reader at Kirkforthir in 1567 or 1568 with a
stipend of xx merkis (*Register of Ministers, Exhorters and Readers*, p. 24) ; but
he was reader at Leslie in 1574 with a stipend of £16 and the kirk-land (*Wodrow
Miscellany*, p. 363) ; and he continued there as reader until 1591 (Scott's
Fasti, ii. 549). [3] *Angid* in MS. [4] *Hym hynself* in MS.

intendent decernis hym to absteyn fra all office and ministracion
in the kyrk quhill he be admittit ;[1] and for his offencis foyrsayd, this nixt Sunday, to accknauledge his offencis foyrsaydis
in the public essemble of the congregacion of Kynglasse, ask
God mercy and the congregacion forgyfnes.

Die tercio mensis Marcii anno quo supra.

*Decretum mat-
rimoniale inter
Zeasteris et
Bunche.*

The quhilk daye, comperis Johane Zeasteris, sumtym monk
in Balmerinach,[2] summond to underly disciplyn for cummyng
in contrar of his promys, mayd in this session upon the xviij
day of Marcii in the lxj year, to absteyn fra cumpany and
carnall dayll havyng wyth Eleyn Bunche, in · havyng of new
carnall dayll agane wyth the said Eleyn, manifestit be procreacion of ane child betuix tham. Quhilk offencis the said
Ihon Zeasteris confessis, offerris hym redy to underly disciplyn
of the kyrk, and also offerris hym redy and wylling to solemnizat
mariaige wyth the said Eleyn; and this nixt Sunday hymself
to compeir, and do his exact deligence to caus the sayd Eleyn
compeir wyth hym at Sanct Talis kyrk,[3] consent to the pro-

---

[1] He was afterwards reader at Kinglassie with a stipend of £10 (*Register of
Ministers, etc.*, p. 24).

[2] The Cistercian Abbey of Balmerino, founded by Ermengarde, the widow of
William the Lion, was burnt, 'with all thyngs that wer in it,' by the English
under Admiral Wyndham, on the night of the 25th of December 1547. Dr.
Campbell says that ' no new monks appear to have entered after that year ;' but,
as he supposes, 'the injury inflicted on the buildings would, no doubt, be par-
tially repaired in the interval between this period and the Reformation,' when
it was practically suppressed (*Balmerino and its Abbey*, pp. 119, 127, 349). On
the 11th of July 1606 the Abbacy, together with the lands of Kirknewton and
Balerno in the sheriffdom of Edinburgh, was erected into a free barony and
lordship of Parliament in favour of Sir James Elphinstone of Barnton. In the
erection it is declared that, ' to the effect foirsaid, his Majestie and Estaittis of
Parliament hes suppressit and extinguischit the memorie of the said Abbacy of
Balmirrenoch that thair sall be na successour provydit thairto, nor na forder
mentioun maid of the same in ony tyme heireftir' (*Acts of Parliaments of Scotland*, iv. 341-343).

[3] No vestige of the chapel of St. Alus or St. Ayle is known to remain, and
even its exact site is somewhat uncertain. Dr. Campbell conjectures that it may
perhaps have survived and been in use as the parish church of Balmerino until
1595 or 1611 (*Balmerino and its Abbey*, pp. 103, 104, 148). The reference in
the text proves at least that it was used as a place of public worship after the
Reformation ; and several entries in 1568 seem to imply that the parish of Balmerino was then known as ' Sanct Teal parrochion.'

clamacion of thar bannis, and wythin xl dayes at the farrest nixt heirefter solemnizat thar mariaige.[1] In respect of the premissis and that the same salbe deuly performit, the Superintendent ordenis the saydis Jhon and Eleyn this nixt Sunday following to compeyr in the public essemble of the congregacion of Sanct Talis kyrk, and thar mak public satisfaccion befoyr proclamacion of thar bannis, and to fulfyll the foyrsayd premissis in all punctis under pane of excommunicacione.

Die xxiiij Marcii anno quo supra.

The quhilk day, Alexander Duncan askis Beatrix Wemys to be decernit to procead to solemnizacion of mariaige wyth hym —as sche that had mayd promys of mariage wyth hym and he in lyik wyis wyth hyr, wythowtyn ony condicione adjecked tharto, thai bayth beand fre personis tym of thar mutuall promys mackyn; quhilk promys the said Beatrix oppynlie confessed and affirmed in presens of hyr frendis, quhen sche wes desyrit of tham to contract mariage wyth Wyliam Ballingall, schawand that be verteu of faythfull and trew promys foyrsayd mayd bethuix tham sche mycht nocht contract wyth ony other—in presens of Beatrix, quhai denyis the sayd clame. And at desyr of Alexander Wednisday nixt to cum [is][2] statut to hym to prev. Parteis heirto warnit be act. *Peticio matrimonialis Duncan erga Wemys.*

Upon the last of Marcii, in the sexty thre year, as in term assignit to Alexander Duncan to prev his clam and promys of mariaige denyed be Beatrix Wemys, comperis Jhon Duncan, *Decretum absolvatorium Wemys contra Duncan.*

---

[1] In a charter granted by the Commendator of Balmerino, and signed at the monastery in 1569, John Yeister, notary public, appears as a witness (*Register of the Great Seal*, vol. iv. No. 2102). In 1574, and down to 1586, the names of Thomas Stevinson and John Yester occur as the two remaining monks who formed the 'convent.' Dr. Campbell also mentions John Yester the Commendator's bailiff, who appears from the *Balmerino Writs* to have been married, and expresses the opinion :—' It is thus probable that he was none other than the *quondam* monk, and that having embraced Protestantism, he followed still further the example of Luther by disregarding his vow of celibacy, and taking to himself a wife ' (*Balmerino and its Abbey*, pp. 138, 139). But it is evident from the text that while the *quondam* monk had little respect for his vows of chastity, he would not have entered into matrimony had it not been for the pains of discipline.   [2] Omitted.

father to the said Alexander, and producis Dauid *D*uncan, Johan Wemys of Pytgrugny, and James Zong: quhilkis ar sworn, admittit and judicialie examinat, and na thing of the clame be thame provyn. Beatrix circumducis the term *quoad non producta;* and Ihon *D*uncan, in nam of Alexander his son, passis fra all farther probacion. The Superintendent, avysed wyth the proces, fyndyng na thing of the clam confessed nor provyn, pronuncis and absolvis Beatrix fra the clam of Alexander; and ordenis Alexander to mak public satisfaction in the essemble of Abyrnethy, this nixt Sunday, for his sclander and wrangus persut.

Die xxiiij Marcii anno etc. lxij.

Decretum matrimoniale inter Henderson et Peblis.

The quhilk daye, Dauid Henderson and Eleyn Peblis, in the session of the Superintendent and ministerie, confessed mutuall promys of mariaige mayd betuix tham befoyr ane curat and famos wytnes. In respect of the quhilk, the Superintendent decernis and chargis the saidis Dauid and Eleyn to compleit and solemnizat thar mariaige wythin xxx dayes nixt heirefter, or ellis in myd tym ether of tham to propon and prev sum ressonabill caws quhy thai may nocht or suld nocht solemnizat thar mariaige, under pan of excommunicacione.

Die quinto mensis Maii anno Domini m°v°lxiij.

Processus et decretum matrimoniale inter Malcolme et Duncan.

The quhilk daye, comperis Dauid Malcom and alleges that Agnes *D*uncan present is his wyff—be verteu of promys mutuall mayd betuix thame, wyth consent of hyr father, fowyr yearis syn bypast, befoir ane preist, accordyng to the use observed for that tym commonly, and carnall dayll betuix hym and hyr followed tharupon—desyris the sayd Augnes to be decernit be the Superintendent to procead wyth hym to the solemnizacion of thar mariaige—in presens of Agnes, quhai confessis the sayd allegacionis, and allegis that the said Dauid sen thar promys foyrsayd wes mayd hes mynted and schawyn his deligence to drown hyr in to ane watter upon the nycht,[1] and also hes gevyn his body in adulterie to Eleyn Allan Mackewyn: offerris hyr to

---

[1] *Mycht* in MS.

prev the sam be wytnes. Quhilk being admittit as ane ressonabyll defence to stop solemnizacion, Agnes producis Dauid
Sanderis and Dauid Clyd and James Clyd, wytnes, quhilkis war
resavit, sworne, admittit, in presens of Dauid, and instantly
examinat. The Superintendent assignis to Agnes the x daye
of Junii nixt to cum for farther probacion. Parteis heirto
summond be act.

The said x day of Junii being cum [and]¹ na deligence don
for other probacion be Agnes, Dauid circumducis the term.
The Superintendent statutis *literatorie* to pronunce.

Upon the xvj day of Junii, *anno etc. lxiij*, Dauid Malcolm
and Agnes *D*uncan being laufully summond to this day be the
Superintendentis² letteres, to heir pronunced in the caus of
procedyng to solemnizacion of mariaige betuix tham, the
Superintendent, avysed wyth the clame of the said Dauid,
ansuer and defens of Agnes, probacionis and deposicionis of
wytnes, and all otheris deduced in the sayd caus, fyndis the sayd
Agnes to have falyeit in probacion of hyr defensis, and heirfor
pronuncis and decernis the said Agnes to procead in solemnizacion of mariaige wyth Dauid Malcolme, wythin xl dayes
nixt heirefter. Pronunced in presens of Dauid and in pane of
nocht comperance of Agnes heirto summond.

Die septimo mensis Julii, anno Domini etc. lxiij.

The quhilk day, efter that Schyr Dauid Donaldson had beyn *Decretum con-*
tra domtnum
summond wyth the Superintendentis letteres, notit *contumax*, *Dauidem Don-*
aldson.
and at he, being apprehendit wythin this cite and had fundyn
caucion for his entering befoyr the Superintendent and falyeit,
wes also summond to have comperit this daye befoyr the Superintendent, personaly apprehendit, to underly correccion and
disciplyn, anent the delacion gevyn in aganis hym for blas-
phemus spekyn aganis the Word of God prechit and religion,
and also for ane huyr-mongar, havand twa syndry women
instantly wyth barne to hym begottyn in hurdom; he oft
tymmis called and nocht comperand, the Superintendent, wyth
avyis of the ministerie of Sanctandrois, decernis inhibicion to

---

Omitted. ² *Superintentis* in MS.

be direct to the minister of Monymayll to be execut thar, com-
mandyng all Cristianis fearyng God to absteyn fra all societie
and cumpany of the said Schir Dauid, declaryng hym to be
fundyn and knawyn to be ane stubburn Papist, blasphemos
spekar aganis the trewth of Goddis Word, and manifest indurit
huyr-mongar, unworthy to hav societe or followschip wyth ony
of the godly, and relacion to be mayd of his vicius lyff and inobedience to [the][1] Justice Clark.[2]

Decretum mat-
rimoniale inter
Lyndesay et
Howasone.

The quhilk daye, Johane Lyndesay, in Reres Myll, in the
session of Superintendent and ministerie of Sanctandrois and
presens of James Howason, father of Cristen Howeson, in
Lathonis, confessis that he hes deflored the virginite of the
said Cristen and hes procreat ane barne wyth hyr, oblesis hym
to solemnizat mariaig wyth the said Cristen, confessis hym to
have mayd ane promys wyth hyr; and the said James Howeson father to the said Cristen consentis that the sayd mariaige
be solemnizat.   In respect of the quhilkis, the Superintendent,
wyth avys of the ministery, ordenis the saydis Johan and
Cristen to compeir in the public essemble of the congregacion
of Sanctandrois, upon Sunday the xij of Julii instant, and mak
public satisfaccion ; quhilk don, thar barne to be baptised efter
nuyn day foyrsayd, and thai to procead and compleit thar
solemnizacion of thar mariaig wythin ane quarter of year nixt
after following, and to decist fra all carnall copulacion of thar
bodeis in the myd tym.

Die quarto Augusti anno quo supra.

Peticio matri-
monii Lyndesay
contra Lynde-
say.

The quhilk daye, Johan Lyndsay, *alias* Kyninmonth, summond be the Superintendentis letteres, at the instance of Elizabeth Lyndesay, to heir hym decernit to procead to the solemnizacion of mariaig betuix hym and the sayd Elizabeth, as he
that is haldyn sa to do be verteu of defloracion of hyr virginite,
and promys of maruge mutuall mayd betuix tham befoyr he
mayd ony other promys to ony other woman, wyth intimacion
to the said Ihon as efferit, &c., as at mayr lenth is contenit in

---

[1] Omitted.
[2] This is the last entry of the *Register* printed in the *Maitland Miscellany*.

the saydis libellat summondis, deuly execut and indorsat. The said Ihon oft tymmis called and nocht comperand, in pan of his nocht comperance Elizabeth producis Archebald Dauidson, Robert Dauidson, Janat Lessellis, Margret Lyndesay, Thomas[1] Trayll; quhilkis ar sworn, resavit, and to examinacion admittit, in pane of nocht comperance of Ihon, &c., and also instantly examinat. And upone the xviij of August Elizabeth produced Thomas Bouy, Janat Smyth and Thomas Lessellis; quhilkis war resavit, suorne, admittit, *in peana contumacii* of Ihon Lindesay herto summond, and war instantly examinat. And upon the fyrst of September, the sayd Ihon being summond and nocht comperand, the Superintendent ordenis Ihon Lindesaye and Cristen Howeson to be summond agan Wednisday nixt to cum, to heir and se procead in this caus; and gyf Cristen or Ihon hes ony excepcion aganis[2] ony of the wytnes, or ony other lawful defence to stop the mariaig betuix Ihon Lindesay and Elizabeth Lindesay, to allege the sam, as sche tyll tyn[3] and wyn.

The quhilk daye, Thomas Cuthbert and Margret Reid *Peticio* Reid delated, called and accused for fornicacion committed betuix *contra* Cuthbert. tham, manifested be procreacion of ane child betuix thame. Thai bayth confes. And Thomas being demandit, Gyf he knew or had ony suspicion aganis Margret that sche wes corruppit befoyr he knew hyr carnaly: quhai ansuered, that he had na suspicion nor knawlege. And now Margret askis Thomas to be decernit to solemnizat mariaige wyth hyr, and tak hyr to his lawfull wyf, according to the law of God, as he that hes deflored hyr virginite. Quhilk to do the said Thomas *simpliciter* denyed, wythowtyn ony resson gevyn be hym. The ministery statutis *literatorie* to pronunce in the clam of mariaig and satisfaccion of parteis; and in the myd tym ordenis[4] Margret to caus hyr father to compeir befoyr tham to schaw his wyl in the sayd caws.

---

[1] This name, which is supplied in the margin, has at first been *Janat*, but has been altered to make it *Thomas*.

[2] *Agns* in MS.　　　[3] Lose.　　　[4] *Ordes* in MS.

Die primo Septembris anno etc lxiij.

Decretum mat-
rimoniale Reid
contra Cuthbert.　The quhilk daye, in the caws and clam of mariaige of Thoimas Cuthbert acclamed be Margret Reid, the Superintendent and ministerie, avysed wyth the said caus and havand the mynd and consent of Thomas Reid, pronuncis and decernis the sayd Thomas Cuthbert to solemnizat mariaig wyth the sayd Margret Reid betuix this and Martymes nixt to cum, and falyeing tharof to pay to the said Margret twenty marchas, to towcher hyr wyth ane other man, at term foyrsayd ; and to bayr his charge of the barn gottyn betuix tham as becummis hym of dewete. Pronunced in presens of the saidis parteis heirto summond.

Die xxix Decembris anno quo supra.

Caucio Paterson.　The quhilk daye, James Brog is becum souerte for Besse Paterson fornicator wyth Andro Baxtar huyrmongar, that sche sall underly disciplyn and obey the ordinance of the ministerie for hyr [1] transgressione.

Die penultimo Septembris anno Domini etc. lxiij, et xx° Octobris anno predicto.

Peticio Kyd
contra Jarden.　The quhilk day, Catren Kyd acclamis mariaige of Mr. Alexander Jarden minister, accordyng to the law of God, becaus the sayd Alexander hes deflored hyr virginite. Mr. Alexander confessis hym to have had carnall dayll wyth Catryne, yit nocht certan gyf sche wes ane virgin befoyr he meld wyth hyr, as also dowtis gyf the barne pertenis to hym quhilk sche hes consavit ; desyris delay of tym, quharby sic tryall may be had as he maw knaw, be the byrth of hyr barne, quhidder the sam appertenis to hym or nocht. In respect of the quhilk clame, ansuer and confession of Mr. Alexander mayd tharto, the Superintendent *Deprivacio* dischergis and deprivis Mr. Alexander Jarden fra his ministerie *Jarden.* of preching and funccion of all office in the kyrk, chargis hym to desist tharfra in all tym cuming fra this hour furth, quhyll he be restored and of new admittit under all heast pane of dis-

---

[1] *His* in MS.

ciplyn.   The ministry ordenis Mr. Alexander Jardeñ to tak to *Decretum*
his wyf Catrin Kyd, and solemnizat mariaig wyth hyr wythin xl *matrimoniale inter Jÿrdeÿ et*
dayes, or ellis in the myd tym to allege and varefy sum resson- *Kyd.*
abyll caws quhy he suld nocht sa do.[1]

Die 3 Novembris anno quo supra.

The quhilk daye, comperis Andro Trayll, sone of Mr. George *Decretum*
Trayll, and offerris hym to underly disciplyn of the kyrk, for *contra Trayll et Anderson.*
fornicacion committit betuix hym and Janat Anderson, desyr-
ing his barne gottyn betuix hym and the said Janat to be
resavit to baptisme.   The ministerie understandyng sum brut of
suspicion to be rased aganis Mr. George Trayll, father to the
sayd Andro, that he suld be father of the said barne, thai
orden the said Mr. George to be called to this nixt Wednisday,
that his part tharin may be tryed and knawyn, and in this myd
tym Andro Trayll and Janat Anderson to fynd caucion to
underly disciplyn and obey the ordinance of the ministerie
wythin xxj dayes, and, the sam fundyn, the barne to be baptised.   And now Andro Trayll is becum caucion for Janat
Anderson, and William Ferre for Andro Trayll, that thai sall
fulfyll the ordinance of the ministerie.   And Mr. George *Purgacio Magistri Georgij Trayll.*

---

[1] On the 31st of December 1563, 'Tuiching the question proponit be the
Superintendent of Fyfe, anent Alexander Jarden, minister of Kilspindie, Inches-
ture, and Rait, wha had committed fornication with a virgine, and therafter had
maried her, and satisfiet the kirk, whither he sould be admittit againe to the
ministrie or not; the Kirk [*i.e.* the General Assembly] suspends the said Alexander fra all functioun of the ministrie within the kirk whill the nixt Assemblie.
and then to receive ansuer' (*Booke of the Universall Kirk*, Ban. Club, i. 45).
Accordingly, on the 29th of June 1564, the matter again came before the General
Assembly, when 'the haill Kirk, in consideratioun of his marriage and public
satisfactioun wher the offence was committed, ordainit to make humble requeist
to my Lord of Murray to be content that the said Mr. Alexander sould be
received againe to his ministrie in respect of the premisses, and therafter that the
Superintendent of Fyffe sould restore him againe to his ministrie as of befor'
(*Ibid.* i. 50).   He became minister of Monimail—a mensal church of the Archbishop of St. Andrews before the Reformation—at Lammas 1568; in 1574 he
had also Collessie, Auchtermuchty, and Abdie under his charge; he removed to
Collessie before 1578, but returned to Monimail in 1579 (Scott's *Fasti*, ii. 501).
One of the offences, with which the commission of the General Assembly was
instructed to charge Patrick Adamson, in July 1579, was that he 'had caused
remove Mr. Alexander Jerdan from the kirk of Monymaill, being his own kirk'
(*Booke of the Universall Kirk*, ii. 433).

Trayll, being called and accused of the suspicion brited aganis hym, purgit hymsilf.

Die xij Januarii anno Domini quo supra.

Decretum contra Stanis et Symson fornicatores.

The quhilk daye, Schir James Stanis, sumtym Papist preist and recanted, being summond to this daye and session, be the Superintendentis letteres dewly execut indorsat and repro-duced, accordyng to the determinacion of the holl Kyrk in thar Generall Essemble, haldyn at Edinburgh in December last wes,[1] and also to ansuer anent his hurdom wyth Maig Symson ; and also the said Maig summond to the sam effect. Thai bayth called and nether of tham comperand, the Superintendent, wyth the avyis of the ministerie, decernis letteres of excommunica-cion in dew forme aganis the said Schir James,[2] accordyng to the determinacion foyrsayd of the holl Kyrk ; and the sayd Maige to be summond agan to certan day wyth intimacion as efferis.

Die viij Marcii anno Domini etc. lxiij.

Decretum matrimoniale inter Bet et Anderson in Flysk.

The quhilk daye, Johane Bet and Besse Anderson in Flysk, fornicatoris, ar ordened be the Superintendent to mak public satisfaccion in the essemble of Flysk this nixt Sundaye. Quhilkis Johan and Besse also confes mutuall promys of mari-aig mayd betuix tham, and wylling to performe the sam ; quhilk thai ar decernit to compleit be solemnizacion wythin fyfty dayes nixt heirefter, under pane of excommunicacionie.

Peticio Tynclar contra Strang.

The quhilk daye, Johane Strang being summond be the Superintendentis letteres, at the instance of Janat Thomson, *alias* Tynclar, to ansuer to hyr clame, as he that mayd promys

---

[1] If the General Assembly, which sat in Edinburgh from the 25th to the 31st of December 1563, took any special notice of Sir James Stanis, their deliverance is not preserved. Perhaps the reference is to the more general statement :— 'The commissioners and brethren of Fyfe presented a row [*i.e.* a roll], wherein war diverse complaints given against the Superintendent of Fyfe : his answere was, That some of these things layed to his charge lay not in his power to amend. The complainers war commended for there zeale in delating things worthie of redresse, and admonished the Superintendent to be diligent in preaching and execution of his office ' (*Booke of the Universall Kirk*, i. 43).

[2] *Janes* in MS.

of mariaige wyth the said Janat in presens of the ministerie of Kynros, and tharefter knew hyr carnale, and sen syn hes jonet hymself in mariaige wyth ane other woman in Flysk, the said Ihon called and nocht comperand is noted *contumax*. The Superintendent decernis letteres of inhibicion upon the sayd Ihon and his pretendit wyf, chergyng tham to absteyn fra all cohabitacion and carnall dayll, unto sic tym that the caus and clame of the said Janat be discussed.

Die xxij Marcii anno quo supra.

The quhilk day, comperis Johan Strang in Burlie and pre- [Strang, sentis the copy of the Superintendentis letteres execut upon Tynclar.] hym, be virteu of the quhilkis he wes comperit to schaw his obedience, wylling to defend the caws layd to his charge be Janat Thomson *alias* Tynclar. And Janat Tynclar nocht present to perseu hyr [clame][1] ànon, the ministerie ordenis Ihon to compeir at the nixt summondis, to quhilk he consentis.

Die xv Marcii anno Domini etc. lxiij.

The quhilk daye, Johane Steynson, readar in the kyrk of *Decretum* Abyrcrumme, and Marion Grymmen, his harlot, summond to *contra* Steynsone and this daye and session be the Superintendentis letteres, as the Grymman secund summondis efter thai had beyn notit *contumaces*, and to forr'i atori have ansuerit upon the delacionis gevyn in upon tham, to wyt, for huyrmongyn inveterat, and also of new manifestit be the being of Marion wyth barne to the sayd Ihon; and also the sayd Ihon for nocht communicateyng at the Lordis Tabyll be the space [of][1] iiij yearis last bypast. The sayd Jhon comperand, his delacion red, he confessis and submittis hym to disciplyn and to obey all charge of the kyrk to be layd to hym. And Marion called and nocht comperand is notet *contumax*. The Superintendent, wyth avys of the ministerie, decernis letteres of excommunicacion aganis Marion for hyr[2] offencis and contempt; and deprivis the sayd Ihon Steynsoun fra the ministracion of readyng and funccion of ony office in the kyrk, ay and quhill his repentance àppeir, and he tharby be of new

---

[1] Omitted.   [2] *His* in MS.

admittit.[1] And also ordenis the sayd Ihon [to compeir][2] this
nixt Sunday, in the public essemble in the kyrk of Anstroyer,
Deprivacio
Joannis
Steynson.
and mak public satisfaccion accordyng to the ordor of the
kyrk, and to absteyn fra all cumpany public or privat of the
said Marione Grymman.

Die viij mensis Marcii anno quo supra.

[Wm. Huntar
and Barbara
Sandelandis.]
The quhilk daye, Wyliam Huntar, of Balcarros, and Barbara
Sandelandis, spows of Ibon Forbes apperand of Reres, summond
be the Superintendentis letteres, deuly execut and indorsat, to
have compered this day, to underly disciplyn of the kyrk for
thar fylthy adulteri committed betuix thame manifestit be
procreacion of ane child betuix tham. Thai called and nocht
comperand, Wyliam is excused be ane diet that he hes befoyr
the Lordis, and Barbara is noted *contumax;* and the summondis
contenewit to Wedinsday nixt to cum concernyng Wyliam
Huntar.

Die xv Marcii anno etc. lxiij.

Decretum
satisfaccionis
Wmi. Huntar
in Balcaros
propter
adulterium.
The quhilk daye, as in term assignit be continuacione to
Wiliam Huntar to compeir and underly disciplyn, for the
offence and sclander rased be his occasion of adulterie committed
betuix hym and Barbara Sandelandis, spows of Ihon Forbes
apperand of Reres, the said Wiliam comperand offerris hym to
underly disciplyn of the kyrk anent the sclander rased of the
said adultery. The Superintendent, wyth the avyis of the
ministerie, decernis the said Wyliam to compeir in the parrochie kyrk of Kylconquhar, upon Sunday the ix daye of Aprill
nixt to cum, in the public essemble of the congregacion, and
thar confes his offences humyll [hym][2]self upon his kneis, fyrst

---

[1] Steynson's place was speedily filled, if the three modern historical writers
may be relied on, who assert that John Ferguson was reader at Abercrombie in
1563 (Scott's *Fasti,* ii. 402; *Selections from the Minutes of the Synod of Fife,*
Abbot. Club, appendix, p. 201; Wood's *East Neuk,* 1887, p. 237); but they
give no authority for the statement. Thomas Young, who had the vicarage, was
reader in 1567 or 1568 (*Register of Ministers, etc.,* Mait. Club, p. 23); and he
was still reader, with a stipend of £16 and the kirk-land, in 1574 (*Wodrow
Miscellany,* p. 361).   [2] Omitted.

ask God mercy, and sa mony particular personis—frendis of the
said Johan Forbas and Barbara Sandelandis—as sall compeir to
resave satisfaccion, and also generaly the holl congregacion
present forgyfnes ; and also, at the sycht and discrecion of the
ministerie of Kylconquhar, ansuer and deliver to thame ane
pecuniall sowm of money, alwayis nocht exceding ten liƀ., to
be distrubuted be tham to the puyr or kyrk work.   And ordenis
the minister or readar of Kylconquhar, ilk Sunday in this myd
tym, to publeis the foyrsayd satisfaccion[1] to be mayd be Wyliam
at the said daye appoynted, requiryng the parteis offendit to
be present.

The quhilk day, James Dot and Margret Fyndlaye delated, *Satisfacio* Dot
called, accused and convict for fornicacion committit betuix *and Fyndlay fornicatoris.*
tham, James for the fyrst falt, and Margret confessyng hyr to
have borne thre barnis of befoyr, gottyn in fornicacion[2] wyth
thre syndry men, sche is ordened to stand ane hour in the jogis
this nixt Setterday, at the marcat croce of Sanctandrois ; and
upon Sunday nixt to cum, the sayd James and Margret, in the
public essemble of the congregacion, to syt upon the penitent
stull duryng the tym of the sermon, and at the end tharof
acknawledge thar offencis on thar kneis, ask God mercy and
the congregacion forgyfnes.

Die xxix Marcii anno Domini m°v° sexagesimo quarto.

The quhilk daye, James Lyell, sumtym Papist prest, confessis *Confessio et*
hymself to have recanted and to hav renuncit all Papistry ; and *obligacio Jacobj Lyell.*
of his awyn proper confession oblesis hym that in tym cuming,
nether in Scotland nor ony other realm or cuntre, he sall, in word
or deid, owtward signe, apparell, or ony other maner or way,
profes Papistry ; bot treuly constantly and manifestly profes the
religion of Crist, according to the doctrin and profession be
hym imbrased and confessed in his recantacione wythin this
cite, utherwayis he to be estemed ane Papist.   The contrary
being provyn, the sayd James to underly all maner of disciplyn alsoweyl of the kyrk as punischiment of the civil magis-

---

[1] *Satisfaccn* in MS.   [2] *Forncacon* in MS.

tratis, and to be cuttit of as ane rannegalt and renunsar of his fayth.[1]

Die xix Aprilis anno Domini m⁰v⁰lxiiij^{to.}

Peticio Bavireg. The quhilk daye, James Gylmor summond to this daye be the Superintendentis letteres, at the instance of Besse Bawerege his spows, to heir hym decernit to adheir to the said Besse as to his lawfull wyff; comperis James, and, for stop of his adherance, *Excepcio* be way of excepcion, allegis that the said Besse laytly, sen *Gylmor.*[2] solemnizacion of thar mariaige, hes gevyn hyr body in fylthy adulterie and incest to Ihon Symson, sister sone to the said James, in presens of Besse quhai denyis the same. And the foyrsayd excepcione being admittit to probacion of James, and gret numer of wytnes be hym produced, resavit, sworne, ad-*Concordia inter* mittit and examinat, the excepcion unprovyn. Finaly, upone *Gylmor et* the xxiiij day of Maii, *anno quo supra*, the parteis being *Bawerege.* movid to concord, the said Besse Bawerege, in presens of James and holl session of Superintendent and ministerie, purgis hyr of the sayd alleged adulterie aganis hyr, and acknauledgis and confessis hyr in tymmis past nocht to have beyn sa obedient to James hyr husband as becam hyr of dewetie toward hyr hus-band and head, quharby sche understandis hym to hav takyn occasion to intent and propon the excepcion of adultery aganis hyr tending to divorcment; and, at desyr of James, one hyr knes askit hym forgyfnes, and hes mayd promys never to be seyn in cumpany wyth Jhon Symson in prevy nor in [public][3] part, and to serve and obey hyr husband as becummis hyr of dewetie. And Robert Bauerege, hyr father, is becumin caucion to James that Besse salbe ane gud and faythfull wyff and servand to the

---

[1] Among those summoned to underlie 'the sensiment off Parliament, for the tressonabill slauchter of umquhile David Cardinale Archbischop of Sanctandrois, Chancellar of Scotland, and for the taking and with-halding of the castell of Sanctandrois,' in 1546, there was a ' Schir James Lyell chaplane' (*Register of the Privy Council*, i. 32). It may be impossible to identify the 'chaplane' with the 'sumtym Papist prest' in the text; but there can be no doubt that the person who came under this new obligation was the same 'Jacobus Lyell' who recanted in February 1559-60 (*supra*, p. 14); and so there must have been some cause for doubting his sincerity.
[2] *Gylnor* in MS.   [3] Omitted.

said James hyr howsband ; and gyf at ony tym sche falyeis, he never sall assist hyr wyth ony help, and heyrupon hes gevyn his hand to James. And James Gylmor remittis all caus and offence to Besse and resavis hyr in his favor and is finaly reconciled wyth hyr.

Die quinto mensis Aprilis anno quo supra.

The quhilk daye, Schyr Nycholl Bawerege, Schyr George Tod, Den Johan Wylson,[1] sa called in Papistry, being[2] summond, be the Superintendentis letteres deuly execut and indorsat, to compeir in this his session befoyr hym and ministerie of Sanctandrois, to underly disciplyn for saying mes and hearyng tharof, and ministracion of sacramentis unadmittit and in privat howsis ; thai, oft tymmes called and non of tham comperand, ar noted *contumaces*. The Superintendent decernis letteres of excommunicacion in dew forme to be execut aganis tham accordyng to the ordor of the kyrk.

Bawerege, Tod, Wylson, excommunicat. Papistis, mesmongaris

The quhilk daye, Thomas Walcar and Margret Mowtray, parrochinaris of Kyngorne, delated for fornicacion committed betuix tham, and summond tharfor, be the Superintendentis[3] letteres deuly execut and indorsat, this day to compeir and underly[4] disciplyn ; and nocht comperand ar notat *contumaces*, and letteres decernit upon tham in forme of excommunicacion to be execut accordyng to the ordor of the kyrk.

Walcar and Mowtray fornicatoris excommunicat.

The quhilk day, Annabell Adeson, nurice to Mr. Robert Ayrth in Couper, and harlot to Schyr Dauid Donaldson,[5] Papist prest, summond to underly disciplyn befoyr the Superintendent ; and nocht comperand is notit *contumax*, and letteres of excommunicacion decernit to be execut aganis hyr accordyng to the ordor of the kyrk.

Adeson, harlot, excommunicat.

The quhilk daye, Schyr Alexander Gaw and Catren Nesche, huyrmongaris and adulteraris, delated to the Superintendent, dwelland in Abyrnethy, summond to this day to underly disciplyn ; and nocht comperand ar noted *contumaces* and letteres

Gaw and Neis adulteraris excommunicat.

---

[1] Dean John Wilson, canon of Holyrood and vicar of Kinghorn, made a public recantation in the parish church of St. Andrews in Februäry 1559-60 (*supra*, pp. 11-13).   *Be* in MS.   [3] *Superintendis* in MS.
[4] *Undrly* in MS.   [5] See *supra*, p. 183.

N

decernit upon tham in forme of excommunicacion, to be execut according to the ordor of the kyrk.

Die x mensis Maii anno Domini 1564.

Obligacio Anderson vicarii de Glesche.

    The quhilk daye, Johane Anderson, sumtym vicar of Glesche,[1] of his awyn proper confession, oblesis hym to solemnizat his mariaige wyth Eufame Pattone upon Sunday the xxviij day of Maii instant, called Trinite Sunday, and to report testimonial to the Superintendent tharupon; and that he and the said Eufam sall underly disciplin, and fulfill the ordinance of the Superintendent as he sall burdyn tham wyth to the uttermost.

    Heir followis the proces led aganis Johane Bycartoun,[2] saidlar, citiner of Sanctandrois, for contempt of the ordor of the kyrk and ministerie, begun the x day of the moneth of Maii, the year of God m°v° sexty fowr yearis.

Causa Bycartoun.

    The quhilk daye, Johane Bycartoun, saidlar, citiner of Sanctandrois, delated for contempt of the establesched ordor of the Reformed Kyrk wythin the citie of Sanctandrois, in procuryng of his barne,[3] laytlie borne wythin this cite, to be presented to baptisme be Mr. Dauid Meldrum, his self being present for the tym wythin the cite wald nocht present his awyn child to baptisme, tharby gevand occasion of offence and sclander to[4] the holl kyrk. Jobane, called befoyr the

---

[1] The parish of Glass in the presbytery of Strathbogie.

[2] In the list of the hammermen of St. Andrews on the 4th of March 1547-8, there is the name of 'Jhone Byccartone'; but, as it is in a different hand from the others and occurs near the end, it has probably been added afterwards. At all events, on the 24th of January 1550-1, there is this plain statement :—' Alexander Powte hes ressavit Johnn Bicartoun in prenteis, and the said Johnn oblessis hym prenteis to the said Alexander for fyif yeris and ane yeir for meit and fee.' His name is also duly mentioned in the list of the brethren of the craft dated 24th July 1560 (*Minute-Book of the Hammermen of St. Andrews*, MS.). He was one of those who befriended the Dominicans in St. Andrews (see *supra*, p. 16, n.).

[3] *Larne* in MS.   [4] *To to* in MS.

ministerie to have beyn accused heirof and comperand, prevenit the accusacione, and, all reverence set asyd, stubburnly,
wyth pertinacite, affirmit and mantenit his contempt of the
said ordor, saying thir wordis in effect following: Quhat is
this ye wald wyth me? I knaw weyll anewch it is becaus I
wald nocht present my awyn barne to baptisme! I never presented ane of my awyn barnis to baptism nor never wyll! I
hav nothing to do wyth yow nor yowr ordor, it is nocht grundit
upon the Scriptur, it is bot idolatre inventit be the braen of
man! And albeyd the said Johan confessed that he had communicat at the Lordis tabyll wyth the rest of this congregacion,
and also that he had assistit the congregacion wyth his body
armit in defence aganis the inimeis impugnoris of the trewth;
nevertheles, being required be the ministerie to remane and
resave ansuer of the foyrsaidis wordis be hym spokyn and to
submit hym to disciplyn, he stubburnly departed, refusand to
heir the voce of the kyrk, and denyed hym to have ony thing
to do wyth the ministerie, or Superintendent, also present for
the tym. In respect of the quhilkis premissis, the ministerye
ordenis ane supplicacione to be put in dew forme under the
sayll of the ministerie, and gevyn up to the magistratis of this
cite, requesting thaim of thar dewetie and office to put sic
ordor to the said Ihone that be thar autorite he be brocht to
obedience of the kyrk: and gyf this sall nocht serve, the ministerie to procead aganis Jhon Bicartoun to excommunicacion, as
to the gretast and last punischement belangand to the spirituall
ministerie.

Followis the tenor of the supplicacione.

Minister, eldaris and diaconis of Cristis kyrk and congrega- *Supplicacio*
cione of the cite and pareson of Sanctandrois, to the honour- [to the Provest,
abyll Provest, ballies and consayll of the sayd citie, Grace, ba^{ll}ies and
mercy and peace frome God the Father, throw Jesus Crist, consayll].
wyth perpetuall incress of the Holy Spirit. We have takyn
occasione bye the contempt and inobedience don and schawyn
befoyr us be Ihone Bycartouñ, saidlar, inhabitant of this cite
of Sanctandrois, to direct this our supplicacione to your honorabyll wysdomis, most ernistly requestyng of your dewetie, and

autorite òf your offices, to attend to the same ; [lest]¹ that be
the evyll exempill of one permitted, otheris and mo at efter
attempt wythowtyn fear to the lyik contempt and inobedience,
and that to the subversion of all godly ordor, and of the commone peace and quietnes we have had be the space of thir last
fyve yearis, granted to us be the gudwyll ànd favor of our God;
nocht dowtyng bot your honorabyll wysdomis wyl do that becummis of dewetye toward the said Johan Bycartoun, to bryng
hym to obedience of the kyrk, that na occasione be left to us
to draw the fearfull swerd of excommunicacion aganis hym,
quhilk of nay way we pretend to do sa lang as ony other hop
of remedy sall appeir. Gevyne under the sayll of the said
ministerie, at Sanctandrois, upon the ten daye of the moneth
of Maii, the year of our redempcione ane thowsand fyve hundreth sexty four yearis.

Die xxiiij mensis Maii anno Domini 1564.

[Bycartoun
still inobedient.]   The quhilk daye, it wes denunced to the ministerie in thar
sessione that ther appered na hop of obedience to be fundyn or
had of Ihon Bycartoun, be meanis of the magistratis of this
cite and thar supplicacione direct to tham for the sam purpos,
nochtwythstanding the magistratis had schawyn tham weyll
myndit tharin. And also be new delacione gevyn in upone the
said Johane Bycartoun to the ministerie, thai fynd that the
sayd Johane Bycartoun, oppynlie befoyr the consayll of the
town, hes impugnit and vilependit the godly establesched ordor
of the kyrk, of examinacion and confession of fayth used and
gevyn be the faythfull befoyr thar admission to the Lordis
tabyll, as ane thing nether godly nor necessar to be used.² In˙

---

¹ Omitted.
² 'All ministeris must be admonisched to be more cairfull to instruct the
ignorant than readdie to satisfie thair appetiteis, and more scharp in examinatioun then indulgent, in admitting to that great mysterie such as be ignorant of
the use and virtu of the same : and thairfore we think that the administratioun
of the Table aught never to be without that examinatioun pass before, especiallie
of those whose knawledge is suspect. We think that none ar apt to be admitted
to that mysterie who can not formalie say the Lordis Prayer, the Articles of the
Beleif, and declair the soume of the Law . . . Everie maister of houshald must
be commandit eathir to instruct, or ellis caus [to] be instructed, his children,
servandis, and familie, in the principallis of the Christiane religioun ; without

respect quharof, the ministerie thocht necessare to desyr the sayd Jhon to cum instantly and confer wyth tham, brotherly wyth quietnes, anent all contraverseis, and to that effect direct fyrst Jhon Motto, ane of the eldaris, and George Blak, ane of the diaconis, to request hym to cum to tham: quhilk return-yng wyth negatyve ansuer resavit fra the said Ihon, thai direct Master James Wylk and Mr. Martyn Gedde, eldaris [and Alex-ander Myller diacon—deleted] to persuad and solyst hym brotherly to cum and speyk wyth the ministerie. Thai also returnand wyth negatyve ansuer, the ministere decernis ane summondis to be lebellat upon his contemptis wyth admonicion[1] in the sam, to be execut in the public essemble of the congre-gacion this nixt Sundaye, to summond the sayd Ihon Bycartoun to compeir befoyr tham upon Wednesday, the last day of Maii, to ansuer to the punctis tharof and to underly disciplyn, under pane of excommunicacion: and so to procead one to the thrid admonicion aganis hym; and gyf he persistis in his contemptis, excommunicacion to be pronunced aganis hym.

Die ultimo mensis Maii anno quo supra.

The quhilk daye, in the session of the ministerie of Sanct-androis, comperis George Blak, readar of the sayd kyrk, and producis ane libellat summondis under the sayll of the said ministerie, deuly execut and indorsat, tharin summond Ihon Bycartoun to this daye and session. Of the quhilk summondis the tenor followis :—

Minister and eldaris of Cristis kyrk and congregacion wythin [Tenor of the fyrst sum-mondis.]

the knawledge whairof aught none to be admitted to the Tabill of the Lord Jesus: for suche as be so dull and so ignorant, that thei can neathir try thame selfis, neathir yit know the dignitie and misterie of that actioun, can not eat and drink of that Tabill worthelie. And thairfore of necessitie we judge it, that everie yeare at least, publict examinatioun be had by the ministeris and elderis of the knawledge of everie persoun within the Churche ; to wit, that everie maister and maistres of houshald cum thame selvis and thair familie so many as be cum to maturitie, before the ministeris and elderis, to gyf confessioun of thair faith, and to ansueir to such cheaf points of religioun as the ministeris shall demand. Such as be ignorant in the Articulis of thair Faith ; understand not, nor can not re-hearse the Commandimentis of God ; knaw not how to pray ; neathir whairinto thair richtuousnes consistis, aught not to be admitted to the Lordis Tabill ' (*First Book of Discipline*, ninth head).   [1] *Admcion* in MS.

the citie of Sanctandrois, to George Blak readar of the said
kyrk, Grace mercy and peace, throw Jesus Christ, wyth perpetuall incress of the Haly Spirit.   Seing it hes pleased the
gudnes of the Eternall, our God, of his meir mercy, to deliver
and reduce us furth of the bondage and yok of Antecrist, to
the lycht of the Ewangell of Jesus Crist be plenteows prechyng
of the same; so that the face of ane perfyt reformed kyrk hes
beyn seyn wythin this cite be the space of fyve yearis, the
sacramentis deuly ministrat, all thingis done in the kyrk be
comly ordor establesched, disciplyn used and resavit wythowtyn
contempt or ony plane contradiccione of ony person; quhill now
laytly, [upon]¹ the x day of Maii instant, Johan Bycartoun—
saidlar, inhabitant of this cite, and membre of this congregacion, adjonit be parttakyng of the Lordis Suppar wyth his
bretheren at the Lordis Tabyll, and assisting the congregacion
wyth his body armit in defence aganis the inimeis impugnaris
of the trewth as ane Protestant, and so haldyn and estemed
hethyrto—being delated, called and to have beyn accused
befoir us for contempt of the godly and comly ordor establesched in the kyrk, in procuryng his child laytlye borne
wythin this cite to be presented to baptisme be Mr. Dauid
Meldrum, his self being present for the tym wythin
this cite wald nocht present his awyn child, tharby gevand
occasione of offence and sclander to the holl congregacion:
the said Johan comperand befoir us prevenit our accusacion,
and, all reverence set apart, stubburnly, wyth pertinacite,
affirmed and mantenit his contempt of the said ordor, and at he
wald never be subject tharunto, and at the sam wes nocht
grundit upon the Scriptur, it wes bot² idolatre inventit be the
braen of man; also refusand to resave ansuer, or to heir the
voce of the kyrk, or to submit hym to disciplyn, being charged
tharto, stubburnly departed.   As also sen syn, he hes nocht
feared oppynly to impugne and vilepend the ordor most godly,
of examinacion and confession of fayth used and gevyn be the
faythfull befoyr admission to the Lordis Tabyll, as ane thing
nether godly nor necessar to be used.   Yit, nochtwythstandyng
all the premissis, we have labored be all meanis to have reduced

_____

¹ Omitted.   ² *Bo* in ms.

the said Johan to hear the voce of the kyrk wyth quietnes, and fyndis our travell as yit to tak non effect toward the sayd Ihon. Heirfor we requir you, in the name of the eternall God, that ye lawfully in the public essemble of the congregacion summond the said Johan Bycartoun to compeir befoyr us, in the consayll hows wythin the said kyrk, upon Wednisday the last day of Maii instant, in the hour of caus at efternuyn, to heir hym decernit to have transgressed the establesched ordor of the kyrk, and to have contempnit the same, and to heir the voce of the kyrk, and tharfor to underly disciplyn as salbe imput to hym for his contemptis and offences foyrsaidis ; wyth certificacion to the said Ihon gyf he compeir nocht, or comperand refusis disciplyn, we wyll procead aganis hym wyth detfull ordor to the finall execucione of excommunicacion as to the gretest and last punischiment belongyng to the spirituall ministerie, and tharefter invocat the assistance of the temporall autorite and civil power. The quhilk to do, we commit to yow power in the Lord be thir presentis, delivering the same be yow deuly execut and indorsat agane to the berrar : gevyn under the sayll of the said ministerie, at Sanctandrois, the xxvj daye of Maii, the year of our redempcion 1564.

Followis the indorsacion : Upon Sundaye the xxviij of Maii, I, George Blak, readar in the parroche kyrk of Sanctandrois, in the public essemble of the congregacion, summond Jhon Bycartoun oppynle, efter the tenor of this summondis retroscript, to daye and place wythin wryttyn, wytnes the holl congregacion and this my subscripsion manuall—George Blak, readar, wyth my hand.

The foyrsayd Jhon Bycartoun oft tymmis called, laufull tym byddyn, and he nocht comperand is noted *contumax.* The ministerie ordenis hym to be summond in maner foyrsayd, for the secund execucion and admonicione, to Wednisday nixt to cum, wyth intimacion as efferis.

Die septimo mensis Junii anno Domini 1564.

The quhilk daye, in the sessione of the ministerie of Sanctandrois, comperis George Blak, reader of the sayd kyrk, and produces ane summondis under sayll of the sayd ministerie, deuly execut and indorsat be the sayd George, readar, tharin summond to this day and session Johane˙ Bicartoun: of the quhilk the tenor followis.

[The Secund
Summondis.]
[Excepting a few slight alterations it is exactly the same as the first summons. The reference to their deliverance from the yoke of Antichrist and the establishment of the reformed kirk is omitted; but there is this addition to the narrative:—' Being constranit of owr dewete, we caused hym to be oppynly summond[1] to . have comperit befoir us, in our session the last day of Maii; wyth certificacion, gyf he comperit nocht, we wald procead aganis hym wyth detfull ordor to the finall execucion of excommunicacion; quhai nevertheles persisting in his contempt hes contumacetly absentit hym.' Then it goes on—' Heirfor, we requir yow, in the name of the eternall God, that ye now, as of befoyr, in this our secund admonicion, laufully, in the public essemble of the congregacion, summond the said Johane Bycartoun to còmpeir' on the 7th of June—and so on as before. ' Gevyn under the sayll of the said ministerie, at Sanctandrois, the secund daye of Junii, the year of our redempcion 1564.']

Followis the indorsacion: Upon Sunday, the ferd day of Junii instant, I, George Blak, reader in the pareis kyrk of Sanctandrois, in the public essemble of the congregacione, summond Johane Bycartoun oppynlie, efter the tenor of ˙this summondis retroscript, to day and place wythin wryttyn, wytnes the holl congregacione, and this my subscripsion manuall—George Blak, readar, wyth my hand.

The sayd Johan Bycartoun oft tymmis called and nocht comperand, lauful tym byddyn, he is notat *contumax* for the secund. The ministerie ordenis hym to be summond and· monest this nixt Sunday in lyik maner, to Wednisday nixt to cum, for the thrid and last admonicion; wyth intimacion that, except he humyll hymself and obey the admonicion, thai wyl procead aganis hym to execucion of excommunicacion the nixt Sundaye tharefter following.

---

[1] *Summond summond* in MS.

Die decimo quarto mensis Junii anno Domini 1564.

The quhilk daye, in the sessione of the ministerie of Sanct-androis, comperis George Blak, reader of the said kyrk, and producis ane summondis under sayll of the said ministerie, deuly executed and indorsat, tharin summond and monest Ihon Bycartoun for the thrid and last monicion to compeyr to this daye and session, as at mayr lenth is contenit in the sayd summondis : of the quhilk the tenor followis.

[It is almost identically the same as the second summons —the only material differences being the merely formal ones necessitated by this being the third summons.[1] 'We have caused the said Johan to be oppynlie summond be twa syndry admonicionis to have compered befoyr us in our session twa severall dayes.' 'Heirfor we requir yow, in the name of the eternall God, that ye now as of befoir in this our last and thrid monicion laufully, and in the public essemble of the congrega-cion, summond and moneis the said Johane Bycartoun to compeir befoyr us,' on Wednesday the 14th of June ; with certification that if he fails, 'wythowtyn ony farther delay, we wyll procead to the finall execucione of excommunicacion,' &c. Given under the seal of the said ministry on the 9th of June 1564.] [The thrid summondis.]

Followis the tenor of indorsacion : Upon Sunday the xj day of Junii, I, George Blak, reader in the parrochie kyrk of Sanct-androis, in the public essemble of the congregacion, summond Johan Bycartoun oppynlye, efter the tenor of the summondis retroscript, to day and place wythin wryttyn, wytnes the holl congregacion and this my subscripsion manuall—George Blak, reader, with my hand.

The sayd Ihone Bycartown, oft tymmis called, laufull tym byddyn,[2] and nocht comperand to obey this thrid and last admonicion, is notit *contumax* ; and be the ministerie decernit worthely to merit the sentence of excommunicacion, and[3] the sam to be execut aganis hym.[4]

---

[1] In one sentence the clerk has omitted an important 'not,' for he has written :—'As also sen syn he hes feared oppynly,' &c.

[2] *Byddy* in MS.   [3] *And and* in MS.

[4] This concluding paragraph has been copied into the *Register* by mistake

Die Veneris decimo sexto mensis Junii anno Domini 1564.

The quhilk daye, the ministerie being convenit and essembled, to consult anent the execucione of the sentence of excommunicacion aganis Ihon Bycartoun, for his trangressionis contempt and inobedience, thretnet aganis hym in the thre public admonicionis, and wordely of hym merit and aganis hym decernit;[1] thai, maturly avysed, efter lang ressonyng, have concluded and ordenis the minister, this nixt Sundaye, the xviij of Junii instant, in his sermone, to declar the danger of excommunicacion, be oppynnyng of the Scripturis and placis tharof most apt for the purpos; and also oppynly to grant to the said Jhon Bycartoun yit awcht dayes of mercy, wylling and desyryng the freindis of the said Johan in the myd tym to travell wyth hym for his amendiment to repentance; and also to signifye and geve place to ony person or personis, offendit wyth thir proceadyngis, to compeir the nixt Wednisday in the olkly session of the ministerie, and geve in be wryt or word the resson and caus of thar offence to be discussed; and gyf nane comperis that day, certyfying tham thar silence to be had for plan consent of the holl congregacione, and ordenis the sentence of excommunicacion to be put in wryt and dew forme, accordyng to the proces deduced aganis the sayd Ihon Bycartoun and rewyll of Sanct Paull wryttyn to the Corynthianis; and the sammyn to be denunced and ·publiclie[2] execut in the essemble, upon Sunday the xxv of Junii instant, except sum occasion ressonabyll of stay occur in the myd tym.

Die vigesimo primo mensis Junii anno Domini 1564.

The quhilk daye, the ministere being convenit in thar sessione, and knawyng the ordor prescrivit this last Frydaye to the minister to use, anent the oppynnyng of Scripturis and declaracion of the danger of excommunicacion, and delay of mercy for awcht dayes granting to Ihon Bycartoun, and desyryng of his frendis to labor wyth hym for reducyng of hym

---

before the 'tenor of indorsacion,' but the clerk has inserted marks to indicate that the order should be changed.

[1] *Decrnit* in MS. [2] *Publie* in MS.

to repentance, and requiryng and place gevyn to ony person
or personis offendit wyth thir procedingis to compeir this daye
and geve in be wryt or word the resson and caus of thar
offences to be discussed, otherwayis thar silence to [be][1] reput
for consent of the holl congregacion : all thir premissis detfully
used be the minister, accordyng to the cherge gevyn to hym,
thai caused to call for ony that wald compeyr to object in
word or wryyt aganis thar procedingis, and seing naine to compeyr, thai accept the silence for consent of the hol congregacion.
And partly be occasion of farther declaracione of the mater
and gravite of excommunicacion to be set furth be the minister,
and partly for other causis movyng the ministerie, thai orden
the execucion and denunsacion of excommunicacion to be con-
tenewed, quhill returnyng of the minister fra the Generall
Convencion of the Kyrk to be haldyn at Edinburgh, the xxvj
of Junii instant, and to be execut wythowt delay the fyrst
Sunday efter his returnyng, except repentance be fundyn in the
sayd Ihon Bycartoun.

> Followis the forme of the sentence of excommunica-
> tione denunced and execut aganis Ihon Bycartoun,
> upone Sunday the ix daye of Julii, anno 1564, in
> public essemble of the congregacion of Sanctandrois.

Wyth incalling of the name of Crist Jesus, Sone of the *Sentencia
eternall God, quho is the way the verite and the lyff, by quhois *excommunica-
mercye and gudnes, we, minister eldaris and diaconis of Cristis *cionis contra
kyrk and congregacion of Sanctandrois, ar called as watchemen *Bycartoun.*
ower his flok, quhilk he[2] hes mercifully delivered and reduced
from the bondage and yok of Antecrist to the lycht of his
Ewangell, be the plenteows preching of the same, so that the
face of ane perfyt reformed kyrk hes beyn seyn wythin this citie
be the space of fyve yearis. [With one or two very slight
variations it now runs on in the same words as the first summons. In recapitulating his assisting the congregation against
the enemies of the truth, the words 'be hym confessed' are
interjected.]   Yit, nochtwythstanding all thir premissis, we did

---

[1] Omitted.   [2] *He he* in MS.

fyrst labor be all meanis to have reduced the said Johan to heir
the voce of the kyrk wyth quietnes; and fyndyng that our
travell to tak non effecct toward hym, we have uttered his
caus and contemptis foyrsaidis to the holl congregacion, be thre
public citacionis and admonicionis mayd thre severall Sundayis
in the public essemble; wyth certificacion to hym, gyf he persistit in his contempt, we wald proceaid aganis hym wyth detful
ordor to the execucion of excommunicacione as to the gretest
and last punischiment belongyng to the spirituall ministerie,
and tharefter invocat the assistance of civill magistratis and
autorite temporall. Efter quhilkis thre public admonicionis
and public prayiris mayd for the said Jobane, at the day
appoynted for execucion of the horribyll sentence of excommunicacion agans hym, we thocht gud be oppynnyng of the
Scripturis of God to have the danger of his stayt declared, to
the fear and terror of the said Ihone and his adherantis qubat-
soever; and also granted awcht dayes of delay and mercy,
wylling his frendis to travell wyth hym in myd tym for his
amendiment; and gevyng place also to ony person offendit
wyth our proceadingis to geve in befoir us the resson and caus
of thar offence to be discussed. Seing non to compeir now,
becaus the said Johane Bycartoun persistis in his contempt,
inobedient to the voce of the kyrk, he wordely meritis and
deservis to be excommunicated, sepirated and cuttit of from the
societie and followschip of the congregacion of Crist Jesus and
all benifites of his kyrk; and to be delivered unto Sathane for
the destruccione of the flesche that the spirit ma be saved in the
daye of the Lord Jesus. Heirfor, havyng God only befoir owr
ees, and the testimonye of his trew and eternall Word, be this
owr sentence, we declar and denunce the said Johan Bycartoun,
for his transgression contempt and inobedience, excommunicat,
seperated and cuttit of from the congregacion and misticall
body of Crist Jesus, and all benefitis of his trew kyrk (the
hearyng of Goddis Word only except); delivering hym oneto
Sathan, for the distruccion of the flesche, that the spirit may
be saved in the daye of the Lord; and at nane of the faythfull
fearyng God, fra this hour furth, accumpany wyth hym in commonyng, talkyn, bying, selling, eating, drynkyn or other way
quhatsoever, except thai be appoynted of the kyrk for his

amendment; wyth certificacion gyf ony do in the contrar thai salbe reput favoraris and fostararis of his iniquite, called and accused tharfor, and, being convict as participant wyth hym, sall resave the lyik sentence wyth hym.   In wytnes heirof the sayll of the said ministerie is heirto affixit, at Sanctandrois, upon the xxiij day of Junii, the year of owr redempcion 1564 yearis, &c.

Upone the ix daye of Julii, anno 1564, I, Cristofer Goodman, minister of Goddis word, in the public essemble of the congregacion of Sanctandrois, execut thir present letteres, and accordyng to the tenor tharof denunced Johan Bycartoun excommunicated, and inhibit all and syndry faythfull to accumpany wyth hym as is abov specifyid.   In wytnes heirof, I have subscrivit this my indorsacion wyth my hand, Cristofer Goodman, minister, &c.

Die xiiij^{to} mensis Februarii anno Domini m^ov^clxiiij^{to.}

Seing it hath pleased the gudnes of the eternall God, to *Penitencia et* move the hart of Johane Bycartoun (efter lang obduracione, *satisfaccio Joannis Bycar-* and lying under the horribill sentence of excommunicacion *town.* pronunced aganis hym be consent of the holl kyrk for his transgressione of godly ordor, obstinacite in the same, inobedience and contempt of the kyrk) to humyll hymself, and compeir befoyr the ministerie the vij day of Februar instant ; and thar, in acknawledgyng of his offences, offer hym willing and obedient to the disciplyn of the kyrk, and to fulfyll thar ordinance in makyng of public satisfaccion to be appoyntit to hym, that he mycht be resavit to the unite of the kyrk and societie of the congregacione of Crist, to the gret rejoysing of the hartis of the said ministerie present at that tym ; quhai knawyng thar dewetie, that as the said Johane was cut of be consent of the holl kyrk, so also he awcht to be resavitt be the holl consent of the same, gyf no occasione of impediment war fund be thame toward hym.   For triall quharof, his foyrsaid desyr, in the public essemble of the congregacione upon Sunday the xj day of Februar foyrsaid, be the minister was publest ; and place gevyn to ony, that wald object impediment to stop the said desyr, to compeir in the session of the ministerie, upon Wednisday this xiiij of Februar, wyth intimacione that otherwayis thar silence wald be had and reput for thar holl consent. And now nan comperand to object, or allege impediment or stop, the ministerie, wyth glad hartis in name of the holl kyrk, declaris the said Johan Bycartoun to be admittit to public repentance and satisfaccione. And understandyng the said Ihon to have sustenit gret dampneg and disays in guddis and body, throw his awyn wyckednes and adheryng to the consall of the ongodlye, and subject instantly to ane disays and maledy that he is nocht habyll to underly sic disciplyn as his demirites justlye doeth deserve, the ministerie tharfor at this present dispensis wyth all rigor, and ordenis the said Jhon, this nixt Sunday, the xviij of Februar, at the end of the sermon befoir nuyn, in the public essemble of the congregacion, his offencis brevely being repetit be the minister, to acknawlege the same and promys obedience in tym cuming to the lawfull ordinance and voce of the kyrk, humyll hymself one his kneis, ask God mercye and the congregacione forgyfnes. This don, the minister sall fyrst resave hym be the hand in the pulpot quhar he standis, and syne sall appoynt hym to pas to sa money of the eldaris as salbe deput to syt together for that purpos; quhilkis in the name of the kyrk sall resave hym and embrace hym as thar brother to the unite of the kyrk. And last of all the minister sall geve thankis to God for his conversione, and mak public prayeris for his continuance, according to the purpos, as the Spirit of God sall move his hart for the tym, &c.

Thir premissis war deuly fulfillit in all poyntis be Ihon Bycartoun [1] the xviij of Februar.[2]

---

[1] On the 28th of April 1567 'the maist part of the bretheren of halmermen' of St. Andrews elected 'Johnne Bicartoun saidlar' as their deacon, until the first of the following March, because another who had been chosen, and who had been previously maltreated in that office, would not accept. Bicartoun only consented to undertake the duties on condition 'that all the haill craftes of the cite of Sanctandrois wald fortifie and defend him, and stand with him in all and syndrie actiones and causes,' concerning the welfare and liberty of the craft. Three days later the brethren again met to confirm his election. On the 23d of August he signs two entries as deacon, the first in a very free bold hand; and in November of the same year he signs other three. His ability to spell was quite equal to his handwriting, for in the five signatures his surname appears in three different forms. Immediately under his last signature, partly written indeed through the lower loop of the 'h' in 'Jhone,' there is this short notice: '*x° die mensis Marcii anno Domini m°v⁶lxvij obitus Jhonnis Bikarton*' (*Bouk off the Statutis and Ordinansis of the Hammermen of Sanctandrous*).

[2] *Januar* in MS.

Die octavo mensis Marcii anno Domini 1563.

The quhilk daye, Robert Boswall and Jonat Wemys, his *Processus inter Boswall et* pretendit spows, being summond be the Superintendentis *Wemys.* letteres to compeyr and heir thamselfis decernit to adheir to other, thai comperand and be the Superintendent requirit to adheir, Jonat allegis that Robert is [1] nocht hyr husband, and gyf he be hyr husband he hes cuttit hymself of fra hyr be committing adultery, and gevyng hyis body to divers and syndry women, as sche sall geve in this day awcht dayes ; quhilk is statut to hyr in presens of Robert herto summond.

Die xvᵗᵒ Marcii anno prescripto.

The quhilk daye, as in term assignit to Jonat Wemys to [Jonat Wemys produce hyr excepcion of adulterie in form aganis Robert Bos- *producis her* uall, to stop hyr adherance to hym, comperis Jonat and pro- *defensis.*] ducis certan wryting; quhilkis, red, seyn and considerit, ar fundyn informall and irrelevant ; and Janat tharfor is ordenit to reform and mak tham relevant, and deliver to Robert Bos- wall ane copy tharof in dew tym, to the effect he may ansuer tharto upon Wednisday in Pasche olk ; and ordenis hym to be summond to that effect.

Die quinto Aprilis anno Domini mᵛᶜlxiiijᵗᵒ·

The quhilk daye, as in term assignit to Robert Boswall to [Robert Bos- ansuer to the defensis proponit be Jonat Wemys to stop hyr *wall ansuers the defenˢⁱs.*] adherance to Robert, comperis Robert and confessis hym to have resavit the copy of Jonatis defensis. And ansuerand to the fyrst part tharof, he admittis and referris hym to the decreit of his divorciment betuix hym and Cristen Awery, and to the decretis of the Lordis of Session. Ansuerand to the secund part, he allegis the contrar tharof is knawyn that he intreted hyr sufficentle. *Item,* to the thrid, he ansueris and allegis that albeid he had committit adulterye sen the depart- ing of Jonat fra hym (quhilk he expresle denyis), in sa far as sche departit fra hym wythowtyn ony just caus, and at he

---

[1] *His* in MS.

requirit hyr bayth in jugment and furth of jugiment to return (quhilk he offerris hym to prev), sche wes the caus tharof; and sa sche, beand culpabill in that caus, awcht nocht to imput ony falt to hym. *Item*, Robert allegis that albeid Jonat wald allege and offer hyr to prev ony adulterye be hym committit in tym of Papistre and blindnes, that suld nocht fall under jugiment of this reformit kyrk. Attowr, albeid it war alleged that he had gevyn his body to ony other woman befoir the last nycht that Jonat departit fra hym, in [sa]² far as thai war reconciled in gevyn of hyr body to hym that last nycht, sche hes no caus to stop hyr adherance. Quhilkis premissis the said Robert desyris to be discussed befoyr ony thing be admittit to probacion of Jonat. The Superintendent, havand respect to the ignorance of the said Jonat, nocht habyll to consave nor mak ansuer to the allegit be Robert, ordenis the copy of this hayll act to be gevyn to hyr, that, be sycht tharof, sche may at hyr plesor have consall to eyk and reforme hyr defensis befoir interlocutor; and Wednisday statuit to the parteis to compeir and heir interlocutor gevyn.

Die xij Aprilis anno etc. lxiiij^{to.}

The quhilk daye, as in term assignit to geve interlocutor in the caws of adherance betuix Robert Boswall and Jonat Wemys, and to Jonat to eyk and reform gyf sche pleased, comperis Jonat and confessis resayt of the copy o hayll act, and refusis to eyk or reforme ony mayr, bot desyris hyr allegacionis admittit to hyr probacion. The Superintendent statutis to the parteis Wednisday nixt to cum and heir interlocutor gevyn.

Die xix Aprilis anno quo supra.

[Jonat passis fra all hyr defensis except that of adultery.]

The quhilk daye, as in term assignit be the Superintendent to gev interlocutor in the caus of adherance betuix Robert Boswall and Jonat Wemys, compiris Jonat and, befoyr inter-

---

¹ Boswell doubtless had an eye on those words of the Reformers, in which, after urging the 'Great Counsall of Scotland' to punish adulterers by death, they say:—'We meane not, that synnes committed in our formar blyndnes (whiche be almost buried in oblivioun) salbe callit agane to examinatioun and judgment' (*First Book of Discipline*, ninth head). ² Omitted.

locutor, passis fra all hyr excepcionis and defensis except the excepcion and defens of adultery allegit be hyr aganis Robert, and be hym committit sen hyr last departing fra his cumpany, and desyris hyr onle to be admittit to prev adultery be Robert committit sen hyr last departur fra hym, in presens of Robert; quhai repetis his fyrst part of ansuer mayd in actis to the thrid part of defensis of Jonat, and [allegis], in respect tharof, na place suld be gevyn to Jonat to prev this sayd pretendit defence of adultery. The Superintendent statutis the twenty of April instant to gev interlocutor upon the pointis of this act : parteis summond to compeyr day foyrsayd in his chalmer and abbay of Sa[nctandrois].

Die xx Aprilis anno predicto.

The quhilk daye, as in term assignit to gev interlocutor in the caws of adherance betuix Robert Boswall and Jonat Wemys, the Superintendent, avysed wyth allegacionis and desyr and ansuer of parteis, admittis the last excepcion of adultery proponit be Jonat agans Robert sen hyr last departur fra hym to hyr probacion, nochtwythstanding the allegit be Robert, provydit that Jonat discend upon the moneth and year of hyr departur last fra Robert, and upon the namis of the personis he committit the adulterie wyth; and statutis to Jonat the thrid daye of Maii nixt to cum to prev the admittit. Parteis heirto sumond be actis. And Robert protestis that he may have place to propon accusacion of adultery aganis Jonat, and other laufull defensis, tym and place : quhilk protestacion is admittit.

[The excepcion of Jonat admittit to hyr probacion.]

Die tertio mensis Maii anno quo supra.

The quhilk day, comperis Jonat Wemys, Lady Claslogy,[2]

[Jonat Wemys producis ane summondis indorsat and execut.]

---

[1] Omitted.

[2] Presumably Carslogie, near Cupar Fife, believed to have been the seat of the Clephanes from the days of William the Lion, and in whose possession it remained until a comparatively recent period. Janet Wemys was probably a widow of one of the lairds; but I can find no trace of her in Sir William Fraser's copious and elaborate *Memorials of the Family of Wemyss.* Lord Campbell writes :—' Soon after my mother's death my father ceased to reside in Cupar,

quhai producis ane summondis of the Superintendentis, direct
to ony minister or reader wythin the bowndis of his office, to
summond wytnes at the instance of the said Jonat, to prev hyr
excepcion of adulterye proponit aganis Robert Boswall to
stop hyr adherance to the said Robert as to hyr lawful husband, and to summond the said Robert to excep aganis the
said wytnes as he mycht of law, as at mayr lenth is contenit
in the saidis letteres, indorsat and execut be Henry Breydfut,
officiar, nether minister nor reader, executor of the saidis
letteres in summonding of the said Robert Boswall in his
maner, as the indorsacion beris. Comperis also James Roger,
servand of the said Robert Boswall, quhai presentit to the
Superintendent ane wrytyng, under sail and subscripsion of
Robert as the sam proportis, of the quhilk [the]¹ tenor
follows :—

[Tenor of the wrytyng sent be Robert Boswell.]

Superintendent of Fyff, and ministerie of the Cristiane congregacion of Sanctandrois, oneto your wysdomis humile schawis
and proponis Robert Boswell, in Ryalye, thir ressonis following, quhilkis being be your wysdomis seyn and considerit,
I awcht nocht, nor may nocht, compeir befoir your wysdomis,
to answer nor defend in the pretendit accion of adherance
intentat befoir your wysdomis for the adherance betuix Jonat
Wemys and me as my spows. Exhortand your wysdomis for
the reward of the eternall God, quhai knawis the secreit of all
hartis, to desist and ceas fra all forder proceding in the said
pretendit accion, and that na proces be deduced nor usit in
the sammyn, aye and quhill I may peaceable have aggres and
regres for defence of the said accion, and that for the causis
following. *In primis*, it is nocht unknawyn to your wysdomis,
namle in your awyn presens in jugiment, that, upon Wednisday the xix daye of April last was, the said Jonat and I
beand befoir your wysdomis pledand in the said caus, the said
Jonat, wyth hecht and presumpteous mynd, cruelly promyst to

---

and moved to Carslogie House, about a mile and a half from the town. This
dwelling was formed out of an ancient fortalice which had belonged to the
Clephanes of Carslogie for twenty generations. I had a room assigned me
scooped out of a wall of immense thickness, and here I took to miscellaneous
reading with extreme ardour' (*Life of Lord Chancellor Campbell*, 1881, i. 19).

¹ Omitted.

caus ding owt all my harnis ;[1] quhilk your wysdomis wyll testefye, and gayf ansuer tharto. And one the morne [she][2] did performe the sammyn, be hyr twa sonnis and servandis wyth otheris divers, to the gret effusion of my blud ; quhilk also is notorlye knawyn to the holl Universite of Sanctandrois. And tharfor I awcht nocht nor may nocht compeir befoir your wysdomis, for feyr of my lyff, to schaw my just defensis in the said accion. Secundlye, I, the said Robert, allegis that I awcht nocht be compellet to adheir to the said Jonat be resson of the causis foyrsaidis, and als in cace we beand together in bed or other place secretlye the said Jonat, or otheris in hyr nam of hyr causing, suld cut my throt. Quhilkis beand hard, seyn and considerit be your wysdomis, thar awcht na process be deducit nor usit in the said accion ; quhilk gyf thar be [I][2] protestis for remeid of law and to have accion aganis your wysdomis, becaus of the notorite of the premissis. And als [I][2] awcht and suld nocht compeir, quhill I be recompansit and satisfyit of dampnege and skayth sustenit be the said Jonat and hyr sonnis, conform to law. *Item*, I, the said Robert Boswall, be the tenor of thir presentis, mackis, con-stitutis, and ordenis James Roger, my servand, for me and in my name to compeir befoir your wysdomis, upon the thrid daye of May instant, in the hour of caus ; and thar, for me and in my name, to produce thir foyrsaidis ressonis in maner above wryttyn be the tenor heirof, subscrivit wyth my awyn hand, and als my sayll is affixit, at the Ryaltie, the secund day of May, the year of God m°v° thre scoyr fowr yearis, befoir thir wytnes, Thomas Dauidson, Johan Mwyr, wyth otheris divers—Robert Boswall wyth my hand, &c.

The Superintendent,[3] efter sycht and consideracion of the execucion of the summondis, fyndis Robert nocht laufully summond ; and for avoyding of nullite of proces, and also in respect of the contentis of the foyrsaid wryting presentit to hym be the servand of Robert Boswall, and notorite of the invasion and hurt don to hym wythin this cite of Sanctandrois in the last diet of this caus, and for otheris divers causis and

[The Superintendent cessis fra forder proceding in this caus.]

---

[1] Brains.
[2] Omitted.   [3] *Superntendent* in MS.

consideracionis moving hym, cessis fra forder proceding in this caus, oneto forder avysiment, and oneto sic tym as suyr access and regres be provydit to the said Robert be ordor of law, and autorite of the juge competent to quhom the provision tharof appertenis. And now, at desyr of the barronis, gentyllmen and frendis of the said Jonat comperand wyth hyr, the Superintendent hes decernit the extract of this act to be deliverit in actentik forme to the said Jonat.

Die xxij mensis Marcii anno Domini m°v°lxiij°·

Processus inter Thomson et Moffat. The quhilk daye, comperis Johane Moffat and Andro Moffat, bretheren german of Gelis Moffat, as narrest havand place of hyr parentis, and, to stop the proclamacion of bannis and solemnizacion of pretendit mariaige betuix Robert Thomson in Langraw and Elizabeth Orkye in Fedinche, allegis that the said Robert suld nocht be admittit to marye wyth the said Elizabeth; becaus, befoir ony promys of maruaige mayd betuix thame, the said Robert hes tyistit the said Gelis Moffat thar sister, sche being ane virgin hes deflored hyr virginite, and tharfor haldyn of the law of God and establesched ordor of this reformit kyrk to mare and tak to his wyf the said Gelis; and heirfor desyris the ministerie to caus stay proclamacion of thar bannis and put inhibicion to Robert to mary quhill this impediment be discussit—in presens of Robert, quhai allegis that Gelis Moffat wyll nocht affirme the sayingis of hyr bretheren. The ministerie assignis Wednisday nixt to cum for forder tryall in this mater; and chargis the said Robert Thomson, [and][1] Jhon and Andro Moffat to compeir the said day, and bryng wyth tham the said Gelis Moffat thar syster; and the proclamacion of bannis to ceas quhill discussing of this impediment proponet.

Die xxix mensis Marcii anno Domini m°v°lxiiij°·

[Forder tryall anent the impediment proponit to stop mariaige betuix Thomson and Orkye.] The quhilk daye, comperis Robert Thomson, Jhon Moffat, Andro Moffat, and wyth thaim Gelis Moffat thar sister, as in term assignit be the ministerie to thaim, for forder and better

---

[1] Omitted.

tryall to be had anent the impediment proponit to stop the proclamacion of bannis and solemnizacion of mariaige betuix Robert Thomson and Elizabeth Orkye. The athis of Robert Thomson and Gelis Moffat takyn. Gelis Moffat, be hyr ayth befoyr God, confessis that sche is deflored be Robert Thomson, and never had carnall dayll wyth ony other man nor the said Robert; and Robert Thomson confessis hym to have had carnall dayll wyth Gelis Moffat. And the saidis Jhon and Andro Moffat, in presens of Gelis Moffat thar sister, as narrest havand place of hyr parentis, allegis and proponis aganis the said Robert Thomson that, the said Gelis Moffat thar syster beand ane virgin, the said Robert, befoir ony promys of mariaige mayd wyth Elizabeth Orky, deflored the virginite of the said Gelis thar sister; and tharfor he is haldyn of the law of God and establesched ordor of this reformit kyrk to marye and tak to his wyf the said Gelis, quhilk thai ask hym to be decernit to performe. And Robert Thomson ansuerand allegis that he hes ressonabyll defensis for hym to allege quhy he suld nocht marye the said Gelis. The ministere, at his desyr, statutis to hym Wednisday nixt to cum to produce his defensis qualefyed in wryt, quhy he suld nocht marye Gelis to his wyf. Parteis heirto sumond be actis.

Die quinto mensis Aprilis anno Domini quo supra.

The quhilk daye, as in term assignit to Robert Thomson to produce his ressonis qualefyed in wryt quhy he suld [nocht][1] mare Gelis Moffat, &c., comperis Robert and producis certan ressonis in wryt, in presens of Gelis Moffat and hyr bretheren; quhilkis beand red, Gelis ratefyis and apprevis all led and don be hyr bretheren in hyr caus of mariaige aganis Robert, and askis the sam to procead and to do hyr justice for sche never knew man carnale bot hym alan, &c.

Followis certan brev and schort ressonis for the part of Robert Thomson, in Langraw, quhilkis being, be your wysdomis, the minister eldaris and diaconis of this Cristian congregacion of Sanctandrois, seyn and rychteouslie considerit, the said [Ressonis producit be Robert Thomson quhy he suld nocht marie Gelis Moffat.]

---

[1] Omitted.

Robert awcht nocht nor may na way be compellit to mary
Gelis Moffat, nochtwythstanding hyr pretendit confession mayd
in ane allegit act befoir your wysdomis the xxix of Marche last
wes, bot he aluterly[1] absolvit fra the pretendit clam of Ihon
[and][2] Andro Moffatis mayd in the said act, as it is conceavit.

In the fyrst, becaus, in the said pretendit act and contentis
tharof, thar apperis na certan perseuar havand or that ony way
may have accion to desyr hym to be compellit to marye the
said Gelis, as may be easely seyn be inspeccion of the sammyn ;
bot onlie that Ihone and Andro Moffatis, allegit bretheren to
the said Gelis, desiris Robert Thomson to be compellit to mary ;
at quhais instance he one na way is haldyn to ansuer in this
cace ; nor yit can̄ thai ony way pretend accion aganis hym
tharfor, nother of the law nor yit practik of this realm, seing
the said Gelis hes institut na accion aganis hym. In respect
quharof he suld be absolvit fra the pretendit clam as it is
conceavyt.

Secundly, gevand that sche had institut ane accion, quhilk
apperis nocht be the said act, thar is na caus nor resson contenit tharin quhy the said Robert suld be compellit to marye
the said Gelis ; bot onlie hyr awyn meir assercion, wythowtyn
ony peticion or clam preceding, or ony allegiance referrit be
the said Robert to hyr ayth ; unto the quhilk be don, he is
nocht haldyn to mak forder ansuer. For hyr pretendit confession, as it is mayd wythowtyn ony peticion preceding as said
is, can na way prejuge hym, nor he tharby be compellit of law
equite nor gud conscience to mary the said Gelis, wythowt sche
wald allege sum laufull promys of mariaige and preve the sam
as accordis.

For, suppos your wysdomis wald think it lawfull, for suppressing of vice, that quhensoever ane man defloris ane virgin
he suld be haldyn to mary hyr wythowtyn ony promis, yit
alwayis sche suld be sic ane as war knawyn to be ane virgin,
wythowt spot or offence notablie knawyn to have beyn don or
committit be hyr ; quhilk is nother allegit nor provyn in this
cace be the sayd Gelis, namly, that sche wes ane virgin undeflorit the tym that the said Robert accumpaneit wyth hyr ; and

---

[1] Wholly. [2] Omitted.

sua, befoir forder proces, he desyris ane qualefyid peticion and
ane[1] competent day to ansuer tharto, utherwayis protestis for
remeid of law tym and place.

Thridly, under protestacion [that][2] the premissis be fyrst
discussit in thar awyn ordor, the said Gelis is haldyn and reput
ane brokyn woman, quhai hes divers tymmis jonit hyr body in
fornicacion and unclenes wyth syndry men, lang befoir that
ever the said Robert knew hyr carnaly ; and is notable knawyn
to have beyn suspect and in suspect placis wyth syndry men,
specialy wyth Robert Dauidson, Thomas Anderson, Dauid
Huntar, Peter Fayrfull, soliter and quiet wyth tham selfis in
ane clos hows, and the dur stekyt one tham be ane lang space ;
sua that it wes vehementle presumit that the saidis personis
knew hyr carnaly and have committit fornicacion wyth hyr ;
quhilk the said Robert belevis sche wyll nocht in hyr conscience
deny, offerryng hym to preve the premissis sa far as thai ar
affirmatyve ; and desyring the affirmatyve of[3] the sammyn, sa
far as thai ar negatyve, to be provyn be the said Gelis, or ellis
to be haldyn *pro confesso*, and desiris ane term heirto.

The quhilk daye, the ministerie, avisit wyth the defencis [The fyrst and
foyrsaydis, the actis of proces, and Buk of Reformacion, and secund defensis
that the saydis Ihon and Andro Moffat in thar peticion repellit : the
allegis tham narrest havand place of parentis of Gelis, repellis thrid admittit.]
the fyrst and secund defensis ; and admittis the thrid defence,
in [sa][2] far as it is relevant, and namly the alleged fornicacion
committit be Gelis, befoir Robert knew hyr, wyth the parteis
specifyed and namit be Robert ; and at desyr of Robert statutis
to hym Wednisday nixt to cum to preve the admittit. Parteis
heirto summond be actis.

Die xij Aprilis anno prescripto.

The quhilk day, as in term assignit to Robert Thomson to [Cottaris pro-
prev his excepcion of defloracion of virginite of Gelis Moffat, duced be Robert
comperis Robert and desyris Thomas Crumblay, Catrin Merns, Thomson
Ihon Gybson, Marion Anderson, Jonat Criste, present, laufully repellit as wytnes suspect :
hys other wytnes
resavit.]

---

[1] *Aie* in MS.   [2] Omitted.
[3] Perhaps *the affirmatyve of* should be deleted in this obscure sentence.

summond, to be resavit wytnes. Aganis the quhilkis personis
Ihon and Andro Moffat allegis that thar cottaris to Robert,
producer, haldis thar howsis and land (quharof thai have thar
lyff) of the said Robert, duelland under hym in Langraw, quhai
may put thaim fra the sam quhen he pleasis; and [in] [1] respect
tharof [2] ar wytnes suspect, and suld nocht be admittit bot
repellit fra wytnes bearyng in his caus and defens. Quhilk
excepcion fundyn relevant of the law, the saidis cottaris confessand the sam, it is admittit and thai repellit. And Robert
Thomson producis Robert Brydy in Prior-lethem, Eleyn Stewart
in Wester Balrymonth, Gressell Peblis thar, Alexander Symson, Alexander Castaris, citneris, Margret Greg, quhilkis ar
sworne resavit and to examinacion admittit, in presens of Gelis
Moffat and hyr bretheren. And Barnard Husband and Wyliam
Brown summond to this daye and nocht comperand, the ministere statutis to Robert Wednisday nixt to cum, to do diligence
for tham and to summond sa mony may wytnes as he wyl use
in this caus. Parteis heirto summond [3] per acta.

Die xix Aprilis anno Domini etc. lxiiij[to]

[Robert Thom-
son producis
thre may wytnes
quhilkis ar
resavit ; and to
do diligence for
other thre nocht
comperand.]
The quhilk daye, as in term assignit to Robert Thomson to
do deligence for Barnard Husband and Wyliam Brown wytnes,
and to warn his wytnes that he wyll use in this caus, comperis
Robert and producis Barnard Husband, Wyliam Brown, James
Hagy, quhilkis ar resavit sworn and to examinacion admittit,
in presens of Gelis Moffat and hyr bretheren. And Dauid
Huntar, Wyliam Fayrfull, and Dauid Mows, provyn laufully
warnit, callit and nocht comperand, the ministerie statutis to
Robert the thrid of Maii nixt to cum to do diligence for the
saidis wytnes. Partibus apud acta citatis.

Die tercio mensis Maii anno Domini quo supra.

[Dauid Huntar
produced and
resavit ; and
Robert Thom-
son to do
dilgence for
Wm. Fayrfull
and Dauid
Mows.]
The quhilk daye, as in term assignit to Robert Thomson to
do dilegence for Dauid Huntar, Wyliam Fayrfull and Dauid
Mows, comperis Robert and producis Dauid Huntar, quhai

---

[1] Omitted.
[2] *Tharo* in MS.   [3] *Summod* in MS.

is resavit sworn and admittit, in presens of Gelis and hyr bretheren. And Wiliam Fayrfull [and]¹ Dauid Mows provyn summond and nocht comperand, the ministere statutis to Robert Wednisday nixt to cum, to do diligence for the saydis Wiliam and Dauid. Parteis heirto summond be actis.

Die x mensis Maii anno quo supra.

The quhilk daye, as in term assignit to Robert Thomson to do diligence for Wiliam Fayrfull and Dauid Mows wytnes : na diligence be hym don, the parteis perseuaris circumducis the term. The ministere statutis *literatorie* to pronunce. [The perseuaris circumdᵉcis the term.]

Followis the deposicionis of wytnes producit in the caus. [Deposicionis of wytnes.]

1 Robert Brydy, cottar in Priorlethem, wytnes, sworn and examinat upon excepcion of fornicacion² proponit be Robert Thomson to stop his mariage wyth Gelis Moffat, deponis that he kennis na thing concernyng the nam and fam of Gelis Moffat. *Item*, he deponis that upon ane tym he com to the bern in Langraw, fand the dur standand oppyn and past in tharat, saw Thomas Anderson lyand in the bern and Gelis Moffat also lyand in the bern, upon ane Sunday efternuyn abowt four houris, at the Lammes tyd in the lxij year. The deponar can nocht tell quhidder thai lay ner together or syndry ; he bald God speid and past his way furth agan, and left tham lyand. The deponar suspect thaim nocht to do ony evyll or have carnall dayll.

2 Eleyn Steward, spows of Robert Caluart in Balrymonth, wytnes, sworn and examinat, &c., deponis that Gelis Moffat dwelt ane half year wyth the deponar. Sche never hard nor saw ony thing to be suspect of hyr womanheid, nor saw na thing as is allegit aganis hyr, bot sum voce of nychtboris. Quhidder thai sayd suth or les³ sche knawis nocht.

3 Gressell Peblis, spows of James Hagy in Balrymonth, wytnes, deponis that Gelis Moffat was servand to hyr ane half year, saw nor kend na thing to be suspect toward hyr womanhead, nor saw na thing allegit aganis hyr be Robert Thomson.

¹ Omitted.   ² *Adultery* in MS.   ³ Truth or lies.

4   Alexander Castaris, inhabitant in Sanctandrois, sworn and
examinat, kennis na thing of this mater.

5   Margret Greg, servand familiar to Ihon Wylson in Fedinche,
wytnes, sworne and examinat upon the defence of Robert
Thomson, deponis that, abowt thre quarteris [of ane][1] year syn,
the deponar and Gelis Moffat war in thar beddis, into ane
symmer mornyng, into ane owtschot of Robert Thomsonis hows
in Langraw, upon fayr daylycht; and Thomas Anderson[2] com
in and all his clathis upon hym and put his hand in the bed,
and the deponar rays and past furth of the bed into the hall,
left the said Thomas Anderson in the chalmer lyand upon the
bed-stok, his hand in the bed quhar Gelis and ane las of ten
year ald or tharby war lyand; and at nan of the thre personis
com furth of the chalmer or owtschot, quhill the deponar had
laset hyr clathis and byggit one the fyir, quhilk tym sche
estemed to ane half hour ; and kennis na mayr in the mater.

6   Alexander Synison, talyour, citiner in Sanctandrois, sworn
and examinat upon the defens of Robert, knawis nathing in
that mater.

7   James Hagy, in Wester Balrymonth, wytnes, sworn and
examinat upon the defence of Robert Thomson, be his ayth
deponis that he never saw suspicione betuix Gelis Moffat and
ony person namit be Robert Thomson nor ony other person.
Item, he deponis that Gelis gat ane evyll nam and wes brutit ;
he[3] can nocht tell nor discend in speciall of ony person sche
wes brutit wyth. *Item*, as concernyng the brut betuix Gelis
Moffat and Peter Fayrfull, James in his ayth and conscience
deponis he never saw tham in naked bed together. *Item*, he
confessis and deponis that he saw Gelis Moffat, wyth hyr clathis
upon hyr, makand ane bed to Peter Fayrfull, brother to the
deponar, in his awyn bern at his command, sche being his servand ; and quhen the deponar com furth to the bern, he saw
Gelis cum furth rynnand fra Peter, he being nakit in the bern,
and otheris his servandis lyand in the sam bern in otheris
heddis ; and kennis na mayr in this mater.

8   Dauid Huntar, couper, citiner, wytnes, sworn and examinat
upon the defence, deponis that he kennis na thing tharof.

---

[1] Omitted.   [2] *Ander* in MS.   [3] *Be* in MS.

9 . Wylzam Brown, servand to Robert Caluart in Balrymonth, wytnes, sworn and examinat upon the defence of Robert Thomson aganis Gelis Moffat and hyr bretheren, be his ayth deponis that he knawis na thing to Gelis Moffat, bot ane gud woman of hyr person 'and womanhead, except hyr falt mayd wyth Robert Thomson. *Item*, examinat upon the alleged being in naked bed with Peter Fayrfull, he ansueris that the sayd Gelis beand in hyr naked bed and ane las wyth hyr, the deponar and other twa yong men, accumpaneid wyth Peter Fayrfull, war playing tham upon New-zear-ewyn, and com altogether quhar Gelis laye in hyr bed ; and Peter in his wantones fell down in the bed abov the clathis, quharof Gelis was rycht discontent. The deponer never saw ony suspicion of hurdom betuix tham than, nor ony other tym, nor kennis na mayr in this mater.

10 ˙ Barnard Hwsband, servand to James Hagy in Balrymonth, wytnes, examinat, sworn upon the sayd defence, be his ayth deponis that he never saw ony thing to Gelis Moffat that was suspect concernyng hyr womanhead other nor wyth Rob Thomson, nor kennis na evyll committit be hyr wyth ony personis namit in defens nor yit wyth ony other. The deponar duelt in Robert Caluartis hows wyth Gelis ane hal year, and never hard nor sawe ony suspicion of hyr body.

Die tercio Januarii anno Domini etc. lxiiij.[1]

The quhilk daye, comperis Andro Moffat, Ihon and Gelis Moffat, efter certain delay and avysiment, grantit to tham to avyis wyth and to schaw thar determinat mynd, quhidder thai wyll abyd at the desyr of mariaige asked and persewed of Robert Thomson, in favoris of the said Gelis for defloracion of hyr virginite. The said personis, wyth ane consent and assent, desyris and requiris of the ministerie to decern Robert Thomson to tak to his laufull wyf the said Gelis Moffat and solemnizat mariaig wyth hyr, according to thar fyrst asking and law of God. Quhilk request being hard and admittit, the ministere

[Andro, Ihon and Gelis Moffat still desyris Robert Thomson to be decernit to tak to his lawfull wyf the said Gelis.]

---

[1] *Lxiij* in MS., which is certainly a mistake.

ordenis the partes to be lawfully warnit to Widnisday nixt to cum,[1] to heir pronuncit in the said caus.

Followis the decreit.

[The Decreit.]   Wyth[2] incalling of the nam of Crist Jesus, Son of the eternall and everlevyng God, quho is the way the verite and the lyff, we, minister eldaris and diaconis of Cristis kyrk and congregacion of the cite and parroche of Sanctandrois, jugis in the caus of impediment opponit, in nam of Gelis Moff[at],[3] to the proclamacion of bannis of pretendit mariaig and promys betuix Robert Thomson in Langraw and Elizabeth Orky in Fedinche, membris of the foyrsaid congregacion ; and mariaig acclamed be Ibon and Andro Moffatis, bretheren german and narrest frendis on lyve to the said Gelis, in hyr nam and [in][4] presens of the said Robert Thomson, for offence done be the said Robert in defloryng of virginite of the said Gelis Moffat ; as in the peticion wryttyn in our act bukis, the xxij day of Marcii, the year of God 1563 yearis, and desyr of the said caus set *literatorie* to pronunce ; the parteis being heyrto laufully warnit, we—being ryplie avysid wyth the said peticion, ansueris, defencis, rychtis, ressonis, allegacionis of parteis, probacionis and deposicionis of wytnes, and all otheris produced and deduced in the said caus ; together wyth the provision and ordinance mayd be consent of the Generall Reformit Kyrk of Scotland, fundit and grundit upon the law of God anent the defloryng of virginis, contenit and wryttyn in the Buk of Reformacion,[5] and be us resavit observit and put in practik be divers decretis of befoir obtemperat be parteis havand interes

---

[1] If the decreet is correctly dated—the 13th of June 1565—the sentence must have been delayed for five months instead of a week.

[2] *Wylht* in MS.

[3] *Noff*[at] in MS. Much of this part of the *Register* is written in a careless, hurried hand ; many of the letters are not half formed.

[4] Omitted.

[5] 'The father, or neyrest freind, whose dowghter being a virgine is deflored, hath power by the law of God to compell the man that did that injurie to marie his dowghtter ; or yf the father will not accept him be reassone of his offense, then may he requyre the dote of his dowghter ; whiche yf the offendar be nott able to pay, then aught the civile magistrat to punishe his body by some other punishement' (*First Book of Discipline*, ninth head).

tharintill; and now havyng God only befoir our ees, and the
testimony of his trew and eternall Word—pronuncis decernis
and declaris the said Robert, for his transgression of the law of
God and offence don in defloryng of the virginite of the said
Gelis Moffat, to marye and tak to his lawfull wyf the said
Gelis Moffat, and solemnizat the band of matrimonye wyth
hyr, according to the ordor of the kyrk, wythin xl dayes [1] nixt
heirefter; nochtwythstanding the excepcion of fornicacion and
unclennes proponit in defence be the said Robert aganis Gelis,
admittit to his probacion and nocht provyn. Pronuncit in the
consall hows of the sayd parroche kyrk, in presens of the sayd
Robert and Andro Moffat, &c., upon the xiij daye of Junii,
the year of God m° v^c lxv yearis, being present in the essemble
Cristofer Gudman, minister, Masteris Ihon Douglas, James
Wylke, Alan Lawmonth, Ihon Moffat, Thomas Wolwod,
James Robertson, Ihon Motto, Stephyn Philp, Thomas Dalgles,
Andro Motto, George Blak, &c.

Die xxiiij^{to} Julii, anno Domini etc., lxiiij^{to}

The quhilk daye, the Superintendent, wyth avyis of his *Decretum inter*
consall, efter tryall takyn anent the public talkyn and evyll *Symson minis-*
terum et Cok-
sayingis betuix Jhon Symson, minister of Kennoquhy, and *burn de Traton.*
Andro Cokburn, of Traton, fyndis that the said Jhon Symson
minister said to the said Andro thir wordis in effect :—It
apperis ye have nocht the fear of God in your hart ! And also
that the said Andro, ansuering to the said Ihon, said thir
wordis in effect :—I have the fear of God in my hart better
nor ye or ony flatterar as ye ar ! Thir [2] premissis provyn be
Wyliam Zowll, Thomas Nylson, citineris, and Thomas Layng,
heirupon examinat; and heirfor the Superintendent ordenis
the said Ihon Symson minister, this nixt Sunday following, in
the public essemble of Kennoquhy, in the pulpot, to acknawlege hymself to have falyeit aganis the said Andro in speakyng
of the foyrsaidis wordis to hym, and his occasion of offence and
sclander tharby gevyn to the congregacion; and tharfor ask
the said Andro (gyf he be present) and also the congregacion

---

[1] *Daye* in MS.   [2] *This* in MS.

forgyfnes, offer hym redy to baptyis the child of the said
Andro, gyf Andro please present his child, according to the
ordor of the kyrk: and also desyris the said Andro to
present his barne to baptisme, and to acknawlege hymself to
have ansuerit raschely in sic wordis spekyn to the minister.

Die secundo Augusti anno Domini etc. lxiiij[to.]

Concordia inter Nycholson et Efflek.   The quhilk daye, Robert Nycholson and Jonat Efflek his
spows summond be the Superintendentis letteres and comperand,
thai ar chergit to adhear as man and wyf, or ellis to allege
ressonabill caws quhy thai suld nocht sa do. Robert allegis he
suld nocht adhear to Jonat, becaus the said Jonat Efflek as he
allegis hes gevyn hyr body to Wiliam Donaldson, mareit man,
duelland in Streweling, at the Rud-daye, beand at the fayr in
Kylconquhar. The said Robert beand demandit gyf he wald
prev his allegacion, and[1] he suld be admittit to prev the sam
befoyr the justice, quhar the said Jonat wald thoyll deid for
hyr offence according to the law, the said Robert—hearand
of the danger, movit of pite toward his wyf, of his awyn fre
motyve wyll—remitted hyr upon this condicion, that sche sall
becum[2] actitat to be ane trew party and servand to Robert in
tym cuming; and gyf at ony tym heirefter sche be fundyn gilte
in gevyng hyr body to ony person by hyr husband, and knawyn
in suspect cumpany and tharof beis conviyct, Robert to have
Obligacio Efflek.   the sam previlege as this falt war nocht remittit: to the quhilk
Jonat consentis, and oblesis hyr be this act tharto, and con-
fessit the allegit be Robert aganis hyr; and one hyr kneis
askit hym forgyfnes, oblesand hyr to be ane trew servand to
hym and never to falye, and consentis to thoyll the deid gyf
sche failyeis to hym in ony tym to cum. And now the
Superintendent committis the woman be supplicacion to the
magistratis of Dysart, quhar sche is resident, to be punist
civile, according to the ordour of that burgh.

Die xxv Julii anno etc. lxiiij[to.]

Lyp, Scot.   The quhilk daye, Ihon Lyp and Elizabeth Scot confessis

---

[1] If.   [2] *Becam* in MS.

mutuall promys of mariage betuix tham mayd, and, beand
commandit to procead to solemnizacion, Johan allegis that
Elizabeth hes brokyn promys, in that sche hes treated James
[*Hayr*—deleted] Thrislay, ressetting hym in hyr hows divers
nychtis, sche and he allan and the dur steakit upon tham : sa
seyn and kend be neyghboris, quharby it is to be understand
and sufficiently supponit that the said Elizabeth hes gevyn hyr
body to the said James sen thar promys mackyn. Quhilk
beand denyed be Elizabeth, the ministerie statutis to Ihon
Wednisday nixt to cum, to prev his allegiance. *Partibus apud
acta citatis.*

Die secundo Augusti anno quo supra.

The quhilk daye, as in term statut to Ihon Lyp to prev his [Lyp, Scot.]
allegacion mayd to stop his maruaige wyth Elizabeth Scot,
comperis Ihon and producis James Smyth, quhai is sworn
admittit and examinat, and in his deposicion previs na thing.
And Michell Smyth, Eleyn Buge, Ihon Smyth [and][1] Bege
Donaldson atteched and nocht comperand, Elizabeth Scot consentis thai be had for resavit and admittit.[2]

Die secundo Augusti anno quo supra.

The quhilk daye, Wyliam Walcar and Jonat Kyninmonth, Walcar,
dilatit for fornicacion committit betuix tham, called and com- Kyninmonth.
perand thai confes the sam ; and for that falt ar monist [to][1]
desist tharfra in tym cuming ; and for thar occasion of sclander
gevyn ar ordenit, this nixt Sunday, in the public essemble of
the kyrk befoyr nuyn, duryng the tym of the sermon, to syt
upon the penitent stull, and at the end tharof, on thar kneis,
acknawlege thar offeuces, ask God mercy and the congregacion
forgyfnes. And besyd this the woman to be committed to
the magistratis be supplicacion, to be punist civile as ane common bard, flytar, banner, suerar and fylthy person.

---

[1] Omitted.

[2] This entry is followed by a blank, reserved, apparently, for the conclusion
of the case, which has never been filled in.

Die xviij Aprilis anno Domini etc. lxv[to.]

[Walcar,
Kyninmonth.]

The quhilk daye, Jonat Kyninmonth of new delatit as suspect wyth Wyliam Walcar, be hanting and frequenting cumpany together, in drynkyn, and wesching his clathis, and tharof accusit, the woman confessis the frequenting of cumpany and drynkyn and wesching of his clathis, purgis hyr of carnall dayll. Thai ar monist, for the secund monicion, that thai be nocht seyn nor knawyn to frequent otheris cumpany ony way in tym cuming.

Die xxiiij[to] *Augusti anno etc. lxiiij*[to.]

Peblis,
Kyninmonth.

The quhilk day, Wyliam Peblis, son of Dauid Peblis in Lammelethem, called and acused for defloracion of virginite of Besse Kyninmonth, dochter of Wyliam Kyninmonth in Kynglasse, in presens of the said Wiliam confessis the sam. And Wiliam refusis *simpliciter* to geve his dochter in mariaige to Wyliam Peblis, and becaus he hes nocht in geyr to paye hyr towcher, it is finale aggret betuix partes that Wiliam Peblis sall resave the barn begottyn betuix hym and Besse Kyninmonth, accept upon hym the burding and charge of upbryingyn of the sam, and relev the sayd Besse and Wiliam hyr father of all coistus and cherge tharof. And Dauid Peblis, fader of the said Wyliam, hes acceppit upon hym the burding and cherge of the sayd barne. The ministerie ordenis the saydis Wyliam Peblis and Besse Kyninmonth to mak public satisfaccion in the essemble of the kyrk, this nixt Sundaye befoir nuyn, according to the ordor of the kyrk, and to absteyn fra all fylthines in tym cuming under pan of disciplyn in saier maner.

Die penultimo Augusti anno prescripto.

Satisfaccion of
Edmond
Cyllok and
Gressell Guthre.

The quhilk daye, it being understand to the ministerie that the parentis of Edmond Haye and Gressell Guthre, now efter divers consultacionis had anent the promys of mariag betuix the said Edmond and Gressell, had gevyn thar consentis to the accompleschment of thar mariage, and at it is desyrit thar bannis to be proclamt; nocht the les, in respect of the carniall copula-

cion had betuix tham efter promys and befoir solemnizacion of
thar mariaige, ordenis tham this nixt Sundaye to compeir in
the essemble of the kyrk befoir nuyin, and thar, duryng the tym
of the sermon, syt upon the penitent stull ; and efter sermon, as *Facta.*
thai salbe requirit be the minister, acknawlege thar offencis,
humyll tham selfis one thar kneis, ask God mercy and the congregacion forgyfnes ; and absteyn fra all carnall copulacion and
suspicion tharof quhill thar mariaige be soliemnizat.

Die xiij Septembris anno Domini etc. lxiiij^{to.}

The quhilk daye, Johan Wyliamson and Cristen *D*yk dilated Satisfaccion of
Ihon Wyliam-
son and Cristen
called and accused for fornicacion committit betuix tham, befoyr
ony laufull promys of mariaige mayd betuix tham knawyn to Dyk.
thar parentis, as is confessed be Robert *D*yk, father to the sayd
Cristein.   Thai ar ordened this nixt Sunday, in the public
essemble of the kyrk, befoir nuyn, duryng the tym of the sermon, to syt upon the penitent stull, and efter sermone acknaw- *Facta.*
lege thar offences, humill tham selfis on thar knes, ask God
mercy and the congregacion forgyfnes.   And the proclamacion of thar bannes and mariaig to ceas, quhill this be
performit deuly.

Die quarto Octobris anno quo supra.

The quhilk day, Bege Gwynd, spows of Alan Steynson baxtar, *Monicio* Gwnd.
delated callit accusit and convict of mys-saying and bannyn of
the said Alan hyr husband, and otherwayis mysbehavying hyr
towardis hym.   Sche is monist to forbear in tym cuming, under
payn of public satisfaccion mackyn tharfor in the essemble of
the kyrk.

Die xxv Octobris anno quo supra.

The quhilk daye, Jonat Smyth askis Jhon Gardinar, servand Satisfaccion,
Gardinar and
to the Lard Carnbe, to be decernit to present ane madyn barn Smyth, forni-
gottyn betuix tham to baptisme, and to concur wyth hyr anent catoris.
the educacion and upbryngyn of the said barn.   Ihon, dowtyng
the barn nocht to be gottyn be hym as he allegit, desyrit the
ayth of Jonat tharupon.   Sche, sworn, and in his presens

examinat deligentlie, deponis that he is father of the said barn ;
and that sche never had carnall dayll wyth ony other man nor
the sayd Ihon. In respect of the quhilkis, the ministerie
ordenis the saidis Ihon and Jonat this nixt Sunday to mak
public satisfaccion in the essemble of the kyrk, be syttyng on
the penitent stull and askyng forgyfnes, &c., and efter nuyn,
Ihon to present thar barn to baptisme. And bayth ar ordenit
to mak public satisfaccion in ony other kyrk quhair thai have
gevyn occasion of sclander, ather be committing of thar fornicacion, or qubair thar barn wes born. And Ihon Sibbald is
causion for Jonat, and Ihon for hymself.

Satisfaccion of Jhon Symsone merchand and Besse Frostrar.

The quhilk daye, Johan Symson marchand and Besse
Frostar, dilated and convict of transgression of the ordor of
the kyrk, in that thai have knawyn other carnaly efter promys
and befoir solemnizacion of thar mariaige, ar ordened to mak
public satisfaccion befoir solemnizacion of thar mariaige, according to the ordor resavit and observit.

Schyr Patryk Fergy *contu-max.*

The quhilk daye, Schyr Patrik Fergy, delated and summond
to this day and session be the Superintendentis letteres to
underly disciplyn for takyng upon hand to prech and minister
the sacramentis wythowtyn lawfull admission, and for drawyng
of the pepill to the chapell of Tulebarne[1] fra thar parroche
kyrk, oft tymmis called and nocht comperand, he is notit
contumax, and ordenit to be summond for the secund monicion
literatorie.

Schyr Ihon Mores is revol-tit and to be excommunicat.

The quhilk day, Schyr Jobane Moreson, efter his recantacion
admittit reader in Mithyll,[2] delated, and summond be the
Superintendentis letteres to underly disciplyn, for ministracion
of baptisme and mariaige efter the Papisticall fasson and that
indifferently to all personis. And also for prohanacion of the
sacrament of the Lordis Supper, abusyng the sam in privat
howsis, as also in the kyrk yard, about the kyrkyard dykis, and
resavyng fra ilk person that communicat ane penne ;[3] and in

---

[1] Tullibardine. [2] Probably Muthil in Perthshire.

[3] Though the charge was illegal it was certainly modest, and Sir John has had
at least one successor in the present century. Lachlan M'Intosh, the priest of
Gairnside, who died in 1846 at the patriarchal age of ninety-three, was in the
habit of charging a penny from each communicant. The light in which some
of his flock regarded the exaction may be inferred from the answer of a young

speciall upon Pasche day last was, in the hows of Ihon Graham in Pannalis, he ministrat to ane hundreth personis. He, oft tymmis called, nocht comperand, and beand of befoir divers tymmis monest to desist tharfra under panis of excommunicacion, now wordely meritis the sam to be execut aganis hym; and sa decretit to be used.

The quhilk day, Schyr Ihon Stephyn delated, and summond be the Superintendentis[1] letteres to this day and session to underly disciplyn, for dayly ministracion of the sacramentis and solemnizacion of mariageis on the Papisticall fasson in the chapell of Sanct Gormoo, ane prophane hous suspendit; and als for mantenyng of ane huyr in his cumpanye, quhai hes born to hym twa barnis, as yit unbaptisit except it be by hymself or sum other Papist prest. He, oft tymmis callit, nocht comperand, is notit *contumax*, and to be summond agane for the secund monicione. Schyr Ihon Stephyn prophanar of sacramentis *contumax.*

Die primo Novembris anno Domini etc. lxiiij^{to.}

The quhilk daye, Thomas Kenzoquhy and Jonat Rynd summond be the Superintendentis letteres to this day and session, to underly disciplyn for adultery committit betuix tham—the wyf of the said Thomas heand one lyve, the said Jonat nevertheles wes fostered in his hows and wyth barn to hym. Thai called and nocht comperand ar notit *contumaces.* Kenzoquhy and Rynd adultereris *contumaces.*

The quhilk daye, Jhon Tod and Jonat Rynd delated, and summond to underly disciplyn, for fornicacion and hurdum wyth contenuance committit be thaim, and kepyn hows together unmaryed. Comperis Ibon Tod and confessis that thar wes mutuall promys of mariaige mayd betuix hym and Jonat Rynd, at Cayr Sunday[2] last wes, he, believyng [hyr][3] at thar contract to have beyn ane fre woman undefamit, tuk hyr haym to his awyn hows; and now is cum to his knawlege sche was consavit wyth child to ane other man befoyr thar contract and Tod, Rynd, fornicatoris.

---

woman, to whom, when catechising in a barn, he put the question: 'Do you pay anything to the priest for pardoning your sins?' Her ready response was: 'Ou aye, sir, a penny!'

[1] *Superindentis* in MS.

[2] The Sunday preceding Palm-Sunday. See Brand's *Popular Antiquities*, 1810, pp. 361-367.   [3] Omitted.

he dissavit; quharfor he hes repudiat hyr fra his hows and
cumpany wyth hyr barne; and Thomas Kenzoquhy, acknawledgyng the barn to be his, hes caused the sam to be baptised
in his nam be [*blank*] Lawson, minister of[1] Mockartse,[2] na
satisfaccion mayd be ony of the saidis parteis. The Superintendent assignis to Ihon Tod to prev his allegacionis this day
xv dayes; and ordenis the sayd Thomas Kenzow,[3] Jonat Rynd,
and Lauson, minister, to be summond to se probacion producit,
and tham to be punist tharfor.

Die xxij Novembris anno Domini etc. lxiiij[to.]

Mont and Scot.   The quhilk day, anent the desyr proponit be Jonat Mont of
mariaige betuix hyr and Jhone Scot, to quhom sche confessis
sche hes gevyn hyr body and consavit barne, efter promys of
mariaige mayd ·betuix tham privatle as sche allegis; the
ministere, understandi ıg thir personis to be sister and brether
barnis and that the man is absent, chargis Jonat to be present
this nixt Wednisday and the man wyth hyr, for tryall to be
had toward his part in this mater.

Die penultimo Novembris anno Domini etc. lxiiij[to.]

Satisfaccion   The quhilk daye, Johan Scot and Jonat Mont, fornicatoris
and inhibecion   and sisteris barns, ar ordened this nixt Sunday for disciplyn to
of Scot and
Mont.   mak public satisfaccion in the essemble of the kyrk, and fra this
furth to seperat tham fra mutuall cohabitacion and societe,
oneto sic tym as thar caus and desyr of maruaige be oppynnit
and discussed in the Generall Essemble of the Kyrk, in December nixt to cum.[4]

---

[1] *Of of* in MS.

[2] The first minister of Muckersey given by Scott is John Row in 1574; the
parish has long been annexed to Forteviot (*Fasti*, ii. 642).   [3] *Sic.*

[4] No reference to this case is preserved among the records of the General
Assembly which met on the 25th of December 1564; but in the Assembly which
met in the following June a very similar case is thus mentioned : ' Whither if a
man abuseing his cousignes, his fathers brothers daughter, sevin yeirs, and
begottin children, and presentlie wald marie her, and underly correctioun, may
marie or not. The degries are second of consanguinitie. Thogh this be not
found contrair to the Word of God, yet because it hes bein publicklie reveilit in
this realme, and that diverse inconvenients are perceivit to enseu of this liberty ;
thinks it good, that it be offerred to the civill magistrate, or els to ane parliament,

Die sexto Decembris anno quo supra.

The quhilk daye, anent the desyr proponit be Ihon Rychard- Satisfaccion of
son in Bonetoun of the admission of his child to baptisme, Rychardson
the Superintendent and ministerie beand certifyed be Master efter excom-
Wyliam Scot, minister of Carnbe,[1] and exhibicion of sentence municacion.
of excommunicacion execut aganis the said Ihon Rychardson,
be ordinance of the ministerie of Carnbe, for his contempt and
inobedience of the said ministere of Carnbe, in the moneth of
December in the lxij year, the said Ihon for that tym beand
parrochinar in Carnbe; and now understanding be purgacion
mayd be the sayd Ihon that the execucion of the said sentence
com never to his knawlege, and seing signis of repentance in
the said Ihon, the Superintendent, wyth avyis and consent of
the ministere and Mr. Wyliam Scot minister foyrsayd, ordenis
the said Ihon Rychardson to compeir this nixt Sunday at the
kyrk of Carnbe[2] ane hour befoyr the prechyn, and thar at the
kyrk dur space foyrsayd stand in the jogis, wyth ane papar
abowt his head, contenyng wryttyn tharupon, Behald the contempnar. And siclyik to stand in sum public place of the
kyrk of Carnbe, wyth the said paper abowt his head duryng
the tym of the prechyng, and at the end tharof confes his
offence, humyll hymself on his kneis, ask God mercy and the
congregacion forgyfnes. And he to be resavit in the bosum of
the kyrk, be the minister and eldaris present in nam of the
holl kyrk; and heirupon procur testimoniall to be presentit to
this ministere of Sanctandrois, and efter sycht tharof his barne
to be admittit and resavit to baptisme.

Die tercio Januarii anno quo supra.

The quhilk day, the clam of mariaige, be verteu of promys Peticio Brown,
                                                            mariage of
                                                            Fowlis.

---

for ordour to be taken therein; in the mean time, that men take not libertie to
themselves according to there fleschly filthie affectiouns; notheles that the persones, in whose name this question was proponit, be joynit in marriage after there
public repentance for the offences bygane, without any hope that uthers have the
like licence, whill farther ordour be tane be the civil magistrat, as said is ' (*Booke
of the Universall Kirk*, Ban. Club, i. 62).

[1] Hew Scott gives no minister of Carnbee before David Spens in 1567 (*Fasti*,
ii. 411).

[2] *Canbe* in MS.

allegit mayd befoyr wytnes, persewit be Mirabell Brown of Ihon
Fowlis, beand denyit be the said Jhon, the Superintendent and
ministere statutis to Mirabell Wednisday nixt to cum to prev
the promys.   Parteis heyrto summond *apud acta.*

Die x mensis Januarii anno quo supra.

Decret of
mariaig betuix
Ihon Fowlis
and Mirabell
Brown.

The quhilk daye, as in term assignit to Mirabell Brown to
prev lawfull promys of mariaige betuix hyr and Ihon Fowlis,
comperis Mirabell and producis James Gowrlay, Margret Kynlowch his spows, and Jonat Kay ; quhilkis ar sworn, resavit,
admittit, in presens of Ihon Fowlis, and instantle examinat ; in
thar deposicionis, deponis and previs that upon Sunday nixt
preceding Michaelmes, in the lxiij year, befoir nuyn, in the
hows of James Gourlay in Lucris, efter that Ibon Fowlis and
the mother of Mirabell war aggreit upon ten marcas of towcher
gude, the said Jhon, be laying his hand in the hand of Mirabell,
promyst to marie hyr, and sche promyst to be gud servand to
hym.   In respect of the quhilk, the ministerie ordenis and
decernis the said Jhon Fowlis to solemnizat mariaig wyth the
sayd Mirabell Brown wythin xl dayes, under pane of excom-

Satisfaccio[1]
Fowlis.

municacion ; and Ihon to mak public satisfaccion in the kyrk
this nixt Sunday, for other promys mackeyn wyth Eleyn
Watson quhilk in the self is null.

Die decimo Januarii anno Domini 1564.

Anent the mari-
aig of Thomas
Moncur and
Lady Lindesay.

The quhilk daye, anent the stop of mariaige betuix Thomas
Moncur and Eleyn Steward, Lady Lindesaye,[2] mayd be twa

---

[1] *Satisfacco* in MS.

[2] Helen Stewart, second daughter of John, second Earl of Atholl, who was
killed at Flodden, and grand-daughter of Archibald, second Earl of Argyll, was
married to John, fifth Lord Lindsay of Byres (see p. 95, n. 2), to whom she had
three sons and six daughters (Wood's *Douglas's Peerage*, 1813, i. 141, 385).
Squire Meldrum pathetically exclaims in his *Testament* :—

> ‘ My Lord Lindesay, adew abone all uther ;
> I pray to God, and to the Virgine Marie,
> With your lady to leif lang in the Struther.’

When Lord Lindsay died in 1563, his widow must have been well advanced
in life, although she so speedily wished to re-enter the married state.

myssyvis of Patrik, Lord Lindesay,[1] hyr sone, send to the
ministeris of Largo and Cowpar, contenyng in generall assercion
that the sayd Lord Patrik is habyll to prev that the said
Thomas is nocht habyll to resave sic benefitis of the kyrk, nocht
discendand in speciall of ony caus, as ane of the said myssyves
presentit befoir the Superintendent beris. The Superintendent,
wyth his consall beand heirwyth avysed, ordenis the ministeris
of Largo and Cowpar this nixt Sunday, the xiiij[2] of Januar
instant, in the public essembles of thar congregacionis, to mak
publicacione : That forsamekyll as Patrik Lord Lindesaye be
his myssyve signefyed to the saidis kyrkis that his Lordschip
had impediment to oppon aganis the mariaige betuix the saidis
parteis, withoutyn ony speciall mencion of the caus and impediment, desyring the said Lord, or ony otheris pretending to
allege ony impediment to stop the said mariaig, to compeir in
the essemble of [*Largo*—deleted] the ministerie of Largo, upon
Sunday the xxj of Januar instant, and thar in speciall geve in
the impediment in wryt, quhilk thai intend to allege ; and the
sammyn being fundyn relevant, the proponar to fynd caucion
for dampnege and expens of parte in cace he falye in probacion.
This being don, term to be assignit to the proponar to prev
the sam, Widnisday the xxiiij of Januar instant, in the essemble
of the Superintendent of Fyff in the parroche kyrk of Sanctandrois, makand intimacion to the saidis Thomas and Eleyn
to compeir and heir and se the sammyn provyn, and deliver
to tham the copye of impediment that salbe proponit to stop
thar mariaige. And in cace na person compeir the said xxj
day of Januar to allege impediment as said is, the sayd mariaige
betuix Thomas and Eleyn to procead, nochtwythstanding the
contentis of the foyrsaidis myssyvis.

The quhilk daye, Wiliam Lawson and Bege Jak, fornicatoris, Lawson, Jak,
fornicatoris.

---

[1] Patrick, sixth Lord Lindsay of the Byres. 'Fiercest and most bigoted of the
Lords of the Congregation, and doomed to unenviable immortality in the pages
of Sir Walter Scott, he was yet an honester man than most of his contemporaries,
and his zeal for the establishment of Protestantism seems to have been sincere,
however alloyed by meaner motives' (*Lives of the Lindsays*, 1849, i. 276). He
died on the 11th of December 1589, 'at a great age' (*Ibid.* i. 311).

[2] *xiiiij.* in MS.

wylling to marie together, ar ordened to mak satisfaccion according to the ordor of disciplin in this kyrk.

Die xxiiij[to.] Januarii anno quo supra.

Ramsay, Zowll, fornicatoris.

The quhilk daye, Rychard Ramsay talyour and Eufam Zowll, fornicatoris, manifestit be procreacion of ane child, ar ordened to mak public satisfaccion this nixt Sunday in the essemble of the kyrk; and Rychard to present the barn after nuyn to baptisme; and Eufam tharefter to resave the barne and ether hyrself foster the said barne or procur to it ane foster mother sufficient; and Rychard to concur in equall expens wyth Eufam anent the educacion of the barne.

Die penultimo Januarii anno quo supra.

Symson and M[c]ke committit to magistratis.

The quhilk daye, Walter Symson and Eufam Macke delated and acused for fornicacion wyth perseverance of huyrmongyn committit be tham. Thai bayth confes the sam, quharfor the ministerie be supplicacion committis tham to be punist civile be magistratis.

Watson and Symson to marye.

The quhilk daye, Henry Watson, cuk to the Bischop of Cathnes,[1] and Gelis Symson delated callit and accusit for fornicacion committit betuix tham. Thai bath confes the sam, and at thai ar under mutuall promys of mariaige mayd betuix tham. In respect of the quhilk confession, the ministerie decernis thame to mak public satisfaccion this nixt Sundaye in the essemble of the kyrk, and paye v s. to the box of the puyr; and wythin xl dayes to procead in solemnizacion of thar mariaige under pane of excommunicacion.

---

[1] Robert Stewart, brother to the Earl of Lennox, was elected Bishop of Caithness in 1542, but was never in priest's orders. He became a Protestant, but still bore the title of Bishop, and enjoyed the revenue of his see. After the murder of the Regent Murray, he also held the Priory of St. Andrews, and was made Earl of March in 1579. His wife, a daughter of the Earl of Athole, divorced him for impotency. He seems to have lived in St. Andrews until his death in 1586, and is said to have left a natural daughter (Keith's *Catalogue*, 1755, p. 128 ; Riddell's *Peerage and Consistorial Law*, 1842, i. 531-542).

Die xxj Februarii anno Domini etc. lxiiij^{to.}

The quhilk daye, anent the delacion gevyn in aganis Andro Duncan and Besse Duncan, tweching the horribill incest committit betuix tham manifestit be procreacion of ane child betuix thaim, the woman beand the reliç of umquhill Dauid Fyff syster son of the said Andro. The parteis beand both summond to this session be Superintendentis letteres to compeyr and underly disciplyn for thar offence foyrsayd, the said Andro comperand . personale he confessis his falt, humely submittis hym to disciplyn; and the woman excused be hyr brother throw impediment of this instant vehement storme of snaw, he in hyr nam confessis hyr offence, offerris hym souerte that sche sall underly and full [fill]¹ the disciplyn to be injineit to hyr. The Superintendent, wyth avyis of the ministerie, ordenis the saidis Andro and Besse thre syndre Sundayes to present thamselfis in the public essembleis of the kyrk of Dron and acknawlege thar offencis, obles thamselfis to absteyn fra all occasion of sclander gevyn in tym cuming, humyll thamselfis on thar kneis, ask God mercy and the congregacion forgyfnes; and, in the sam maner, thre Sundayes, mak the lyik satisfacion in the kyrk of Sanct Iohnstoun,² and pay to the box of the puyr of every ane of the saidis kyrkis x s.

Satisfaccion of Duncan and Duncan for incest.

The quhilk daye, anent the question of mariaige betuix Ihon Makcullo and Catrin Angus, and impediment to stop the sam proponit be Jhon aganis Catrin, the Superintendent and ministerie, advysed wyth the allegacionis and confessionis of parteis, findis the promys of maruaig betuix the saidis Ihon and Catrin to be lawfull, in respeç of the tym it wes mayd in and carnall copulacion following thar upon; and tharfor the saidis Ibon and Catrin to procead to thar solemnizacion and mariaige wythin xl dayes, under pan of excommunicacion, nochtwythstanding the allegit be Ihon, admittit [to his probacion]¹ and nocht provyn.

Decretum matrimoniale inter M^{c}cullo et Angus.

---

¹ Omitted. ² Perth.

Die xxij mensis Augusti anno Domini 1565.

Proces betuix
Beynstoun
[and]¹ Hep-
burn.

The quhilk daye, James Beynston, apperand of Lammelethem,²
and Joanna Hepburn, dochter and naturall of Patrik, Byschop
of Murray,³ laufully summond to this daye and session be the
Superintendentis letteres, to heir and se tham decernit to procead to solemnizacion of thar mariaige, contract betuix tham
detfully wyth consent of thar parentis and publeist be proclamacion of thar bannis, or ellis to allege ane ressonabill caus
quhy⁴ the sam suld nocht be don, &c. The saidis parteis
comperand, Joanna Hepburn allegis sche suld nocht be decernit
to compleit and solemnizat mariaig wyth James Beynstoin,
becaus that in the mayntym of the allegit contract, promys, or
gevyng of consent to the proclamacion of bannis tharof, the
said Joanna wes constranit and compellit be just fear and dredor
that mycht fall in ane constant mai, and that be Patrik Hepburn, parson of Kynoyr,⁵ my brother, wyth sic wordis, pronuncit
be hym wyth ane vehement and aufull contenance, sayand, Gyf
I consentit nocht to the said promys and completing tharof, he
sudd drown me in the watter of Erne as I past to Perth. And
I beand bot ane yong woman of xiij or xiiij yearis of aige,
destitut of knawlege, fearing my said brother that thar sudd
ane gret inconvenience follow heirefter, wyth sorowfull mynd

---

¹ Omitted.

² Lamboletham, now in Cameron, was then in the parish of St. Andrews.

³ Patrick Hepburn, son of Patrick, first Earl of Bothwell, succeeded his uncle,
John Hepburn, as Prior of St. Andrews in 1522, and was advanced to the See
of Moray in 1535, with which he held the Abbacy of Scone *in commendam.* He
persecuted Alesius with brutal cruelty, and had a chief hand in the martyrdom
of the aged Walter Mill. His zeal against heresy was only surpassed by his
shameless profligacy. Besides Joanna he had at least other ten natural children,
and these apparently by different mothers (Laing's *Knox*, i. 40, 41, 360; Anderson's *Annals of the English Bible*, ii. 447-449; *Register of Great Seal*, iii. Nos.
1329, 3169; iv. No. 460). 'He outlived and braved the Reformation, and continued his former mode of life in his palace and castle of Spyny, and his profuse
alienation of church lands, till his death, 20 June 1573' (*Registrum Episcopatus
Moraviensis*, Ban. Club, p. xvi.).

⁴ *Quhy quhy* in MS.

⁵ From 1562 to 1566 Patrick Hepburn was prebendary of Kynor and Dun-
hennan, which now form the parish of Huntly (*Illustrations of the Antiquities of
Aberdeen and Banff*, Spald. Club, ii. 164, 168). Three of the Bishop's bastards
bore the name of Patrick.

and sayr hart, bursting owt wyth tearis throw the aufull and
terrebyll fear and threatnyng of my said brother, beand far fra
my freindis at that tym, in cace of inconvenience as said is, wes
compellit to consent to quhat thing my said brother wald have
me to do or say.   And sua I awcht nor suld nocht be decernit
to compleit the said band, bot fred of the sayd James, lyikas
I am bayth of mynd and deid afoir God and man, lyikas I
never consentit tharto befoir in ony tym, bot constantle sted[1]
at the compulsion foyrsayd, lyikas I do yit and ever sall in that
mater.   Quhilkis premissis the sayd Joanna offerrit hyr to
prev, desyring hyr to be admittit tharto.   The Superintendent
requirit the sayd Joanna[2] to geyf hyr ayth of calumpne, gyf sche
hes just caus to propon and allege the foyrsaidis defensis; quhilk
desyr the sayd Joanna obeyit and fulfillit in gevyng hyr ayth,
and be the sam affirmit sche had just caus to propon and allege
the sam, and at thai war most trew.   The Superintendent, in
presens of James Beynstoin, admittis the saydis defensis to probacion of the sayd Joanna, and statutis to hyr at hyr desyr
Wednisday nixt to cum to prev the sam.   Parteis heyrto summond *apud acta.*   And James Beynstoun confessis that at the
pretendit contract and promys mackyng betuix hym and the sayd
Joanna, his father commandit hym to consent tharto, or ellis he
suld never get[3] gud of hym nor nan of his heretaige; and sua
fearing the foyrsayd thretinyng of his father, rather compellit
nor myndit wyth his hart to perform, he consentit, albeid the
sayd Joanna apperit to hym to have als lytell wyll of hym as
he had of hyr.   Quhilk confession Dauid Bowey, prolocutor for
Joanna Hepburn, acceppis sa far as mackis for the probacion of hyr defens, and repetis the sam in probacion tharof.

Die xxix Augusti anno Domini etc. lxv[to.]

The quhilk daye, as in term assignit to Joanna Hepburn to
prev hyr defensis proponit to stop hyr proceding to solemnizacion of mariaig wyth James Beynstoun and admittit, comperis[4]
Andro Bowey, hyr procurator be hyr mandat, and producis

---

[1] Stickled.
[2] *Ihon* in MS.
[3] *Gud* in MS.
[4] *Comperis comperis* in MS.

Wyliam Cwnygham of West Bernis, Thomas Wod sumtym
monk in Lundoris, Wiliam Lermonth in Scone, Wiliam Monepenny citiner in Sanctandrois, Issobell Mortoun Lady of Bernis,
Elizabeth Monepenny relict of Andro Wod, quhilk ar resavit,
suorn and admittit, in presens of James Beynstoun, and
instantle examinat.   Of the quhilkis thar deposicionis followis.

[Deposicionis of wytnes.]

1   Wyliam Cwnygham of West Bernis, wytnes, sworn and
examinat, be his ayth deponis that he hard Patrik Hepburn
speyk scharp and hard wordis to Joanna Hepburn to persuad
hyr consent to the contract and promys of mariaig wyth James
Beynstoun; hard and saw Joanna mak mony sunyeis [1] and say
sche wald nocht consent to na mariaig, quhill sche knew the
mynd of hyr father; and saw hyr burst and gret wyth mony
tearis, and be hyr plane contenance and behavor schawyn at
the pretendit promys mackyng wyth James Beynstoun, it
apperit planlie to the deponar Joanna gave na expres nor plan
consent in word nor contenance.   *Item*, the deponar hard
Patrik Hepburn say to Joanna, his syster, gyf sche wald nocht
consent to contract and promys mariaig wyth James Beynstoun, sche suld never get gud of hyr father bot gang lyik ane
huyr.

2   Thomas Wod, wytnes, sworn and examinat upon the saydis
defensis, be his ayth deponis that he wes present in Strawethey [2]
at the fyrst cuming thar of Joanna Hepburn, thar hard, be hyr
rehers and spekand wyth hyr awyn mowth, that sche wes
brocht thar agans hyr wyll, and at sche knew nathing of ony
maruaige to be talkit betuix hyr and James Beynstoin.   This
hard, the deponar departit furth or onything procedit, and
kennis na mayr.

3   Wyliam Lermonth, familiar servand to Patrik, Bischop of
Murray, wytnes, sworn and examinat anent the maner of
cuming of Joanna Hepburn to Strawethe and otheris defensis
proponit for hyr part, be his ayth deponis that he knawis
perfytlye that Joanna Hepburn, at hyr cuming fra Sanct

---

[1] Excuses.

[2] 'The castle of Stravithy, a little west from the centre of the parish' of
Dunino, 'was a regular fortalice, situated in a bog with ditch and drawbridge';
but 'the bog has been drained, and the site of the castle converted into corn-
land' (*Statistical Account of Fifeshire*, 1845, p. 365).

Jhonstoun to Strawethy, had na consent of hyr father and wes
dissavit be Patrik Hepburn hyr brother that brocht hyr.
Causam sciencie reddit, the deponar hymself wes send be Patrik,
Bischop of Murray, father to the said Joanna, sa son as he gat
wyt to stop the contract ; and also he hard the mater tryed
befoyr the said Bischop, and sa fund that all procedit wythowt
his consent, and wythowtyn knawlege of Joanna, quhai wes
browcht in Fyff wythowt hyr knawleg or consent to mary
thar. *Item*, the deponar examinat upon the manesyng of
Patryk toward Joanna, specifyed in the defensis, the deponar
affirms the sam to be trew. *Causam sciencie reddit*, he wes
present in Strawethy in ane ower chalmer, alan in cumpany
wyth Patrik and Joanna, in ane nuyk of the sayd chalmer
besyd ane chymnay, hard Patryk bost Joanna to droun hyr in
Ern, gyf sche consentit nocht to mary wyth James Beynstoun.
Item, the deponar affirmis the greting and tearis of Joanna,
mayd bayth befoyr the pretendit promys and in tym tharof.
He wes present hard and saw as he deponis.

4   Wyliam Monepenny, citner of Sanctandrois, wytnes, sworn
and examinat, be his ayth deponis that he wes present quhen
James Beynstoun, Joanna Hepburn, and frendis war convenit
to se and heyr promys of mariag betuix James and Joanna ;
saw Patrik Hepburn tak Joanna Hepburn be hyr alan and
spak wyth hyr the space of ane hour ; saw Joanna in that tym
greit veray sayr, and at lenth saw hyr cum wyth ane drery and
sad contenance, [with][1] tien,[2] and waykly wyth law voce consent, and be support of Patrik gev furth hyr hand : and kennis
na mayr in this caus.

5   Jssobell Morton, Lady of Bernis, wytnes, sworn and examinat,
be hyr ayth deponis that sche hard Joanna Hepburn say[3] to
the deponar, in Strewethy, that Patryk Hepburn hyr brother
brocht hyr thar aganis hyr wyll fra Sanct Ihonstoun upon ane
hors behynd hym. *Item*, sche deponis that sche hyrself wes
present quhen James Beynstoun, Joanna Hepburn, and frendis
war convenit to heir and se promys of mariag betuix James
and Joanna ; and the deponar saw at that self sam tym Joanna
Hepburn burst owt wyth greting and tearis ; quhilk seyn be

---

[1] Omitted.   [2] Sorrow, vexation.   [3] *Sayd* in MS.

the deponar, sche departit fra tham, beand disparit of ony
gud succes to follow upon sic begynnyn. *Item*, the deponar
deponis that befoyr ony pretendit promys betuix parteis, sche
hard Joanna Hepburn say oppynly that sche wald never mary
wyth James Beynstoun, and[1] thai suld harll hyr at ane hors
tayll : and kennis na mayr in this mater.

6   Elizabeth Monepenny, relict of Andro Wod, wytnes, sworn
and examinat, be hyr ayth deponis, and is conform to Issobell
Mortoun wytnes immediet preceding.

Declaracion of nullite of pretendit promys betuix Beynston and Hepburn.

The quhilk daye, the Superintendent and ministerie, avysit
wyth this proces preceding, findis and understandis that the
pretendit promys of mariaig̅ betuix James Beynston, apperand
of Lammelethem, and Joanna Hepburn, namit naturall dochter
of Patrik, Bischop of Murray, and of Jonat Vrquhart, of the
part of Joanna Hepburn is nor wes no fre nor lawfull promys
nor wylling consent, bot mayd throw fear of thretnyngis, wyth
wepying and lamentabyll contenance, dissavit be meanis of
Patrik Hepburn, parson of Kynoyr, hyr brother, unratefyed be
hyr in ony sort sen syn, and tharfor in the self nul and *non
effectum* :[2] and heirfor pronuncis and declaris the sam null, and
the saidis James Beynstoun and Joanna Hepburn, and every
ane of tham, to be fre for ony caus foyrsayd preceding, and at
liberte to mare in the Lord wyth ony lawfull parte, and heirupon decernis testimoniales to the parteis, &c.

Die septimo Februarii anno Domini etc. lxiiij^{to.}

Cognicione anent the barn of Cristen Flukar allegit to perteyn to Mr. Dauid Meldrum.

The quhilk daye, Cristen Flukar, servand sumtym to Mr.
Dauid Meldrum, delated to be wyth barne, sche nocht mareit
and the father unknawyn, and fugytyve efter knaulege had of
hyr being in Scottiscrag, and sche, hyr father, mother, and
James Chesolme in Scottiscrag hyr resettar, summond be the
Superintendentis letteres to this daye and session, comperis
James Chesolm personaly, and excused Cristen be bodely seyk-
nes. And the sayd James, being examinat upon certan headis,
ansuered as efter followis. The said James in his ansueris, in
his conscience, confessis that his brother, Thomas Chesolme,

---

[1] Although.   [2] *Offectum* in MS.

dwelland in Strolsownd, arryved at Dundei furth of Ducche
land at the Rud-day,[1] in Maye last wes, or tharby, and
remanit in Scotland the space of ane moneth, and than departit
toward Strolsownd; and in the tym of his being heir his sayd
brother resorted to the hows of Master Dauid Meldrum, quhar
Cristen Flukar dwelt for the tym, and thar knew the said
Cristen carnaly; and heirefter abowt viij dayis efter the nixt Chesolm,
Flukar.
Lammes, the said Thomas his brother returned in Scotland
and departed estward at Mychaelmes; and befoyr that his last
departyng, he confessed to the deponar that the said Cristen
Flukar was wyth child to hym, and ordenit hym to caus baptyis
the child, and mak expensis tharupon: quhilk child wes borne
upon Sanct Stephins daye,[2] this instant year of lxiiij. Quhilk
deposicion wryttyn, the Superintendent monest James Chesolm
to compeyr this day xv dayes, befoyr hym and the ministere in
thar essemble, quhen Cristen Filukar wes hayll, and caus hyr
cum wyth hym: to the quhilk he consentit.

Die xxj Februarii anno quo supra.

The quhilk daye, as in term assignit to James Chesolm to Chesolm,
compeir and wyth hym Cristen Flukar, comperis James Chesolm Flukar.
and excusis the absence of Cristen be impediment of instant
tempest and storme of snaw. Quhilk excus considerit and
admittit, the Superintendent monest James to compeyr this
day xv dayes and bring Cristen Flukar [3] wyth hym.

Die septimo mensis Marcii anno Domini etc. lxiiij[to.]

The quhilk day, as in term assignit to James Chesolm to Chesolm,
compeir and bring wyth hym Cristen Filukar, comperis James Flukar.
and allegis he hes put the said Cristen furth of his hows; and
be his ayth deponis he wayt nocht quhar sche is at this present
tym, and at na other person nor Cristen Flukar required hym
to treat the said Cristen, nor to be wytnes at baptisme to hyr
barne; and confessis that thar war wytnes at baptisme wyth
hym—ane called Barclay in Nether Corbe, and ane Flukar
father to the said Cristen, and ane woman brother wyf of the

---

[1] The 3d of May.   [2] The 26th of December.   [3] *Fluk* in MS.

said Cristen. The Superintendent monesis James to compeir this day viij dayes, and bryng wyth hym the said Cristen Flukar, according to his promys mayd the vij of Februar last wes, under pan of excommunicacion.

Die xiij Juni anno Domini m⁰v^clxv^to.

Chesolm,
Meldrum,
Flukar.

The quhilk day, efter that knawlege wes gottyn that Cristen Filukar, sa lang fugityve, wes duelland in *D*unde, and had confessed to Ihon Kynlowch, hyr master, that the barn be hyr borne wes begottyn betuix hyr and Master Dauid Meldrum, the said Master Dauid beand warnit to ansuer for hymself; and also James Chesolm, understand to be convoyar of the mater, summond to this daye and session and comperand, and the said James re-examinat upon the headis that he mayd ansuer to the vij of Februar last wes, contenit in the act of dayt foyrsayd, and accused of the sam to be knawyn now untrew, in his ansueris is becum repugnant to his formar deposicionis. And fyrst, he now deponis that Thomas Chesolm arryvit at Leyth abowt Pasche, and sua contrary to his fyrst deposicion in twa puntis, to wyt, anent the place and also anent the tym. Quhilk is ordenit to be ingrossit in the actis, quhill forder tryall be had in this caus, that be the sam he may be convict of perjure and underly disciplin, and [be]¹ committit to the Justice be supplicacion to be punest as the crym of fals wytnes deservis of the law. And the sayd Master Dauid Meldrum comperand and accused of adulterye committit be hym, he beand the husband of Cristen Thomson his lawfull wyf, hes gevyn his body to Cristen Flukar, manifestit be procreacion of ane child gottyn betuix tham, as the said Cristen hes confessed; . quhilk Mr. Dauid stowtly denyis hym to be gilte of the sayd accusacion, and offerred hym pron and redy to geve his ayth of calumpne. The Superintendent and ministere ordenis the said Mr. Dauid and James Chesolm to compeir this nixt Wednisday, and se forder triall takyn in this mater; and decernis supplicacion to be direct' to the ministerie of *D*unde be thar ordinarie meanis [to]¹ caus Cristen Flukar to compeyr the sayd Wednisday.

---

¹ Omitted.

Die xx mensis Junii anno Domini quo supra.

The quhilk day, as in term assignit for forder tryall to be takyn anent the barn born be Cristen Flukar for knawlege of the father tharof, the sayd Cristen comperand, hyr ayth of verite takyn to declar the trewth of the thingis to be demandit of hyr, and sche examinat, hyr deposicion follouis. In the fyrst, being demandit upon hyr ayth, quhai is father of hyr barne laytle borne upon Sanct Stephinis day last wes, sche ansueris and deponis Master Dauid Meldrum present to be fader tharof. *Item*, Cristen deponis that Master Dauid Meldrum beand in his bed in[1] ane mornyng, his wyf beand at Sanct Leonardis prayeris,[2] he called upon the deponar to gyf hym his clathis, at quhilk tym the said Master Dauid fyrst knew hyr carnaly, and that wes in the begynnyn of Lentron in the lxiij year; and siclyik the said Master Dauid knew hyr carnaly twa syndry mornyngis in his awyn bed, his awyn wyff ane of the sayd tymmes beand in Dunde. *Item*, the deponer confessis that efter sche wes knawyn to be wyth barne, Master Dauid schew to hyr that his wyff endlit upon hyr, and desyrit hyr to depart of the town; and also deponis that the wyf of Mr. Dauid, knawing hyr wyth barn, sperit at hyr quhai wes father to hyr barn; and the deponar ansuerit that the father of hyr barn was nocht in Scotland; and sa be that meanis sche bayd still in hows of Mr. Dauid quhill Martymes at hyr term com. *Item*, sche deponis at the term of Martymes beand cum, at consayll and desyr of Master Dauid, sche past haym to hyr fatheris hows; and befoyr hyr departing resavit fra Master Dauid xxx s. to mak hyr expensis, and sustenit hyr tharwyth quhill sche wes lychtar; and xiiij dayes efter sche wes lychtar, the deponar caused the vicar of Crech wryt ane byll in hyr

---

[1] *An* in MS.

[2] In speaking of the second year of his course at St. Leonard's College, 1572, James Melvill says: 'The graittest benefit I had of him [James Wilkie] was his daylie doctrine at the prayers in the kirk, everie morning; for he past throw the twa buiks of Samuel, and twa of the Kings, very pleanlie and substantiuslie' (Melvill's *Diary*, Wod. Soc., p. 27). It may be inferred from the incidental reference in the text that there was morning prayer in St. Leonard's Kirk while Duncanson was Principal, and that the attendance was not confined to students. See *supra*, pp. 76, and 103, n.

Q

nam to send to Master Dauid, wythowtyn mencione of his nam
tharin, and send the sam byll to Master Dauid wyth hyr father;
and efter Mr. Dauid had resavit the byll fra hyr father, James
Chesolm in Scottiscrag com to Cowpar, and thar sowcht hyr
father and met wyth hym, and sperit at hym gyf he had ane
dochter lyand in child-bed, quhai confessied sa to be. And the
sayd James requirit hyr father to caus the deponar cum and
meit hym the nixt Sunday, at Sanct Talis kyrk[1] wyth hyr
barne, and he suld gar baptyis the barne; and forbad hyr
father or ony other belangyn to hyr to ken or speik ane word
to Master Dauid Meldrum anent the mater, for he wald nocht
ken tham, for he had byddyn the said James do all thingis that
nedit to be don and he wald perform the sam. Quhilke foyrsaidis talkyn, the sayd Cristen deponis hyr[2] father tald to
hyr. *Item*, the said Cristen [deponis][3] that sche and Cristen
Patton, hyr brother wyff, com to Sanct Talis kyrk at day feyrst
appoynted, quhar sche met James Chesolm ane lytill bewest
the kyrk-yard; quhai excused hym be absence of the minister
of that kyrk that the barn wald nocht be gottyn baptised that
daye; and bald hyr be of gud comfort for sche knew the father
of hyr barne had na may barnis, and he wald do[4] weyll to hyr
barin and to hyrself. *Item*, the said James Chesolm, tym foyrsaid, in presens of the said Cristen Patton, hyr brother wyf,
duelland in Corbe-hyll, requirit the deponar to father hyr barne
upon Thomas Chesolm, his brother; and tackis upon hyr conscience and saull, sche never sawe the said Thomas Chesolm in
hyr lyftym, that sche kend hym be ane other man. Efter this
talkyn, the deponar departit to hyr father hows, remanit thar
quhill the nixt Sunday, and com agane to Sanct Talis kyrk;
quhar James Chesolm met hyr, and be hyis meanns and convoy ·
caused hyr to be admittit to ask that congregacion forgyfnes
and hyr barn to be baptised. And the deponar beand instruckit be James Chesolm, quhen sche wes required be the
minister quhai awcht hyr barn, sche ansuerit Thomas Chesolm
wes hyr barnis father. *Item*, efter baptysing of hyr barn, the
deponar returned wyth hyr barn to hyr faderis hows, and
remanit thar quhill the Lard of Kynayr send for hyr to inquir

---

[1] See *supra*, p. 180, n. 3.   [2] *His* in MS.   [3] Omitted.   [4] *To* in MS.

of hyr barnis father. And sche adverteist James Chesolm tharof, quhilk James causit hyr wyth hyr barn cum fra hyr fatheris hows to the hows of James, quhar the deponar remanit ane moneth. In quhilk myd tym James Chesolm wes summond to cum to Sanctandrois befoyr the Superintendent, and he desyrit the deponar to cum wyth hym, and to gev ane ayth thar that Thomas Chesolm, brother to the said James, wes father to hyr barn; and instruckit hyr of mony thingis that he desyrit hyr to say and sweir. And becaus the deponar refusit and grudgit to sweir the thing that sche knew to be fals, James put hyr away fra his hows, and wythheld hyr barne in his hows; and efter that the deponar com agan to the hows of James Chesolm, and desyrit hyr barn to be deliverit to hyr, the sayd James refusit to deliver to hyr hyr awyn barn, bot wythhaldis and mantenis the sam. *Item*, the sayd Cristen deponis that befoyr sche wes lychtar, sche revelit to Cristen Patton, hyr gud-sister, that Master Dauid Meldrum wes father of hyr barne. *Item*, the sayd Cristen deponis that Rychart Mar and Thomas Gulen, servandis to James Chesolm, knew and kend that Master Dauid Meldrum was fader to hyr barn, or sche com to the hows of James Chesolm.[1]

Die septimo Februarii anno etc. lxiiij [to.]

The quhilk daye, Dauid Trumbull and Agnes Peblis delated, called, accused, and convict of fornicacion committit betuix tham, manifestat be procreacion of ane child betuix tham and confessed. Thai ar ordened[2] to mak public satisfaccion in the essemble of the kyrk, and pay x s. to the box of puyr, and thar child to be resavit tharefter to baptisme. *Satisfaccion of Trumbull and Peblis fornicatoris.*

The quhilk daye, Baltasar Spens,[3] exortar in Kynowll, delated and summond to this session be the Superintendent letteres, to heyr hym decernit to underly disciplyn for abusing of his office and vocacion, in baptising of al barnis indifferently, *Deprivacion of Spens exoratar in Kynowll.*

---

[1] The remainder of the page is blank in the *Register*, as if left for the conclusion of the case.

[2] *Orden* in MS.

[3] *D. Balthasare Spens, notario publico*, witnesses a charter at Rossye, on the 3d of December 1556 (*Register of Great Seal*, iv. No. 1130).

and divers others notorus and wechty offencis, and nocht comperand, is worthely deprivit fra his office be Superintendent.[1]

The quhilk daye, James Myllar and Jonat Lauder delated
callit and accused for fornicacion committit betuix tham.
The woman confessis, and allegis secret promys of mariaige
preceding the carnall copulacion. James denyis all. The
woman for hyr part referris all to his ayth, and delay grantit
to hym to avyis wyth his ayth. The daye cumand he confessis
carnall deyll, and denyis and purgis hym of promys. The
personis are committit to the magistratis be supplicacion to be
civile punist.

Die xxviij Marcii anno Domini m°v^clxv^{to}.

The quhilk daye, Niniane Smart and Catrin Scot, summond be
the Superintendentis letteres, delated and accused for transgressing of the ordor of the kyrk, and occasion of sclander gevyng to
otheris, in that thai, after mutuall promys of mariaige befoyr
solemnizacion tharof, hes kepit and haldyn hows together at
bed and burd, and nether causis thar bannis be proclamit nor
mariaige solemnizat. Quhilk confessit, thai ar chergit to gev
thar namis, and caus thar bannis be proclamit, and procead to
solemnizacion of thar mariaige befoyr this nixt Wytsundaye,
under pan of excommunicacione.

Die xj mensis Aprilis anno quo supra.

The quhilk daye, James Adeson in Arneill and Elizabeth
Bowy delated called and accused of fornicacione, manifestit
be procreacion of ane child betuix tham. Thai confes. Elizabeth clamis mariag of James, according to the law of God, for
defloracion of hir virginite; finale, sche, behaldyng he culd
nocht be persuadit wyllingle tharto, grantis to accep ane porcion of hys gayr to help to dot hyr, and quitis and renuncis
mariage of hym, sche being dischergit of the burdyng and
educacion of thar barne. And James oblesis hym to resave
the barn, and accept upon hym the educacion and expens of
the barn, and to pay[2] x liɓ. to Elizabeth, tharof v liɓ. in hand,

---

[1] The contraction for *per* is repeated in MS.   [2] *To pay to* in MS.

and fynd caucion for the other v lib. accitat: quhilk Elizabeth acceppis and exoners James of mariaige. And bayth the saidis parteis ar ordenit to mak public satisfaccion in the assemble of the congregacion this nixt Sundaye.

Die xxv^{to} Aprilis anno quo supra.

The quhilk daye, Robert Watson, servand to the Bischop of Caytnes,[1] and Margret Greiff, servand woman to Thomas Meffen, dilated for fornicacion and warnit to this essemble; and nocht comperand, thai ar notit *contumaces*, and committit be supplicacion to the Provest and balles of Sanctandrois to be punist civile, hayth for thar fornicacion and inobedience. *Xij Septembris*, Margret Greif is resavit and admittit to public satisfaccion for hyr fornicacion committit wyth Robert Watson, and hyr barn resavit to baptisme.

Watson and Greiff fornicatoris committit.

Greif admittit to satisfaccione.

Die secundo Maii.

The quhilk daye, Jhon Leis and Margre Walcar delated called accused and convict of adultere committit betuix tham, manifestit be procreacion of ane child, the said Ihon Leis, smyth, inhabitant of Sanctandrois, being the husband of Bege Scot. Thai ar committit to the Provest and balles of Sanctandrois be supplicacion to be punist civile, according to the ordor resavit and observit.

Leis, Walcar, adultereris committit.

Die x Octobris anno quo supra.

The quhilk daye, Bege Scot, spows of Ihon Leis, in presens of the ministerie, confessis that it com to hyr knawlege, at the Senze-fayr[2] of Sanctandrois last bypast, that Jhon Leis hyr

Reconciliacion of Leis and Scot.

---

[1] See *supra*, p. 232.

[2] In 1581, 'oure Soverane Lord and thrie estaitis of Parliament, understanding that the Provest, bailleis, counsall and communitie of the cietie of Sanctandrois, and thair predicessouris, hes bene in use and possessioun of ane publict fair and mercat callit the Seinzie fair, beginnand upoun the Mononday efter Pasche Mononday yeirlie, and continewand to the space of xv dayis nixt therefter, within the said cietie and cloister of the Abbay situate within the samin, in all tymes bigane past memorie of man . `. . ratefiis, apprevis, and confermis the foirsaid prevelege of the said mercat and fair' (*Acts of the Parliaments of Scotland*, iii. 239). It was held in the cloister of the Priory (Martine's *Reliquiae Divi Andreae*, p. 188).

husband had committit adultery wyth Jonat Walcar, quhilk
offence for hyr part sche hes remittit wyth hyr hart and is
reconcilit wyth hym.

Die secundo mensis Maii anno etc. lxv.

Benns and
Smyth monest.

The quhilk daye, Thomas Beins and Besse Smyth his spows
ar monest be the ministere to adhear in mutuall cohabitacion
incontinent, under panis of excommunicacion.

Die xxv mensis Maii anno quo supra.

Wyliamson
absolvit fra
adherance to
Scot.

The quhilk daye, Dauid Scot and Eufam Wyliamson, beand
delated to the Superintendent in his visitacion for nocht adherance nor proceding to solemnizacion of thar mariaige, beand
under promys of mariaige and carnall copulacion following
tharupon, laufully summond be the Superintendentis letteres
to this session, to adheir and proceaid to thar solemnizacion of
mariaig and mutuall cohabitacion, or ellis to schaw sum ressonabill caus quhy thai suld nocht sa do ; and comperand, the
sayd Eufam, in presens of Dauid, allegis sche suld nocht adheir
to hym, becaus, efter the sayd promys of mariage and carnall
copulacion betuix the sayd Dauid and hyr, and now sen reformacion of religion, the said Dauid hes gevyn his body to
Beatrix Henderson and Besse Dicson, manifestit be procreacion
of twa children betuix hym and the saidis Beatrix and Besse
respective; and sua be adultre committit be the said Dauid he
hes cuttit hymself of fra hyr; and tharfor askis hyr to be
absolvit fra adherence, and liberte to mary in the Lord. The
sayd Dauid confessis the allegacion of gevyng his body and procreacion of children befoyr mencionat as is allegit, and for his
defence allegis the occasion tharof wes gevyn be Eufam, quha
absentit hyr fra his cumpany, na occasion mayd be hym to hyr.
The Superintendent, avysed wyth the defens and ansuer and
confession, absolvis Eufam fra adherance and proceding to
solemnizacion of maruage wyth the sayd Dauid, and committis
the said Dauid to be punist be the magistratis accordyng to
the law.

Die xiij mensis Junii anno Domini quo supra.

The quhilk daye, the Superintendent, in takyng cognicion anent[1] the clam of mariaige perseuit. be Issobell Rynd of Ihon Gardinar, parrochinaris of Forgown, fyndis sufficiently provyn that thar bannis war proclamit in Forgon kyrk be bayth thar consentis befoyr carnall copulacion, quhilk sen syn is followit tharupon betuix tham ; and heirfor the Superintendent decernis and monesis the saydis Ihon Gardinar and Issobell Rynd to proceaid in solemnizacion of thar mariaige wythin xl dayes under pan of excommunicacion. *(margin: Gardinar and Rynd decernit to marye.)*

Die xv^{to} Augusti anno quo supra.

The quhilk daye, Thomas Dwry is becum caucion for Ihon Castaris, extranear, that he sall compeir in this citie and underly disciplyn of the kyrk and correccion of the magistratis betuix this and Alhallow-day[2] nixt to cum, for his fornicacion committit wyth Catrin Smaw; and, gyf he falyes sa to do, Thomas to pay fyve marcas to the box of the puyr. And the said Catrin Smaw oblesis hyr to underly disciplyn and correccion quhen sche salbe requiret. Heyrfor thar barn to be baptised. *(margin: Castaris and Smaw fornicatoris have fund caucon v marcas. No^t a.)*

Die xxix Augusti anno Domini etc. lxv^{to.}

The quhilk daye, Andro Weland, in Kylrynne, and Anne Anderson, inhabitant in Sanctandrois, delated, callit and accused as huyrmongaris. Thai confes thar offensis, schawing signis of .repentance, ar contract be mutuall promys of mariaige, and oblest to procead to solemnizacion betuix this and Sanct Lucas day[3] nixt to cum. Thai ar ordened to mak public satisfaccion in the essemble of congregacion of Sanctandrois, this nixt Sunday befoir nuyn, and thar barn to be resavit to baptisme efter nuyn. *(margin: Weland, Anderson, contract.)*

Die quinto mensis Septembris anno Domini etc. lxv^{to.}

The quhilk daye, Patrik Lokarid and Cristan Thalland beand summond be the Superintendentis letteres laufully to compeir *(margin: Lokard, Thalland.)*

---

[1] *Anent anent* in MS.   [2] 1st of November.   [3] 18th of October.

in this essemble, to heir tham decernit to proceid to solemnizacion of mariaige contract betuix tham, or ellis ether of tham
to schaw ane ressonabill caus quhy thai sudd nocht sa to do;
wyth certificacion that quhidder thai comperit or nocht the
Superintendent wald do justice to the parte comperand, as at
lenth is contenit in the said letteres deuly execut, indorsat and
reproducit: thai 'called, comperis Patrik and 'for his part confessis thar wes mutuall promys of mariaig mayd betuix hym
and the said Cristen Thalland, upon the secund daye of Aprill
last was, in presens of the minister and sum of the eldaris of
Kyngorn Ester and otheris wytnes; according to the quhilk
promys he for his part is wylling to procead to solemnizacion
of mariaige, and that thar bannis be proclamit according to
the ordor of the kyrk. And seing thar is na caus allegit for the
part of Cristen to stop thar proceding, Patrik desyris the premissis be hym rehersit and confessit to be admittit to his probacion, and competent term statut to hym to prev the sam;
and the sam being provyn the Superintendent to decern the
sayd Cristen to procead to solemnizacion of mariaige wyth
hym. The Superintendent admittis the allegacion of Patrik
to his probacion, and statutis to hym *literatorie* to prev the
sam as accordis of law.

Die xij Septembris anno quo supra.

Lokard,
Thalland.

The quhilk daye, according to the term set *literatorie* to
PatrikLokard to prev mutuall promys of mariaige betuixt hym
and Cristen Thalland, as in the act Wednisday last was, comperis Mr. Alexander Sibbald, procurator, admittit for Patrik,
and producis ane lettre of summondis of Superintendentis,
deuly execut and indorsat, tharin summond the sayd Cristen
to this session and desyr foyrsaid; and also for desyr of
term producis ane testimoniall subscrivit be Thomas Byggar,
minister,[1] Wyliam Boswall, Ihon Kyrkaldy, eldaris of Kyngorn,
and James Nycholson, of dayt the x day of September instant.

---

[1] Biggar, who had been a member of the chapter of St. Andrews before the
Reformation, was admitted minister of Kinghorn in 1564, and died in 1605.
His son Mr. Thomas, reader in the same parish, suffered for non-conformity in
1621 (*Booke of the Universall Kirk*, Ban. Club, i. 222 ; Scott's *Fasti*, ii. 543).

In payn of nocht comperance of the said Cristein, the Superintendent, avysed wyth the testimoniall[1] and twa generall impedimentis specifyed tharin obecke[2] be Cristen, in respect of the
generalite tharof and that thai ar inept and irrelevant, ordenis
the bandis to be proclamit; and gyf Cristen allegis and offerris
to prev relevantle ony laufull and speciall caus, sche to be
hard and term to be assignit to hyr to prev the sam deuly as
efferis. And gyf na relevant nor speciall caus salbe allegit be
hyr, or falyes in probacion, monicionis to procead aganis hyr
anent thar solemnizacion. And gyf sche disobeis, the sentence
of excommunicacion to be fulminat wyth detfull ordor.

Followis the tenor of testimoniall producit.

Master Thomas Byggar most ernistlye wysseth, Grace
mercy and peace, from God the Father and from our Lord
Jesus Crist, be verteu of the Holy Spirit, unto the Superintendent of Fyff, and to the minister eldaris and diaconis of Sanctandrois, for salutacion. Forsamekyll bretheren as ye have
requirit ane testimoniall of me, quhidder this berrar, Patrik
Lokart, wes contract wyth Cristen Thalland befoir me and
sic elderis, sic ane day of Aprill, as allegit befoir yow. I
assur yow bretheren that the saidis Patrik and Cristen mayd
mutuall promys of mariaig in Wyliam Boswallis hows, befoir
me and the said Wyliam and Jhon Kyrkaldy, both eldaris, and
James Nycholson ane of the diaconis, wyth otheris quhilkis
war present for the tym, evyn the sam day that he allegit,
quhilk wes upon Moninday, the secund of Aprill *anno* 1565.
The quhilk day also, Patrik and Cristen being contract, thai
passit ower the watter togidder, bot to quhat end I knaw
nocht; and wythin two or thre dayes thai cuming agane to
Kyngorne, the said Cristen send Wyliam Boswall and James
Nycholson to inquir me for Gods saik that I wold nocht
proclam thar bannis, for Cristen had hard sic thingis of Patrik
be report of otheris that sche wald rather suffer dead than

---

[1] *Testioall* in MS.
[2] Objected. It occurs in almost the same form on p. 83.

perfyt mariaig wyth hym. Than I causit Patrik and Cristen cum befoir me and the elderis and diaconis, and thar I askit of hyr the caus quhy sche wald nocht perfyt hyr promys mayd to Patrik. Hyr ansuer wes, befoyr us all, that Patrik wes brutit to have takyn at his awyn hand mor than justle appertenit to hym, for the quhilk caus sche fearit that he suld be cut of from this present lyff. And morower that he wes nocht cleyn of his body, and sic other thingis as thyr. Quhilk I never culd be persuadit that sic causis war sufficient to stop mariaige ; yit nochtwythstanding all the eldaris and diaconis war in my contrary, and so stoppit the proclamacion of bannis as yit. And tharfor I am glayd that the Superintendent and ye have takyn the accion from us, becaus we culd nocht aggre upon the sam. And lat the Superintendent and the Rector call to mynd quhat I spak to tham of this mater, for I remember I askit consall of tham both in the sam accion : of the Superintendent into his awyn chalmer, and of the Rector cuming ower the watter in ane boyt. So fayr ye weyll in the Lord. Of Kyngorn, the ten deye of September 1565, be youris at command, Wiliam Boswall, Thomas Byggar minister of Kyngorne, Ihon Kyrkaldy, Iames Nuchalson, wyth my hand at the pen.

Die septimo Novembris anno etc. lxv^{to}.

Decretum
matrimoniale
inter Lokard et
Thalland.

The quhilk daye, efter that the ordinance of the Superintendent specifyed in the act *xij Septembris* wes send to the ministerie of Kyngorne, and answer tharof resavit this day be the Superintendent, contenyng, in effect, that Patrik Lokard of his part hes desyrit the proclamacion of bannis betuix hym and Cristen Thalland to ceas, and wylling to quit hyr of mariaige, the Superintendent, avysed tharwyth, ordenis ane cherge to be put in wryt and dew forme to the minister of Kyngorne, requiring hym to proclam the bannis betuix the saidis Patrik and Cristen, and to moneis tham bayth to procead to solemnizacion of thar mariaige wythin xl dayes, under pane of excommunicacion to be fulminat aganis tham or ony of tham that contempnis to procead in mariag, nochtwythstanding ony thing allegit or spokyn be ony of the saidis parteis.

Die xij Septembris anno quo supra.

The quhilk daye, Jhon Cornfut is absolvit fra the clam of mariaig persewit of hym be Jonat Wylson, and the sayd Ihon set at liberte to marye in the Lord wyth ony lawfull partye.

Die xxvj Septembris anno quo supra.

The quhilk daye, Master Dauid Meldrum beand admittit to procur in the caus of Elizabeth Payt, in hyr clam of mariaige of Ihon Wemys, for this diet to save hyr caus fra paresing, becaus sche is seik and maye nocht compeir; and the said Mr. Dauid in his ressonyng injurit Dauid Wollwod [2] ane of the eldaris, saying to hym in the essemble and audience of the holl session, that thai wald be accused befoyr God that admittit sic ane ignorant to be upon this sayt. In respect of the quhilk, the Superintendent, wyth avys of the ministerie, repellis the said Mr. Dauid fra procuryng befoir thame in the said caus or ony other in tym cuming; and ordenis hym also to be called, accused tharfor, and to underly disciplyn of the kyrk as efferis for the offence.

Meldrum admitat [1] [to procur.]

Repelled.

The quhilk daye, Besse Paterson requiris Andro Baxtar as father to hyr barne laytle borne to present the sam to baptisme; and the said Andro, dowtyng gyf the barn be his, requiris the ayth of Besse in declaracion of the verite, quhidder he be father of the said barne or nocht. Besse sworne, and in his presens examinat upon syndry headis, sche deponis the barne alwayis to be gottyn wyth hyr be the said Andro, and nan other to have mayd caws wyth hyr bot he allone. In respect of the quhilk, the saidis Andro and Besse, for disciplyin of the kyrk, ar ordenit to mak publict satisfacion this nixt Sunday in the essemble of the congregacion, thar barn to [be][3] baptised efter nuyn, referryng civil punischment to be execut aganis the saidis personis, be the magistratis, as huyrmongaris.

Baxter, Paterson, huyrmongaris.

Satisfaccione.

Committit.

---

[1] *Admotat* in MS.

[2] David Welwod was the son-in-law of John Motto, having married his daughter Janet (*Abstract of the Writs of St. Andrews,* No. 139).

[3] Omitted.

Die x Octobris, anno Domini etc. lxv^{to.}

Russell,
Kynnmonth,
Ledop.

The quhilk daye, Thomas Russell and Cristen Kynnmonth accused for fornicacion committit betuix tham. Thai bayth confes carnall [dayll][1] had betuix tham, and that efter mutuall promys of mariaige privatle mayd betuix tham alan wythowtyn knawlege or consent of thar parentis, the woman wyth child to Thomas. And Cristen also confessis (at demand of the Superintendent) that, efter hyr fyrst promys foyrsaid and carnall dayl following tharupon betuix hyr and Thomas Russell, sche hes mayd mutuall promys of mariaige wyth Dauid Ledop, and tharefter hes gevyn hyr body to the said Dauid ; quhilk sche allegis don be hyr throw fear and thretnyng mayd to hyr be hyr father, to quhom sche schew befoyrhand hyr formar privat promys mayd wyth Thomas Russell, bot conceled the carnall dayll that followit the sayd formar promys betuix hyr and Thomas. Quhilk Wyliam Kyninmonth, father of the sayd Cristen, beand examinat upon his knawlege of the sayd formar promys reveled to hym be Cristen his dochter, confessis the sam trew as sche hes rehersit. The Superintendent ordenis the saidis Thomas Russell, Cristen Kynnmonth, and thar fatheris, to compeyr befoyr hym [on][1] Wednisday the xxiiij of October instant ; and Dauid Ledop to be summond to compeyr the sayd day, for farder tryall to be had in this caus. And Thomas Russell for his part acceppis the confession of Cristen Kynnmonth sa far as it mackis for hym, and, namely, that part quharin sche confessis mutual promys of mariaige wyth Dauid Ledop and carnall deyll following tharupon, sen the promys mayd betuix hym and the sayd Cristen ; and seing be hyr confession sche heis committit adultery sche hes cuttit of hyrself fra hym, and tharfor desyris the Superintendent to decern hym to have liberte to mary wyth ony other laufull parte and protestis tharfor.

Die xxiiij^{to} Octobris anno quo supra.

*Decretum
divorcii
Kynnmonth et
Russell.*

The quhilk daye, as in term assignit to Dauid Ledop to be summond, and to Thomas Russell and Cristen Kyninmonth

---

[1] Omitted.

wyth thar fatheris to compeyr, for forder tryall to be takyn anent dowbyll promys of maruaige wyth carnall dayll following tharupon, confessed be .Cristen Kyninmonth, mayd the former wyth Thomas Russell, confessit the later wyth Dauid Ledop, the saidis personis comperand, the ayth of Dauid Ledop takyn be the Superintendent[1] upon thes declaracion of the verite concernyng his part. The sayd Dauid, dilegentle examinat, be his ayth deponis and declaris that thar wes promys of maruage laufully mayd one his part betuix hym and the sayd Cristen, wyth consent of his frendis and hyr father. At quhilk promys mackeyn, the said Cristen, beand requirit, mayd fayth sche had nether don nor sayd, in word nor deid, bot that sche mycht laufully contract mariaige wyth hym the said Dauid; and he, tharby understandyng and belevyng the said Cristen to have beyn ane virgin, knew hyr carnaly as hys wyff. Nevertheles, sen syn, the said Cristen is knawyn (lyikas sche hes confessit wyth hyr mowth spekand) to be wyth barne to Thomas Russell, wyth quhom sche wes contracked be mutuall promys of mariaige; and sua the said Dauid dissavit be hyr falt hyd and[2] concelit be hyr, unknawyn to hym, sche being ane huyr quhom he belevit to have resavit for ane madyn and virgin to his wyff; and tharfor of the law of God he suld be mayd fre of hyr and [have][3] liberte in the Lord to mary ony other lawfull parte. The Superintendent, wyth the avyis of the ministerie, avised wyth the holl proces and confessionis of parteis, findis that Cristen Kyninmonth, be gevyng of hyr body to Dauid Ledop, efter promys and carnall deyll mayd and had betuix hyr and Thomas Russell, hes committit adulterie, and tharby cuttit of hyrself fra the sayd Thomas; and that the said Dauid is dissavit be conceling of the verite fra hym be the said Cristen, he belevyng to have resavit ane virgin to his wyf, and otherwayis knawyn be hyr and the said Thomas Russell confessionis, and be hyr person beand sa far gayn : and heirfor pronuncis and decernis the sayd Thomas Russell and Dauid Ledop, and every ane of tham, liberte to marie in the Lord and fred of the said Cristen, provydit that the saidis Thomas Russell, Dauid Ledop and Cristen Kyninmonth, this nixt

---

[1] *Superintendet* in MS.　　[2] *And and* in MS.　　[3] Omitted.

Sunday in the public essemble. of the congregacion of the kyrk
of Dininno, mak public satisfaccione and schaw signis of repentance, for thar offencis and sclander gevyn ; and oneto the tym
the sam .be deuly done na ministracione of sacramentis nor
mariaige to be ministrat to the parte falyeing. This satisfaccione wes deuly mayd and decreit obeyit. . And efter obedience
Reconsiliacio gevyn to thir decreit, the saydis Dauid Ledop and Cristen
Ledop et Kynn- Kyninmonth war reconsiled. Dauid remittit Cristen and re-
month. savit hyr in favor and solemnizat the band of mariaige wyth
hyr, requirand and obtenand the consent of the kyrk tharto.

Die xxviij mensis Novembris, anno Domini 1565.

Lawson,   The quhilk daye, Jhone Lawson, baxtar, and Bege Powerd
Powerd, forni-
catoris com-   delated, callit, and the man accused of fornicacion committit
mittit.   wyth Bege manifestit be procreacion of ane child, the woman
accused of hurdom and huyrmongyn, that sche of befoir wes
delatit and convict as ane fornicatorix wyth Dauid Layng, and
now wyth Ihon Lawson. Thai hayth confes thar offensis foyrsaydis, and ar committit to the magistratis to [be][1] punist
civile according to the law, quhilk being put in execucion thar
barne to be baptised.

Die quinto Decembris, anno Domini quo supra.

Watson,   The quhilk daye, Wyliam Watson, cordinar, and Bege
Cowpar, forni-
catoris com-   Coupar delated, callit and accused[2] for fornicacion committit
mittit.   betuix tham. Thai confes. The woman allegis promys
mutual of mariaige betuix tham. Wyliam denyis the sam,
referrit to his ayth and he sworne, purgis hym, and is absolvit.
Bayth the parteis committit to the magistratis, to be punist
civile according to the law for thar fornicacion foyrsayd.

Die xij mensis Decembris, anno Domini etc. lxv[to.]

Duplyn   The quhilk daye, Mathow Dwplyn, cordinar, inhabitant in
adulter,
Angus fornica- Sanctandrois, efter mutuall promys of mariaug mayd betuix
tris.

---

[1] Omitted.   [2] *Accised* in MS.

hym and Eleyn Smyth and carnall dayll follouing tharupon,
is delated for gevyng his body as ane adulterar to Gressell
Angus. The saidis Mathow and Gressell callit, singularle
examinat, and at the lenth confrontit, finale, be thar[1] athis thai
singularlie, and ilk ane also in presens of other, confessis
carnall dayll betuix thaim, befoyr Wytsundey in the lxiij
year, in the hows of Dauid Bell, lang efter the departing of
Eleyn Smyth fra the cumpany of Mathow. In respect of the
quhilk, the sayd Mathow, as ane·adulterar, and Gressell, as ane
fornicatrix, ar committit to the magistratis of this cite, to be
punist civile according to the municipall lawis of this realm.
And the sayd Eleyn Smyth at hyr desyr decernit fred of hyr   Smyth divorciat
promys fra the said Mathow, and liberte to marye in the Lord   fra Dwplyn.
wyth ony lawfull parte.

Die xix Decembris anno quo supra.

The quhilk daye, Walter Flemyng and Margret Layng,   *Peticio* Layng
beand summond be the Superintendentis letteres for discussing   *contra* Flemyng.
of impediment proponit be Margret to stop the mariaige
of the said Walter, comperis. Margret allegis mutuall
promys of mariaug mayd betuix hyr and Walter befoir wytnes
in the kyrk of Monymayll, at the baptising of ane barne
gottyn betuix tham abowt sex yearis syn. Quhilk denyed be
Walter, the Superintendent statutis to Margret Wednisdaye,
the xvj of Januar nixt to cum, to preve the said promys. And
Walter allegis that the barne last borne be Margret fatherit
upon hym, the said Margret, wyth hyr awyn tung spekand,
confessit the sayd last barne to be the barne of George Clapan,
vicar of Keremuyr, quhom sche requirit divers tymmis to caus
the sam to be baptised as his barne: quhilk Margret denyed.
The Superintendent admittis the sam to probacion of Walter,
and foyrsaid xvj daye of Januar assignit to Walter to prev his
allegacion. Parteis heirto summond be this act.

---

[1] *Gar* in MS.

Die xvj Januarii anno quo supra.

[Layng,
Flemyng.]

The quhilk daye, as in term assignit to Margret Layng to prev mutuall promys of mariaig betuix hyr and Walter Flemyng, and to Walter to prev the fathering of the last barne borne be Margret upon George Clapan be hyr awyn tung spekand, the parteis called, comperis Walter [and,]¹ in payn of nocht comperance of Margret, producis ane certificacion subscrivit be Peter Ramsay, minister, contenyng [in]¹ effect that Margret is content to discherg Walter of the promys foyrsayd. Quhilk, being considerit and sentence tharof, is understand to mak the caus dubius, and tharfor the Superintendent ordenis ane summondis to summond bayth the parteis to certain daye, the woman ether to prev the promys allegit be hyr or ellis to underly disciplyn for stop mayd of the bannis of mariaige of Walter, and inhibicion to both the parteis that nan of thaim procead in mariaig wyth ony other parte, quhill discussing of the premissis.

Die xx Februarii anno Domini m°v°lxv^{to·}

*Absolvatorium
Flemyng a
clameo Layng.*

The quhilk daye, Margret Layng provyn lawfully summond be the Superintendentis letteres, deuly execut and indorsat, at the instance of Walter Flemyng, this daye to compeirr befoyr the Superintendent and ministerie of Sanctandroiš to prev the impediment proponit be hyr for stop of mariaige of the said Walter, and sche nocht comperand, Walter circumducis the term, protestis sche be na forder hard, and he to be absolvit fra hyr clam and [have]¹ liberte to procead to solemnizacion of his mariaige. The Superintendent for tryall of the verite caused the ayth of Walter to be takyn, quhai, be his ayth examinat, deponis that he never at ony tym maid promys to marye the said Margret, nether prevely nor oppynlie; nor hes mayd ony promys to Margret of ony bud² or gayr,³ nor gevyn ony to hyr, to ceas fra persut of mariaige or discherge hym of promys; and that he hes nocht mayd caws wyth hyr in procreacion of this last barne be Margret borne. In respect of the quhilk,

---

¹ Omitted.   ² Bribe.   ³ Gear.

the Superintendent ordenis the bannis of Walter to be proclamit wythowtyn prejudice of the accion of Margret, providit
that Walter fyrst mak satisfaccion in the kyrk for fornicacione
confessit be hym, committit wyth Margret sen[1] procreacion and
byrth of the fyrst barne born to hym be Margret.

Die nono mensis Januarii anno Domini m°v°lxv^{to.}

The quhilk daye, in presens of the Superintendent and his *Protestacio ballivorum* collegis, commissaris deput be the Generall Kyrk, and ministerie *burgi de Crayll.* of Sanctandrois, comperis Jhon Reid, allegit ballie of the burgh of Crayll, and Mr. Alexander Mortoun, allegit clark of the said burgh, for tham selfis and in name of the kyrk of Crayll, and protestis quhat the said Superintendent and his collegis and assessoris dois, in the accion betuix Robert Arnot and Effe Crostrophyn[2] anent the clame of mariaige persewit be Effe, prejuge nocht thame in thar previlege nor kyrk, and siclyik thar minister, in that accione; and forder allegis bayth the contrackyng of mariaige and divorciment is provydit, be the King and Quenis Maieste and Secreit Consall, to be discussit and tryed befoir the commissaris of Edinburgh, deput tharto, and tharfor the Superintendent nor his collegis, commissaris, awcht nocht nor suld nocht sit nor proceid in this accion, nether concernyng the minister nor parteis.

The quhilk daye, Robert Arnot induellar in Crayll summond *Kaye contra Arnot.*

Se in MS.

[2] In the General Assembly, on the 27th of December 1565, 'Anent the complaint givin in be the Superintendent of Fyfe agains John Melvill, minister of
Craill, alledging the said John to preceid to the solemnizatioun of mariage
betuixt Robert Arnot and Euphame Corstarphin, notwithstanding that ane
uther woman claims the said Robert ; the haill kirk assemblit ordainit ane inhi-
bitioun to passe agains the said Johne, that he in no wayes solemnize the said
mariage untill sick tyme as Mr. John Dowglas, Rector of the Universitie, and
Mr. James Wilkie regent, heare the complaints to be givin in be the said
Superintendent, and alse any uther partie haveand entresse, and the same to be
discussit be them ; giveand power to them to give foorth sentence according to
Gods Word, and to use the censures of the kirk agains the dissobeyars' (*Booke
of the Universall Kirk*, Ban. Club, i. 73). Calderwood, after giving the substance of the above, exclaims :—'Heere yee may see, the Superintendent's
complaints were tried by others than superintendents' (*History of the Kirk of
Scotland*, ii. 303).

be the Superintendentis letteres, at the instance of Eufam
Kaye,[1] to ansuer anent the clame of mariaige to be persewit be
the said Eufame, and bayth the saidis parteis comperand,
Robert allegis the said accione and clame alredy discussit befoir
the ministerie of Crayll, and decreit absolvator gevyn in favor
of hym, and for verificacion tharof producis ane decreit in
forme, under the sail of office, subscrivit be the minister Ihon
Malwyll, Jhon Reid, Wiliam Bowsye, Dauid Bane, ballies of
Crayll, M. Alexander Mortoun, scrib and notar, in nam of
the rest of eldaris of Crayll, of the quhilk the tenor followis :—

[Tenor of the decreit absolvator by the ministerie of Crayll in favor of Arnot.]

Decimo octavo mensis Decembris anno Domini 1565. The
quhilk day, Robert Arnot and Eufame Crostrophyn lawfully summond and warnit to compeir this day befoir the
minister, eldaris and diaconis of the burgh of Crayll, anent the
allegacion of ane promys of mariaig to be mayd betuix the
said Robert and Effe, as the summondis usit tharupon at mayr
lenth proportis, the saides Robert and Eufame comperand personaly be tham selfis, the said Robert expreslie denyed that ever
he mayd ony promys to marie the said Effe, and mayd his ayth
of fidelite tharupon ; the said Effe allegiand his promys of
mariaig be word alanerly ; nether promys provyn befoir minister,
eldaris, diaconis of Crayll, nor yit befoir ony other wytnes.
And the said Robert producit ane act, of dayt the xix of
Marcii, the year of God m°v°lxiij yearis, mayd be the minister,
eldaris, diaconis of the burgh of Crayll, quhilk tenor of the act

Statut of the ministerie of Crayll.

followis :—Becaws the holy band of mariaige is sa ordenit of
Almychty God, excluding the wyckit in thar wyckitnes, and
that becaws thai have nocht the inwart wyrkyng of the Holy
Ghost, the wyckit huyrmaster dissembling, and the harlot mor
prone and redy to syn than becummeth the reverent auditor to
heir ; heirfor we, the ballies, minister, eldaris and diaconis,
expell, nichillat and mak of na avayll the promys of the fylthy
huyrmaster and harlot quhar wycketnes is voluntaryelye committit of both the parteis, except laufull wytnes be producit of

---

[1] Twice called *Crostrophyn* and twice *Kaye*, evidently by mistake. *Corstarphin* or *Crostrophyn*, it clearly appears, was the name of the woman Arnot
wished to marry ; while *Kaye* was the 'uther woman' who claimed him. The
session-clerk probably confounded them through both bearing the same Christian
name.

the sammyn befoir the kyrk, quhois jugimentis tweching disciplin the wyckit sall abyd.—And in respect of the said Robertis
ayth and confession, and act foyrsaid, and of the dayly ordor
and consuetud of this sayt, and the said Effe nocht produsand
nor allegiand ony wytnes in the said caus bot hyr awyn allegiance be word onlye, tharfor, and for causis foyrsaidis, the saidis
ballies, minister, eldaris and diaconis, that is to say, Ihon
Maleyn, minister, Wiliam Bowsy, Edward Bane, Ihon Reid,
ballies, Dauid Kay, Wyliam Annand, Jhon Crostrophyn, efter,
Ihon Dyngwall, Andro Bycartoun, Thomas Dauidson, Thomas
Crostrophyn, Thomas Martyn, George Lyell, Patrik Gedde,
hes ordenit and decernit, and be thir present ordenis and
decernis, the said Robert Arnot to be fre of the said Effe and
to marye ony other at his awyn plesur; and in lyik maner
ordenis the said Effe to be fre of the said Robert and to marie
ony other that plesis hyr at hyr plesur; and ordenis and
decernis all allegit promys bygayne to be of nane effect force
nor avayll, and that for the caus above wryttyn; and in tym to
cum na impediment to be mayd betuix the saidis personis or
parteis, in ony bannis or proclamacionis[1] used be ony of tham
for solemnesing of the band of mariaige, quhom it sall happyn
ether of the parteis, that is to saye, nother sall sche gayn call
hym nor he gayn call hyr; and this to be extendit in mayr
ample forme, and to be extract under our sayll of office wyth
our subscripsionis. Followis the tenor of subscripsionis, *per me
Joannem Malwill, concionatorem verbi Dei in Crayll,* Jhon Reid,
ballie, wyth my hand, Wiliam Bowsy, wyth my hand, Eduard
Bane, wyth my hand, M. Alexander Morton, wyth my hand,
for the hayll eldaris and diaconis abone wryttyn, at thar command.[2] Extract and drawyn furth of the buk of the eldaris be
me, clark of Crayll, of the eldaris sayt, and notar public, requirit
tharto, [M. Alexander][3] Morton.

The Superintendent, efter sycht of the sayd decret[4] red in
presens of the sayd Effe Kaye, schawis to hyr that, the said
decreit standing in strenth unreducit, he can nocht procead

---

[1] *Exclamacionis* in MS.

[2] From this it may be inferred that while the minister and three bailies could
sign their names, none of the ten elders and deacons could do so.

[3] Omitted.   [4] *Decret decret* in MS.

forder in hyr caws, reservyng liberte to the said Effe to apprev
the said decreit or to perseu for reduccion tharof, as sche and
hyr frendis sall think gud. Upon the quhilk Robert Arnot
requiris act.

Die xxiij Januarii anno etc. lxv^{to.}

Layng, Criste,
fornicatoris,
committit.

The quhilk daye, Henry Layng and Mariory Cristy delated,
callit and accused for fornicacion betuix thaim committit, comperand and confessand, thai ar committit to the magistratis of
this cite as inhabitantis tharof, to be punist civile according to
the law.

Die penultimo mensis Januarii anno Domini etc. lxv^{to.}

[Mr. Ihon
Dalgles and
Jonat Wemys
summond bot
compeir nocht.]

The quhilk daye, M. Ihon Dalgles[1] and Jonat Wemys,
Lady of Claslogy, inhabitantis of the cite of Sanctandrois,
beand lawfully summond to this daye and sessione be letteres
of the ministerie, deuly execut and indorsat be Alexander
Rowch ane of the diaconis, to ansuer anent the delacione gevyn
in upon tham, of occasion of sclander gevyn be tham be committing of hurdome, manifestit be procreacion of ane child
betuix tham laytle wythowtyn ony solemnizacion of thar
mariaige, and of nocht presenting of thar said child to baptisme, quharby thai ar reput contempnaris of the sacrament of
baptisme ; and thai, and ilk ane of tham, to resave and underly
disciplyn of the kyrk for the premissis, or ellis deuly to purge
tham of the foyrsaidis offences, quharby the said sclander may
be repressed and avoydit ; wyth certificacione to thame gyf
thai compeir nocht, the said daye and place, to the fulfilling of .
the premissis, the ministerie wald proceid wyth detfull ordor
be public monicionis to the finall executing of the sentence of
excommunicacion agans tham, for thar offencis and contempt
of the voce of the kyrk, wyth incalling of the assistance of civil
magistratis and autorite temporall ; as at lenth is contenit in
the sayd letteres under sayl of the said ministerie, datit at
Sanctandrois the xxv of Januar, *anno* &c. lxv, reproducit, lau-

---

[1] Mr. Johne Dalglesche was one of those who joined the congregation by
approving the 'Generall Band' of the 13th of July 1559 (*supra*, p. 9).

fully execut [1] and indorsat be the sayd Alexander, and copeis
tharof deliverit to the saidis personis *respective*; the saidis Mr.
Ihon and Jonat ofttymmis callit, laufull tym byddyn, and
nocht comperand, the ministerie, in pane of thar nocht comperance and contempt of the voce of the kyrk, ordenis letteres
of monicione aganis thame to be put in deu forme, and to be
deuly execut in the public essemble of the congregacione upon
Sunday, the x of Febriar nixt to cum, except thai compeir and
obey in myd tym, be purgacion of thar selfis or resavyng and
underlying of disciplyn.

Die sexto Februarii anno Domini m°v°lxv^{to.}

The quhilk daye, comperis Mr. Ihon Dalgles and proponis
certan excepcionis, dilatoris in his maner, and thareftir producis the sam wyth otheris in wryt; quhilkis beand resavit be
the ministerie to be red in thar audience and be tham to be
considert, and cherge gevyn to the said M. Ihon to remane
and resave ansuer, he departit, disobeying the said charge.
The ministerie, efter sycht of the saidis excepcionis and inobedience of the said M. Ihone, quhai nether be word nor wryt
mayd purgacion nor submittit hym to disciplyn, ordenis the
monicionis to procead aganis hym and Jonat Wemys this nixt
Sunday, according to thar deliverance Widnisday last wes,
nochtwythstanding the excepcionis producit, quhilkis ar repellit
as thai ar notit.

Die xiij Februarii anno Domini etc. lxv^{to.}

The quhilk daye, George Blak, readar of the parrochie kyrk
of the cite of Sanctandrois, producit ane lettre of monicione
under sayll of the ministerie of [Sanctandrois],[2] deuly execut
and indorsat be hym, of the quhilk the tenor followis :—

Minister, eldaris and diaconis of Cristis kyrk and congregacione of the cite and pareson of Sanctandrois, to the redar of
the said kyrk, Grace, mercye and peace throw Jesus Crist, wyth
perpetuall incres of the Haly Spirit.   Forsamekill as M.

---

[1] *Execeit* in MS.   [2] Omitted.

Ihon Dalgles and Jonat Wemys, Lady of Claslogy—inhabitantis
of the said cite and membris of the said congregacion, sa reput
and haldyn, being delated to us for hurdom committit be
tham, manifestit be procreacion of ane child betuix tham furth
of the band of matrimonye, na solemnizacion preceding; and
for nocht presenting of thar child to baptisme, quharby thai
ar reput and haldyn contempnaris of the sacrament; tharthrow
gevand occasion of offence and sclander to the holl congregacion
—war lawfully summond, personaly apprehendit be our patent
letteres and copeis of the same deliverit to tham, to have
comperit befoir us, in owr olklie essemble of the kyrk haldyn
the penult day of Januar last wes; to have resavit disciplin of
the kyrk for thar foyrsaid offence or ellis to have purged tham
deuly tharof, quharby the said sclander mycht have beyn
repressed and avoydit; wyth certificacion to tham gyf thai
comperit nocht to fulfill the premissis, we wald proceid wyth
detfull ordor be public monicionis to the finall sentence of
excommunicacion aganis tham for contempt of the voce of the
kyrk.   And becaws thai comperit nocht the said daye, we
decernit public monicionis to be put in forme and to be execut
in the essemble of the congregacion upon Sunday, the x of
Febriar instant, gyf thai comperit nocht in myd tym to obey
and fulfill the desyr of the said summondis.   And albeid the
said M. Ihon comperit befoir us this last Wednisday, the sext
of Februar instant, he nether wald acknawlege his falt and
resave disciplyn, nor yit mak lawfull purgacione, bot contenewit in his contempt of the voce of the kyrk.   Heirfor we
requir you, in the name of the eternall God, that ye lawfullye
in the public essemble of the kyrk summond the saidis Mr. Ihon
Dalgles and Jonat Wemys to compeir befoir us, in the parroche
kyrk of the cite of Sanctandrois and consall hows tharof, upon
Widnisday the xiij day of Februar instant, at efter nuyn in
the hour of caus; to resave and underly disciplyn of the kyrk
for thar demeritis foyrsaidis, or ellis deuly to purge tham as
accordis of the sam; wyth certificacion to tham gyf thai
compeir nocht, or comperand refusis disciplyn and purgacion
of tham selfis, we wyll procead wyth detfull ordor to the finall
execucion of excommunicacion aganis tham, as to the gretest
and last punischiment belangand to the spirituall ministere;

and tharefter invocat the assistance of the civil power and
autorite temporall. The quhilk to do we commit to you
power in the Lord be thir presentis, delivering the sam be yow
deuly execut and indorsat agane to the berrer. Gevyn under
the seyll of the said ministerie, at Sanctandrois, the vij of
Februarii, the year of owr redempcion 1565.

Followis the tenor of indorsacion. Sunday, the x of Februar
instant, I, George Blak, reader wythin wryttyn, execut thir
presents in the public essemble of the said congregacion the
tym of the sermon, conforme to the tenor heirof, the holl
congregacione beand wytnes. George Blak red[er.]

The foyrsaidis M. Ihon and Jonat oft tymmis callit and
nocht comperand, lawfull tym byddyn, the ministerie ordenis
letteres in the secund form of monicion to be put in forme and
execut[1] this nixt Sunday following, and the saidis M. Jhon and
Jonat to be summond to compeyr the nixt Wednesday as
of befoir.

[Letteres in the secund form of monicion to be execut aganis thⁱ'anⁱ.]

Die xx mensis Februarii anno Domini etc. lxv[to.]

The quhilk daye, M. Jhon Dalgles and Jonat Wemys, Lady
of Claslogy, beand monest for the secund monicion, and summond in the public essemble of the congregacion be patent
letteres, under seyll of the ministerie, reproducit deuly execut
and indorsat be George Blak, readar of this kyrk, to compeir
in this session of the ministerie, and thar ether to purge tham
selfis deuly as efferis, or ellis acknawlege thar offences and resave
disciplyn for occasion of offence and sclander gevyn be tham to
thes congregacione be thar hurdom committit, manefestit be
procreacion of ane child betuix tham furth of the band of
matrimony, and nocht presenting of thar said child to baptisme,
tharby haldyn contempnaris of the sacrament of baptisme:
quhilkis Mr. Ihon and Jonat callit and comperand, thai desyr
that word hurdom contenit in the saidis letteres to be interpret
to tham, quhat kynd of hurdom is tharby menit and signifyied.
For satisfying of the said desyr, the ministerie declaris to tham
that be that word hurdom is signifyed and to be understand

[M. Ihon Dalgles and Jonat Wemys c[l]anat bⁿ peyr.]

. [1] *Execit* in MS.

fylthye lechery, committit wyth contenuance, and perseveryng
in the said filthy vice to the gret sclander of this congregacion.

Efter quhilk interpretacion, at desyr of the saidis M. Ihon and
Jonat, contenuacion and delay is grantit to tham, quhill
Wednisdaye nixt to cum, to gyf thar ansuer quhidder thai wyll
purge or acknawlege. The saydis M. Ihon and Jonat summond
and monist be this act to compeyr the sayd Wednisdaye, wyth
certificacion as of befoir.

Die xxvij Februarii anno Domini etc. lxv^{to.}

The quhilk daye, as in term assignit be contenuacion to M.
Ihon Dalgles and Jonat Wemys to ansuer to the delacion, and
ether be acknawlegyng of thar offensis, resavyng of disciplin
tharefor, or ellis to purge tham deuly as efferis; thai oft tymmis
callit and nocht comperand, lawfull tym of court byddyn, the
ministerie, in pane of thar nocht comperance, decernis and
ordenis the thrid monicion to be put in forme and execut in
the public essemble this nixt Sundaye as efferis; quhilk be
request of the Lard Craghall, under hop of obedience, wes con-
teneuit quhill the vij of Aprill.

Die x mensis Aprilis anno Domini m°v^{c}lxvj^{to.}

The quhilk daye, George Blak, readar, producit ane lettrei
of monicion of the ministerie of Sanctandrois under sayll of
the said ministerie, be hym execut and indorsat deuly, of the
quhilk the tenor followis:—

Ministeris, eldaris and diaconis of Cristis kyrk and congregacion of the citie and pareson of Sanctandrois, to the redar
of the said kyrk, Grace mercye and peace throw Jesus Crist,
wyth perpetuall incres of the Holy Spirit.   Forsamekyll as
M. Ihon Dalgles and Jonat Wemys, Lady of Claslogy, inhabitantis and membris of the said citie and congregacion, sa haldyn
and reput hytherto, war laufully summoind, personaly apprehendit be our patent letteres, to compeir befoir us at certan
day and place assignit to thame; to ansuer to delacion gevyn
in to us upon tham, anent the fylthy hurdom wyth unscham-
full perseverance committit betuix tham, manifestit be pro-

creacion of ane child, and contempt of the sacrament of baptisme now be the space of ane half year and may in nocht presenting of thar said child to baptisme, and occasion of offence and sclander tharby gevyn to this hol congregacion; and tharof to purge tham deuly as efferis, or ellis to acknawlege thar saidis offences and resave and underly disciplyn of the kyrk tharfor, that tharby the sclander foyrsayd mycht be repressed and avoydit; wyth certificacione to tham as efferit: and becaus thai comperit nocht the said day, bot contumacetly absentit tham and contempnit the voce of the kyrk, we caused owr otheris letteres of monicionis in the fyrst and secund formis be execut in the public essembleis of our congregacion twa severall sundayes, quharby the saidis M. Ihon and Jonat war monist and summond to compeir befoir us at certan dayes and placis to the effect foyrsaid, and to resav and underly disciplyn of the kyrk for thar foyrsaidis offensis and contemptis, wyth certificacion as efferit; quhai nevertheles temerariowslye persistis in thar contempt of the voce of the kyrk: heirfor we requir yow, in the nam of the eternall God, that ye now as of befoir, in this our last and thrid monicion, lawfully, in the public essemble of the congregacion, moneis and summond the saidis M. Ihon Dalgles and Jonat Wemys to compeir befoir us in our olklie essemble of the kyrk, wythin the foyrsaid parroche kyrk of Sanctandrois and consall hows tharof, upon Wednisday, the ten daye of April instant, efter nuyn in the hour of caus; to resav disciplyn for thar foyrsaidis offences and contemptis, or ellis deuly to purge tham in sic sort as tharby the foyrsaid offence and sclander may be repressed and avoydit; wyth certificacion to tham, gyf thai falye and contempnis to heir the voce of the kyrk, wythowtyn forder delay we wyll proceid to the finall execucion of the sentence of excommunicacion aganis tham, as to the gretest and last punischment belangand to the spirituall ministerie, and tharupon invocat the essistance of the autorite temporall. The quhilk to do we commit to you power in the Lord be thir presentis, delivering the sam be yow deuly execut and indorsat agane to the berrer. Gevyn under the sayll of the said ministerie at Sanctandrois, upon the thrid day of April, the year of our redempcion m°v°lxvj yearis.

And followis indorsacion: Upon Sunday, the 7 of April, I,

George Blak, readar wythin wryttyn, execut thir presentis in the public essemble of the congregacion, in tym befoir the sermon, the holl congregacion beand wytnes. Ge. Blak redar.

[M. John Dalgles and Jonat Wemys nocht comperand thar contempt to be publist in the congregacion, &c.]

The foyrsaidis M. Ihon and Jonat oft tymmis callit, lawfull tym byddyn, thai nocht comperand, the ministerie, in pane of thar nocht comperance and for thar contempt of the voce of the kyrk, ordenis and decernis publicacion of the sam to be mayd in the congregacione essemblit this nixt Sundaye be the minister; and prayeris to be mayd for the saidis personis for thar amendiment, befoyr the horribyll sentence of excommunicacion be fulminat and execut aganis tham; and to grant to thame viij dayes of mercy, wylling and desyring thar frendis in myd tym to labor and travell wyth tham for thar amendiment to repentance and obedience. And also to signify and gev place to ony person or personis, offendit wyth thir procedingis, to compeir this nixt Wednisday, the xvij of Aprill, in the olklye session of the ministerie, and gev in be wryt or word the caus and resson of thar offence to be discussed; wyth certificacion, gyf nane comperis that daye thar silence to be had for plan consent of the holl congregacion to the execucion of the sentence of excommunicacion aganis the saidis M. Ihon and Jonat.

Die xvij mensis Aprilis anno Domini m°v°lxvj^{to.}

[M. Ihon Dalgles and Jonat Wemys to be excommunicat on the v of Maii.]

The quhilk daye, the ministerie, being convenit in thar olkle essemble, understandyng the ordor prescrivit Wednisday last wes to the minister to use this last Sundaye bypast in the essemble of the congregacion, anent thar procedingis be monicionis aganis M. Ihon Dalgles and Jonat Wemys, for thar contempt of the voce of the kyrk, in nocht compering to purge tham nor acknawlege thar offence and underly disciplyn, for [1] the occasion of sclander and offence be thaim gevyn be filthy hurdom [2] wyth contenuance tharintill, &c.; and of execucion of excommunicacion be thaim merit tharfor; and public prayeris to be mayd for thaim and thar amendiment to repentance and obedience; and grantyng to tham viij dayes of mercy, wylling and requiring thar frendes to travell wyth thaim in myd tym

---

[1] *Fra* in MS. [2] *Hurdon* in MS.

for amendiment ; and to signify and geve place to ony persone
or personis offendit wyth thar procedingis to compeyr this daye,
to gev in be wryt or word thar resson and caus to be discussit,
wyth certificacion as efferit gyf nain comperit this daye that
thar silence wald be had for plan consent of the holl congregacion to execucion of the sentence of excommunicacion aganis
the saydis M. Ihone and Jonat: quhilkis premissis, knawyn to
have beyn detfully usit be the minister, thai causit to call gyf
ony wald compeyr to gyf in, ether in wryt or be word, ony
caus or resson to stop the execucion of the said sentence, laufull tym byddyn, nan comperant, the ministerie ordenis the
sentence of excommunicacione to be put in wryt and forme,
according to the proces deducit and doctrin of Sanct Paul to
the Corrinthianis ; and the ministeris thir twa nixt Sundayis to
caus public prayeris to be mayd for thaim and thar repentance ;
and, gyf thai persist wythowtyn signis of repentance, the
sentence to be execut upon Sunday the v day of Maii nixt
to cum.

> Heir followis the defensis for the part of M. Ihon
> Dalgles and Jonat Wemys, Ledy of Carslogy, yongar,
> aganis the pretendit byll persewit be the allegit
> ministeris, eldaris, diaconis of the citie of Sanctandrois
> aganis tham, anent the delacion gevyn in upon tham
> of sclander of allegit hurdom committit be tham, as
> at mayr lenth is contenit in the pretendit byll ; in
> respect of the [quhilk, the]¹ saidis M. Ihon and
> Jonat awcht nocht to enter in pley befoir [tham]¹ in
> this caus as jugis incompetent to tham, bot suld be
> remittit to thar awyn jugis competent, for the causis
> and ressonis following, &c.

In the fyrst, the saidis M. Ihon and Jonat allegis that [the]¹ [Defensis of M.
allegit minister, eldaris and diaconis of this citie, ar na juge Ihon Dalgles
and Jonat
competent to cognosce in the said accione of delacion, becaus Wemys repellit
as thai ar not't.]
thai ar mer layik and ignorant personis for the maist pairt,
havand na commissione or power gevyn to thaim be our

---

¹ Omitted.

Soweranis Lord and Lady or thar Session, nor ony other
ordinar juge havand power to gyf the sammyn; bot gyf ony
power thai have, the sammyn is ane usurpit power and autorite
tane at thar awyne handis, makand dirogacion to other
ordinarie jurisdiccione, in hie contempt of the King and
Quenis Maiesteis autorite, and[1] expres aganis thar ordinancis
and inhibicionis laytle mayd, statut, and publist, be oppyn
proclamacion, at the marcat croces of all burrowis and citeis
wythin the reallm : That nan thar liegis nor subjectis suld tak
upon hand or usurp ony jurisdiccion of thais causis, quhilk
wes wont to be tretit, cognoscit and decidit befoir be the
spirituall jugis.[2]   Lyikas this pretendit caus and utheris siclyik

---

[1] *And and* in MS.

[2] This proclamation must have been made after the Queen's marriage to
Darnley, 29th July 1565, and before Dalgles presented his defences on the 6th
of February 1565-6. In all probability it was the same proclamation that was
referred to by the bailie and clerk of Crail (*supra*, p. 257). When on the 24th
of August 1560, Parliament abolished the Pope's jurisdiction, and declared 'that
na bischop nor uther prelat of this realm use ony jurisdictioun in tymes to cum
be the said Bischop of Romeis autorite' (*Acts of Parliament*, ii. 534, 535), 'the
jurisdiction of the Church in consistorial matters,' as Riddell states, 'returned
to the Crown'; and 'the necessary consequence was their remaining for a time
in an untoward predicament, subject to no statutory or express defined jurisdiction' (*Peerage and Consistorial Law*, 1842, i. 426, 427). But Joseph Robertson
has shown that, although 'the consistorial courts of the old church were shut,'
yet 'in rare and exceptional instances, trial of consistorial causes was still taken,
and sentence given, under authority of the ancient hierarchy' (*Concilia Scotiae*,
vol. i. p. clxxiv. n. 1). Besides the examples given by Robertson of the exercise
of this old authority by the Archbishop of St. Andrews, at least one other may
be added. On the 9th of November 1556, he granted a dispensation for the
marriage of John Macmoran and Elizabeth Quhitefurd, both of the diocese of
Glasgow (Original in the Moredun Collection). Immediately after the Reformation—and, as this *Register* shows, for several months before the 24th of
August 1560, in St. Andrews at least—the kirk sessions took over part of the
consistorial work, especially that relating to matrimonial causes. Indeed, on
the 4th of July 1562, the General Assembly resolved 'to make supplicatioun to
the Secreit Counsell, that either they give up universallie the judgement of
divorce to the Kirk and their sessiouns, or els to establish men of good lyves,
knowledge and judgment, to take the ordor thereof' (*Booke of the Universall
Kirk*, i. 19). Perhaps it was in tardy response to this desire that in December
1563 the Queen and Privy Council, 'undirstanding that the caussis quhilkis the
prelattis of this realm had decidit in the consistoriis of befoir, be lang delay of
justice, ar frustrat, . . . thocht gude that jurisdictionis be erectit in sindrie partis
of this realme for discussing of the saidis caussis, and that commissaris be
appointit to gif attendence thairon' (*Register of Privy Council*, i. 252). The

war wont, in all tym bypast, to be treatit and decidit befoir
tham, as ordinarie jugis, tharto havand sufficient power, bayth
of the spirituall and civil magistrat to that effect and be tham
apprevit, be the lawis of this realm and actis of Parliament
maid tharupon, standand as yit unrevocat, reducit, or tane

royal charter, however, constituting the commissaries of Edinburgh, was not
granted until next February (Balfour's *Practicks*, 1754, pp. 670-672). The Queen's
attempt, by a writ under her sign-manual, on the 23d of December 1566, to restore
Archbishop Hamilton to his former jurisdiction, and the consequent discharging
of the commissaries ' of thair offices forder in that pairt,' proved abortive ; ' and
the only use which he is known to have made of his recovered power was to carry
through, with scandalous haste, the scandalous divorce which removed the last
obstacle to Mary's marriage with Bothwell' (*Concilia Scotiae*, vol. i. pp. clxxviii.-
clxxx). On the 31st of December 1562, the General Assembly had ordained,
' that no minister, nor others bearing office within the Kirk, take in hand to
cognosce and decide in the actiouns of divorcement, except the superintendents,
and they to whom they sall give speciall commissioun, and betwixt speciall persons ;' on the 27th of December 1566, in resolving to oppose Hamilton's
restoration, the Assembly declared that the ' causes for the maist pairt judgeit
be his usurpit authoritie pertaines to the true kirk,' then glancing back to the
appointment of the commissaries, they add that it was ' for hope of good things
the Kirk oversaw the Queens Majesties comissioun givin therintill to sick men,
who for the most part was our brethren ;' and on the 6th of March 1570.1, the
Assembly included among their articles ' to be proponit to the Regents Grace
and Secreit Counsell,' the following, ' Because the conjunctioun of marriages
pertaines to the ministrie, the causes of adherents and divorcements aught also
to pertaine to them, as naturallie annexit therto' (*Booke of the Universall Kirk*,
i. 30, 88, 187). On the 16th of the following June, the Commissary Court
'reduced a decree of solemnization of marriage . . . pronounced by Mr. John
Wynrame, Superintendent of Fife, the previous 8th of February, at the instance
of Barbara Johnstone against Henry Moreis, " becaus" it was given by him
" wranguslie, he nawayis being judge to cognosce, or decree therintill on ony sik
actione,"' in respect that, many years before, the commissaries had been appointed
to cognosce in all such causes, and had ever since done so as the only competent
judges (Riddell's *Peerage and Consistorial Law*, i. 431, 432). In the *Second
Book of Discipline*, which was presented to the King in 1578 and engrossed in
the records of the Assembly in 1581, complaint is lodged against ' the mingled
jurisdictioun of the commissaris, in sa far as they mell with ecclesiastical materis,
and have no commissioun of the Kirk therto, bot war erecit in tyme of our
Soveranes moder, quhen thingis wer out of ordour' (*Booke of the Universall
Kirk*, ii. 507). The special grievance mentioned then was that the commissaries
should judge ministers, 'and depose thame fra thair rowmes'; but the other matters
of dispute still rankled, for Riddell refers to a decision of the Presbytery of
Edinburgh, which was reversed by the commissaries on the 24th of February
1581-2. Parliament ratified the commissariat of Edinburgh in 1592, but on the
establishment of Episcopacy restored it to the bishops and archbishops in 1609
(*Acts of Parliament*, iii. 574 ; iv. 430).

away be ony contrar statut or law, be ony havand power to do the sammyn. And sua the saidis pretendit minister, eldaris and diaconis of this citie, being bot certan pryvay and ignorant personis for the maist part, ar na wayis jugis competent to cognosce in this caus, havand na power tharto, as said is, bot onlye usurpit in hie contempt of the King and Quenis Maiesteis autorite and utheris mennis jurisdiccione, *mittentes falcem in messem alienam*. And tharfor the saidis M. Ihon and Jonat awcht and suld be remittit to thar jugis ordinar and competent in this caus, vidz., the commissaris of Edinburgh, quhai ar speciall deput to that effect, as said is : protesting, gyf ye, allegit minister eldaris and diaconis, procedis forder heirintill, for nullite of your procedingis ; and that ye incur crym of leismajeste, for the usurpyn of your pretendit autorite wythowtyn ony power or commission gevyn or grantit to yow be thaim to that effect ; and for thar Graces accion aganis yow for usurpyn of the sam.

This fyrst excepcion be the ministerie is repellit, in respect of the generall proclamacion of owr Soweran,[1] set furth in approbacione of owr relegion fundyn at hyr Gracis arryvall to stand, the sam standing undischargit ; and that disciplin is ane part of owr relegion, and we in possession tharof at our Soweranis arryvall, to quhom we ar obedient subjectis and na usurparis of autorete.

---

[1] On the 25th of August 1561, 'Hir Majestie ordanis lettres to be direct to charge all and sindrie, liegis, be oppin proclamatioun at the mercat croce of Edinburgh, and utheris places neidfull, that they, and every ane of thame, contene thame selffis in quietnes, keip peax and civile societie amangis thame selffis ; and in the meyntyme, quhill the States of hir realme may be assemblit, and that hir Majestie have takin a finall ordour be thair avise and publict consent,—quhilk hir Majestie hopis salbe to the contentment of the haill,—that nane of thame tak upoun hand, privatlie or oppinlie, to mak ony alteratioun or innovatioun of the state of religioun, or attempt ony thing aganis the forme quhilk hir Majestie fand publict and universalie standing at hir Majesteis arrivall in this hir realme, under the pane of deid : with certificatioun that gif ony subject of the realme sall cum in the contrair heirof, he salbe estemit and haldin a seditious persoun and raser of tumult ; and the said payne sal be execute upoun him with all rigour, to the exemple of utheris' (*Register of Privy Council*, i. 266, 267). The Queen states, on the 23rd of May 1567, 'that na thing hes sa effectualie nurissit and intertenyt the publict quietnes amangis hir Hienes subjectis, nor contenit thame in hir dew obedience,' as the above proclamation, which had been renewed several times (*Ibid.* p. 513).

Secundly, protesting alwayes that the formar allegiance be weyll and degestle avysit and discussit, for caus[1] the saidis M. Ibon and Jonat allegis that gevand and nocht grantand that the saidis pretendit minister, eldaris and diaconis had ony jurisdiccion, gevyn to tham be ony havand power tharto, to cognosce or tak dilacion in sic causis, lyikas thai have nane; yit thai[2] are na jugis competent to the saidis M. Ihon and Jonat, be sa mekyll as the said M. Ihon is presentlie, lyikas he hes beyn lang befoyr the intenting of this pretendit accion, familiar servand to the Lard of Craghall, makand continuall residence wyth hym wythin the parrochyn of Seres be the space of twa yearis last bypast, or at the lest the maist part tharof; and siclyik the said Jonat parrochinar of the parrochyn of Disart, and be the space foyrsaid or at the lest the maist part tharof remanyng thar, havand fyir and flet wythin the samyn.   And swa the pretendit minister, eldaris and diaconis of this cite are na jugis competent, nor hes power or naem in this caus; bot [the defendaris][3] awcht and suld be remittit to thar jugis competent as said is; and that in respect that gyf the pretendit minister, eldaris and diaconis hes in ony tym by-past usurpit ony power or autorite to cognosce in sic causis, that wes onlye upon the parrochinaris of Sanctandrois and na utheris, lyikas the defendaris ar nocht: pretesting, gyf ye proceid, as of befoir, for remeid tym and place.

This secund excepcion repellit, in respect of the offence committit wythin this cite, and offence and sclander gevyn to this congregacione, fyir and flet instantle kepit wythin this cite be Jonat, and dayly resorting of Mr. Ihon wyth hyr.

Thridlye, the saidis M. Jhon and Jonat allegis that thar suld be na proces nor jugiment had upon the pretendit sum-mondis rasit aganis tham, becaus the sammyn beris na certan parte perseuar tharof; lyikas all summondis bayth in criminall and civil accionis awcht and suld conteyn alsweil the perseuaris as the defendaris.   And als the pretendit summondis is generall and informall, obscur and inept, in that part berand that the delacion [wes][3] gevyn in upon the defendaris, upon occasion of sclander gevyn be tham be committing of hurdom, &c.; nocht

---

[1] Because.   [2] *Thar* in MS.   [3] Omitted.

specifying quhai gave in the delacion, nor yit condiscendant quha tharby is sclanderit be thar occasionis, quhar and quhat tym, place, daye, year and moneth the sammyn allegit hurdom wes committit, and quhat kynd of hurdom it wes, quhidder *simplex* fornicacion or adultery, quhilk awcht and suld have beyn specifyed in the pretendit summondis, gyf the sammyn had beyn relevant. And tharfor the sammyn is inept, irrelevant, generall, obscur, capcious; and sua the sammyn suld be rejeckit and repellit, &c. And sua protestis, gyf thar be ony forder proces heirin, as of befoir.

This thrid excepcione is repellit in respect of the summondis.

Ferdly, the said M. Ihon and Jonat allegis that, gevand and nocht grantand thai had ony carnall dayll together, yit the sammyn wes na hurdom nor yit can be callit so, becaus the said M. Ihon knew that the said Jonat had allegit sum ressonis befoir the Superintendent, ministeris, eldaris and sayt of Sanctandrois, to stop hyr pretendit adherance to Robert Boswall, be verteu of ane wyckit and ungodlye promys mayd betuix the said Robert and Jonat, beand of the law of God and man null of the self; and the said Jonat desyrand the kyrk to declar the sammyn to be null and hyr to be fre tharof, becaws, in [1] the tym of the mackyn tharof, sche mysknew that the said Robert wes jonit in mariaige wyth ane uther callit Cristen Awerye yit alyve. [2] And the said Jonat—beand surly persuadit in hyr conscience, be verteu of the hearyng of the Word of God, that, sa lang as sche wes in the said Robertis cumpany, sche lay in manifest adulterye, in gret perrell of hyr awyn saull, he bavand ane uther lawfull wyff of his awyn yit on lyve, as said is—desirit the Superintendent, ministeris and eldaris of Sanctandrois for the tym, for the causis foyrsaidis and utheris contenit in hyr ressonis producit befoir thame to stop hyr adherence foyrsaid, that thai wald declar the sammyn null. The Superintendent and sayt foyrsaid, fyndand the sammyn ressonabyll, admittit hyr foyrsaidis ressonis to hyr probacion, and direckit summondis to summond wytnes for prevyn of the sammyn, and lyikwyis xxx wytnes comperand befoir thaim to prev the sammyn, &c. The said M. Ihon—beand sercerat [3] of

---

[1] *Of* in MS.　　　[2] *Supra*, pp. 207-212.　　　[3] ? Certified.

hyr ressonis dependand and admittit to hyr probacion, and
that hyr pretendit promys to Robert Boswall wes wycket
wrangus and ungodlye, and of na wayis culd stand wyth the
law of God—contractit wyth the said Jonat in the fear of God,
wyth lawfull consent everilk ane to other, for evading of adultery, and procreacion of children, and sua ar jonit be God.
And the premissis of the law ar tolerabill and lesum, and
tharfor can nocht induce ony kynd of hurdom, bot rather
honest and lesum consummacion of mariaugie.

This ferd repellit, becaws the maner of asserseracion[1] of Mr.
Ihon, nor the ordor of contract and maner of conjunyng of
tham, is nocht qualefyed conforme to the ordor of the kyrk.

Attowr, gyf the saidis M. Ihon and Jonat had fallyn in ony
kynd of hurdom, as aluterly thai denye, yit the sammyn awcht
nocht to be imput to tham, nor yit awcht thai to resave ony
correccion tharfor; bot rather the Superintendent and sayt of
Sanctandrois awcht to be punist, for the causis followand.
Becaus, lang affoir the said M. Ihone and Jonat contrackit
togedder, the said Jonat schew and manifestit to M. Ihon
Wynram, Superintendent, minister, eldaris and diaconis of the
kyrk of Sanctandrois, that sche had jonit hyrself wycketly, in
manifest adultery aganis the law of God and man, to Robert
Boswall, desyrit the Superintendent and kyrk of Sanctandrois
to seperat hyr tharfra, quhilk of the law of God thai awcht
to have don, and nocht to suffer sic devillis promys to stand
betuix ony man or woman. The Superintendent in that cace
beand ane necligent pastor, and the ministeris, eldaris and
diaconis of Sanctandrois siclyik, nocht havand respect to the
fregilite and facilnes of the said Jonat, beand ane woman
fregill and facill of natur, nor yit myndfull of thar deweteis
according to the law of God, postponit and deferrit the said
Jonattis allegiance, and wald nocht resave hyr wytnes to prev
the sammyn; the Superintendent and kyrk foyrsaid beand
maist humely requirit, in the nam of God be the said Jonat
and hyr frendis, nocht onlye anis twys or thryis bot continualy
be the space of fyve yearis last bypast, to procead and do
justice to the said Jonat in the said mater. The said M. Ihon

---

[1] ? Certification.

Wynram nocht alanerly postponit the said mater, as said is,
bot one his maner persuadit the said Jonat be all meanis
possible to return agane to the said Robert, in that dampnable
band of adulterye, aganis hyr conscience. And he seand that
sche wald nocht be persuadit tharto, nocht alanerly postponit
hyr caus as said is, bot cessit from all forder proceding tharintill, and sua planly refusit to do the said Jonat justice, or at
the lest *tacite* refusit the sammyn, quhilk is ane sufficient caus
of the law to repell the Superintendent, ministeris, eldaris and
diaconis of Sanctandrois, that thai, nor nocht ane of tham,
cognosce in ony caus pertenand to the said Jonat: concludand
as of befoir, &c.

This last repellit in respect of the place it is proponit, and
also in respect that the Superintendent wes only juge in the
caus mencionat in the defence, and that the minister and eldaris
cognoscis in this present caus.

Sentence of excommunica-tioun aganis M. Johne Dalglesche and Jonet Wemis.

Wyth incalling of the name[1] of Crist Jesus, Sone of the eternall and everlevyng God, quhai is the way the verite and the
lyff, throwcht quhois gudnes and mercy we, ministeris, eldaris
and diaconis of Cristis kyrk and congregacion of the cite and
parochyn of Sanctandrois, ar callit as watchemen ower his
flok, quhilk he hes mercifully deliverit and reduced from blindnes ydolatrie and supersticion, to the lycht of his Ewangell be
the plenteows preching of the sam, so that the face of ane perfyt reformit kyrk hes beyn seyn wythin this cite be the space
of sex yearis, disciplyn usit and resavit; and now occasion being
offerrit be delacione gevyn in befoir us upon M. Ihon Dalgles
and Jonat Wemys, Lady of Claslogye, inhabitantis of this cite
and membris of this congregacion, so haldyn and reput hytherto,
tweching the offence and occasion of sclander be tham gevyn
be fylthy hurdom, wyth continuall perseverance, committit
betuix tham, manifestit be procreacion of ane child, and thar
contempt of the sacrament of baptisme in nocht presenting thar
said child to baptisme; [quhilkis][2] war lawfully summond be
our patent letteres, personaly apprehendit, to have comperit
befoir us, at certan day and place to tham assignit, to ansuer to
the said delacion, and to purge thaim tharof deuly as efferit, or

---

[1] *Nane* in MS.   [2] Omitted.

ellis to acknawlege the same and tharfor to resave disciplyn of
the kyrk and fulfill the same, quharby the said offence and
sclander mycht be repressed and avoyded; wyth certificacione
to tham as efferit.   And becaus thai comperit nocht the said
day and[1] place, bot contumacetly absentit tham and contempnit the voce of the kyrk, we decernit and causit our otheris
letteres of monicionis in the fyrst, secund and thrid formis to be
execut thre severall Sundayes, in the public essembleis of the
congregacion, quharby the saidis M. Ihon and Jonat war
monest and summond to compeir befoyr us, at certan dayes and
place assignit to tham, to the effect foyrsaid; wyth certificacion to tham, gyf thai comperit nocht to purge thaim of the
foyrsaidis offensis and occasion of sclander, or ellis to acknawlege the same, resave and underly disciplyn tharfor, we wald
proceid aganis tham wyth detfull ordor to the finall execucione
of the sentence of excommunicacion, and invocat[2] the assistance of the autorite temporall.   And albeid the said M. Ihon
at the last comperit befoir us, he nether wald deuly purge hym,
nor acknawlege his offence, resave and underly disciplyn tharfor as efferit, bot persistit temerariouslie in contempt of the
voce of the kyrk and continuall reparyng to the said Jonat
Wemys.   Efter quhilkis thre public monicionis and public
prayeris mayd for the saidis M. Ihon and Jonat, at daye appoynted for execucion of the horribill sentence of excommunicacione aganis thame we grantit awcht dayes of delay and
mercye, wylling thar frendis to travell wyth tham in myd tym
for thar amendiment; and grantit and gave place also to all or
ony offendit wyth owr procedingis to compeir befoir us, at
certan day and place to tham assignit, to produce and geve
in befoir us be word or wryt the resson and caus of thar offence
to be discussit; wyth certificacion, gyf nane comperit we wald
accept and reput thar silence for plane consent of the holl con-
gregacio[n] to the execucione of the excommunicacion.   And
becaus nan comperit, and that the saidis M. Ibon Dalgles and
Jonat Wemys persistis and contenewis in thar fylthy wicketnes,
evyll exempill, and contempt of the voce of the kyrk, thai
wordely merit and deservis to be excommunicated, seperated

---

[1] *And and* in MS.   [2] *Ivocat* in MS.

and cuttit of from the societe and followschip of the congregacion of Crist Jesus and all benefitis of the kyrk, and to be
deliverit unto Sathane for distruccion of the flesche that the
spirit may be saved in the daye of the Lord Jesus, according
to the doctrin of Sanct Paul. Heirfor, havyng God onle befoir
owr ees, and the testimonie of his trew and eternall Word, be
this owr sentence we declar and denunce the saidis M. Ihon
Dalgles and Jonat Wemys, for thar grevos offencis, occasion of
sclander, and contempt of the voce of the kyrk, excommunicated, seperated and cuttit of from the congregacion and mys-
ticall body of Crist Jesus, and all benefitis of his trew kyrk (the
hearyng of the Word of God onlye except); delivering tham
to Sathan for destruccion of the flesche, that, thai being
eschamit and brocht to repentance, thar spirit may be savit in
the day of the Lord Jesus; and that nan of the faythfull fearing God fra this hour furth accumpany wyth ony of tham in
commonyng, talkyn, bying, selling, eating, drynkyn, or other
way quhatsumever, except thai be appoynted be the kyrk for
thar amendiment; wyth certificacion gyf ony dois in the contrar
thai salbe reput favoraris and fostararis of thar iniquiteis, callit
and accused tharfor, and, being convict, as participant wyth
tham, sall resave the lyik sentence wyth tham. In wytnes
heirof the saill of the said ministerie is heirto affixit, at Sanctandrois, upon the fyrst daye of the moneth of May, the year
of our redempcioun m°v°lxvj yearis. Followis the indorsacion of
the minister executor of the excommunicacion.[1]

Die xxvij Marcii anno Domini etc. lxvj.

Fayrfull, Cunnyne, for-nicatoris.

The quhilk daye, Peter Fayrfull and Catherin Cunnyne[2]
callit and accusit for fornicacione committit betuix tham,
manifestit be procreacion of ane child, thai confes thar offensis.
Catrin allegis mutuall promys of mariaige betuix Peter and
hyr, quhilk he denyis. The sam referrit to his ayth be Catrin;

Fayrfull absol-vit of mariaige.

he, sworne, purgis hym be his ayth, and is absolvit fra the said

---

[1] A blank has been left in the *Register* for the indorsation, but it has never
been filled in.

[2] An old form of *Cunninghame.*

clam and promys. Bayth the saidis Peter and Catrin ar[1] ordenit to[2] conveyn this nixt Sunday in the public essemble of the kyrk, and mak public satisfaccion, according to the ordor of the kyrk, &c.

The quhilk daye, Robert Zowll, maltman, inhabitant of this cite, and Cristen Hagy, parrochinar, in Strykynnes, delated, callit and accusit for fornicacion committit betuix tham, manifestit be procreacione of ane child. Thai confes thar offens, and ar ordenit this nixt Sunday to mak public satisfaccion in the essemble of the kyrk, according to the ordor observit; thar barn tharefter to be resavit to baptism; the man committit to the magistratis to be punist civile, according to the law, as thar citiner. *Zowll, Hagy, fornicatoris.*

Zowll committit.

Die xvij Aprilis anno quo supra.

The quhilk daye, Schyr Ihon Dauidson, in Crayll, summond be the Superintendentis letteres, callit, comperand and accusit for pretendit ministracion or rather prophanacion of the Sacrament of baptisme, in the kyrk of Crayll, wythowtyn admission or preching of the Word; he confessis his falt. The Superintendent, wyth avyis of the ministerie, ordenis the said Schyr Ihon Dauidson to compeir this nixt Sundaye, in the public essemble of the congregacion of Crayll, and thar confes and acknawlege his offence, ask God mercy and the congregacion forgyfnes, and absteyn fra the lyik doing in tym cuming under pane of excommunicacion. *Dauidson prophanar[3] of baptisme inhibit.*

Die xxiiij[to] Aprilis anno quo supra.

The quhilk daye, Walter Skaythlok, walcar,[4] inhabitant in Sanctandrois, and Begis Watson, in the new myll upon Edyn, delated as fornicatoris, summond, callit and accusit. Bayth the parteis confessis carnall dayll; and Begis allegis the sam to have beyn under mutuall promys of mariaig mayd betuix tham befoyr famos wytnes, and for verificacion of the sam exhibit *Skaythlok and Watson monest to marye.*

---

[1] *As* in MS.

[2] *In to* in MS.

[3] *Prophanat* in MS.

[4] A fuller.

ane sufficient testimoniall[1] in wryt recognoscit. In respect of the quhilk, the Superintendent, wyth avyis of the ministerie, monesis bayth the parteis to procead in solemnizacion of thar mariaige wythin xl dayes under pane of excommunicacion.

Die primo Maii anno quo supra.

Liddell fornicator.

The quhilk daye, Dauid Lyddell, fornicator wyth Eleyn [*Lyddell*—deleted] Harpar fugityve, is ordenet to mak public satisfaccion, in the essemble of the congregacion, this nixt Sunday befoir nuyn, and at efter nuyn his barn to be baptised.

Die xv[to] Maii anno quo supra.

Decretum ab-solvatorium Skyrlyng.

The quhilk daye, anent the clame of mariaige persewit be Jonat Huntar of Jhon Skyrling, be resson of promys and defloracion of hyr virginitie *respective*, as desyr set to pronunce, and Jonat to geve hyr ayth of calumpne befoir pronunciacion, bayth the parteis comperand the ayth of Jonat requirit, sche refusit to sweir, and of hyr awyn motyve wyll renuncit the clam of mariaige be resson of defloracion. In respect of the quhilk, and at na lawfull promys betuix parteis is confessit nor provyn, the Superintendent absolvis Ihon fra the clam of mariaige of the said Jonat; and, becaus of carnall dayl confessit be beyth the saidis parteis, ordenis tham bayt to mak public satisfaccion, in the essemble of the congregacion of Lathrisk, this nixt Sunday, the xix of Maii instant. As also the Superintendent, in consideracion of the confession and

[*Satisfaccio* Ihon Hutson.]

deposicione of Ihon Hutson confessing hym to hav had carnall dayll wyth Jonat Huntar, ordenis that the sayd Ihon mak public satisfaccion in the kyrk of Kylgowr, upon Sunday the xxvj of Maii instant.

Die xxij Maii anno Domini etc. lxvj[to.]

Beton, Arnot.

The quhilk daye, anent the impediment mayd be Cristen Beton to staye the proclamacion of bannis of mariaige betuix Thomas Arnot and Jonat Anderson, parrochinaris of Lathrisk,

---

[1] *Testioall* in MS.

the saidis Cristen Betoin and Thomas comperand befoyr the
Superintendent, in the essemble of the ministerie of Sanctandrois, the said Cristen allegis that the sayd Thomas Arnot
tistit hyr be his foyr promisis, namly, of mariaige (sche being
ane virgin undeflorit [1] or difamit wyth ony spot concernyng hyr
virginite); he deflorit hyr virginite and tharfor haldyn of the
law of God for the forisayd offence to tak hyr to his lawfull
wyf, and is nocht fre to mare wyth ony other; and desiris and
askis hym to be decernit be the Superintendent to tak hyr to
wyf, and the proclamacion of bannis and solemnizacion of the
mariaig betuix hym and Jonat Anderson to be stayed and
cease—in presence of Thomas Arnot; quhai, for his defence,
allegis the sayd Cristen wes deflorit and lost hyr virginite befoyr
he knew hyr carnalye.   Quhilk defence the Superintendent
admittis to probacione of the sayd Thomas, and statutis to hym
Wednisdaye, the v of Junii nixt to cum, to produce the sam
relevantle articulat, and to prev the sam daye foyrsaid : parteis
heirto summond be actis.

Die tercio Julii anno Domini etc. lxvj[to.]

The quhilk daye, Thomas Arnot beand summond at the
instance of Cristen Beton to compeir this daye, to heyr the
caus and clame of mariaige persewit be the sayd Cristen of hym
suscitat and to proceid, and comperand, the caus suscitat,
according to desyr of last term, to hym to produce his defence
qualefyit in articulis, anent the allegit defloracion of Cristen
befoyr he knew hyr carnale, and to prev the sam.   The Superintendent decernis letteres to the said Thomas to summond his
wytnes to ony lawfull daye in this moneth ; and Thomas refusis
to resave ony letteres, or to prev the allegit be hym.   And
Cristen desyris Thomas to be decernit to tak hyr to his wyf,
becaus he hes grantit that he had carnall deyll wyth hyr, and
can nocht prev sche wes ane spilt woman befoir he meld wyth
hyr.   The Superintendent statutis Wednisday nixt to cum to
pronounce.   Partes heirto warnit be act.   And Thomas allegis
that he hes mayd satisfaccioṇ to the kyrk and congregacion of

Beton, Arnot.

---

[1] *Umdeflorit* in MS.

Lathrisk for his offence and falt, at command of the kyrk;
offerris hym to prev the sam; and allegis, in respect tharof, he
suld be absolvit.   And Cristen allegis that wes na mendis to
hyr, for the falt he had mayd to hyr.[1]

Die xix Junii, anno Domini m°v^clxvj^{to.}

Decretum matrimoniale inter Gedde et Suntar.

The quhilk daye, Andro Gedde and Jonat Suntar, dochter
of Ihon Suntar, citiner, callit befoir the ministerie for staying
of thar solemnizacion of thar mariaige efter mutuall promys
mayd betuix tham; the mater tryed, it is fundyn that efter
persuasion mayd be Elizabeth Watson, mother of the said
Jonat, sche fyrst privatle grantit to mak promys wyth the said
Andro befoyr hyr awyn frendis, and tharefter, wyth [2] consent of
hyr father and mother,[3] oppynly in presens of thaim and otheris
hyr frendis, George Blak, diacon and readar of the kyrk, and
divers otheris famos wytnes, the sayd Jonat willingle and frely
consentit and mayd promys mutuall of mariaige wyth the said
Andro Gedde and he wyth hyr.   And the said Jonat being
demandit be the said George [4] Blak, gyf sche wes compellit or
frely consentit to makyn of the said promys, sche confessit hyr
consent wes fre wythowtyn compulsion.   In respect of the
premissis, the ministerie declaris the foyrsayd mutuall promys

---

The following decree has been cancelled, and the more formal one of the
same date inserted almost immediately after it :—

' Die x Julii anno quo supra.

' Decretum matrimoniale inter Beton et Arnot.'

'The quhilk daye, as in term set to pronunce be the Superintendent, in the
caus of impediment mayd be Cristen Betoun to the proclamacion of bannis of
pretendit mariaig betuix Thomas Arnot and Jonat Anderson, and mariaig
acclamit be the said Cristen Betoun of the sayd Thomas Arnot, for offence don
to hyr be said Thomas in defloracion of hyr virginite throw his tyisting of hyr,
the Superintendent, avysit wyth the peticion of the said Cristen, ansuer of the
said Thomas, pronuncis and decernis the said Thomas Arnot to mary and tak to
his wyf the said Cristen Beton, in satisfaccion of the offence don to hyr be hym
in defloryng of hyr virginite, nochtwythstanding the defence allegit be Thomas
admittit to his probacion and nocht provyn ; and to proceid to solemnizacion of
thar mariaige wythin xl dayes under pane of excommunicacion, thar bannis to be
proclamit *interim*.   Pronuncit in presens of parteis.'

[2] This has at first been written *in presens and wyth;* but the clerk, in deleting
presens and, has neglected to draw his pen through *in.*

[3] *Nother* in MS.   [4] *Cherge* in MS.

of mariaig betuix Andro Gedde and Jonat Suntar to be lawfull
promys, and tharfor the parteis to abyd tharat, and to procead
to solemnizacion of the sam betuix this and Michaelmes, under
panis of excommunicacione to be execut upon the inobedient:
thar bannis to be proclamit *interim*.

Die x mensis Julii anno quo supra.

The quhilk daye, in the caus of impediment mayd be Cristen *Decretum*
Beton to the proclamacion of bannis of mariaige betuix *Betoin contra* Arnot.
Thomas Arnot and Jonat Anderson, parrochinaris of Lathrisk,
and mariaige clamit be the said Cristen of the said Thomas,
for offence be hym don to hyr in defloracion of hir virginite,
according to the law of God, as desyr of term set to pronunce
in the said caws, the Superintendent, avysit wyth the impediment mayd be Cristen, and hyr clam of mariaige of the said
Thomas Arnot, for his offence done to hyr in defloring of hyr
virginite, according to the law of God, and peremptor excepcione
proponit and allegit be the said Thomas for his defence in the
said caus, to wyt, that the said Cristen wes deflorit and had
lost hyr virginite befoir he knew hyr carnalye, admittit to his
probacion, and all otheris deducit in the said caus, findes that
the said Thomas be proponyng of the said peremptor defence
hes confessit the intencion of the said Cristen perseuar; and
heirfor, having God only befoir his ees and the testimone of
his trew and eternall Word, pronuncis and decernis the said
Thomas Arnot gilte in defloracion of the verginite of the said
Cristen Beton, and for his foyrsayd offence don to hyr he is
haldyn to tak the said Cristen Beton to his lawfull wyf; and
tharfor na bannis nor mariaige to proceid forder betuix the
saidis Thomas Arnot and Jonat Anderson, nor yit wyth ony
other woman bot the said Cristen Betoun; nochtwythstanding
the said peremptor excepcion proponit, admittit and nocht
provyn. Pronuncit in the consall hows, wythin the parroche
kyrk of the cite of Sanctandrois, in presens of the parteis, year,
day and moneth abov wryttyn, &c.

Die xvij Julii anno Domini mᵒvᶜlxvjᵗᵒ.

Blacatar parson of Methell inhibit fra ministracion of baptisme.

The quhilk daye, M. Wyliam Blacatar, parson of Methell,[1] callit and accused be the Superintendent for baptising of ane barne gottyn in hurdom betuix M. Ihon Dalgles and Jonat Wemys Lady of Claslogy, na satisfaccion mayd be the parentis for the offence and sclander gevyn be thaim to the congregacion of Sanctandrois, quhar thar hurdom wes committit in procreacion of the said barne. The said M. Wyliam confessis hym to have baptist the said barne of necligence and be persuasion of Capitan Wemys, belevyng the barne had belangit to hym. The Superintendent, in respect of the said confession, inhibitis the said M. Wyliam Blacatar fra this tym fordwart to mak ministracion of baptisme, except he be of new admittit tharto: quhilk inhibicion Master Wyliam acceppit, ansuerand and sayand he suld obey.

Die Sabbati[2] xxᵒ Julii anno quo supra.

[Caucio Dwdyngstown for Frostair and Anderson.]

The quhilk daye, James Dwdyngstown is becum caucion for James Frostair and Jonat Anderson, fornicatoris, that thai sall underly and obey disciplyn of the kyrk for thar fornicacion quhen thai salbe requirit, and that thai sall solemnizat thar mariaig betuix this and Martymes nixt to cum; and gyf thai falye heirin James to payie, in nam of pane as sowm liquidat,

---

[1] Mr. William Blacater, rector of the Parish Church of Methil, is mentioned on the 1st of February 1536-7 (*Register of Great Seal*, iv. No. 1656). The notarial instruments in the Wemyss charter-chest show that, 'in 1545, the installation of. Robert Swyne, a priest of St. Andrews, as rector of Methil, took place. The former rector, Mr. William Blackadder, had resigned office. Friar John Grierson, father of the provincial order of Friars preachers in Scotland, presented the Pope's bulls on the occasion' (Sir William Fraser's *Memorials of the Family of Wemyss of Wemyss*, i. 143). In 1574 Robert Swyne was reader at Methil, with a stipend of £13, 16s. 8d. and the kirkland (*Wodrow Miscellany*, p. 362). In 1661 Parliament ratified to the Earl of Wemyss 'the right and title of the patronage of the personage and viccaradge of the kirk of Methill' (*Acts of the Parliaments of Scotland*, vii. 120); but the parish seems to have been incorporated with that of Wemyss about the period of the Reformation, and was not constituted a *quoad sacra* by the General Assembly until 1839 (Scott's *Fasti*, ii. 563).   [2] Saturday.

the sowm of ten marcas to the box of the pur; and James
Frostar oblesis hym to relev James Dudyngstoun of the said
caucion and pane.

Die sexto Novembris anno Domini etc. lxvj^{to.}

The quhilk daye, comperis Eufam Ogylwy and producis ane *Absolvatorum* Clark.
lettre of summondis under signet of the Superintendent, deuly
execut and indorsat be Mr. Robert Paterson minister of Crech,
tharin summond Robert Clark at hyr instance to heyr[1] promys
of mariaige provyn betuix hyr and the sayd Robert; as also
tharin summond Jhon Paterson, Andro Schethom, Lorence
Cant and Dauid Ogylwy, wytnes, comperand be verteu of the
summondis to testefy in the sayd caus; and certan objeccionis
proponit aganis the saydis wytnes. At lenth the sayd Eufam,
wyth consent of hyr brother present, referris hyr clam of mariaige and promys be hyr allegit to the ayth of Robert Clark.
He sworn and examinat in his deposicione purgis hym. The
Superintendent heirfor absolvis Robert fra the clam and mariaig of Eufam and [decernis][2] liberte to Robert to mary ony
othir laufull parte wythowtyn impediment of the sayd Eufam.

Die Marcurii xiij Novembris anno quo supra.

The quhilk daye, Nycholl Zong, parrochinar in Stramyglo, Nycholl Zong
summond be the Superintendentis[3] letteres and comperand, is convict of
in^cest.
delated, accused of committing insest wyth Cristen Spyttell,
naturall and lawfull dochter of his awyn mareit wyf. He confessis his offence and that ane barne[4] is gottyn betuix hym and
the sayd Cristen his dochter in law. Quhilk confession the
Superintendent ordenit to be notit and actitat in this buk.

Die quarto Decembris anno quo supra.

The quhilk daye, Wyliam Huntar, spows of Besse Aytkyn, Satisfaccion of
Huntar and
and Bege Scot summond, callit, comperand and accusit of adul- Scot adulteraris.

---

[1] *To the heyr* in MS.   [2] Omitted.
[3] *Superintendis* in MS.   [4] *Borne* in MS.

tery committit betuix thaim, manifestit be procreacion of ane
child betuix tham, and for contempt of baptisme in nocht
desyrng thar barn to be baptisied.   The sayd Wylliam and
Bege confessis thar adultery, schauys[1] owtward signis of repentance, offerrs thaim redy and wylling to underly disciplyn of the
kyrk for thar offencis; and Wyliam confessis that he put the
barn be hym gottyn in adultery to fosteryng to the wyf [of][2]
Ihon Collfe, callit Besse Aleson, in Cassyngray;[3] and his sayd
barn be his awyn procurment and consall of the sayd Iho Colfe
wes baptist, in the hows of Ihon Colfe in Cassingray, be ane ald
dayf prest, callit Schyr Alexander Broun, sumtym curat in Kylconquhar, quhai baptist the barne for ane testan[4] in the nam of
the Father the Son and the Holy Gayst, wythowtyn ony prayer
redyng or other cerimone, beand present Henry Greg, Ihon
Colfe, and Besse Aleson, gossopis and cummer.   The Superintendent ordenis the saydis Wyliam Huntar and Bege Scot twa
syndry Sunday to compeir, cled in sack-clayth, in the essemble
of the congregacion of Sanctandrois; and syt in sic place as
salbe appoyntit to thaim duryng the tym of the sermonis; and
at the end tharof acknaulege thar offensis, ask God mercy and
the congregacion forgyfnes.

Reconciliacion
betuix Huntar
and Aytkyn his
wyff.

The quhilk daye, Besse Aytkyn, in presens of the Superintendent and ministere, remittis Wyliam Huntar hyr husband
the offence don in gevyn his body to Bege Scot in adulterie:
quhilk Wyliam solemple hes mayd his ayth, and be the sam
promyst to intreat the sayd Besse his wyf as the Word of God
requiris, and never to falye aganis hyr; and is be the Superintendent and ministerie monest to keip gud part to hyr, certefy-
ing hym gyf heirefter he falye aganis his band and promys to
his wyf be adulterie, he salbe deliverit to the temporall magistrate be supplicacion as [ane][2] incorrigibill adulterar.

Die xv^{to.} Januarii anno Domini m°v^clxvj.

Processus inter
Wm. Cristesone
et Issobellam
Lyndesay ejus
sponsam.

The quhilk daye, Wyliam Cristeson and Issobell Lyndesay[5]
beand summond be the Superintendentis letteres to heir thaim

---

[1] *Schauyn* in MS.   [2] Omitted.
[3] Cassingray is in the parish of Carnbee.   [4] A small silver coin.
[5] Isabell Lindsay was the eldest daughter of John Lord Lindsay of Byres and

decernit to adheir in bed and burd as becummis the husband and wyf, or ellis ether of tham to schaw ane ressonabill caus quhy the sammyn suld nocht be don ; bayth the saidis parteis comperand, the said Issobell allegis sche suld nocht be compellit nor decernit to adheir to Wyliam as to hyr lawfull husband, becaus thar nether is nor was ony promys of mariaige betuix Wyliam and hyr—in presence of Wyliam ; quhai affirmative allegis lauful promys and mariaige betuix hym and Issobill, vidz., that betuix Martymes and Zowll in the year of God 1554 yearis, abowt fyve howris at evyn or tharby, in the land of umquhill Robert Macke, in the burgh of Coupar, in presence of famos wytnes and Schyr James Mortoun prest, according to the ordor of the kyrk of Scotland for that tym, thar wes mutuall promys of mariaige mayd betuix hym, the said Wiliam, and the said Issobell, quharupon followit thar carnall copulacion wyth continuance ay sen syn betuix tham, thai haldyn and reput mareit personis wyth all thar nychboris. Efter quhilk mutuall promys foyrsayd, certen gentillmen, send be the Lord Lyndesay father to the said Issobell in his nam, requirit the said Issobell to 'cum fra the said Wyliam and lev hym, and hyr said father suld caus hyr be weyll marieit ; the said Issobell, in hyr ansuer gevyng to the saidis gentellmen send fra hyr father, in thar presence, ratefyed and affirmit the foyrsayd mariaig, sayand, and in cherge gevand to the saidis gentilmen to say to hyr father, That he suld provyd for the rest of his dochteris unmareit for sche was alredy mareit wyth the said Wyliam, and gyf sche war to mary sche wald yit marye wyth the said Wiliam. In respect of the quhilkis Wiliam is wylling to adheir to Issobell as to his wyff, and desyris hym to be admittit to preve the premissis, and term statut to hym to prev the sam, and the sammyn provyn Issobell to be decernit to adheir to hym. The Superintendent

---

Helen Stewart (see p. 230, n. 2), and was married to Norman Leslie, the Master of Rothes, in or before February 1540-1 (Wood's *Douglas's Peerage*, i. 385). The bold and daring Norman Leslie, so well known in connection with the prominent part he played in compassing the death of Cardinal Beaton, distinguished himself by his matchless bravery, in fighting for the French King at Renti, in the autumn of 1554, but there he was so severely wounded that he died fifteen days afterwards (Sir James Melville's *Memoirs*, Ban. Club, pp. 25, 26).

admittis the affirmatyve allegacion of Wiliam to his probacion,
and at his desyr Wednisday nixt to cum statut to hym to prev
his alligacion.   Parteis heirto summond *apud acta.*

Die Mercurii xxij° Januarii anno Domini etc. lxvj.

The quhilk day, as in term assignit be the Superintendent
to Wiliam Cristeson to prev the admittit to hym anent the
mariaige betuix hym and Issobell Lyndesay, comperis Wyliam
and producis ane eik to his formar allegacionis in presens of
Issobell, of the quhilk the tenor followis.

[Eik to Wyliam   *In primis*, I, Wiliam Cristeson burges of[1] Cowpar, offerris me
Cristesonis
former allega-   to prev ane solempt contract and promys of mariaige to be
cionis.]   mayd betuix me and Issobell Lyndesay, Mastres of Rothesay,
in verba de presenti, owr handis conjunit be Schyr James Mortoun, in Cowpar, in Robert Mackeis hows, twelve year bypast
in November.

Secindlye, that the said Issobell my spows and I, in the Lady
Brakmonthis hous, at begynnyn of the relegion, desyrit to communicat at the table of the Lord, Paull Meffen[2] heand minister.
At the quhilk tym, the foyrsaid promys and contract of mariaige be the said Issobell and me wes ratefyed, sche confessing
(in presence of the kyrk thar essembled) us to be man and wyff;
and requirit gyf forther solemnizacion war requisit that the
minister wald use it.   To the quhilk he ansuerit that owr ratificacion thar was sufficient, exhorting us to leve in Godis fear,
and upon this war we resavit to the table ; and since that tym
ever hes kepit hows and bed together.

Quhilk eik beand red in audience of the sayd Issobell, and
be hyr denyed as is consavit, and to probacion admittit, and to
be discussit wyth the proces ; Wyliam for desyr of term producit ane lettre of summondis of the Superintendentis under his

---

[1] *Of of* in MS.
[2] Paul Methven took a prominent part in the Scottish Reformation, but, after
being appointed minister of Jedburgh, fell into adultery, for which he was so
severely dealt with by the Church that, ' overwhelmed with shame, and despair-
ing to regain his lost reputation,' he stopped in the midst of the 'humiliating
penance' prescribed to him, and retired to England (M'Crie's *Knox*, 1861,
pp. 250, 251).

signet and subscripsion, deuly execut and indorsat be M. Dauid
Fressar, readar in Cowpar, tharin summond to this diet, to
beyr wytnes in the said caus of allegacionis of the said Wiliam,
thir personis underwryttyn comperand, and be the said Wiliam
for probacion of his intent producit, vidz., Dauid Lyndesay of
Piatstown, Master Robert Nycholl, M. Robert Ayrth, Jhon
Lyndesay, burges of Coupar, Margret Lanbart, Thomas
Flescher, Schyr Dauid Lowson, Dauid Welaind, Dauid Peterson, Dauid Baxtar, Andro Thomson, quhilkis ar resavit, sworne
and to examinacion admittit in presence of Issobell.   And also
the said Wiliam producis Dauid Wat, James Anderson, scrib,
and Eleyn Cristeson, summond as said is, in presence of Issobell,
quhai allegis the saidis personis suld nocht be resavit as wytnes
in this caus : and fyrst aganis Dauid Wat sche allegis that the
producer and the said Dauid ar brether and sister barnis ; and
James Anderson and the producer ar thrid and ferd in kyn ;
and Eleyn Cristeson is syster to the producer.   And Wiliam,
ansuering, allegis that in respect that he producis tham to prev
contract promys of mariaige (quhilk commonle is don befoir
frendis) the saidis wytnes suld be resavit, nochtwythstanding
the allegacion of Issobell.   The Superintendent ordenis thaim
to be resavit *cum nota*, and the allegacionis of parteis to be
discussit wyth the proces.   Quhilkis Dauid Wat, James Anderson, and Eleyn Cristeson ar resavit, sworn, and to examinacion
admittit, *cum nota*, in presence of Issobell.   Mayrower, the
sayd Wyliam producis[1] ane testimoniall,[2] under sayll of Dauid
Ayrth, ballie of the burgh of Coupar, and subscripsion of
James Anderson, notar, of dayt the xiij day of December, *anno
Domini* 1556, contenyng sasing gevyn to the saidis parteis in
conjunct fe as husband[3] and wyff ; and the rolment[4] and actis
of court haldyn be Issobell Lindesay and Wyliam Cristeson hyr
spows, under subscripsion of Thomas Flescher, notar, of deyt
$xv^{to.}$ *Julii, anno lvj* ; wyth ane act of the sam court of creacion
of Andro Ballingall in thar officiar ; and ane prothogoll subscrivit be James Anderson, notar, of deyt $xxvj^{to.}$ *Julii anno
Domini etc. lxiiij^{to}*, contenyng resignacion of certan landis mayd

---

[1] *Pro producis* in MS.
[3] *Husbad* in MS.
[2] *Testioall* in MS.
[4] Register, record.

be Wiliam Cristeson and Issobell Lyndsay his spows, &c.; and
ane precept of warnyng of the said Issobell wyth consent of
[Wyliam][1] Cristeson hyr spows, subscrivit wyth hyr awyn hand
be hyr recognoscit, and hyr seyll, of deyt the thrid of[2] *Marcii
anno etc. lvij.* Wȳliam renuncis all forder probacion. The
Superintendent statutis *literatorie* to pronunce in the sayd
caus.

Followis interrogatoris of Issobell.

[Interrogatoris
of Issobell.]   It mot be sperit at every ane of the wytnes, gyf thai be of
kyn or allia[3] to the said Wyliam producent, or gyf thai have
gevyn hym parciall consall in this caus, or is rewardit, or in
hop to resave gud deid fra hym for thar deposicion, and gyf
thai favor the ane parte mayr nor the other, by equite and
justice.

Item, it salbe sperit at every ane of tham, gyf thai war present at the allegit mariaig makyng, quhar the sam was mayd,
in hall or chalmer, befoyr nuyn or efter nuyn, at quhat howris,
quhai was minister tharat, quhidder ane Papist preist, or ane
other laufull minister, and gyf mariaige wes mayd in Inglis or
in Latyn, quhat the preist or minister said, or yit the parteis
at that tym, quhai wes present tharat, quhar sat the allegit
bryd and brydgrum, and the Papist preist or minister for the
tym. And that every wytnes geve ane relevant and concludand
caus of thar knawlege, gyf thai depon the mater to be of
trewth, &c.

Followis the depocicionis of wytnes producit.

[Deposicionis
of wytnes.]   Dauid Lyndesay of Pyatstown,[4] wytnes, summond, resavit,
sworne, admittit and examinat upon the allegacionis of Wiliam
[1] Cristeson and interrogatoris. In his deposicione purgis hym of
all parcialite, and deponis that he was nocht present at the

---

[1] Omitted.   [2] *Of of* in MS.   [3] Allies.
[4] David Lindsay was in 1561 served heir to his father, William Lindsay of
Pyetstone, the second son of Patrick, fourth Lord Lindsay of the Byres (*Lives
of the Lindsays,* i. 444).

allegit promys mayd betuix parteis. *Item*, efter the tym of the allegit promys, the deponar knawis and saw the parteis keip and contenew in mutuall cohabitacion at bed and burd, haldyn and reput mareit folkis. *Item*, concernyng the messag send fra the Lord Lindesay to Issobell Lyndesay and ansuer gevyn and confession of promys articulat, he deponis the sam trew. Examinat upon his caus of knawleg, the deponar confessis he wes messinger send be the Lord Lyndesay, did his messeg articulat, resavit the ansuer articulat, and confession of Issobell in speciall, sche granting the allegit promys and handfasting mayd be Schyr James Mortoun prest. Examinat upon the secund part of the eyk, he deponis the sam trew: he wes present hard and saw as the same bearis, and wyth hym mony otheris faytfull; and amangis the rest M. Wiliam Ramsay ane of this ministerie. Examinat upon the place quhar he resavit the ansuer of his messege, he deponis it wes in the hows of Robert Macke : and purgis hym of the rest of interrogatoris.

2   Master Robert Nycholl, wytnes, summond, sworne, and examinat upon the allegacionis of Wyliam Cristeson, deponis that he was present tym and place articulat, hard and saw promys of mariaig betuix parteis, thar handis layd together be Schyr James Mortoun prest, accordyng to the Papisticall ryt usit for that tym ; and that tharefter carnall copulacion betuix parteis followit tharupon, and thai reput and haldyn be common voce and fame as mareit folkis. Examinat upon the interrogatoris, he purgis hym of all parcialite and all puntis of the interrogatoris, and kennis na mayr in this mater except the place wes in the hows of Robert M^cke, in Cowpar, tym articulat. He remembris nocht quhai wes present nor quhow thai sat.

3   Jhon Wat, wytnes, sworn, admittit *cum nota etc.*, examinat upon the allegacionis of Wyliam Cristeson, he is conforme to Master Robert Nycholl, wytnes preceding, in all punttis, except he grantis hym secund in kyn wyth the producer.

4   Eleyn Cristeson, sister to the producer, wytnes, sworn, resavit *cum nota*, examinat, &c., be hyr ayth deponis and is conforme to Mr. Robert Nycholl, wytnes preceding, concernyng the handfasting of parteis be Schyr James Mortoun. Examinat upon the interrogatoris, sche ansuers that sche is sister to the producer and purgis hyr of all parcialite, wald justice triumphit,

and is conform to the said Mr. Nycholl in ansueryng to the interrogatoris twechyn the prest, hows, tym, and daye.

5   Robert Trumbull, coupar of his craft, burges in Coupar, wytnes, summond, sworn, examinat upon the allegacionis of Wiliam Cristeson, be his ayth deponis that he, be the space of twelve yearis last bypast, hes, in his office as coupar, wrocht to the parteis, beyn in thar hows and chalmer, seyn thaim in bed together naked, and that thai war haldyn and reputt mareit folkis, the woman kepand his marchand buth as his wyff and sa haldyn; and kennis na mayr, and purgis hym of interrogatoris.

6   Margret Lambart, spows of James Anderson marchand in Cowpar, wytnes, summond, sworne, admittit and examinat, &c., deponis that sche nether hard nor saw ony thing articulat, bot alanerly that the parteis war haldyn and reput wyth thar neyghboris mareit folkis, hes seyn tham divers tymmes in naked bed, and Issobell kepand the marchand buth of Wiliam as his wyff; and purgis hyr of the interrogatoris.

7   M. Robert Ayrth, burges in Coupar, wytnes, summond, sworn, admittit and examinat[1] upon the allegacionis of Wiliam, and in speciall upon the last part of his eyk, deponis that at the communion ministrat in the hows of Lady Brakmonth be Paul Meffen, tym articulat, he wes present, hard the ratificacion and confession articulat be Wyliam and Issobell, hes seyn the parteis thir mony yearis keip cumpany as man and wyf, sa haldyn and reput be thar neyghboris. Attowr, the deponar beand send to Issobell be hyr mother, as messenger to desyr hyr to cum fra Wyliam Cristeson producer, he resavit hyr ansuer and cherg to say to hyr mother, That sche had mareit hyr anis and now sche hes mareit hyrself wyth the producer; and wald never leyf hym. Examinat upon the interrogatoris, he purgis hym.

8   Johan Lyndesay, burges of Cowpar, wytnes, summond, sworne, admittit and examinat, &c., be his ayth deponis that, be the space of twelve yearis or tharby, the parteis hes kepit cumpany as man and wyff, sa haldyn and reput be thar neyghboris. He hes seyn tham in bed, hes hard Issobell divers tymmis in

---

[1] *Examinat examinat* in MS.

presens of Wyliam and divers otheris personis confes hyr his
wyff, and hym confes to be hyr husband, hes seyn tham in
naked bed. He resortit in thar hows wyth tham thre yearis,
saw gret cherite betuix tham quhill now laytle; and kennis na
mayr, and purgis hym of the interrogatoris.

9   James Anderson, scrib in Cowpar, wytnes, summond, resavit
cum nota, sworne and examinat, &c., be his ayth deponis that
he kennis nathing articulat, except that thir mone yearis the
parteis hes kepit mutuall cohabitacion, haldyn and reput for
mareit folkis, hard Issobell confess Wyliam Cristeson to be hyr
husband divers tymmis in his presens; and at divers resigna-
cionis of landis, mayd be Issobell, Wyliam wes present as hyr
husband, gave his consent tharto, the sammyn mencionat in
the instrumentis of saisingis, to the quhilkis the deponar is
notar. He knawis na mayr in this mater; and purgis hym of
the interrogatoris, except he confessis hym to atteyn to the
producer in ferd and thrid of kyn.

10   Thomas Flescher, burges in Cowpar, wytnes, summond,
sworne, admittit, and examinat, &c., be his ayth deponis and
is conform to James Anderson, wytnes preceding. He hes
beyn notar and scrib in makyng of instrumentis and asseda-
cionis to the parteis wyth bayth thar consentis, quharin the
consent of Wyliam husband to Issobell[1] wes all tymmis mencionat; and quhar subscripsion wes requirit Wyliam subscrivit
in takyn of his consent: and kennis na mayr in this mater;
purgis hym of the interrogatoris.

11   Schyr Dauid Lowson, wytnes, summond, sworne, admittit,
and examinat, &c., be his ayth deponis that he kennis nocht
the promys nor handfasting betuix parteis articulat, he wes
nocht present. *Item*, concernyng the carnall dayll and reputa-
cion of mareaige betuix parteis, he deponis the sam trew; he
hard and kend the sam be reparyng to the parteis. *Item*, concernyng the messege send be Lord Lyndesay to Issobell and
ansuer be hyr geivyn articulat, the deponar deponis the sam to be
trew: examinat upon his knawlege, the deponar wes messenger
send, dyd his messege, resavit ansuer as is articulat. Examinat
upon the interrogatoris, he purgis hym: and kennis no mayr.

---

[1] *Wyliam* in MS.

12   Dauid Weland, burges in Cowpar, wytnes, summond, sworn,
admittit, and examinat, &c., be his ayth deponis that he wes
nocht present at the promys mayd in the hows of Robert M^cke
articulat. *Item,* sen syn he hard Issobell divers tymmis confes
Wyliam to be hyr husband, and at sche had takyn hym to hyr
husband, and wald keip promys wyth hym so lang as sche levit.
The deponar examinat upon the secund part of the eik, he
deponis the sam trew ; he wes present at the communion in
[the][1] hows of Lady Brakmonth, hard and saw as is articulat :
and purgis hym of the interrogatoris, and kennis no mayr.
13   Andro Thomson, servand to Issobell Lyindesay, sworn and
examinat, kennis nathing articulat.
14   Dauid Peterson, burges in Cowpar, wytnes, summond, sworn,
admittit, and examinat, &c., be his ayth deponis that be the
space of twelv yearis or tharby he hes seyn and kend Wyliam
Cristeson and Issobell Lindesay keip mutuall cohabitacion as
mareit folkis, sa haldyn and reput be all neyghboris ; and divers
tymmis, the deponar beand syttand in jugiment as ballie and
juge in Cowpar, have comperit befoir hym bayth the parteis
Wyliam and Issobell in proper personis, producit billis of
compttentis aganis divers dettoris, contenyng the complaynt set
furth in nam of Issobell and in nam of Wyliam hyr husband
for his interres : and kennis na mayr in this mater, and purgis
hym of interrogatoris.
15   Dauid Baxtar, burges of Coupar, wytnes, summond, admittit, sworne, and examinat, &c., be his ayth deponis, and is
conform in all thingis to Dauid Peterson, wytnes preceding ;
and forder he hes seyn the parteis in naked bed together.

Die quinto Februarii anno Domini etc. lxvj^{to.}

The quhilk day, comperis Wyliam Cristeson in the session of
the Superintendent and producis ane lettre of summondis under
signet of Superintendent, deuly execut and indorsat be Andro
Angus reader in the kyrk of Lesle,[2] tharin summond Wyliam
Cristeson and Issobell Lindesay to compeir befoyr the Superintendent in his session this day, to heir decernit and decreit

---

[1] Omitted.   [2] See p. 179.

gevyn in the caus foyrsayd of adherence. The saydis parteis callit upon to heir pronuncit, the decreit wes pronuncit and red as folles.

Wyth incalling of the nam of Crist Jesus, Sone of the eternall and everlevyng God, quhai is the way the verite and the lyff, M. Ihon Wynram, Superintendeint of Fyff, juge in the caus of adherence of Wyliam Cristeson and Issobell Lyndesay his spows in bed and burd as man and wyff, beand avysit wyth the negatyve defence proponit for the part of Issobell to stop the said adherence, and wyth the affirmatyve of the said negatyve defence mayd and allegit be the said Wyliam and to his probacion admittit, and wyth wrytis, deposicionis of wytnes producit for the part of Wyliam in probacion of his affirmatyve, and wyth all producit and deducit in the said caus, the consall of the ministere of Sanctandrois in the sayd caus had and followit ; and fynding the sayd affirmatyve sufficientle provyn, pronuncis and decernis the saidis Wyliam Cristeson and Issobell Lyndesay laufully conjunit in the band of matrimonye; and tharfor as mareit man and wyf to adheir ilk ane to other in mutuall cohabitacion, bed and burd, every ane to intreat other as accordes man and wyf to do of the law of God, under panis of excommunicacion to be execut aganis the parte inobedient to this decreit. Pronuncit in our consistoriall place, wythin the parrochie kyrk of the cite of Sanctandrois, upon Wednisday, the fyft daye of the moneth of Februarii, the year of God 1566, in presens of Wyliam Cristeson and in pane of nocht comperance of Issobell Lyndesay heirto laufilly summoind ; and befoir thir wytnes M. Robrt Hammyltoun, minister, M. Wyliam Ramsay, M. James Wylke, M. Alan Lawmonth, M. Thomas Balfour, eldaris and citineris of the cite and congregacion of Sanctandrois.

Die Marcurii, quarto mensis Februarii, anno Domini 1567.

The quhilk day, anent the supplicatioun maid to the seat be Johne Kircaldy to desire licence that Maister James Lermontht, Provest of Kirkhill, and Margrat Kircaldy, the said Johne dochter, may solemnizat the band of matrimonie contractit betwix thame outwytht this parrochioun, nochtwytht-

standing that thair bannis was laufullie proclamit wythtin the
sam upon thre several Sondaiis. The seat in consideratioun
that nethir the said Johne nor Maister James ar indwellaris
nor fremen of this citie, bot remanis for ane seasoun; and in
respect that the said Johne desyrit the same to be performit
wythtout ryoutesnes on ane honest quiet maneir, and being
desyrit be freindis to cum furtht of the towne and resort to
thame, quba promist to mak expensis of the brydell and swa
wald releve thame in that part; the seat, in consideratioun of
the said Johne resonable desyre, gevis licence to the said Johne,
Maister James, and the said Johne dochtir to pas and marie
in the Lord quhair it sal pleas them; providing, in respect of
the thyngis foirsaid and cais of the caus, this be nocht ane
preparative or drawn in exemple for utheris.

Die Marcurii, tertio mensis Martii, anno Domini 1567.

Ramsay,
Symsoun.

The quhilk day, Richart Ramsay and Alexander Symsoun,
travellaris, ar monesit be the Superintendent and seat to
abstein in tyme cuming fra going to merkattis and makking of
merchandice on the Sabbat day, undir paine of excommunicatioun.

Die Marcurii, decimo mensis Martii, anno Domino 1567.

Wallace,
Hakstoun, rij.[1]

The quhilk day, Dauid Hakstoun, in the parrochioun of
Dunboug, being somound to this day to heir and see hym
decernit to proceid in mareage wytht Isobell Wallace be resoun
of promis and defloration of hir virginite, the Superintendent, .
in paine of non comperence of the said Dauid, decernit hym to
be somound of new to proceid in the said mareage, wytht intimation gyf he comperis nocht the Superintendent will proceid
to pronuntiation of his decreit; and the said Dauid to be
somound to this day aucht dayis.

[Jonet Bathe-
son testis.]

The quhilk day, Jonet Bathesoun in Forther examinat upon

---

[1] The meaning of this word, or more probably contraction, is uncertain.
After this it occurs frequently in the margin, and generally, if not always, in
such cases, the matter is delayed for a definite time.

the last birtht of ane[1] bairn, borne be Jonet Hakstoun in
Forther wythtin the parrochioun of Lawthreis.

The quhilk day, anent the inquisitioun takin upon the Law, Makke,
father of the bairn begottin upon Maige Law, the Superin- *rij.*
tendent ordani[t] Dauid Makke in 'Crail, quhom the said
Maige allegit to be father of the bairn, to preve his allegeance,
to wit, that the said Maige confessit the [father of the][2] bairn
to be ane callit Petir Ramsay ; and that the said Petir grantit
the bairn to be his, and upon ane day borrowit sylver in Craill,
and cam a gait wart to Sanctandrois to tak with the bairn and
to caus the sam to be baptized ; and to preve the sam this day
aucht dayis.

Die Marcurii ultimo Martii 1568.

The quhilk day, Elene Forbes, spous to Nichol Pertht, and Forbes, Forbes.
Margrat Forbes, spous to James Hendersoun, sisteris, ar becum
bund and oblist, of thair awn propir confessiounis, that quhilk
of thame beis fund, in word or deid, to offend to utheris in
tyme cuming sal pay to the collectour of the puris of this citie
xl s. unforgevin. And in lik maneir Andro Duncansoun and *Duncansoun*
his wyf, and William Moreis yownger and his wyf, obligat in *Moreis et*
maneir abuif expremit. *sponsa.*

Die Marcurii, secundo die mensis Junii, anno Domini 1568.

The quhilk day, Johne Dayis servand to Andro Crastaris, Dayis, Walcar.
smytht, being callit befoir the seat to heir hym decernit to
solempnizat the band of matrimonie wytht Agnes Walcar, be
resoun of promis of mareage maid be hym to hir, the saidis
parteis comperand be thame selvis, the said Johne denyit ony
promis, and becaus the said Agnes could nocht preve the
promis [sche][2] referrit the sam to the said Johne aitht ; and
he being sworn denyit that evir he maid promis, albeit he had
carnall deal wytht hir as was confessit be thame baytht. In
respect of the quhilk, the seat, becaus na promis was provin
nor that athir of the saidis parteis parentis consentit tharto,
gaif tham licence to marie quhom they plesit in the Lord.

---

[1] *And* in MS.   [2] Omitted.

Die Marcurii ultimo Junii 1568.

Rolland,
Dischington,
[callit to geve
confessioun of
thair faitht.]

The quhilk day, the kirk, according to the Word of God and practice of utheris reformat citeis and townis wythtin this realme, callit M. Dauid Dischingtoun, M. James Rolland, procuratoris, requiring them of the confessioun of thair faitht, that, according to Act of Parliament, we mycht understand quha kepit ane uthir face of religioun then God of his mercye now, eftir our lang blyndnes, had offered unto us, resavit and universalie apprevit in Parliament;[1] quhay comperand declarit that they could nocht gyf haesty ansueir and wythtout forthir

[Delay grantit
to] *xiiij*^{to} *Julii*.

delay subscrive our articlis, and tharfoir requirit the copie of the articlis; and the xiiij day of Julii wytht thair awin consent was gevin to them, to gyf thair answeir in write to the saidis articlis.

Die Marcurii xiiij^{to} Julii 1568.

Rolland.
[Forther delay
grantit to]
xxiij^o *Julii*.

The quhilk day, in the terme assignat be the kirk to Maisteris James Rolland and Dauid Dischingtoun to gyf thair ansueris in wryte to the articlis of Confession of Faitht, the said M. Dauid comperit nocht, and the said M. Jaimes compering be hymself said he was nocht throlie avisat, and desyrit forthir dilatioun. The seat, being avisat and willing to wyn hym, assignat to hym Fryday the xxiij day of Julii instant.

Die Marcurii xxj^{mo} Julii 1568.

[Forther delay
grantit to]
xxiij^o *Julii.*
Dischington.

The quhilk day, Maister Dauid Dischingtoun comperit befoir the seat, alleging the caus of his absence in the last diet to be becaus the Superintendent, Rectour and minister was absent in Edinburght; and desyrit Fryday the xxiij day of Julii instant, to gyf his ansuere in write to the articlis gevin in to hym; quhilk the seat grantit to hym.

---

[1] On the 20th of December 1567, Parliament ratified the Reformation Acts of 1560, and approved anew the *Confession of Faith*, which was then re-engrossed among the Acts of Parliament.

Die Veneris xxiij° Julii 1568.

The quhilk day, Maister James Rolland comperit and Rolland. according to his promis gaif in sum ansueris in write to the articlis gevin in to hym; and desyrit forthir dilation to gyf in moir full ansueir to every head of the articlis be thame selves; to quhom the seat assignat Wedinsday the xxviij day of Julii xxviij Julii. instant, to gyf in the saidis ansueris, willingly desyrit be hym.

The said day, in the terme assignat be the seat to Maister Dischington. Dauid Dischingtoun to gyf his ansueris in wryte, subscrivit wytht his awn hand, to the articlis gevin in to hym concerning the religion, the said M. Dauid, comperand be hymself, ansuerit that he wald nocht gyf his ansueir in wryte nochtwythtstanding the former promis, nor yit acknawlege us to be the kirk, nor yit acknawlege this to be the trew religioun that we have resavit and preachit; allegeing that gyf he gaif his ansuere in wryte that it wald be blaudit upon every mannis teitht, and forther he wald be blawdit in the pulpet quhair the preacheris ralis by thair text: and sa departit wytht fume and anger; nochtwythtstanding the seat promist that his writting sould nocht be blawdit, bot he sould have sufficient ansuere in wryte wytht quietnes. Nocht the les the seat, yit being of mynd to repres his stubburnes and be al meanis posseble to wyn hym, ordanis yit hym to be warnit to Wedinsday the xxviij of Julii xxviij Julii. instant, to compeir befoir the seat and to gyf in his ansueris in wryte subscrivit wytht his hand: and gyf he comperis nocht the minister to proceid to public admonesing of hym, according to the ordour appointed be the Kirk, into the General Assemblye haldin at Edinburght in Junii last bipast.[1]

---

[1] No meeting of the General Assembly was held in June 1568, but on the 8th of July of that year: 'Anent the excommunicatioun of Papists, and separatioun of them fra the societie of Chrysts bodie, after due admonition refuseing to joyne themselves to the Kirk; it is concludit, that after they have receivit sufficient admonitioun according to the ordour establishit in particular kirks, and they yet remaining obstinate, they sall be declarit publicklie in all congregations necessar to be out of the societie of Chrystis bodie, and to be excommunicat' (*Booke of the Universall Kirk*, Ban. Club, i. 126, 127).

Die Marcurii, undecimo mensis Augusti, anno Domini millesimo quingentesimo sexagesimo octavo.

Alexander,
Alexander,
Wischart.

The quhilk day, Robert Alexander elder in Montflovry,[1] Robert Alexander yownger thair, and Agnes Wischert thair, being somound be the Superintendentis lettres to compeir befoir hym and his ministerie of Sanctandrois this day, to heir hym[2] decernit to be punisched for using and usurping of the office of ane minister or redar in the Kirk of God, having no vocatioun tharto nor lauful admissioun, &c., as at mair lyntht is contenit in the citatioun deuly execut and indorsat; the said Robert Alexander, elder, comperand be hymself, desyrit the Superintendent to certifie hym quha was informar of the Superintendent, or dilatour of hym of the causis contenit in the somoundis. And the Superintendent refusit to advertis hym quha was informar or dilatour, for it was nocht necessar; and desyrit hym to ansuere to the pointis of the somoundis. And now the Superintendent hes continuat the somoundis to the

Primo Septembris.

first day of September nixt to cum, to the effect that the said Robert elder, Robert yownger, and Agnes Wischart compeir thameselves in thar awin propir personis to ansueir to the pointis of the somoundis, or ellis proces to be had according to justice.

Wilson,
Gourlay.

The quhilk day, in the terme assignat to Margaret Wilsoun to produce witnes for probatioun of promis of mareage betwix hir and Patrik Gourlay, producit Richart Leis in Balmerynocht, Alexander Gyllet in Kilbyrnis, syster sone to the mother of the said Margaret, Johne Brown in Coultray, William Gourlay in Souththeild, William Gourlay in Lucheris, Dauid Grig in Fordell, Henry Gourlay in Lucheris. And Johne Michel · in Balmerynocht, and Thomas Stevinson thair, somond and

Primo Septembris.

nocht comperand, the Superintendent sett the first day of September nixt to cum, to do diligence for Johne Michel and Thomas Stevinson; and to produce utheris witnes sa mony as

---

[1] Probably in the neighbourhood of Leven. It was part of the 'tenandry of Scoonie,' which Sir Alexander Gibson of Durie acquired from Lauder of the Bass (Wood's *East Neuk of Fife*, 1887, p. 33).

[2] That is the elder Robert Alexander : the others were summond on quite a different charge. See *infra*, pp. 299, 300.

the partie plesis, and Christen Braed and Patrik Gourlay
warnit to compeir the said day.

1   Richart Leis, witnes in the caus abuif wryttin betwix [Deposicionis
Margaret Wilsoun and Patrik Gourlay, deponis that, upon ^{of witnes.]}
the x day of Junii last bipast, the saidis Margaret and Patrik
being in Christen Braed hows in the Demins of Balmerynocht,
the deponent write the contract of mareage betwix the saidis
parteis, and referris hym thairto ; and forthir, befoir diverss
famous witnes, saw thair handis layit togethir ; and being
requirit quhat wordis war pronuncit, the deponent can nocht
tell.

2   Johne Brown, witnes in the said caus, deponis and sayis, that
the deponent layit the twa parteis handis togethir and said ilk
ane of them was content of utheris to go to mareage ; and the
deponent sperit at Patrik Gourlay, Ar ye nocht content ? And
he ansuerit and said, And[1] I war nocht content the mater had
nocht cum sa far fordward ! And [they][2] kissit utheris ; and
the deponent thareftir said, Ye maun[3] mary wythin xl dayis.

3   William Gourlay in Souththeild, witnes, deponis that he
kennis the contract maid betwix the parteis, bot kennis nocht
the promis of mareage.

4   William Gourlay in Lucheris conform to William Gourlay
in Souththeild.

5   Alexander Gillet in Kilbyrnis, syster sone to Margaret
Wilson, conform to William Gourlay in Souththeild.

6   David Grig in Fordell conform to William Gourlay in
Souththeild.

7   Henry Gourlay in Lucheris conform to William Gourlay in
Souththeild.

Die Marcurii, primo die mensis Septembris, anno Domini
j^mv^clxviij^o, per dominum Superintendentem et sedem.

The quhilk day, comperit Robert Alexander yownger in *Decretum Sup-*
erintendentis
Montflowrye, and Agnes Wischert thair, on the ane and uthir *penes Robertum*
Alexander
partis. Askit and demandit of the Superintendent, gyf they *juniorem et*
war contractit in mareage, or solempnization of mareage maid *Agnetem*
Wischart.

---

¹ If.   ² Omitted.   ³ Must.

betwix tháme: quhilkis ansuerit, in ane voce and severalie, that thair was na solemnization of mareage betwix thame. And thairfoir the Superintendent inhibit the solemnization of mariage betwix thame, quhill the said Robert Alexander yownger war fourtein [yeris][1] of aige compleit;[2] becaus the said Robert Alexander yownger confessit hymself to be bot of threttein yeris of aige at Sanct Laurence[3] day last bipast.

Superintendent, Alexander in Monflovry.

The said day, in the terme of continuation of the citation rasit at the instance of the Superintendent of his office aganis Robert Alexander elder in Montflowrye, comperit the said Robert be hymself and denyit the pointis of the citation sa far as concernis hym, and appealit to the General Assemblie of the Kirk. The Superintendent nevirtheles assignat this day aucht dayis to the said Robert to heir probation led upon the pointis of the said citation: and the said Robert warnit *apud acta* to heir probation led, &c., wytht intimation and certification, &c.

[Gourlay, Wilson.]

The said day, in the terme assignat to produce ma[4] witnes in the action and caus of promis of mareage betwix Patrik Gourlay and Margarete Wilson, war producit [*Johne*—deleted] Thomas Stevenson in Balmerynocht and Johne Michelson thar.

8   Thomas Stevinson, sworn, resavit and examinat, deponis that he was present at the contract making betwix thame and saw Johne Brown, walcar, ane of the eldaris of Sanct Teal parrochion, lay the parteis handis togethir; bot Patrik Gourlay spak nocht ane word: and forther kennis nocht in the caus.

9   Johne Michelson, witnes, deponis that he was present at the contract making betwix Patrik Gourlay and Margaret Wilson, and saw thair handis laid together be Johne Brown, ane of the eldaris of Sanct Teal parrochion; and [it][5] being demandit be hym of them, gyf they war content of utheris, hard them say that they sa war.

Gourlay, Wilson.

The said day, Andro Barthlhlat, in Sanct Teal parrochion, is decernit to be somound be the Superintendent lettres, to bear witnessing in the action and caus of promis of mareage

---

[1] Omitted.

[2] 'We affirm that bairns and infantis can nocht lauchfullie be mareid in thair minor aige, to wit, the man within fourtene yeiris of aige, and the woman within twelf yearis, at the least' (*First Book of Discipline*, ninth head).

[3] August 10th.   [4] More.   [5] Omitted.

betwix Patrik Gourlay and Margaret Wilson, to this day xv
dayis, viz., xv of September instant. *Patricio apud acta citato,* xv^{to} *Septembris.*
etc., wytht powar to the said Margaret to somound utheris wit-
nessis as sche pleasis to the said day peremptourlye.

*Die Marcurii, decimo quinto Septembris, anno Domini millesimo
quingentesimo sexagesimo octavo.*

The quhilk day, in the terme assignat to Andro Barclaytht *Decretum*
solemnizationis
to compeir to bear witnessing in the action and caus of promis *matrimonii*
of mareage betwix Patrik Gourlay and Margaret Wilsoun, *futuri inter*
Patricium
wytht ony utheris to be nominat be the said Margaret, comperit *Gourlay et*
Margaretam
Andro Bartclaytht and Robert Thomsoun in Balmerynocht, *Wilson infra*
somound be the Superintendentis lettres, in presence of *x*^{ta} *dies.*
Margaret Wilson, quha war resavit and sworn: and forthir
probation renuncit in presence of Patrik Gourlay. The Superintendent, in respect of the depositiounis of witnes producit of
befoir and this day, fyndis the promis of mareage betwix Patrik
Gourlay and Margaret Wilsoun sufficientlie provin; and thairfoir decernis and ordanis thame to proceid to the solempnization of mareage betwix thame wytthin fourty dayis undir paine
of excommunication; and letteris to be gevin furtht heirupon
als oft as neid beis.

10   Robert Thomsoun, in Balmerynocht, witnes, sworn, resavit
and examinat, deponis that, upon the day of the contract
making and promis of mareage betwix Patrik Gourlay and
Margaret Wilsoun, he was present in Christen Braed hows;
qubair he saw and hard Patrik Gourlay cry on Margaret
Wilson, being at the burn-syde weschyng claitht, and said,
Margaret, sen we sould eik and end of this mater lat us go til it.
And thaireftir incontinent they cam into the hows; and Johne
Brown in Cowtray sperit at Patrik Gourlay, Ar ye content to
have this woman to your wyf? And he said, Ye! And [in][1]
lik maneir sperit at Margaret gyf sche was content to have
Patrik to hir[2] husband, and she[3] said, Ye! And then the said
Johne Brown, ane of the eldaris of Balmerynocht said, I sal lay
your handis togethir, lay your hyppis quha wil!

---

[1] Omitted.   [2] *Your* in MS.   [3] *He* in MS.

11   Andro Barclaitht, quha and Margaret Wilson ar sister bairnis, conform to Robert Thomsoun.

Decretum Thomson, Gilchriste.

The quhilk day, the seat decernis and ordanis William Gilchriste to adhere to Jonet Thomson his spous, and intrait hir in bed and buird as becummis ane man his wyff continualie in tyme cuming, wythtin aucht dayis, undir paine of excommunication; and letteres to be direct heirupon als oft as neid beis: and siclik ordanis the said William Gilchriste, upon Sunday nixt to cum, to cum to the penitent seat wythtin this citie in the parroche kirk in sek-claitht, to resave penence for nocht presenting of his bairn to baptisme, bot suffiring[1] the sam to dee and depart wythtout baptisme, undir siclike payne of excommunication.

Die Marcurii, decimo quarto mensis Octobris, anno Domini millesimo quingentesimo sexagesimo octavo.

Agnes Thomsoun.

The quhilk day, anent the petitioun gevin in be Agnes Thomsoun, desyring hir to have licence to marye of new, nochtwythtstanding that sche was divorsit of befoir fra Archibald Philp hir husband for adulterie committit be hir, and sufferit discipline ecclesiasticall and was realye punesit thairfoir; the seat refusit to gyf licence to hir, and referrit the jugement thairof to the Assemblie of the General Kirk[2] nixt to be haldin.[3]

---

[1] *Suffir* in MS.   [2] *Kir* in MS.

[3] The Reformers held that adulterers should suffer death, and if foolishly spared by the civil sword ought to be excommunicated; but in answer to the question if they might not marry again after reconciliation with the Church, they state :—'That yf thai can not leve continent, and yf the necessitie be suche as that thai fear farther offence of God, we can not forbid thame to use the remeady ordayned of God. Yf the partie offended may be reconcilled to the offendar, then we judge that in nowyse it shall be lauchfull to the offendar to mary any other, except the partie that befoir hath bene offended' (*First Booke of Discipline*, ninth head). It was probably in connection with the reference in the text, that one of the Articles, which the General Assembly resolved, on the 5th of March 1568-9, to present to the Regent, was :—'That the questioun of adulterie may once take effect; at least a decision in that heid, quhither the adulterer sall be admitted to the benefite of mariage or not' (*Booke of the Universall Kirk*, i. 140). In 1574 the Assembly ordained that all those married men who had committed adultery with other men's wives and after the death of their own

The said day, Johne Sourdy is becumin souerte for Henry Rymour, for satisfactioun to be maid for fornication committit be hym wytht Elizabeth Wallace, undir paine of xl liƀ. And siclik the hornar[1] in Ergail[2] souerte for the said Elizabetht undir paine foirsaid.

The said day, Maister William Sanderis and Thomas Buddo ar becum souerteis for satisfaction to be maid be Johne Gairdnar, for fornication committit be hym wytht Besse Scot, undir paine of xl liƀ. actitat.

The said day, Dauid Mylis and Andro Colyne ar becum souerteis for Henze Leythe, cuik of the Auld Colleage, and Mareoun Dik, for satisfactioun to be maid be thame for fornicatioun committit be thame, undir paine of xl liƀ.

The quhilk day, as the day appointed and assignat to al maneir of personis having vote wytthin this citie to compeir to object aganis the personis nominated to be eldaris and deakinnis for this yeir inncuming; na persoun nor personis comperand to object, the Superintendent and seat findis the personis nominated elegible, and thairfoir ordanis the electioun to pas fordward.

Die Marcurii xxvij° Octobris 1568.

The quhilk day, the seat hes creat and ordinat Maister Alane Lawmontht and Maister Thomas Balfour thair procuratouris, to perseu Dauid Wemis and utheris personis quhatsumevir, for thingis concerning the seat for help of the puir, befoir the commissaris of Sanctandros, Provest and ballies, or utheris jugis competent quhatsumevir, *cum permissione de rato, etc.*

---

wives had married those whom they had polluted should 'separate themselves and abstaine fra uther, untill the tyme it be decydit be the Judge Ordinar, whither the said mariage be lawfull or not' (*Ibid.* p. 308). And in 1576, they would 'not presently resolve the question, whither if a man or woman divorcit for adulterie, ought to be admitted to the second mariage;' but they forbade ministers and readers to marry any such persons under pain of deprivation *simpliciter*, and ordained the parties so joined to separate themselves (*Ibid.* p. 377).

[1] A worker in horn; but the name was also applied to an outlaw, one at the horn.

[2] A suburb of St. Andrews, immediately outside the city gates.

Marginal notes: Rymour, Wallace. / Gairdnar, Scot. / [Leythe,] Dik. / Elderis, deakinnis. / Constitucio procuratorum edis.

Brown, Turpie,
rij.

The quhilk day, William Turpie, ansuering to the complent gevin in be Margaret Brown aganis hym, allegit that the said Margaret was corrupt and had carnal deal wytht ane uthir man or he knew hir. This allegeances denyit be Margaret. The seat ordeined the said William to preve, this day aucht dayis.

Die Marcurii, tertio Novembris, anno Domini jᵐvᶜlxviijᵒ.

Fleming,
Ramsay.

The quhilk day, anent the promis of mareage allegit maid to Jonet Fleming be James Ramsay marinar in Sanct Monanis and defloring of hir virginite, the seat, eftir cognitioun takin heirintill, wytht consent of parteis and for stencheing of forthir pley betwix thame, fyndis and ordanis the said James to tak the bairn gottin betwix thame, to be resavit be hym incontinent, and to be brocht up be hym upon his expensis in tyme cuming; and the said Jonet to bear na chairge thairof: and forthir the said James to content and pay to the said Jonet for defloring of hir virginite five merkis, thairof twa merkis and ane half or he be mareit wytht the woman that he hes laetlye maid [promis]¹ to, and utheris twa merkis and ane half wythtin yeir and day nixt thaireftir. And to this effect to be actitat in the Stewarttis bukis of the Regalite of Sanctandrois, undir quhais jurisdictioun he dwellis.

Williamson,
Parke.

The quhilk day, the seat hes fund and ordinat Johne Williamsoun, fleschear-boy wythtin this citie, to caus nuris and bryng up the bairn begottin betwix hym and Elene Parke, fra this furtht upon his expens, or ellis to appoint wytht the said Elene thairfoir, undir paine of excommunication.

Mylson, Pittillo,
Sym.

The quhilk day, Thomas Myilsoun, smytht, is becum souerte of his awin propir confessioun for² Thomas Pittillo in Anstroyer, that he sal cum to this citie and mak satisfactioun in presence of the congregation for fornication committit be hym wytht Effe Sym, and that wythtin xv dayis eftir the said Thomas [*Syms*—deleted] Myilson be requirit upon xv dayis warning to caus the said Thomas Pittillo entir to that effect, quhow sone the said Thomas Pittillo may guidlie cum to this citie

---

¹ Omitted.   ² *That* in ᴍꜱ.

wythtout suspicion of pest, undir paine of excommunication
and xx liƀ.

The quhilk day, in the term assignat to William Turpie to Turpie, Brown,
preve Margaret Brown to have bein corrupt or to have had *rij.*
carnal deal wytht ane uthir man or he knew hir, producit be
William, Archibald Dexten, Dauid Stein, Robert Fermour,
quha, being sworn resavit and examinat, deponit that they
knew no thyng of William allegeances bot be report of utheris.
The seat set to preve for the secound dilation this day aucht
dayis.

Die Marcurii, decimo die mensis Novembris, anno Domini
millesimo quingentesimo sexagesimo nono.

The quhilk day, in the terme assignat to William Turpie to Turpie, Brown.
preve Margaret Brown to have bein corrupt or he had carnal
deal wytht hir, comperit William, quba[1] producit Jonet
Symson, spous to Dauid Symson, in presens of Margaret
Brown, quha deponit that, this tyme thre yeir or thairby, sche
hard Margaret Brown say that sche had departit of bairn, bot
quhom wythtall sche cald nocht tell. And siclik Jonet Brown,
spous to Thomas Robertson, examinat sworn and resavit,
deponis conform to Jonet Symson, except that sche sayis it
was this tyme twa yeir. And siclik producit Margaret
Waucht, spous to Alexander Ansteane,[2] sworn resavit and
examinat, deponis conform in al thyng to Jonet Brown, except
that sche sayis that sche hard Margaret Brown say that the
bairn sche partit wytht was to William Turpie.

Die Marcurii, vigesimo quarto mensis Novembris, anno Domini
millesimo quingentesimo sexagesimo octavo.

The quhilk day, Jonet Calland dwelland in Kilconquhar, [Calland, Wil-
dochtir to umquhill Johne Calland in Kilconquhar, Thomas soun, Mont,
Law son[3].]
Wilsoun in Brvmesyde, Margaret Mont his spous, and Agnes
Lawsoun in Balbuthye, being somound to this day to heir
thame and ilk ane of them decernit to be punnesit for gaetting

---

[1] *Qua* in MS.   [2] Perhaps *Austeane.*

U

of ane bairn borin be the said Jonet Calland, ilk ane for thair
awn part, &c., comperit the said Thomas Wilsoun; and being
inquirit be the Superintendent to schaw the trewtht, in sic
thingis as the Superintendent sal speir at hym, upon his grite
aitht, in presence of the seat, in the first being inquirit, gyf he
knew Jonet Calland, sayis that he knawis hir nocht; and siclik
being inquirit, gyf he kennis Alesoun *alias* Ele Calland, spous
to Martine Dischington, ansueris that he kennis Aleson, bot
nocht hir spous, Martine Dischington; and confessis and
grantis that he coft[1] this yeir ane kow fra ane callit Toddie,
servand to Martine Dischington. And being demandit, gyf
thair was ane madin bairn puttin to hym and his wyf in nures-
ing, at the first Marie day[2] last was or thairby, quha ansueris
at the tyme foirsaid thair was ane madin bairn[3] put in fostering to his wyf, he nocht being at hame at that tyme [bot][4] in
Newbyggen selling ane hors to Andro Fairful. And being
demandit, quha was the bairn father and mother, and quha[5]
pat the bairn to his wyff, ansueris he kennis nethir the bairn
father nor mother, and belevis ane callit Margaret Ramsay in
Kilconquhar and ane uthir woman of aige brocht the bairn to
his hows. And being demandit, quhow lang the bairn was
wytht hym in howseld, ansueris, fra the said Marimes quhil
Monenday was aucht days, the xv day of November instant;
quhilk day sche departit and was bured in the kirk yaird of
Kembak befoir thir personis, Jsobel Gilchriste, and Margaret
Mont spous to the said Thomas Wilson, and at the said
Thomas maid the graiff quhairin the bairn was bureid. And
being demandit, quba was present at the bairnis departur
ansueris,[6] hymself, his wyf, Jsobel Gilchriste, and Jonet Rogear;
and sayis that he kennis nocht quhethir the bairn was baptised
or nocht. And attour sayis that Margaret Ramsay, and the
agit woman abuif wryttin, payit to the said Thomas Wilson
wyf Ls. for the first quartar for fostering of the bairn.

Agnes Lawsoun, meadwyf in Balbuthie, witnes, sworn in the
caus abuif wryttin, deponis that sche kennis perfitlie that
Jonet Calland buir ane madin bairn, about the sext day of

---

[1] Bought.   [2] August 15th.   [3] *Born* in MS.
[4] Omitted.   [5] *Quhat* in MS.   [6] *Sayis ansueris* in MS.

Julii last bypast or thairby, in Kilconquhar in James Grig hows; and sayis that the said Agnes, deponent, was mydwyf at the tyme; and sayis thair was na creatur present at the bairn bering bot the deponent, Margaret Ramsay and twa bairnis; and sayis that the common bruit was that Martine Dischington was the bairn[is] father, quha is guid brother to Jonet Calland.

Marcurii, octavo Decembris, anno Domini j^{m}v^{c}lxviij°.

The quhilk day, Jonet Calland being summond wytht the Superintendentis letteres to this day to heir trial takin of the bairn that sche buir this last somyr, comperit the said Jonet, quha, being inquirit quha was the bairnis father, deponit as sche wald ansueir in the presence of God that George Dischingtoun, brother to the Laird of Ardros, was the bairnis father; and that the bairn departit wythtout baptisme. The Superintendent ordanit the said George to be somond for forthir tryall to be takin heirintil. Calland, Dischingtoun.

The quhilk day [*George Blak denuncit to the assemblie that—* deleted] Johne Gairdner and Besse Scott upon Sunday the xij day [*of d—*deleted]. *Non tenet.*

Non tenet. Sunday the xij day.[1]

Marcurii, decimo quinto mensis Decembris, anno Domini 1568.

The quhilk day, it was decernit be the assemblie, becaus, on Sunday the xij day of December instant, Johne Gardnar and Besse Scott, in presence of the hail congregatioun, confessit promis of mareage betwix thame and ratifiit the same, decernit that they sould proceid furtht to accomplescheament of the mareage betwix thame. Gairdnar, Scott, to proceid to m^{a}reage.

The quhilk day, Johne Smal and Agnes Thomsoun, being dilatit to the Superintendent as fornicatoris relapsit, and being accusat thairof, confessit carnal deal betwix them and sche to be wytht childe. The Superintendent and assemblie hes referrit thame to be puneschit be the magestratis. Smal Thomson, commjtt to be punesit be the magestratis.

---

[1] These imperfect entries seem to show that no scroll minute-book was kept at this period.

Rait, Jnglis, *rij xxij do Decem- bris.* The quhilk day, the seat hes ordanit Elene Jnglis to be warnit agane this day aucht dayis, to compeir to heir the objectiounis, proponit be hir aganis the witnes producit betwix hir and Alane Rait, discussit.

Geddy, Rykard. The quhilk day, Christen Geddye clamit mareage of Dauid Richard, be resoun of promis maid to hir [1] be the said Dauid, and referrit the promis to the said Dauid aitht, quha sweir that he nevir maid hir promis, and thairfoir [the seat] [2] absolvit the said Dauid of the said clame.

Die Marcurii, vigesimo secundo Decembris, anno Domini j^m v^c lxviij.

The quhilk day, anent the complent and clame gevin in be
Wallace. Rymour. Elspet Wallace aganis Henry Rymour, tweching the said Elspet desyre to caus the said Henry to marie hir be resoun he deflorit hir and gat hir virginite, or ellis to tochir hir. The Superintendent, wytht avis of the assemblie, decernis the said Henrie to marie hir or content hir wytht gear. And now the saidis parteis hes referrit thame to Johne Motto and Dauid Gibson for the part of the said Elspet, and James Robertson and Charles Geddie for the part of the said Henrye, alsweill tweching the mareage or gevin of gear to hir to help hir to mareage; and to end the said mater betwix this and Newar day [3] nixt to cum.

Roull, Dauid- son. The quhilk day, Niniane Rowll and Eufame Dauidson, being dilatit to the Superintendent as fornicatoris, hes purgit thair self [is] thairof, and monesit under paine of cursyng to abstein in tyme cuming out of all suspect places.

Galbraitht, Brown. The quhilk day, Johne Galbraitht and Jonet Brown ar decernit be the Superintendent and seat to adhere to utheris, and to intrat utheris as becummis faithtful spousis in bed and buird, and to remane thairintil, wythtin viij dayis, under paine of excommunication.

Rait, Jnglis. The quhilk day, the Superintendent and seat, taking cogni- tioun in the allegeances maid be Elein Jnglis, quhairfoir sche aucht nocht to adhere to Alane Rait hir husband, to wit, that

---

[1] *To hir to thir* in MS.   [2] Omitted.   [3] New-Year's day.

Alane sould say that he wald haif hir in howseld that he mycht
be fulfillit of hir bluid and flesche, fyndis the said Elene to
have failyeit in probation of hir allegeances ; and thairfoir
ordanis and decernis the said Elene wythtin viij dayis to adhere
to hir said spous, to be intrated be hym in bed and buird as
efferis, undir paine of excommunication ; and public monitionis
to be direct heirupon gyf neid beis.

The quhilk day, Christein Lyall is decernit to cum to the *Decretum
contra Lyall*
kirk twa Sundays, to mak repentance in the penitent seat in *adulterum.*
sekclaitht, for adultre committit be hir and haldand hir bairn
unbaptizat be the space of thre yeris, undir paine of excommunication.

*Die Marcurii, vigesimo nono Decembris, anno Domini
j^m v^c lxviij^o.*

The quhilk day, Katharine Neische, dilatit to the Superin- Neische
tendent as ane usurar, comperit and purgest hir self thairof ; *usuraria.*
and is decernit the seat to desist and ceas fra using of
usurie in tyme cuming, undir paine of excommunicatioun.

The quhilk day, Maister Johne Todryk,[1] dilatit to the Super- Todryk,
intendent of fornication wytht Margaret Ramsay, comperit and Ramsay.
purgist hym self be his grite aitht ; and monesit to abstein fra
hir in tyme cuming, *et ab omni loco suspecto*, undir paine of
excommunication.

The said day, Jsobel Bonar, spous of Archibald Mwir, dilatit *Bonar sponsa
Archibaldi
Mvir.*
to the Superintendent for nocht cuming to the kirk to heir the
Word of God upon the Sunday, is monesit to cum to the kirk
upon the Sunday to the effect foirsaid in tyme cuming, undir
paine of excommunicatioun, she being in hir heal.[2]

The said day, James Broig, Hev Lokart, Johne Blak and Barbouris of
George Nairn, barbouris, dilatit to the Superintendent[3] for this citie.
using of thair craf upon the Sabbat day, ar monesit to abstein
in tyme cuming undir paine of excommunication.

The quhilk day, Henry Blak and Margaret Moreis, dilatit of Blak, Moreis.
fornication to the Superintendent, comperit and confessit the
sam ; and Margaret, now being wytht childe, and referrit to hir

---

See pp. 28, 29.   [2] Health.   [3] *Superintendit* in MS.

aitht gyf it was to the said Henry, swir that it was to hym and that he gat hir virginite, and that sche nevir knew nor had carnal deal wytht ony uthir man : and ar baitht monesit that, wythtin xx dayis efter hir birtht, [thai ar][1] to cum to mak satisfaction, &c.

Die Marcurii, quinto die mensis Januarii, anno Domini j^mv^clxviij°.

Ramsay, Duncan.

The quhilk day, the seat hes ordanit Patrik Ramsay and Christen Duncan to be somound upon Sunday nixt cuming opinlie, to compeir befoir the seat to gyf his testification that gyf the madin bairn allegit begottin betwix hym and the said Christen be his or nocht ; wytht certification gyf he comperis nocht the bairn salbe decernit to be his and haldin as confest, and Patrik to be somound to this day aucht dayis.

Thowles, Christe.

The said day, Maige Thowles allegis ane madin bairn born be hir to Thomas Christeis in Lang Raw, thairfoir the seat ordanis the said Thomas to be somound opinlie upon Sunday nixt to cum, to compeir this day aucht dayis to gyf his testification thairof, wytht intimatioun gyf he comperis nocht it sal be haldin as confessit.

Die Marcurii, duodecimo Januarii, anno Domini millesimo quingentesimo sexagesimo octavo.

Malwil, Lermontht.

The quhilk day, Agnes Malwill confessit that sche hes born ane sone to Maister James Lermontht, Provest of Kirkhill, quhilk bairn is ane yeir auld and sumthyng mair ; and desyris the said Provest to resave the said bairn fra hir to be brocht up and nurischeid upon his expensis. And Agnes allegis that sche maid satisfaction for hir offence in Marie Kirk of Aberluthnot in the Mearnis, in presence of the heal congregation thair.

Die Marcurii, vigesimo sexto mensis Januarii, anno Domini j^mv^clxviij°.

Citatio Christe ad instantium Catharine Gourlay.

The quhilk day, Thomas Christe, indwellar in Sanctandros,

---

[1] Omitted.

is somound and ordanit be the seat to compeir this day aucht
days befoir the seat, to ansueir at the instance of Catharine
Gourlay, undir paine of excommunication.

Wytht incalling of the name of Christe Jesus, Sone of the *Decretum*
eternal and evirleving God, quba is the way verite and lyffe, *ecclesie pro*
Alano Rait
throucht quhais guidnes and mercye we, minister eldaris and *contra Helenam*
Jnglis.
deacanis of Christe kirk and congregatioun of the citie and
parrochioun of Sanctandros, ar callit as watchemen owre his
flok, quhilk he hes mercifullie delivered and reduceid from[1]
blyndnes idolatrie and superstitioun, to the lycht of his
Euuangel be the plentuus preaching of the samine ; swa that the
face of ane perfite and reformit kirk hes bein sein wythin this
citie be the space of nyne yeris or mair, ecclesiastical discipline
usit and resavit in the same ; and now occasioun being offered
be trew dilatioun gevin befoir us upon Helene Jnglis, spous of
Alane Rait, that quhair the said Alane and Helene, being
laufullie cuppilled togethir in the holie band of matrimonie,
remanit thairintil thir monie yeris bigane and had procreation
of children betwix thame, nochttheles the said Helene, aganis
the doctrine of Paule the Apostole of Jesus Christe, hes
divorced and separated hir self fra mutual cohabitation societie
and cumpanie of the said Alane hir spous, and be na way wil
returne, nor remain wytht hym in familie hous bed and buird,
bot wikedlie and stubornlie uterlie refusis to do the sam, in
grite and dangerus perrell of hir awin saule, and havie sclander
of the membris of this our congregation ; we, heirfoir, being of
will and mynde to have the said sclander removit extinguesed
and avoded, callit baitht the saidis parteis befoir us, and tuik
diligent cognition and inquisition of the sclander [and] offenc
foirsaid. And the parteis foirsaidis comperand befoir us, the
said Helene allegit and proponit sum defensis and causis quhy
sche sould nocht adhere nor accumpanie wytht the said Alane
hir spous. Quhilkis defensis, we thynking to be resonable
admittit the same to the said Elene probation, and gaif
sufficient dilation to hir to preve the sam ; and in terme
assignat to hir to preve hir saidis defensis, sche producit and

_____
[1] *Frorm* in MS.

brocht in befoir us certane honest and famous witnes, quba
being resavit admittit sworn and diligentlie examinat in our
presence, thaireftir trial takin be us of the said Elene heal
allegeances, reasonis, causis, defensis, and hir probationis
deducit thairupon, fand and decernit the said Helene to have
succumbit and failyeit in probation of hir saidis defensis; and
nochtwythtstanding the same ordanit and decernit hir to adhere
to the said Alane hir husband, and to remain wytht hym in
hous, bed, buird and mutual cohabitation as becummis faithtful
spousis to do; and to this effect hes divers and sundrie tymis
be our selves, and utheris myd personis of guid fame and conversation, admonised the said Helene meikle gently and als
wytht threaetining of the paine of excommunication; quhilkis
admonitiounis sche hes stubburnle refusit to obey, and be na
way wil adher[e] to hir said husband; bot contemptueslie dis-
pisis the admonitionis of the Kirk, and wil nocht herkin to the
voce thairof, and persistis and contineuis in hir said wikednes,
geving evil exempil[1] to utheris to the grite sclandir of the
membris of this hole congregation; and thairfoir mereittis
worthelye to be excommunicated, separated and cuttit of from
the societie and felouschip of the congregation of Christe Jesus,
and all benefitis of his Kirk, and to be deliverit to Sathan for
destruction of the flesche, that the spirite may be saved in the
day of the Lord Jesus, according to the doctrine of Paul :
heirfoir, having God onlie befoir our eis, and the testimonie of
the trew and eternal Word, be this our sentence declaris and
denuncis the said Helene Jnglis, for hir grevous offens, occasioun
of sclandir and contempt of the voce of the Kirk, excommunicated, separated, and cuttit of from the congregation and
mistical bodie of Christe Jesus and secludit from al benefitis of
his trew Kirk (the hering of the Word of God onlie except[ed)];
delivering hir to Satan for destruction of the flesche that the
spirit may be saved in the day of the Lord Jesus; and that
nane of the faithtful that fearis God fra this furtht accumpanie
wytht the said Helene in commoning, talking, bying, selling,
eating, drynking, or uthirwaiis quhatsumevir (except they be
appointed be the Kirk for hir amendment); wytht certification

*Decretum
ecclesie pro
Alano Rait
contra Helenam
Jnglis.*

---

[1] *Exepil* in MS.

gyf ony dois in the contrair they salbe reput favoraris and
fosteraris of hir iniquite, callit and accusat thairfoir, and being
convict, as participant wytht hir, sal resave the lik jugement
and sentence wytht hir.   In witnes heirof the seal of the said
ministere is affixt heirto at Sanctandros, &c.

*Per   dominum   Superintendentem[1]   et   ministerium   civitatis
    Sanctiandree, die Marcurii, secundo die mensis[2] Februarii,
    anno Domini j^mv^clxviij^{o.}*

The quhilk day, Elizabetht Forret, spous to M. Dauid Gaw, *Forret, Gaw.*
producit ane libellat somound of the Superintendentis rasit at
hir instance aganis the said M. Dauid, for causis conten   n
the somoundis.   The said Elizabetht comperand be hir self,
and the said M. Dauid being laufullie somound oft tymis callit
and nocht comperand, the Superintendent and ministerie
assignat Wedinsday the nynte day of Februar instant to the *Nono Februarii.*
said Elizabetht, to preve hir somoundis in paine of non comperence of the said M. Dauid, and he to be somound to heir
probation led for the first dilation. ΄

The quhilk day, Dauid Nicholsoun, burges of Cowper, is *Decretum
decernit be the Superintendent and seat to be somound to heir Rauff.*
and see hym decernit to proceid in mereage wyth Grissil Rauff,
according to promis maid be hym to the said Grisil and defloring of hir virginite, or to allege ane resonable caus in the
contrar, &c.

The said day, Thomas Christe, in Lang Raw, is decernit be *Decretum
                                                              contra*
the Superintendent and seat to present ane madin bairn, *Christe in
begottin betwix hym and Maige Thowles, to baptisme on Lang Raw.*
Sunday nixt to cum, under pane of excommunication, and that
in the parroche kirk of this cite.

*Per dominum Superintendentem et ministerium civitatis Sancti-
    andree, die Marcurii, nono die mensis Februarii, anno
    Domini j^mv^clxviij^{o.}*

The quhilk day, Andro Alexander, *alias* Gossept Andro, is *Decretum
                                                            contra*
admonisched be the Superintendent and seat that in tyme *Andream
                                                          Alexander.*

---

[1] *Superindentem* in MS.   [2] *Mensis J.* in MS.

cuming he suffer na opin cairting and dysyng, nycht walking
and drynking, in his hows, under paine of excommunication
and impresoning of his persoun.

Per dominum Superintendentem et ministerium civitatis Sancti-
andree, die Mercurii, xvj^{to} mensis Februarii, anno Domini
j^{m}v^{c}lxviij^{o}.

Decretum contra
Jacobum Dud-
ingston.
The quhilk day, James Dudingstoun, maltman, being dilatit
for using of cumpany in eating, drinking, and resaving in howss-
ald Helene Jnglis eftir sche was excommunicated, and chargeit
to compeir befoir the Superintendent and ministerie to heir
hym punesit thairfoir, comperit and confessit that Helene
Jnglis hes bein in his hows sen sche was excommunicated, and
hes eattin and drunkin wytht hir: quhairfoir the said James
is decernit be Superintendent and ministerie and als admonesed
to desist and ceas fra doing siclik in tyme cuming, under paine
of excommunication.

Scrimgeour,
Robertson,
Scot, rij xxiij^{o}
Februarii.
The quhilk day, Johne Scot is becum souerte to entir Male
Robertson his sister befoir the Superintendent and seat this
day aucht dayis, to ansuere at the instance of James Scrimgeour
hir spous, undir paine sic as salbe layit to his charge.

Die Mercurii, xxiij^{o} mensis Februarii, anno Domini j^{m}v^{c}lxviij^{o}.

Scot,
Scrimgeour,
Robertsoun.
The quhilk day, Johne Scot, as souerte to entir Male Robertson this day, to ansuere at the instance of James Scrimgeour
hir spous, undir sic panis as the Superintendent sal lay to
his chairge, oft tymis callit and nocht comperand, [the seat][1]
remittit the injunction of the paine to Johne Scot to the
Superintendent and modification thairof in like maneir.

Die Marcurii, penultimo mensis Martii, anno Domini j^{m}v^{c}lxix^{o}.

Wenesoun in
Kincaple.
The quhilk day, Thomas Weneson, in Kincaple, accusat for
using of the fleschear craft in slaying and selling of flesche
upon the Sabbat day, quhilk gevis hym occasion to abyde fra
hering of the Word of God, is admonesed to desist and ceas

---

[1] Omitted.

fra sic like in tyme cuming, quha hes promittit to do the
sam.

The quhilk day, James Thomsoun, dwelland in Balmerynocht, Thomson,
being somound wytht my Lord Superintendentis lettres, to heir Smytht.
him decernit to complet and perform the band of matrimonie
wytht Jonet Smytht, according to his promis maid to hir thairupon, the saidis parteis compering be thame selves the said
James denyit al promis. The seat assignat this day aucht
dayis to preve the sam. *Partibus apud acta citatis.*

The said day Katharine Awat, dwelling in Balmerynocht, Awat,
being somoind wytht my Lord Superintendentis lettres, dilatit Maltman.[1]
for commiting of incest wytht hir guidfather callit Andro
Malcom,[1] be ane child of twa yeris auld, and presentlie being
wytht childe to hym, confessis the offence ; heirfoir ordenis hir
to stand thre Sundaiis in sek claytht in the maest patent kirk
dur of Balmerynocht ; and in the last Sunday to be resavit to
the kirk. And forthir ordenis thame to be committit to the
magistratis of the reylm, to be punesed according to ordour
takin.

Marcurii die sexto mensis Aprilis 1569.

The quhilk day, anent the often tymis calling of George Decretum Su-
Dischingtoun and Jonet Calland for ane procreatioun of ane perintendentis
childe gottin betwix thame, quhilk departit unbaptizat, and Dischjngton et
nocht comperand, except the woman anis comperit ; in respect Calla'id.
of thair grite inobedience and lang contempt be the space of
ane yeir or thairby, the Superintendent, wytht avis of the seat
and ministerie, ordanit monition wytht excommunication thairintil to be gevin aganis them, in cais they continew in disobedience.

The quhilk day, in the terme assignat to Jonet Smytht to Smytht,
preve promis of mareage maid betwix hir and James Thomsoun Thomson.
in Balmerynocht, producit, be the said Jonet, Dauid Kay in
Southt Ferritoun of Portin Craig, Thomas Kay his brother
thair, and Simon Adam thair, in presence of the said James,
nathyng being objectit aganis them, &c.

In primis, the said Dauid Kay, sworn resavit and admittit, *Primus testis.*

---

[1] *Sic.*

deponis that, foure yeris syne or thairby, the deponent was present in Simon Adam hows quhen James Thomson and Jonet Smytht maid mutual promis of mareage ilk ane to uthir, and at that tyme ilk ane content of uthir, in presence of Sande Mathow in Kilburnis, Henry Boytour, Simon Adam, and Thomas Kay, and was contentit that thair bannis sould bein proclamat on Sunday nixt thaireftir.   And in verification heirof the deponent promittit of his gear to the said James iiij lib., and Simon Adam promittit iiij bollis malt.

Secundus testis.   Thomas Kay secundus testis conformis Dauidj Kay primo testi.

Tertius testis.   Simon Adam, father of law to Jonet Smytht, witnes, sworn resavit and admittit, deponit conform to the first witnes; and forthir deponis that he hard and saw the promis maid, and held up handis for performing of the premissis.

Rij.   The Superintendent and seat set to the said Jonet, to preve for the secound dilation, this day aucht dayis, *partibus apud acta citatis.*

Kenlowy.   The quhilk day, Johne Kenlowy is decernit to desist and ceas fra accumpaniing wytht Margaret Gibson, dochtir to Stevin Gibson, in the said Johne chalmer and all utheris places suspect, under panis to be injonit be the Superintendent and seat.

*Die Mercurii, xxvij° mensis Aprilis, anno Domini j*ᵐ*v*ᶜ*lxix°,*
per Superintendentem et sessionem.

Jamesoun, Staig, *rij.*   Anent the pley of promis of mareage be Elspet Jamesoun aganis Thomas Staig, and they being somoind to this day the said Thomas and Elspet grantis that they [had][1] carnail deal togethir, upon the first Marye-day last was and syndry uthiris tymis sen syne; and the said Elspet was haldin and reput ane virgine at the said tym.   And quher the said Elspet allegis promis of mareage maid to hir be the said Thomas, he denyis al promis; and the said Elspet, becaus sche hes nocht probation, referris the promis to his aitht *simpliciter*.   And Thomas being sworn denyis al promis.   And as to the defloring of the said Elspet virginite, he sais he kennis na thing of

---

[1] Omitted.

hir bot guid and honestie quhill the tyme he had deal wytht hir. Bot he allegis that thre yeris syne or mair, he maid ane secrete promis of mareage to Besse Dudingston, and sone thaireftir begat ane bairn of hir; and at baptising of the said bairn he maid ane opin promis of mareage to the said Besse, in presence of the parrochionaris being present for the tyme, and Stevin Dudingston of Sandfurde. And the said Stevin, at that tyme, becam souerte for the said Thomas that he sould perform his said promis wytht the said Besse. And sen syne the said Thomas confessis that he hes had carnal deal wytht the said Elspet Jameson, quhilk Elspet allegis hir to be wytht bairn to the said Thomas. The Superintendent set this day aucht dayis to gyf his decrete heirintil, and ordanis ane somoundis to be direct to somound Stevin Dudingston of Sandfurd and Besse Dudingston and utheris to be nominat, for declaration of the verite in the premissis.

The quhilk day, Maister Johne Dalglesche being accusat for having in cumpany wytht hym Jonet Wemis quha is ane persoun excommunicated, M. Johne confessis mutuall societe wytht hir this lang tyme bygain, and now allegis the said Jonet to be deidlie seik, and quhow sone [it][1] sal pleas God to restoir the said Jonet to hir heal, oblesis hym that he and sche sal cum and submit thame to correction of the Kirk in sa far as the Kirk is offendit wytht thame, and satisfie the Kirk thairfoir. Dalgles, Wemis

The quhilk day, Maister Thomas Methtwen[2] being callit and accusat for nocht assemling wytht the rest of the congregatioun to the communion, according to the ordour tane, and thairfoir in respect of his absence to pay xl s. to be distributit to the puir for nocht compering to examination and communioun. M. Thomas ansuered, nocht for ony contempt or that he was nocht persuaded of the religion acceptat, and forme and maneir of the ministration of the sacramentis used, bot movit of necessite to pas to his freind the Laird of Pomais quha was in extrimite of deatht; and opinlie protestat that he imbrased alreddye the religion now resavit and mentenit, and promittit faithtfullie to communicat wytht the rest at ministration of the communion; and abhorrit and detestit al Appreving of religion be M. Thomas Methtwen and imbreassing thairof in al points.

---

[1] Omitted.

[2] For his accusation, proud answers, and decreet against him, see pp. 135-138.

superstition and Papistre and abusing of the sacramentis in tyme bipast, wytht transsubstantiation, imparation, and al utheris erroris in tyme bipast.

Die Mercurii, primo Junii, anno Domini j^mv^clxix^o.

Resaving of Laurence Dalgles to religion. | The quhilk day, Laurence Dalgles comperit befoir the assemblie, and being desyrit to imbrace and resave the religioun offerit to us be the grite favour and mercy of God, imbrased and resavit the sam, and apprevit it in all pointis, wytht the maneir and form of administration of the sacramentis observit and resavit, renuncing idolatrie superstitioun and Papistrie, befoir authorized in tyme of the Paip and the Antechristis kingdome; and promittis faithtfullie to gyf opin testimonie and confession thairof, be communicating wytht the rest of the brethrin the nixt tyme the communion beis ministrat. In witnes of the quhilk the said Laurence hes subscrivit thir presentis frelie, and wythtout fear or compulsion, day and yeir abuif writtin, wytht his awin hand.

Laurence Dalglesche.

Decretum Skirling. The quhilk day, the Superintendent, wytht avis of the assemblie, hes ordinat and decernit Andro Lamb to compleit the band of matrimonie wytht Besse Skirling, according to the promis thairof maid be hym to the said Bessie wytht carnal deal following[1] thair upon, nochtwythtstanding the pretendit contract of mareage maid betwix hym laetlie and Margaret Lamb, undir panis to be injunit thairintil.

Thir actis and ordinances following sould have bein inserit[2] in thir bukis, upon Wedinsday the xviij day of Maii last bipast.

Die Mercurii decimo octavo Maii 1569.

Dischingtoun, Calland. The quhilk day, in respect of the promis of mareage, confessit in presens of the Superintendent and assemblie, maid

---

[1] *Followit* in MS.   [2] Inserted.

betwix George Dischingtoun and Jonet Calland wytht carnal dail following thairupon, the Superintendent, wytht avis of the assemblie, hes decernit the saidis George and Jonet, willinglie consenting heirto and of thair awin propir confessiounis, to proceid and perform mareage, according to thair promis, betwix this and the xv day of August nixt to cum, undir paine of excommunicatioun ; and hes differrit the satisfactioun to be maid to the kirk to the day of thair mareage ; and ordanis the bannis to be proclamat betwix the saidis personis the thre nixt Sundaiis immediatlie and nixt following.

The said day, in respect of the grite transgressiounis doin be Maister Andro Kircaldy and Sir Johne Bowsye, and of thair grite contempt and inobedience, the seat ordanis thame to compeir twa several Sundays in the kirk of Wemis clethit wytht sek-claitht, and thair in presence of the hael peple sal stand in sum opin place of the kirk, as the minister sal appoint, in tyme of preching ; and eftir the preaching the secound Sunday sal upon thair kneis ask God and the congregatioun forgevenes, quhom they have offendit and sclanderit. And Maistir Andro sal pas to Kilconquhar upon ane Sunday immediatlie thaireftir, and thair sal ask God and the congregation forgevenes, for solemnizing of mareage of Johne Wemis and Effem Wemis umquhill Lady of Kilconquhar, by al guid ordour and wythtout proclamation of bannis, &c.[1]

Kircaldy, Bowsye.

I, Maister Dauid Dischingtoun, am content and promittis faithtfullie be thir presentis that, gyf the Superintendent of Fyiff and Maister Robert Hammiltoun minister of Sanctandros wil assure me on thair consciences that the ordour now usit be thame in the kirk of God concerning the ministratioun

M. Dauid Dischingtoun promᵗˢ of joning to religᵒᵘn.

---

[1] In the General Assembly, on the 25th of December 1565, 'Mr. Johne Winram complainit upon the said Mr. Johne Frude [minister of Dalmeny], that by his counsell and perswasion the Ladie Kilconquhar and Johne Weymis had contractit mariage [*per*] *verba de presenti*, notwithstanding that ane woman, called Elizabeth Pot, had claimed the said Johne Weymes before the Superintendent, whilk clame was not yet justified ; and that Mr. Andro Kirkadie had maried the saids persouns, after the minister was departed out of the kirk where they were maried.' It was ordained that the parties should answer to the complaint before the end of that Assembly, but the result is not clear (*Booke of the Universall Kirk*, i. 66). Andrew Kirkcaldy is mentioned as a notary in 1529 and 1534, and also as a presbyter in 1545 ; and Bowsey as a notary in 1572 (Sir William Fraser's *Memorials of the Family of Wemyss*, ii. 156, 170, 209, 278).

of the body and bluid of Christe is treulie usit and ministrat, according to Christis institutioun in his lettir supper; and that at resaving of the bread and wyne, I resave spiritualie be faitht the body and blude of Christ, and my saule is nuresed thairby to lyff eternal lyke as my body is nuresed be braed and wyne, quhilkis ar signis and sealis of Goddis promis to al men that worthelie communicatis, in maneir abone wryttin; and gyf they wil assuir me heirof as said is, I sal, God willing, compeir on Wedinsday nixt to cum in the counsal hows befoir the assemblie of the kirk and jone me thairwytht, and promit treulye to be participant of Christis communione at the nixt ministration thairof. And this I promis me to do be this my hand wryte, at Sanctandros the xv day of Maii 1569. And this promis is subscrivit in maneir following :

> M. Dauid Dischingtoun wytht my hand.
> Maister Dauid Russal promittis the sam in name of my broder abone writtin.

The xviij day of Maii 1569.

The quhilk day, Maister Dauid Dischingtoun comperit befoir the assemblie, and, eftir the Superintendent and minister had satisfiit hym as is abone wryttin, adjunit hym faithtfullie to the religioun and imbrased the sam, &c. wytht the maneir and form of the ministration of the sacramentis now used, renuncing and refusing the contrary, and promittit opinlie as is befoir wryttin.

Die Mercurii, decimo quinto mensis Junii, anno Domini millesimo quingentesimo sexagesimo nono.

The quhilk day, the Superintendent and ministerie hes ordanit and decernit ane citatioun to be gevin furtht upon Patrik Ramsay, to compeir befoir this seat upon Wedinsday the xxij of Junii instant, to gyf his declaration upon the trewtht of ane madin bairn allegit gottin betwix hym and [blank], and gyf he be the father of the bairn or nocht; and confessing the sam, he to be decernit to present the bairn to baptisime ; wytht intimation gyf he comperis nocht, the bairn sal be haldin his awin, and proces of excommunication to be led aganis hym, becaus he hes bein often tymis of befoir admonesed twa yeris bigane and maid continual disobedience.

Die Mercurii, vigesimo secundo Junii, anno Domini 1569.

The quhilk day, Elizabetht Crychttoun Lady of Carmurie and Patrik Gray hir servand, being somound be the Superintendentis lettres deulie execut and indorsat to compeir this day, as they that, upon Sunday the twelf day of the monetht of Junii instant, at proclamatioun of the bannis for the thrid tyme betwix George Dischingtoun and Jonet Calland, interponit thame selves allegeand that they had sum resonable causis to propone and allege quhy the saidis parteis mycht nocht nor sould nocht proceid to completing and solemnizing of the band of mareage: the saidis Elizabetht and Patrik being diverss and syndre tymis callit to propone and allege the saidis resonis and causis and nocht comperand, the[1] sessioun—quhom to the Superintendent committit the triall and discussion of the saidis causis gyf ony had bein proponit in his absence—becaus na cansis war allegit nor proponit, decernit and ordainet the minister of Kilconquhar to proceid to the solemnizatioñ of mareage betwix the saidis parteis, at the tyme ellis prefixit thairto, to wit, the xv day of August nixt to cum, or sonar gyf it sal pleas thame, and charge to be gevin to the said minister to that effect gyf myster be.

Decretum solemnizationis matrimonii Dischington Calland.

Die Mercurii, sexto Julii anno Domini 1569.

The quhilk day, Jonet Smytht producit the Superintendent lettres deulye execut and indorsat upon Alexander Mathow in Balmerynocht and Henry Boytour in the Byris thairof, to bear witnessing in the action and caus of promis of mareage perseuit be the said Jonet aganis James Thomson in Balmerynocht, and als upon the said James to heir the said witnes sworn resavit and admittit to examination, al personlie apprehendit as the indorsation bearis. Na persoun comperand the

Smytht, Thomsoun.

---

[1] *The the* in MS.

seat referrit the ordour to be takin thairintil to the Superintendent.

Walcar, Daiis. The said day, anent the clame of promis of mareage perseuit
be Agnes Walcar aganist Johne Daiis smytht, hayth [1] parteis
comperand be thame selfis, the said Agnes of hir fre motive
will dischargit and be the tenour heirof dischargis the said
Johne of al promis of mareage maid to hir; and als wytht hir
awin consent and in ful contentatioun for defloring of hir virginite, to hir support and help hes resavit Thomas Layng in
Eleine Hill souerte and ful dettour for the said Johne, to content and pay to hir five merkis usual money of this realm, or
evir the said Johne be mareit wytht ony uthir person.

Die Mercurii, vigesimo Julii 1569.

Dischingtoun. The quhilk day, Maister Dauid Dischingtoun being callit
and accusat for nocht presenting hym self to the last communioun, according to his promis quhen he adjunit hym self
to religioun, Maister Dauid comperand allegit partlie for veseing
of his freind Maister Dauid Gaw, quhom to he was gritlie
addettit, quha then was extreimlie handillit wytht seiknes, and
partlie for seiknes and alteration of his bodie that he incurrit
in the mean tyme he could nocht cum to the communioun;
and testifiit befoir God that this was the just caus of his
absence and absentit nocht hym self hipocritaclie nor *subter-
fugii causa*. The seat hes decernit and ordinat this excusa-
tioun to be publist be the minister on Sunday nixt to cum, and
Maister Dauid to be present [2] and confes the sam and appreve
his adjunction and imbreassing of our religion.

Die Marcurii, decimo mensis Augusti, anno Domini j^{m}v^{c}lxix^o.

Jnglis, Rait. The quhilk day, Elene Jnglis spous to Alane Rait comperit
in presence of the assembly, and for hir offences hes referrit hir
and offered hir to correction and discipline. The seat hes
ordanit hir offir to be publist be the minister upon Sunday

---

[1] *Be* in MS.   [2] *Presentlie* in MS.

nixt to cum, and continewat the decreit of correction to be pronuncit upon Wedinsday the xvij day of August instant.

Die Mercurii, xxiiij^{to} mensis Augusti, anno Domini millesimo quingentesimo sexagesimo nono.

The quhilk day, the sessioun hes ordeined Laurence Dalgles to cum to the parroche kirk upon Sunday nixt to cum, and to remain to[1] the sermon be finisched ; and thaireftir the minister for the tyme sal publis the act subscrivit be the said Laurence of his adjunction to religioun and imbrasing of the sam, and to ratifie and appreve the said act and his adjunctioun ; and als the minister sal publis the caus and excusation maid be Laurence of his remaning fra the last communioun and testifie[2] the sam to be of verite, and that he baid nocht fra the communioun of set purpos nor hypocriticallie, nor yet sal absent hym self thairfra in tyme cuming, undir paine of excommunication. · Laurence Dalgles.

Die Veneris, decimo quarto mensis Octobris, anno Domini j^{m}v^{c}lx nono.

Eldaris electit and chosin.

Maister Johne Dowglas, Rectour	Maister Martine Geddye
Maister Thomas Balfour	Maister William Cok
Maister William Ramsay	Johne Motto, Johne Muffat
Maister Alane Lawmontht	Charles Geddye
Maister James Wilke	Maister Johne Bonkil
Thomas Walwod	James Forret in Polduff.

Diaconis electit and chosin the said day.

William Gifferd	George Blak
William Zwill	Charles Guthre
Alexander Myllar	Robert Murray
Alexander Roucht	Thomas Layng in Elein-hil
William Main	Dauid Froster in Kincaple.

---

[1] *Remain t* in MS.   [2] *Testitifie* in MS.

Die Mercurii, secundo Novembris 1569.

Dilatioun to be gevin up be the seat. The said day, it was devisit statut and ordinat that gyf thair be ony of the sessioun that kennis ony adulteraris fornicatoris or [persounis][1] culpable of ony uther crymis, that they sould gyf up thair dilation this day aucht dayis.

Die Mercurii, nono Novembris 1569.

Maling. The quhilk day, the sessioun hes ordinat Agnes Maling to be warnit to compeir befoir the assemblie this day[2] aucht dayis, to ansueir to sic thingis as sche salbe accusat of.

Dischington. *Item*, siclik Maister Dauid Dischingtoun to be warnit in lyke maneir.

Ramsay. *Item*, siclike Patrik Ramsay of Culluthye to be warnit in like maneir.

Die Mercurii, decimo sexto mensis Novembris, anno Domini 1569.

Maling. The quhilk day, Agnes Maling is decernit be decreit of the sessioun to bryng ane sufficient testimonial that, the bairn begottin betwix hir and Maister James Lermontht, Provest of Kirkhill, was baptizat in Marie-kirk of Abirluthtnot, and **Septimo Decembris.** that sche maid satisfaction to the kirk thair as sche allegis, the vij day of December nixt to cum.

Darny, Patersoun. The said day, Petir Derny and Marioun Dande *alias* Patersoun dilated, and callit befoir the sessioun, of fornication, comperit and confessit thair offence; and the seat referrit the punition of them to the magistratis.

Die Mercurii, vigesimo primo Novembris, anno Domini millesimo quingentesimo sexagesimo nono.

Confessio Read. The quhilk day, Marable Ryad,[3] in Byrhillis, being dilatit to the seat of fornicatioun, confessit that sche buir ane bairn to

---

[1] Omitted.   [2] *Dayis* in MS.
[3] Altered from *Read*, probably meant for *Rynd*.

Johne Corstorphine cowper, brother to Martine Corstorphine in Byrehillis, at Martimes was twa yeris; and the seat ordanis Jonet Annel in Pukie, Jonet Paterson and Jonet Brown thair, quha was wytht the said Mirable the tyme of hir birtht, to be somound to testifie quhom on the said Mirable fatherit hir bairn the tyme of hir birtht.

Die Mercurii, septimo die mensis Decembris, anno Domini 1569.

The quhilk day, the session hes continuat the action and caus intentat be the Superintendent of his office aganis Dauid Betoun off Creicht and [*blank*] Lesly his spous, in presence of the said Laird and Lady, undir hoip of concord, to ferd day of Januar nixt to cum. The saidis personis warnit *apud acta.* *Superintendent, Beton, Leslye.* *Quarto Januarii.*

Die Mercurii, xiiij^{to} Decembris 1569.

The quhilk day, Jonet Paterson in Pukye, and Jonet Brown thair, witnes, warnit at command of the seat to testifie in sa far as they ken quha was the father of the bairn borne be Marable Rynd in Byrehills, twa yeris syne or tharbi, quba, comperand and sworn, deponit they war present wytht the said Mirable the tyme of birtht, and, incontinent eftir sche was deliverit, hard hir say, God let hir nevir be bettir nor sche was sche head nevir carnail deal wytht man bot wytht Johne Corstorphine, Beiggis Fermour sone, and the bairne was his. *Depositionis. Paterson, Brown.* *Rynd, Corstorphine.*

Die Mercurii, xxj^{mo} Decembris 1569.

The quhilk day, Andro Lawson, in Nethir Mawgis, sworn, deponis that he was present quhen Jonat Lawsoun, now nurice in Lathokir, pat the bairn begottin betwix Johne Chaeplen in Ladedey and the said Jonet to ane mylk [1] woman in Strakinnes, quhilk woman name the deponent kennis nocht, nor qubat sche promised to the said mylk woman the deponent kennis nocht; and [the seat] [2] ordanis the said Jonet to cal Catherine Mvir in Bwnfeild and witnes, to this day aucht dayis, to bear witnes *Chaeplen, Lawson, rij.*

---

[1] *Myk* in MS.   [2] Omitted.

and testifie that sche deliverit the bairn to the said Catharine in nurisching, &c.

Durye, Wobstar, *rij*.

The said day, anent the Superintendentis somondis rasit aganis Dauid *D*urie, at the instance of Johne Wobstar, for the allegit interruption maid be the said Dauid to the said Johne for reding of the prayeris on Sunday was aucht dais, comperit Dauid and grantis that he tuik the said Johne prayer buik and laid it bi, and said, Ye sal nocht reid heir sa lang as the parrochion plesis me! and allegis that the Superintendent[1] admittit hym to be redar be word at the kirk style of Monimeal, upon Moninda eftir Sanct James day last bipast, the Superintendent then being in Monimeal at his visitation: and forder allegis that Johne Wobstar maid nocht the prayeris in the kirk of Monimeal sen Al-hallowmes was ane yeir. And Johne allegis that he offered hym syndry tymis to reid the prayeris and was stoppit. *Ad probandum hinc inde allegata hodie ad octo.*

Die Mercurii, xxviij° Decembris, 1569, *presente Superintendente.*

[Wobstar, Durye.]

The quhilk day, in the caus of allegeances maid be Johne Wobstar aganis Dauid *D*ury, in the terme assignit to preve the allegeance, being somond Johne Spens in Lethem, Dauid Duncan in Monimeil, William Mylis, William Paterson, Alexander Anderson, Johne Hew, Henry Mathye, and Dauid Anderson, comperit Johne Hew and Henry Mathye, admittit and sworn in presence of Dauid Dwry. The rest of the witnes decernit *contumaces.*

Henrye Mathye, witnes, producit sworn resavit and admittit, examinat, deponis that he kennis perfitlie and saw Johne Wobstar cum syndry tymis to the parroche kirk of Monimeal to say the prayeris, and offered him to say the prayeris, and saw nevir impedment maid to hym be Dauid Durye.

Johne Hew, conform to Henry Mathye, and ekis that Dauid Dwry said to Johne Wobstar, Ye sal say na prayeris heir, quhill ye schaw[2] the Superintendent writing to dischairge me and that ye ar admittit.

---

[1] *Superintendit* in MS.   [2] *Ye schaw the schaw* in MS.

The said day, in the terme assignit to Dauid *D*ury to preve [Durye,
his allegeance aganis Johne Wobstar, producit Alexander ^{Wobstar.]}
Sibbald of Rankelo,[1] Florence Auchtmowty, Johne Spens,
William Mylis, Dauid Dwn, Thomas Schewes : quhairof com-
perit Alexander Sibbald, Florence Auchtmowty, and Thomas
Schewes. The rest decernit *contumaces.*

Alexander Sibbald, sworn resavit and admittit, deponis
that he was present and hard the Superintendent admit Dauid
Dury redar of Monimail be word.

fflorence Auchtmowtye deponis that he hard nocht the
Superintendent admit Dauid *D*ury to be redar be word.

Thomas Schewes, resavit sworn and admittit, kennis na
thyng in the mater.

The said day, the Superintendent hes decernit Johne Wob- Wobstar,
star and[2] Dauid *D*ury to [do][3] diligence for thair witnes, Dury, *rij.*
somond and nocht comperand, this day aucht dayis, and to
somond utheris witnes gyf they pleas for the second dilation.

Die Mercurii, quarto Januarii anno Domini 1569.

The quhilk day, anent the somoundis rasit at the instance *Wemis de*
of the Superintendent of his office aganis Johne Wemis of *eodem, Trail.*
that Ilk and Jonet Trail his spous,[4] anent thair adherence in
bed and buird as man and his wyf aucht to do of the law of
God, and anent sic thingis as he was to inquire of them, at
thair compering befoyr[5] hym, of his office, &c., [as][3] at mair

---

[1] Over-Rankeillour belonged to the Sibbalds, cadets of the Sibbalds of Bal-
gonie, for several centuries, and from them Sir Robert Sibbald, the 'eminent
physician, naturalist, and antiquary,' was descended (*History of Fife*, 1803,
pp. 393, 394; Anderson's *Scottish Nation*, iii. 450).

[2] *And and* in MS.   [3] Omitted.

[4] In 1556 Sir John Wemyss of that Ilk divorced Margaret Otterburn, whom
he had married in 1534 ; and, before the 21st of February 1557-8, he married
Janet Trail, daughter of Alexander Trail of Blebo, and widow of John Ramsay
of Ardbekie. She is called Lady of Lumbeny in March 1569. Sir John died
in the end of January 1571-2. He had a family by each of his wives ; and five
sons and one daughter besides, of whom three were legitimated. 'Janet Trail
was still alive in June 1575, when her step-son, David of Wemyss, paid her
£1000 Scots, in full satisfaction of all her claims of terce or conjunct infeftment'
(Sir William Fraser's *Memorials of the Family of Wemyss*, i. 150-155).

[5] *Be* in MS.

lyntht is contenit in the somoundis; becaus nane of the parteis comperis to schaw ane resonable caus quhy they sould nocht adheir togethir, and becaus the Superintendent is nocht desyrus to do ony wrang or be ower heasty in proceding aganis ony of the parteis, bot rather to gyf to them sufficient tyme to produce thair defensis, and in hoip of concord be mediation of freindis, [he][1] ordanis the saidis personis to be somound to

xxv^o Januarii. compeir personlie upon Wedinsday the xxv day of Januar instant, to produce al thair defensis quhy they sould nocht adheir; wytht certification gyf they compeir nocht in thair awin propir personis to the effect foirsaid, the Superintendent wil decerne them *simpliciter* to adheir.

[Durye appelis.]   The quhilk day, Dauid Durye, allegeing hym to be hurt be the Superintendent and assemble of Sanctandros, appellat to the General Assemblie of the Kirk.

[Wobstar, Durye.]   The said day, Johne Spens, witnes, producit for Johne Wobstar, sworn resavit and examinat, deponis that he saw Johne Wobstar offir hym to say the prayeris in the kirk of Monimail, and was stoppit be Dauid Dwry.

William Mylis conform to Johne Spens.

William Paterson conform to Johne Spens.

Alexander Anderson conform to Johne Spens.

Wobstar, Durye. *xj^o Januarii.*   The said day, the Superintendent assignit Wedinsday the xj day of Januar instant to pronunce in the action persewit be Johne Wobstar aganis Dauid Dury, and ordinat Dauid Dury to be warrint be ane somoundis to the said day.

Beton, Leslye.   The quhilk day, anent the adherence betwix the Laird of Creicht and his wyffe, the Superintendent, wytht avis of the assemblie, assignit Wedinsday the xxij day of Februar nixt to

Dauid Beton of Creicht. cum to gyf in and schaw al thair causis and resonis quhy they sould nocht adheir; wytht intimation gyf they compeir nocht

xxij^do Februarii. that day to the effec foirsaid, the Superintendent wil decerne them *simpliciter* to adheir. *Partibus predictis apud acta citatis.*

Superintendent, Symson.   The quhilk day, Johne Symson, wrycht in Monimaill, somond to this day, and accusat be the Superintendent for having carnal deal wytht Maige Burd and Maige Colein, he being mareit wytht Maige Pryde, denyis adulterie committit

---

[1] Omitted.

wytht Maige Burd; and[1] confessis he hes had carnal deal wytht Maige Colein. The Superintendent deferris the carnal dail wytht Maige Burd to forthir trial, and somoundis hym to compeir befoir the General Assemblie of the Kyrk the second day *Secundo Marti.* of Marche nixt to cum, to resave his injunctionis of the Kirk for adulterie committit wytht Maige Colyne; and admonesit be the Superintendent to absten fra forthir deal having wytht the said Maige Colyne, undir paine contenit in actis[2] of Parliament.

Die Marcurii, decimo octavo mensis Januarii, anno Domini j^{m}v^{c}lxix$^{no.}$

The said day, Maister Johne Dalglesche is decernit, be[3] sens- *Rij* Dalglesche, ment of the Superintendente and assemblie, to remuif Janet Wemis. Wemis persoun excommunicated furtht of his cumpany and mutual cohabitation wytht hym in hows bed and buird wythtin xv dayis, or ellis this day aucht daiis to preve sufficientlie that the said Jonet is his mareit spous, undir paine of excommunication.

Die Mercurii, xxv^{to} mensis Januarii, anno Domini j^{m}v^{c}lxix$^{no.}$

The quhilk day, in the terme assignit to Maister Johne Dalglesche, Dalglesche to compeir this day to preve sufficientlye that Jonet Wemis. Wemis is his mareit wyffe, becaus Maister Johne comperis nocht the session ordanis and decernis the said Maister Johne to remuif the said Jonet Wemis furtht of his cumpany, according to the ordinance of the last act maid thairupon, under paine of excommunication.

The quhilk day, comperit Besse Ballingal, relict of umquhill Ballingal, George Myllar, and complenit upon Johne Myllar, hir sonne, Myllar. that quhair upon Setterday the xxj day of Januar instant, undir silence of nycht, the said Johne schot hir and possit[4] hir wytht his feit, and ruggit the curche of hir head, and callit hir blarit carling, wytht mony utheris injuries wordis, then and of befoir; and desirit the session that sche mycht have remeid. And the said Johne, being warnit be Alexander Roucht and

---

[1] *And and* in MS.   [2] *Actistis* in MS.   [3] *Ba* in MS.   [4] Pushed or pounded.

Alexander Myllar deakinnis to compeir this day befoir the
session, contenualley disobeyt, thairfoir the session committit
hym to the magistrattis.

*Die Mercurii, primo Februarii, anno Domini millesimo
quingentesimo sexagesimo nono.*

Ogilwy, Zwill. The quhilk day, Christen Zwil, dochtir to William Zwil in
Ergail, deponis, in the presence of God and the assemblie, that
upon the sextein day of October last bipast, eftir commoning
of contract of mareage betwix William Zwill hir father and
Patrik Ogilwy and they nocht aggreand thairupon, the said
Patrik cam to the said Christen, and said to hir, Christen thair
is bot ane litle distance betwix your father and me, and yit I
trow we sal aggre.   And the said Christen being sorye thairat,
the said Patrik said, Christen I promit I sal nevir have uthir
wyf bot yow.   Quhilk promis the said Christen was and is yit
content of, and William Zwil hir father apprevis the sam, and
attour the said Patrik sayis and affirmis that he maid promis
of mareage to the said Christen be gevin his hand to hir that
he sould marye hir, and als swearis that he nevir maid promis
to ony uther woman.   And the said Christen swear that the
thingis deponit be hir is of [tr]utht and veritie, as sche wil
ansuere in presence of God upon the day of jugement.   And
forthir the seat ordanis William Stevinson and his dochtir to
be warnit to compeir this day aucht dayis, to ansueir to sic
thingis as salbe inquirit of them ; wytht certification gyf they
compeir nocht, they sal nocht be hard eftirwart to oppone or
object aganis the promis of mareage maid be Patrik Ogilwy to
Christen Zwill.

Decretum ses-
sionis contra M.   The quhilk day, the sessioun hes ordanit public admoni-
Johannem   tiounis to be gevin furtht upon M. Johne Dalgles, to remuif
Dalglesche.   Jonet Wemis persoun excommunicated furtht of his cumpany
and mutual cohabitation,[1] under paine of excommunicatioun,
conform to the ordour ellis takin in the kirk.

---

[1] *Excommunication* in MS.

Die Mercurii, octavo die mensis Februarii, anno Domini 1569.

The quhilk day, Maister Johne Dalgles producit his com- Dalglesche
plent to the seat; the assemble, being present wanting ane *rij xxij^{do} Februarii.*
grite numbir thairof and in spetial the Superintendent and
minister, continuat ansuere to the complent to this day xv
dayis, to wit, the xxij day of Februar instant.

Die Mercurii, vigesimo secundo Februarii, anno Domini
j^{m}v^{c} sexagesimo nono.

The quhilk day, the seat, in respect of Jonet Patersoun Decreit of the
aitht gevin and depositiounis of witnes maid anent the bairn seat for bap-
tising of John
born be the said Jonet to Johne Corstorphine, ordanis the said Corstorphine
bairn.
Jonet to cum to the parroche kirk of this citie and mak hir
repentance, and that being doin the bairn to be presentit to
baptisme be sum of the said John freindis.

The quhilk day, in the terme assignit be the Superintendent Beton, Lesly.
to Dauid Betoun of Creicht and Beterage Lesly his spous, to
gyf in al thair resounis and causis in write quhy athir of them
aucht nocht to adheir to utheris, to remain in the band of
matrimonye contractit and solemnizat betwix them; the saidis
personis comperand be thair selves, the said Dauid allegit
that he had na caus nor resoun to produce or schaw quhy he
aucht nocht to adhere, and is content to adheir. And Beterage
desyrit aggreance wytht avis of freindis and in spetial of hir
brother, my Lord of Rothes, quha is presentlie of the realm,
and belevis hym schortlie to cum hame; and thairfoir desyrit
continuation of the caus to my Lordis hame cuming. The
Superintendent, wytht avis of the assembly and consent of
parteis, continuat the caus to the xv day of Marche nixt to *xv^{to} Martii.*
cum; wytht certification gyf Beterage producis nocht hir resonis
and causis, the said day, quhy sche sould nocht adhere, the
Superintendent wil decerne hir *simpliciter* to adhere under
paine of excommunication. *Partibus apud acta citatis.*

Die Marcurii, decimo quinto mensis Martii, anno Domini
j^{m}v^{c} sexagesimo nono.

The said day, in the terme assignat to Beterage Leslye to Betoun of
gyf in all hir causis and resonis in write, quhy sche sould nocht Creich, Leslye.

adhere to Dauid Betoun of Creicht, hir spous, in bed buird and
mutual cohabitation, according to the last act of this caus,
maid upon the xxij day of Februar last bipast, the assemblie,
in absence of the Superintendent, wytht consent of parteis, continuat the said caus, in the sam stait form and effect as it is
now, to the xij day of Aprile nixt to cum.   *Partibus apud acta
citatis.*

Zwil, Ogilwy.   The said day, William Zwil, father to Christiane Zwil, schew
to the seat the grite infirmite and seiknes of Patrik Ogilwy, his
guid sone, contractit wytht the said Christiane, ellis handfast be
promis of mareage maid betwix them and thair bannis laufullie
proclamit ; in respect of the said Patrik deadlie infirmite,
requirit and desyrit of the seat that the solemnizatioun of the
mareage betwix them mycht be solemnizat this day, nochtwythtstanding the act and ordinance maid that na solemnization
sould be maid publiklie in face of the congregation [bot][1] upon
ane Sunday.[2]   In respect of the premissis and utheris circumstances moving the seat for the tyme, the seat condescendit and
grantit the said request.

*Die Mercurii, vigesimo secundo mensis Martii, anno Domini
j^mv^clxix^no, in presentia domini Superintendentis ministri et
sessionis.*

Decretum   The said day, the sessioun ordanis Maister Johne Dalgles,
sessionis contra
M. Johannem   this nixt Sunday the xxvj of Marche instant, to be publiclye
Dalgles.   admonesed to remove Jonet Wemis persoun excommunicated
furtht of his cumpany and mutual cohabitatioun wythtin viij
dayis, under paine of excommunication, in respect of diverss ·
admonitionis maid of befoir quhilk he hes nocht obtemperat.

Spens, Kairnis,   The quhilk day, anent the somoundis rasit at the instance
rij.   of Margaret Spens spous to Henry Kairnis aganis the said
Henry, the sessioun decernis and ordanis the said Henry to
be somound of new to this day aucht dayis, and in the mean

---

[1] Omitted.
[2] 'The Sunday befoir sermon we think most convenient for mariage, and it
to be used no day ellis without the consent of the hoill ministerie' (*First Book
of Discipline,* ninth head).

tyme the Rectour, minister, M. Thomas Balfour and Maister
Martine Geddye to speak the said Henrye, to se gyf he may
be reconciled wytht the said Margaret.

The said day, Robert Braed, being dilatit to be ane Papist *Decretum*
and mentenar of Papistrie, is decernit be the sessioun that gyf *sessionis contra*
Robertum
evir he be fund dilatit of the premissis again [he][1] sal pay to *Braed.*
the collectouris to the puris ten lib. to be takin up wythtout
forgyfnes, and nocht to be admittit to the nixt communioun
wythtout he gyf confession of his faitht.

Die vigesimo nono mensis Martii, anno Domini millesimo quin-
gentesimo septuagesimo.

The said day, the sessioun, in respect of Jonet Wemis Ordinance of
obedience schawing, ordanis hir, upon Sunday nixt to cum, to the session
anent Jonet
cum to this parroche kirk, and thair to resave sic discipline Wemis.
and correction as salbe injuned to hir, for hir heicht contemp-
tioun in lang lying under excommunicatioun be the space of
foure yeris or thairby; and intimation heirof to be maid to
the peple in the doctrine on Fryday nixt to cum; and this
dispensatioun for this present the seat hes grantit to [hir][1] be
reasoun of the said Jonettis grite seiknes and infirmite.

The said day, anent the complent of Margaret Spens aganis *Decretum*
Henry Kairnis hir spous, the sessioun hes thocht expedient that *sessionis penes*
Kairnis et
the Rectour, the minister, Maister Thomas Balfour and *Spens conjuges,*
rij.
Maister Martine Geddye to speak the said Henry, and gyf he
wil nocht use thair counsal anent resaving of the said Margaret
to hows bed buird and mutual cohabitation, &c., he to be
publiclie admonesed to that effec in write, under paine of
excommunication, &c.; and to be summound to that effect to
this day aucht dayis.

Die Mercurii, decimo nono mensis Aprilis, anno Domini j^mv^c
septuagesimo.

The said day, the sessioun ordanis ane writing to be direct Dalgles,
to Robert Boswel in Ryallie, to compeir befoir the session this Wemis.

---

[1] Omitted.

day aucht dayis, to propone and allege caus gyf he ony hes to
stop mareage betwix Maister Johne Dalgles and Jonet Wemis ;
wytht intimation gyf he comperis nocht, command sal be gevin
to George Blak redar to proclame the bannis on Sunday nixt
to cum betwix the said Maister Johne and Jonet.

Die Mercurii, vigesimo sexto mensis Aprilis, anno Domini 1570.

Decretum pro-
clamationis
bannorum inter
M. Joannem
Dalgles et
Jonetam
Wemis.

The said day, in the terme assignat to Maister Johne Dalgles
to reproduce Robert Boswel ansuere of the writing direct be
the session to hym befoore the proclamation of bannis of mareage
betwix the said Maister Johne and Jonet Wemis, comperit the
said Maister Johne Dalgles, quha schew to the seat ane decrete
absolvitour of the commissaris of Edinburght, pronuncit betwix
the said Jonet Wemis and Robert Boswel, subscrivet be Johne
Johnestoun, the saidis commissaris scribe, of the dait the xxvj
day of Marche yeir of God j^{m}v^{c}lxviij yeris.   In respect of the
quhilk, the seat ordanis and decernis George Blak redar to
proclame the bannis betwix the saidis Maister Johne and Jonet
Wemis.

Nota.
Licence gevin
to the minister.

The quhilk day, the sessioun, wytht avis of the Superintendent,
in respect of the ministeris infirmite, hes licentiat hym for sex
oulkis *in totum* to desiste fra preaching, to the effect that he may
gyf hym self to be curit be medicine for reporting[1] of his
healtht ; and the beginning of the licence to be on Wedinsday
nixt to cum, and forthir to indure then the tyme abuif speci-
fiit according to the discretion of the seat.

Requisitio
ministrorum.
Hamilton,
Ramsay.

The said day, Maister Robert Hammilton, minister of Sanctandros, and Maister William Ramsay, secound principal
maister of Sanct Saluatoris Colleage, requirit M. Johne Winram,
Superintendent of Fyiffe, and the session of Sanctandros (in
consideration of ane accusacion gevin in aganis them *respective*
be Maister James Carmichel and his complices, in the sinodal
convention last haldin in Sanct Leonardis scolis, the fyft day
of Aprile instant, and conclusion of the said Superintendent
and his sinodal assemblie then convenit, be his and thair commissionaris and mediatouris, to wit, M. Johne Row and Maister

---

[1] Obtaining.

William Clark, ministeris, quhair it was concludit that the
trial of the said accusatiounis sould be remittit to the Superintendent and session of Sanctandros, and sa mony of them
that wil purge thame selffis of partial counsal, wytht concurrence of sex gentilmen and als mony ministeris as the partie
defendaris and mediatoris foirsaidis condescendit on) to proceid
in the said mater this day as in the day appointed thairto ;
and to gyf sentence absolvitour or condemnatour according
to justice, upon the pointis of the accusaton, for removing
of sclandir and pacefiing of the present devision in this
kirk.[1]

---

[1] There is a blank after this entry, but on the 21st of June the session granted
testimonials in favour of Ramsay and Hamilton at their request (*infra*, pp. 338,
339). Richard Bannatyne gives a most interesting account of the disagreement
which then existed in St. Andrews, but it is much too long to be quoted in its
entirety. Hamilton, who formerly 'wald not spair to reprove, most seveirlie,
whatsoever he knew to be done amiss, ather be the Queine, in the court, or
utherwayis,' had begun ' to grow cauld in his sermondis, and never spake a word
of these materis, as gif thei never aperteinet unto him.' According to Bannatyne, the regents of St. Leonards complained to the General Assembly—not to a
'sinodal assemblie'—and Ramsay took it so much to heart that he died soon afterwards (*Memoriales*, Ban. Club, pp. 228, 259). The matter, however, was brought
before the General Assembly in July 1570, and it was in view of that Assembly
that Hamilton specially requested the testimonial on the 21st of June. Petrie,
in his account of that meeting of Assembly, says that ' James Carmichell school-
master of Santandrews accuseth Rob. Hamilton, minister there, of some
points of doctrin delivered in a sermon. The Clark-Register and the Justice-
Clerk and another Lord of the Session shew, in the L. Chancellors name, that
he had heard of that controversy, and it containes some points tending to treason
and against the King's authority : and therefore they require, that the Assembly
would not decide in that matter concerning the King's authority until the nobility
conveen, which will be within few dayes : but in such things as concern heresy,
or properly belong unto their jurisdiction they may proceed. Unto this protestation the Assembly agreeth ; and went on in discussing the complaint in so
far as it concerned doctrine and slander that may arise thereupon ' (*Compendious
History*, 1662, second part, p. 368). Petrie adds within brackets—'But I finde
not the particulars.' The existing records of the Assembly, which are extremely
meagre on the case, bear out Petrie's statement to a certain extent, but say
nothing about the Lords of the Session (*Booke of the Universall Kirk*, i. 179).
Principal Lee conjectures that Hamilton's 'collegis' there mentioned were not
his colleagues in the New College, although most of them were men of his own
class, but the members of the kirk-session, because in this *Register* they formally
approve his doctrine (*Lectures on the History of the Church of Scotland*, i. 303).

Die Mercurii, tertio Maii 1570, *per Superintendentem et sessionem, ministro presente.*

Pryide,
Luklaw.

The quhilk day, anent the somoundis rasit be the Superintendent of his office upon Dauid Luklaw yownger in Cowper and Maidge Pryide, to inquire quha is the father of the bairn quhilk sche buir upon Zwil-ewin last was, &c., as at mair lyntht is contenit in the somoundis, comperit the saidis Dauid and Maidge. And Maidge being inquirit quha is the said bairn father, sche ansueris, upon hir conscience and in the presence of God, that the said Dauid is the bairnis father; and offeris hir to swear the sam. And Dauid [in][1] the contrar denyis that he is the bairnis father; and offeris hym to gyf his aitht thair upon, gyf it sal be thocht expedient the sam to be tane. The Superintendent, befoir accepting of athir of the saidis parteis aitht, be resoun of thair contrarius sayingis, ordanis the witnes somond to this day[2] to be examinat, that was present at the byrtht of the said bairn. And befoir examinatioun of witnes, the said Maidge being demandit quhair and in quhat place the bairn sould be gottin be the said Dauid Luklaw, sche ansuered that befoir Sanct James day at last was, be the space of sex oulkis Dauid hantit to hir be nycht and day, and spetialie that he com to Thomas Fleschear hall twyss or thryis on syndry nychttis, and sche opinnit the dur to hym, and[3] scho helpit hym of wytht his clathis and [he][1] lay doun besyde hir in ane langsadil. And at utheris tymis wythtin the said space, he cam to the loft abuif the brew hows in Thomas Fleschearis and lay wytht hir, wythtin the quhilk tyme sche alledgis the bairn was gottin; and offeris hyr to gyf hir aitht thair upon. And the said Dauid denyis the hail premissis, and offeris hym to swear the sam. Attour, comperit Jonet Ademsoun and Male Abirnethye, witnes, somound be the Superintendent to testifie in the said action. And Dauid Luklaw, being inquirit gyf he had ony thyng to object aganis them, sayis they ar bot wemen and aucht nocht of the law to be resavit to bear witnes in sic casis. And the Superintendent, in respect of the practik of this session, ordanis them to be sworn ressavit and examinat.

---

[1] Omitted.   [2] *Thay* in MS.   [3] *And and* in MS.

Jonet Ademsoun, witnes abone writtin, somound sworn resavit and examinat, deponis that as sche remembris upon Zwil-ewin[1] last bipast, sche was in Male Abirnethy hows, quhair Maidge Pryde was extremely seik as woman mycht be in hir byrtht; and the deponent askit of Maidge quha was the bairn father: sche ansuered, I warrand it is yowng Dauid Luklawis.

Male Abirnethy *citata jurata recepta et examinata conformis in omnibus Jonete Adesoun priori testi.*

And now the Superintendent diferris the takin of athir of the saidis parteis athis, quhil he prevent them be ane somoundis of new to that effect.

Die Mercurii, vigesimo quarto mensis Maii, anno Domini j{m}v{c} septuagesimo.

The quhilk day, in respect of the adulterie manifestlie com- mittit[2] be Thomas Christie wytht Jonet Rynd, and they being accusat thairof and confessit, the sessioun hes committit thame to be punesit be the majestratis of this citie as adulteraris, and fra this furtht that nane of them accumpanie wytht utheris in bed nor buird.

Christe, Rynd, decretum sessionis.

Die Mercurii, decimo quarto mensis Junii, anno Domini j{m}v{c}lxx{mo}.

The quhilk day, James Bisset is decernit be the Superintend- ent to remove Catharine Ferry furtht of his hows, and [to abstein][3] fra forthir cohabitatioun wytht hir in tyme cuming in bed or buird, wythtin xxiiij howris, undir paine of excommunication.

Decretum Superintendentis contra Bissett et Ferry.

The said [day],[3] Robert Grub is decernit in al tyme cuming to observe and keip his paris kirk, for herying of the Word of God and public prayeris, undir pane of excommunication.

Decretum contra Grub.

The quhilk day, anent the clame of mareage betwix Besse Bruce and Michel Geddie, in respect of the mannis aitht gevin upon the promis of mareage referrit be Besse to his aitht, the

Brwce, Geddve, rij.

---

[1] *Zwil Zwlis-ewin* in MS.   [2] *Confessit* in MS.   Omitted.

Superintendent and session absolvis the said Michel of the said promis. And as to the secound part of the said Besse bil, quhair sche allegis that he gat hir virginitie, and be reson thairof sould marie hir or tochir hir, the Superintendent and session assignis this day aucht dayis to the said Michel to preve the said Besse to be ane corruppit woman, or he had knawledge of hir, for the first dilation.

Decretum Symson, Kempt.

The said day, anent the complent gevin in be Dauid Symson aganis Andro Kempt, comperis Andro Kempt and denyis the pointis of the bill; and Dauid Symson offeris hym to preve the sam instantlie, and to that effect producit [*Johne Schare*— deleted], Alexander Scharp, Niniane Rowl, Dauid Stevin and Johne Mwir. The Superintendent, in respect of the depositionis of the witnes, ordanis and decernis Andro Kemp, upon Fryday nixt cumms eftir sermon, to ask Dauid Symson and his mother forgevenes upon his kneis, for the offens committit be hym aganis them, and gyf he committis sic lik in tyme cuming to be deprivat of his office: and M. Robert Winram collectour to pay to Dauid Symson mother in first end of his stipend xx s.

Peablis, Grub.

The said day, Alexander Peablis and Johne Grub decernit to keip the kirk on the Sabbat day in tyme cuming, undir paine of excommunication.

Die Mercurii, xxj*mo* Junii 1570.

Bruce, Geddie, *rij.*

The said day, the session hes continuat the action and caus movit betwix Besse Brwce and Michel Geddie, wytht consent of the said Besse, to this day aucht dayis.

Decretum testimonialium M. Willelmj Ramsay ministri verbi Dei.

The said day, the sessioun, al in ane voce, eftir Maister William Ramsay had desyrit ane testimonial of the verite of his doctrine lyiff and conversatioun, sen he begoutht to travel in this citie in the Word of God and explication thairof, testifiis his hail doctrine continualie sen syne to be trew and sound in all sortis, and his lyf and conversation to have bein haly guid and wythtout reproche: and heirupon decernit testimonial to be gevin in dew form as efferis.

Decretum testimonialium M. Robertj Hammilton ministri.

The quhilk day, the assemblie of eldaris and deakins of the sessioun of the citie of Sanctandros being requirit be thair

minister, Maister Robert Hammiltoun, as they wald ansueir to
God, gyf that sen the beginning of his ministratioun amangis
them, ethir in preaching of the Word forme of prayer or out-
ward and external maneir of leving, he had transgressit the
limitis of his vocatioun or left ondoin that becam ane trew and
faithtful minister, or gyf ony abuse was cropin in in this congregatioun be his negligence, or be hym mentenit sen the beginning of his ministratioun, that they[1] wald ansueir in the premissis according to the trewtht, and to have thair testimonial
thairintil in dew form as efferis, quhairby his part mycht be
knawin in this lettir aige and pirelus dayis to al quhatsumevir,
bot specialie to the brethrin of the General Assemblie of this
realm, to be haldin at Edinburght the fyifte day of Julii nixt
to cum.   The quhilk petitioun the assemblie, understanding to
be resonable, willing to bear testimonie to the trewtht, testifiis
and declaris al in ane voce, That the said minister baitht in
preaching of the Word and doctrine, form and maneir of
prayer, external conversatioun of lyiffe, to have behad[2] hym self
as becummis the trew minister and servand of God; swa that
as yit, by his travel, the purite of the Euuangel, form of ministratioun of the sacramentis, and ordour of discipline, offerit to
us of the mercies of God sen the beginning of reformatioun, by
his notable and excellent instrumentis, is yit kepit amangis us;
and swa na abuse, prasit be God, cropin in in our kirk be his
negligence, nor yit mentenit be hym, or ony thing tawcht
quhairof we consavit sclandir or the godlie justlie mycht be
offendit.

The said day, the minister requirit that he mycht have the *Nota.*
tyme and licence grantit to hym of befoir for recovering of his Prorogation of
the miniſter
healht, be reson that he being impedit sen syne wytht preach- licenſe to gyf
hym ſelf to be
ing of the Word, exercising of fastein, public prayeris, and curtt of his
ministration of the Lordis supper to the landwart, that he healtht.
mycht use it quhen he thocht tyme maest convenient.   The
session, al in ane voce, consentit to the prorogation of the said
license.

---

[1] *The* in MS.   [2] Demeaned or behaved.

Die Mercurii, decimo nono mensis Julii, anno Domini j^{m}v^{c}
septuagesimo.

Decretum
Derny.

The quhilk day, Mareoun Dande exonerat, quit-clamit
and dischargit Petir Dairny of al promis of mareage betwix
them and defloring of hir virginite, or ony thing that sche may
alledge to stop the said Petir to mary wytht ony uthir, and
thairfoir [the seat]¹ ordanis the said Petir bannis to be proclamit
this nixt Sunday.

Die Mercurii, vigesimo sexto mensis Julii, anno Domini
millesimo quingentesimo septuagesimo.

Betoun de
Creycht, Leslye.

The quhilk day, anent the somoundis rasit at the Superintendentis instance of his office aganis Dauid Betoun of Creich
and Beterage Leslye his spous, tweching thair adherence, &c.,
as Christiane man and wyffe, or to allege caus, &c., comperit
the said Beterage, quha allegit that sche aucht nocht to be
compellit to adheir to Dauid Betoun of Creicht, becaus thair
dependis befoir the commissar of Edinburght ane actioun of
divorciament at hir instance aganis hym, for adulterie committit
be hym, as the libel thairupon at mair lentht proportis : quhilk
sche offerit hir to preve sufficientlie be write, as accordis of the
law, and desyrit ane terme to be assignat to hir to preve the
sam. Comperit the said Dauid, quba desyrit ane terme to

Penultimo
Augusti.

be assignat to hym to ansuere to the saidis allegeances, quhom
to the Superintendent assignat the penult day of August nixt
to cum. *Partibus apud acta citatis.*

Die Mercurii, nono die mensis Augusti, anno Domini
millesimo quingentesimo septuagesimo.

Nota.
Nota.
Decreit of the
seat anent the
puiris.

The quhilk day, it is decernit and ordanit be the seat, that
fra this furtht, that the deaknis of the quartaris mak na distributioun of the almis to na puris, bot to theis that frequentis
and cummis to sermoundis, public prayeris, examinatioun and
communioun, presenting of thair bairnis to baptisme, and wil

---

¹ Omitted.

gyf compt of thair faitht, and can say the Lordis Prayer, Beleve, and Commandementis of God, or at the least sal learn the sam wythtin ane monetht ; and als to mak it knawin and congregation thair mareage.[1]

Mercurii, die penultimo mensis Augusti 1570.

The quhilk day, in the terme assignat to Dauid Betoun of Creicht to ansueir to the allegeances of Beterage Leslye maid upon the xxvj day of Julii last bipast, the saidis parteis comperand be them selves, and the Superintendent being absent be reason of quhais absence the cause slepis.

Betoun, Leslye, *dormit.*

Die Mercurii, decimo tertio Septembris, anno Domini millesimo quingentesimo septuagesimo.

· The said day, the sessioun hes ordanit ane supplicatioun to be direct to the magistratis of this citie for guid ordour to be takin in tyme cuming, for reformatioun of the grite abuse usit be new mareit personis in violatioun of the Sabbat day ; and in spetial quhen, the day of thair mareage eftir nuin,[2] they resor[t] nocht to hering of the doctrine, and at evin eftir supper insolentlie, in evil exemple of utheris, perturbis the town wytht rynning thair throw in menstralye and harlatrye.

Nota. For repressing of the insolentcye of new marett folkis wythin this citie in brekking of the Sabbat.

Mercurii, die quarto mensis Octobris, anno Domini j^{m}v^{c} septuagesimo.

Patrik Myllar and Catharine Donaldson hes agnoscit thair fail of fornication, and the said Catharine to be wytht childe to hym, and submittit them to discipline of the kirk, and to absten in tyme cuming, and gyf they be fund relaps to be punesit accordinglye.

Millar, Donaldson.

---

[1] This clause is unintelligible, probably through the omission of some words.
[2] Marriages were then solemnised on Sabbath forenoon (*infra*, p. 345, n. 1).

Die Veneris, decimo tertio Octobris, anno Domini j^m v^c
septuagesimo.

Eldaris chosin be commoun voit and consent of the kirk.

Maister Johne Dowlglas, Rector	Mr. Martyne Geddye
Mr. Thomas Balfour	Mr. William Cok
Mr. Johne Ruthirfurd	Johne Motto
Mr. Alane Lawmontht	James Robertsoun
Mr. James Wilke	Johne Martine, elder
Dauid Walwod	James Forret in Polduf
Thomas Walwod	Mr. Johne Bonkil.

Diaconis electit in maneir foirsaid.

Charles Guthre	George Blak
William Gifford	Andro Motto
Johne Levingstoun	Andro Watsoun
Alexander Winchestir	Thomas Layng in Elenehill.
Alexander Roucht	

Die Mercurii, decimo octavo mensis Octobris, anno Domini
j^m v^c septuagesimo.

Nota.
Ratificatioun of the Act for convening.

The quhilk day, [*the maest part of*—deleted] the sessioun being assemblit ratifiit and apprevit the Act maid of befoir, tweching the convening to the assemblie at twa eftir nuin ilk Wedinsday, and quha failyeis to incur the panis contenit thairintil, and siclik of remaning to the end of the assemblie wythtout leve be askit and grantit.

Die Mercurii, decimo quinto mensis Novembris 1570.

Decretum sessionis contra Forret[1] et Wallace.

The said day, the seat decernit Andro Forret and Agnes Wallace to desist and ces fra forthir mutual cohabitatioun in bed and buird, ay and quhill he gaet ane testimonial of the deatht of Mareoun Dowglas his wyf, and gyf they cum in the contrar to be punesed as accordis of the law of the realm.

---

[1] *Forrret* in MS.

Johne Wilsoun, baxter, dilatit for ane common blasphemar, *Decretum sessionis contra Wilson pistorem.* swearare, bannar and ane common drunkat, admonesed to desist in tyme cuming, uthirwaiis he sal nocht be admittit to the communioun nor his bairnis to baptisme, and gevin in the handis of the magistratis to be punesed.

Gelis Symsoun, spous to George Vtein baxter, decernit to *Decretum sessionis contra Symson sponsam Georgj Vtein.* desist and ceas in tyme cuming fra selling of candil and braed on Sundays, and nocht resorting to the kirk for heryng of Goddis Word, missaying and disobedient to hir husband, undir pane of ten lib., and to sit in the joiggis xxiiij howris; and lykwys dilatit for fliting wyth hir nychtbouris, and selling of bread tyme of sermon on Sunday.

Die Mercurii, vigesimo secundo mensis Novembris, anno Domini j^mv^clxx^{mo.}

[There is a blank after this heading.]

Die Mercurii, decimo tertio mensis Decembris, anno Domini j^mv^clxx^{mo.}

The quhilk day, Jonet Smytht, lauful dochtir of Patrik Smytht, Martine. Smytht maltman citenar of Sanctandros, in presence of the Superintendent minister and sessioun-ecclesiastical of the said citie, exponit and declarit that it was nocht unknawin to them that quhow, in the monetht of November last bipast, undir silence of nycht, sche was ravissed and violentlie reft fra hir fathir and mother, and maisterfullie, aganis Goddis lawis and lawis of this realm, tane away fra hir saidis parentis aganis hir and thair willis be Stevin Martine, secound sone to William Martine of Giblestoun,[1] desyring heirfoir sic remedy of the Superintendent[2] minister and sessioun mycht of Goddis law mak to hir thairfoir. The Superintendent, wyth avis of the session and minister, offered to gyf hir ane citatioun as sche and hir parentis pleasit to libell. And the said Jonet being askit and demandit be Johne Martine, citenar and ane of the

---

[1] The Martines owned the half of Gibliston from 1494 to 1622 (Wood's *East Neuk of Fife*, 1887, pp. 268, 269).

[2] *Superindent* in MS.

ballies of the citie of Sanctandros, gyf the said Stevin deflorit
hir or did ony harme or skaitht to hir in hir persoun that may
redound to the corrupping of hir virginite. Sche ansuered and
confessed that sche kapit[1] na herm thair throw, bot was als
cleine and pure thairof as sche was quhen sche was borne of hir

Instrument
Martein.

mother. And heirupon the said Johne Martine, in name and
behalf of the said Stevin Martine, askit act and instrument.

Declaratioun of
M. Robert
Hammiltoun
minister to the
assemblie and
sessioun.
Nota.

The said day, Maister Robert Hammiltoun, minister of the
citie of Sanctandros, schew to the sessioun quhow that it was
nocht unknawin to them quhat travel and[2] labour he had tane
sen his entre to the ministerie; and quhow evil he had bein
handillit, nocht onlie in wanting of his stipend the space of
twa yeris and mair, bot also of that support and releve in
preaching of the Word, quhilk Maister Guidman and utheris
had befoir, being ministeris, and he hym self likwis befoir the
daitht of my Lord Regentis grace[3] of guid memorie; quhair-
throw they mycht perceave that he was becum waik and debilitat
in his bodie, and so unhable to sustein sic grite. chairgis as
befoir:[4] requiring heirfoir the sessioun and kirk, in consideratioun of the premissis and cheiflie that he lakit the concurrence
and support in preaching the Word that utheris had befoir,
that na falt sould be fund wytht hym eftirwart, albeit he kepit
nocht the ordinarie days of preaching as of befoir; bot they
wald be content wytht that resonable travell quhilk he offerit
to undirly in tyme to cum, according as his body mycht reson-
ablie sustein; and imput the laik unto them that tuik up the
teindis and gaif nocht hym sic assistence as they gaif to utheris
befoir, in preaching the[5] Word and administratioun of the
sacramentis, and nocht to hym. The quhilk the sessioun and
kirk, al wytht ane voce and wytht uniform consent, thocht verry
resonable, lamenting he sould be sa evil handillit baitht in the
ane and the uthir, and wald be content wytht that travel and

---

[1] Received.   [2] *And and* in MS.
[3] The Regent Murray was murdered on the 23d of January 1569-70.
[4] In compliance with the desire of the General Assembly, in 1565, that the
St. Andrews congregation should choose a minister 'out of their own Universitie' (see p. 28, n.), Hamilton had been elected; but he still held his Divinity
Chair in St. Mary's College.
[5] Here this entry is turned over the leaf, but the scribe has inserted the next
entry—relating to Zowng and Myles—at the bottom of this page.

labour quhilk he wald undirlie in tyme to cum, in preaching
of the Word according to his awin discretioun; exhorting hym
moest gentelye in the menetyme, quhil forthir ordour be tane,
that he wald keip Sunday and Wedinsday ;[1] and sa, in respect
of the premissis, albeit the ordinarie dayis be hym war nocht
kepit, wald nocht imput to hym as ane offence or fault worthye
of reprove or correctioun on his part.

Die ultimo mensis Januarii 1570.

Comperit Mr. Antone Zowng and confessit ane bairn borne Zowng, Myles.
be Gelis Myles to be his, and promittit to present the bairn to
baptisme and submit hym to discipline ecclesiastical.

Die Mercurii, vigesimo primo die mensis Februarii, anno
Domini millesimo quingentesimo septuagesimo.

The quhilk day, the sessioun hes decernit Elene Jnglis [2] to *Decretum*
bring ane sufficient testimonial fra Alane Rait hir spous that *sessionis penes Elenam Jnglis.*
sche hes adherit to hym in bed buird and mutual cohabita-
tioun, and is content to remain wytht hym oure .alquhair, at

---

[1] 'Some churcheis may convene everie day; some thryise or twise in the
weeke ; some perchance bot onis. In these and such like must everie particular
churche, by thair awin consent, appoint thair awin polecie. In greit tounis we
think expedient that everie day thair be eathir sermon, or ellis Common Prayeris,
with some exercise of reiding the Scripturis. What day the publict sermon is,
we can neathir require or gretlie approve that the Commoun Prayeris be publictlie
used. . . . In everie notable toun, we require that one day, besydis the Sunday,
be appointed to the sermone and prayeris ; whiche, during the tyme of sermone,
must be keipit fre frome all exercise of laubour, alsweill of the maister as of the
servandis. In smaller tounis, as we have said, the commoun consent of the
churche must put ordour. But the Sunday must straitlie be keipit, both before
and efter noon in all tounis. Before noon, must the Word be preached and sacramentis ministered, as also mariage solempnissed, yf occasioun offer : after noon
must the young children be publictlie examined in thair catechisme in audience
of the pepill. . . . At efter noon also may baptisme be ministered, whan occasioun is offered of great travell before noon. It is also to be observit, that
prayeris be used at after noon upoun the Sunday, whair thair is neathir preching
nor catechisme' (*First Book of Discipline*, ninth head).

[2] She had been excommunicated for stubbornly refusing to adhere to her husband and for contemptuously despising the voice of the kirk ; but had afterwards
offered to submit to discipline (*supra*, pp. 311, 312, 322).

his plesure. The sessioun is content to resave hir as ane
membir of Christis Kirk, sche satisfiing the kirk according to
ordour of discipline usit thairintil, or ellis to find sufficient
cautioun that sche sal adheir to hir husband at his hamecuming, or to pas to hym quhair evir he be gyf he sendis for
hir.

Die Mercurii ultimo Februarii 1570.[1]

Nota.
Myllar.

Patrik Myllar, cowper, dilatit that he said publiclie, that
sum of the eldaris and dakinnis of the seat,[2] that he was dilated
be sum of the seat of malice and invy ; and he, comperand and
being accusat thairof, spak heichtlye prowdlye and irreverend-
lie, wytht grite banning swering and blaspheming the name of
God, and contemning the seat.

Layng, rij.

The said day, Alexander Laing being accusat that he said to
the minister, Schyr I cam to yow of befoir of my awin head,
bot now I am send to yow be sum of the eldaris and decanis,
be commissioun, to declair that William Geddye aucht to sit
on the stuil als weil as I ; and gyf ye do it nocht ye wil be
accusat of parcialite ; and sum of the eldaris and decanis wil
avow this in your face ! And Alexander being demandit and
askit quha [3] war the eldaris or decanis, or gyf he wald byde at
accusation thairof, he wald do nethir the ane nor the uthir.
The seat ordanis the said Alexander to gyf his aitht heirupon
this day aucht dayis.

Decretum
sessionis penes
Robertum Hew
officiarium.

The said day, the seat hes ordanit Maister Thomas Balfour
to deliver to Robert Hew officer of the session xx s., in compleit
payment of al thingis bigane, and quhill Michaelmes nixt to
cum to deliver to hym sic accidentis as may fal in the mein·
tyme.

Die Mercurii, quarto die mensis Aprilis, anno Domini, $j^{m}v^{c}$ septuagesimo primo.

Decrete of the
sessioun to the
Superintendent
chartour of
reces.

The quhilk day, anent the chartour of reces of the Superintendentis presentit to the assemblie, the assemblie resoning

---

[1] This entry is very faint, especially the words in the margin.
[2] Probably this clause should have been deleted.   [3] *Quhat* in MS.

thairwytht thinkis guid that the Superintendent be present
wytht them according to the accustumed maneir in trying and
examinating of the personis gevin up be hym, and also that he
present the inquest and dilatoris names, quhairby the transgressoris may be punisched, according to the ordour of this
kirk ; uthir waiis the seat can nocht meĺ thairwytht, becaus
they war nocht participant of taking up of the dilatiounis
contenit in the said chartour ; bot ar, likeas they have bein
continualie sen beginning of Reformation of thair kirk, in use
of resaving of dilatiounis wythtin thair jurisdiction thair selves,
according to the Buik of Discipline.

Die Mercurii xviij° Aprilis 1571.

The said day, Elene Jnglis, spous to Alane Rait, comperit *Decretum*
befoir the sessioun and desyrit hir as sche hes doin oft tymis of ^{Elene Jnglis.}
befoir to be resavit as ane membir of the congregatioun, and
to injoy the benefitis thairof ; and hes maid faitht, in presence
of the sessioun, that, unfeingyeitlie and wythtout dissimilatioun,
sche craiffis this of the kirk for eschewing of the fearful and
terrible sentence of excommunicatioun led aganis hir ; and hes
promittit faithtfullye that sche sal willinglye adhere to hir
said spous at his hame cuming in thir partis, or to pas to hym
in ony part of this realm, and to remain wytht hym in bed
buird and mutual cohabitatioun, quhen evir sche salbe requirit
thairto be hir said husband, sa that na fail thairintil salbe
fund in hir in tyme cuming ; and als promittis that sche sal
satisfie the kirk, and submit hir to sic discipline and correctioun as [1] salbe requirit of hir, and to find sufficient cautioun
heirupon undir paine of fourtie liƀ. The seat—in consideratioun heirof, and in respect of the said Elene humiliatioun and
unfenyeid repentence as apperis, and that sche hes sworn, in
presence of God and sessioun, that sche dois thir thingis wythtout dissimilatioun and nocht to dissave the kirk ; and that ane
repentand synner should be resavit and imbreassit, and nocht to
be castin of—hes ordanit and decernit hir to be resavit again,
and to bruik and jois the ƀenefit of Christis Kirk, as ane livelye
membir thairof.

---

[1] *As as* in MS.

Die Mercurii, vigesimo tertio mensis Maii, anno Domini j^mv^c septuagesimo primo.

Decretum sessionis, rij.

The said day, the brethir of the sessioun assemblit hes ordenit the officiar of the assemblie to warne the heal brethir of the sessioun and membris thairof, to wit, minister eldaris and diaconis, to compeir this day aucht days, to intrait upon sic thingis as sal be offered and proponit, and to request the Superintendent to cum to that effect.

Hammiltoun, Scot.

Memorandum, that upon Wedinsday the xvj day of Maii instant Elspet Hammiltoun, dochtir to Thomas Hammiltoun in this citie, dilatit of fornicatioun wytht Thomas Scot cuik of the New Colleage, comperit and confessit that sche had carnall deal wytht the said Thomas Scot befoir Candilmes last was: quhilk confessioun the seat acceptat, and ordinat the said Thomas Scot to be callit to resave ecclesiastical discipline, and to bring to remembrance the aitht he gaiff of befoir, and to re-examinat hym again.

Die Mercurii, penultimo mensis Maii, anno Domini 1571.

Vote of sessioun anent fasting.

The quhilk day, it is voted be the sessioun [or[1] *at least be the maest part thairof*—deleted] that thair was na public fasting desyrit of the seat to be injunit and proclamit for ony occasioun or caus occurring befoir this day; nocht the les the hael sessioun, in respect of grite trublis apperand, hes thocht expedient public fasting to be inditit, wytht avis of the Superintendent, and that conform to the act of the last General Assemblie[2] haldin in Edinburght the x of Marche last bipast, and personis to be appointed be hym to occupie the stuil of praeching and prayeris during the said tyme.

Decretum sessionis.

The said day the seat hes ordenit the names of them that presented nocht thame self to the last communioun to be schawin to the seat.

---

[1] In deleting the other words the scribe has neglected to draw his pen through *or.*

[2] In the sixth session of the General Assembly held in March 1570-1, ' the Kirk ordaines all superintendents, and commissioners to plant kirks, in their first synodall conventious heirafter following, with the advyse of their ministers, to reason [upon the necessity of publick fasts,] and appoint publick fasting, if it sall be thocht necessar ' (*Booke of the Universall Kirk,* i. 193, 194).

The said day, the seat hes ordenit Alexander Roucht and *Decretum sessionts penes Magistrum Dauidem Dischingtoun, rij.* Alexander Winchestir, deaconis, to warne Maister Dauid Disch-ingtoun to compeir this day aucht dayis, to ansueir to sic thingis as salbe proponit to hym.

Die Mercurii, xxvij° mensis Junii, anno Domini j'''v'lxxj''°.

The quhilk day, comperit Elspet Hammiltoun and confessit *Confessio Hammiltoun, Scot.* that, according to the notatioun maid in thir bukis upon the xxiij day of Maii last was, it is of veritie that sche refusit to swear that sche had carnail deal wytht Thomas Scot cuik of the New Colleage, befoir Candilmes immediatlie preceding.

Die Mercurii, undecimo Julii, anno Domini j'''v'lxxj''°.

The quhilk day, Johne Authinlek and Jsobel Forret confessit *Authinlek, Forret.* them to have had carnal deal or they war mareit. The seat decernit them on Sunday nixt to cum to mak satisfactioun in presence of the congregation.

Die Mercurii, decimo octavo mensis Julii, anno Domini
j'''v'lxxj''°.

The quhilk day, the fleschearis of this citie being attachit *Decreit of the session anent fleschearis.* and warnit to this day, to heir them accusat for brekking and selling of flesche upon the Sabbat day, and to resave dis-cipline thairfoir, comperit Martine Lumisden and Johne Andersoun, fleschearis, and confessit that thair servandis sauld sum smal fleschis and drawchtis to puir folkis on the Sabbat day. Comperit lykwys James Herman and confessit hym to have doin the sam be hymself. Johne Williamson confessit selling of flesche in litle quantite upon Sunday, tyme of prayeris and nocht of preaching. Thomas Cuthtbert conform to Johne Williamson, James Myllar, James Dempstertoun, Patrik Paw-toun, Alexander Watson, James Cuik, Jonkein Mernis, Alex-ander Lumisden servand and [*blank*].[1] The seat ordenis the saidis personis to be offered up to the majestratis be supplica-tion, that ordour may be takin according to actis of Parlia-me[nt][2] and statutis of this citie.

---

[1] This blank extends to nearly a line and a half.
[2] In 1526 and again in 1540, Parliament ordained that there should be thiec

Die Mercurii, xxij^{do.} mensis Augusti, anno Domini j^mv^clxxj^{mo.}

Admonitio Loquhoir, Logye. The quhilk day, Mariory Loquhoir, spous to James Logye, comperand and accusat upon the dilatioun castin in at the counsal hows dur, anent ane alegit bardal haldin in thair hows, denyit the sam, and admonesed be the sessioun to abstein fra al occasion of suspitioun in sic cases, undir al panis that eftir may follow.

Die Mercurii decimo nono Septembris 1571.

Lawmontht, Rolland, rij. The seat, in respect that Henry Lawmontht hes bein diverss tymes socht be the officiar of the assemblie at his dwelling place wythtin this citie, to charge hym to compeir befoir the assemblye to ansueir anent the grite brute of hym of adulterie and incest committit be hym wytht Effem Rolland, and could nocht obtein his personal presence; the seat yit ordanis the officiar to warne hym to compeir on Wedinsday nixt to cum, wytht intimation that, gyf he comperis nocht, on Sunday nixt thaireftir he sal be somound opinlie be writing in the kirk.

The names of eldaris and diaconis chosin upon the xij day of October 1571.

Eldaris.

Mr. Johne Dowglas, Archibischop and Rector of Sanctandros [1]
Mr. Thomas Balfour
Mr. Johne Ruthirfurd
Mr. William Cok
Mr. James Wilke
Mr. Alane Lawmontht
Mr. Alexander Sibbald
Mr. Martine Geddye
Johne Motto
Dauid Walwod
Charles Geddy
Mr. Johne Bonkil.

Diaconis.

William Zwill
William Gyfferd
Johne Walcar
William Maine
Johne Levingstoun
Andro Watsoun
Alexander Hay
George Blak.

weekly markets in Edinburgh for selling flesh, namely, on Sunday, Monday, and Thursday (*Acts of the Parliaments of Scotland*, ii. 314, 378). In 1568 an Act was made 'anent the keiping of the Sabaoth day,' but its terms are not given (*Ibid.* iii. p. 56).

[1] Douglas was nominated Archbishop of St. Andrews on the 18th of August

Die Mercurii, xxiiij° Octobris, anno Domini j^m v^c lxxj^mo.

The said day, the seat concludit and ordinat Henry Law- *Decretum sessionis penes* montht to be wairnit to compeir befoir the sessioun this day *Henricum* aucht dayis, to wit, Weddinsday the last day of October instant, *Lawmontht.* to ansueir to sic thingis as is contenit in the act of this sessioun maid upon the xix day of September last bipast; and the said Henry to be warnit be twa of the brethrin of this sessioun that war appointed to warn hym to this day; and he being brotherly warnit and admonesed to compeir as said is and compeir nocht, the seat ordeinat and decernit the said act of the dait the xix day of September to have ful stryntht and effect.

Die Mercurii, ultimo Octobris, anno Domini j^m v^c lxxj^mo.

The said day, in respect that the brethir of the sessioun, Lawmontht, *rij* appointed to admonische and warne Henry Lawmontht to this *vij° Novembris.* day to compeir befoir the sessioun, could nocht apprehend hym to that effect, [the sessioun][1] hes yit requestit the said brethir to warne hym to this day aucht dayis, to wit, the vij of November nixt to cum, to compeir befoir the session to the effect mentionat in the act immediatlie abuif wryttin, wytht intimation contenit in the sam.

Heireftir fallowis certane notis, concerning Maister Dauid Dischingtoun accusatioun for absenting hym fra the communioun, callit be the seat to remembrance and ordenit to be insertit in the bukis.

Upon Sunday callit Palme Sunday last bipast, in the public Mr. Dauid assemblie of the congregatioun of this citie, the minister maid Dischington.

1571, but was not inaugurated until the 10th of next February (Richard Bannatyne's *Memoriales*, Ban. Club, pp. 178, 223). He was present, however, as Archbishop of St. Andrews, in the Parliament which met at Stirling on the 5th of September 1571 (*Acts of the Parliaments of Scotland*, iii. 65). The troubles of his new office had already begun. 'The Superintendent of Fyfe inhibited the Rector of Sanct Androis to voit as ane of the Kirke, till he sould be admitted be the Kirke, undir the paine of excommunicatioune. Mortoun commandit him to voit (as Bischope of Sanct Androis), undir the paine of treasone' (Bannatyne's *Memoriales*, p. 183).   [1] Omitted.

publicatioun of administratioun of the Lordis supper to the brethrin of this citie, and requirit al theis that had promised to cum to the communioun on Law Sunday, that they sould cum to examinatioun in myd tyme and alsua to the communioun. And Maister Dauid Dischingtoun being in this town remanit furtht of this citie and absentit hym self fra the communioun.

Item, upon the xix day of Junii last was, immediatlie befoir the landward communioun, Mr. Dauid Dischington was callit and comperit to the assemblie, quba was accusat that he wald nocht keip his promis to cum to the last communioun, albeit he was opinlie warnit in presence of the heal congregation, desyring hym to cum upon Myd Sounday to the communioun wytht his brethrin : quhilk Mr. Dauid Dischington ansuered, viz., Quhen I maid the promis I lukit for ane uthir thing nor I see, for ever ilk ane of thame wald cut utheris throtis quha gaes to that communioun, and thairfoir I wil nocht keip promis.

Mr. Dauid Dischington.

Die Mercurii, septimo Novembris 1571.

Lawmontht, decretum sessionis rij q. xxjmo Novembris.

The quhilk day, anent the bruit and sclandir of adulterie and incest committit be Henry Lawmonth wytht Eufame Rolland, in respect of Henry declaration in presence of the sessioun, the seat hes ordenit inquisitioun and trial of the bruit and sclandir to be takin, quhairof, gyf na certentie may be had, the said Henry aitht to be takin upon his innocency for removing of the sclandir. And to that effect the seat hes ordenit ane citatioun to be direct upon certane witnes, and Henry to be chargit to heir the witnes sworn and resavit to this day xv dayis.

Decretum sessionis penes Magistrum Dauidem Dischington.

The quhilk day, Maister Dauid Dischingtoun, warnit, comperit befoir the seat, and being demandat and askit be the minister and seat, qubat was his occasioun of byding fra the last communioun of the Lordis supper celebrat last in this citie, alsweil to the inhabitantis thairof as to the landward folkis, by[1] promis maid be hym of befoir that he sould be participant

---

[1] Against.

thairof, &c. Quha ansuered, for causis moving his conscience at that tyme he could nocht communicat: and now hes promittit faithtfullie that he sall communicat, and be participant of the nixt communioun to be celebrat in this citie, and sal nocht absent hym thairfra; of quhilk promis gyf he sal failye thairintil, the seat hes decernit that it sal be procedit aganis hym to excommunicatioun, wythtout forthir calling.

Die Mercurii, xiiij^to Novembris 1571.

The said day, the seat hes ordenit ane citatioun to be gevin furtht upon Dauid Orm, Elene Lawmontht his spous, Maister Alane Lawmontht, Mr. William Skein, Waltir Makeson, Grisel Wod his spous, to compeir upon Wedinsday, the xxj day of November instant, befoir the seat, to bear leal witnes upon the brute and sclander of adulterie and incest committit be Henry Lawmontht wytht Effem Rolland. And Henry to be warnit at his dwelling place to heir the witnes resavit and sworn. *Decretum sesstonis penes Henricum Lawmontht rij xxj^mo Novembris.*

The said day, anent the request of Thomas Scot, desyring hym joined in matrimony wytht Elspet Hammilton, offering hym to mak satisfaction, the seat hes committit hym to the magistrattis to be punesed as ane fornicatour; and satisfaction being maid the said Thomas to proceid to mareage, and the bairn begottin betwix hym and the said Elspet to be baptized. *Scot, Hammiltoun*

Die Mercurii xxj^mo mensis Novembris 1571.

Depositiounis of witnes in the inquisitioun and trial of adulterie, allegit committit be Henry Lawmontht wytht Eufame Rolland.

Maister William Skein, commissar of Sanctandrois, resavit sworn and examinat, deponis that he hard ane brute and common fame throught the town, and forthir kennis nocht. *[Lawmontht, Rolland: depositiounis of wytnes.]*

Maister Alane Lawmontht, sworn resavit and examinate upon the pointis of the articlis of inquisitioun, deponis that he kennis perfitlie his sone Henry Lawmontht and Jsobel Orm to be mareit, and Effem Rolland to be Jsobel Orm syster dochter; and gyf evir his sone had carnel copulation wytht the said

z

Effem or nocht he kennis nocht, bot of brute thairof risen, &c.:
and forthir knawis nocht in the mater.

Waltir Makkesoun deponis that Henry Lawmontht cam to
hym upon ane day, and desyrit ane chalmer of his to put sum
gear in, and he granted hym ane chalmer; and he brocht ane
pakkat of gear furtht of Henry Anderson, and pat in the said
chalmer: and forthir knawis nocht, &c.

Grisel Wod, spous to Waltir Makeson, deponis that Henry
Lawmontht cam to hir, and said that he had ane heretrice of
the northtland to bring to this town, and sperit of hir gyf he
mycht have ane chalmer to keip hir in, and sche granted ane
chalmer; and thaireftir Henry cam furtht of Dunde, and upon
ane nycht at evin brocht Effem Rolland and ane las wytht hir,
and put them in ane chalmer quhair they remanit xvj dayis;
bot al the tyme, nethir be day nor nycht, saw nevir Henry
Lawmontht wytht the said Eufame in chalmer thair alane, nor
knew hym to ly wytht hir: and forthir knawis nocht.

Die Mercurii, vigesimo octavo Novembris 1571.

Lawmontht,
Rolland, *rij
quinto Decem-
bris.*

The seat hes ordanit Dauid Orme, Elene Lawmontht his
spous, [*James*—deleted] Patrik Ramsay, Margaret Ballone his
spous, William Ademson tailyowr, Henry Anderson, Jsobel
Methtwen his spous, Dauid Loutheane and Beiggis Corby
servandis to Dauid Orm, to be warnit to compeir befoir the
session upon Wedinsday the v day of December nixt to cum,
to bear witnessing in the caus of inquisition abone wryttin.

Die Mercurii, quinto Decembris anno Domini 1571.

Lawmontht,
Rolland, *rij
xij° Decembris.*

In the terme assignat be the sessioun to Dauid Orm, Elene
Lawmontht his spous, Patrik Ramsay, Margaret Ballone his
spous, William Adamsoun tailyowr, Henry Andersoun, Jsobel
Meffen his spous, Dauid Lawtheane and Beiggis Corby servandis to the said Dauid Orm, to compeir to testifie in the
action of inquisition of adultery betwix Henry Lawmontht and
Eufame Rolland, comperit Patrik Ramsay; and for the rest
nocht comperand, the sessioun ordeins thame, togethir wytht
James Ramsay tailyowr, Elizabetht Myilson his spous, and

Male Kengzow thair servand woman, to be warnit to this day aucht dayis ; wytht certification, gyf thay compeir nocht, they sal be warnit opinlie and [be][1] public admonition in write in the kirk.

1   Patrik Ramsay, sworne in presence of the session and examinat, deponis that he kennis na thing, except that he hard be bruit wythtin this citie, that Henry Lawmontht brocht Eufame Rolland to Waltir Makkeson hows,[2] and that he convoyit hir out of Dunde to the said Waltir hows, and out of that to Crawmound.

2   William Adamsoun tailyowr kennis na thing in the mater, except of bruit and sayingis wythtin this citie, quhilk of na way he wil affirme to be of veritie.

Die Mercurii, duodecimo Decembris 1571.

In the terme assignat be the sessioun to Dauid Orm, Elene Lawmontht his spous, [*Patrik Ramsay*—deleted,] Margaret Ballone spous to Patrik Ramsay, Henry Andersoun, Jsobel Meffen his spous, Beiggis Corby and Dauid Lowdeane servandis to Dauid Orm, James Ramsay tailyowr, and Elizabetht Myilson his spous, and Male Kengzov thair servand, to compeir to testifie in the caus of inquisitioun of adulterie betwix Henry Lawmontht and Eufame Rolland, comperit James Ramsay, Beiggis Corby, Besse Myilson, and Male Kengzow. The seat assignat this day aucht dayis to do diligence for the witnes nocht comperand, be opin admonitioun in the kirk for the witnes nocht comperand. Lawmontht, Rolland, *rij*.

3   James Ramsay, tailyowr, witnes, sworn, deponis that he saw Henry Lawmontht at syndry tymis pas up to Waltir Makesoun foir chalmer, quhair Eufame Rolland as he hard say was, and as he hard say that Henry borrowit the chalmer fra Waltir Makeson til byng up sum graitht that cam furtht of Flanderis to dry ; and als he hard Thome Layng say that Henry Lawmontht servand cam to the Elenehill to borrow ane hors, and horsit Eufame Rolland ; bot quhair he had hir to kennis not.

---

[1] Omitted.   [2] *Hows hows* in MS.

4   Beiggis Corby, servand to Dauid Orm, witnes, sworn and
    examinat, deponis conform to Patrik Ramsay witnes abone
    wryttin.

5   Besse Myilson, spous to James Ramsay tailyowr, witnes,
    sworn, deponis that sche knew nevir that Effe Rolland was in
    Waltir Makeson quhil sche was away; and then hard be com-
    moun voce that sche had bein thair: and forthir knawis nocht
    in the mater.

Wilson in Lam-   The quhilk day, Thomas Wilson in Lambelathem, being
melathem *rij*.   accusat for getting of ane bairne in adulterie with Beiggis Cow-
    den, ansueris, Gyf sche or ony uthir wil affirm in his presence
    that he gat ane bairn wytht hir or ony uthir by his wyf he is con-
    tent to suffer the dead; and denyis the accusatioun *simpliciter*.
    The seat ordanis hym to compe[ir] this day aucht dayis.

6   Male Kenzow, servand to James Ramsay tailyowr, witnes,
    sworn, deponis that sche saw Henry Lawmontht syndry tymis
    pas up Henry Anderson stair; and as sche hard say it was to
    se sum gear that was in Wat Makeson loft of Henry dryand;
    and hard Henry Anderson servand woman tel that Effe Rolland
    was in Wat Makeson heicht chalmer.

*Die Mercurii, decimo nono mensis [Decembris],[1] anno
Domini j^m v^c septuagesimo primo.*

Lawmontht,   The quhilk day, in the terme assignat be the sessioun to
Rolland, *rij*   Dauid Orm, Elene Lawmontht his spous, Henry Anderson,
xxvj^to Decem- Jsobel Methtwen his spous, and Dauid Lowtheane servand to
bris.   Dauid Orm, to compeir to testifie in the actioun of inquisition
    of the adulterie and incest betwix Henry Lawmontht and
    Eufame Rolland, comperit Robert Hew officiar of the seat, and
    verifiit that he warnit al the personis abone wryttin, except
    Henry Anderson quha is presentlie of the cuntre, to compeir
    this day to the effect foirsaid, quhairof comperit Jsobel Metht-
    wen and Dauid Lowdeane.   The seat ordanit Dauid Orm, and
    Elene Lawmontht his spous, to be warnit be officiar of session
    to compeir this day aucht days, failyeing thairof to be warnit
    be public admonition in the kirk.

_____

[1] Omitted.

7   Jsobel Methtwen, spous to Henry Andersoun, examinat,
deponis that sche knew nevir that Eufame Rolland was in
Waltir Makesounis; bot, eftir sche passit and departit furtht
of Waltir Makeson hows, hard say that sche was thair, and
saw Henry Lawmontht cum at sum tymis to Waltir Makeson
hows, bot quhat was his erend the deponent kennis nocht; and
forthir knawis nocht.

8   Dauid Lowdeane, servand to Dauid Orm, knawis na thing in
the mater, bot, eftir Eufame Rolland[1] passit fra Dauid Orm
hows, hard say that sche was in Waltir McKeson hows.

The said day, Margaret Gibsoun producit hir complent *Gibsoun, Ken-*
aganis Johne Kenlowy, desyring hym, according to his promis *lowye, rij*
of mareage to hir maid and defloring of hir virginitie be pro- *xxvjᵗᵒ Decem-*
creation of ane man child betwix them, to compleit the band of *bris.*
matrimonie wytht hir. The said Johne confessit that he begat
ane bairn wytht hir, and desyris the bairn to be admittit to
baptisme, and aucht dayis to ansueir to the rest of the complent. The seat assignat this day aucht dayis, to wit, the xxvj
day of December instant, to ansueir to the clame.

Die Mercurii xxvjᵗᵒ Decembris 1571.

In the terme assignat to Johne Kenlowy to ansueir to the *Gibsoun, Ken-*
clame of Margaret Gibsoun aganis hym, the seat asinnis this *lowy, rij.*
action to this day aucht dayis, wytht consent of parteis under
hoip of concord.

In the terme assignat to Dauid Orm and Elene Lawmontht *Rij Law-*
his spous, to compeir to ansueir to sic things as salbe sperit at *montht, Rol-*
them in the caus of inquisition of adulterie and incest betwix *land.*
Henry Lawmontht and Eüfame Rolland, and gyf they compeir
nocht to be warnit be public admonition in the kirk, comperit
Dauid Orm and, sworn, deponit as eftir fallowis. The seat
assignat this day aucht dayis to Elene Lawmontht, Jsobel
Straquhin, and Thomas Layng in Elene-hyl, to compeir this
day aucht dayis under panis foirsaid.

9   Dauid Orm, sworn and examinat, deponis that he kennis
na thing in the mater bot be bruit; and he, hering say that

[1] *Lowdeane* in MS.

Eufame Rolland was in Grantoun, send to see gyf that was of trewtht, and sche was fund to be thair.

Die Mercúrii, secundo Januarii 1571.

Kenlowy,
Gibsoun.

The said day, in the terme assignat to Johne Kenlowy to ansueir to the complent of Margaret Gibson aganis hym, comperit Johne, declaring that it was of trewtht that Margaret buir ane bairn to hym, and that he deflorit hir virginite ; and thairfoir, according to the law of God, promittit to tochir hir at desyire of hir parentis, and to accept the cuir and cair on hym for upbrynging of the bairn.

Lawmontht,
Rolland, *rij.*

The said day, in the terme assignat to Elene Lawmontht, spous to Dauid Orm, Jsobel Straquhin, ahd Thomas Layng in Elene-hyll, to compeir to ansueir to sic thingis as salbe sperit at them in the trial and inquisition of adulterie and incest betwix Henry Lawmonth[t] and Eufame Rolland, comperit Thomas Layng, quha was resavit, sworn and deponit as eftir fallowis.   And as for Elene Lawmonht and Jsobel Straquhin,

Nono Januarii. they war decernit to compeir this day aucht dayis, uthir wayis to be warnit be public admonition in the kirk.

10   Thomas Layng, in Elene-hill, resavit and sworn, deponis that trew it is he lent ane hors to Henry Lawmontht servand, as he hes doin at syndry utheris tymis, being requirit be his maister ; bot to quhat purpos it was, ethir to convoy Eufame Rolland or uthirways, he kennis nocht.   And of the allegit adulterie and incest committit he kennis na thing, bot be bruit and fame.

Scot,
Hammilton.

The said day, comperit Elspet Hammiltoun and desyrit the bairn begottin betwix hir and Thomas Scot to be resavit to baptisme, becaus he being absent, submittit hir to discipline of the kirk.   The seat, in consideration [that][1] be his bil gevin in befoir, [he][1] confessit hir to be wytht bairne to hym, and desyrit befoir his deperture that the bairn in his absence be resavit to baptisme, and in respect of hir obedience, ordenis that eftir hir impresonment, and satisfaction to the kirk, the bairn to be resavit to baptisme, providing that at the said

---

[1] Omitted.

Thomas resorting to this citie to mak satisfaction, according to the ordour, of impresoning viij dayis, and satisfaction to the kirk.

Die Mercurii, nono Januarii 1571.

In the terme assignat to Elene Lawmontht and Jsobel Straquhin to compeir to ansueir to sic thingis that salbe sperit at them, anent the allegit adulteri[e] and incest committit betwix Henry Lawmontht and Eufame Rolland, comperit Jsobel Straquhin, quha deponit as eftir fallowis. And [the seat]¹ ordanis Elene Lawmontht to compeir this day aucht days, wytht intimation gyf sche comperis nocht sche sal be publiclie admonesed; and forthir, the seat to devis quhat forthir trial salbe takin in the mater, be inquisition to be takin be witnes, or uthir wayis. Lawmontht, Rolland, *rij*.

11   Jsobel Straquhin, sworn and examinat, deponis that sche knawit na thing in the mater bot of voce and fame.

The said day, comperit Johne Kenlowy and desyrit the bairn begottin betwix hym and Margaret Gibsoun to be resavit to baptisme. The seat, nochtwythtstanding that he hes promittit to tochir the said Margaret according to the law of God, nocht the les to tak away the sclandir of fornication committit, ordenis them to be impresoned according to the ordour of fornicatouris, and to mak repentance in the kirk; quhilk being don the bairn to be resavit to baptisme. Kenlowy, Gibson.

Die Mercurii, decimo sexto mensis Januarii 1571.

The quhilk day, in the terme assignat be the seat to Elenc Lawmontht spous to Dauid Orm, to compeir to ansueir to sic thingis as salbe sperit at hir, anent the inquisition of the adulterie and incest allegit to be committit be Henry Lawmontht wytht Eufame Rolland, and the seat to decerne qubat forthir maneir of proces sal be takin in the said caus of inquisition, comperit Elene Lawmontht and ansuerit as eftir fallowis. [Lawmontht, Rolland.]

---

¹ Omitted.

Non tenet.

12   Elene Lawmontht, spous to Dauid Orm, examinat, deponis [that sche][1] kennis nothing, bot that hir gudman, undirstanding that Eufame Rolland was to depart from hym and furtht of his hows, desyrit hir to remain ; and gyf scho wald nocht remain, he sould gar convoy hir honestlie to hir freindis ; and thaireftir the guidman passit to his bed, and he being in bed Eufame past furtht of the hows ; and saw hir nevir sensyne, and hard say sche was in Waltir Makeson hows sex oulkis : and forthir deponis that Dauid Orm, being advertesit be Stevin Orm of hir departour, callit hir and desyrit hir to confess.

12   Elene Lawmontht, spous to Dauid Orm, sworn and examinat, deponis that Eufame Rolland is Henry Lawmontht wyffis sistir dochtir, and as to the rest of the articlis knawis nocht, except that hir husband, being advertesit be Stevin Orm his brother that the said Eufame was to depart furtht of his hows, as the deponent was informit, hir said husband wythtout hir knawledge callit the said Eufame befoir hym in his galrye, desyring hir to remain quhill he send hir away to hir freindis, and gyf sche departit uthirwaiis, they sould na hows in Sanctandros hald hir, and he sould gyf hir up to the town as ane evildoar ; and upon that suspition wythtout thair knawledge sche departit that sam nycht at nyne howris at evin, the guidman being in his bed ; and forthir sayis that sche and hir husband was nocht content wytht the suspition at they at tymis tuik of luking betwix Henry Lawmontht and the said Eufame befoir hir departour ; and mair deponis that sche hard say that the said Eufame was sex oulkis in Waltir Makeson hows eftir sche departit of Dauid Orm hir husband hows ; and forthir kennis nocht in the mater.

13   Henry Andersoun, witnes, sworn resavit and examinat, kennis na thing in the caus except of sum bruit that he hard.

Die Mercurii, penultimo mensis Januarii, anno Domini
$j^{m}v^{c}lxxj^{mo.}$

Confessio Catharine Wilsoun.

The quhilk day, Catharine Wilsoun, servand to Thomas Bredfute, accusat be the seat for fornicatioun committit wytht

---

[1] Omitted.

Thomas Wod, confessit the fail, and als confessit hir to be wytht childe to the said Thomas. In respect of the quhilk the seat committit hir to the magistratis to be punesed according to the ordour.

The quhilk day, Bessy Bawdy confessis Jonet Bawdy hir sister to be presentlie wytht childe to Alexander Kinninmontht in Craighal, spous to Cristen Wilsoun ; and this sche hard of confession of the saidis Alexander and Jonet in hir awn hows, wythtin thir xv days last bipast ; and thairfoir the saidis Alexander and Jonet to be callit to be punesed as adulteraris. *Kinninmontht, Bawdy, adulteri.*

Die Mercurii, sexto die mensis Februarii, anno Domini j^m*v^{c}lxxj*$^{mo.}$

The quhilk day, Mareoun Schewes and Henry Dikesoun being somound wytht the Superintendentis letteres to compeir befoir hym and the seat, to heir and see them decernit to proceid to mareage be resoun of mutual promis of mareage and carnal deal following betwix them, as is contenit in the somoundis, or ellis to alledge ane caus quhye they sould nocht do the sam ; the saidis personis comperand be thair selffis the said Henry passit fra the allegeance of carnal deal and allegit that at Witsunday, in the lxviij yeir, thair was mutual promis of mareage maid betwix them. The said Mareon denyit the sam. And for probatioun the said Henry producit certane famous witnessis, sworn resavit and admittit wytht consent of parteis, and incontinent, being examinat in presence of the Superintendent and seat, deponit they knew na thing of the promis. In respect of the quhilk, the Superintendent and seat absolvit the said Mareon of the said promis, and decernit hir to proceid in mareage wytht James Forret, according to promis thairof laufullie maid betwix them. *Decretum Absolutorum Schewes, Dikison.*

Die Mercurii, vigesimo die mensis Februarii, anno Domini j^m*v^c septuagesimo primo.*

The said day, for guid ordour to be observit, as hes bein of befoir, tweching the tyme of sermone als weil in teaching as hering, alsweil on the Sabbat day as on utheris oulk wark Decrete of the session anent the tyme of the doctrine, alsweil on the Sabbat day as oulk wark dayis.

dayis, the Superintendent, wytht avis consent and assent of the seat, hes ordeined that in tyme cuming the minister sal begin to teache upon Sunday ane litle befoir ten howris befoir nune, and end his teaching sone eftir elevin howris ; and on the oulk wark day to begin at nyne howris befoir nune and end at ten howris, or ellis to compas the houre sa sone as he may guidlie.

Die Mercurii, xxvij° Februarii, anno Domini j^mv^clxxj^mo.

Lawmontht. The said day, the seat ordenis the proces of Henry Lawmontht to be vesiit and sein, and gyf neid beis forthir trial to be takin thairintil, as the seat sal think best.

Die Mercurii, 1571, xij° Martii.

For convention of the eldaris, deakonis, rij. The said day, the seat hes ordeined, wytht consent of Johne, Archibischop of Sanctandros, the heal eldaris and deaconis of this citie to compeir this day aucht dayis, for ordour to be takin in tyme cuming, and remeid to be had for the slaw convening of eldaris and deaconis to the oulklye assemblye, and warning to be maid be the officiar of the assemblie.

Die Mercurii, decimo nono mensis Martii, anno Domini j^mv^clxxj^mo.

Cautio pro Dauide et Jsobella Balfowris. The said day, Mr. Thomas Balfour, in presence of the assemblie, and Mr. Alexander Sibbald, bailye, is becum bund and obligat as cautionar for Jsobel Balfour and Dauid Balfour, that the said Jsobel sal mak satisfaction, for the bairn consavit and born betwix hir and the said Dauid in fornication, wythtin viij dayis eftir sche be convalescit of hir seiknes and risin furtht of hir cheilbedlair ; and siclik the said Dauid, presentlie being of the realm, wythtin aucht days eftir his returning to this citie of Sanctandros ; undir the paine of fourtie pundis, thairof of xx lib. for the said Jsobel, and xx lib. for the said Dauid.

This act concerning Jsobel Balfowr[1] deletit in respect that sche hes alreddy maid hir repentance, and swa M. Thomas Balfour cautionar relevit becaus Jsobel was impresoned. Jo. Bonkil.[2]

---

[1] *Balfowr* is interlined over *Dwry.*

[2] Bonkil was clerk at this time. His entries begin on p. 293. It will be observed that he has a contemptuous disregard for the form of the possessive case, and that he adds a final 't' to all words ending in 'h.'

Die Mercurii, vigesimo sexto Martii, anno Domini j^mv^clxxij^{do.}

The said day, the seat—in respect of the present necessitie Kennethy, that Gilbert Kennedy, quha begat ane bairn wythtin the partis Balcasky. of Carrik wytht Elene Balcasky, and maid satisfactioun and repentence in the parroche kirk of Stratoun wythtin the partis foirsaid, and producit his testimonial thairof of the minister of Stratoun, togethir wytht his fatheris testimonie of his consent to the mareage betwix hym and the said Elene, and that the bannis ar ordourlie proclamit betwix them, and that he may nocht remain fra his maisteris service—hes ordenit hym and Nota. the said Elene to be mareit on Sunday nixt to cum, the penult day of Marche instant, the said Elene the said day makking first hir satisfaction and repentance; providing that this ordinance be nocht prejuditial to the membris of our congregation, nor brocht in use to them that hes nocht the said necessitie in ony cais, bot repentence and mareage to be on several dayis.

The said day, Thomas Wod confessit fornication betwix Wod, Wilson. hym and Catharine Wilson befoir his mareage, and becaus he is nocht nor was indwellar in this towne, the seat decernit hym to be resavit to repentence wythtout impresonment.

The quhilk day, James Makke, walcar, dilatit and accusat *Decretum* for violating and brekking of the Sabbat day, and nocht re- *sessionis contra* sorting to the sermoun and praieris, is decernit be the seat *Makke ful-* *lonem.* that, gyf he beis fund committing siclike in tyme cuming, he sal pay xl s. to the collectour of the puiris almes.

Die primo mensis Aprilis, anno Domini j^mv^clxxij^{do.}

The said day, comperit Henry Kilmoun, cuik, servitour to Kilmovn, my Lord Bischop of Caithnes,[1] and desyrit the bairn gottin Methtwen. betwix hym and [*blank*] Methtwen in fornication to be admittit to baptisme. The seat, in respect of present necessite, hes ordened the bairne to be resavit to baptisme, and gyf evir the said Henry salbe fund to commit fornication again wytht the said [*blank*] Methtwen in tyme cuming, to be cut of fra this

---

[1] See p. 232, n.

congregation, and his offence to be publicat to my said Lord
his maister; providing that [*blank*] Methtwen entir in preson
and mak satisfaction according to the ordour, and that being
doin, the bairn to be baptizat, becaus the man hes alreddy
maid repentence.

Die Mercurii, nono die mensis Aprilis, anno Domini j^mv^clxxij^{do.}

Decretum sessionis penes [Jsobell—deleted] Jonet Balfour.

The quhilk day, the seat hes ordenit [*Jsobel*—deleted] Jonet
Balfour to mak satisfaction according to the ordour, for the
bairn begottin betwix hir and Dauid Balfour in fornication,
and satisfaction maid accordinglie Maister Thomas Balfour to
be fred of xx^{ti} lib. that he becam cautionar for in cais the said
[*Jsobel*—deleted] Jonet maid nocht satisfaction, according to
the act maid in thir bukis, upoun the xix day of Marche last
bipast.

Decreit of the session anent bairnis begottin in adultery or fornication.

The said day, the seat hes decernit and ordeined that in
tyme cuming na bairne, begottin in adulterie or fornicatioun
outwytht [*this citie of Sanctandrois and par*—deleted] this parrochioun of Sanctandrois, be resavit to baptisme, and albeit the
sam be borne in the citie of Sanctandros.

Die Mercurii, xxiij° mensis Aprilis, anno Domini j^mv^clxxij^{do.}

Dewar, Schifwrycht. Storme.[1]

The quhilk day, George Dewar, wobstar, is becum souerte
wytht his awin consent to entir Lucas Schifwrycht, in Ergail, to
ansueir in the seat to sik thingis as sal be inquirit of hym
quhenevir he[2] beis requirit thairto, undir paine of twenty lib.
money of this realm. And the said Lucas is becum obligat
and actitat wytht his awin consent to releif his said sonerte
of the premissis undir paine foirsaid.

Die Mercurii, ultimo mensis Aprilis, anno Domini j^mv^clxxij^{do.}

Decrete of the sessioun anent the fleschearis.

The quhilk day, the fleschearis of this citie undirwryttin
comperit befoir the ministerie, and in thair presence the auld

---

[1] *Storme* has been added.   [2] *Be* in MS.

actis contenit in the bukis of this assemblie was red, quhairin
the saidis flescheris war admonesed to keip the Sabbat day
haly, according to the fourt commandemand of almychty God,
and als the dilatiounis of this instant yeir was red in thair
presence; qubair the saidis fleschearis war dilatit as eftir fallowis, to wit, Martine Lumisden and Alexander Lumisden, and
thair servandis, brekkaris of flesche and sellis the sam upon
Sunday, the saidis Martine and Alexander standand besyid
thair servandis, brekking and selling the said flesche at thair
command; Johne Andersoun, Johne Blak, James Myllar,
Androv Myllar, Thomas Cuthtbert, Patrik Pawtoun, Johne
Williamson, James Herman, James Dempstertoun, Alexander
Watson, and James Cwik, be thair selves brekaris of flesche
and sellaris of the sam, upon the Sunday, in public markat,
violating the Sabbat day; albeit the saidis fleschearis war oft
tymis dischargit be the ministerie and hes nocht obeyit the
sam, bot contemptuusly refusit to obey; and becaus the saidis
fleschearis be continuation of tyme lang bipast hes violatit the
Sabbat day, being yeirly callit and admonesed, and hes nocht
hard the voce of the kirk: heirfoir the ministerie, in presens of
the saidis fleschearis, hes commandit and chargit al and hail the
fleschearis of this citie present for the tyme, and alswa al utheris
that sal succeid in thair place, in the name of the eternal God,
thair selves and thair servandis to abstein fra violating of the
Sabbat day in tyme cuming; and that they nor nane of thair
servandis in tyme cuming slay brek nor sel flesche, privatlic
nor opinlie, upon the Sunday, undir paine of excluding and
debarring of them and thair servandis fra al benifit of the kirk
in tyme cuming, to wit, mareage, baptising of thair bairnis,
and participatioun of the Lordis table, wythtout they mak
public repentence for thair faill, quhilk sal be injoined to them
be the ministerie.

Die Mercurii, septimo Maii, anno Domini j^{m}v^{c}lxxij^{do}.

The quhilk day, the seat hes ordeined that in tyme cuming
nane sal present thair selves to the communion wythtout tikat
resavit fra the clark of the quartar quhair they dwel or
minister. And quha that dois the contrar sal mak public

Nota.
Decreit of
session aganis
them that
presentis thame
selves to the
communion
wythtout tikat.

satisfactioun, and upon thair kneis ask God and the congregation forgifnes.

Die decimo quarto Maii, anno Domini $j^{m}v^{c}lxxij^{do}$.

Ramsay,
Smytht.

The said day, anent the complent gevin in be Jonet Smytht aganis Andro Ramsay, cordonar, makking mentioun that he hes deflorit hir virginite be mutual and carnal copulation wytht hir, and hes promittit mareage to hir, quhilk he refusis to perform ; comperit Andro Ramsay, quha confessit the promis of mareage and carnal copulation as is contenit in the complent, and befoir carnal copulation he desyrit his fatheris consent to marie according to his promis, and could have na ansueir of his father thairof. The seat ordeined Patrik Ramsay and his spous to compeir this day aucht dais, to ansueir to sic thingis as salbe sperit at them.

Die Mercurii, xxj^{mo} Maii, anno Domini $j^{m}v^{c}lxxij^{do}$.

Rekye, Coling.

The quhilk day, Thomas Rekie, in the parrochioun of Logye, and Margarete Coling thair, somoind wytht my Lord Archibischop of Sanctandros letteres to compeir befoir hym, to ansueir to sic thingis as sould be sperit at them anent ane bairn gottin betwix [them][1] in adulterie ; the said Thomas compering be hym self confessit and granted that he had carnail deal wytht the said Margaret, bot yit sayis the bairn is nocht his. Comperit also the said Margaret, and allegit the said Thomas to be the bairnis fathir and na uthir, and for verification thairof that, at the tyme of birtht, in presence of Beiggis Orknay in Kilmany, Besse Mason in Forret Myll, and Cristen Jngrame thair, sche confessit the bairn to be the said Thomas and na utheris.

Ramsay,
Smytht, *rij.*

The said day, in the terme assignat to Patrik Ramsay and his spous to compeir to ansueir to sic thingis as sal be inquirit of thame, anent the promis of mareage maid be Androw Ramsay thair sone and Jonet Smytht, they being verifiit warnit to compeir be Robert Hew officiar of the seat and nocht comperand, the seat ordeined them to be warnit of new to compeir

---

[1] Omitted.

this day aucht dayis to the effect foirsaid, wytht intimation gyf they compeir nocht the seat wil proceid as efferis.

Die vigesimo octavo mensis Maii, anno Domini j^{m}v^{c}lxxij^{do}.

The said day, in the terme assignat to Patrik Ramsay to compeir befoir the sessioun to ansueir to sic thingis as sould be sperit at hym, anent the promis of mareage maid be Andro Ramsay his sone to Jonet Smytht; comperit the said Patrik, quba being demandit be the seat, gyf evir he gaif his consent to the said promis of mareage or was requirit thairto; quha deponit and ansuered that his sone requirit hym to gyf his consent; and Patrik refused aluterlie to gyf his consent thairto. In respect of the quhilk, the seat ordined the said Andro to travel alwais to have his father consent for performing of his promis, uthirwayis to use the libertie that God hes gevin to hym, according to the ordinance of the kirk and privilege grantit in sic casis be the samin kirk.[1] *margin: Ramsay, Smytht.*

Die Mercurii, undecimo Junii 1572.

The said day, Lucas Storme confessit adulterie committit be hym wytht Elizabetht Drowmoind, spous to Thomas Stevinson, and also incest wytht Elspet Wallace his wyffis sistir, or he mareit his wyffe; and thairfoir George Dewar wobstar is becum souerte for the said Lucas that he sal fulfil the heal injunctiounis to be injoined to hym, be my Lord Archibischop of Sanct-andros the kyrk and the assemblie, undir the paine of twenty lib. *margin: Confessio adulterii et incestus Storm. Cautio Storme Dewar.*

Die Mercurii, penultimo die mensis Julii, anno Domini j^{m}v^c septuagesimo secundo.

The quhilk day, the session thinkis expedient ane commis-sion to be gevin to Mr. Robert Hammilton, minister, and Mr. *margin: Decreit of the seat of the commission to commissionaris to the General Assembly of the Kirk[2] to be*

---

[1] While the Reformers insisted that those under the power of others should consult their parents or curators regarding marriage; yet they held that, if these should object on worldly grounds, the matter might be brought before the ministry or the civil magistrate, who, if they found no sufficient cause for object-ing, might 'enter in the place of the parent,' and 'admit thame to mariage' (*First Book of Discipline,* ninth head).   [2] *Kir* in MS.

haldin at Pertht the vj of August nixt to cum. William Cok, ballie, to compeir in the Assemblie General to be haldin at Pertht the vj of August nixt to cum.

Die xxvij⁰ Augusti, j^m v^c lxxij^o.[1]

Decretum Prat, Tullos. The said day, William Prat is decernit be the seat to resave Gelis Tullos his spous in bed and buird, and to intrait hir as becummis ane Christiane man to intrait his spous ; and als the said Gelis to serve hir said spous as becummis in al tyme cuming, undir paine of excommunication.

Die Mercurii, vigesimo secundo Octobris, 1572.

Myllar et Monipenny fornicatores. Gelis Monipenny confessis hir to be wytht childe to James Myllar, sum tyme servand to Dauid Orme, and James confessis hym to have had carnal deal wytht the said Gelis.

Pittillo, Johneson, fornicatores. Jonet Johnestoun confessis hir to be wytht child to Johne Pittillo, servand to Mr. Alexander Jarden.

Brown, Howeson, fornicatores. Agnes Brown confessis hir to be wytht childe to George Howeson, chaepman, in this citie, and als confessit be George Howeson to the dilation foirsaid.

Tweddell et Zowng, fornicatores. Effe Tweddel confessis hir wytht childe to Robert Zowng, servitour to the Laird of Kinkell.

Die Mercurii, quinto die mensis Novembris, anno Domini j^m v^c lxxij^do.

Eldaris.

Mr. Johne Ruthirfurd, Provest of Sanct Saluatoris Colleage
Mr. James Wilke, Principal of Sanct Leonardis Colleage
Mr. Archibald Hammiltoun,[2] professour in the New Colleage
Mr. Alane Lawmontht
Mr. Thomas Balfour

James Robertsoun	Charles Geddy
Mr. William Cok	Mr. Johne Bonkil
Johne Motto	Mr. James Wemis of Lathokir
Dauid Walwod	Andro Wod of Strathtwethye
Thomas Walwod	James Forret of Polduff.

---

[1] *lxxvij⁰* in MS., evidently by mistake, as otherwise the entry would not only be misplaced, but misdated, for in 1577 the 27th of August was a Tuesday.

[2] Archibald Hamilton was one of the five Hamiltons who entered St. Mary's

Diaconis.

James Brydie	William Main
Alexander Crastaris	Alexander Hay
William Zwill	George Blak
William Gyfferd	Thomas Layng in Eleinhill
Alexander Myllar	Andro Lawson in Nethir Magas
	Dauid Foster in Kincaple.

The form of the aitht gevin be eldaris and diaconis, wytht certaine particular actis and ordinances concerning the ministerie and sessioun.

We sweir and promisis, conform to the chairge this day injoined to us, to stay remove and wythtstand according to our power al idolatrie blasphemie disordour, and al uthir thingis contrar the Word of God, reformatioun of the Euuangel, and form of discipline resavit conform to the Word of God, and to advertis thame to quhom it sal appertein as occasioun salbe offered. *Nota.* [The aitht gevin be eldaris and diaconis, wytht certaine actis concerning them.]

Item, quhen we sal undirstand ony thing worthie to be reportit to the seat, that we sal, wythtout hetred favour or affectioun particular, declair the sam ethir be word or write to the minister or redar, that this parrochioun may be haldin clein, and ordour of discipline in the fear of God observit.

Item, that al thingis, enterit in and disputat amangis us, to the end off the final conclusioun, salbe kepit secrete ; and then being askit of ony persoun tweching the equite thairof and quhat was thair part, we sal refer us semplie to the decreit wythtout ony excuse of our awin persoun, undir paine of infamie and depositioun of the seat.

Item, wytht guid conscience we sal dischairge in al pointis

College in 1552. He was appointed a regent in that college in 1558, and 'was promoted from the professorship of Rhetoric to the station of third master in 1569, and to that of second master in 1575' (Lee's *Lectures,* i. 228, 345, 346). For a long time during Knox's last visit to St. Andrews, Hamilton, 'who at that time made the highest pretences to religion and piety' (Laing's *Knox,* vi. 651), would not attend his preaching, 'bec us that he affirmed, in his teiching, that Hammiltounes wer murthereris ' (Bannatyne's *Memoriales,* p. 262). He afterwards went to France, recanted his Protestantism, and wrote two virulent works against the Scottish Reformers (M'Crie's *Knox,* n. G G G). In connection with the eldership, he will be met with again in this *Register.*

and keip the statutis and ordinances that ar devisit be the
brethir, seat, and General Assemblie, and word of God,[1] and
procuir the sam according to our power.

Item, we, all befoir sworne, assemblit, subscrivis to the act
concerning the tyme of our convening and howre, and promissis
to continew in the sam fra our entre quhill it be absolvit;
providing alwayis that na actionis, ethir of the Superintendentis or ony uthir, be presented befoir us quhill the effaris of
oure awin kirk be decernit and concludit, and thaireftir it be
lesum to depart, gyf that willinglie we find nocht guid to
remain.

Nota.

Item, that na persoun sal remain wytht us, electit eldaris and
deaconis,[2] at voting, wythtout they be tacheris wythtin our
congregatioun, and hes promisit to reveil nothing intrated in
this privat assemblie.

Item, last, that all thingis may be doin wytht guid ordour
and discretioun, we promis that ane onlie sal speak, and everilk
ane sal speak as they sal be requirit, wytht reverence frelie his
jugement, according to his conscience.   And gyf ony conten-
tioun throucht heat of disputatioun ryis amangis the brethrin,
he sal be brotherlye admonesed be the minister, that wytht ane
cumlie ordour all thingis may be concludit.   And gyf the
minister brekkis this ordour that he be admonesed be the
eldaris wytht modestie.   *Lecta et approbata.*

Jo. Bon[kil.]

Die xxj° Mai lxj°·

[Here the entry, ' Anent the absens fra the sait,' already
printed on p. 72, is re-inserted, with a few very slight and
unimportant variations.   There is most difference in the final
clause, which here reads :—' for ilk falt to the box of the puir
onforgevin.']

---

[1] The words *and word of God* are in the margin, and are indicated by marks
to come before *General Assemblie*, thus throwing both the *ands* together.

[2] The words *electit eldaris and deaconis* are added in the margin.

*Die Mercurii, decimo nono mensis Novembris, anno Domini
millesimo quingentesimo septuagesimo secundo.*

The said day, the sessioun hes statute and ordinat the towne *Nota.* to be quartered, to the effect that trial may be takin of the Statut of confession of thair faitht befoir the public fasting and com- cerning trial, munioun nixt to be celebrat. And the inhabitantis namis of &c. this citie to be rollit, according to the act statut red and approvit yerlye in this kirk.

Die Mercurii, tertio Decembris, anno Domini j^{m}v^{c}lxxij$^{do.}$

The quhilk day, the sessioun statut and ordeined the names *Nota.* of them that wilfullie absentit thame fra the last communioun Statut for trial to be presentit to the seat, and to that effect trial to be takin of th^{e}m th^{at} of everilk quarter be the ministeris and examinatoris thairof: absentit thame and siclik that inquisitioun be takin be dilatioun of them that munion and ar commoun bidars from the doctrine and preachingis the fra the doctrine dayis appointeid thairto; and to begyn the premissis this day and preaching, aucht dayis, to wit, the tend day of December instant.

Die Mercurii, decimo Decembris, anno Domini j^{m}v^{c}lxxij$^{do.}$

The said day, in the term assignat to tak trial of them that [Absentis abaid fra the last communioun and to gyf up thair namis in communion.] write—

Comperit James Brebner and confessit that he nevir communicated sen the beginning of the religion.

Thomas Wobster confessis that he was nevir at the communion bot anis, and then was admittit in hoip that he sould have lernit.

James Donald, seeman, confessis hym nevir to have bein at the communioun.

Alane Steil, wobstar, confessit hym to have bein fra the last communion, and communicated nevir bot twys, and cam nevir to examination bot twys.

Johne Lundy, servand to the Ladyis of Culuthy and Ardre, nevir communicated, and confessis that he was warnit be

George Blak and William Main to cum to the last communioun and gyf confession of his faitht.

Thomas Orok confessis hym nocht to [1] have communicated thir sevin yeris bygain, and can nocht say the Lordis Prayer.

Confessio Ade, and approbation of our relegion.

Stevin Ade, masoun, being callit and accusit for nocht cuming to the last communioun, nor yit sen beginning of Reformation, ansuered that he was nocht evir remanent heir, yit in Brechein hes twys communicated wyth M. Johne Helpburn; and promisit to bryng ane testimonial thairupon betwix this and the first of Aprile nixt to cum; and ratifiis and apprevis our religion, renuncing the Pap, mes, purgatorie, wytht the hael rest of utheris abominatiounis, and he being present promittit to communicat at the nixt celebration of the Lordis Suppir, &c.

Confessio Myllar.

Patrik Myllar, cowper, being dilatit for hurdom wytht Jsobel Ramsay quha buir ane barne to hym at Alhalowmes last was, Patrik confessis hym to have had carnal deal wytht hir at Candilmes last was. Jonet Gibson being present tyme of birtht of Jsobel Ramsay [*and also Katerine and Wiliam*—deleted] and fathered the bairn upon Patrik Myllar.[2]

Hardy, Mark, fornicatoris.

Jsobel Hardy confessis hir to be wytht childe to Dauid Mark servand to Henry Wilsoun maltman.

Die Mercurii, vigesimo quarto mensis Decembris, anno Domini millesimo quingentesimo septuagesimo secundo.

Confessio adulterii Mark.

The said day, Margaret Mark, spous to Androw Brown tailyowr, grantis hir to have bein absent fra cohabitatioun of hir said spous thir five yeris bygaine, and committit adulterie wytht Gilber Hay, brother sone to the Laird of Langnedrye, in Edinburgh, in Dauid Lowsoun hows, tailyowr, and usit the said Gilbertis cumpanye be the space of ane quartar of yeir, twa yeir syne. The ministerie, in respect of the adulterie confessit, ordenis the said Margaret tō be punesit as ane adulterar in sekclaitht, according to the ordour of the Kirk.

Johne Tailzowr.

The said day, Johne Tailzowr, seeman, confessit hym nevir to have bein at the communioun thir tuelf yeris bygain, and

---

[1] *t* in MS.

[2] This entry has been roughly scored out.

confessis that he imbrases the religioun, and was absent of the
realm tyme of celebration of communioun.

Johne Bell, cuik, nevir communicat bot twis, alleging hym Johne Bel.
to be absent of the town tyme of the celebration of the communion, and promittis in tyme cuming to hant the communion,
and is nocht knawing to be ane contemnar.

[Johne—deleted] George Craik nevir communicat and can George Craik.
say no thyng.

Nicol Howat nevir communicated.   Nicol Howat.

Die Marcurii, vigesimo primo Januarii, anno Domini
j^m v^c lxxij^do.

Androv Law presentit his bairn to baptisme, and gaif con- Confessio Law.
fessioun o[f] his faitht, and apprevit the religioun and ministratioun of the sacramentis usit in this congregatioun; and
promittit in tyme cuming to frequent the preaching and
prayaris, and to communicat quhen tyme servit; and this
promis was maid in presence of the congregatioun.

The quhilk day, the seat concludit and ordinat that the Nota.
personis off and membris of this sessioun that absentis thame Decretum
selves in tyme cuming, and cummis nocht the oulk day sessio'ti^. p^en es
appointed to sitt, that they be punisched according to the act absentes a
maid of befoir, wythtout exceptioun of personis and forgeving sessione.
to ony man, wythtout the absent have lawful impediment and
the sam apprevit be the sessioun.

Item, siclik,[1] it is statut and ordinat, anent the punischement Nota.
of adulteraris and fornicatoris in tyme cuming, that the session Statutum
send thair supplication to the magistratis of this citie, to execut sessionis penes
the actis and ordinances of the seat, and also to tak ordour adulteros for-
wytht thame that ar warnit to compeir befoir the seat and com- njcatoris et
peris nocht; and George Blak to present the supplication and c^ntuma^es
to report ansueir to the seat. And siclik the sessioun desyris violatores Sab-
the actis aganis the brakeris of the Sabbat day to be put to bati et non
executioun be the magistratis in general and particular, and frequententes
aganis nocht frequentaris to the sermonis, and decane of gild publicas con-
ciones.

---

[1] *Item, it is siclik* in MS.

to do his deutie conserving the sam, [as well as][1] utheris magistratis and maisteris of howsis.

Die Mercurii, vigesimo octavo Januarii, anno Domini
j^mv^clxxij^{do.}

Lumisden *rij.* Margaret Lumisden, relict of umquhill Alane Brown skinner, is dilatit to the seat as ane commoun resetter of Thomas Tullos in Hilcairnie, nycht and day, and to have carnal deal wytht hym and utheris diverss person[is]; and thairfoir the seat ordenis hir to be callit and accusat thairfoir this day aucht dayis.

Admonesit to eschew al sclandir in tyme cuming.

Howeson, Brown, *rij.* *Item,* Johne Howesoun, chaepman, in mutual cohabitation wytht Johne Brown merchand dochtir, keping bed and buird wythtout mareage, to be callit and accusat this day aucht dayis.

Scott, Meffen, *rij.* *Item,* Henry Scot, cuik, dilatit for mutual cohabitation wytht [*blank*] Meffen his harlot of auld, to be callit as said is.

Leyis, Walcar, *rij.* *Item,* Johne Leyis, in Kincaple, frequentis Margaret Walcar his auld harlot, to be callit *ut supra.*

Mark, Hardy, fornicatoris. Dauid Mark, servand to Henry Wilson, confessis Jsobel Hardy to be wytht childe to hym; and committit to the magistraitis to be punisched as fornicatoris.

Die Mercurii, decimo octavo mensis Februarii, anno Domini
j^mv^clxxij^{do.}

Tweddel accusat for brekking of the Sabbat day for thresching of corne. The quhilk day, Hannis Tweddell, accusat for brekking of the Sabbat day in thresching of corne fra fowre howris in the morning quhil foure howris at evin, confessit his offence; the correctioun committit be the seat to the magistratis.

Wallace, Wallace, Storm. The quhilk day, Elspet Wallace, being askit upon ane grite aitht gyf sche schow to Beterage Wallace hir sister, befoir sche was mariit wytht Lucas Storm, that he had carnal deal wytht hir, quha ansuered that sche said to the said Beterage cuming to be mariit [*blank*]. And Beterage ansuered, Now is tyme to speak gyf thair be ony impediment quhy I may nocht mary hym, and said na mair. Also the said Elspet confessis that

---

[1] Probably omitted.

sen the mareage he hes had diversis tymis carnal dail wytht hir, and hes solistit hir to pas wytht hym. Also Beterage sayis, in hir grite aitht, that sche nevir gat knawlege of Elspet hir sister befoir the mareage, that evir Lucas had carnal dail wytht hir; and Beterage requirit, befoir the mareage, al that was in the hows for the tyme gyf they knew ony impedment that they sould schaw the sam, quba said they knew nane.

The quhilk day, the sessioun hes decernit the bairn begottin betwix Patrik Myllar and Agnes Patersoun to be resavit to baptisme, becaus the bairn is seik and waik, and that the said Agnes hes submittit hir to mak satisfactioun at the kirkis desyre and will; and to that effect Dauid Walwod is becum cautionar undir paine of xl liᵬ. And als in respect that the said Patrik hes confessit the bairn to be his befoir us, and oft-tymis of befoir admonesit to present the said bairn and refusit to do the sam, thairfoir in the said Agnes obedience hes ad-mittit the bairn to be baptizat; remitting the said Patrik to be punesed be the magistratis of this citie. *Myllar, Patersoun.*

The quhilk day, M. Johne Ruthirfurd, Charles Geddy, M. George Leslye, and Johne Scot, chosin wytht avis of the sessioun betwix Jonet Dauidsoun and Margaret Mylis, fand falt wytht Margaret Mylis and appointed hir so frelye to mak ane mendis, quhilk the said Margaret did conform to appoint-ment; and thairfoir decernit, that gyf athir of the saidis per-sonis heireftir injure utheris ᵬe wordis, that the falter salbe punesched maist rigorouslie, athir be opin repentence upon the Sabbat day, or gritar as the kirk and sessioun sal thynk ex-pedient, conform to the cryme and circumstances thairof. *Dauidson, Mylis.*

Die Mercurii, vigesimo quinto Februarii, anno Domini jᵐvᶜlxxijᵈᵒ.

The quhilk day, befoir sermoun, Johne Forret, sumtyme callit Schir Johne Forret,[1] Vicar of Swentoun in the Mers *Recantacio Forret.*

---

[1] Perhaps the same John Forret who acted as procurator for John Forret of that ilk (*supra*, p. 117). There can be no doubt, however, as to his identity with the 'Popish priest called Sir John Forret,' whom the Bishop of St. Andrews was charged, in the General Assembly, on the 6th of March 1572-3, with admitting 'to minister the sacrament of baptisme in the Merce in Swinton,

wythtin the diocy of Sanctandros, recantit in maneir eftir
following, willinglie offering hym self as ane subject of the
Archibischoprie of Sanctandros.

Die Mercurii, decimo octavo mensis Martii, anno Domini $j^{m}v^{c}lxxij^{do.}$

Nota.
Statut of the
session anent
Papistis.

The quhilk day, it is statut and ordinat be the sessioun that
the namis of the Papistis wythtin this congregatioun be serchit
and gevin in bil to the minister, that ordour ma be takin wytht
them according to Act of Parliament betwix this and the aucht
Octavo Aprilis. day of Aprile nixt to cum; and siclik the names of al thais
that hes alterages or fundatiounis wythtin the parroche kirk of
this citie of Sanctandros.

Die Mercurii, vigesimo quinto mensis Martii, anno Domini millesimo quingentesimo septuagesimo tertio.

Nota.
Anent the
preistis wythtin
this citie, rij. q.

The quhilk day, that all suspitioun of Papistrie in this
reformat congregatioun be removit, it is ordenit: That the
heal preistis that brukis ony fundatioun wythtin this citie
compeir this day xv dayis, of new to gyf confession of thair
faitht, and to ansueir to sic thingis as sal be sperit and askit of
them, concerning the pointis of religion and observing of the
preaching and doctrine.

Nota.
Ladiis of Ardre
and Culuthie.

The Lady Ardre and Lady of Culuthye and Johne Lundye
thair servand dilatit and suspectit of Papistrie.

Nota.
Besse Brown.

Besse Brown, servand to Schir George Read, Papist and
nevir cam to the communioun.

Nota.
Dauid Mwir.

Schir Dauid Mwir, ane of the fundatioun of our Lady alter
wythtin the parroche kirk of the citie of Sanctandros, ane
Papist unrecantit and obstinet.

---

to whom the Superintendent of Lothian had of before given certain injunctions
which the said priest had not yet fulfilled.' Douglas answered, 'That the fore-
said priest recanted all Papistrie in the Kirk of Sanct Andrews; and thereafter
he admittit him to administer the sacrament of baptisme.' 'The Assembly
ordained the said Popish priest to repair to the Superintendent of Lothian to
receive his injunctions; and in the meantime to be discharged of all office and
function in the Kirk' (*Booke of the Universall Kirk*, Ban. Club, i. 255).

Die Mercurii, anno Domini j^mv^clxxiij^{o.} decimo quinto Aprilis.

The quhilk day, Lucas Storme, schifwrycht, callit befoir the *Confessio incestus et adulterit* session, and accusat[1] of adulterie and incest committit wytht *Storm,* Elspet Wallace, sistir to Beterage Wallace his wyffe, divers and *Wallace.* sindry tymis sen he was mareit wytht the said Beterage, and eftir he was admonesed be the kirk to desist thairfra be public admonitioun in the presens of the heal congregation ; the said Lucas, being of grite penetence as apperit, confessed the said accusation fail and cryme befoir my Lord Archibischop of Sanctandros and sessioun. In respect of the quhilk, the session remittit the punitioun thairof to the magistratis. And the said Elspet confessit the said cryme of befoir in presence of the session, upon the xviij day of Februar last bipast.

The quhilk day, Christen Geddye, dilated to the seat to be *Accusacio Geddy, Eliston,* wytht childe be committing of fornicatioun, denyit the sam ; *fornicatoris.* and gyf it be fund uthir waiis sche to be punesched for the said denyal according to the ordour.[2] And yit, upoun the xxiiij day of Junii 1573, Christen, callit befoir the assemblie, confessit hir to have borne ane woman bairn to Dauid Eliston, quhilk the said Dauid confessit.

Die Mercurii, vigesimo secundo Aprilis, anno Domini j^mv^clxxiij^{o.}

The quhilk day, it is statut and ordeined be the sessioun *Decretum sessionis Storm,* that Lucas Storm and Elspet Wallace be[3] publiclie somound *Wallace.* to cum to repentence for adulterie and incest committit betwix them—to wit, the said Lucas, being mareit wytht Beterage Wallace, committit adulterie and incest wytht the said Elspet —undir pane of excommunication.

Die Mercurii, sexto Maii, anno Domini j^mv^clxxiij^o

The quhilk day, anent the fornicatioun committit be *Nota. Decreit of the* servandis wythtin mennis howsis, alsweil to burght as land *session anent* wytht[in][4] this parrochion of Sanctandros, the seat ordenis *servandis fornicatoris and thair maisteris.*

---

[1] *Accasat* in MS.
[2] The concluding sentence of this paragraph has been added afterwards.
[3] *To be* in MS.   [4] Omitted.

ane supplicatioun to be offered up to the magistratis to consent [to][1] ane act to be maid that quhatsumevir servand committis fornicatioun, the servand maister sal pay the servandis half ffee quhithir it be hael yeir or half yeir to be deliverit to the collectour of the puuir almes, and that the act of xl s. maid on the maister be put to execution, wythtout derogatioun of the punischement of impresoning maid off befoir.

Celebratioun of the communion : examination and dilatiounis befoir the communion.

The quhilk day, tweching the celebratioun of the communioun nixt to be, [it][1] is appointed to be upon Sunday the last day of Maii instant, and the first day of examinatioun to be upon Twisday the nynetein day of Maii instant, and dilatiounis to begin to be takin up upon Furisday the xiiij day of Maii instant.

Die Mercurii xiij° Maii 1573.

Pittillo, Johneson.

The said day, anent the fornicatioun committit betwix Johne Pittillo and Jonet Johnesoun, it is concludit be the seat that they sal mak satisfactioun upon the penitent stuill and mid gre thairof, for the fornication ellis committit. And becaus promis of mareage is alreddy maid betwix thame befoir the redar, and the said Jonet being now in nurischip bund in service, the seat ordenis them to find souertie undir[2] paine of xl lib. to compleit the band of matrimonie betwix them, betwix this and mydsomer in anno etc. lxxiiij.

Die Mercurii, vigesimo Maii, anno Domini jᵐvᶜlxxiij°.

Angus, Dauidsoun, fornicatores.

The quhilk day, Nannis Angus confessis hir to be wytht childe to Thomas Dauidsoun, sone to Agnes Wilsoun, and Nannis confessis na promis of mareage betwix hir and the said

Rogear, Just.

Thomas. And James Rogear and Christen Just confessis ane childe gottin betwix them in fornication, and offeris them to discipline of the kirk, and the kirk remittis them to the magis-

Mair, Gray.

tratis. And Margaret Mair confessis hir wytht childe to Malcom Gray chaepman.

---

[1] Omitted. [2] That undir in MS.

Die Mercurii, tertio Junii, anno Domini j^mv^clxxiij^{o.}

The quhilk day, it is denuncit and schawin to the sessioun Cristell.
that Johne Christal, indwellar in the burght of *D*unde, is ane Nota.
excommunicat persoun, and hantis and resortis to this citie, and sion anent
resavit thairintill and mentenit, to the grite sclandir of the person excom-
sam; quhairfoir the sessioun, for evading of the said sclandir, Dundee.
hes fund and decernit the premissis to be opinlie publist in
pulpet; and, publication being maid, gyf ony persoun or personnis, inhabitantis of this citie, resavis hym in thair hows, bys
or sellis wytht hym, or communicatis or usis cumpany wytht
hym, qubil he be reconsilit to his awin kirk, [they]¹ sal be
giltie of his cryme and excommunicated.

The quhilk day, James Portarfeild is denuncit to the ses- James Portar-
sioun, to absent hym self wilfullie fra the communion and ane feild.
public contemnar of the religioun.

And [*Johne*—deleted] Stevin Robertson, *alias* Sowtar, and Stevin Robert-
his twa sisteris, nevir communicated; and he and his mother son *alias* Sow-
and saidis sisteris lyis in bed togethir.

Item, it [is]¹ denuncit to the sessioun that Alexander Naper Alexander
hes separated hym self fra his wyffe, esteming and allegeing hir Naper.
to be ane harlat and huir, quhilk is ane grite sclandir in this
citie.

The said day, it is decernit be the session that the act maid *Nota.*
in thir bukis, anent them that presentis them selves to the com- Anent them that
munion wythtout tikatis, or wytht fengyeit tikatis, of the dait selves to the
the vij day of Maii 1572, be put to executioun; and likwis the wythtout tiketis
act and statut maid on them that cummis nocht to examina- or feingyeit
tion and communioun.

Die Mercurii, xxiiij^{to.} Junii, anno Domini j^mv^clxxiij^{o.}

The quhilk day, anent the allegit promis of mareage betwix Ednem, Pittillo.
Thomas Pittillo, smytht, and Catharine Ednem, the parteis
comperand be them self, the said Catharine allegit the said
Thomas to have maid promis of mareage to hir *simpliciter* and
now hes rejectit hir be contracting hym wytht ane uthir woman.

¹ Omitted.

Quhilk promis the said Thomas denyit, and allegit that he maid na promis to hir, bot this commoning was betwix them,[1] that gyf the said Thomas fathir and mothir wald be content that he sould marye hir, and that hir freindis wald support hir thairto, he sould be content thairwytht. And the said Catharine, being requirit gyf sche wald preve hir allegeances of promis, said sche could nocht preve the sam; and referrit the said Thomas allegeance of promis *simpliciter* to his aitht, quha sweir his allegeance to be of trewtht and rejectit hir of na wyss, and kennis na thing of hir bot all guid and honestie; and gyf his father and mother wald have consentit he sould mareit[2] hir by ony uthir woman. In respect of the quhilk the seat absolvit them of premissis *hinc inde* geving licence to them to mary in the Lord.

Myllar, Moni-
penny.
Nota.

The quhilk day, William Gyfferd and Thomas Playfeir ar becum souerteis for James Myllar and Gelis Monipenny, that they and ilk ane of them sal fulfill the injunctiounis of the kirk quhenevir they salbe requirit thairto, under paine of xx^{ti} liƀ. In respect of the quhilk, the sessioun hes ordeined the bairn gottin betwix them in fornication to be resavit to baptisme.

Die Mercurii, secundo Septembris, anno Domini j^{m}v^{c}lxxiij^{o}.

Bred.

The quhilk day Robert Bred being accused for brekking of the Sabbat day in leading of his cornis confessit the said fail.

Moreis, Parke,
rij ix Septem-
bris.

The quhilk day, William Moreis, wrycht, is decernit be the sessioun, in respect that he allegis the bairn fathered be Beiggis Parke on hym is nocht his, bot ane uther mannis in the parrochioun of [*blank*] callit;[3] ordanis the said William to preve the sam this day aucht days, the nynte day of September instant, uthir waiis to tak wytht the bairn.

[Guidlat.]

The said day Johne Guidlat maltman, accusat for brekking of the Sabbat day binding of benis, confessit the sam.

---

[1] These words *commoning was betwix them* are added in the margin, and the relative marks indicate that they should be inserted before *this*, not after it; but that order would mar the sense.

[2] *Nevir mareit* in MS., but as the words *ane uthir* have been deleted after *mareit* so should *nevir*.

[3] The name is omitted.

Die Mercurii, decimo sexto mensis Septembris, anno Domini
j^mv^clxxiij^{o.}

The quhilk daye, Johne Gourlay marinar confessis Jonet Myllar to be wytht childe to hym, and the said Jonet confessis the sam, and submittis them to discipline of the kirk.   And Johne Lawsoun baxter is becum souerte for Johne Gourlay, for satisfaction to be maid to the kirk, undir paine of xl. lib., and Johne Gourlay oblist to releve the said Johne Lawson.   And Simon Myllar cowper souertie in like maneir for Jonet Myllar, and the said Jonet to releve the said Simon.

Confessio Gourlay, Myllar.

The quhilk day, my Lord Archibischop of Sanctandros, wytht consent of the seat—nochtwythtstanding the promis of mareage betwix George Neilsoun in the parrochioun of Seres and Elspet Swan, in respect that the said George hes gevin his body and contractit wytht ane uthir woman callit Jsobell Kinsman, and mareit wytht hir in the face of the congregation of Cowper, and efter hir deatht hes contractit of new wytht Jonet Grig and gevin his body to hir—decernit the said Elspet Swan to be fre of hym, and nocht to be compellit to adheir to hym; and als ordenis the said George Neilson to desist and ces fra al forthir adherence wytht the said Jonet Grig, undir paine of excommunication.[1]

Neilson, Swan, Kinsman, Grig.

Die septimo mensis Octobris, anno Domini j^mv^clxxiij^{o.}

Elene Florymound *alias* Oliphant dilatit to the seat to be ane commoun barlat, and to be callit, and the magistratis to tak ordour wytht hir be ordour of ane assis; and now comperit the said Elene and grantit and confessit hir to have had carnal conversation wytht Johne Anderson, servand to Robert Scheves my Lord of Caithnes [2] servand, and that scho hes promis of mareage of hym; and in likwis confessis and grantis hir to have had carnail conversatioun wytht Johne Betoun, servand to George Dowglas, in myd September last was or thairby, wythin the citie of Sanctandros.

Fornicatoris. Oliphant, Andersoun.

Oliphant, Betoun.

---

[1] *Excommunicatio* in MS.   [2] See *supra*, p. 232 n.

Die decimo sexto mensis Octobris, anno Domini ɉᵐvᶜlxxiijᵒ·

The quhilk day, the personis undir wryttin, wytht commoun consent of the inhabitantis of the citie of Sanctandros, war electit and chosin eldaris and diaconis.

Eldaris.

Maister Johne Ruthirfurd, Provest of Sanct Saluatouris Colleage

Maister James Wilke, Principal of Sanct Leonardis Colleage

Maister George Gillespie, regent in the New Colleage

Maister Alane Lawmontht

Maister Thomas Balfour, bailye	Dauid Walwod
	Charles Geddy
Maister William Cok	Maister Johne Bonkil
James Robertsoun, bailye	Andro Wod of Strawethie
Johne Motto	James Forret of Smyddie
Charles Guthre[1]	Grein.

Diaconis.

Alexander Crastaris	William Main
James Brydie	George Blak
William Zwill	James Alane
William Gyfferd	Dauid Foster in Kinkaple.
Alexander Myllar	

Die xxjᵐᵒ mensis Octobris anno 1573. The quhilk day, the actis concerning the ai[tht],[2] hour of assemblie appointed to convein, allowit and red of befoir, war th[is] day red publesed and apprevit.

Die Mercurii, quarto die mensis Novembris, anno Domini ɉᵐvᶜlxxiijᵒ·

Mont, Hagye. The quhilk day, Marioun Dawsoun maedwyf in Ladeddye and ʹJames Mont in Strakinnes being somound to compeir

---

[1] In this year Charles Guthrie is described as master of the fabric of the parish church (*Abstract of the Writs of St. Andrews*, Nos. 140, 147).

[2] The oath taken by the elders and deacons after their election. See p. 369.

befoir the seat to ansueir to sic thingis as sould be sperit at ^{The sessioun} them, comperit the said Marioun. And being examinat anent ^{differris deci-
sioun of this} ane bairn begottin in adulterie betwix the said James and Chris- ^{mater quhil
consultation be} ten Hagye, the said Marion, comperand be hir self, deponis that ^{takin wytht the} sche was wytht the said Christen in the extremitie of hir birtht, ^{General Assem-
plie of the} and demandit of hir quha was the bairnis father, and Christen ^{Kirk.} ansuerit, the said James was the bairnis fathir, in presence of Jonet Lawson in Strakinnes, Jonet Dury thair, Jonet Moreis in Gogston, and Gelis Bawn in Strakinnes, and al this don in Strakinnes. And becau[s] the said James Mont being somound, personlie apprehendit be George Blak redar be word, comperit nocht, the seat ordeined hym to be somound opinlye in the kirk be sundry admonitionis, as use is, to compeir befoir the seat to ansueir for the cryme of adultery in gaetting of the said bairn, undir paine of excommunication.

The said day, anent the soum of iij lib. iiij s. xj d. collectit ^{Ordinance of} be Maister Thomas Balfour and Maister Martine Geddye, to the ^{the seat for
support of} support of Jsobel Adesoun, relict of umquhill Andro Kemp, ^{Jsobel Adesoun
relict of Andro} being in grevous seiknes, at desyre of the assemblie; the said ^{Kemp.} sylvir being presentit to the assemblie, the assemblie decernit the sam to be deliverit to William Main to dispone the sam to the said Jsobel support, to wit, viij d. ilk day sa lang as the said sowm lestis, quhilk sowm the said William resavit to the effect foirsaid.

Die Mercurii, undecimo die mensis Novembris, anno Domini
j^mv^clxxiij^o.

The quhilk day, the membris of the seat having considera- ^{Nota.} tioun of the multitude and grite numbir of infantis wythtin the ^{Decretum ses-
sionis penes} parrochioun of Sanctandros, als weill to Burgh as land, born ^{parentes non
baptizatorum.} of auld and yit unbaptized throwcht necligence and slewtht of thair parentis, quhairby and throw occasioun thairof ane grite numbir of the saidis infantis departis and decessis wythtout baptisme, quhairfoir it is statut and ordinat be the seat that the minister, upon Sunday the xv of November instant, sal publiclie, tyme of assemblie of the hail congregatioun to the sermon, wairn and chairge in general all thais wythtin the parrochioun of Sanctandros, als weil to burgh as land, that hes thair bairnis yit unbaptized, that they present thair bairnis and children unbaptized in the communioun iile[1] wythtin the parroch kirk of the citie of Sanctandros, wytht intimatioun and certificatioun that quha failyeis heirintil they salbe haldin and reput as contemnaris of the holie sacrament of baptisme, Christis verry institution and ordinance, and salbe callit accused and punisched thairfoir accordinglie.

Die Mercurii, decimo octavo mensis Novembris, anno Domini millesimo quingentesimo septuagesimo tertio.

Sibbald, Bred, rij.

The quhilk day, William Sibbald producit his complent and clame aganis Robert Bred, the copie of the clame decernit, the seat assignat this day aucht dayis to answeir, and the parteis warnit to the said day.

Die Mercurii, vigesimo quinto Novembris, 1573.

[Sibbald, Bred.]

The said day, in the terme assignat to Robert Bred to ansueir to the complent gevin be William Sibbald aganis hym,[2]

Nicol, Burell.

The said day, Margaret Nicol, presentlie dwelling in Nydie ground wytht ane woman callit Jsobel Fischear, comperit and desyrit ane woman bairn begottin betwix hir and William Burell in Cairskirdo to be baptized ; and allegit the bairn to be gottin aucht dayis befoir Fasterennis evin last was, and born viij dayis befoir Alhalowmes last was ; and gottin in William Geddyes hows wythtin this citie of Sanctandros, and borne in the said Jsobel Fischearis hows ; and Besse Watsoun in Nydye mydwyffe for the tyme of hir birtht. Comperit the said William Burell and denyit the bairn *simpliciter* to be his, and allegit hym nevir to have had ca[r]nal deal wytht the said Margaret. In respect of the quhilk the seat ordennis forthir t[ri]al to be takin in the mater, and George Seage souerte to entir the said William, sa oft as neid beis and as he sal be chargit, undir pane of xl lib.

---

[1] The south transept of this parish church is still known as the communion-aisle.

[2] This entry here ends abruptly, a blank space being left after it.

The said day, for trial of the allegit adulterie committit Mont, Hagye.
betwix James Mont in Strakinnes and Christen Hagye thair,
the seat thocht gude to call certane maest famous an[d] honest
of lyfe and conversation nychtbouris to the said James Mont,
to testifie alsweil of the lyff and conversation of the said James
as quhat they ken of the bairn born be the said Christen,
allegit to be the said James gottin in adulterie, and letteres to
be direct to somond witnes to that effect.

Die Mercurii, secundo die mensis Decembris, anno Domini
j^m v^c lxxiij^o.

The said day, anent the trial of adulterye committit betwix Mont, Hagie.
James Mont in Strakinne[s] wytht Christen Hagye thar, comperit somound be the seat *ex officio* William Oliphant in Strak-
ynnes, James Crastaris thar, Thomas Minneman thar, Johne
Read thar, Jonet Lawson thar, Alexander Nylson[1] in Grigs-
toun, and Jonet Moreis in Gokstoun; quba being sworn and
severalie examinat, Jonet Moreis and Jonet Lawso[n] deponit
that they hard Mareoun Dawsoun inquire Christen Hagye, in
the tyme of the extremite of hir birtht, quha was the bairnis
fathir; sche ansuerit and said, God lat hir nevir be bettir then
sche was at [that][2] howr bot the said James Mont was the
bairnis father and na uthir.

Die Mercurii, nono de mensis Decembris, anno Domini
j^m v^c lxxiij.

The said day, William Moreis is decernit be decreit of *Decretum*
sessioun, for non presenting the bairn to baptisme begottin *sessionis contra*
betwix hym and Beiggis Parke, and in respect that the said *Moreis.*
William confessèd hym to have had carnal deall wytht the said
Beiggis Parke and suffered the bairn to depart wythtout baptisme, the said William twa several Sundaiis, ilkane eftir
uthir, to sit upon the hieest of the penitentis saiet in sek-
claitht, and to pay to the collecto[ur] of the puir almes xxx s.

The quhilk day, anent the trial of the bairn[3] begottin as is Burel, Nicol.

---

[1] Perhaps *Mylson.*   [2] Omitted.   [3] *Borun* in MS.

2 B

allegit in adultery betwix William Burell in Karskirdo and
Margaret Nicoll sum tyme servand to William Geddye maltman, comperit the said William Geddye, Beterage Gudlat his
spous, and Robert Geddy the said William sone, witnessis,
somond to testifie quhat they ken in the said mater. The said
William examinat deponit he knew nathing. Beterage deponit that sche hard William Burrel brother say that sche lay
ane nycht wyth them : and asking hir quhy sche lay wyth them,
sche ansuered, It was better to ly in cumpany nor in ane cauld
bed. And Robert Geddy deponit that, ane day in the morning,
he hard William Burel and the said Margaret Nicol hand-
speking in thair bed togethir, in the chalmer nixt the hal ; and
the said Margaret Nicol confessed that the said William Burel
had nevir carnal dail wytht hir bot anis, and that viij dayis
befoir Fasterennis-ev[in] last was, in ane bed betwix the brew
hows and the hal. And Johne Bur[el] witnes examinat deponis he kennis nathing in the mater.

Nota.
Decretum of the
session for con-
temnaris of the
sacrament of
baptisme.
The said day, the seat ordeined the minister to mak public
admonitioun upon Sunday nixt to cum, to al theis that hes
thair bairnis to be baptised, and hes nocht gevin up thair
names in the day appointed nor yit presented thair bairnis,
that fra this furtht they be accusit and punisched as contemnaris of the sacrament of baptisme.

Die Mercurii, xvj^{to} Decembris, anno Domini j^{m}v^{c}lxxiij^{o.}

Zowng,
Tweddell.
The quhilk day, comperit Robert Zowng, servand to the
Laird of Kinkel, desyring the bairn begottin betwix hym and
Effe Tweddel to be baptised, allegeand that he knew nocht the
admonition maid to them that presented nocht thair bairnis to
baptisme. [The seat] [1] hes ordeined the saidis Robert and Effe
to present thairselves to the penitent stuil of the parroche kirk
of this citie, and the said Robert to pay to the collectour of
the puir almes v s., and that being doin the bairn to be baptised ; and for performing heirof Johne Moreis baxter souertie
for Robert, and the said Effe hes fund M. Thomas Balfour
cautionar that [at] [1] the furtht rinning of hir nurischep sche sal

---

[1] Omitted.

cum to be impresoned, according to the ordour undir paine [of]¹ xx liᵬ.

Die Mercurii, vigesimo Januarii, anno Domini jᵐvᶜlxxiijᵒ·

The quhilk day, Patrik Myllar cowper is decernit be decreit of the sessioun to marie Catharine Donaldson, his handfast wyf, betwix this and Fasterennis-ewin, and to gyf to the puir x s. For payment of the quhilk William Main is cautionar, and Patrik to releve his cautionar. *(margin: Myllar, Donaldson.)*

The said day, George Saige in Ergail is becum souerte and cautionar for William Burell in Kairskirdo, to fulfil the ordinance of this sessioun anent the bairn begottin be hym as is allegit in adulterie wytht Margaret Nicoll, eftir consultation be takin in the General Assemblie of the Kirk, undir paine of ane hunderitht merkis, and the said William to releve the said George undir pain foirsaid, and William Muffat baxter cautionar for Margaret Nicoll to releve hir cautionar. *(margin: Burell, Nicol, Saige. The General Assemblie.)*

The said day, the sessioun hes ordeined the bairn begottin betwix Andro Weland and Agnes Andersoun to be resavit to baptisme, in respec that Besse Law mydwyf, Elen Hwnyman and Besse Lawson, deponit that they² war present wytht the said Agnes the tyme of hir birtht, and hard hir confess the bairn to be Andro Welandis. *(margin: Decrete of reset of Agnes Andersonis bairn to baptisme.)*

Die Mercurii, vigesimo septimo Januarii, anno Domini jᵐvᶜlxxiijᵒ·

The quhilk day, it is ordinat be my Lord Archibischop of Sanctandros³ and the heal membris of sessioun to be in- *(margin: Nota. Anent the superstitius keping of Zwillday haly.)*

---

¹ Omitted.　　　　² *The* in MS.

³ It is somewhat remarkable that this, the last occasion on which Douglas is mentioned as being present in the Session, is in connection with the suppression of the observance of Yule or Christmas. On the 6th of March 1573-4, Douglas was charged in the General Assembly with various faults, and among others, ' That he was not only Bishop, but Rector of the University, and Provest of the New Colledge; that he preached not in Sanct Andrews, where he made his residence.' In his defence he urged that since the previous Assembly he had been continually sick, and ' promised to preach in time coming according to his .ability,' and said that he was content to demit ' the Rectory and Provestry,' ' how soon my Lord Regents Grace and Commissioners shall come to Sanct

serit[1] in thir bukis, *ad futuram rei memoriam*, that quhow upon Sunday the xxiiij day of Januar instant Waltir Ramsay lorymar, Waltir Lathangye cultellar, and Johne Smytht blaksmytht in Ergail, being accusat and convictit of befoir for observing of superstitious dayis and spetialie of Zwil-day, becam penitent and maid opin satisfactioun thairfor in presence of the heal congregation then being present. And thairfoir the minister, at command of the assemblie, publiklie denuncit the said Sunday that al personis, wythtin this parrochioun, that observit superstitiouslie the said Zwil-day or ony utheris dayis, sould be punnischeid in lik maneir; and siclik sould be punished in like maneir gyf they abstenit fra thair wark and lawbour that day, mair then ony uthir day except Sunday, quhilk only sould be kept haly day.   And heirupon the session interponit thair decreit.[2]

Andrews for visiting of the Colledges' (*Booke of the Universall Kirk*, i. 286, 287). Petrie relates that 'within some weeks after that Assembly John, called Archbishop of Santandrews, went into the pulpit to preach, and falling down died' (*Compendious History*, part ii. p. 384). But James Melvill speaks of him in August 1574 as 'newlie departed this lyff' (Melvill's *Diary*, Wod. Soc. p. 47); and the date of his death is more exactly fixed as the last day of July in that year (*Diurnal of Occurrents*, Mait. Club, p. 341).   Martine and Lyon erroneously place it in 1576. 'The disastrous ends of all the promoters of prelats in these days,' namely, Morton, Douglas, Arran, and Adamson, says a keen Covenanter, 'may justly cause their course the rather to be shunned and detested' (*Naphtali*, 1667, pp. 41, 42).   To this warning Honeyman replies: 'If Mr. Douglas, Archbishop of St. Andrews, dyed (as he saith) in the pulpit, some perhaps may think that a glorious end, while a faithful preacher was drawing others to Heaven to slide in himself' (*Survey of Naphtali*, part ii. 1669, p. 239).

[1] Inserted.

[2] For much interesting information concerning the pagan origin and superstitious customs of Yule, see Jamieson's *Dictionary* and Brand's *Popular Antiquities*, and, for its religious observance, Bingham's *Antiquities*. In *The Gude and Godlie Ballates* (Laing's ed. pp. 43, 45, 61, 66) there are four pieces which may be described as Christmas songs or carols, and another (P. 63) is entitled—'Ane Ballat of the Epistill on Christinmes Evin'; but in the forefront of the *First Book of Discipline*, ' the keeping of holy dayis of certane sanctis commandit by man, suche as be all those that the Papistis have invented, as the feistis (as thai terme thame) of appostillis, martyres, virgenis, of Christmess, Circumcisioun, Epiphany, Purification, and uther fond feistis of our Lady,' is included among those things which should be ' utterlie suppressed as damnabill to mannis salvatioun.'   The General Assembly, in 1566, in approving of the later *Helvetic Confession*, excepted that part which allowed the observance of saints' days and days dedicated to Christ (*Booke of the Universall Kirk*, i. p. 90); but it was no easy task to suppress the old customs even in Scotland, and the Assembly was

The said day, James Clwny cultellar and Waltir Zownger being accusit for violating of the Sabbat day be superstitius keping of Zwill-day haly day, and abstening fra thair wark and lawbour that day, James Clwny promittit to desist and ces·fra keping of Zwil-day haly in tyme cuming, undir pain contenit in the act immediatlie preceding. And Waltir Zownger, attour the premissis, being accusat that he did that was in hym to mak his nychtbouris disobedient to the kirk, sayand, in the Gallowlaik,[1] that it becam nocht honest men to sit upon the penitent stule; quhilkis wordis he confessit: and als said that he is ane yowng man and saw Zwil-day kepit halyday, and that the tyme may cum that he may see the like yit; and thairfo[r] wald nocht becum oblist nor astrictit in tyme cuming to work or abstein fra wark that day, bot at his awn plesure. In respect of the premissis, the session decernis and ordenis hym to be admonesed be public admonitioun to mak satisfactioun upon the penitent stuil undir pain of excommunication, and als in respect that he being requirit wald gyf na uthir ansueir nor yit submit hym to the voce of the kirk.

Die Mercurii, tertio Februarii, anno Domini j^mv^c
septuagesimo tertio.

The quhilk day, Johne Sourdie, accused for keping of Zwil- day, confe[ssit] the sam; and being chargit that he sterit up

---

exercised over the matter in 1575, 1577, and 1596 (*Ibid.* pp. 334, 339, 389, 874). The Presbyterian reasons for rejecting those days have been ably stated by Calderwood, in his *Perth Assembly*, 1619, pp. 63-86, and in his *Re-Examination of the Five Articles*, 1636, pp. 139-144, 187-209; and by Gillespie in his *Dispute against the English-Popish Ceremonies*, 1637, part i. pp. 20-36, part iii. pp. 1-15. A curious commentary on the entries in the text is furnished by one who in the following October was elected an elder of this session. In speaking of the ministers of Scotland he says—' In contempt of the uther halie dayes observit in England, thay cause thair wyfis and servants spin in oppin sicht of the people upon Zeul day; and thair affectionat auditeurs constraines thair tennants to yok thair pleuchs on Zeul day in contempt of Christs nativitie, whilk our Lord hes not left unpunisit; for thair oxin ran wod and brak thair nekis, and leamit sum pleugh men, as is notoriouslie knawin in sindrie partes of Scotland' (John Hamilton's *Facile Traictise*, 1600, pp. 173, 174).

[1] The *Gallowlaik*, or, as it is sometimes called, the *Gallow-hill beside the citie*, was the general meeting-place of the crafts.

the uthir brethrin accused for the said caus till have disobeyit
the kirk, denyis the sam al u[t]terlie ; in the menetyme submittis hym self to correction of the kirk g[yf] he sal nocht use
Zwil-day as ane uthir warkday in tyme cuming, and to mak
public repentence in face of the congregation gyf evir he cum-

Obedientia
Days fabri.

mis in the contrar.   And likewis Johne *D*ays, smytht, being
accused for superstitious keping of Zwil-day, confessed the
sam and oblesit hym to absten in tyme cuming undir pain foir-

Crastaris.1

said.   And Andro Crastaris, smytht, accused as Johne Dayis,
denyit *simpliciter*, and admones[ed] to absten fra keping of

Alexr. Smytht,
Thomas Pla-
feir,

Zwil-day haly day undir pain foirsaid.   Alexander Smytht and
Thomas Plafeir hes promittit to obey the voce of the kirk,
and to abst[en] in tyme cuming fra the superstitius keping of

Io. Thomson.

Zwil-day : and s[ic] like Johne Thomson wrycht.

Die Mercurii, decimo Februarii, anno Domini j^{m}v^{c}lxxiij^{o}.

Obedientia
Zownger.

The quhilk day, Waltir Zownger cam to agnitioun of his
disobedience, and offered hymself to undirlye the correction
quhatsumevir the ministerye wil injone to hym, for his non
comperence being twis admonesed and stubborn ansueir gevin
be hym, accused for the superstitious keping of Zwil-day, as is
contenit in the act of thir bukis the xxvij day of Januar last
was.

Obedientia
Brown, Scharp,
Pittillo,
Cuthtbert,
Bruce smytht,
Muffatt smytht.

The said day, Dauid Brown tailyeor, Alexander Scharp
baxter, Thomas Pittillo smytht, Charles Cuthtbert smytht,
denyis al keping of Zwil-day, nor yit that they gaif counsel to
the disobedience to the kirk,[2] and promittit nevir to do the sam
in tyme cuming, bot evir to be obedient to the voce of the kirk,
and cheiflie Charles Cuthtbert.   Dauid Brwce smytht promittis
obedience in lik maneir.   Andro Muffat smytht promittis obedience in tyme cuming.   Dauid Blair saidlar, Charles Hageye
smytht, Alane *D*ewar smytht, William Swyne cowper, Patrik
Brown cultellar, Dauid Brwce and his eldest sone wobstaris,
James Murdo smytht, Johne Jakson smytht.

---

[1] *Dayis* in MS.   [2] *Kir* in MS.

Die Mercurii, vigesimo quarto Martii, 1573.

The decisioun of the General Assemblye of the Kirk.   *Nota.*

It is thocht that quha lyis wyth ony woman and the sam *Fathering of bairnis.* woman *tempore partus* layis the bairn on hym, he sal be haldin father to the bairn, the man confessing hym to have carnal dail wytht the woman wythtin the yeir; and for moir verificatioun thairof thinkis the midwyffis and wemen being wytht hir for the tyme athis to be takin.

Item, it is thocht resonable that quhen ony bairn is fatherit *Fathering of bairnis.* upon ane man, les nor he confes carnal dail wytht the woman, or ellis be sufficientlie provin, that the man be absolvit tharfra, he purgen hym self of carnal deal; and gyf athir he confes carnal dael or yit be provin, sche laying the bairn upon hym the tyme of birtht, that he be the father tharof.

Die Mercurii, ultimo Martii, anno Domini j^{m}v^{c}lxxiiij$^{to.}$

The quhilk day, according to the determinatioun of the *Burell, Nicol, adulteri.* General Assemblie of the Kirk, William Burel in Karskeirdo and Margaret Nicol being confronted anent the bairn begottin betwix them in adulterie, the said Margaret constantlie affirmit the bairn was gottin be the said William and na uthir; and the said William als constantlie denyit the sam. The seat heirfoir hes superseid thair determination in the said mater quhil forthir consultation be takin; and the said William souerte, to wit, George Seage to stand stil. And the sam to be doin *Mont, Hagye.* James Mont in Strakinnes and Christen Hagye; and James now confessis that on Lames day befoir the said Christen birtht he bald the said Christen pas of the cuntre, for the suspition that rais and brute that he was the bairnis father, &c.

Die Mercurii, quinto Maii, anno Domini 1574.

Nota.

The quhilk day, the seat ordenis ane supplicatioun to be *Anent wemen adultrices* direct to the magistratis of this citie to mak thair decrete and *nocht to be ad-* ordinance, that fra this furtht, for cleingeing of this citie of *mittit to be nurices and to* filthie harlottis and adulterices, that na woman harlot or adul- *that effect* trice be sufferit to be nurices in this citie in tyme cuming. *supplicatiounis to be direct.*

Lawsoun,
Wischart, adul-
teraris.

The quhilk day, Johne Lawsoun, baxter, and Margaret Wischart, spous to Alexander Layng, dilatit to the seat for adulterie committit be them, comperand be thame selves, confessit the committing of the said cryme, and submittit them selffis to correction and discipline of the kirk, and promittit to fulfil the heal injunctiounis to be injoned to them be the kirk and the heal ordinance thairof.

Lawsoun,
Chaeplen, *rij.*

The quhilk day, Jonet Lawsoun producit hir clame aganis Johne Chaeplen, the clame being red Johne denyit the sam. The seat assignit this day aucht days to preve the sam.

· *Mercurii, duodecimo Maii,* 1574.

Lawson,
Chaeplen.

The quhilk day, in the terme assignit to Jonet Lawson to preve hir clame aganis Johne Chaeplen, comperit the said Jonet and allegit sche had done diligence for witnes, and could nocht have them. The seat assignit hir this day aucht dayis, to wit, the xix of Maii instant to do diligence for hir witnes, or nocht to be hard in tyme cuming.

Die Mercurii, decimo nono Maii, 1574.

Lawson,
Chaeplen, *rij.*

The quhilk day, in the terme assignit to Jonet Lawson to do diligence for hir witnessis for probation of hir clame of mareage aganis Johne Chaeplen, the said Jonet producit Maister Johne Winram, Andro Lawso[un], and Andro Crastaris smytht. M. Johne Winram, examinat, deponis that he hes lukit his bukis and can find nathing tharintil, and forthir kennis na thing of the promisses of mareage betuix the saidis parteis, and forthir referris to his awn bukis and bukis of this assemble, quhilk sal be patent quhen reson sal be requirit. Andro Lawson repellit fra bearing of witnes becaus he is solistar[1] in the caus. Andro Carstaris, examinat, deponis that he hard Johne Chaeplen say in the Superintendentis chalmer that ethir he sould marie Jonet Lawsoun or satisfie hir. And the seat assignit this day aucht days to do diligence for probation of hir clame as sche wil be servit.

---

[1] Solicitor or agent.

Die Mercurii, xxvj^{to.} mensis Maii, anno Domini j^m v^c lxiiij^{to.}

The seat decernit and ordeined the examinatioun, preced- Anent examina-tors to be chosin:
ing the celebratioun of the communioun nixtocum, to begin fasting and
upon Moninday the vij day of Junii nixt to cum; and Wedins- communioun : *rij.*
day the secound of Junii nixt to cum appointed to cheis the
examinatoris, and to tak ordour anent the fasting and celebration of the communioun.

The said day, in the terme assignit to Jonet Lawson to do Lawsoun,
diligence for probati[on] of promis of mareage betwix hir and Chaeplen, *rij.*
Johne Chaeplen, comperit [Wil]liam Oliphant in Strakinnes for
the said Jonet Lawson, and allegit the m[a]est part of probation of the said promis to consist in ane instrument tak[in] in
Mr. Thomas Zowng notar public hand, quha at this present is
in Lo[w]theane wytht my Lord Lyndesay his maister, and
desyris ane competen[t] day to be assignit for production of
the said instrument, and to do diligence th[air]foir. The seat
assignis this day aucht dayis to do diligence for the said instrument and to produce the sam, and als the said Johne Chaeplen
the sai[d] day to gyf his aitht upon the said promis.

Die Mercurii, nono Junii, 1574.

The quhilk day, Elene Anstroder in Strakinnes denuncit and Colsy, Myllar,
complenit to the seat that Dauid Colsy, hir mareit husband, Anstroyer.
hes, by al godlie ordour, repudiat hir and joned hym self in
adultery wytht Jsobell Myllar, and remanis wytht hir in Rum-
gallye. Baitht the saidis Dauid Colsy and Jsobel Myllar
accusat of the said adulterie, in presence of the seat, confessit *Cautio* Myllar.
the said cryme and fand souertie to obey the injunctionis of the
kirk. Petir Roucht souertie for Jsobel Myllar undir pain of
xl lib.

The said day, Margaret Fowles confessed hir to be wytht Fowles,
childe to Robert Methtwen, and fand caution [*blank*] to fulfil Methtwen.
the ordinance of the kirk.

Mirable Nicol confessed hir to have borne ane mai childe in Nicol, Skadowy,
adulteri wytht William Skadowye in Clattie, and Mirible Nicol adulteri.
now dwellis wytht Robert Tailzeor merchand in this citie of
Sanctandros.

Decretum
Chaeplen *con-*
tra Lawson.

    The said day, in the terme assignit to Johne Chaeplen to compeir to gyf his aitht anent the promis of mareage alledgit maid be hym to Jonet Lawsoun, the said promis being *simpliciter* referrit to his aitht, comperit [the said Johne Chaeplen][1] and swair and maid faitht that he nevir maid promis of mareage to hir, bot onlie promittit to hir ane kow. In respect of the quhilk, and instrument of Maister Thomas Zowng schawn and red, the [*judge*—deleted] seat absolvit the said Johne Chaeplen fra the said promis.

Die Mercurii, xxiij° Junii, anno 1574.

Ordour eftir the
communioun,
rij.

    The quhilk day, the seat ordenis the heal quarteris to be tryit according to the ordour, to have intelligence quha[2] cam nethir to examination nor communioun. And the trial of the first quartar to be takin this day aucht dayis, and the keparis of the bukis to produce the sam, and swa ilk Wedinsday to proceid quhill ending of the said triall.

Corstorphine,
Rudeman,
fornicatoris.

    Beterage Corstorphine in Ergail confessis hir to be wytht childe to Alexander Rudeman servand to [*blank*] Corstorphine in Parkhill.[3]

Die Mercurii, ultimo Junii, 1574.

Nota.
Ordour anent
persons conven-
ing to sermond.

    The quhilk day, for gude ordour to be observit in convening to heir the Word of God upon the Sabbat-day, and uthiris dayis in the oulk quhen the Word of God is preachit, als weill of the studentis wythtin colleageis as inhabitantis wythtin this citie, and utheris wythtin this parrochionis quhatsumevir, the seat hes statut and ordinat captouris to be chosin to vesy the hail town according to the division of the quarteris of the sam ; and, to that effect, every Sunday thair sal pas and vesy ane bailye, ane elder, twa diaconis, and twa officeris inarmit wytht thair halbartis, and the rest of the ballies and officeris to be in redines, gyf they be requirit to assist to them to appre- hend the transgressoris, to be punisched conform to the actis

---

[1] Omitted.   [2] *Qua* in MS.
[3] There has been added in the margin—*Dead, and the bairn baptized.*

of the kirk, and this ordour to begin on Sunday, viz., the xj day
of Julii nixt to cum, and Mr. Thomas Balfour· to begin the
ordour and to continew.

Die Mercurii, septimo die mensis Julii, anno Domini j^mv^clxxiiij^{to.}

Memorandum: of the iij liḃ. iij s., ane hard-head [1] les, gatherit *Adeson relict of Kempt.*
be Mr. Alexander Sibbald and Alexander Crastaris to Jsobel
Adeson, relict of Androw Kempt, thair was deliverit to [2] the
said Jsobell iij s. The rest this day was deliverit to Beterage
Walcar to the support of the said Jsobell, quhairof sche sal *Walcar.*
mak compt quhen sche sal be requirit; and the seat to be na
forthir burdenit to mak support to the said Jsobell.

The quhilk day, anent the supplicatioun gevin in be Marioun *Cok, Boytour.*
Boytour, anent the resaving of the bairn to baptisme begottin
betwix hir and Thomas Cok, the saidis Thomas and Marion
findand sufficient souerte to fulfil the ordour to [be] [3] injoned
to them be the kirk, to resave the bairn to baptisme.

Die Mercurii, decimo quarto mensis Julii, anno Domini j^mv^clxxiiij^{to.}

The quhilk day, the auld Ladiis of Ardre and [*Balgoun—* *Ladiis of Cuilethie*
deleted] Culluthie ar decernit, be decreit of sessioun, to present *and Ardrie.*
thair selffis to examination wytht the landwart folkis in the
nixt oulk, and to cum to the communioun wytht them on
Sunday cum aucht dayis, undir paine of excommunication.

The quhilk day, the seat hes thocht expedient ane writting *Colsy, Myllar.*
to be send to George Scot minister of Kircaldy, to advertis
hym that Dauid Colsy in Bukhawin hes left Elene Anstroyer
his mareit wyffe, and joined hymsel[f] in adulterie wytht Jsobell
Myllar.

---

[1] The value of the base coinage authorised in 1554, and called ' Lions ' or
' Hard-heads,' was ' iij half pennyis ilk pece ' (Cochran-Patrick's *Records of the
Coinage of Scotland,* vol. i. pp. çxxxviii. 98).

[2] *To to* in MS.   [3] Omitted.

Die Mercurii, vigesimo primo Julii, anno Domini j^mv^clxxiiij^{to.}

Nota.
Anent the con
vention to the
assemblye, *rij
xxviij^o Julii.*
The quhilk day, the minister, in respect of the slaw convening o[f] the brethir of sessioun to the oulklie assemblie, hes
denuncit and schawin to the seat that gyf they keip nocht
ordour in tyme cuming to the assemblie, he wil publiclie gyf
them admonitioun in the pulpet t[o] observe the ordour undir
paine of excommunication, according to the actis of [the] kirk.
The sessioun presentlie convenit thinkis expedient the heall
membris of the seat to be warnit to convene this day aucht
days, to hei[r] this protestatioun of the ministeris publist, and
decreit òf the seat gevin, [or]¹ the protestation to tak effect.

Nota.
Anent the
comede askit
to be playit be
M. Patrik
Authinlek upon
Sunday the first
of August nixt
to cum.
The said day, anent the supplicatioun gevin be Maister
Patrick Authinlek for procuring licence to play the comede
mentionat in Sanct Lucas Euuangel of the forlorn sone, upon
Sunday the first day of August nixt to cum, the seat hes
decernit first the play to be revisit be my Lord Rectour,
Minister, M. Johnne Rutherfur[d] Provest of Sanct Saluatour
Colleage, and Mr. James Wilke Principal of San[ct] Leonardis
Colleage, and gyf they find na falt thairintill the sam to be
play[it] upon the said Sunday the first of August, swa that
playing thairof be nocht occasioun to wythtdraw the pepil fra
heryng of the preaching, at the howre appointed alsweil eftir
nune as befoir nune.²

---

¹ Omitted.

² It would have been interesting to know whether this play was well attended
so soon after the sudden death of the first appointed reviser. One thing is certain, the session was soon taken to task for the liberty thus granted. The
General Assembly which met at Edinburgh, on Saturday the 7th of August,
required Robert Hamilton to appear before them, to answer *super inquirendis ;·*
but he excused himself ' be the business of the *Colledge*,' and Wynram's declaration to him ' that the Assembly was to dissolve incontinent.' Instead of letting
the matter lie over, ' The Generall Assembly of the Kirk giveth commission to
Mr. John Spotswood, Superintendent of Lothian, Mr. Robert Pont, Provest of
the Trinity *Colledge*, Mr. David Lindsay, minister at Leith,·John Brand and
the Kirk of Edenburgh, with any three of the fornamed persons, conjunctly to
summon the ministers, elders and deacons of Sanct Andrews to compear before
them, and to try the cause, why the fast was not keeped among them according
to the Act of the said Assembly ; and of the violation of the Sabbath day by
profane playes, and such other things as they shall inquire of them at their
coming ; and what beis done be them hereinto, to certify the brethren in their
nixt Assembly ' (*Booke of the Universall Kirk*, i. 312). On the 17th of February

Die Mercurii, xxviij° Julii, 1574.

The quhilk day, the seat hes ordinat the heal seat to convein this day aucht dayis, and to be warnit to that effect; and triall to be takin of the first quartar of this citie quha cam nocht to the examination and communioun, that ordour may be takin thairintil, and ane tikatt to be gevin to the officer of [*court—* deleted] kirk to warn the heal seat to the effect foirsaid.

The seat to be warnit to this day aucht dayis' rij quarto Augusti.

The quhilk day, the seat ordenis ane supplicatioun to be offered up to the magistratis for reparing and mending of the kirk or the winter season cum in, and the supplication to be presentit be George Blak and William Gyffort in the tolbuitht upon Fryday nixt to cum.

Supplication for reparing and mending of the kirk.

1574-5, these commissioners met and ordained 'ane precept to be direct to sumond the said minister, eldaris, and deaconis;' and on the 24th of that month Robert Hammilton, appearing for himself and as commissioner of his kirk, desired delivery of the heads on which he was to be questioned. These were, why the Act of the General Assembly was not kept anent the fasting; why 'at that tyme Robin Huidis playis wes sufferit to be playit, and thair throw prophanand the fasting;' and if 'ane clark play was playit at the tyme of the preching, at the marrage of Mr. Thomas Balfouris dochter.' In his answer concerning Robin Hood's plays, Hamilton admitted that 'certane servands and young children plaid them certane days,' but,;he added, 'alwayis the kirk bayth prevatlie in thair assemble, and I publiclie in tyme of preching, dischargeit the samen, as it is notorious knawn, and desyrit the magistrattis to tak ordour thairwith.' He further stated that—'Ane clark play wes plaid be the scollouris of the grammar-scull, bot not at the tyme of preching, and yit for causes moving us we dischargeit the mais[ter again?] to play the samin' (Lee's *Lectures*, i. 313, 314). A fortnight later, the 7th of March 1574-5, the General Assembly again met at Edinburgh, and considering 'that the playing of clerk playes, comedies or tragedies upon the canonical parts of Scripture, induceth and bringeth with it a contempt and profanation of the same,' concluded, 'That no clerk playes, comedies or tragedies be made of the canonicall Scripture, alsweill new as old, neither on the Sabboth day nor worke day, in tyme comeing; the contraveiners heirof, (if they be ministers) to be secludit fra thair functioun, and, if they be uthers, to be punischit be the discipline of the Kirk: and ordaines ane article to be given in to sick as sitts upon the policie, that, for uther playes, comedies, tragedies, and uthers profane playes as are not made upon authentick partes of the Scripture, may be considderit befor they be proponit publicklie, and that they be not playit upon the Sabboth dayes' (*Booke of the Universall Kirk*, i. 322, 323). In October 1576, the Assembly peremptorily refused to grant the petition of the town of Dunfermline, asking liberty to play on a Sabbath afternoon 'a certain play which is not made upon the canonical parts of the Scripture' (*Ibid.* p. 375).

Die Mercurii, decimo octavo Augusti, anno Domini millesimo quingentesimo septuagesimo quarto.

Burel, Nicoll,
rij xxv^{to} Augusti.

The quhilk day, William Burell in Kairskirdo is decernit be decreit of the seat to be warnit to compeir this day aucht dayis, to purge hym of the bairn allegit begottin betwix hym and Margaret Nicoll, and his purgatioun being takin in presence of the seat, to mak his purgation opinlye in presence of the congregation on Sunday nixt thaireftir.

Confessio adulterii Rynd, Smytht.

The said day, Margaret Rynd, being accusat of adulterie committit be hir wytht Richart Smytht in Kinninmontht, confessis that in the first oulk of Lentroun last was, the said Richard and scho being cuming fra Baldinny Myll to Kinninmontht to the said Richard hows, [he][1] keist hir down be the way and had carnal deal wytht hir.

Die Mercurii, xxv^{to} Augusti, 1574.

Tailzeor, Robertsoun, in adulterie.

The quhilk day, comperit Jonet Robertsoun, in Kinnaldy, and confessit hir to be wytht childe to Henry Tailzeor, schiphird in Strawethie, spous to Beiggis Myllar.

Purgatio Burel in Karskirdo.

The said day, comperit William Burell in Karskeirdo, and purgit hym be his aitht, in presence of the seat, of the bairn allegit begottin in adultery betwix hym and Margaret Nicol, and decernit be the seat to cum on Sunday nixt to cum, or Sunday cum aucht dayis, to mak the like purgation in presence of the heal congregation, tyme of sermon.

Purgatio Burell in Kairskirdo.

Memorandum. Upon Sunday the xxix day of August 1574, William Burell in Kairskirdo maid his purgatioun opinlye in the parroche kirk of Sanctandros, tyme of sermon, in presence of the heal congregatioun being thair for the tyme, of the alledgit adultery committit be hym wytht Margaret Nicol, according to the ordinance abone writtin.

Die Mercurii, sexto Octobris, 1574.

Nota.
Mr. Archabald Hammiltoun.

The quhilk day, in nominatioun of the eldaris and diaconis to be chosin, Maister Archibald Hammiltoun,[2] professour in the

---

[1] Omitted.   [2] See p. 368, n. 2.

New Colleage, was nocht nominat to be ane elder, becaus he,
being of befoir nominat and electit, refused to accept the office
of eldrie on hym, and nocht to be nominat quhil he mak
repentence thairfoir, and to be callit to that effect.

The said day, Elene Jnglis confessed in presence of the *Jnglis, Nairn,*
sessioun that sche was wytht childe to George Nairn, sone to *fornicatoris,*
Alexander Nairn, undir promis of mareage maid to hir as sche *rij.*
allegis be the said George. And the said George to be called
to this day aucht dayis; and comperit George confessing the
formar allegeance except promis of mareage, and promisis to
observe the ordour concerning his repentence to be maid.

Die Mercurii, decimo tertio Octobris, anno Domini j^m v^c lxxiiij^to.

The quhilk day, anent the complent of sclandir gevin in to *Decretum*
the seat be Besse Wylie, spous to Andro Stwit, aganis Margaret *Wylye contra*
Colyne, spous to Patrik Wylie, the seat, eftir triall and cogni- *Colyne.*
tion takin in the mater, hes fund the said Margaret Colyne to
have havely sclanderit the said Besse Wylye; and thairfoir the
said Margaret Colyne, in presence of ane or twa of the ballies
eldaris and diaconis, [to]¹ cum to Besse Wylye yeat, and thair
to cognosce and confes hir offens and ask the said Besse Wylie
forgivenes; and gyf evir sche do siclik in tyme cuming, to
sitt in the gokstuil duryng the magistrattis will.

*Die Mercurii, vigesimo die mensis Octobris, anno Domini mille-
simo quingentesimo septuagesimo quarto.*

Maister Robert Hammilton minister.

Eldaris votit electit and chosin.

Maister Johne Ruthirfurd, Provest of Sanct Saluatoris Colleage
Mr. James Wilke, Principal of Sanct Leonardis Colleag
Mr. Johne Hammiltoun,² regent in the New Colleage

---

¹ Omitted.

² This is the John Hamilton who, like Archibald Hamilton, was trained in
St. Mary's College, turned Protestant, but returned again to Popery, and became
one of the most violent opponents of that faith he had once professed. For

Maister Thomas Balfour, bailye
George Brown, bailye
Mr. William Cok, bailȳe
Dauid Walwod
James Robertson
Johne Motto

Charles Guthre
Charles Geddye
Mr. Johne Bonkil
Mr. James Wemis
Andro Wod
James Forret.

Diaconis.

Alexander Crastaris
James Brydye
William Gyfferd
Alexander Myllar
William Main
George Blak
James Alane

Johne Lewingston
Thomas Layng
Waltir Kinninmontht
Dauid Foster
Thomas Weneson
Martine Corstorphine.

Nota.
Ratification and approbation of the statutis maid of befoir.

The quhilk day, minister eldaris and diaconis abone writtin affirma[t] ratifiit and approvit the heal statutis and ordinances of the sessioun, maid upon the fyft day of November, year of God· j^{m}v^{c}lxxij, and swear of new to observe the sam in all pointis.

Dilation to be takin up.

The said day, the seat appointis dilatioun to be takin up again this day aucht dayis, also that the actis of the kirk be red upon Sunday nixt to cum, and ane assis to be warnit of every quartar of the town.

Nota.
Decretum sessionis contra Alanem Watson pro selatione xl. s.

The quhilk day, the seat concludit Alane Watsoun to pay xl s. to the collectour of the puiris alms, becaus he revelit nocht to the sessioun the fornicatioun committit in his hows betwix Thomas Cok and the said Alane servand woman ; and cheiflye in respect that he confessed that, eftir it was schawin to hym that his servand woman was wytht bairn, he pat hir

Andro Gibson to pay xl s. to the puir.

furtht incontinent out of his hows. And also Andro Gibsoun to pay xl s., becaus he revelit nocht to the seat that it was schawin to hym that his dochter was wytht bairn be his awin gude-sone on Twisday was xv dayis.

---

notices of his career in St. Andrews, see Lee's *Lectures*, i. 345-348 ; and for his chequered, aspiring and adventurous life on the Continent, his return to Scotland, and his death in the tower of London, see Hailes's *Sketch of the Life of John Hamilton.*

The said day, the seat being requirit be the ministerie of Testimonial
Dunde, quhethir gyf they had ony caus, deducit and provin Rolland, Plai-
befoir them, quhy Eufame Rolland sould nocht resave the feir.
benefit of the kirk in mareage to be celebrat betwix Thomas
Plafeir and hir; the seat, eftir they had considerat the proces
and depositiounis of witnes in trial taking of the suspitioun of
adulteri betwix Henry Lawmonht and the said Eufame, fand
nocht the adultere sufficientlie provin, and thairfoir ordinat
ane testimonial to be send to the kirk of Dunde in favoris of
the said Eufame, requiring them to tak hir purgation in hir
conscience, and send the sam to us again that we may tak
ordour for the weil of our kirk and removing of sclandir.

Die Mercurii, xxvij° Octobris, 1574.

The quhilk day, the seat hes ordeined Johne Lewingstoun to Johne Leving-
be warnit to compeir this day aucht days, to gyf his reasoun ston to be
quhy he being electid diacon wal nocht accept the office on warnit, rij.
hym; and gyf he comperis nocht, it wil be procedit aganis hym
publiclie according to the actis.

The said day, Johne Lawsoun is appointed to cum to the Johne Law-
kirk dur and penitent stuill as of befoir, on Sunday nixt to soun.
cum, and thaireftir to be resavit, undir conditioun that he sal
present hym self to the nixt sinodal assemblye, or quhen he
salbe chargit, in lynnyng clothis, according to the actis of the
General Assemblie.

The said day, Nannis Methtwen confesses hir to be wytht Scot, Methtwen,
childe to Henry Scot, cuik to my Lord Bischop of Caithnes,[1] et fornicatoris.
relapsis, and Henry to be callit again Wedinsday nixt to cum.

Die tertio mensis Novembris 1574.

The quhilk day, the seat ordenis Henry Forsytht and Chris- Forsytht, Tur-
ten Turbane, dilatit as fornicatoris, to be confrontit this day bane, rij.
aucht dayis, in presence of the seat, for trial to be takin, becaus
Henry denyis the bairn to be his.

The said day, the seat, in respect that Margaret Wischart Margaret
Wischart to be
absolvit.

---

[1] See p. 232, n.

2 c

hes sufficientlye maid hir repentence in presenting hir self to the penitent stule, ordanis hir to be absolvit and to resave the benefit of the kirk on Sunday nixt to cum.

Nota.
Purgatio
Lawmontht.

The quhilk day, comperit Henry Lawmontht, and, being demandit of the seat gyf he wald mak his purgation in his conscience of carnal deall wytht Eufame Rolland, ansuered that, in presence of this seat, he purgit hym thairof in his conscience of befoir, and yit affirmis in his conscience the said purgation to be of verite. In respect of the quhilk, the seat ordanis George Blak to proceid in the proclamation of bannis betwix Thomas Plafeir and the said Eufame Rolland.

Purgatioun of
Ewfame Rolland.

The ansueir of the ministerie of *D*unde concerning the purgatioun takin be them of Eufame Rolland at desyre of this sessioun fallowis :—[1]

Die Mercurii, xvij° Novembris, 1574.

Tailzeor in
Strawethye.

The quhilk day, anent the supplicatioun gevin in be Henry Tailzeor in Strawethye, the seat hes ordeined the said Henry, becaus he hes sittin upon the penitent stuill bot ten Sundais, yit to sit ten several Sundayis, and, or he pas to the seat, to stand in the kirk dure in sik-claitht every Sunday, quhill the said ten Sundayis be compleit.

Admonitio
Thomson cordonar, *violator*
Sabbati.

The said day William Thomson cordonar dilatit for nocht keping of the Sabbat day admonesched to absten in tyme cuming.

Blak *violator*
Sabbati.
Confessit be
Blak.

Item, James Blak walcar dilatit as said is, and sindry admonitionis gevin to hym of befoir abstenit nocht, the seat heirfoir decernit hym to have incurrit the[2] panis of the act, and the ballies requirit to put the act to execution.

Die Mercurii, xxiiij° Novembris, 1574.

Distributioun of
the xl s. takin
fra Richart
Smytht.

The quhilk day, George Blak granted hym to have resavit fra Dauid Crastaris, in name of Richart Smytht, xl s., becaus the said Richart revelit nocht the harlatry committit in his

---

[1] A space has been left for the answer, but it has never been copied in.
[2] *The the* in MS.

hows; and the sait ordeined the said George to deliver to
Skipper Lessillis wyffe,' callit Besse Forbes, twenty schillingis,
and utheris twenty schillingis to Duncan Dauidsoun officiar of
the sessioun.

Die Mercurii, primo Decembris, 1574.

The quhilk day, anent the bairn alledgit to be gottin in *Methtwen*
fornicatioun betwix Robert Methtwen and Margaret Fowles, *Fowles.*
Robert Methtwen is content the said Margaret makking faitht
and geving hir aitht in presence of the session that the bairn
is the said Robertis, he is content to tak thair wytht, and to
satisfie the kirk.   And the said Margar[et] cam in, and in
presence of the sait maid faitht and swear that the bairn is
Robert Methtwen[is].

The said day, Robert Bred, dilatit of druknes and working *Monitio* Bred.
on the Sabbat day, admonesed to desist and ces thairfra in
tyme cuming, undir al hiest paine that the kirk may lay to his
chairge.

Die Mercurii, octavo Decembris, 1574.

The said day, Dauid Adesoun, indwellar sum tyme wytht *Adesoun, Rynd,*
Richart Smytht in Kinninmon[ht], desyrit ane bairn, begottin *Smytht.*
in fornication betwix hym and Margaret Ry[nd] in fornicatioun, to be baptized : quhilk was refused, becaus the said
Margaret [con]send the bairn to be Richart Smytht in Kinnin-
monht, and he and Margaret cuming to repentence the bairn
sal be resavit to baptisme.

The said day, in respec that Robert Methtwen, upon the *Robert Meffen*
first day of December instant, promittit to satisfie the kirk *to satisfie the*
for fornication committit be hym wytht Margaret Fowles, [the *kirk.*
seat][1] ordanis hym to be requirit to mak satisfaction, wytht
certification gyf he dois nocht he sal be procedit aganis to
excommunication upon Sunday nixt to cum.

---

[1] Omitted.

Die Mercurii, duodecimo Januarii, anno Domini j^mv^clxxiiij^{to.}

Decretum sessionis contra Jacobum Thomson latanium. [1] The quhilk day, James Thomsoun masoun, being dilatit and accusit for superstitious keping of Zwil-day last was haly day, and that he said that quba wald or wald nocht he wald nocht work on Zwil-day, and was nocht in use of the sam ; and, being again askit quhethir he wald stand be that or not, promittit that, in tyme cuming, during his remaning in this citie, he sould nevir keip the said Zwil-day haly day, bot sould work on that day as on [2] ony uthir day to ony man that wald offir hym wark ; and to this effect was actitat of his awin propir confession, undir paine of presenting of hym self to the stuil of repentence, according to the ordour, and payment of xl s. to the puir. And gyf na man chargis hym wytht wark, he sal wirk sum riggen-stanis [3] of his awin.

Sessio Bell. The said [day], [4] William Bel baxter dilatit for keping of Zwil haly, and in spetial on Newar-day [5] last was, in his hows, the sam being ful of lychtis and mony in cumpany, hymself cryit wyth lowd voce, superstitiously, Zwil! Zwil! Zwil! William denyit the sam. The seat ordanit the dilation to be provin this day aucht dayis, and William Bel to be warnit to oppone and object aganis the witnes.

Die Mercurii, nono Februarii, anno Domini j^mv^clxxiiij^{to.}

Reid, M^cky, rij. The quhilk day, the sessioun appointis this day aucht dayis to Elizabetht M^cky, dochtir to umquhill Robert M^cky, to preiff the compulsion allegit be hir in hir defensis producit be hir aganis Thomas Reid.

---

[1] Probably meant for *laterarium.*
[2] *Of* in MS.
[3] The stones forming the ridge of a roof.
[4] Omitted.
[5] Prior to 1600, the civil, ecclesiastical and legal year began in Scotland on the 25th of March, and the entries in this *Register* are dated accordingly ; but this reference in the text seems to show that popularly the year was supposed to begin at Yule. The Anglo-Saxons began their year on the 25th of December (E. W. Robertson's *Historical Essays,* 1872, p. 82) ; and the Icelanders are said still to do the same (Jamieson's *Dictionary*).

Die Mercurii, decimo sexto Februarii, $j^m v^c lxxiiij^{to.}$

The quhilk day, in the terme assignit to Elizabetht M^cky, M^cke, Read, dochtir to umquhill Robert M^cky, to preiff the alledgit compulsion contenit in hir defensis producit aganis Thomas Read, and now producit Robert Read, sone to George Reaid in Brownhyllis, [quha,]¹ sworn and examinat, deponis that he knawis not nor hard ony compulsion; and siclik producit Robert² Read and George Richartson, servandis to Mr. Thomas Balfour, and Thomas Beanis tailyeor. Robert Read, servand to Mr. Thomas Balfour, sworn resavit and examinat, deponis that, on Sunday befoir the handfasting, he hard Robert M^ckye say to Elspet M^cky his dochtir, Gyf thow wil not be content to do my counsal thow sal have na geir of myne: and sche ansuered, I desyre to mary na man. George Richartsoun deponis that nethir was he at the contract making nor handfasting, and hard nocht hir father compel hir to mary. Thomas Beanis, sworn resavit and examinat, deponit that he hard nevir hir father compell Elspet M^cky to mary Thomas Read. Schir Robert Smytht³ resavit and sworn kennis not the compulsion alledgit. The seat assignit this day aucht dayis to Elspet to do diligence for Robert Baxter.⁴ And now Robert Baxter, comperand, deponis that upon the Sunday eftir nuin umquhill Robert M^cke said to Elspet his dochtir, I have spokin wytht Thome Read, qubat thinkis thow of it? [And Elspet ansuered,]¹ Fathir, quhat alis yow at me? Ye ar tyrit of me! Gyf ye wil gyf me ony thing, gyf me it, and ye sal hald it to your self qubil ye leiff. And Robert Makke ansuered, Quein! quhat auchtis to the? Gai seik thy motheris testament, truly ony thing thow aucht to have of it thow sal have!

---

¹ Omitted.   ² Interlined over *Thomas.*

³ Probably the Robert Smyth who signed the General Band and also the Recantation in February 1559-60 (*supra*, pp. 11, 14). He had a son, John, who became a hammerman, and who, in 1584, is described as lawful son of 'umquhill Sir Robert Smyth curat'; and in a list of the brethren of the craft in the following year, he is entered as 'curat,' èvidently to distinguish him from other two John Smyths in the same craft (*Bouk of the Hammermen of Sanctandrous*).

⁴ The remainder of this paragraph has been inserted afterwards.

Die Mercurii, secundo Martii, 1574.

Commission to the Assemblie of the Kirk.

The quhilk day, the seat hes votit commission to be gevin to Maisteris Thomas Balfour and William Cok, commissionaris of the seat, to compeir in Edinburght in the General Assemblie of the Kirk, to be haldin the vj day of Marche instant.

Nota. Forbidding of the play of Roben Hwid.

The said day, the seat ordenis the minister, on Sunday nixt to cum, or uthirwayis as he sal be chargit and warnit, in the name of the eternal God, to command and chairge all and quhatsumevir personis indwellaris in this citie and spetialy yowng men in general, and als in spetial as he salbe informit, That nane of them presume nor tak upon hand to violat the Sabbat day, be using of playis and gemmis publiclie as they war wont to do, contrafating the playis of Robein Huid, expres defendit and forbiddin be Act of Parliament,[1] undir all biest pane that the seat may injone to them.

---

[1] In 1555 it was 'statute and ordanit that in all tymes cumming na maner of persoun be chosin Robert Hude, nor Lytill Johne, Abbot of Unressoun, Quenis of Maii, nor utherwyse, nouther in burgh nor to landwart' (*Acts of the Parliaments of Scotland*, ii. 500). Latimer, in a well-known passage of a sermon preached before Edward the Sixth in 1549, complains that although he 'sent word over night' to a town that he would preach there next morning because it was a holiday, yet on his arrival 'the church was fast locked;' and when at length the key was found, he was told they could not hear him because it was Robin Hood's day. 'I thought,' he says, 'my rochet should have been regarded, though I were not; but it would not serve, it was fain to give place to Robin Hood's men . . . all this hath come of unpreaching prelates' (Latimer's *Sermons*, Parker Soc. p. 208). Despite the Act of Parliament and later Acts of the General Assembly Robin Hood's play was long popular in Scotland. A riot was occasioned by an attempt to suppress it in 1561, see Laing's *Knox*, ii. 157-160; *Diurnal of Occurrents*, pp. 283-285. Perhaps the manner in which the session had been recently taken to task (*supra*, p. 396, n. 2) may have quickened their zeal at this time. While James Melvill was a student in St. Andrews, plays were included among the 'solemnities' then used when the students attained their 'Bachlar art;' and he mentions one play specially, which was made by John Davidson at the marriage of 'Mr. Jhone Colvin,' and which he saw played in Knox's presence in 1571, 'wherin, according to Mr. Knox doctrin, the Castle of Edinbruche was beseiged, takin, and the captan, with an or twa with him, hangit in effigie' (Melvill's *Diary*, pp. 27, 28). The chief opposition to Robin Hood probably arose not only from the impropriety of celebrating the exploits of a robber, but because, in 'gathering' for it, his admirers were too ready to copy his example; and the General Assembly alleged that the observance caused the profanation of fasts as well as of the Sabbath (*Booke of the Universall Kirk*, ii. 407, 410, 784).

Die Mercurii, xxiij° Martii, 1574.

The quhilk day, Henry Tailzeor in Strawethie is admittit to [Heury
be resavit again to the kirk, becaus occording to the ordour he Tailzeor.]
hes maid satisfaction in sekclaitht mony Sundayis, conform to
the actis of kirk, and this to be don on Sunday nixt to cum.

Die Mercurii, penultimo mensis Martii, anno Domini j^mv^clxxv^{to.}

The quhilk day, George Grig and Jonet Myllar, dochtir to Grig, Myllar.
Alexander Myllar cultellar, being dilatit as fornicatoris and the
said Jonet to be witht childe to the said George, comperit the
saidis George and Jonet; and the said George[1] confessit hym
to have had carnal dail witht the said Jonet, bot quhethir the
bairn sche is withtall be his or not, he knawis not; and
referris *simpliciter* to the said Jonet aitht gyf the bairn[2] be his
or not. The said Jonet, being sworn be invocation of the
eternal God, deponis in hir aitht that sche nevir had carnal
dail witht man bot witht the said George onlye, and the bairn
to be the said Georgis and na utheris.

The said day, Christen Tuirbane confessis that sche buir Forsytht,
ane bairne in fornication to Henry Forsytht, and oblesis hir Turbane.
to satisfie the kirk quhen evir sche sal be requirit; and Maister
Johne Scot, hir maister, souerte for hir to fulfil the ordinance
of the kirk.

The quhilk day, Johne Kirk confessit Margaret Ednem to Kiik, Ednem.
be witht childe to hym, and hes promittit to mak satisfaction
to the kirk, and decernit to do the sam.

The said day, James Brenche tailyeor decernit witht his [Brenche, Bell.]
awn consent to ma[k] his repentence, upon Sunday cum aucht
dayis, for brekking of the ordour in lying witht his partye
befoir solemnization of mareage betwix hym and [*blank*]
Bell.

The said day, Johne Robertsoun seeman confessit and *Nota.*
grantit hym to have had carnal dail witht Christen Zwill, Robertson,
dochtir to Johne Zwil baxter, he being not divorsit fra Zwill.
Mariory Waed, and offeris hym to mak repentence according

---

[1] *Jonet George* in MS.   [2] *Bairn bairn* in MS.

to the ordinance of the kirk ; and Dauid Robertson fleschear cautionar for the said Johne [to][1] fulfil the sam undir paine of xl lib.

[The puir.]   The quhilk day, the seat ordenis and appointis the personis undir writtin, to tak trial and vesy the puris of ilk quartar withtin this citie, that the puir and agit, yowng and auld, may be supportit witht the common almes as efferis, and the personis able to be removit thairfra.

The first quartar.

Anent trial to be takin of the puir.   The Southt-gaet fra the Abbay to the parroche kirk on baitht the sydis of the gait : Maister Thomas Balfour, bailye, Mr. Martine Geddy, Mr. William Cok, George Brown, ballies, to vesy the said quartar ; and the heal rest of the quartaris, togethir witht Johne Motto, Dauid Walwod, James Robertson, Charles Geddye, witht the rest of eldaris and diaconis ; and this visitation to be maid witht al expeditioun ; and also to try, conform to ane act maid of befoir, quhow mony of them can say the Lordis Prayer, the Beleve, and the Commandementis of almychty God.[2]

Nota.
Anent the burial of the puris.   The said day, it is statut and ordenit be the seat that, in tyme cuming, the puris be convoyit to the burial witht the inhabitantis of the town als weil as the riche, according [to][1] the ordinances maid of befoir, and the transgressouris of the said ordinance to be punisched conform to the act.

Myllar, Grig,
rij quarto Maii.   The said day, Alexander Myllar producit ane clame aganis George Grig, tweching the defloring of the said Alexander dochtir.   The seat ordenis the copy of the bill to be gevin to the said George, and assignit this day aucht dayis, to wit, the fourt day of Maii nixt to cum.

---

[1] Omitted.
[2] Those who could not repeat the Lord's Prayer, the Creed, and the Commandments, were not to be admitted to the Lord's Table (*supra*, p. 196, n. 2).

Die Mercurii, quarto Maii, anno Domini j^m v^c lxx quinto.

The said day, the seat hes appointed and thocht gude the communioun be celebratit upon Witsunday nixt to cum, to wit, Sunday cum xv dayis, the xxij day of Maii instant. Celebration of the communion.

And swa examinatoris to the first quartar, Maister James Wilke, Principal of Sanct Leonardis Colleage, Mr. Martine Geddy, Mr. William Cok, William Gyfford, Johne Bonkil.

The secound quartar, Mr Patrik Authinlek, Mr. Alexander Jarden, Mr. Thomas Balfour, James Brydie, [*Mr. William Cok* —erased] James Robertsoun.

The thrid quartar, the minister, Mr. Robert Jncheoth, Johne Motto, Charles Guthre, Dauid Walwod, James Alane, Johne Levingston.

The fourt quartar, Mr. Johne Ruthirfurd, George Brown, George Blak, William Main, Alexander Myllar.

Item, the examination to begyn upon Moninday the nynte day of Maii instant.

The quhilk day, in the terme assignit to George Grig to ansueir to the bil producit be Alexander Myllar aganis hym, comperit George and producit ansueris in wryte in presence of the said Alexander, and the mater continuat to this day aucht dayis. Myllar, Grig, ^{rij.}

Mercurii, xxv^to Maii, 1575.

Absentis fra the communioun last celebrat upon the xxij day of Maii 1575.

Robert Brown in the Este-burn-wynd, George Philp [*blank*]. James Gilrwitht refusing to joine handis witht Johne Cwik wyff, being desyrit be George Blak to be reconciled witht the said Johne Cwik wyffe, and now reconciled. [Absentis fra the communion.]

Robert Bred nethir presentit hym self to examinatioun nor the table of the Lord, and accusit to be ane commoun drunkat subject to drunkienes. The seat hes ordeined Robert Bread to pay xl s. to the collectour of the puris almes, for his absence fra the examinatioun and communion ; and gyf he beis fund dilated again for drunkinnes he sal sit upon the umest[1] penitent Bred.
Act aganis drunkattis.

---

[1] Uppermost, highest.

stuil, witht ane paper about his head, and his falt writtin
thairintil; and this to strek upon al drunkatis.

Thomas Hwsband, being unreconciled witht Andro Colyne,
cam to the table of the Lord, and was participant thairof;
and Thomas, being accusit heirof, maid faitht, in presence of
God and the seat, that he had na invy at Andro Colyne, nor
buir malice in his hart aganis hym. And the seat commandit
hym to pas to Andro Colyne, and bryng hym in presence of
the seat, that they mycht knaw the sam; quhilk was done in
presence of the seat, &c. Maister Alexander Jarden and
George Philp being at inamite [1] and now reconciled.

Die Mercurii, primo Junii, 1575.

[Read, M^cke.]   The quhilk day, the seat appointed this day aucht dayis, the
viij day of Junii, to pronunce and gyf furtht decreit in the
actioun of [*Robert M^cky*—deleted] Thomas Read aganis Elizabetht M^cke.

Die Mercurii, octavo Junii, 1575.

Nota.
Decretum
solemnizationis
matrimonii
inter Thomam
Read et Eliza-
betht M^cke.

The quhilk day, in the terme assignit to pronunce and gyf
furtht decreit in the actioun of Thomas Read aganis Elizabetht
M^cke, dochtir of umquhill Robert M^cke in the West-burn-
wynde, the seat, in respect that Elizabetht M^cke allegit hir
compellit be hir fathir to mary the said Thomas and failyeit in
probation thairof, decernit hir to proceid in mareage witht
Thomas Read undir paine of excommunication.

Die Mercurii, penultimo mensis Junii, anno Domini
j^mv^clxxv^{to.}

Catharine [2]
Ramsay and
Thomas Wat-
son fornicatoris.

The quhilk day, Christen [2] Ramsay, servand to Catharine
Rettray, relict of umquhill Johne Wilsoun, grantis hir witht
childe to Thomas Watsoun brother to Alane Watsoun; and
that the bairn was gottin in the said Catharine hows, and the
said Catharne undirstude not this bot withtin this monetht,
and that scho schew the sam to Alane Watsounis wyffe xiiij

---

[1] *Janimite* in MS.   [2] *Sic.*

dayis syne; and als confessis that sche had carnal dail witht the said Thomas in Alane Watsonis hows.

Die Mercurii, vigesimo quarto mensis Augusti, 1575.

The quhilk day, Beterage Rantoun confessis hir to be witht childe to Johne *alias* Schir Johne Kenlowy; and Johne Kenlowy allegit that at the tyme the said Beterage allegis the bairn to be gottin, to wit, in the Passio[n] oulk befoir Pasche last was, he offeris hym to preif sufficiently that ane uthir man lay and had deal witht the said Beterage, and confessis that he lay witht the said Beterage bot not the tyme foirsaid; and gyf the said Johne previs not sufficientlye his saidis allegeances that he sal tak witht the bai[rn], and submit hym to the correction of the kirk; and gyf the bairn cumm[is] not to the said raknyng that he wil not tak witht it and protestis the sam, &c. *(margin: Kenlowy, Rantoun.)*

The quhilk day, William Ferry, for George Gryg baxter, producit the dischairge of the General Assembly discharging the kirk of Sanctandros to proceid aganis the said George Grig, compelling hym athir to mary or tochir Jonet Myllar. The seat appointed this day aucht dayis to gyf thair deliverance [*quhethir they wald obey the said chairg or not, or ellis to see quhat they think best to be don in the mater*—erased]. *(margin: Gryg, Myllar. Ultimo Augusti.)*

Die ultimo mensis Augusti, anno Domini j^{m}v^{c}lxxv^{to}.

The quhilk day, in the terme assignit to delyver be the seat gyf they wil obtempir and obey the chairge of the General Assemblye, forbidding to proceid in the action of Jonet Myllar aganis George Gryg anent the mareing or tochoring of hir, or at least to see quhat they think best to be don in the mater; and comperit George Grig and desyrit ansueir of the seat, and desyrit hym to be admittit to mak his repentence according to the ordour of this seat and kirk. The assembly presentlie convenit continuis the ansueir qubil this heal assemblye be convenit, and ordenis the heal assemblye to be warnit to that effect to this day aucht dayis. *(margin: Myllar, Gryg, rij vij° Septembris.)*

Die Mercurii, xxj^{mo.} Septembris, 1575.

*Decretum
sessionis penes
Margaretam
Moncur.*

The quhilk day, Margaret Moncur is ordeined be decreit of the seat to abstein fra cumpany of Schir Johne Kenlowy and al uthiris, quietly, in al suspect places, in tyme cuming; and gyf sche be fund to do the contrare to be punisched accordinglye, and sche being dilatit it sal be haldin *pro confesso.*

Eldaris and diaconis for the yeir in to cum.

Eldaris.

Maister Johne Ruthirfurd, Provest of Sanct Saluatoris Colleage
Maister James Wilke, Principal of Sanct Leonardis Colleage
Maister Johne Robesoun, regent in the New Colleage
Maister Thomas Balfour
Johne Martine elder ⎫
Maister William Cok ⎭ Ballies.

George Brown   Upaland.
Johne Motto   Maister James Wemis of Lathokir [1]
James Robertson   James Forret in Smydde-Grein.
Mr. Martine Geddy
Mr. Johne Bonkil
Charles Guthre.

Diaconis.

William Zwill	Alexander Smytht	
Alexander Castaris	Alexander Myllar.	
Johne Scott	Thomas Layng	⎫
George Blak	Martine Costorphine	⎬ Upaland.
William Gyfferd	Waltir Kinninmontht	⎭
William Main	Dauid S[co]t in Kincaple	
James Schewes		

---

[1] About five years after this, ' Mr. James Wemyss of Lathocker had obtained service of himself as heir to the office of Constable of the castle and town of St. Andrews, which had been granted to his great-grandfather, John Wemyss of Kilmany, by Henry Wardlaw, Bishop of St. Andrews, in 1440, when he married Janet Wardlaw, the Bishop's niece. Archbishop Adamson impugned the documents on which the service was based, alleging them to be forged, and cited "the gud man of Lathokar" before the Lords of Session to prove the authenticity of the writs. . . . It is probable the Wemysses had allowed the exercise of it [the office] to fall into abeyance, and the Archbishop, deeming "it hurt and

Die Mercurii, vigesimo sexto Octobris, anno Domini
j^m v^c lxx quinto.

The quhilk day, the seat ratifiit and apprevit the statutis of
this session maid upon the v day of November 1572, the saidis
statutis being red, &c.

The quhilk day, Johne Robertson seeman and Christen Zwill *Nota.*
adulteraris ar decernit be decreit of the seat to mak thair re- Robertson,
pentence in sek-claitht, upon Sunday the sext day of November Zwil, adulteri.
nixt to cum, undir paine of excommunicatioun.

The said day, Johne Zwil baxter is ordeined that in tyme *Decretum*
cuming he resate not in howsald Johne Robertson seeman, and *sessionis contra*
gyf Christen Zwill his dochtir wil not forbeir cumpany of the *Johannem*
said Johne Robertson [that][1] he put hir furtht of[2] his hows, *Zwil.*
undir pain of excommunication.

Die Mercurii, nono mensis Novembris, anno Domini
j^m v^c lxx quinto.

The quhilk day, comperit Beatye Strang, sumtyme servand Strang, Ler-
to the Laird off Balcolmy, witht hir mother kepar of the Laird monht.
of Balcolmy hows, being askit quha was fathir to the bairn that
sche buir upon Moninday was thre oulkis, to wit, the [*blank*]
day of October last was, in Christen Strangis hows, the mydwyffe callit [*blank*] being present, togethir witht Duncane
Dauidsonis gude-dochtir callit Aleson Myilsoun, the tyme of
hir birtht, and affirmis constantlye the bairn to be William
Lermontht, servand to the Laird of Balcolmy, quhilk he begat
in the first heal oulk of Lentroun last was as sche belevis, or the
said William passit in France, and now allegis the said William
was seik at Fasterennis-ewin and befoir the seiknes the bairn
was gottin.

The said day, Thomas Wilsoun, servand to Johne Wilson, Wilsoun,
Bwikles.

---

dishonour to be abusit in ane office of sick consequens, quhilk," he says, "their
predecessours hes nocht bruikit, and quhairof I se na autentik ground," was not
prepared to yield the point. Very probably the dispute was compromised, and
the office yielded up to Adamson for some consideration, as it never seems to
have been possessed by the Wemysses, at least subsequent to this date ' (Sir
William Fraser's *Memorials of the Wemyss Family*, i. 177).

[1] Omitted.   [2] *Of of* in MS.

confessis and grantis that he had carnal deal witht Agnes
Bwikles, upon ane Sunday foure oulkis befoir Witsunday last
was. And the said Agnes confessis hir to be witht qwik childe
to the said Thomas Wilson, and as sche affirmis the bairn was
gottin viij dayis eftir the Seingze-day last was.

Die Mercurii, xxviij° Decembris, 1575.

**Forman,
Clwnye.**
   The quhilk day, Besse Forman grantis and confessis hir to be
witht childe to Mathow Clwnye, and Mathow confessis the sam,
and that he hes maid promissis of mareage to the said Besse,
and to perform the sam witht al diligence, and baytht to absten
fra mutual societe quhil they be mareit, undir pain of excommunication. And Dauid Kynneir, cautionar for Besse Forman
to mak satisfaction to the kirk, and to absten fra mutual copulation quhill they be mareit, undir pain of ten merkkis. And
Johne Sowrdy souerte for Mathow Clwny undir pain foirsaid.

**Murray,
Cordye, fornica-
tores.**
   The said day Jonet Murray, hantand witht Nannis Schewes,
confessis hir witht childe to Alane Cordye in Cossingray.

Die Mercurii, xviij° Januarii, 1575.

**[Mariorye
Smytht dilatit
of wichecraft :
deposicionis of
wytnes.]**
   The quhilk day, Robert Grub, yownger in Baalye, witnes,
examinat upon the dilatioun and accusatioun of Mariorye
Smytht, spous of Johne Pa, dilatit and accusat of wichecraft,
sworne, deponis that he hard be his awin wyffe, Jsobel Johnestoun, and Nannis Michell, report that the said Jsobel Johnesoun, being in traveling of hir childe, Pais wyffe cam to hir
and Nannis Michel being thair layit hir hand on the said
Nannis, and sche becam seik incontinent thaireftir; and the
deponentis wyffe being laid up in hir bed, sche tuik the said
Nannis be the hand, and sche becam weil again, and eat and
drank witht the rest of the wemen [that][1] war thar; and
attour, deponis that viij or nyne dayis thaireftir his spous foirsaid, being verry seik, send for the said Pa wyffe, and sche
refusit to cum quhil the deponent yeid hym self and compellit
hir to cum, and at hir cuming sche tuik the deponentis wyffe

---

[1] Omitted.

be the arme, and grapit hir, and pat up hir fyngaris betwix the scheddis of hir hair, and incontinent thaireftir sche cryit for mait: and attour, deponis his wyffe was sa seik that nane trowit hir lyffe being oppressit witht swait and .womyng,[1] qubil Pa wyffe cam and handillit hir, and this was fowre yeir syne cum Witsunday.

Christiane Methtwen, spous to Waltir Padye, cowper, witnes, sworne and examinat in the said caus of accusation, deponis in hir aitht that tyme foirsaid sche was present in Grub hows, quhen his wyffe was travelling in hir childe-evill, and Nannis Michel cam in, and eftir sche had askit at Grub wyffe hir ant quhow sche did, Pa wyffe said sche wald be weil belyffe, and incontinent thaireftir the said Nannis Michel becam verry seik, and Grub wyffe was lychtar incontinent and softer of hir seiknes; and Grub wyffe being laid up in hir bed the said Nannis becam the better: and confessis that they war all fleyit, and ane myst cam ower the deponent ein, that sche could not see quhat Payis wyffe did to Grub wyffe: and forthir deponis that ix dayis eftir the said Grub wyffe was lychter and being verry seik, the deponent and Robert Grub yeid for Pa wyffe, and compellit [hir][2] to cum and vesy Grub wyffe, and eftir sche tuik Grub wyffe be the hand sche becam the bettir and eit and drank.

Die Mercurii, xxv[to] mensis Januarii, anno Domini j[m]v[c]lxxv[to].

The quhilk day, Mariory Smytht, and [3] Johne Pa hir spous [Smytht, Pa.] for his interes, being somound to heir witnessis sworne resavit and admittit in the action of wichecraft persewit aganis the said Mariory, thir witnessis undir-writtin war resavit sworn and admittit to examinatioun, in pain of non comperence of the saidis Mariory and hir spows.

William Balfour, baxter, witnes, somound sworne resavit and admittit, deponis the pointis contenit in the Superintendentis chartour of reces of dilation to be of trewtht and veritie.

James Gilrwitht, witnes, confessis that his kow gaif na mylknes, and his dochtir repruffit and accusit Mariory Smytht that hir fathir kow gaif na mylk, and thaireftir his dochtir

---

[1] Moist heat   [2] Omitted.   [3] *And and* in MS.

becom seik, and Mariory being[1] callit to James Gilrwitht hows
to vesy his dochtir, sche said nathyng wald aill hir scho wald be
weil aneucht.[2]

Item, Andro Sellar and Thomas Christie, examinat in the
said mater, deponis that they desyrit Johne Pay nocht to
depart of the town gyf his and his wyffis caus war gud. He
ansuered that he feared, and thairfoir he and his wyffe yeid
thair wayis. And Besse Hereis confessed the sam, and forthir
[that he][3] said that for hym self he durst byde, bot yit his
wyffe feared, and thairfoir they[4] durst not byde : also that Pay
desyrit hir gude-man to pas to the coles witht Dauid Robertson, becaus he was ane sonsy man ; and sen Pa and his wyffe
dwelling undir them, he was xl merkis bettir.

Mareoun Dawsoun, mydwyffe, witnes, sworn, takkis on hir
sowll that sche knawis nathing of the dilatioun. Alexander
Ade, witnes, knawis nathyng of the dilation. Maige *D*awson
knawis na thyng bot be relatioun of utheris, &c.

*Die decimo quinto mensis Februarii, anno Domini
j^mv^clxx quinto.*

<table>
<tr><td>Murray and
Campbel, for-
nicatores.</td><td>The quhilk day, Margaret Murray, servand to Hew Lynde-
say, confessis hir witht childe to Coline Campbel, sumtyme
student in the New Colleage.</td></tr>
<tr><td>*Nota.*
For brekking
of the Sabbat
day.</td><td>The said day, Thomas Read, Andro Hog, Johne Sourdy,
Robert Murray, and Simon Wellis, Arche Wischart, Johne</td></tr>
</table>

Blak walcar, Johne Fairful, Johne Paterson, Johne Muffat,
George Methtwen [*merchandis*—deleted], Alexander Myllar
cultellar servand, Andro Myllar fleschear, Dauid Robertson
fleschear, James Dempstertoun fleschear, Johne Nicolsoùn
fleschear, Johne Kelle fleschear, Johne Furde chaepman, Andro
Trymlay chaepman, James Myll chaeplen, Andro Trymlay
merchand dochtir, Andro Mynneman, Alexander Ramsay tailyeor dochtir, James Bawerage cordonar, accusat for using
merchandice upon the Sunday in Carrail aganis Goddis Word,
and brekking of the cumlye ordour of this citie ; admonesit to

---

[1] *Be* in MS.   [2] *Aneththt* in MS.
[3] Omitted.   [4] *Th* in MS.

desist and ces fra siclik doing in tyme cuming, undir pain of excommunication and incurring of the panis contenit in Actis of Parliament; and ane supplication to be gevin up to the magistratis to punesche them according to the saidis Actis.

Die Mercurii, decimo octavo mensis Aprilis, anno Domini j^mv^clxx sexto.

The quhilk day, it is statut and ordinat be the session that fra this furtht that al transgressoris, sic as fornicatoris and adulteraris, be impresoned in the steple of the parroche kirk of this citie, thair to remain according to the ordour, and this statut to be publist be the minister in the pulpet.

Nota. Decreit of the Se^ssion anent the impresoning of transgres- souris.

Die Mercuri, xiij° Maii, 1576.[1]

The quhilk day, it is appointed be the seat that the communion be celebrat upon Sunday cum xx dayis, to wit, the xvij of Junii; and the examination to begyn upon Moninday cum aucht dayis, the fourt day of Junii.

[Communion and examination.]

The quhilk day, Johne Smytht gun-makkar is becum cautionar that Thomas Traill and Margaret Smytht sal fulfil the ordinance of the kirk, to be injoned to them for alledgit brekking of the ordour of the kirk, quhenevir they salbe callit thairfoir, undir pain of ten lib. And Alexander Smytht obligat and actitat to releve the said Johne Smytht.

Traill, Smytht, Smytht. Nota.

Die xxiiij^{to} mensis Junii, anno Domini j^mv^clxxvj^{to.}

The quhilk day, Johne Blak in Raderny is becum souerte for Beiggis Blak thair, now lyand in cheildbed-lair, that how sone sche beis restoryit to hir heal [sche sal underly disciplin][2] quhen sche sal be requirit thairto undir paine of x lib.

Nota. Blak, Blak. Nota.

Die quarto mensis Julii, 1576.

The quhilk day, it [is][2] statut that na prevy subscriptionis

Nota. Nota. Of the consent of the assemblye.

---

[1] The 13th of May was not a Wednesday, but the date of this entry has been altered, having originally been *xxiij°*; and in the entry *xx* has been substituted for *xv*, and *cum aucht dayis* for *nixt to cum*.   [2] Omitted.

of ony personis of the assembly, withtout heal consent of the assemblye, have effect in tyme cuming.

Die Mercurii, undecimo Julii, 1576.

Wilsoun, Arthour.

The quhilk day, Johne Wilsoun, sone of umquhill Henry Wilson, citenar of Sanctandrois, being callit befoir the sessioun, and askit gyf Henry Forsytht his gude-fathir had usit hym hardlye in ony sort, quhairby he was constranit to johne hym self in mareage and so seik the assistence of his alya,[1] and also gyf his mother had not doin hir dewty to hym, ansuered that he could fynd na falt witht athir of them bot thocht it was for his awin weil to joine hym self witht sic ane partye, and wald stand constant at the promis maid be hym to [blank] dochtir to Henry Arthour, befoir George Blak redar. And Maister Andro Wilson, being callit be the seat, allegit curatour to the said Johne, being askit gyf the said promis was maid witht his consent, ansuered that he was incertane gyf he was chosin curatour to the said Johne or not, bot gyf he was chosin he nevir accepted the office of curatory on hym.

Die vigesimo primo mensis Julii, anno Domini $j^m v^c lxxvj^{to}$.

Nota. Clwnye, fforman.

The quhilk day, James Sourdy armorar is becum souerty for Mathow Clwny cultellar,[2] that he sal mary solemplye, in presence of the congregation of this citie, Besse fforman, betwix this and Zwil nixt to cum, undir paine of xx lib. ; and the said Mathow to releve the said James his cautionar undir paine foirsaid, so oft as neid beis, de mandato ministri.

Die Mercurii, octavo Augusti, anno $j^m v^c lxxvj^{to}$.

Lermontht, Strang.

The quhilk day, Beaty Strang being callit to depone hir aitht quhethir the bairn alledgit to be gottin betwix hir and William Lermontht was the saidis William or not, becaus the said William referrit simpliciter to the said Beaty aitht gyf the bairn was his; the said Beaty ansuering in hir conscience that

---

[1] Alliance.
[2] Evidently the same individual who is mentioned p. 169, n. 4.

the bairn was not the said William, and affirmis the bairn gottin be ane Frencheman, servand to the Laird of Ramorny, callit Rinnie, and the bairn to be his.

Die Mercurii, xxix° mensis Augusti, anno etc. lxxvj[io.]

The quhilk day, William Elistoun confessit hym to have Elistoun, had carnal deal witht Elspet Fairly, presentlye being witht Fairlye, fornicatoris. childe; and that the first tyme he lay witht hir was on Sunday befoir Fasternnis ewin, the fourt of Marche last was, and the last tyme in the Seingze oulk nixt thaireftir, to wit, in the monetht of Maii. The said Elspet examinat thairupon aggreis witht the sam in al pointis, and forthir the said Elspet alledgit promis of mareage maid be hym to hir, and referris the sam to his aitht.

The said day, Colyne Campbel grantis hym to have gottin Campbel, ane childe in fornication witht ane Margaret Murray, and Murray. offeris hym to accomplische the discipline of the kirk quhatevir beis injoned to hym, and thairfoir desyris the bairn to resave the benefit of baptisme.

The said day, the seat, for consideratiounis moving them, *Nota.* decernit in tyme cuming na cautioun to be taking of them *Decretum sessionis.* That that ar dilatit for fornication or adulterie, bot incontinent to na caution be suffir[1] ecclesiastical discipline eftir the offence be provin. tar̂e.

Electioun of eldaris and diaconis, upon Fryday, the twelt day of October, yeir of God j[m]v[c]lxxvj yeris.

Eldaris.

Maister Johne Ruthirfurd, Provest of Sanct Saluatoris Colleage
Maister James Wilke, Principal of Sanct Leonardis Colleage
Maister Johne Robeson, regent of the New Colleage
Maister Thomas Balfour ⎫ Ballies.
Maister William Cok ⎭

Johne Martine, elder   Mr Martine Geddy
Maister Patrik Authinlek   Mr Johne Bonkle
Johne Motto   Charles Guthre
James Robertson   James Forret in Smyddie-grein.

---

[1] *Suffit* in MS.

Diaconis.

Non subscribitur.

William Zwill
Alexander Castaris
Johne Scot
George Blak
Charles Watson, writar
David Blair
Alexander Smytht
Alexander Myllar
Thomas Layng in Elene-hill.

Approbatioun of the statutis maid of befoir.

Die Mercurii, septimo Novembris, 1576.—The quhilk day, the seat ratifiit and apprevit the statutis maid upon the fyft day of November j^m^v^c^lxxij yeris, and hes promittit faithtfully to observe the sam in tyme cuming.

Die Mercurii, xxviij° Novembris, anno Domini j^mv^clxxvj^to.

Nota. Zwil, Cwnyng, Robertson.

The quhilk day, Johne Zwil and [*blank*] Cwnyng his spous ar decernit, on Sund[ay] nixt to cum, to mak thair repentence for resaving of Johne Robertson seeman in thair hows, quha committit adultery witht Christen Zwil thair dochtir, undir pain of excommunication.

Die decimo nono mensis Decembris, 1576.

Decretum sessionis penes Egidiam Symson.

The quhilk day, Gelis Symsoun is decernit of hir awin propir confessioun, that gyf evir sche sal in tyme cuming be dilatit to be ane bannar or blasphemar of hir husband, or not to cum to the sermon on the Sabbat day, to sit in the gok stule xxiiij howris.

Die xxvj^to mensis Decembris, 1576.

Lawson, Christie.

Thomas Lawson and Catharine Christie grantis ane childe begottin betwix them in fornication. Dauid Zowng, deakin of the wobstaris, cautionar for Thomas Lawson to entir upon Settirday nixt to cum, to entir to mak his repentence according to the ordour, undir pain of xx lib.

Decretum sessionis penes Jonetam Elder.

Item, Jonet Elder, in respect of hir confession of hir evil tung, is thocht, gyf sche committis siclike in tyme cuming, to be banesed the town be decreit of the magistratis.

Die Mercurii, secundo Januarii, anno Domini j^mv^clxxvj^{to.}

The quhilk day, Richard Smytht in Kinninmontht is decernit Smytht,
be decreit of session to compleit [the][1] band of matrimonye *Nota.*
betwix hym and Jonet Ramsay, on Sunday cum aucht daiis,
undir pain of x lib., to be takin up be the ballies to the use of
the puiris; and this nixt Sunday to mak satisfaction for
brekking of ordour, on Sunday nixt to cum.[2] [*Patrik*—
deleted] Thomas Galloway cautionar, and Richard Smytht to
releve his cautionar Thomas foirsaid.

The said day, Margaret Mar, spous to George Richartson, *Decretum*
decernit in tyme cuming to desist fra keping of taverine upon *sessionis contra*
the Sabbat day in tyme cuming, undir pain of xl s., and to *Margaretam*
mak public repentence upon the penitent stule. Quhilk *Mar.*
decreit was gevin furtht witht consent of the saidis Margaretis
and hir spous.

Die Mercurii, sexto Februarii, 1576.

Memorandum : this day aucht dayis appointed to consult *Rij.*
gyf promis of mareage in tyme cuming sal be *per verba de* *Nota.*
presente vel de futuro, and siclik quhair the transgressouris salbe impressoned.

Item, anent the sermone to be maid on Fryday in tyme
cuming.

Die Mercurii, decimo tertio mensis Februarii, 1576.

The quhilk day, anent the supplication gevin in be Margaret [Margaret
Clapen to have hir bairn baptized, it is thocht gude that my [Clapen.]
Lord of Sanctandros[3] direct ane somoundis, to call hir husband

---

[1] Omitted.

[2] These five superfluous words are added in the margin.

[3] According to James Melvill,' when John Douglas was created Archbishop of
St. Andrews, Patrick Constantine, or Adamson, was so disappointed at not
being preferred, that he 'becam a zealus preatchour against bischopes. I hard
a sermont of his,' continues Melvill, 'the ouk efter the Bischope was maid, upon
ane extraordinar day, that he might haiff the graitter audience; wherin he maid
thrie sorts of bischoppes : My Lord Bischop, My Lord's Bischop, and The Lord's
Bischope. "My Lord Bischope," said he, "was in the Papistrie : My Lord's
Bischope is now, when my Lord getts the benefice, and the Bischope serves for

to compeir befoir my said Lord Bischop in this seat, to ansueir
to sic thingis as sal be sperit of hym.

[Robert Mal-
will.]

The quhilk day, it is ordeined be the saet that Robert
Malwill, upon Sunday nixt to cum, cum to the penitent stuill
and mak his public repentence, for the sclandir[1] committit be
the murthering of Dauid Martine; and to submit hymself to
ony forthir thyngis that the kirk sal injone to hym, and to
fynd caution thairto gyf the kirk thynkis expedient.

Nota.
[Anent promis
of mareage.]

The said day, it is thocht gude that the parteis that ar to
mak promis of mareage cum befoir the seat, and gyf up thair
names in wryte, quhilk salbe deliverit to the redar, and the
promis to be maid *per verba de futuro* in tyme cuming.

Nota.
[Lentht of
sermon.]

The said day, it is ordeined that in tyme cuming the sermon
begyn on the Sunday at half howre to ten, and to be endit at
the farrest at elevin howris.[2]

Die Mercurii, vigesimo Februarii, anno Domini 1576.

Elistoun, Fairly.

The quhilk day, William Elistoun confessis and grantis that
the childe laitlye born be Elspet Fairly to be his, gottin in

---

na-thing bot to mak his tytle sure : and The Lord's Bischope is the trew minister of the Gospell"' (Melvill's *Diary*, Wod. Soc. p. 32). And when it was
announced in the General Assembly, in October 1576, that the Regent Morton
had presented Adamson as Douglas's successor he was publicly asked, ' Giff he
wald receave that bischoprik?' To which he answered, 'He wald receave na
office judgit unlawfull be the Kirk'; and as to that bischoprik, he wald na wayes
accept of it without the advyse of the Generall Assemblie.' But Melvill adds,
' Nevertheless, or the nixt Assemblie [April 1577], he was seasit hard and fast
on the bischoprik ' (*Ibid*. pp. 56, 57).

[1] In 1565 the General Assembly clearly distinguished between the slander,
for which the Church was to deal with notorious malefactors, and the crime
for which the magistrate was to judge them (*Booke of the Universall Kirk*, i.
74-76).

[2] Some interesting notes on the length of sermons will be found in Dr. Edgar's
Old Church Life, first series, pp. 103-106. A more extraordinary example than
any there mentioned occurred towards the close of last century, when James
Thomson of Dunfermline preached an action sermon of two hours in his
ninetieth year (*Old Statistical Account*, xiii. 445). People evidently loved long
sermons in those days and plenty of them. An old man, who died fifty years
ago, remembered when, in the parish church of St. Andrews, both a lecture and
a sermon were included in the forenoon service on Sabbath ; yet numbers of the
members, when the service was ended, went straight to the Burgher church,
arriving in time to hear the sermon there.

fornication, and offeris hym to mak his repentence according to the ordour. The seat desyris the magistratis to tak ordour witht the saidis persounis, and thaireftir they sal be resavit be the kirk.

Mercurii, xiij° Martii, 1576.

The quhilk day, comperit befoir the seat Johne Mwdy [Bannis of tymmir-man and Beterage Kyng, and siclike Nicol Johneson Mwdy and and Jsobel Jak, and desyrit thair bannis to be proclamit to the son and Jak.] effect that they may be mareit.

Kyng, of Johne-

Mercurii, decimo Aprilis, anno Domini j^mv^clxxvij°.

The quhilk day, it is statut and ordinat be the seat that na *Nota.* committaris of public offensis, as fornicatioun, &c., sal be Anent commit-admittit to the communion,[1] quhill the nixt communion eftir offensis. makking of thair repentence, that thair gude behaviour may be knawin.

taris of public

The said day, William Smytht baxter and Meg Brown ar Smytht, Brown. admoneseid in tyme cuming fra convenyng in ony suspect place : gyf they do the contrar to be haldin as fornicatoris.

Die Mercurii, xxiiij^{to} Aprilis, anno Domini j^mv^clxxvij°.

The quhilk day, Dauid Cowper and Jsobel Ray his spous ar Cowper, Ray, ordein[ed] and decernit be the seat to intreat utheris honestly Rosse. and godly, in mutual societie, in bed and buird, in al tyme cuming ; and siclike the said Dauid to abstein fra cumpany and hanting of Christiane Ros hows ; and siclik the said Christiane Ros to resave not the said Dauid Cowper in hir hows ; and ilk ane of them to conten thair mowthis fra al fylthye and ungodlye speaking, undir pain of excommunicatioun.

Mercurii, octavo Aprilis, 1577.

The quhilk day, William Clark seeman confessit hym to Clark, Blyitht. have had carnal deal witht Elspet Blytht, eftir promis of mareage betwix them and thair bannis laufully according to

---

[1] *Nixt communion* in MS.

the ordour proclamit; and thairfoir [the seat][1] ordenis hym
to solemnizat the band of matrimony witht hir on Sunday nixt
to cum, undir paine of excommunication.

Die Mercurii, vigesimo sexto mensis Junii, anno Domini
j^mv^clxxvij^{o.}

Myllar, Cwik,
Hay.

The quhilk day, Johne Myllar in Baldinny-myln and Elspet
Cwik his spous accusat for the doun putting of ane woman
bairn, begottin betwix them in band of matrimonye, the thrid
day of October last bipast, be byrnyng of the said bairn to the
daitht. The saidis Johne and Elspet confessis that the bairn
[was][1] deliverit be thame to thair servand, Elspet Hay, at
aucht howris at nycht or thairby, sche passit out of the spens
to the hows witht the bairne; and witht[in][1] ane half howre
thaireftir hir guidman and sche hard the bairn greit, and the
said Johne past out of the spens from his awin bed, and fand
the bairn lyand be the fyire, and Elspet Hay slepand withtout
al clathis bot the sark, quhilk al was brynt the sleiffis except,
quhen the bairn was brocht be the said Johne Myllar to the
said Elspet Cwik. And Johne Myllar confessis the bairn
was brynt upon the bak and rycht schulder in spetial, and deit
upon the xiiij day eftir contracting of the byrnyng. Attour,
the said Johne Myllar grantis hym to have had carnal deal
witht the said Elspet Hay at Lames immediatlye preceding;
and as for the bairn that the said Elspet Hay is presently
witht, the said Johne Myllar referris to the said Elspet Hay
aitht gyf the bairn be his or not.

Oliphant,
Guthre.

The said day, Margaret Oliphant grantis and confessis hir
to have borne ane madin bairn in this citie to ane callit Patrik
Guthre, servand to my Lady Oliphant, as sche allegis; and,
becaus sche committit na offens in gaetting of the said bairn
in this citie, allegis hir not to be punisched heir, and yit desyris
the bairn to be baptized. The seat decernis the said Margaret
Oliphant to pas to the minister of Carnbe to caus hir bairn to
be baptizit.

---

[1] Omitted.

Die septimo mensis Augusti, anno Domini etc. lxxvij°·

The quhilk day, Jonet Leiche confessit hir to be witht Cok, Leiche, fornicatoris.
childe in fornicatioun witht William Cok, and that he had
knawledge of hir[1] carnaly betwix Pasche day, the vij day of
Aprile, and the xvij day thairof callit the Seingze day. And
the said William being accusat confessit that he lay witht hir
in his fatheris barne, upon Twisday eftir Pasche day, and nevir
knew hir carnaly eftir nor befoir. The quhilk the said Jonet Gr g, Sourdy, fornicatoris.
aggreit thairto. And lykewys Catharine Sourdy confessit hir
to be witht childe to Alane Gryg, quhilk the said Alane did
confes. And als Margaret Straquhin grantit hir to be witht Straquhin. *Confessio* Jak.
childe to Dauid Jak now in Noroway. And Dauid Jak eftir-
wart comperand confessit the sam.

Die decimo quarto mensis Augusti, anno Domini j^mv^clxxvij°.

The quhilk day, Patrik Hammiltoun being callit be the Hammiltoun, Arthour.
officiar of the sessioun, and his fathir, as he alledgit, Robert
Hammiltoun, being requirit that the said Patrik sould obey
the kirk, comperit Patrik obeying the voce of the kirk, and his
fathir ; being accusit that he hes begottin ane childe witht
Nannis Arthour, confessit the sam to be of trewtht, and promittit to be obedient and fulfill the command of the kirk in al
thyngis to be injoned to hym.

The quhilk day, Gelis Mylis desyrit to be mareit witht *Nota.*
Robert Lawson, sone to umquhill Dauid Lawsoun. The seat Mylis, Lawson.
dischargit them to procead forthir thairintil, qubil it be knawin
gyf the bairn sche buir of befor to Antone Zowng was baptizat as scho alledgit, and gyf the said Antone confessit hym
to be fathir to the said bairn ; and also quhil sche mak hir
repentence in this kirk for the fail committit be hyir.

The quhilk day, Johne Myllar, sone to Johne Myllar in Bal- Myllar, Hay, adulteri.
dinny myll, confessit hym to have gottin ane childe in adul-
terye witht Elspet Hay in Kairskeirdo in Seres parrochion,
and referris to the woman conscience gyf the bairn be his, bot
alwayis confessis that he had carnal daill witht hir, and hes

---

Acknawledge hir in MS.

offered hym to mak his repentence according to the ordour, and
to begyn on Sunday nixt to cum.

Die Mercurii, xxj^{mo} Augusti, 1577.

Petir Eviot,
Castaris, forni-
catoris.

The quhilk day,[1] Christen Castaris confessis and grantis hir
to be witht childe to Petir [2] Ewiott, and the said Dauid confessis
the sam, and confessis baitht promis of mareage betwix them.

Nota.
Smytht.

The quhilk day, the seat ordenis officiar of the assembly to
warne and charge Johne Smytht, cordonar, to celebrat the band
of matrimony witht [blank], betwix this and Michaelmes, under
paine of excommunication.

Die Mercurii, xxv^{to} mensis Septembris, j^mv^clxxvij^{o.}

Decretum ses-
sionis penes
Hugonem Frew.

The quhilk day, Hew Frew in Pewkye being accusat for presenting ane utheris mannis bairn gottin in fornicatioun, he
being admonesed privelye be George Blak that the fornicatour
hym self wald not gaet the bairne baptizät without repentence
passing afoir ; and als compering upon Sunday thaireftir pre-
sentand the said harlottis bairn, being admonesed to depart,
he wald not gaet the bairn baptizat, contemptuuslye remanit
and wald not obeye the admonition ; and forthir being chargit
for the said offence to compeir the nixt Wedinsday befoir the
session, be the said George, obeyit not : quhilk premissis he
confessit, and thairfoir the session injunis the said Hew to sitt
upon the umest [3] stuil of repentence for the offenc[e] committit, the sam day the harlot fathir to the said bairn witht his
harlot makkis thair repentence for the fornication be thame
committit, according to the ordour undir paine of excommunication.

Die Mercurii, secundo Octobris, 1577.

[Fowlis, Bel.] ·

Margaret Fowlis[4] confessis hir to have borne in fornication
ane woman bairn to Alane Bel servand to William Stevinson.

Bel, Thowles.

Alane Bel confessis hym to have had carnal dael witht Mar-

---

[1] *Dauid* in MS.
[2] *Petir* interlined over *Dauid* erased.
[3] Uppermost, highest.
[4] *Sic*.

garet Thowles[1] quha hes borne ane childe, and Alane referris to the said Margaret aitht, gyf the bairn be his; and gyf sche confessis the bairn to be his he sal tak thairwitht, and allegis promis of mareage betwix them.

Die Mercurii, decimo sexto mensis Octobris, 1577.

The namis of eldaris and diaconis electit upon Frydaye the xj day of October 1577.

Maister James Wilke, Principal of Sanct Leonardis Colleage
Mr. James Martein, Provest of Sanct Saluatouris Colleage
Mr. Johne Robeson, ane of the principall maisteris of the
    New Colleage
Mr. Thomas Balfour
Thomas Walwod, ballie

Alexander Castaris, ballie	Alexander Nairn
Mr. William Cok	James Forret in Smyddye-greyn
Johne Motto	William Monipenny
Mr. Marten Geddye	Mr. Johne Bonkle.

*D*iaconis.

William Zwill	Alexander Smytht
Johne Scot, merchand	Alexander Myllar
George Blak	Andro Watson
Charlis Watson, writar	Thomas Layng
James Ade	Waltir Kinninmontht.

The quhilk day, minister eldaris and diaconis abone writtin ratifiit and apprevit the heal statutis and ordinances of this sessioun maid of befoir, and in spetial the statutis and ordinances maid upon the fyfte day of November, yeir of God j^m v^c lxxij yeris. *Ratificatio statutorum sessionis.*

The quhilk day, the sessioun having consideration of James Steill, biddel and officiar of the session, gude service in keping of the presoun hows, the seat hes ordeined and decernit the said James to have twa schillingis off every person, man or woman, *Nota. Ordinance of the seat are it James Steill.*

---

[1] *Sic.*

[quha]¹ sal happin to be impresoned in tyme cuming, or they be relevit of preson.

Die xxvij° Novembris, 1577.

Williamson,
Johneson.

The quhilk day, Jonet Johneson confessit hir to be witht childe to William Williamson, quha being callit granted the sam ; and Jonat Johneson confessit that sche [is]¹ clethit witht ane husband, quha is passit to Flanderis as scho allegit to the wearis, callit Johne Spynk.

Die Mercurii, xxvᵗᵒ Decembris, 1577.

Dauidsone,
Downye.

The quhilk day, Thomas Dauidson and Mariorj Downy confessit thame in fornication to have had carnal deal, and the said Mariorj to be witht childe to the said Thomas.

Lermontht,
Strang.

The said day Beterage Strang confessis hir to be witht childe to James Lermontht of Balcolmy yownger.

Die Mercurii, decimo nono Februarii, anno Domini 1577.

Nota.
For preaching.

The quhilk day, the seat hes ordeined and decernit that, at the minister nixt hame cuming, ordour be takin quhow the kirk sal not be defraudit for inlaik of teaching in tyme cuming, nethir in his presence nor absence.

For reparatioun
of the kirk.

The said day, the seat ordenis ane supplication to be direct to Provest ballies and counsal of this citie, for reparation of the kirk, and taking of compt of the kirk geir, that the sam may be bestowit as efferis.

Die Mercurii, quarto Maii, anno Domini jᵐvᶜlxxviijᵒ·

Williamsoun,
Johnesoun.
Nota.

The quhilk day, William Williamsoun is decernit be the seat to mak his repentence as ane fornicator, becaus he maid faitht in presence of the seat that he nevir knew to this howre that Jonet Johnesoun, quhom witht he had carnal deal, was spowsit or wedded witht ony person. William Stevinson baxter cautionar for William Williamson to fulfil the heal injunctiounis of the kirk, and the said William to releve his cautionar.

---

¹ Omitted.

The quhilk day, Henry Fairfull, in presence of the seat, con- *Confessio* *Fairfull.*
fessit that he cam cautioun to Thomas Walwod balye, to entir
Thomas Dauidson *alias* Thomas Rawffye this day befoir the
seat undir paine of xl s.

Die Mercurii, undecimo mensis Junii, anno Domini millesimo
quingentesimo septuagesimo octavo.

The quhilk day, Thomas Plaifeir is becum souertye for Johne *Nota.*
Robertsoun and Christen Zwil, that they sal absten in tyme *Robertson,* *Zwill.*
cuming fra carnel copulation, and to be obedient to fulfil al *Nota, nota.*
the injunctionis of the kirk ; and the said Christen to begyn
hir public [repentence]¹ upon Sunday nixt cumin[g], and Johne
Robertson at his hame ² cuming, undir paine of xl liþ. : and at
the beginning of Christen repentence, the bairn begottin betwix
them to be resavit to baptisme.

Die Mercurii, xxvᵗᵒ Junii, anno etc. septuagesimo octavo.

The quhilk day, the seat hes ordeined Margaret Clapen to *Nota.*
rays the Bischoppis letteres to somound [*blank*] Auchtmowty, *Clapen,* *Auchmowtye.*
hir husband, to present the bairn begottin betwix them to bap-
tisme, witht al diligence, and to bryng the saidis letteres
indorsat.

Die Mercurii, nono Julii, 1578.

The quhilk day, Jonet Hagy confessit that William Geddy, *Confessio* *Hagye.*
seeman, in winter last was eftir supper in William brother hal,
he and his wyffe being furtht of the hows, lay witht hir and
had carnal deal witht hir.

The said day, Catharine Kelly confessis hir to have had *Confessio* *Kelly, Lowrye.*
carnal deal [witht]¹ Johne Lowrye at twa syndry tymis ; and
Johne Lowyr confessis the sam.

The said day, Henry Scot *alias* Kilmoun grantis and confessis *Scot alias* *Kylmoun,* *Methw°n.*
hym to have maid, and be the tenour heirof in presence of the
seat makkis, promis of mariage to Agnes Meffen, be deliverance of his hand to the said Agnes ; and to solempnizat the

---

¹ Omitted.　　　² *Heal* in MS.

band and promis of mareage maid be hym to hir in face and
visage of the kirk, opinlye, withtin yeir and day, or soner as
sal pleas the kirk, quhen he sal be requirit thairto ; and to mak
his repentance at the sycht of the kirk according to the ordour
quhenevir he salbe requirit thairto, undir al hiest paine and
chairge that eftir may fallow : and heirfor the seat ordenis the
bairn, last begottin and borne betuix the saidis Henry and
Agnes,[1] to be resavit to baptisme upon Sunday nixt to cum.

Die Mercurii, decimo sexto Julii, 1578.

Adam,
M^cknair,
fornicatoris.

The quhilk day, Jonat Adam confessis hir to be witht childe
begottin in fornication betwix hir and Donald M^cknair, servand
to Maister Dauid Carmichel, and offeris hir to mak hir repentance according to the injunctiounis of the kirk.

Die Mercurii, penultimo Julii, 1578.

Oliphant.

The quhilk day, Margaret Oliphant is decernit be the seat
to bryng ane sufficient testimonial of the minister of Abirdaigy,

xxj dies.

that the bairn alledgit that sche hes unbaptizat was baptizat,
this day thre oulkis.

Dalgles,
Browne,
fornicatores.

The said day, Margaret Browne confessit hir to be witht
childe to Dauid Dalgles, sone of umquhill Thomas Dalgles.

Brown, Read,
fornicatoris.

Item, Beaty Browne verifiit the bairnis father that sche desyris to be baptizat is callit Thomas Read, sumtyme servand to
the Laird of Kinkel and now past to Camdy, and is content to
mak hir repentance ; and thairfoir the seat ordenis the bairn to
be baptizat on Sunday nixt to cum.

Stevinson,
Mykeson,
Cwnynghame.

The said day, Catharine Stevinsoun grantis hyir to have ane
woman childe of twa yeris auld, gottin betwix hir and Stevin
Mikeson, yit unbaptizat ; and siclik, ane uthir woman childe
of nyne oulkis ald, begottin betwix hir and Alane Cwnynghame.

Die Mercurii, decimo tertio Augusti, 1578, in presentia ministri seniorum et diaconorum civitatis Sanctiandree.

Robertson,
Suthirland,
fornicatores.

Agnes Robertson confessis hir witht childe to Donald Suthirland, servitour to my Lord Bischop of Caithnes.[2]

---

[1] *Henry and Henry* in MS. [2] *Supra,* p. 232, n.

The said day, Jonet Ryngane was decernit to bryng ane suf- *Ringane,*
ficient testimonial that the bairn gottin betwix hir and Dauid *Schewes. Nota.*
Schewes was baptizat. And now, upon the thrid day of Sep-
tember 1578, was producit ane testimonial of Petir Ramsay,
minister of Dairsy, of the baptizing of the bairne.[1]

The said day, comperit Robert Awchmowty, spous to Mar- *Nota.*
garet Clapen, being askit gyf the bairn borne be the said Mar- *Auchmowty, Clapen.*
garet was his lawful sone, confessit the sam ; and had na caus
to lay to the said Margaret, and sayis that his and hir stubburnes was caus that the bairne was unbaptizat. And the said
Robert offered to present his bairn to be baptizat, swa the said
Margaret wil adheir to. hym ; and swa the matir continuat
quhill Michaelmes nixt to cum, undir hoip of ful reconciliation. J. B.

Die Mercurii, decimo quinto Octobris, anno Domini j^mv^clxxviij^{o.}

The quhilk day being appointed to al personis to compeir, *Nota.*
to alledge ony thyng aganis the personis nominat to be eldaris ·
and diaconis, being thriis callit na person comperit to object.

Eldaris and deaconis electit the penult day of October 1578.

Eldaris.

Maister James Vilkie, Rector of the Universitie of St Androis
Maister James Mairtyne, Provest off the Auld College
Maister Johne Robertsoun, ane of the principall maesteris off
    the New College
Maister Thomas Balfour
Maister Martein Geddye

Maister Villiam Cok	Villiam Ferrye
Maister Dauid Meldroum,	Johne Mutto
baillie	James Robertsoun
Dauid Balfour, baillie	Maister Johne Bonkle.

---

[1] Under this entry there is a special heading: ' *Die Mercurii tertio Septembris*
1578 '; but the minute concerning Auchmowty and Clapen is begun above that
heading, extends below it, and even under the heading of 15th October.

*D*iaconis.

George Blak	Alexander Millar
Johne Scot	Andro Vatsoun
Charlis Vatsoun, wretar	Johne Levingstoun
James Scheues	Thomas Laing
Alexander Smith	Valter Kynninmounth.

Ratificatioun of the Statutis[1] of the sessioun. The quhilk day, minister eldaris and diaconis ratifiit and apprevit the heal statutis and ordinances of this session, maid upon the fyfte day of November, yeir of God j^m v^c lxxij yeris.

Wedinsday, the xij day of November, 1578.[2]

Wedinsday, the xix of November, 1578.

Decreit of the session aganis Johne Smytht. The quhilk day, Johne Smytht being dilatit to the assemblye for abusing of hym self, and resaving in his hows playaris at cairtis and dyce nycht and day, and haldaris of drunkattis in his hows nycht and day. The said Johne is decernit be the seat that gyf evir he beis fund in tyme cuming, to abuse hym in tyme cuming, [he][3] sal mak his public repentence upon the penitent stuill, and to pay to the pure at the will of the seat.[4]

Decretum sessionis contra William Moreis. The said day, William Moreis wrycht beyng dilated to the seat as ane commoun player at cairtis and dyce, the said William decernit as Johne Smytht immediatlye abone writting.

Kengzow, Schewas, fornicatores. The said day Male Kengzow confessis hir to be witht childe to William Schewes merchand.

---

[1] *Statuis* in MS.   [2] There is no entry under this date.
[3] Omitted.
[4] John Smyth was perhaps too thoroughly wedded to cards and dice to be so easily persuaded to discard them, for in 1598 the deacon and council of the Hammermen dealt with a John Smyth, their officer, for neglecting his duties 'and abusing of his awin persone in playing at cards and dys.' It was decerned, that 'if evir he beis fund disobedient to the craft or playing at cards and dys, or uther extraordinar games at ony tyme heirefter, that the said John sal incur the censuris of the kirk, and to pay to the craft x li., or els deprivit of his fredome and libirtie of the craft : to the quhilk the said John willingle consents '. (*Bouk of the Hammermen of Sanctandrous*).

Wedinsday, the xxvj day of November, 1578.

The quhilk day, the seat hes appointed, the xvij day of *Nota.*
December nixt to cum, Margaret Clapen to bryng hir freindis Clapen, Aucht
to consult upon the baptizing of the man childe, gottin betwix mowty, *xvij*
hir and[1] Robert Auchtmowty hir spous ; and lykewys the said *Decembris.*
Robert to gyf his ansueir wyth avis of his freindis.

Wedinsday, the xvij of December, 1578.

The quhilk day, comperit Margaret Clapen accumpaniit wyth *Nota.*
certane of hir freindis, to the effec expremit in the act abone Clapen,
immediatlye writtin. The session, becaus of non comperence Auchmowtye.
of Robert Auchmowtye, quhom they knaw not to have bein
advertesed, appointis, the last day of December instant, the
said Margaret to compeir to the effect foirsaid, and also the
said Robert, and hym to be advertesed to that effect be my
Lord of Sanctandrois, Bischop and Superintendent.

Die ultimo mensis Decembris, anno Domini jᵐvᶜlxxviijᵒ·

The said day, my Lord of Sanctandrois hes direct ane *Nota.*
somoundis aganis Robert Auchtmowtye, conform to the desyre Auchmowtye,
of the formar act, to compeir the vij day of Januar ; witht inti- Clapᶜn.
mation, gyf he comperit not, he wald caus the bairne gottin
betwix hym and Margaret Clapen to be baptizat.

Die Mercurii, septimo Januarii, anno Domini jᵐvᶜlxxviijᵗᶜ·

The quhilk day, the somoundis of the Bischop of Sanct- *Nota.*
an[dros] being producit, execut and indorsat, chergeing Robert Auchmowty,
Auchmowtye spous to Margaret Clapen to compeir peremp- Clapen.
tourlye befoir hym and the session, to present his bairn, gottin
betwix hym and the said Margaret in matrimonye as the said
Robert confessit, as the said somoundis, of the dait the secound
of Januar 1578, at mair lyntht proportis, witht intimation he
wald caus the said bairn to be baptizat, and to proceid aganis

---

[1] *And and* in MS.

2 E

hym as ane contempnar of the ordinances of the kirk : the said Robert, being laufully somound, oft-tymis callit and nocht comperand the Bischop of Sanctandros, witht avis of the session, decernit the bairn to be baptizat. And the said Margaret, as[1] ane member of this congregation, submittis hir to the said kirk and discipline thairof in al tyme cuming, of hir awn propir confession.

Die Mercurii, quarto Februarii, 1578.

Read, M^cke.

The quhilk day, anent the exceptioun alledgit be Elizabetht M^cke aganis Thomas Read, allegeand hir be compulsioun of hir fathir to have maid promis of mareage witht Thomas Read, and thairfoir that sche aucht not to proceid in mareage witht the said Thomas ; becaus the said Elizabetht failyeit in proba- tion of hir saidis allegeance, the seat ordenis and decernis the said Elizabetht to proceid to mareage witht the said Thomas, undir sic pains as the kirk may lay to hir chairge.

Arthour,
Seaton, *rij.*

The quhilk day, James Arthour and Jonet Seitoun being dilatat to the seat as fornicatoris, and the said James being demandit, gyf thair be ony promis of mareage betwix hym and the said Jonet,[2] James denyis the sam. The seat assignat this day aucht dayis to the said James, to compeir to gyf his aitht gyf he had carnal copulation witht the said Jonat or not; and, gyf he confessed, gyf he wald submit hym to discipline or not; witht certification, gyf he comperis not to gyf his aitht and to mak his purgation, the feal to be haldin as confessed.

Die Mercurii, undecimo Februarii, 1578.

Arthour,
Seitoun.

The seat continuat geving of James Arthour aitht upon the thingis expremit in the act immediatlye preceding to this day aucht dayis, an he warnit *apud acta* to the said effect.

Die Mercurii, decimo octavo Februarii, anno Domini 1578.

Greyff, Kellye.

The quhilk day, Alexander Myllar, cultellar, in presence of Dauid Balfour bailye and the seat, is becum cautionar

---

[1] *Is as* in MS. : has originally run *is becum.*   [2] *James* in MS.

that Dauid Greyff sal marye Margaret Kellye, dochtir to
Johne Kelly fleschear, withtin five oulkis nixt to cum, undir
paine of xx lib.; and the said Johne to releve the said Alexander undir paine foirsaid.

The said day, in the terme assignat to James Arthour to Arthour,
compeir befoir the seat to gyf his aitht and mak his purga- Seitoun.
tioun, gyf he had carnal deal witht Jonat Seetoun or no, and
gyf he comperit not to be haldin *pro confesso* that he had
carnal copulatioun witht hir, and thairfoir to be decernit to
mak his repentence opinly, according to the ordour; the seat,
in respect that the said James comperit not to gyf his aitht,
hes haldin the said deid *pro confesso*, and thairfoir decernis the
saidis James and Jonet to mak thair repentence opinlye according to the ordour.

Die *xviij° Martii*, 1578.

The quhilk day, Christen Vtein confessis hir to be witht Ramsay,
childe to Johne Ramsay, sone to James Ramsay tailyeor, undir Vtein.
promis of mareage; and thairfoir [the seat]¹ ordenis the saidis
Johne and Christiane to be warnit as efferis.

The said day, Jonet Gifferd, dochtir to umquhill William Moreson,
Gyfferd, grantis hir to have had carnal deal witht [*blank*] Gyfferd.
Moreson, tailyeor to my Lady Maisteris Forbes, undir promis
of mareage, and they be baitht to be warnit to this day aucht
dayis.

Die *xxv*ᵗᵒ *Martii*, 1579.

The quhilk day, the seat ordenis Christiane Stewart, sister Stewart.
to William Sinclair wyffe, to be callit to compeir this day
aucht dayis, to ansueir to accusatioun to be laid to hir concerning hir being witht childe.

Item, the seat appointis dilatioun to be takin up befoir the
communioun nixt to be celebrat upon Law Sunday nixt to cum,
to the xxvj day of Aprile nixt to cum. Mr. Robert Hammiltoun minister, Dauid Balfour baillie, Johne Motto, George
Blak.

---

¹ Omitted.

Die Mercurii, xxij^{do.} Aprilis, 1579.

Schewes,
Keingzow.

The quhilk day, William Schewes confessis hym to have had carnal conversatioun witht Male Kengzow, and yit grantis the bairne that sche is laetly deliverit of not to be his becaus sche hes passit ower the tyme, xx dayis ower the tyme, and thairfoir desyris the said Male to gyf hir aitht gyf the bairne be his or not.

Die Mercurii, xiij° Maii, 1579.

Nota.
[The heal town
to be vesyit.]

The quhilk day, the seat hes ordeind and desyrit that the heal town quartarlye be vesyit be sum of the ballies and sum of the sessioun, to the effect they that ar not mareit may be knawin, and gyf ony bairnis be unbaptizat, and for tryal of ony notable crymis.

The first quartar, fra the parroche kirk [eastward][1] on baitht the sydis of the gait : Mr. Thomas Balfour elder, and Dauid Balfour ballie, Andro Watson, writar.

The secound quartar, the rest of the Sowtht Gaet and Ergyle : Ballie Alexander Winchestir, James Robertson, William Ferry Dene-of-Gild.

The thrid quartar, the heal Merkkat Gaet: Mr. Dauid Meldrum balle, Mr. Martine Geddy, Charles Watson scribe.

The fourt quartar, the heal Northt Gaet and Fischear Gaet:[2]

---

[1] Omitted.

[2] This division of the four quarters of the town shows that there were only three main streets in St. Andrews in those days. The first and second quarters comprehending South Street, and its continuation, Argyle ; the third, Market Street ; and the fourth, North Street and the Fisher Gate. But according to an old tradition there were four large streets. Writing in 1728 William Douglass [? De Foe] says, ' The northmost of these four streets, call'd the Swallow Street, is now entirely ruinous, and not one house to be seen, though it was formerly the principal street where the chief merchants and traders resided, having in it the great hall built over piazzas, where the people of business met daily about the affairs of trade' (*Some Historical Remarks on the City of St. Andrews,* pp. 7, 8). Bishop Pococke also refers to this fourth street (*Tours in Scotland,* Scot. Hist. Soc. p. 266) ; and Dr. Johnson links its loss with the gradual decay, which, he says, set in when the city lost her archiepiscopal pre-eminence (*Journey to the Western Islands,* 1819, pp. 6, 7). The statement in the text, however, and the old map of the town, *c.* 1530, conclusively prove, at least, that such a street did not exist in Reformation times.

Ballie Johne Martyne elder, Alexander Castaris, George Blak, Johne Scot.

Christen Bawdy, servand to Dauid Kynneir baxtar, grantis hir to be wytht childe to James Brown, servand to Alane Thomson in Cowper; and now confessis the fathir of the bairn to be Thomas Henderson, servand to Dauid Kinneir, and confessis the said Thomas to have had first carnal deal wytht hir in the West Burn Wynde, in David Kynneir barn.

Bawdy and Brown fornicatoris.

Die Mercurii, primo Julii, 1579.

The quhilk day, James Prowd yownger is becum bund and obligat, wytht his awin consent, to pay to George Blak collectour of the puris almis xl s., betwix this and Michaelmes nixt to cum, for certane faltis that he was dilatit for to the seat.

James Prowd yownger. Nota.

The said day, the seat decernit and ordinat Johne Scot merchand to be somound upon Sunday nixt to cum, to resave the injunctiounis of the kirk for the alledgit adultery committit be hym wytht Grisel Motto.

Nota. Scot, Motto.

Die Mercurii, octavo Julii, 1579.

The quhilk day, Margaret Clapen spous to Robert Auchmowty confessit hir to be wytht childe to Johne Schewes, brother germane to Patrik Schewes of Kembak, and the childe to be consavit sen Peace last was, and the bairne consavit eftir the departing of the said Robert hir spous and that sche sould [send ane][1] testimonial tharof.

Nota, nota, nota. Confessto Margarete Clapen.

The quhilk day, Johne Scot merchand—being callit befoir the seat be ane libellat somoundis, rasit at the instance of Jonet Murray his[2] spous aganis hym, tweching the alledgit adultery committit be hym wytht Grisel Motto, spous to William Anderson mercha[nd], in his absence—comperit personlye and confessit the said cryme, lamented the sam, submitting hymself to the discipline of the kirk and cravis hym to be

Moray, Scott.

---

[1] These words are somewhat doubtful, being faint and indistinct.
[2] *Hir* in MS.

admittit to the sam. *Item*, the said Johne, ansuering to the
byl of William Andersoun, submittis hym to the discipline of
the kirk and cravis the sam.

Walcar, Pater-
son.

The said day, Alexander Walcar confessis hym to have had
carnel copulation wytht Nannis Paterson, quha is presentlye
wytht childe, and referris to the said Nannes aitht gyf the
childe be his or not.

Die Mercurii, decimo quinto mensis Julii, anno Domini 1579.

Johne Scott
resavit to
repentance.

The quhilk day, Johne Scott comperit befoir the sessioun
upon his kneis, bewaling his adulterie, craving for Goddis saik
to be admittit to repentence, and [promitting that][1] quhat the
kirk wald presentlie injone to hym, presently or in tyme cuming to fulfil the sam, at plesure of the kirk. The sessioun hes
resavit the said Johne to repentence, and ordenis hym on
Sunday nixt to cum to begyn his repentence, according to
the ordour takin wytht commoun adulteraris.

*Die Mercurii, vigesimo secundo Julii, anno Domini millesimo
quingentesimo septuagesimo nono.*

Henderson,
Bawdy.

The quhilk day, Thomas Henderson grantis hym to have
begottin ane childe in fornication, wyth Christen Bawdye
dwelling in James Gifferd hows.

Scott.

The said day, fforalsmekle as Johne Scot, upon Wedinsday
the xv day of Julii instant, promittit to enter on[2] Sunday last
was to mak his repentence and hes failyeit thairintil, [the seat][1]
ordeneid the said Johne to be summoned upon Sunday nixt to
cum, to entir to mak his repentence conform to the last act,
undir paine of excommunication.

Mvtto, Scott.

The said day, Grisel Motto is ordeined to be warned to this
day aucht dayis, to ansueir to sic thingis as sal be sperit at hir
anent the adultery committit be hir wyth Johne Scot.

Die Mercurii, vigesimo nono Julii, 1579.

Grisel Motto,
Johne Scott.

The quhilk day, Grisel Motto, being callit and accused for

---

[1] Omitted.   [2] *Om* in MS.

adultery committit be hir witht Johne Scot merchand, confessis that, be persuasion of the said Johne Scot, the first
familiarite betwix them was upon Thurisday eftir Michaelmes
day last bypast, and [he][1] lay wytht hir that nycht; and his
persuasioun to induce hir to commit the said cryme wytht hym
was fyve yeris befoir the said Thurisday eftir Michaelmes day;
and hes continewit wytht hir sen syne as he pleasit, and cheiflye
com to hir hows tyme of common prayeris usit in the kirk.
And the said Grisell, confessing hir adultery and the bairne to
be the said Johneis, cravit Goddis mercy and pardone; and
desyrit wytht all humilite the kirk to resave hir to repentence.
The kirk appointed this day aucht [dayis][1] to gyf hir ansueir. *v^{to} Augusti.*

The said day, the seat hes ordened Margaret Clapen, this [N]*ota,' nota,*
day nyne oulkis, to produce ane sufficient testimonial of the *nota.*
deatht of Robert Auchtmouty hir spous. Clapen,
Auchmowtye.

The said day, Elspet Dik confessis hir to be wytht childe to Dik, Jameson.
Nichol Jameson, servand to the yowng Laird of Dairsy, in fornication; and this is the secound bairne that sche is wytht to
the said Nichol.

The said day, the seat callit Johne Thomson baxtar and Thomson,
William Turpy, quha hes respeit for the slawchtir of umquhill Turpye.
Dauid Symson, and desyrit them to acknauledge thare offence,
and tak away the sclander, to mak thar publice repentence,
according to the act of the General Assembly, quha compering
desyrit this day aucht dayis to gyf thar ansueir, quhilk the seat *Mercurii* the
appointed to them.[2] v. of August.

Marcurii, die quinto mensis Augusti, 1579.

The quhilk day, minister eldaris and diaconis hes ordeined *Nota, nota.*
and decernit that, in tyme cuming, nane be resavit to compleit *Decretum ministerii.*
the band of matrimonye, wythtout they rehers to the redar the
Lordis Prayeris, Beleve, and the Commandementis of God.

The said day, William Schewes, comperand, desyrit his bairn Schewes,
gottin in fornication betwix hym and Male Kengzow to be Kengzow.
baptizeid, undir caution that he sal satisfye the kirk at sic Ordinance
tyme as he may be lasered.[3] The seat, in respect of the anent fornicatouris to be
observit in al
tyme cuming.

---

[1] Omitted.   [2] *They* in MS.   [3] At leisure.

ordinance concerning fornicatoris and baptizing of thar bairnis
establesched and practized of befoir, injunis to the said William
to satisfye the majestratis according to the ordour, and thareftir publiklye to obey the kirk, and his bairn then to be
resavit to baptisme ; and gyf the said William obeyis not
this ordinance, he to be admonesed undir paine of excommunication opinlye ; and the said ordour to be observit in al tyme
cuming aganis sic lik.

Decretum sessionis penes Turpye et Thomson. The said day, the seat hes ordeined William Turpy and
Johne Thomson, upon Sunday nixt to cum, opinlye to be
admonesid to mak thar repentence, for the slauchtir of umquhil
Dauid Symson.

Die vigesimo quinto Augusti, 1579.

[Murray, Scot.] The quhilk day, Jonet Murray producit hir [1] bill of complent
of injuris and sklandir againis Johne Scot sumtym hir spous ;
and efter the same being red, and denyit be the said Johne,
the sessioun admitted the complent to probatioun. And the
said Jonet, incontinent thaireftir, producit James Bennat
merchand, Margareit Maen and Jonat Balfour, witnes ; quha,
being sworne and severalie examinat, deponit the haell pointtis
off the clame to be of trewth. The seat assignit this day viij
dayis to pronunce.

[Scot, Murray.] The quhilk day, Johne Scot producit his clame of complent
againis Jonet Murray. The seat ordenit this day viij dayis to
him to preiff the same.

Die Mercurii,[2] secundo Septembris, 1579.

[Murray, Scot.] The quhilk day, in the terme statut to pronunce in the
actioun of Jonet Murray againis Johne Scot, becaus the seat is
not full and compleit number, continowat the pronunciatioun
of the said complen[t] to the xxiij day of September.

The said day, in the terme assignit to Johne Scot to preiff
his bill againis Jone[t] Murray, compeirit the said Johne
and allegit that he cawsit James Steill warne Malie Kelso[t],

---

[1] *His* in MS.   [2] *Mercurei* in MS.

spous to James Brog, Margareit Heriot, relict off umquhill
Johne Traell, Dauid Myllis youngir, and Christiane Barcley
his spous, witnes; quhom James Steill allegit was warnit.
The seat becaus the said Jonet was absent, the minister and
witnes not compeirand, ordenit the parties to be warnit to this
day viij dayis.

Die Mercurii, xxiij° Septembris, 1579.

The quhilk day, the seat, in respect off the probatioun Decretum Murray.
deducit upone the clame of Jonet Murray aganis Johne Scot,
ordenis the said Johne upon Sounday nixt to cum, in presens
off the congregatioun off this citee, to sitt down upone his kneis,
confes his offence maed aganis the said Jonett, and pronunce
thir wordis, haldand his awin tung in his hand, Fals[1] tung
thow leid! and confes that he knawis na thing to the said Jonet
bot gud and honestie.

Item, siklyk[2] the said Johne is ordenit and decernit be the Decretum contra Scot.
seat to cum everie Sounday to the little kirk dure at the
secund bell, thair to remane—beirfutted, baer haed, and face
uncoverit—to the thrid bell, and thareftir to pas to the penitent seat, and ascend and discend thairupone moderatlie; and
siklyk is decernit to compeir everie preatching day within the
owk, in his awin appaireil, and sitt undir the powpet during
the tym off sermounth, and als daylie to frequent the morning
and evening prayaris.

The quhilk day, Thomas Huntar and Johne Scot, according Accusatio Scot, Huntar.
to the desyr of the seat, being accused be Mr. James Vilkie,
Mr. Johne Watsoun, and Dauid Balfour bailyee, upone that
point of Jonet Murrayis clame, to wit, that quhair the said
Johne Scot requeistit and desyrit the said Thomas to pas ower
to Edinburgh, and thar before the commissaris affirme and say
before thame that he had carnell dael with the said Jonet:
quhilkis parsonnis being confronted, the said Thomas confessit
that within thir vj owkkis, Johne Scot and he being gaun[3]
abowt the feildis, the said Johne said to him thir wordis, Will
ye pas ower to Edinburgh before the saidis commissaris, and

---

[1] *And fals* in MS.   [2] *Siblyk* in MS.   [3] *Gang* in MS.

thar tak upone yow and afferme that ye lay with my wyff Jonet Murray and had carnall dæll with hir? Ye will do me gryt plesour! Quhilk petition the said Thomas thinking maest vyld and ungodlié refusit the same. Quhilk accusation the said Johne on his conscience culd not deny, bot confessit the sam to be off trewth, saying that it was in mowis[1] that he desyrit him.[2]

Die decimo quarto Octobris, 1579.

Bell.

The quhilk day, the sessioun ordenis Catharine Bell to be summonit upon Sonday nixt to cum, to compeir upon Wedinsday nixt to cum befoir the said sessioun, and thar confess in thair presens to quhom scho is wyth chylde; in respect that oft and diverss tymmes scho hes bein serschit and socht wythin this citie, to the effect foirsaid and culd nocht be apprehendit.

Meldrom.

The quhilk day, the sessioun, in respect off the commoun and odious bruit past upon Mr. Dauid Meldrom and Catharine Bell for fornication committit be thaime, ordenis the said Mr. Dauid to compei[r] befoir the said sessioun and mak his purgatioun off the said sclandir, befoir anye testimoniall be granted to him for mariage.

Anent all fornicatouris.

Item, siclyk the sessioun ordenis Catharine Pittillok to be summond opinlie, to compeir upon Wadinsday nixt to ressave hir injunctionis for fornicatioun, becaus scho hes alredye personallie, and as yit contemptuouslie disobeyis; and siclyk ordeinis all personis, delated for fornicatioun and dissobeying, to compeir the said day to the effect foirsaid.

Die vigesimo quinto mensis Novembris, anno Domini millesimo quingentesimo septuagesimo nono.

Maister Robert Hammilton minister.

Eldaris votit electit and chosin upone the xviij day off November 1579.

Mr. James Wilkye, Rector off the Universitie off St. Androis
Maister Jaimes Martine, Provest off St. Saluatour

---

[1] Jest.   [2] *Hir* in MS.

Mr. Jhone Robertsoun
Mr. Thomas Balfor
Mr. Martine Geddye   Deaconis.
Mr. William Cok   George Blak
Mr. Dauid Russell, baillie   Alexander Millar
Jaimes Mortoun, baillie   Alexander Smith
Jhone Martine, eldar   Charlis·Watsoun, notar
Jaimes Robertsoun   Jhone Levingistoun
Thomas Walwod   Jaimes Alane
Jhone Mutto   Dauid Blair
Mr. Jhone Bonkle.   Jaimes Ade.

The quhilk day, minister eldaris and deaconis abone specefeit *Ratificatioun and approba·tioun off statuttis maid off befoir.* affirmat ratifeit and approvit the haill stattuttis and ordinances off the sessioun maid upone the fyft day off November, the yeir off God jajv^{c}lxxij yeris,[1] and swoir to observe the sam in all pointtis.

The quhilk day, comperit William Watsoun and Christen *Watsoun, Craig. Secundo Decembris.* Craig fornicatoris, quha being accusat confessit thair fornicatioun, and submitted thaime to the discipline off the kirk, according to the accustomed ordour observit.

The quhilk day, Margaret Nicoll allegit hir, in presens off *Nicoll, Aldye.* the sessioun, to be wyth bairne to Jhone Adye, as he confessit him selff. The sessioun ordenit thaime to compeir this day *Secundo Decembris.* aucht dayis for triall to be takin thairanent.

The quhilk day, Catharine Pittillok, in presens off the *Confessio Pittillok.* sessioun, allegit hir to be wyth bairne to Thomas Lawdeane, and yit granttis he nevir confessit the sam to anye persoun. The session ordenit hir to bring testificatioun to thaime be the meid-wyffe that the bairne is the said Lawtheanis.

Die secundo mensis Decembris, anno Domini millesimo quingentesimo septuagesimo nono.

The quhilk day, the sessioun, in respect off Jhone Scottis *Ordinance con·cerning Jhone Scot.* absence thir diverss Sondayis from penitence contrar the desyre

---

[1] Frequently the *m* for *millesimo* is written extremely like *aj*, but this clerk removes all dubiety by putting a dot over the *j*.

off the injunctionis imput to him, thairfoir hes thocht it expedient that[1] the said Jhone be advertissit wyth all diligence
quhairevir he bies apprehendit, that he compeir befoir the
sessioun and fulfill the decreit pronuncit and prescrivit to him,
or ellis to allege ane ressonable caus quhye he suld nocht do the
sam ; wyth certificatioun and[2] he compeir nocht at the day
appointed, the sessioun will proceid conforme to the ordour.

Meldrum, Bell.
The quhilk day, Mr. Dauid Meldrom, being in presens off
the assemblie and desyrit, according to the desyre off the act
maid upone the xiiij day off October last bipast, to mak his
purgatioun off the sclander past upon him and Catharine Bell,
ansuerit he belevit he wes innocent off the sclander : and being
desyrit to giff[3] his grit aith thairupon, answerit, he was na
wayis haldin to giff[3] his aith, becaus the sam redounded to his
awin turpitude and infamie. And the session assignit this
day *xx^{ti}* dayis, to wit, the xxij day off December instant, to
avise upon his purgatioun.

xxij^{do}. Decembris.

*Die nono mensis Decembris, anno Domini millesimo
quingentesimo septuagesimo nono.*

Methwne,
Andersoun,
Methwne.
M.[5]
The quhilk day, comperit Jsobell Methwne, and Henrye
Andersoun hir spous for his interes, and producit [hir][4] claime
aganis Margaret Methtwn hir sister. The sessioun, in respect
off hir non comperance, assignit this day viij dayis to the said
defender, to compeir personallie to heir probatioun led.

Decretum contra Aldye, Nicoll.
The quhilk day, Jhone Aldye and Margaret Nicoll ar
decernit be the sessioun to enter in prisoun upon Setterday
nixt, thairin to remaine viij dayis nixt thaireftir, and to mak
thair publict repentance according to the accustomit ordour
observit.

Decretum contra Mutto.
The quhilk day, Grisell Mutto is decernit be the sessioun to
enter, upon Sonday nixt, upone the penitent stule, cled in the
gown maid for adultereris, wyth certificatioun contenit in the
actis preceding in this actioun.

This com to na effect.

---

[1] *That that* in MS.			[2] If.			[3] *Iff* in MS.
[4] Altered and blotted, perhaps *thair.*
[5] *M* is probably used by this clerk as equivalent to *rij.* See p. 294, n.

Die decimo sexto mensis Decembris, 1579.

The quhilk day, in the term assignit to Henrye Andersoun and his spous to preiff thair claime and bill aganis Margaret Methwne, the parties comperand, the saidis persewaris producit Bessye Walwod, spous to Jaimes Smith, Robert Wylie, tailyeor, Jhone Millar and Jonet Gorlay, witnessis, sworne and examinat, nathing aganis thaime opponit. The session ordenit the persewar to do forder diligence for the witnessis accaipit, to this day[1] viij dayis.

Andersoun, Methwnnis.

Die xiij° Januarii, 1579.

The quhilk day, Maister Dauid Meldrum is decernit be the voetis of the sessioun to compeir this day aucht dayis, to gyf his aitht upon his purgatioun of the fornicatioun, allegit committit be hym wytht Catharine Bell.

Meldrum, Bell, rij.

Die vigesimo mensis Januarii, 1579.

The quhilk day, in the terme appointed be the sessio[n] to Mr. Dauid Meldrom to compeir, to giff his aith upon his purgation off the fornication allegit committed be him with Catharine Bell sumtyme his servand, comperit the said Mr. Dauid, and, being sworne be his[2] grite aithe, deponit, as he wald answer in the presens off almichtie God upon the day off jugement, he nevir had carnall copulatioun nor daill with the said Cathari[ne].

The quhilk day Jsobell Hardye[3]

Nota. Purgatio Meldrom, &c.

Die vigesimo octavo mensis Januarii, 1579.

The quhilk day, the sessioun hes ordenit Margaret Clapen to report ane faithfull testimoniall off the deces off Jhone Auchtmowtye hir husband, betwix this and Pasche day nixt to cum.

Clapen, Auchtmoowtye.

Nota. Clapen.

---

[1] *This day this day* in MS.

[2] *His his* in MS.

[3] This entry, which here stops so abruptly at the foot of a page, is probably that which is entered in full at the bottom of the next page of the *Register.*

Die tertio mensis Februarii, anno Domini 1579.

Confessio
Crawfuird.

The quhilk day, comperit Mariorye [*Sibbald*—erased] Craw-fuird, and confessit and granted hir to be wyth chylde to Alaster Robertsoun, servand to my Ladye Leuenox.

Confessio
Hendersoun.

The quhilk day Mariorye Hendersoun confessit and granted hir to be wyth chylde to Jaimes Cambell hiland-man.

Confessio
Scherpe,
Zoung.

The quhilk day Elizabeth Zoung confessit and granted hir to be wyth chylde to Jhone Scharpe. The said Jhone present in assemblie confessit he had daill wyth hir, and nocht the les allegit the bairne wes Dauid Thomsonis, quha had carnall daill wyth hir, thre or foure dayis befoir the tyme that he lay wyth

Decimo
Februarii 1579.

hir in the myln. The session ordenit the said Jhone Scharpe to compeir, to declair in his conscience at quhat tyme he had to do wyth the said Elizabeth Zoung.

Confessio
Pittillok.

The quhilk day, Margaret Brown, maid-wyffe in Strawethie, and Agnes Fuird, being appointed be the session to comper this day to report the confessioun off Catharine Pittillok the tyme off hir birth, quha being sworne deponit the said Catharine confessit the bairne wes Thomas Lawthean. And now the said Catharine, sworne be hir grite aith, deponit the bairne is Thomas Lawtheane. The session ordenit hir to enter in preson upone Setterday nixt, conforme to the ordor.

Die decimo mensis Februarii, 1579.

Andersoun,
Hardye.

The quhilk day, Jsobell Hardye, being accusat for fornica-tioun committit be hir wyth Jhone Andersoun littistar,[1] con-fessit the sam committed be hir baith in the hows scho payis maill for, and in the said Jhonis awin hows. The sessioun

xvij° Februarii.

ordenit the said Jhone to depone upone the premissis this day viij dayis, on his aith alreddye gevin.

Die decimo septimo mensis Februarii, 1579.

Confessio
Thomsoun.

The quhilk day, comperit Dauid Thomsoun baxter and con-fessit and granted that[2] he had carnall daill wyth Effie Zoung,

---

[1] A dyer.   [2] *Hat* in MS.

and the first tyme thairoff xiiij dayis befoir Witsunday, and the
last tyme in tyme off Zwill last wes.

The quhilk day, comperit Agnes Orok and confessit and *Confessio*
granted the bairne borne off hir wes begottin be Mr. Murdo *Orok.*
Murchesoun, student in St Leonardis, and that the bairne wes
gottin and engenderit at Mid Lentron last wes.

Die vigesimo quarto mensis Februarii, 1579.

The quhilk day, comperit Jaimes Fuird in Craill and con- *Confessio*
fessit and granted he had begottin ane woman bairne wyth *Fuird,*
Wentoun.
Margaret Wentoun, lykas the said Margaret confessit hir selff.

Die nono mensis Martii, 1579.

The quhilk day, comperit Jonett Hagye and confessit and *Confessio*
granted fornicatioun comittit be hir wyth Alane Hendersoun, *Hagye.*
and that scho wes wyth bairne [unto]¹ the said Alane.

Die vigesimo mensis Aprilis, anno etc. octuagesimo.

The quhilk day, comperit Jonett Gordoun and confessit and *Confessio*
granted hir to be wyth chylde to Jhone Kirk, servitor to the *Gordoun,*
Kirk.
Superentenden[t]; lyk as the said Jhone present confessit and
granted him selff.   And now the said Jhone confessit that
he promittit faithfullie to the said Jonett, that quhow sone it
suld happin hir to be wyth bairne, that he suld accomplische
the band off matrimonye betuix thaime.

The quhilk day comperit Bessye Gorlay and confessit and *Confessio*
granted hir to have boirne ane bairne to Jhone Vrquhat. *Gourlay.*
Nota.

The quhilk day, comperit Mawse Balcanquell and confessit *Confessio*
and granted hir to be wyth chylde to Duncane Kenloquhye; *Kenloquhye,*
Balcan{}{}ell.
lykas the said Duncane confessit him selff.   And als the said
Duncane confessit him to haiff had daill wyth Christen Tor-
beane, quha is presentlie wyth bairne to him, in lyk maner.

The quhilk day, Jaimes Lerman being acusat be the sessioun *Lerman.*
for streking and misusing off his wyffe, and schuitting hir to *M.*

---

¹ Deleted.

the yeat ; comperit the said Jaimes and denyit the said accusatioun.   The sessioun assignis this day viij dayis to pruiff.

Die quarto mensis Maii, anno Domini millesimo quingentesimo
octuagesimo.

Sessio Zwill.
Zowl.
Nota.[1]

The quhilk day, the session ordenit and decernit Cristen
Zwill to be warnit to compeir this day viij dayis, to wit, the xj
day off Maii instant, to heir injunnctionis gevin to hir for adulterie committed be hir wyth Jhone Robertsoun mariner ; wyth
certificatioun, and scho compeir nocht, the sessioun will proceid
in excommunicatioun aganis hir.

[Moncur.]

The quhilk day, the sessioun, in respect Margaret Moncur
being warnit and attachit to this day be Jaimes Steill officiar, to
compeir befoir the sessioun to answer to sic thingis as they
have to lay to hir chairge, and in respect off hir disobedience,
ordenit and decernit hir to be remittit to the secular magistrat,
for ordor to be takin wyth hir for hir inobedience foirsaid.

Die undecimo mensis Maii, anno Domini j^m v^c octuagesimo.

Sessio Zwill.
xviij^o Maii.
[*N*]*ota.* Zowll.[1]

The quhilk day, the sessioun ordenit Christen Zwill to be
warnit to this day aucht dayis, to wit, the xviij day off Maii
instant, to heir injunnctionis gevin to hir for adulterie committit be hir wyth Jhone Robertsoun mariner ; wyth certificatioun,
and scho compeir nocht, the sessioun will proceid in excommunicatioun aganis hir.[2]

Die primo mensis Junii, anno Domini millesimo quingentesimo
octuagesimo.

Moncur.[3]

The quhilk day, Agnes Robertsoun, servand to Margaret
Moncur, witnes, being demandit giff evir scho hard the said
Moncur say thir wordis, eftir that scho wes demandit be Alex-

---

[1] The words *Zowl* and *Nota* have been added in another hand, and on the
outer side of the margin.

[2] Fully half a page is left blank after this entry.

[3] *Mocur* has been afterwards written outside of this.

ander Lundye hir husband, quha wes aucht the bairne scho wes wyth, answerit, it wes Dauid Watsonis, and in telling tharoff grat verye sair ; and this the said Agnes deponis the said Margaret sayid thir sam word[is].

Ultimo Augusti, 1580.

The quhilk day, comperit Agnes Angous and confessi[t] and granted hir to be wyth bairne to Jhone Buge younger, and submitted hir to the discipline off the kirk.

Confessio Angous, Buge.

Die decimo mensis Augusti, 1580.

The quhilk day, comperit Beteraige Bredfute and confessit and granted scho wes delyverit [1] off ane maidin bairne to Jaimes Wemis, sone to Jaimes Wemis off Cask-barrine.[2]

Nota.
Confessto Bredfute, Wemeis.

Die ultimo Augusti, 1580.

The quhilk day, comperit Agnes Angous and confessit and granted hir to be wyth chylde to Jhone Buge younger, and submitted [3] hir to the discipline off the kirk ; and siclyk confessit this to be the thrid tyme scho committed fornication.

Confessio Angous.

Die septimo mensis Septembris, 1580.

The quhilk day, Margaret Clapen is ordenit, conforme to the desyre off the act maid upone the xxviij day off Januar last bipast, to present to the session off this citie ane testimoniall off the departure off Jhone Auchtmowtye hir husband, upone Wadnisday nixt to cum, as scho was appointed upone the said xxviij off Januar to present the said testimoniall betwix that [and] [4] Pasche day nixt tharefter ; wyth certification, and scho

Clapen.
Last act of Clapin.

xiiij⁰ Septembris.

---

[1] *Delyver* in MS.

[2] James Wemyss, ancestor of the family of Wemyss of Caskieberran, was one of the three sons of David of Wemyss of that Ilk. James married Janet Durie, Lady of Carden, who died in 1578, and by whom he had eight sons and three daughters, the eldest being James (Sir William Fraser's *Memorials of the Family of Wemyss*, i. 298, 299).

[3] *Smitted* in MS.   [4] Omitted.

failyie heirintill, the kirk will proceid aganis hir conforme to the ordor observit in the lyk caice.

Die decimo quarto mensis Septembris, jajv^c octuagesimo.

Confessio Andersoun.

The quhilk day, comperit Jhone Andersoun littistar and confessit and granted that he had carnall copolatioun wyth Jsobell Hardye, and that the bairne scho wes wyth wes his, and tharfoir submittit him to the discipline off the kirk.[1]

Sessio, Angous. Nota.

The quhilk day, Jhone Buge younger being attachit to this day to compeir befoir the assemblie, quha comperand, and being accusat for fornication committed be him wyth Agnes Angous, denyit that he evir had carnall daill wyth hir. The

xx^{mo} Septembris.

session ordenit him to compeir this day aucht dayis, to be confrontet wyth the said Agnes.

Die xxvij^{mo} Septembris, 1580.

Confessio Vrquhart. Nota.

The quhilk day, comperit Jhone Vrquhart, indwellar in Aberdein, and confessit and granted him to have begottin ane [2] man chylde wyth Bessye Gourlay, and submittit him to the discipline of the kirk, and desyrit eirnestlie his bairne to be baptisit, according to the ordor observit in the lyk caice. And becaus he is schortlie, God willing, to depart to his guid voyage, for satisfaction off the kirk he offeris Andro Moreis cowtion and souertie.

Decretum contra Millar. Nota, nota, nota.[3]

The quhilk day, Mr. Robert Hammiltoun minister and George Blak exorter exponit and declarit to the session that Jaimes Millar, servitor[4] to Dauid Orme, confessit and granted him to have begottin ane bairne wyth Catharine Bell, desyring thaime for Goddis caus to ressaiff his bairne to baptisme, and siclyk granted the sam be ane bill producit this day befoir the said session desyring his bairne to be baptisit. The session in respect it is theirbe understand to thaime that this is the thrid tyme that he hes committed fornication, they remit him to the

---

[1] *Kir* in MS.
[2] *Ane ane* in MS.
[3] The triple *nota* has been added afterwards, as many of the marginal words are in this part of the *Register*, and are inserted between *contra* and *Millar*.
[4] *Servit* in MS.

secular juge, and to be punischit be thaime according to Act off Parliament.[1]

The quhilk day, comperit Jsobell Duncane and confessit and granted hir to be wyth chylde to Wyliam Zwill mariner, and submittit hir to the discipline off the kirk. *Nota. Confessio Duncane.*

Die secundo Novembris, 1580.

The quhilk day comperit Elene Wemis and confessit hir to be wyth chylde to the Laird off Giblistoun eldar. *Nota. Confessio Wemis.*

Item, comperit Walter Zounger and confessit and granted that he had committit fornication wyth Margaret Killoch, and submittit him to the correction and discipline of the kirk. *Confessio Zounger. Nota, nota. Satisfeiit.*

The quhilk day, anent the claime off sclander and infamie gevin in be Alison Brown, spous to Nicoll Cwik, aganis Catharine Kynnier, the session, be sufficient tryall taikin be thaime thairupon, findis the said Catharine to have havilie sclanderit and diffamit the said Alisoun ; and thairfoir ordenis and decernis hir to sit down upone hir knyis, confes hir offence, and pay instantlie x s. to the puir ; and giff evir scho be fund in tym cuming to injure the said Alisoun, to pay x merkis to [be][2] emplo[yed] to the commoun wark off this citie. *Decretum contra Kynneir. Nota, nocht execut.*

---

[1] In 1567, Parliament ordained that those convicted of fornication should, for the first fault, as well the man as the woman, pay £40, or be imprisoned for eight days, ' thair fude to be breid, and small drink,' and afterwards be presented to the market-place of the town or parish bare-headed, there to stand fastened that they may not remove for two hours. For the second fault the penalty was one hundred merks, or the term of imprisonment to be doubled, ' thair fude to be breid and watter allanerlie,' ' to be presentit to the said mercat place, and baith the heidis of the man and the woman to be schavin.' For the third fault the penalty was £100, or the imprisonment tripled, their food to be bread and water, ' and in the end, to be taine to the deipest and foulest pule, or watter of the towne, or parochin, thair to be thryse dowkit, and thairefter baneist the said towne or parochin for ever.' In all future convictions the third penalty was to be re-inflicted. Those who preferred the ' pecuniall panis' were to be allowed the privilege of escaping from the humiliating penalties, but the latter were to be executed on all who were unable or unwilling to pay, and the money thus obtained was to be used for pious purposes in the places where the crime was committed (*Acts of the Parliaments of Scotland,* iii. 25, 26).

[2] Omitted.

Die xiiij[to] mensis Decembris, 1580.

Nota.
Preching upone
Sonday at twa
howris.
The quhilk day, the session hes ordenit and decernit, for diverss honest and guid respectis, that, in all tym cuming, the preching upone the Sonday efternune to begyn at twa howris efter nune, and swa furth to continow.

Nota.
Mariage upone
Wadnisday.
Item, siclyk that it salbe lesum to marie in all tym cuming upone Wadnisday, swa that the three severall Sondayis befoir the personis to be mariit thair bandis be proclamit.

Die xxj[mo] mensis Decembris, 1580.

Nota.
Confessio Ade.
The quhilk day, the session hes ordenit and decernit Stevin Ade maissoun to report ane testimoniall fra the Laird off Dwn, that he hes communicat wyth the Christiane congregation thre yeris bipast, and to present the sam wyth all diligence, and to find caution to that effect.

Confessio Brog.
Nota.
The quhilk day comperit Bessye Brog and granted and confessit hir to be wyth chylde to Dauid Stevin baxter.

Die xxvijj[vo] Decembris, 1580.

Confessio
Stevin.
Nota.
The quhilk day, Dauid Stevin baxter confessit and granted him to have committit fornication wyth Bessye Brog, and the bairne scho is wyth to be his awin.

Die vigesimo nono mensis Martii, anno Domini millesimo quingentesimo octuagesimo primo.

Nota.
Anent the com-
plent off the
buriall, &c.
The quhilk day, anent the complent offerit to the sessioun be Mr. Thomas Buchannan, Commissionar off Fyffe, concerning the buriall off certen personis maid off lait wythin the parroche kirk off this citie, contrar to ane certen act and ordinance maid in the Generall Assemblie,[1] the session, in respect the said com-

---

[1] The General Assembly, in 1576, declared that burials should not be in the kirks, 'and that the contraveiners be suspendit fra the benefites of the Kirk, quhill they make publick repentance' (*Booke of the Universall Kirk,* i. 378). In 1560 the Reformers had expressed a decided opinion on this point, believing burial in churches to be unseemly, and, evidently on sanitary grounds, desiring that a convenient place, 'lying in the most free air,' be appointed for that use

plent is necessar to be intreatit befoir the Provest and counsell off this citie, hes continowit all forder proceding heirintill, quhill this day xv dayis, to the effect foirsaid.

Die septimo mensis Junii, anno Domini millesimo quingentesimo octuagesimo primo.

The quhilk day, the session hes ordenit and decernit the clerk off everye quarter off this citie to pas throwch ilk quarter, and[1] thair to enroll the haill naimes off evir ilk howshald, and speciall off theis quhilk salbe off perfect aige, chairging thame to compeir wythin the communion ile off this parroche kirk off this citie, and thair to bé answerable to the said session to sic thingis as salbe proponit unto thaime, upone Tysday nixt to cum, at sevin howris in the morning; and everye day thairefter to compeir as they salbe chargit, to sic tyme as the haill town be compleitlie tryit and examinat; and siclyk everye ane off the said session to be present at the day they salbe chairgit to, under the paine off viij s. *Concerning the entrie off the haill inhabitantis off this citi'e to examination.*

The quhilk day, Jonett Robertsoun confessit and granted hir to be wyth chylde to Alexander Hendersoun in Hadingtoun, and submittis hir to the discipline off the kirk.[2] *Confessio Robertsoun. Nota.*

Die Veneris, decimo tertio mensis Octobris, anno Domini millesimo quingentesimo octuagesimo primo.

Eldaris electit and chosin.

Mr. James Wilkie, Rectour of the Universite of Sanctandrois
Mr. James Martine, Provest of the Auld College
Mr. Jhone Robertsoun, ane of the maisteris of the New College
Mr. Thomas Balfour, bailye
Mr. William Cok, bailye
Mr. Dauid Russell
Mr. Martine Geddy
Jhone Motto

---

exclusively, and that it 'be weill walled and fensed about' (*First Book of Discipline*). And the General Assembly, in December 1563, in certain regulations for country funerals, state that the dead should be buried six feet deep.

[1] *And and* in MS.   [2] The next page is blank.

James Robertsoun   Up on land.
Dauid Balfour   Androw Wod of Straythvethy
William Ferry   Mr. Androw Aytoun of Kynnaldy.
James Smyth.

Deaconis electit and chosin the same day.

George Blak
Charlis Watsoun, notar
Alexander Smyth
- James Ade   Up on land.
Androw Watsoun   Martine Carstrophein in Byrhillis
Jhone Hagy   James Calvart in Over Kenlovy
Alexander Dayis   Walter Kynnynmonth in Baldwny
Dauid Blair.   Dauid Forester in Kincapill.

Die Mercurii, decimo octavo mensis Octobris, anno Domini
j^mv^{centesimo} octuagesimo primo.

Ratificatioun of the statutis maid of befoir.

 The quhilk day, eldaris and deaconis aboif specifyt affirmit ratifyt and apprevit the haill statutis and ordinances of the sessioun, maid upon the fyft day of November, the yeir of God j^mv^clxxij yeiris, and ar all suorn and oblist to observe and keipe the same.

 The quhilk day, the sessioun ordanis that dew ordour be takin be thame this day aucht dayis, for ane sufficient clerk to this assemblie and his stipend yeirlie.

Die xxvj^{to} mensis Octobris, anno octuagesimo primo.

Electioun of the clerk.

 The quhilk day, the haill sessioun and seniouris, all with ane voce, hes electit and chosin Jhone Motto and Charlis Watsoun clerkis and scribis to this assemblie and sessioun, and in thair absens Mr. Dauid Russell, quha hes all acceptit the sam[e] in and upon thame ; and the sessioun to direct thair supplicatioun to the Bischop of Sanctandrois, Provest bailyeis and counsall of the said citee, for the clerkis yeirlie stipend, and gude ordour to be takin for the samyn at the Bischopp[is] returning fra the Parliament.

Wilsoun, *rij.*

 The quhilk day, Elspot Quariour, Cristane Carstaris, Petir

Eviot, Margaret Ramsay, Dauid Ade, Margaret Berclay, Jonet Dik, and Agnes Andersoun, to be warnit be the officiar to compeir befoir the sessioun this day aucht dayis, to testifie qubat thai knaw twiching the fornicatioun allegit committit betuix Mr. Thomas Wilsoun and umquhill Cathrin Schankis.

The quhilk day, Nicholl Hay in Kynnynmonth dalatit to the sessioun for allegit gatting of ane madin barne in fornicatioun wyth Margret [*blank*] in Kynnynmonth his servand; he ordanit to be warnit be the redar, upon Sonday nixt to cum, oppinlie in the parroche kirk, to ansuer to the sessioun this day aucht dayis. *Delatio* [1] Hay, *rij.*

The quhilk day, Cristene Turbane delatit for nevir cuming to kirk nor communioun; and also Bessy Robertsoun, mother-in-law to Cuthbert Mores, delatit also for nevir cuming to the kirk nor communioun; and siclyke the said Bessy delatit for witchcraft; as also Begis Dayis delatit for being at discentioun and hetred wyth the said Besse Robertsoun. The sessioun ordanis thame all to be oppinlie warnit in the kirk be the redar, upon Sonday nixt to cum, to compeir on Weddinsday nixt to ansuer befoir the sessioun. *Delatio* [1] Robertsoun, Turbane, Dayis, *rij.*

Die primo mensis Novembris, anno lxxxj[o.]

The quhilk day, in the terme assignit to warne Elspot Quarioir, Cristene Carstaris, Petir Eviot, Margret Ramsay, Dauid Ade, Margret Berclay, Jonet Dik, and Agnes Anderson, to testifie the treuth quhat thai knaw tuiching the allegit fornicatioun committit be Mr. Thomas Wilsoun with umquhill Cathrine Schankis, comperit Margret Ramsay, witnes, suorn ressavit and examinat, with the haill remanent witnes befoir specifyt except Agnes Anderson [2] also comperand, ressavit suorn and examinat, deponis, all with ane voce aggreand, that, thre or four dayis befoir the departure of umquhill Cathrine Schankis, thai hard hir say that hir barne suld nevir haif ane uther father bot Mr. Thomas Wilsoun, bot at the tyme of hir extremite of *Wilsoun, Schankis.*

---

[1] *Confessio* in MS.

[2] The words *except Agnes Anderson* are in the margin, and there are marks to indicate that they should be taken in here, and also after *aggreand* in the next line.

hir seiknes deidle hard hir say na thing of him. And [the session] [1] ordanis Mr. Thomas to be warnit, and to gif his aith upon the premissis this day aucht dayis.

Die octavo mensis Novembris, anno Domini j^{m}v^c octuagesimo primo.

Wilsoun,
Schankis.

The quhilk [day], [1] being laidfullie warnit Mr. Thomas Wilsoun to gif his ayth upon the allegit fornicatioun committit betuix him and umquhill Cathrin Schankis, comperit the said Mr. Thomas, quha being suorn maid faith, and on his conscience denyit that evir he hed carnall daill wyth the said umquhill Cathrin.

Die decimo quinto mensis Novembris, anno octuagesimo primo.

Adulterii.
Confessio
Robertsoun,
rij.

The quhilk day, Jhone Robertsoun, mariner, being warnit to this day and accusit for haifing carnall daill with Cristene Zwill ane excommunicat person, and for nocht making publict repentance as ane adultrar, conforme to the act maid in this auditorie the xj of Junii, lxxviij yeris, comperit the said Jhone, quha confessit he hes hed carnall daill with the said Cristene sen the dait of the said act, and within this tolmonth last wes. The sessioun, in respect of his confessioun, ordanis Thomas Playfeir to be warnit to this day aucht dayis, to heir decrete pronuncit aganis him upon the sowme of xl ħ. conforme to the tenour of the said act ; and ordanis Jhone Robertsoun to abstein in tyme cuming fra having carnall daill wyth the said Cristene, and to compeir on Sonday nixtt to cum, and begyn agane his repentance in sekclayth upon the penitent stuill, undir the pane of excommunication, and that publict admonition be maid to him to that effect in kirk be the redar.

Brwntoun,
Logy, *rij.*

The quhilk day, the sait ordanis [*CristaneBransche*—deleted] Jonet Brunton to be warnit to this day aucht dayis, for allegit fornication and cumpane with the Laird of Logeis bruther.

Confessio
Brausche, Cok.

The quhilk day, Cristane Bransche confessis sche is with barne to William Cok, sone to Mr. William Cok, bailye, and that sche hed carnall daill with him thre oulkis or thairby

---

[1] Omitted.

befoir Witsonday last wes, in the said Mr. Williamis cros-hall,
ane nycht, and ane tyme in the nakit bed, be hir awin faut
cumand to his bed; and sayis the barne wilbe borne thre
oulkis eftir Zwill nixttocum or thairby. Conperit also the said
William Cok, quha, being inquirit upon the treuth of the said
Cristenis confessioun and if the samyn wes of treuth, denyis the
samyn and that he nevir knew the said Cristane carnalie.

The quhilk day, becaus Margret Clepen and Jhone Scheves Clepen,
adultraris wer warnit to this day and comperit nocht, as wes Scheves.
verefyt be the officiar, the sessioun ordanis thame to be warnit
to this day aucht dayis agane, undir the pane of excommunication and of publict admonition in the kirk.

The quhilk day, being warnit Patrik Quhyte mariner and Quheit, Spens,
Jonet Spen[s] his spous for nocht adherand togidder being reconcelit.
mariit, comperit the said Patrik and Jonet and eftir that thair
caus and ressonis wer hard thai att the pl[an] consall and desire
of the sessioun wer reconcelit as appirrit.

The quhilk day, the sessioun ordanis Elene Wemes to be Wemes,
warnit to this day aucht dayis, for to receave injunction for the Martine.
fornication committit be hir with the Laird of Giblatson. rij.

The quhilk day, the sessioun ordanis the act to be extractit Mwffet,
out of the townis buikis quhair William Mwffeit wes actit Wemes,
cautioun for Jame[s] Wemes of Kaskebaren younger, undir ane Caskebarreane.
pand[1] &c. and the act to be deliverit to the bailyeis to be put
to executioun.

Die xxij° mensis Novembris, anno lxxxj°·

The quhilk day, the sessioun ordanis Jhone Robertsoun Robertsoun,
adultrar yit as of befoir to begyn his repentance, in sek claith Zwill.
upon the penitent stuill, upon Sonday nixttocum, and sa furth Decretum
to continew conforme to the ordour for the adultrie com- contra Playfeir.
mittit betuix him and Crestene Zwill now excommunicat; and Adulterii.
to abstein fra carnall copulation with hir in tymes cuming
undir the pane of excommunicatioun: and also decernis Thomas
Playfeir to pay the sowme of fourty lib. as cautioun for the
said Jhone Robertso[un], conforme to the act maid in this
sessioun thairanent the xj of Junii, lxxviij, in presens of the

---

[1] Pledge.

said Jhone Robertsoun and Thomas Playfeir baith present laidfully warnit to this day, to the effect aboif writin.

Confessio
Leiche.
Adulterii.

The quhilk day, Beatrix Leiche confessis hir to be with barne
to Thomas Mwir, servand to the yowng Laird of Balcomy, sche
being yit mariit with Alexander Wrycht ondivorsit.   The seat
ordanis hir to begyn hir repentance as ane adultrice on Sonday
nixttocum, and to abstein in tymes cuming fra cumpanie with
Thomas, and to continew in repentance conforme to the ordour.

Bruntoun,
Wemes.
rij.

The quhilk day, Jonet Bruntoun being warnit to this day
comperit, and allegi[t] sche hes maid satisfactioun in the kirk
of Logy for the fornication committit be hir with Normond
Wemes, and that hir barne is baptezit.   The sait ordanit hir
to report Mr. Thomas Dowglas ministeris testimoniall thairupon this day aucht dayis: also being accusit for haifing carnall
daill with the said Normond sen hir barne wes borne, denyit
the samyn, bot refusit to mak faith thairupon; thairfor the
sait ordanis hir to advys with hir conscience and to declair the
samyn this day aucht dayis.

Confessio
adulterii[1]
Scheves,
Clepen, *rij.*

The quhilk day, comperit Jhone Scheves and Margret Clepen
adultraris as thai quha wer laidfully warnit to this day, quba
confessit thair adultrie togiddir.   The sessioun ordanis the
said Jhone and Margret to abstein fra haifing carnall copulatioun togiddir in tymes cuming, and to find cautioun to that
effect; and to mak publict repentance as adultraris quhen the
sessioun sall require thame, under the pane of excommunication, and that ather this day aucht dayis, or at the leist this
day xv dayis at the farrest.

Die Mercurii, penultimo Novembris, anno lxxxj°·

Confessio
Bruntoun,
Wemes.

The quhilk day, Jonet Brwntoun producit ane testimoniall
subscrivit be Mr. Thomas Dowglas minister that hir barne wes
baptizit, and denyit that sche hed carnall daill with Normond
Wemes sen Pasche last wes, quhilk wes the tyme that sche com
to this citee to duell, bot confessis that sche hed carnall daill
with him about Fastronisevin last wes in Lastarrik.   The
sessioun ordanis hir, in respect that sche duellis now within this

---

[1] *Adulerii* in MS. In many of the marginal notes in this part of the Register,
adulterii has been added afterwards, by another hand.

citee and that sche hes maid na repentance as yit for hir fault
committit in Lastarrik, to produce testimoniall of hir repentance and satisfaction within the parrochin of Lastarrk, of the
minister thairof, befoir this sessioun betuix this and Zwill nixt *xxv^to Decem-*
to cum, or ellis betuix this and the samyn tyme to mak repent- *bris.*
ance within this kirk thairfor, or than to depart hirself furth
of this parroche.

The quhilk day, the sessioun ordanis Jhone Scheves and Scheves,
Margret Clepen adultraris to compeir upon Weddinsday nixt *Adulterii.* Clepen, *rij.*
to cum and receave injunctionis, in respect that it is notorous
that Jhone Scheves freindis ar now cum hame furth of Edinburgh, with quhome he allegit he wald counsall, quhairupon
the last delay wes grantit; and ordanis the officiar to warn
thame to that effect: and siclyke supplicatioun to be direct
aganis Beatrix Leiche adultrice and reporttit as said is with [Leiche.]
Thomas Mwir.

The quhilk day, the sessioun ordanis Mr. Alexander Jarden, Jarden, Geddy,
minister, and William Geddy to be warnit to this day *rij.*
aucht dayis, to ansuer to sic thingis as salbe proponit aganis
thame.

The quhilk day, the sessioun ordanis Androw Baxter and Baxter, Robert-
Jhone Robertsoun belmen to be warnit be the officar to this soun, *rij.*
day aucht dayis, to heir and see gude ordour takin tuiching
the baptisme and buriall.

The quhilk day, the sessioun ordanis ane supplicatioun to be Robertsoun,
direct to the majestranis of this citee, to require Jhone Robert- *Adulterii.* Zwill.
soun adultrar and Cristane Zwill excommunicat to obey the
voce of the kirk, and mak satisfactoun and repentance for
thair offencis conforme to the ordour; and the samyn supplicatioun to be presentit be ane of the sessioun and reportit
agane with ansuer with all diligence: and siclyke supplicatioun
to be direct aganis Beatrix Leiche aduiltrice.   [Leiche.]

Die sexto mensis Decembris, anno lxxxj^o.

The quhilk day, Mr. William Cok, bailye, and being com- The presenta-
missioner for this citee to the Generall Assemblie to procure of Generall tioun of the act
ane pastore for the kirk of St. Androis, comperit befoir this Assemblie for
assemble of St. Androis; and for declaratioun of his diligence minister. electioun of ane

producit this act of the Generall Assemble quhilk followis in effect. *Acta sessione* 19, *xxx° Octobris*, 1581. Anent the provisioun of the kirk of Sanctandrois[1] of ane pastore,[2] the kirk hes tocht it meit that the Priour and town of St. Androis nominat ane of the brether quhome thai haif best lyking of to serve the cure, and to propone him unto the ministeris of the Kingis hous, ministeris of Edinburgh, Mr. Dauid Lindesay, Jhone Brand, Mr. Adam Jhonesoun, Dauid Ferguisoun, Mr. Andrew Melvill, William Christesoun, the Lairdis of Braid, Pilrig, Culluthy, and Lundy; to quhome the kirk gevis commissioun, or to ony aucht of thame, to gif assent in thair name thairto, and place him thair, providing thai find na laidfull and ressonabill impediment proponit that may stay thair placing thair, or that thai be nocht of ane of the collegis, quhome the kirk exemis for considerationis heirfra. And siclyke that with thair avys the minister[3] presentit be sufficientlie providit, as als his kirkis quhairfra he is takin if he be

Rij.

---

[1] *S'anctandrois* in MS.

[2] In the General Assembly, in April 1576, it was objected against Robert Hamilton that he was Provost of St. Mary's College as well as minister of St. Andrews, when 'the said matter beand long debaittit with reasons on every syde, and rypelie advysit, the present Assembly, in respect of the circumstance of place and congregation of Sanct Androes, finds and declares the twa offices joynit in his person to be incompatabill in him. Mr. Patrick Auchinleck, commissioner for the toun of Sanct Andrews, protested in name thereof, that this sentence prejudge not the toun of Sanct Andrews, nor ingender any prejudice to them touching their minister, without they be called and heard' (*Booke of the Universall Kirk*, i. 351). In October of the same year, the matter again came before the Assembly, and Hamilton was then ordered to 'cast off the said office and charge of Provestrie of the New Colledge, as an impediment, stay, and hinderance to his office and calling of the ministrie;' but William Skene in name of the New College dissented, and to this dissent Hamilton adhered, alleging that 'the Kirk could not discharge him of the Provestrie, and that he could not beare the burden of the haill kirk of Sanct Androes in his awin person' (*Ibid.* p. 375). He seems to have held tenaciously to both offices, for the case came before the Assembly in October 1578 and also in July 1579 (*Ibid.* ii. 422, 433). Soon after the latter date, he had to relinquish the Provostry, in which he was succeeded by Andrew Melville (M'Crie's *Melville*, 1824, ii. 473; Melville's *Diary*, Wod. Soc. p. 122); and he died at Edinburgh on the 16th of April 1581 (Scott's *Fasti*, ii. 388). The stipulation in the text, that his successor in the ministry was not to be chosen from 'ane of the collegis,' was probably prompted by the difficulty of getting Hamilton to cease being a pluralist. When he was elected, the Assembly had advised the congregation to choose a minister 'out of their own Universitie' (*supra*, p. 28, n.). [3] *Ministeris* in MS.

transportit be alsua stakit.[1] Extract furth of the Register of
the Actis of the Generall Assemblie of the Kirk be Mr. James
Riche clerk thairof.   J. Riche.[2]—The sessioun, for performeing
of desyre of the said act, ordanis Mr. Patrik Adamsoun,
Bischope of St. Androis, Mr. Androw Melvill, Principall of the
New College, Mr. James Wilkye, Rectour, Mr. James Martine,
Provest of the Auld College, Mr. Jhone Robertsoun, Mr.
Thomas Balfour, Jhone Motto, Mr. Dauid Russell, Mr. William
Cok, James Robertsoun, Mr. Martine Geddy, William Ferry,
James Smyth, Thomas Welwod, Jhone Wod, Dauid Wemes,
Dauid Balfour, with the Provest of this citee, to pas all togidder
to my Lord Erle of Marche, Priour of St. Androis, upon
Satterday nixttocum, [at ix houris befoir none,][3] and travell
with his lordschip for ane ressonabill stipend to Mr. Robert
Point, quhome the sessioun thinkis meit to be minister of this
parroche, and to report ansuer heirof agane this day aucht
dayis.

The quhilk day, the sessioun hes concludit that my Lord Supplicatioun
Bischop, accumpanei[t] with Jhone Motto and Mr. Dauid Robertsoun,
Zwill, Clepen,
Russell, elderis, present, upon Friday nixttocum in the tolbuith Leiche, &c.
Adulteraris.[4]
of this citee, to the majestrattis of the samyn, ane supplicatioun Miller.
for gude ordour to be takin with Jhone Robertsoun, Cristene
Zwill, Margret Clepen, and Beatrix Leiche, adultraris, and with
James Miller thrys ellis committit in fornicatioun, and to
report ansuer tharof agane[5] this day auch[t] dayis.

The quhilk day, the sessioun continewis thair determinatioun *Admonitio*
aganis Jhone Schevis, for his adultrie committit with Margret Scheves,
Clepen, *rij. q.*
Clepen, in hope of amendiment and humiliatioun, to this day
xv dayis; and presentlie admonisis the said Jhone personalie
to abstene fra forder cumpanie with the said Margret in tyme
cuming, under the panis contenit in the act of Parliament: and
also admonisit the said Margret present to abstein fra cumpanie
with the said Jhone, in all tyme cuming under the samyn pane.

---

[1] Accommodated.   [2] See *Booke of the Univ. Kirk*, ii. 539, 546.
[3] These words are in the margin. The scribe has omitted the mark in the
text to show where they should be taken in.
[4] *Adulteraris*, which has been added afterwards, is inserted between *Zwill*
and *Clepen*.
[5] *Agae* in MS. In this part of the *Register* some words have been hurriedly
written, the letters occasionally not being half formed.

Jarden, Geddy,
rij.

The quhilk day, becaus Mr. Alexander Jarden and William Geddy comperit nocht, being warnit to this day, the sessioun ordanis thame to be warnit agane *de novo* to this day aucht dayis.

Andersoun,
confessio
Patersoun,
rij.
Satisfeit.

The quhilk day, Barbary Patersoun confessis sche is with barne to Jhone Andersoun litster. The sessioun ordanis thame baith to be warnit to this day aucht dayis.

Die decimo tertio mensis Decembris, anno lxxxj°·

Jarden, Geddy,
rij.

The quhilk day, the sessioun ordanis Mr. Alexander Jarden and William Geddy to be warnit to this day aucht dayis, and also Jhone Pittillow, Cathrine [*blank*], servand to William Geddy, Jhone Williamsoun, Cristene Dick, his spous, to beir trew testimonie tuiching the dilatioun of sklander offerrit up to the sessioun upon the said Mr. Alexander and William Geddy.

Adulterii.
Injunctionis
gevin to Beatrix
Leiche.

The quhilk day, the sessioun ordanis Beatrix Leiche adultrice to begyn hir repentance upon Sonday nixttocum, cled in sek claith, to begyn at the secund bell to the sermon befoir none, and stand beir-futtit at the [*blank*] kirk dur, quhill the thrid bell to sermon be sessit, and thaireftir to sitt upon the penitent stuill in the adultraris place and gre, quhill the sermon and prayaris be done and benedictoun gevin, and sa furth ilk Sonday to continew quhill the kirk be satisfeit, conforme to the ordour.

Confessio
Andersoun,
Patersoun.

The quhilk day, comperit Jhone Andersoun litstar and Barbarry Patersoun, quha baith confessis wyth ane voce that thai haif hed carnall daill togidder viij dayis befoir Lammes last wes, and Barbarry confessis sche is with barne to Jhone Andersoun. The sessioun, in respect that Jhone Andersoun is

Satisfeit.
Satisfeit baith.

relappis in fornicatioun, and that this is his secund falt, ordanis him to enter in pressoun upon Satterday nixttocum, and to remane thair nurisit onlie upon bread and watter be the space of xv dayis; and the xv dayis endit the said Barbary to enter in pressoun and continew thairin viij dayis nurisit upon bread and small drink alanerlie; and thairefter thai baith togidder to mak publict repentance conforme to the ordour.

Cluny, *rij.*

The quhilk day, the sessioun ordanis Margret Cluny adultrice to be warnit to this day aucht dayis, and ressef new injunctions conforme to the ordour.

Die Mercurii, vigesimo mensis Decembris, anno Domini j$^{m}v^{c}$
octuagesimo primo.

The quhilk day, Mr. William Cok bailye takis the burding upon him to convein the counsall of the town to morne, for sending of ane honest man to Edinburgh with my Lord of Marche letter, and ane uther letter from the town, to Mr. Robert Point to be pastor of this congregatioun, that the said Maister Robertis uter mynde may be hed thair anent with diligence, or him self to cum heir in propir persoun. *Mr. Robert Point to be send for.*

The quhilk day, the sessioun ordanis and decernis Jhone Scheves and Margret Clepen adultraris to begyn thair repentance in sek claith upon Sonday cum aucht dayis, to stand at the kirk dur fra secund bell to sermone beir-futtit quhill the thrid bell be cessit, and thaireftir to sitt on the adultraris place of the penitent stuill, quhill the sermone be endit, and sa furth ilk Sonday to continew quhill the kirk be satisfeit; and ordanis the officiar to warne thame heirto, and if thai failye that publict admonitioun be maid to thame in the kirk Sonday cum aucht dayis, conforme to the ordour. *Decretum Scheves, Clepen.*

The quhilk day, William Zwill mariner and Bessy Duncane fornicatouris present ar decernit to be impressonit and mak satisfactioun conforme to the ordour, for fornicatioun confessit be thame; and William to enter in presson Satterday nixttocum, and Bessy, Satterday cum aucht dayis. Bessy allegis promis of mariage maid to hir be William Zwill, quhilk being referrit be hir to his aith, he deniit the samyn on his conscience. *Duncane, Zwill. Duncane satisfeit and mariit with [blank.]*

The quhilk day, becaus Margret Cluny hes bein oft and diveris tymes warnit to mak satisfactioun for hir adultrie and contempteuslie disobeyit, thairfor the sessioun comittis hir to the secular majestratis to be handlit conforme to hir dimerittis. *Cluny.*

Die Mercurii, xxvij Decembris, anno lxxxj$^{o.}$

The quhilk day, Robert Nicholl seyman grantis he hes hed carnall daill with Jonet Andersoun ane yeir sensyne or thairby. Becaus Jonet comperis nocht the sessioun ordanis hir to be warnit to this day aucht dayis, and Robert present warnt to the samyn day *apud acta.* *Robert Nicholl, Andersoun, rij.*

Scheves,
Clepen,
Robertsoun,
rij.

The quhilk day, for gude caussis the sessioun hes tocht gude to advis to morn with the generale ministrie convenit at the exerceis for gude ordour to be hed with Jhone Scheves, Margret Clepen, and utheris adultraris, as also to advys anent the baptisme of Jhone Robertsonis barne; and the Bischope to propone the mater, and reportt thair jugement thairintill this day aucht dayis; and Jhone Scheves personalie warnit be the officiar to this day aucht dayis.

Die tertio mensis Januarii, anno octuagesimo primo.

Scheves,
Clepen,
Robertsoun,
rij.
Adulterii.

The quhilk day, in absens of the Bischop, Mr. James Martine maid relatioun that the Bischop of St. Androis, upon the xxviij day of December last wes, exponit[1] the mater and questioun of the punisment of Jhone Scheves and Margret Clepen for adultrie, and of the baptisme of Jhone Robertsonis barne, &c., to the generall assemblie of the kirk of St. Androis convenit to the exerceis, quba tuik to advys thairwith to Thuirsday the ferd of Januar instant; and be resson thairof the saidis materis ar continewit to this day aucht dayis, the tent of Januar instant, and ordanit Jhone Scheves present [and Margret][2] Clepen to be warnit to the said day.

Anderson,
Thomson,
rij.

The quhilk day, [Elene—deleted] Jonet Andersoun, delatit for committing fornicatioun, confesses hir to haif hed carnall daill with Robert Thomsoun, and alsa with Robert Nicholl, na maner [of][2] satisfactioun maid thairfor as yet within this citee, decernit thairfor[3] be the session to enter in presson on Satterday, according to ane relaps; and Robert Thomson to be warnit agane this day aucht dayis.

Die decimo Januarii, anno octuagesimo primo.

Robertson,
rij.

The quhilk day, the declaratioun of the baptisme of Jhonc Robertsonis barne is continewit to this day aucht dayis.

Scheves,
Clepen,
adulterii.

The quhilk day, the sessioun with ane voce ratifeis thair decrete pronuncit aganis Jhone Scheves and Margret Clepen adultraris, pronuncit the xx day of December last wes, and

---

[1] *Exonit* in MS.   [2] Omitted.   [3] *Thairto* in MS

ordanis thame as of befoir to begin thair repentance upon
Sonday nixttocum, and thairefter to continew quhill the kirk
be satisfeit, conforme to the ordour observit aganis adultraris
in this congregatioun in tymes bygane, [and if thai] [1] failye that
publict admonitioun be maid to thame in the kirk.

The quhilk day, becaus that Robert Thomsoun, being delatit Thomsoun
for fornicatioun committit be him with Jonet Andersoun, as remittit to the majestratis.
Jonet confessit, be procreatioun of ane cheild, nather comperit
befoir the session nor yit enterit in presson, being oftimes
thairto chargit, the sessioun remittis him to the secular majestrattis.

Die decimo septimo mensis Januarii, anno lxxxj°.

The quhilk day, Patrik Smalum mariner and Cristene Lyell, *Confessio*
being warnit to [2] this day and accusit for keping cumpanie Smalum, Lyell.
togidder and haifing carnall daill onmariit, comperit baith and
confessit carnall daill togidder ; and Patrik allegit promis of
mariage betuix thame, if Cristene be ane fre woman, and is content to performe the samyn if sua be, and to satisfie according
to the ordour thairfor.

The quhilk day, the sessioun ordanis Jonet Bruntoun to be Bruntoun,
warnit to this day aucht dayis, to ansuer to the ordinance maid *rij*
in the act the penult of November last wes.

The quhilk day, the sessioun ordanis the dakinis of ilk *Decretum*
quarter collectour to the puir, to gif ilk ane thair ouk about Aitchesoun.
sex d. to Thomas Aitshesoun, in all tymes cuming during his
dayis.

The quhilk day, anent the supplicatioun gevin in to the Admissioun
sessioun, desiring ane man cheld now of xv yeir auld procreat in of Karnis to
adultrie betuix umquhill Henry Carnis [3] and umquhill [*blank*], baptisme.

---

[1] Deleted.   [2] *To to* in MS.

[3] The Session was exercised in 1569-70 concerning the reconciliation of Karnis
and his wife (*supra*, pp. 332, 333) ; and on the 17th of August of that year, 'Andro
Greif citienar of Sanctandrois become souertie and lawborrowis that Andro
Cowpar cannonar in Dunde salbe harmeles and skaythles of Henry Cairnis,
citienar of Sanctandrois, and all that he may let, bot as law will, but fraude or
gyle, under the pane of twa hundrith merkis' (*Register of Privy Council*, ii. 12).
In March 1570-71, Mr. Robert Wynram, Collector of Fife, appeared in the
General Assembly, 'and shew how he was purgit be ane condigne assyse befor

desiring the said cheld yit onbaptizit to be ressavit to baptisme and ane of Christis Jesus kirk; the session ordanis the said man cheld to cum to the kirk, and craif at the minister or redar for the tyme baptisme for Goddis saik, and in Christ Jesus name, and thairefter to be ressavit to baptisme.

Andersoun, Sellar, to enter agane. The quhilk day, Jonet Andersoun, being aucht dayis impresonit for relappis in fornicatioun, wes at command of the sessioun relevit, in respect of the vehemensie of the storme of wedder, and hes fund [*William Dewar maltman*—deleted]
Satisfeit. Androw Sellar cautioun for hir; quha is oblist of his awin propir confessioun to entir the said Jonet in presson betuix this and Pasche nixttocum, to reman uther aucht dayis impresonat, and that sche sall satisfie according to the ordour, under the pane of xl s. to be applyit to the use of the puir onforgevin.

Nicholl actitat upon Dewar. The quhilk day, William Dewar maltman is oblist cautioner for Robert Nicholl seyman, to enter the said Robert in presson
Satisfeit. and to reman thair and satisfie the kirk conforme to the ordour as ane fornicatour, betuix this and Pasche nixttocum, under the pane of xl s. to the use of the puir onforgevin, and Robert Nicholl oblisis him to releif the said William.

Die ultimo mensis Januarii, anno octuagesimo primo.

Confessio Dalgleis, Macnab. The quhilk day, comperit Jonet Dalgles and confessis that sche hes borne ane barne in fornicatioun to Jhone Makniab trumphiter, offerring hirself to discipline, desiris the[1] barne to be baptizit. The sessioun ordanis hir to report testimoniall fra the Kingis gracis minister, or ministeris of Edinburgh, that Jhone Macnab confessis the barne to be his, and thaireftir to deliver ane sufficientt plege that thei sall satisfie this congregatioun for this offence, quhilk being done the barne thaireftir
Decretum contra Thomsoun, Andersoun. to be baptizit.

The quhilk day, the sessioun ordanis Robert Thomsoun to

the civill magistrate, for the slaughter of Henrie Kairnes, citizen in St. Androes: not the les because the blood was shed against his will, always he willinglie offerit to the Kirk to underly quhatsoevir uther thing they wold lay to his charge for satisfaction of the Kirk ' (*Booke of the Universall Kirk*, i. 194).

[1] *The the* in MS.

entir in presson upon Satterday nixttocum, for fornicatioun committit be him with Jonet Andersoun, and to satisfie the kirk thairfor conforme to the ordour ; in respect that it is sufficiente verefyt be the sessioun that he comperit befoir thame personalie and confessit his offence, and submittit him self to discipline of the kirk.

The quhilk day, the sessioun ordanis the officiar to warne Arduthy, *rtj.* Bessy Arduthy to this day aucht dayis, to ansuer befoir thame tuiching the departure of ane boy leatle in Mr. Martine Geddeis wel[l] ; it being delatit to the sessioun the boy to haif bein hir awn barne, gottin in adultrie or fornicatioun and nevir baptizit.

The quhilk day, the sessioun ordanis Jhone Scheves and Scheves, Margret Clepen adultraris to be warnit be the officiar to begyn Clepen, adulteraris,[1] *rij.* thair repentance upon Sonday nixttocum, conforme to the ordinance maid thairanent the xx day of December last wes, and ane tikket to be gevin to the officiar thairupon ; and if thai failye that the officiar report the tiket with his charge verefyt to the sessioun this day aucht dayis.

The quhilk day, the sessioun ordanis George Small and Small, Gardner, Merrabill Gardner his spous to be warnit to this day aucht *rij.* dayis, to ansuer befoir thame tuiching the sudden departure of thair barne in the bed.

Die septimo mensis Februarii, anno octuagesimo primo.

The quhilk day, becaus Robert Thomsoun being be the Thomsoun reofficiar at command of the sessioun chargit to entir in pressoun mittit to the majestratis. upon Satterday nixttocum and disobeyit, as wes verefyt be the officiar, the sessioun remittis him to the secular majestrattis.

The quhilk day, Margret Clepen adultrice being warnit per- Scheves, sonale be the officiar (as the officiar verefyt) to begyn hir Clepen, adulteraris.[1] repentance for adultrie, committit be hir with Jhone Scheves, upon Sonday the ferd day of Februar instant ; with certificatioun, if sche failyeit, publict admonition suld be usit aganis hir to that effect, nocht the les the said Margret disobeyit contempteuslie.   And becaus Jhone Scheve[s] wes furth of this

---

Aduleraris in MS.

realme and culd nocht be hed to mak his repentance for the
cryme foirsaid, the session continewis the mater aganis him
quhill his hamecuming; and with ane voce ordanis the said
Margret yit as of befoir to be warnit agane to mak satisfaction
conforme to the ordour upon Sonday nixttocum, with certification if sche failye that publict admonitioun sall be usit aganis
hir.

Arduthy, *rij.*   The quhilk day, comperit Bessy Arduthy as sche that wes
laidfullie warnit to this day, and accusit be the sessioun quhais
aucht the boy that drownit laitly in Mr. Martine Geddeis well,
and quhidder he wes hir awin barne or nocht, and quha wes his
father, and if he wes evir baptizit and be quhome. The
sessioun committis full power to Mr. Dauid Russell, ane of the
elderis and memberis of this kirk, to try the said Bessy, and to
feill hir trew testimony in the premissis, and to report and
declair the samyn to the sessioun this day aucht dayis.

Small, Gardner,   The quhilk day, George Small and Mirabill Gardner, his
rij. q. spous, comperand befoir the sessioun as thai that wer laidfullie
warnit to this day, to ansuer anent the sudden departure of
thair barne wyth thame in the bed, confessit that the said
barne wes haill and levand wyth thame at fyve houris in the
morning, and or half hour to sevin wes deid be the sleuth of the
said Mirabill. The sessioun continewis thair determinatioun
heir anent to this day xv dayis, and the said day Masteris
Thomas Balfour and William Cok bailyeis, baith present, promis to report the consell of the townis advys, and determinatioun in that mater.

Mane, Bruce,   The quhilk day, Nicholl Mane and Jonet Bruce being warnit
rij. to this day to ansuer for the fornicatioun committit betuix
thame, comperit Jonet Bruce, quha confessis sche is wyth barne
to the said Nicholl. The sessioun ordanis Nicholl to be warnit
to this day aucht dayis.

Die xiiij^{to} mensis Februarii, anno octuagesimo primo.

Die xiiij^{to} mensis Februarii, anno octuagesimo primo.

Clepen, adul-   The quhilk day, the sessioun ordanis Margaret Clepen to
terie.[1] begyn hir repentance for adultrie committit be hir wyth Jhone
Rij.

---

[1] *Adulerie* in MS.

Scheves, upon Sonday nixttocum, the xviij of Februar instant, conforme to the ordinance maid [heir][1] anent of befoir, wyth certificatioun if sche failye that publict admonitioun be maid to hir in the kirk upon Sonday cum aucht dayis, and in the meanetyme to be warnit to compeir befoir the sessioun this day aucht dayis.

The quhilk day, the sessioun ordanis Mr. Dauid Russell to Arduthy, *rij.* be warnit to this day aucht dayis, to declair befoir thame the depositioun of Bessy Arduthy upon the dilatioun and ordinance maid in the act the vij of Februar instant, and Bessy to be warnit to that effect agane the said day.

The quhilk day, comperit Nicholl Mane quha confessis he *Confessio* hes hed carnall daill wyth Jonet Bruce, and that[2] the barn *Mane, Bruce.* quhilk Jonet is presentle wyth is his barne, confessis also promis of mariage betuix thame, and submittis him self to the discipline of the kirk ; he is content also to marie hir sua that his freindis be content. The session continewis thair ordinance aganis Nicholl for ane moneth nixttocum, wythin the quhilk space Nicholl promisis to report his frendis consent to the mariage, utherwys to satisfie the kirk as ane fornicatour quhen the kirk plesis.

Die vigesimo primo mensis Februarii, anno octuagesimo primo.

The quhilk day, Margret Clepen adultrar, being chargit to Clepen, haif comperit upon Sonday last, to haif maid satisfactioun for adulterie. hir adultrie oppinlie in the kirk, disobeyit and thairfor being chargit to this day to compeir befoir the sessioun, comperit personalie ; and sche, being personalie present befoir the session this day, chargit to begin hir repentance on Sonday nixttocum as of befoir, wyth certificatioun if sche refusit sche suld be publiclie admonisit on Sonday nixttocum. Sche, in presens of the haill sessioun convenit for the tyme, planlie refusit.

The quhilk day, comperit Dauid Horne elder for Dauid Horn Horn, Criste, younger his sone, and William Cristie mariner for Anabill contractit. Cristie his sister, and desirit licience to contract the said Dauid younger and Annabill uponland be George Blak redar, becaus

---

[1] Altered.   [2] *That that* in MS.

the parteis duellis out of this citee.   The samyn wes refusit be
the sessioun, thairfor the parteis comperit befoir the session
and wer contractit.

Confessio Kellie,   The quhilk day, comperit Margret Kellie, quha confessis sche
Cwnnghame,
Stevinsoun.   ressavit ane madin bairn thre yeir sensyne cum Witsonday fra
Cathrine Stevinsoun mother to the said barn, and fra the
minister of Craillis wyfe togidder, out of the said ministeris
hous in St. Androis for the tyme, in Henry Lawmonth far[1]
chalmer.   And the said Margret sayis that the said barn is the
barne of Alane Cwninghame, gottin in the Iland of Maij ; and
that the said Alane sumtyme payit to hir ane part of the said
barnis buird, and the said[2] Cathrine sumtymes ane uther part
thairof.   The sessioun ordanis supplicatioun to be direct to
the minister of Craill[3] for said mater and triall to be takin
thairintill.

Arduthy, *rij. q.*   The quhilk day, the sessioun conteinewis the caus of Bessy
Arduthy to this day xv dayis, and that the haill sessioun be
warnit to that effect aga[ne] the said day.

Die vigesimo octavo mensis Februarii, anno lxxxj[o.]

Clepen, *rij.*   The quhilk day, Margret Clepen adultrice being opon Son-,
Adultery.[4]
day last wes oppinlie be the redar callit upon in the publict
assemblie in the kirk to compeir and mak humiliatioun
conforme to the desire of the last act, as wes sufficientlie
verefyt ; and becaus sche comperit nocht the sessoun desirit
Mr. James Wilkye, Rectour, Mr. Thomas Balfour, balye, and
George Blak, redar, memberis of the sessioun,[5] to confer with
the said Margret, if thai culd be ony meni[s] persuade hir to
be obedient to the voce of the kirk, and to report hir ansuer
to the sessioun this day aucht dayis.   .

---

[1] Perhaps *foir*.   [2] *And the said and the said* in MS.
[3] John Edmestoun was minister of Crail at this time (Scott's *Fasti*, ii. 416).
[4] *Adullery* in MS.
[5] As George Blak was a deacon—not an elder—the expression in the text
shews that, even after the adoption of the *Second Book of Discipline*, deacons
were still regarded in St. Andrews as members of the session.

Die septimo Martii, anno lxxxj°

The quhilk day, as ane terme appointit to Mr. James Clapen,
adulteri.
Wilkye, Rectour, Mr. Thomas Balfour, bailye, and George
Blak, redar, to report Margret Clepenis ansuer, conforme to
the desire of the last act, conperit the said Mr. James and
George Blak, quha declare to the sessioun that the said
Margret promis[it] to gif ane ansuer betuix that and Sunday
last wes, quhidder sche wald obey or nocht. And Mr. James
and George present declarit that the said Margret geif thame
na ansuer ; lykeas also James Steill officair being sen[t] to Mr.
Thomas Balfour, seklie and absent for the tyme, to inquire if
he gat ony ansuer fra the said Margret, the said James, returning agane to the session wyth the said Mr. Thomas mynd, said
that the said Mr. Thomas gat na ansuer fra the said Margret.
Thairfor the sessioun ordanis the first public admonitioun to
be execut upon Sonday, the xj day of Marche instant, aganis
the said Margret for hir contempt.

The quhilk day the caus of Besse Arduthy continewit to Arduthy, *rij.*
this day aucht dayis.

The quhilk day the sessioun ordanis Margret Moncur and Bruntoun,
Moncur, *rij.*
Jonet Bromton to be warnit to this day aucht dayis.

The quhilk day, the sessioun ordanis the communioun to be The tyme ap-
pointit to mines-
minestrat be the grace of God to the inhabitantis of this citee tration of the
upon Palme Sonday nixttocum, the viij day of Aprile nixtto- communioun :
dilationis.
cum ; and dilationis to be takin befoir examinatioun, and
answer of the dilationis to be reportit this day aucht dayis.

Die decimo quarto mensis Martii, anno lxxxj°

The quhilk day, comperit Jhone Tod and Issobell Guild, *Confessio* Tod,
Guild. Satisfet.
quba confessis thai haif hed carnall daill togidder, and the
said Issobell sayis sche is wyth barne to the said Jhone ; thairfor thai submit thame selfis to discipline, and thairfor the
sessioun ordanis[1] the woman to enter in pressoun on Satterday
nixttocum, and the man on Satterday cum xv dayis, and to
satisfie conforme to the ordour.

---

[1] *Ordanis ordanis* in MS.

Arduthy, *rij.*

The caus of Bessy Arduthy is continewit to this day aucht dayis, and than sche is ordanit to declair hir conscience to the haill sessioun.

Confessio Monipenny, Gulen, *rij.* Baith satisfeit.

The quhilk day, Gelis Monipenny [1] confessis hir to be wyth barne to Jhone Gulen in Darsy, and allegis hir to be contractit wyth him in mariage in [*Darsy*—deleted] Carnebe be Michell Ramsay [2] redar thar, and grantis that it is [3] the fourth tyme that sche hes committit fornication, and submittis hir self to discipline. Mr. James Martine, Provest of the Auld College, is desyrit be the sesson to signifie the premissis to Mr Jhone Rutherfurd, minister of Darsy, that ordour may be takin wyth Jhone Gulen, and to report ansuer thairof to the sessioun this day aucht dayis.

Confessio Methven, Skirling, *rij.*

The quhilk day, Agnes Methven confessis that sche buir ane barne to Robert Skirling, servand to the Laird of Cambo, yit onsatisfeit, submittis hir self to discipline. The sessoun ordanis Skirling to be warnit to this day aucht dayis.

Reif, *C*luny, *rij.*

The quhilk day, the session ordanis Margret Cluny to enter agane on Sonday nixttocum, and continew in satisfaction as ane adultrice, conforme to the ordinance, quhill the kirk be satisfeit, and also ordanis Thomas Reif adultrar wyth hir to be warnit to this day aucht dayis.

Moncur *rij.*

The quhilk day, Margret Moncur, being warnit to this day and accusit quha is hir barnis father, desirit delay quhill this day aucht dayis to advis thairwyth, and sche is decernit wyth hir awn consent to compeir and declair quha is hir barnis father. -

Examinatioun befoir the communioun : wyth examina-touris.

The quhilk day, ansuer of the dilationis being producit be the clerk befoir the session, the sessioun ordanis the examinatioun to begyn upon Mononday nixttocum, according to the ordour usit and observit of befoir. Examinatouris in the first quarter, Mr. James Wilkie, Rectour, Mr. Martine Geddy, Wiliam Ferry, and Andro Watson scribe [thair] [4] to. The secind quarter, Mr. James Martine, James Robertsoun, Dauid Balfour, Jhone Hagy, scribe. The thrid quarter, Mr. Jhone Robertsoun, Mr. Henry Leiche, James Smyth, Mr. Dauid

---

[1] *Monipennipenny* in MS.
[2] Michael Ramsay was reader at Carnbee in 1574 with a stipend of £20 (*Wodrow Miscellany*, p. 361).   [3] *Is is* in MS.   [4] Omitted.

Russell, Charlis Watson, clerk. The ferd quarter, George Blak.

The quhilk day, in the sessioun of the ministrie of St. Androis, comperit George Blak redar of the said kirk and producit ane libellat summondis under the sele of the said ministrie dewlie execut and indorsat, thairin summond Margret Clepen adultrice to this day and sessioun, of the quhilk the tenour followis :—

Minister elderis and deaconis of Christis[1] kirk and congregatioun, wythin the citee of St. Androis, to George Blak redar of the said kirk, Grace mercy and peace, from God the Father, throw Jesus Christ our Saluiour. fforsamekill, as, upon Weddinsday, the xxij day of November last wes, Jhone Scheves and Margret Clapen adultraris, being callit and comperand befoir us in the consull hous, confessit thair adultrie togidder be procreatioun of ane madin barne; and for the samyn, upon the xx day of December last wes, wer be our decrete decernit to mak publict humiliatioun and satisfactioun, conforme to the godly ordour inviolablie observit in this kirk and congregatioun aganis adultrairis continewalie frome[2] tyme to tyme sen Reformatioun in religioun, as our actis in assemblie maid thairupon at lenth testifeis. And it is of verite that the said [Jhone—deleted][3] be himself[4] and utheris in his name at diveris tymes comperit personalie befoir us in our assemblie, promising to fulfill our ordinance and to mak humiliatioun and satisfactioun as said [is];[5] and we willing to wyn synneris wyth quietnes rather nor sevirite to repentans, evir hoping from day to day willing obedience and satisfaction to haif bein done as is aboif rehersit, (albeit the contrar wes menit) and na thing ellis socht bot drift and delay of tyme quhill the said Jhone micht pas to saill furth of this realme to evacuat discipline, and gude ordour in the meane tyme frustrat, as we haif now sen syne fund in experiance be the said Jhonis departure wythout satisfactioun; and yit, understanding the said Margret to remane presentlie obstinat and sklandrous wythin this citee, causit call hir befoir us

Citacio Clepen, adulterii.

---

[1] *Chrstis* in MS.   [2] *Forme* in MS.

[3] *Margret* has been interlined over *Jhone*, but her name too is deleted.

[4] Altered from *himself* to *hirself*. In the second summons it reads—*Jhone be himself and utheris in his name*.   [5] Omitted.

in our assemblie, travelling ernestlie wyth hir to humbill hirself
and to mak satisfactioun publict for hir hienous crime, as said
is, as we also diveris utheris tymes be certane godlie and zelous
memberis of our ecclesiasticall sait travellit and conferrit wyth
hir to the samyn effect, culd find nathing bot inobedience and
contempt in hir. Heirfor we require yow, in the name of the
Eternall our God, that ye laidfullie, in the publict assemblie of
the kirk and congregation, summond the said Margret to compeir befoir us in the consall hous wythin the said kirk, upon
Weddinday, the xiiij of Marche instant, in the hour of caus at
efter none, to heir hir decernit to haif contempnit and transgressit the godly ordinance and voce of the kirk; and thairfor
to underly discipline[1] as salbe imput to hir for hir contempt
and disobedience; wyth certificatioun to hir, if sche compeir
nocht, or comperand refusis discipline, we will proceid aganis
hir wyth detfull ordour to the finall executioun of the feirfull
sentence of excommunicatioun, as the greatest and last punischment belangand to the spirituall ministrie; and thaireftir invocat the assistance of the temporale authorite and civile
power. The quhilk to do we commit to yo[w] power in the
Lord be thir presentis, delivering the samyn be yow dewlie
execut and indorsat agane to the berar. Gevin undir the sele
of the said ministrie at St. Androis, the vij day of Marche, the
yeir of God j^{m}v^{c}lxxxj yeris.

Rij.

Followis the indorsatioun: Upon Sonday, the xj day of
Marche 1581, I, George Blak, redar in the parroche kirk of
St. Androis, in the publict assemblie of the congregatioun,
summond Margret Clepen oppinlie eftir the tenour of this summondis retroscript, to the day and place wythin writin, witnes
the hoill congregatioun, and this my subscriptioun manual, *sic
subscribitur*, George Blak, redar.

The foirsaid Margret oftimes callit, laufull tyme biddin,
and sche nocht comperand is notit *contumax*. The ministrie
ordanis hir to be summond in maner foirsaid, for the secund
executioun and admonitioun, to Weddinsday nixttocum, wyth
intimatioun as efferis.

Dalglesche, xxj. The quhilk day, Jonet Dalgles decernit to report testimoniall

---

[1] *Disciplince* in MS.

this day xxj dayis, conforme to the ordinance [and][1] the act, the last of Januar last wes, and the copy of the act decernit to hir.

Die vigesimo primo Martii, anno lxxxj°·

The quhilk day, Barbaray Wod confessis hir to be wyth barne to Dauid Oliphant, servand to my lord of Newbuttill, and that the said barne wes gottin in Jhone Hekleins hous wythin this citee. The sessioun ordanis hir to depart furth of this [citee— deleted] parrochie wythin xv dayis ; and supplicatioun to be direct to the majestratis to that effect. The sessioun ordanis also Jhone Heklein to be warnit to this day aucht dayis, and accusit for sufferring harlotrie to be committit in his hous. And also Androw Miller, undir quhome Barbaray Wod now duellis, and to be accusit for setting of ane hous to ane harlott. *Confessio Wod.* *Heklein, Miller, rij.*

The quhilk day, the sessioun ordanis Henry Quisme present to compeir agane befoir thame this day aucht dayis, to ansuer to the dilatioun movit aganis him for contracting mariage wyth Elspot Rikkert and haifing carnall daill wyth hir, he haifand ane mariit wyfe of his awin levand ondevorsit ; and also ordanis William Muffett and Androw Carstaris, dilatouris of him, to be warnit to the said day for forder triall. *Quisme, rij.*

The quhilk day, Elspot Fairlie confessis sche is wyth barne to William Pitcane,[2] and submittis hirselfe to discipline, and allegis promis of mariage maid to hir be William. *Confessio Fairlie.*

The quhilk day, it is delatit that Issobell Zwill[3] is lichter of ane barne in Niniane Lowis hous. It is supponit to be the Laird of St. Monanis barne gottin in fornicatioun. The sessioun ordanis for triall thairof the meidwyfe, and als the maister of the hous, to be warnit heirto this day aucht dayis. And Gelis Mylis, witnes, being suorn and examinat upon the same mater, declaris that sche wes wyth the said Issobell [in][1] tyme of hir burth, and hard hir say that the barin wes the Laird of St. Monanis barne. *Zwill, rij.*

The quhilk day, Thomas Reif younger, confessand him to haif committit adultrie wyth Margret Cluny, is decernit to *Decretum contra Reif.*

---

[1] Omitted.   [2] Perhaps *Pitcarne.*
[3] The words *it is delatit that* having been omitted are supplied in the margin, but there the name *Issobell Zwill* has been unnecessarily repeated.

compeir upon Sonday nixt to cum, wyth the said Margret, cled
in sekclaith, bair heddit and bair futtet, and stand at the kirk
dur fra the secund to the thrid bell to sermone befoir none;
and thaireftir to compeir upon the adultraris place of the penitent stuill wythin the kirk, and sitt thairon quhill the sermon
be endit; and sa furth to continew ilk Sonday quhill the kirk
be satisfeit, conforme to the ordour.

The quhilk day, in the sessioun of the ministrie of St.
Androis comperis George Blak redar, and producis ane summondis undir the sele of the said ministrie dewlie execut and
indorsat aganis Margret Clepen adultrice, of the quhilk the
tenour followis :—

[This begins in the same way and runs on in the same form
as the previous summons, a few words and phrases are altered,
and others om$_{itt}$e$_d$, and a very few added. None of these are
of any importance, except the changes rendered necessary by
this being the second summons. To the narrative there is
added :—' And thairby, being constranit of our dewetie, causit
hir be oppinlie summond to haif comperit before us in our
assemblie upon Weddinsday the xiiij of Marche instant; wyth
certificacioun if sche comperit nocht we wald proceid aganis hir
wyth detfull ordour to the finall executioun of the fairfull
sentence of excommunicatioun, quha nevertheles persisting in
hir contempt hes contempteuslie absentit hir.' And then it
proceeds :—' Heirfor we require yow, in the name of the eternall
God, that ye now as of befoir, in this our secund admonitioun,
laidfullie in the publict assemblie of the congregatioun, summond the said Margret Clepen to compeir befoir us, in the
consall hous wythin the said kirk, upon Weddinsday the xxj
day of Marche instant, at efter none in the hour of caus. . . .
Gevin under the sele of the said ministrie, at St. Androis, the
xiiij day of Marche, the yeir of God j^{m}v^{c}lxxxj yeris.']

ffolowis the indorsatioun : Upon Sonday the xviij day of
Marche 1581, I, George Blak, redar in the parroche kirk of St.
Androis, in the publict assemblie of the kirk of St. Androis,
summond Margret Clepen oppinlie eftir the tenour of this
summondis aboif writin. Witnes the hoill congregatioun, and
this my subscriptio[un] manuall—George Blak, redar, wyth
my hand.

The said Margret oftimes callit and nocht comperand, laid[full][1] tyme biddin, sche is noted *contumax* for the secund. The ministrie ordanis hir to be summond and admonist this nixt Sonday in lyke maner, to Weddinsday nixttocum, for the thrid and last admonitioun; wyth intimatioun that, except sche humill hirself and obey the adm[o]nitioun, thai will proceid aganis hir to the finall executioun of excommunicatioun the nixt Sonday thaireftir following: and now continewis the executioun of the last summondis, in respect of the communion to be ministrat, quhill Sonday the viij day of Aprile nixttocum.

Die quarto mensis Aprilis, anno octuagesimo secundo.

The quhilk day, anent the complantis of injuris gevin in *Reconciliatio Quhyte, Spens, Dauidsoun.* befoir the sessioun be Dauid Quhyte and Jonet Dauidson his spous[2] aganis Cathrine Bron and Jonet Spens hir dochter, and be the saidis Cathrine and Jonet upon the saidis Dauid and his spo[us]. Thai ar all, in presens of the sessioun, in the luif and feir of God, reconcelit togidder; an[d] with thair awin consentis decernit be the session that quhilk of thame first failyis to utheris agane heirefter, in word or deid, the falter to mak publict satisfactioun to the persoun that beis offendit in the kirk oppinlie in presens of the pepill, upon ane Sonday; and to pay to the persoun that the offens beis don to ten merkis onforgevin, providing that the offence be first tryit and verifyt.

The quhilk day, Mr. Jhone Rutherfurd minister of Darsy *Confessio Gulen.* haifand power of the session to tak the aith of Jhone Gulen, if the barne Gelis Monipeny is presentle with be his barn or nocht, conperit the said Mr. Jhone and declaris that the said Jhone Gulen grantis the barin to be his barn. Thairfor the session decernis Gulen to mak satisfactioun in this kirk for his offens, on Sonda[y] the sext of Maii nixttocum; and, becaus he *Sexto Maij.* duellis in the parrochin of Darsy, requestis Mr. Jhone Rutherfird minister thairof [to][1] require Gulen to obey thair decrete, and to remember the puir for his impresonment.

The quhilk day, Dauid Caid is decernit to mak publict *Dauid Caid.*

---

[1] Omitted.   [2] *Spois* in MS.

satisfactioun in the kirk, for his offens and sklander done to the kirk and congregation in the tuilze betuix him and Jhone Heklein.

Die undecimo mensis Aprilis, anno Domini j^mv^c octuagesimo secundo.

Clepen.

The quhilk day, in the sessioun of the ministrie of St. Androis, comperit George Blak redar thair and producit ane summondis dewlie execut and indorsat upon Margret Clepen adultrice, quhair sche is summond and admonisit for the thrid and last admonitioun to compeir to this day, as at mair lenth is contenit in the said summondis. The said Margret being oftimes callit, nocht comperand, laidfull tyme biddin, is notat *contumax*; and be the ministrie decernit worthy to mereit the sentence of excommunicatioun, and the samyn to be execut aganis hir.

Rij.

The quhilk day, it is thocht gude that the haill memberis of the sait be warnit to this day aucht dayis, for electing commissioneris to the Generall Assemble, and to treat upon sic heidis as suld be proponit thair.

Rij.

The quhilk day, it [is][1] concludit that the haill flescheouris and utheris mercheandis within this citee be warnit to this day aucht dayis, for travelling to Craill mercat on the Sabboth day, and accusit thairfor.

Thomson, Downye.

The quhilk day, Cathrine Thomson proponit hir actioun of injuris aganis Jhone Downy. The session remittis the injurie done agans Cathrin to the civile majestratis; and to preif the blaspheme spokin aganis the sacramentis *literatorie*, and Downy to be warnit[2] thairto.

Die Mercurii, xviij° Aprilis,[3] anno lxxxij°·

Commissioneris electit to the Generall Assemblie.

The quhilk day, the sessioun thinkis meit and expedient that ane commissioun be gevin to Mris. William Cok, Dauid Russell and Martine Geddy, or ony tua of thame, as commissioneris to

---

[1] Omitted.   [2] *Warn* in MS.

[3] *Decimo xviij° Aprilis* in MS.

compeir in the Generall Assemblie of the Kirk, to be haldin in this citee the xxiiij day of Aprile instant.

The quhilk day, Martine and Alexander Lummisdanis, James Dempstar, Thomas Cuthbert, Jhone Blak, Thomas Logy, Jhone Mernis, James Cuik, James and Androw Millaris, James Herman, Androw Andersoun, and Jhone Kellie, flescheouris; and siclyke, Archibald Wischert, Androw Hog, Robert Mwrray, Androw Miniman, Jhone Fairfull, William Andersoun, Alexander Wod, Alexander Caid, smyth, and Thomas Zoung, mercheandis, being all personale befoir the ministrie, as thai quha wer laidfullie warnit to this day and accusit for keping of the mercat of Craill on the Sabboth day, and for violating of the said day aganis the fourt commandiment of Almychtie God; and in thair presens the auld gude and godlie actis of this sessioun being red publiclie to thame anent the keping bolie the Sabbath day, and speciale ane act maid anent the said flescheouris upon the last day of Aprile, lxxij yeris; [1] quhilk act the saidis flescheouris ratifeis and apprevis, and promissis to keip the samyn under the panis thairin contenit. And lykewyis the saidis flescheouris, and the haill remanent [2] personis mercheandis aboif writin, ar be the voce of the ministrie and sessioun, with thair awin consentis, decernit according to the Word of God to keip holy the Sabboth day in all tymes cuming; and that the saidis flescheouris nor nane of thame, nather be thame selfis nor thair servandis, slay brek nor sell flesche, nather in this citee nor yit in Craill, nor in na uther part within this realme, upon the Sabbot day; and als that the saidis mercheandis, nor nane of thame, nather be thame selfis nor thair servandis, travell to Craill mercat, nor to nane uther mercat, on the Sabboth day, [3] nor that thai sall na kynd of geir, in na mercat

Decrete of the sessioun anent the flescheouris and dreparis and mercheandis.

---

[1] *Supra*, pp. 364, 365.   [2] *Remament* in MS.

[3] In England, Henry the Eighth's monastic commissioners 'had been directed to enforce an abrogation of the superfluous holydays; they had shown such excessive zeal that in some places common markets had been held under their direction on Sundays' (Froude's *History of England*, iii. 98). The Scotch Reformers on the other hand were anxious from the first to suppress Sabbath markets, and resolved in 1562 to supplicate the Queen to that effect (*Booke of the Universall Kirk*, i. 19, 30); and approached the Regent on the same matter in 1575 (*Ibid.* i. 339). At length in 1579, Parliament ratified an Act of James the Fourth, forbidding the holding of markets or fairs on holydays, or in churches

within this realme, on the Sabboth day; bot that thai, and
ilk ane of thame, keip the samyn holy according to the Word
and commandiment of the eternall God, under the pane of
excluding and debarring thame selfis, thair wyfis, barnis and

---

or church-yards on any day, and, 'seing that the Sabboth dayis ar now com-
mounlie violat and brokin alsweill within burgh as to landwart, to the greit
dishonour of God, be balding and keiping of the saidis mercattis and fairis on
Sondayis, using of handy laubor and working thairon,' &c., ordained that no
markets or fairs be held on that day under pain of escheating of the goods to the
use of the poor, and that no work be used on that day, nor gaming and playing,
passing to taverns and alehouses, selling of meat or drink, nor wilful remaining
from the parish kirk in time of sermon or prayers on that day. The penalty for
working was ten shillings, for the other breaches twenty. Those who refused or
were unable to pay these sums were to be put in the stocks for twenty-four hours
(*Acts of the Parliaments of Scotland*, iii. 138). In October 1581, because no
execution had followed the Act against Sabbath markets, the Assembly desired
that the Parliament then sitting might take further order, and that some punishment be appointed to the magistrates who did not execute it (*Booke of the Universall Kirk*, ii. 536); and on the 29th of the following month, in ratifying the
liberties of the Kirk, Parliament ratified the Act of 1579 (*Acts of Parliament*, iii.
211).   In 1587 Parliament changed the market of Crail, which had been held
on Sunday since the days of Robert the Bruce, to Saturday (*Ibid*. iii. 507).
The old habits were not so easily eradicated, for in March 1589-90, in August
1590, and in July 1591, the Assembly were constrained to return to the charge
(*Booke of the Universall Kirk*, iii. 748, 749, 769, 776, 784). In 1592 Parliament
declared it lawful for those towns and parishes whose markets had been previously held on the Sabbath to choose other days of the week (*Acts of Parliament*,
iii. 548) ; and in 1593 and 1594 ratified the former Acts, and made more stringent
provision for their observance (*Ibid*. iv. 16, 63). But in 1596, the Assembly
had still to lament that the 'keiping of mercatts' was one of the common forms
of Sabbath profanation (*Booke of the Universall Kirk*, iii. 874). For the better
observance of the Sabbath, Parliament ordained in 1598 that each Monday
should be kept as a pastime day (*Acts of Parliament*, iv. 160). Even when the
markets were held on Monday they led to Sabbath desecration. Baillie says :—
'For remedie heerof, many supplications have been made by the Assembly to
the Parliament : but so long as our bishops satte there, these petitiones of the
Church were alwayes eluded : for the praelats labour in the whole iland was to
have the Sunday no Sabbath, and to procure by their doctrine and example
the profanation of that day by all sorts of playes, to the end people might be
brought back to their old licentiousnes and ignorance, by which the Episco-
pall Kingdome was advanced.   It was visible in Scotland, that the most
eminent bishops were usual players on the Sabbath, even in time of divine
service. And so soone as they were cast out of the Parliament, the Churches
supplications were granted, and acts obtained for the carefull sanctification of
the Lords day, and removing of the mercats in all the land from the Munday
to other dayes of the week' (*Review of Bramble's Faire Warning*, 1649, p. 42).
The Acts to which Baillie refers were passed in 1640, 1644, and 1646.

servandis fra all benefete of the kirk in tyme cuming, to witt,
[fra]¹ baptisme of thair barnis, fra the Lordis Supper and fra
mariage, and forder under the pane of excommunicatioun, as
the kirk sall pleis injune to thame for thair faill.

Die secundo mensis Maii, anno lxxxij°·

The quhilk day, the sessioun ordanis Margret Clepen to be Clepen.
warnit to compeir befoir thame this day aucht dayis, to ansuer
anent hir obedience; uther wyis, if sche compeir nocht, the
kirk will proceid aganis hir with detfull ordour to excommunicatioun.

Die Mercurii, nono Maii, 1582.

The quhilk [day],¹ it is thocht meit be the sessioun that the Anent Mr.
Bischop, Mr. William Cok, Mr. Dauid Russell, Mr. Martine minister.
Geddy and Alexander Wynsister pas and confer with my Lord *Rij.*
of Marche, for gude ordour to be takin for Mr. Robert Pont
minister, and for his stipend, that he may be hestit to cum
hame, and to report ansuer this day aucht dayis.²

---

¹ Omitted.

² Robert Pont, who had been one of the early elders of the St. Andrews
congregation, was now a Senator of the College of Justice, and held the
Provostry of Trinity College Edinburgh, as well as the first charge of St.
Cuthbert's or West Kirk. The Earl of March was Commendator of the Priory
of St. Andrews (P. 232, n.), and, according to James Melvill, he 'colluded with
the rewallars of the town to hald the ministerie vacand, and in the mean tyme
tuk upe the stipend, and spendit the sam, with the rest of the kirk-rents of the
Pryorie, at the goff, archerie, guid cheir, &c.' (Melvill's *Diary*, Wod. Soc. p.
126). Scott enters Pont among the ministers of St. Andrews at this date (*Fasti*,
ii. 388). At the end of April 1583, in the General Assembly, 'Mr. Robert Pont
declairit, that, with lose of his heritage and worldlie commoditie, he had proponit
to sitt down in Sanct Androes, and had served on his awin charges a whole year,
and could not have any equall conditiouns of living, no, not the least provisioun
that any had that past befor, and now altogither his heart is abstractit from
them; praying the Kirk not to lay the charge upon him against his will' (*Booke
of the Universall Kirk*, ii. 620). This declaration seems to bear out Scott's
statement; but there is nothing in the *Register* to show that Pont served as
minister here; indeed, there is one entry, which will appear in the second part,
from which it may at least be inferred that he did not serve here for a whole year.
For more information about Pont than is contained in the works mentioned on
p. 2, n. 4, see Wodrow's *Collections upon the Lives of the Reformers*, Maitland
Club, vol. i.

Tikket of har-
lottis to the
majestratis.
. The quhilk day, the sessioun ordanis the clerk to gif ane
tikket to the Bischop, to be gevin to the majestratis of this
citee, of Margret Clepen and utheris inobedient adultraris, and '
of utheris wicket harlottis within this citee, that the majestratis
may tak ordour with thame ; and the Bischop to report ansuer
this day aucht dayis. The tikket is deliverit. Mergret Clepen
wes warnit to this day, and contempteuslie disobeyit.

Rij.

Confessio
Sowter *alias*
Robertsoun,
Walker, *rij.*
The quhilk day, Agnes Sowter *alias* Robertson confessis sche
is with barne .to. Patri[k] Walker, and that the first tyme sche
hed to do with him wes ane yeir syne in Margret Moncurris
hous, and that the barne wes gottin about Zwil[l] last wes, in
the said Margretis hous. Sche confesis also that sche buir ane
madin barne befoir in fornication to *D*onald Sutherland, now
servand to the young Laird of Blabow. Sche submittis hirself
to discipline. The sessioun ordanis Patrik Walker and *D*onald
Sutherland to be warnit to this day aucht dayis.

Thomsoun,
Downy.
The quhilk day, in the caus persewit be Cathrine Thomson
aganis Jhon[e] *D*owny, anent injuris, the sessioun remittis the
injurie done to the said Cathrine to be decidit befoir Provest
and bailyes of this citee as civile majestratis ; bot this day .
being assignit to preif the blasphemy spoki[n] aganis the holy
communion and sacrament of Christ Jesus, the said Jhone being
also laidfullie warnit to this day to heir probationis deducit
thairupon, and he, oftimes callit, comperit nocht, ressavit
Alexander Ramsay tailyeour, witnes, suor[n] and examinat,
deponis on his conscience that he hard the said Jhone speik
na blasphemy aganis the sacrament. Cristene Thomson, being
also ressavit suorn and examinat, deponis on hir conscience
that sche hard Jhone *D*owny say, tyme libellat . . . .[1] with
mony utheris injurous words odious to be hard or put in
wreit. Beatrix Pratt, Margret Brabanar and Beatrix Gibsoun,
witnes, also being all ressavit, suorn and examinat severalie,
deponis ilk ane, on thair consciences, conform to Cristene
Thomson witnes in all thingis. The sessioun statut to pronunce *literatorie*, and ordanit the haill sait to be warnit to this .
day aucht dayis, with the majestratis to advys heirupon.

---

[1] The expression is very coarse.

Die Mercurii, decimo sexto Maii, anno lxxxij°·

The quhilk day, the sessioun hes concludit that na mariage proceid betuix Henrie Quisme and Elspot Rikkert, quhill productioun of ane sufficient testimoniall of the departure of Margret Bowsy, Henreis first spous.

Na mariage to proceld betuix Quisme and Rikkert.

The quhilk day, Agnes Sowtar and Patrik Walker fornicatouris being confrontit, Patrik denyis the barne that Agnes is with to be his, becaus he denyis on his conscience that he hed evir carnall daill with hir bot anis, that wes in Margret Moncurris hous tua yeir sensyne. And Sowtar being inquirit, in Patrikis presens, howft sche hed to do with Patrik, ansueris money sindry times, and in diveris places, quhen he plesit, and spetialie amangis the craigis at the partane sey, and in Jhone Martinis yaird, and the last time sche hed to do with him wes a litill eftir harvest last wes. Margret Moncur, witnes, being ressavit, suorn and admittit, and examinat for triall of the mater, and inquirit how lang it is sen Sowtar duelt in hir hous, ansueris tua yeir cum Witsonday. The parteis submittis thame to discipline. The sessioun continewis the mater quhill forder triall may be hed in this mater.

Walker, Sowtar. Lettres.

Die penultimo mensis Maii, anno lxxxij°·

The quhilk day, comperit Jhone Scheves and Margret Clepen adultrates personilie befoir the sessioun, quha promist faithfullie to mak satisfactioun and humiliatioun for thair adultrie conforme to the ordinance of the kirk, to witt, the said Jhone Scheves promist to begyn his humiliatioun upon Sonday nixttocum, and the said Margret promist to begyn upon Sonday cum aucht dayis, and sa furth to continew ilk Sonday, thair owk about, in humiliatioun, according to the ordinance of the kirk, quhill the kirk be satisfeit.

Jhone Scheves and Margret Clepennis promis of humiliatioun.

Die Mercurii, decimo tertio Junii, anno octuagesimo secundo.

The quhilk day, Jonet Dewar confessis hir to be with barin

Confessio[1] Dewar, Caid. Baith satisfeit.

---

[1] *Confesso* in MS.

to Alexander Caid smyth. Sche submittis hirself to discipline. Alexander is ordanit to be warnit to this day aucht dayis.

Die Mercurii, xx° mensis Junii, anno octuagesimo secundo.

Downy, *rij.*   The quhilk day, the sessioun ordanis Jhone Downy to be warnit to this day aucht dayis, to ansuer befoir thame for the blaspheme spokin be him aganis the sacrament of the Lordis Supper, and to ressaif injunctionis thairfor; with certificatioun, if [he][1] compeir nocht, he salbe oppinlie admonisit in the kirk, Sonday cum aucht dayis.

Walker, Stewart, *rij.*   The quhilk day, becaus Patrik Walker and Elspot Stewar, [quhilkis][1] wes warnit to compeir befoir the sessioun to this day, to haif ansuerit upon the dilation gevin in aganis thame, as wes verefyt be the officiar, comperit nocht, the sessioun ordanis thame to be warnit to this day aucht dayis, with certificatioun if thai failye publict admonition to pas agans thame.

Caid, Dewar.   The quhilk day, Jonet Dewar and Alexander Caid fornicatouris, being confrontit, thai confess carnall copulation togidder, and that the barne Jonet is with is Alexanderis barne. Thai submittand thame selfis to discipline, Jonet to entir in presson, Setterday nixttocum, and Caid Satterday cum aucht dayis; and thaireftir on Sonday cum aucht dayis, thai baith togidder to mak humiliation conforme to the ordour.

Lawsoun, *rij.*   The quhilk day, Jhone Lawsoun baxter is ordanit to be warnit to this day aucht dayis, to ansuer *super inquirendis.*

Die Mercurii, quarto Julii, anno lxxxij°.

Satisfactio Downy.   The quhilk day, Jhone Downy, at decrete and command of session for blasphemy spokin be him aganis the sacrament of the Lordis supper, upon his knewis, in presens of the sessioun convenit for the tyme in counsal hous, maid humiliatioun, and promist to mak forther satisfaction, als great and oft as the kirk sall injune and pleis require.

The land communioun to be ministrat.   The quhilk day, it is concludit be voit of sessioun that the land communioun be ministrat upon Sonday, the penult of Julii

---

[1] Omitted.

instant, and that examinatioun begyn Mononday cum aucht
dayis, the xv of Julii instant.

Die Mercurii, undecimo Julii, 1582.

The quhilk day, Patrik Walker and Elspot Stewar, being Walker,
baith present befoir the sessioun, confessit carnall copulatioun Sowtar, *r·it·*
togidder under promis of mariage, and wer baith content to
marie togidder. The sessoun continewis thair mariage quhill
the parentis consentis be obtenit and schawin thairto; and
als, thai, submittand thame to discipline, ar decernit to mak
satisfactioun for thair offence befoir the mariage, conforme to
the ordour; and also ordani[t] Patrik Walker befoir all uther
thingis to mak publict repentance as an[e] fornicatour for
harlotrie committit be him with Agnes Sowtar. And the
session ordanis Sowtar with hir maidwyfe to be warnit to this
day aucht dayis, for triall to be takin betuix Patrik and
Sowtar; and forder Patrik and Elspot Stewart ar commandit
be the session to abstein fra utheris carnall societie quhill the
marage be endit.

Die xiiij^{to} mensis Augusti, anno lxxxij^{o·}

The quhilk day, the sessioun ordanis Issobell Duncane to Duncane.
mak humiliatioun upon Sonday nixttocum, upon the penitent
stuill, for fornicatioun committit be hir with William Zwill,
and thaireftir to be marriit with [*blank*].

Die Mercurii, duodecimo [1] Septembris, anno lxxxij^{o·}

The quhilk day, Patrik Walker confessis he hes hed carnall Walker, Hillok,
daill with Bessy Hillok in Sanctnicolais, upon Weddinsday *rij·*
befoir the sengze day last wes. The sessioun ordanis him and
the said Besse to be warnit agane to this day aucht dayis.

---

[1] *Duodecmo* in MS.

Die Mercurii, vigesimo sexto Septembris, anno lxxxij°·

Monitio
Angous,
Budge.

The quhilk day, Jhone Budge younger is oblist and actitat, of his awin propir consent, to pay ouklie to Agnes Angous quhill this tyme tuelf moneth, for sustentatioun of the barne procreat betuix thame, twelf penneis; and siclyke to pay for the said Agnes housmaill quhill this day tuelf month, quhair evir sche duellis, quhat evir it be.

END OF VOL. I.

Printed by T. and A. Constable, Printers to Her Majesty.
at the Edinburgh University Press.

REPORT

SECOND ANNUAL MEETING

OF THE

SCOTTISH HISTORY SOCIETY.

———

THE Second Annual Meeting of the Society was held on
Tuesday, October 30th, 1888, in the Professional Hall, George
Street, Edinburgh,—Professor Masson presiding.

The SECRETARY read the following letter from Lord Rosebery,
who had been announced to preside at the meeting :—

'DALMENY PARK, EDINBURGH, *29th October* 1888.

' DEAR MR. LAW,—I am extremely annoyed to find that, owing
to a confusion of dates, I cannot be with you to-morrow. A
month ago I accepted an engagement to go into Lanarkshire
for a day and two nights. I was under the impression that our
meeting of the History Society was fixed for to-day. I cannot
forego my other engagement at the last moment, and am convinced that you will easily find a better chairman than myself to
preside at to-morrow's meeting. Nor is any chairman necessary to
demonstrate the vigour and vitality of our Society, which opens
out such prospects of usefulness, and which will, I hope, not lay
down its arms without having made an unrivalled contribution to
the history of Scotland. The great point is to attract the notice
and the confidence of owners of MSS. and other historical materials

2

who may be disposed, by intrusting them to us for printing, to put them beyond the chances of fire and time. I must end by adding how real is the disappointment I feel at not being with you to-morrow.—Yours very truly, ROSEBERY.'

The SECRETARY next read the Report by the Council, as follows:—

Since the original list of 400 subscribers was completed, there have been 18 vacancies. These have been filled up, and there still remain 34 names on the list of applicants waiting for admission. All the new members have up to this date been supplied with the volumes of the first year's issue on payment of a double subscription. There are, however, no remaining copies of *Pococke's Tours*, and only three copies of *Cunningham's Diary*.

The first volume due for the current year, *The Grameid*, edited by the Rev. Canon Murdoch, is now ready for issue. Some apology is due to members for the slight delay which has occurred in the completion of the *Register of the Kirk Session of St. Andrews*. The delay, however, is due only to the extreme care which the editor, Mr. Hay Fleming, has taken to ensure accuracy by collating his proof-sheets with the original manuscript, letter by letter. The text is now in print, and the volume only awaits the editor's preface. It will be in the hands of members in a few weeks.

On the other hand, two of the three volumes announced for next year are in a forward state. Mr. Goudie has collected some valuable materials to illustrate the local history of Dunrossness, etc., in the Shetlands, in reference to the diary of the Rev. John Mill, which is ready for the press. The narrative of Mr. James Nimmo, the Covenanter, is also transcribed and ready for the printer. These will be followed in the course of the year by a second volume of the *St. Andrews Register*.

The first publication of our fourth year will be Mr. Archibald Constable's translation of Major's History of Scotland. A portion of the work has already been done, and makes most interesting reading. The promised introductory memoir of Sheriff Mackay is now in the editor's hands. 'Major' will be accompanied by a volume of *Glamis Papers*, to be edited by Mr. A. H. Millar (author of *The Burgesses of Dundee*) from the archives at Glamis Castle, which have been placed at the disposal of the Society by the kindness of Lord Strathmore. These papers consist of the *Book of Record*, written by Patrick, first Earl of Strathmore (died in 1695), giving an account of his restoration and decoration of Glamis Castle and Castle Lyon, now Castle Huntly, in the Carse of Gowrie, under the direction of Inigo Jones; a diary or household book of Lady Helen Middleton, afterwards Countess of Strathmore; an account-book of the Earl's valet, and other documents bearing on the social life or on the state of trade and the industrial arts in Scotland at the close of the seventeenth century.

Among other works in contemplation may be mentioned the *Diary* of Andrew Hay of Stone, near Biggar, afterwards of Craignethan. Hay was a zealous Presbyterian, and a constant correspondent of Johnston of Warriston at the time when General Monck was on his march towards England. The diary is written in an original and quaint style, and is interesting for its local allusions, which will be elucidated by the editor, Mr. A. G. Reid of Auchterarder.

Sir George Clerk of Penicuik has been good enough to permit the Society to publish an autobiography of his ancestor, Sir John Clerk, Baron of the Exchequer and Commissioner for the Union. This autobiography, made up from journals kept regularly by the writer from his twenty-sixth year, is carried down to within a few months of his death, which took place in 1755. The book deals largely with domestic and family matters, but it is also the record, by an eminent Scotsman, of an active life spent in literary and antiquarian pursuits as well as in public affairs, and as such cannot fail to be welcome to the Society. Members are to be congratulated on having secured for an editor of this volume Mr. J. M. Gray, the Curator of the National Portrait Gallery.

The Council have also resolved to publish from a manuscript in the Advocates' Library a translation, with the original Latin, of an inedited treatise on the Union of the Crowns of Scotland and England, written by the famous Scottish lawyer, Sir Thomas Craig, who was appointed by the Parliament of Scotland as one of the Commissioners for the treaty of Union of 1604. Though not strictly historical in form, this learned work treats of a most important moment in the national history from the point of view of a Constitutional lawyer and statesman, and abounds in historical illustration. It appears, therefore, to the Council to very properly fall within the scope of the Society's work.

The Rev. A. W. Cornelius Hallen undertakes to edit a volume of extracts from the diaries and household books of Sir John Foulis of Ravelston (1679-1707), and of Dame Hannah Erskine, wife of John Erskine of Balgownie (1675-99).

The Society will also be glad to learn that Professor Mitchell of St. Andrews will write an historical introduction to the *Minutes of the Commission of the General Assembly*, 1646-1662, and otherwise assist in the preparation of this work, which is under the editorial care of Dr. Christie.

Lastly, the Council have great pleasure in announcing that Lord Rosebery has signified his intention to print and present as a gift to the members of the Society some valuable papers on the Rebellion of 1745. These will consist of official lists of rebels furnished to the Government by the officers of Excise in the various districts of Scotland. In these lists there are no less than 2520 names of rebels, with descriptions of their rank or occupation, and occasionally the value of their property, together with the acts of rebellion of which they were accused, and in some cases the names of the informers against them. No lists of this character and extent have hitherto been made known. The special thanks of the Society are due to Lord

5

Rosebery for this appropriate and valuable gift. No copies of this work will be printed for sale or reserved for future members. The gift will be strictly limited to the existing members of the Society at the date of publication.

Three members have, according to the rules, retired from the Council, viz. Mr. Omond, Mr. Russell, and Sir Arthur Mitchell. It is proposed that the Rev. Dr. Sprott and the Rev. A. W. Cornelius Hallen take the places of the first two, and that Sir Arthur Mitchell be re-elected.

The TREASURER, in submitting the financial statement for the year (hereto appended), suggested that £150 of the balance should be set aside to form a reserve fund to meet contingencies.

The CHAIRMAN, in moving the adoption of the Reports, said the condition of the Society was extremely prosperous in every way. He thought their publications were such as not only to justify the existence of the Society, but to prove that there existed material for valuable operations on the part of the Society. They were about to issue *The Grameid* and *The Register of the Kirk-Session of St. Andrews* as the volumes for the second year. The only thing that need be noted about the companionship of these two was that it was a proof that the Society was not a partisan society. It aimed at representing Scottish feeling and Scottish fact because it was Scottish feeling and Scottish fact, and not because they agreed with it or did not agree with it. Next year they would have a diary of Shetland, and the narrative of a Covenanter, the latter of which he had read and found extremely curious. To look forward another year, they had that admirable book, *Major's History of Scotland*, which was the first-fruits of a modification made in their constitution last year, when Lord Rosebery was present, by which they were enabled, when they found an important book illustrative of Scottish history in any other tongue than the English, and rather inaccessible, to bring such a volume within their scope. Mr. Constable was translating it for the first time. It was really amazing that so curious a book, by a man of

such peculiar temperament, jocosity, and advanced ways of thinking, should have been left for that Society to make accessible.
With that volume would be issued a new volume of the Glamis
Papers, and he thought they ought not to pass from that without
expressing their indebtedness to Lord Strathmore for consenting
to the publication of these domestic records. There was also the
diary of Andrew Hay of Stone; and Sir George Clerk of Penicuik
had very handsomely placed at their disposal a very interesting
autobiography of an ancestor of his. Then they had a treatise on
the Union, which had never appeared before, by Sir Thomas Craig,
who, he thought, had the best brain among the lawyers of his day.
It was unfortunate that the ablest Scottish intellects at that time,
and for a century or two, employed Latin in their writings. The
state of the Scottish mind would have been very different if it had
not happened that, following the example of the great George
Buchanan, people did not write in the vernacular. The consequence was that a number of excellent themes that should be
flowing in our veins as natural traditions, remained as lumps upon
the wayside. Lord Rosebery, whose absence they regretted, was
to present to the Society an excellent volume on the Rebellion of
1745. It was additionally valuable as a proof that Lord Rosebery
was not merely the nominal founder of the Society, but had his
heart, and when necessary his purse, at the centre of their affairs.

Dr. George Burnett, Lyon-King-of-Arms, seconded the motion,
and the Report, with the proposal of the Treasurer to form a
reserve fund, was unanimously adopted.

The Rev. Dr. Sprott, the Rev. A. W. Cornelius Hallen, and
Sir Arthur Mitchell, K.C.B., were elected Members of Council.

THE LORD PROVOST (Sir Thomas Clark), in proposing a vote of
thanks to the Secretary, Treasurer, and Chairman, mentioned that
there was a large amount of valuable matter to be found in the
archives of the Town Council, and suggested that the Society
might devote some attention to it. Mr. SKINNER, Town-Clerk,
intimated his willingness to render what service he could to the
Society in that connection, and the CHAIRMAN said the suggestion
should not be lost sight of.

CHARGE.

Balance from last year, . . .	£66	17	7
47 Subscriptions in arrear, for 1886-7, . .	49	7	0
400 Subscribers for 1887-8, at £1, 1s., . .	420	0	0
2 New Members admitted during year to supply vacancies, ...	2	2	0
34 Libraries at £1, 1s., ...	35	14	0
Copies of previous issue supplied to new members, .	18	18	0
	£592	18	7
Interest on Bank Account and Deposit Receipts, .	6	13	11
Sum of Charge, . .	£599	12	6

DISCHARGE.

I. *Incidental Expenses*—

Printing and posting Circulars, .	£6	7	1			
Stationery (including Receipt-book),	3	15	6			
Postage, addressing, and delivery of copies, . . .	14	19	10			
Stamps for lettering of cloth covers,	4	17	6			
Copies of Major's *Historia* (1521, 1740) for editor, . . .	2	6	6			
Hire of room (Dowell's), . .	1	1	0			
Postages of Treasurer and Secretary,	2	18	8			
Clerical work, . . .	4	15	9			
List of members and report (bound with the *Grameid*), . .	9	10	0			
Charges on Cheques, .	1	0	6			
				51	12	4
Carry forward, .				£51	12	4

Brought forward,   £51 12 4

II. *The Grameid*—

Composition, press-work, and paper, £80   9   9
Proofs and corrections,   .   .   38   6   0
Drawing and lithographing of
    the Philp monument,   .   .   5   7   0
Binding and back-lettering of 480
    copies, ...   18 10   0
Transcripts,   .   5   0   0
                                    147 12 9

£199   5   1

III. *The St. Andrews Register* (expenses incurred to
    date)—

Composition, press-work, and paper, £82   7   0
Proofs and corrections,   .   .   26   3   0
Transcript of MS.,   .   .   .   28   0   0
                                    136 10 0

Total Expenditure,   £335 15 1

IV. 18 Subscriptions in arrear, .   18 18 0
Balance in Treasurer's hands—
    Deposit Receipts, with interest, £205   5   3
    Bank Balance, with interest,   .   42 17   2

                         £248   2   5
Less 3 Subscriptions received in
    advance for 1888-9,   .   .   3   3   0
                                   244 19 5

Sum of Discharge,   £599 12 6

EDINBURGH, 10*th November* 1888.—The Auditors have examined the
Treasurer's Accounts for the year ending 1st November current, and find them
correct and properly vouched, with a balance of two hundred and forty-four
pounds nineteen shillings and fivepence at the credit of the Society.

                             RALPH RICHARDSON.
                             WM. TRAQUAIR DICKSON.

Scottish History Society.

THE EXECUTIVE.

President.
THE EARL OF ROSEBERY, LL.D.

Chairman of Council.
DAVID MASSON, LL.D., Professor of English Literature, Edinburgh University.

Council.
Sir ARTHUR MITCHELL, K.C.B., M.D., LL.D.

Rev. GEO. W. SPROTT, D.D.

Rev. A. W. CORNELIUS HALLEN.

W. F. SKENE, D.C.L., LL.D., Historiographer - Royal for Scotland.

Colonel P. DODS.

J. R. FINDLAY, Esq.

GEORGE BURNETT, LL.D., Lyon-King-of-Arms.

J. T. CLARK, Keeper of the Advocates' Library.

THOMAS DICKSON, LL.D., Curator of the Historical Department, Register House.

Right Rev. JOHN DOWDEN, D.D., Bishop of Edinburgh.

J. KIRKPATRICK, LL.B., Professor of History, Edinburgh University.

ÆNEAS J. G. MACKAY, LL.D., Sheriff of Fife.

Corresponding Members of the Council.
OSMUND AIRY, Esq., Birmingham; Very Rev. J. CUNNINGHAM, D.D., Principal of St. Mary's College, St. Andrews; Professor GEORGE GRUB, LL.D., Aberdeen; Rev. W. D. MACRAY, Oxford; Professor A. F. MITCHELL, D.D., St. Andrews; Professor W. ROBERTSON SMITH, Cambridge; Professor J. VEITCH, LL.D., Glasgow; A. H. MILLAR, Esq., Dundee.

Hon. Treasurer.
J. J. REID, B.A., Advocate, Queen's Remembrancer.

Hon. Secretary.
T. G. LAW, Librarian, Signet Library.

RULES.

1. The object of the Society is the discovery and printing, under selected editorship, of unpublished documents illustrative of the civil, religious, and social history of Scotland. The Society will also undertake, in exceptional cases, to issue translations of printed works of a similar nature, which have not hitherto been accessible in English.

2. The number of Members of the Society shall be limited to 400.

3. The affairs of the Society shall be managed by a Council consisting of a Chairman, Treasurer, Secretary, and twelve elected Members, five to make a quorum. Three of the twelve elected members shall retire annually by ballot, but they shall be eligible for re-election.

4. The Annual Subscription to the Society shall be One Guinea. The publications of the Society shall not be delivered to any Member whose Subscription is in arrear, and no Member shall be permitted to receive more than one copy of the Society's publications.

5. The Society will undertake the issue of its own publications, *i.e.* without the intervention of a publisher or any other paid agent.

6. The Society will issue yearly two octavo volumes of about 320 pages each.

7. An Annual General Meeting of the Society shall be held on the last Tuesday in October.

8. Two stated Meetings of the Council shall be held each year, one on the last Tuesday of May, the other on the Tuesday preceding the day upon which the Annual General Meeting shall be held. The Secretary, on the request of three Members of the Council, shall call a special meeting of the Council.

9. Editors shall receive 20 copies of each volume they edit for the Society.

10. The owners of Manuscripts published by the Society will also be presented with a certain number of copies.

11. The Annual Balance-Sheet, Rules, and List of Members shall be printed.

12. No alteration shall be made in these Rules except at a General Meeting of the Society. A fortnight's notice of any alteration to be proposed shall be given to the Members of the Council.

PUBLICATIONS.

Works already Issued.

1887.

1. BISHOP POCOCKE'S TOURS IN SCOTLAND, 1747-1760. Edited by D. W. KEMP.

2. DIARY OF AND GENERAL EXPENDITURE BOOK OF WILLIAM CUNNINGHAM OF CRAIGENDS, 1673-1680. Edited by the Rev. JAMES DODDS, D.D.

1888.

3. PANURGI PHILO-CABALLI SCOTI GRAMEIDOS LIBRI SEX. — THE GRAMEID: an heroic poem descriptive of the Campaign of Viscount Dundee in 1689, by JAMES PHILIP of Almerieclose. Edited, with Translation and Notes, by the Rev. A. D. MURDOCH.

4. THE REGISTER OF THE KIRK SESSION OF ST. ANDREWS. Part I. 1559-1582. Edited by D. HAY FLEMING.

In Preparation.

DIARY OF THE REV. JOHN MILL, Minister of Dunrossness, Sandwick, and Cunningsburgh, in Shetland, 1742-1805, with original documents, local records, and historical notices relating to the District. Edited by GILBERT GOUDIE, F.S.A. Scot.

A NARRATIVE OF MR. JAMES NIMMO, A COVENANTER. 1654-1708. Edited by W. G. SCOTT MONCRIEFF, Advocate.

THE REGISTER OF THE KIRK SESSION OF ST. ANDREWS. Part II. 1583-1600. Edited by D. HAY FLEMING.

LIST OF PERSONS CONCERNED IN THE REBELLION (1745), with Evidences to prove the same, transmitted to the Commissioners of Excise by the several Supervisors of Excise in Scotland. Presented to the Society by the EARL OF ROSEBERY.

GLAMIS PAPERS; including the 'BOOK OF RECORD,' written by PATRICK, FIRST EARL OF STRATHMORE (1647-95), the DIARY OF LADY HELEN MIDDLETON, his wife, and other documents, illustrating the social life of the seventeenth century. Edited from the original manuscripts at Glamis Castle by A. H. MILLAR.

JOHN MAJOR'S DE GESTIS SCOTORUM (1521). Translated by ARCHIBALD CONSTABLE, with a Memoir of the author by ÆNEAS J. G. MACKAY, Advocate.

THE   RY OF ANDREW HAY OF STONE, NEAR BIGGAR, AFTERWARDS CRAIGNETHAN CASTLE, 1659-60. Edited by A. G. REID, .A. Scot., from a manuscript in his possession.

THE RECORDS OF THE COMMISSION OF THE GENERAL ASSEMBLY, 1646-1662. Edited by the Rev. JAMES CHRISTIE, D.D., with an Introduction by the Rev. Professor MITCHELL, D.D.

In Contemplation.

'THE HISTORY OF MY LIFE, extracted from Journals I kept since I was twenty-six years of age, interspersed with short accounts of the most remarkable public affairs that happened in my time, especially such as I had some immediate concern in,' 1702-1754. By Sir JOHN CLERK OF PENICUIK, Baron of the Exchequer, Commissioner of the Union, etc. Edited from the original MS. in Penicuik House by J. M. GRAY.

SIR THOMAS CRAIG'S DE UNIONE REGNORUM BRITANNIÆ. Edited, with an English Translation, from the unpublished manuscript in the Advocates' Library.

THE DIARIES OR ACCOUNT BOOKS OF SIR JOHN FOULIS OF RAVELSTON, (1679-1707), and the ACCOUNT BOOK OF DAME HANNAH ERSKINE (1675-1699). Edited by the Rev. A. W. CORNELIUS HALLEN.